Microeconomics

GRADE BOOSTER SERIES

ELIJAH M. JAMES PhD

8TH HOUSE PUBLISHING

First Edition

Published worldwide by 8th House Publishing
www.8th House Publishing.com

Front Cover Design by 8th House Publishing

Set in Raleway, Adobe Garamand Pro and Adobe Caslon Pro.

ISBN 978-1-926716-44-2

'Microeconomics - Grade Booster Series' by Elijah M. James Ph.D.

LIBRARY AND ARCHIVES CANADA CATALOGUING IN PUBLICATION DATA
A catalog record of this book is available from Library and Archives Canada.

BabalonBOOKS is a division of 8th House Publishing, Montreal, Canada.
www.8thHousePublishing.com

8th House Publishing
Montreal, Canada

Microeconomics

GRADE BOOSTER SERIES

Dedicated to my grandchildren:

Sabrina

Josephine

Ariana

Isabel

Robert

Do not forsake wisdom, and she will protect you;
love her, and she will watch over you.
The beginning of wisdom is this:
Get wisdom. Though it cost all you have, get understanding.

(Proverbs 4:6, 7).

ACKNOWLEDGEMENTS

A work of this magnitude is not usually accomplished by any single individual. In the case of the Grade Booster Series (GBS)—Microeconomics, I have received a great deal of help and support from many different quarters. My dear friend and colleague, the late Matlub Hussain, was a staunch advocate of student success. He read an earlier draft of the manuscript and made many suggestions for improving it. Dr. Alaka Ganguli with whom I share an office, was always available for discussions, and gave freely of her time and expertise. Alaka, I am greatly indebted to you. I must thank the members of the Department of Economics at Dawson College for creating a friendly environment that fosters scholarship.

My children Ted, Jennifer, Andrea, Kapil, and my niece Bernadette have encouraged me throughout the entire process of preparing the manuscript. They have served as sounding board for my ideas.

I owe a debt of gratitude to my students at McGill University, Concordia University, John Abbott College, and Dawson College who opened my eyes to some of the problems that students face in their study of economics.

Finally, I would like to thank Mr. Emery Moreira and his hard-working staff at 8th House Publishing for the excellent job they have done in transforming my manuscript into such a fine product.

I thank you all.

PREFACE

The idea of a grade booster series in economics originated with my own observation of my students. I noticed that on numerous occasions, students obtained low grades, not so much because they were unfamiliar with the relevant material, but more so because of their inability to utilize the information they had to solve problems and answer questions. Discussions with colleagues quickly confirmed that they too were witnessing the same phenomenon. It was clear then, that if students could be taught how to harness the information they possess and use it to answer questions and solve problems, their grades would improve significantly.

The main purpose of the Grade Booster Series (GBS)—Microeconomics is to help you, the student taking an introductory course in microeconomics, improve your grade. By studying the problems contained in the Grade Booster Series, you will acquire confidence in attacking problems, your fear of economics will diminish, you will better understand the principles and concepts discussed in your textbook, you will be able to apply them in different circumstances, and you will learn how to answer economic questions and solve problems in tests and examinations.

Through the GBS—Microeconomics, you will learn to properly organize economic information into answers to questions; you will learn a step-by-step procedure to solving economic problems; you will develop the ability to think clearly; and all these will translate into a better grade in your microeconomics course.

The GBS—Microeconomics gives you access to more than 2,250 economics problems/ questions with full answers and explanations, including:

548 Essay problems
624 Multiple-choice questions
590 True/False questions
405 Completion questions

Pedagogical Features

The GBS—Microeconomics is loaded with pedagogical features, including the following:.

1. *The Essay Questions:* Not only do we provide answers to the essay questions, but we provide a section referred to as ***Requirement and Clue*** under which we point out what is required for a good answer or solution, and give some hints as to how you should proceed.
2. *Multiple-choice Questions:* After indicating the correct choice, we provide a *reason* for making that choice.
3. *True-False Questions:* If a statement is false, we provide an *explanation* as to why it is false.

So, if you want to boost your grade in microeconomics, the GBS—Microeconomics is what you need. Welcome to the Grade Booster Series—Microeconomics

Keyed to Your Textbook

The *Grade Booster Series (GBS)—Microeconomics* is designed to be used with any traditional textbook in introductory microeconomics. For the convenience of students taking an introduction to microeconomics course, we have provided this key to some of the major microeconomic textbooks. It would be impractical to list all the major textbooks used in microeconomics courses, so only a sample is represented.

Using the *Key* is rather simple. For example, if you are studying Elasticity and you are using Mankiw, the relevant chapter is Chapter 5 (*Elasticity and Its Application*). This is Module 6 (Elasticity and Its Uses) in the GBS. What if your textbook is not listed? Not a problem! Note the title of the chapter you are studying, turn to the index of the GBS and see which module matches the material you are studying. It's that simple.

GBS	BA	CA	COL	HUB	JAM	MAN	MCC	MIL	RAG	SAY
Mo1	1	1	1	1	1	2	1	1	1	-
Mo2	-	-	2A	1A	1A	2A	-	-	2	TK
Mo3	3	2	-	2	2	2	1	2	1	1
Mo4	-	-	3	2	-	-	2	-	-	-
Mo5	4	3,4	4,5	3	3	4	3	3	3	2,3
Mo6	5	5	6	6	4	5	6	19	4	4
Mo7	13	6	19	10	6	21	7	20	6	5
Mo8	-	-	-	8	-	-	-	21	-	-
Mo9	14	7	11	11	7	13	9	22	7	6
Mo10	14	8,9	11	11	8	13	9	22	8	6,7
Mo11	15	12	13	12	9	14	10	23	9	8
Mo12	16	13	14	15	10	15	12	24	10	10
Mo13	17,18	15	14,15	13,14	11	16,17	13	25,26	11	11
Mo14	19	-	17	17	12	18	-	28,29	13-15	12
Mo15	19	10	17W	17	12	18	-	28,29	15	12
Mo16	20	18	18	18	13	19,20	-	30	-	-
Mo17	10,11	16	8	5	15	10,11	4	31	17	-
Mo18	-	-	8W	-	-	-	-	-	-	-
Mo19	8	19	7	4	-	12	5	5	18	-
Mo20	-	20	9	9	14	3,9	-	32	32	13
Mo21	-	20	10	-	14	-	-	-	33	-

Key:

GBS = *Grade booster series*; **Mo** = *Module*; **Tk** = *Toolkit*

BA = Robin Bade & Michael Parkin, *Foundations of Microeconomics*, 8th Edition, Pearson, 2018

CA = Karl E. Case, Ray C. Fair, and Sharon E. Oster, *Principles of Microeconomics,* 12th Edition, Pearson, 2017

COL = David Colander, *Microeconomics*, 10th Edition, McGraw Hill, 2017

HUB = R. Glen Hubbard & Anthony Patrick O'Brien, *Microeconomics*, 6th Edition, Pearson, 2017

JAM = Elijah M. James, *Microeconomics*, 2nd Edition, Pearson, 2012

MAN = N. Gregory Mankiw, Ronald D. Kneebone, & Kenneth J. McKenzie, *Principles of Microeconomics*, 7th Edition, Nelson, 2017

MCC = Campbell McConnell, S. Brue, and S. Flynn, *Microeconomics*, 20th Edition, McGraw Hill, 2015

MIL = Roger LeRoy Miller, *Economics Today: The Micro View*, 19th Edition, Pearson, 2018

RAG = Christopher T. S. Ragan, *Microeconomics*, 15th Edition, Pearson, 2017

SAY = John Sayre and Alan Morris, *Principles of Microeconomics*, 8th Edition, McGraw Hill, 2015

Look for the ***Grade Booster Series--****Macroeconomics!*

TOPIC

1 THE SUBJECT MATTER OF ECONOMICS - MICROECONOMICS

SYNOPSIS

An understanding of economics is extremely important in any modern society. It is a fact that many of the critical problems and issues that members of society face are somehow related to economics. The decisions that consumers, businesses, and the various levels of government make determine how society uses its scarce resources.

Economics is the discipline that studies how a society uses its scarce resources to satisfy the unlimited wants of its customers. Because it studies a particular aspect of human behavior, economics is considered a **social science** in the same sense that social psychology, sociology, and political science are social sciences.

Human wants are unlimited while the means available to satisfy those wants are limited. This problem of **scarcity** is the fundamental economic problem. We must find ways of using our scarce resources to satisfy as many wants as possible.

Economists employ the scientific method. They construct models and use them to help them understand how the economy works. **Positive statements** are factual. They deal with what is, was, or will be. **Normative statements** are opinions or value judgements. They deal with what ought to be. **Positive economics** is concerned with how the economy actually works, while **normative economics** is concerned with how the economy ought to function. Economists are more likely to disagree over the normative aspects of economics than over the positive aspects.

A **variable** is anything that can assume different values. **Endogenous variables** are those whose values are determined in the model, whereas the exogenous variables are those whose values are determined by factors outside the model. The **exogenous variables** affect the endogenous. A **flow** (or flow variable) has a time dimension while a **stock** (or stock variable) does not have a time dimension.

The *post hoc ergo propter hoc* fallacy is the false conclusion that a cause-effect relationship exists because events may occur in sequence. The ***ceteris paribus*** (other things being equal) assumption is important in economics. It allows the economist to isolate the effects of certain variables. The assumption allows the economist to hold other factors constant while he or she examines the effects of the variable that is of current interest.

The two main branches into which economics is divided are *microeconomics* and *macroeconomics*. **Microeconomics** studies the behaviour of individual economic units, while **macroeconomics** studies the behavior of broad economic aggregates. A good understanding of how the economy functions requires a knowledge of both microeconomics and macroeconomics.

LEARNING OBJECTIVES

In connection with this module, you should be able to:

1. Formulate an adequate definition of economics.
2. Discuss the subject matter of economics.
3. Discuss the importance of economics.
4. Identify and classify the resources of the economy.
5. Discuss the incomes derived from various resources.
6. Explain what economists do in terms of employment.
7. Discuss the nature of scientific inquiry.
8. Explain economic methodology.
9. Distinguish between positive and normative economics.
10. Explain why economists sometimes disagree.
11. Distinguish between microeconomics and macroeconomics.

DEFINITIONS & CONCEPTS

You should be able to define the following terms and concepts:

social science
scarcity
scientific method
economic goods
free goods
producer goods
consumer goods
capital goods
scientific method
hypothesis
model
definitions
assumptions
ceteris paribus
positive economics
normative economics
variable
endogenous variable
exogenous variable
stock variable
flow variable
resources
rent
profit
wages and salaries
interest & dividends
land
labour
capital
entrepreneurial services
microeconomics
macroeconomics
positive statement
normative statement

1

THE SUBJECT MATTER OF ECONOMICS

Concepts, Definitions & Problems

Problem 1-1

Distinguish between absolute scarcity and relative scarcity. Why does scarcity exist?

Requirement and Clue: *Recognize that this is a two-part problem. Your solution should address both parts. The two concepts are different and it is your task to illustrate that difference.*

Solution:

Economists distinguish between *absolute* scarcity and *relative* or *economic* scarcity. Ordinarily, when we say that something is scarce, we mean that only a small quantity of it exists, or that it is difficult to obtain. For example, one may say that fresh vegetables are scarce during a drought, or that a 1945 coin is scarce or rare, meaning that it is seldom seen. That concept of scarcity is referred to as *absolute scarcity*. However, when economists talk about scarcity, they mean the extent of availability of something in relation to how much of it is wanted. This is the concept of *economic* or *relative* scarcity. The following table illustrates the difference.

Absolute scarcity versus relative scarcity

Situation	Amount available	Amount wanted	Condition
A	60	40	No economic scarcity
B	100	150	Economic scarcity

Let us look first at absolute scarcity. In situation A, 60 units of an item are available, while in situation B, 100 units are available. In an absolute sense, the item is scarcer in situation A than in situation B. Absolute scarcity can be determined solely by looking at the amounts available.

Let us now look at relative scarcity. In situation A, 60 units of an item are available, but only 40 units are required. In this situation economic scarcity does not exist since more of the item is available than is wanted. In situation B, 100 units of the item are available but 150 units are wanted. The amount that is wanted exceeds the amount that is available. In this situation, the item is relatively scarce. Relative scarcity is determined by comparing the amount available with the amount that is wanted.

Scarcity exists because quantities of goods and services are limited while desires for these goods and services are unlimited.

Problem 1-2

What is the meaning of the term scarcity in economics? Does scarcity really exist?

Requirement and Clue: *This is a two-part problem. The first part is definitional. You are required to demonstrate that you understand the concept of scarcity as it is used in economics. You are not asked to write an essay or a term paper on scarcity. Just say what scarcity means in economics. The second part of the problem requires a demonstration of the existence of scarcity.*

Solution:

In economics, scarcity is the condition that exists when the goods and services available are insufficient to satisfy our wants for them. Thus in economics, scarcity is always relative—the quantities available in relation to wants. Quantities of most goods and services are limited, whereas wants or desires for those goods and services are unlimited.

By definition, scarcity is a reality. It does exist. A few goods, such as air and sunlight (in most circumstances) are not scarce. But in the vast majority of cases, scarcity is a fact of life. We just don't have enough resources to enable us to produce all the goods and services that we want.

Problem 1-3

What is the difference between "economic goods" and "free goods"? Give examples of each.

Requirement and Clue: *Say what economic goods are and what free goods are. Your examples should support your definitions.*

Solution:

Economic goods are goods that are relatively scarce, that is, they are not available in sufficiently large quantities to satisfy people's wants for them. Such goods are produced using scarce resources and therefore have a positive price. Examples of economic goods are oil, computers, hospital beds, and automobiles.

Free goods, on the other hand, are goods that are readily available in sufficiently large quantities to satisfy people's wants for them. Free goods are not the result of the use of scarce resources. Even at a price of zero, there are sufficient quantities of free goods to satisfy all wants. Examples of free goods are air, sunlight, and sea water.

Problem 1-4

Explain each of the following terms:

(a) *Free good*

(b) *Producer good*

Requirement and Clue: *You are expected to define each concept clearly. Although the problem does not specifically ask for examples, you should provide them nonetheless.*

Solution:

(a) A free good is a good that is so plentiful that no one has to pay for it. If you were on a river and you wanted water to wash your hands, you would not have to pay for the water since there would be so much of it available. In this case, the water would be a free good. Note that a free good in one situation may not be a free good in another situation. For example, the water that flows out of the faucet in your bathroom is not a free good. If a government provides elementary education "free of charge", it does not mean that elementary education is a free good. Although the recipients do not pay for it directly, it is paid for out of taxation.

(b) A producer good is any good that is used by the producer in the process of production. They are the inputs or factors of production that producers use to produce their output of goods and services. They are distinguishable from consumer goods in that consumer goods are not intended for further processing. Examples of producer goods are raw material, fuel, equipment and plant.

Problem 1-5

What is the difference between consumer goods and capital goods? Can a good be both a consumer good and a capital good?

Requirement and Clue: *Notice that this is a two-part problem. Address each part in order. Your solution should include examples of consumer goods and capital goods. For the second part of the problem, think of a good that is used by both consumers and producers.*

Solution:

Consumer goods are goods that are intended to satisfy the wants of consumers directly. They are the goods that consumers buy for final use. Examples of consumer goods are clothing, home computers, television sets, food, furniture, and kitchen appliances. Capital goods on the other hand, are goods that are produced and used to produce other capital goods and consumer goods. Capital goods satisfy consumer wants only indirectly. Examples of capital goods are farm implements, machine tools, printing presses, and factories.

It is possible for the same item to be both a consumer good and a capital good. For example, a farmer may use his pickup truck to haul produce to market and for personal and family transportation. When the truck is used to haul produce it is a capital good, and when it is used for personal or family transportation it is a consumer good. Similarly, a personal computer in a business office is a capital good, but when it is used at home by a student it is a consumer good.

Problem 1-6

Economics is often defined as a social science. Sociology, psychology, and political science are also social sciences. How does economics differ from each of the social sciences listed above?

Requirement and Clue: *Say why these disciplines fall into the category of social science. Mention what each deals with and how economics differs from them.*

Solution:

Economics, sociology, psychology, and political science are all social sciences because each studies some aspect of human behavior. Economics studies how society uses its scarce resources to satisfy unlimited wants; sociology studies the development, organization, and functioning of a society and its institutions; psychology studies the mental characteristics or attitude of an individual or group to understand behavior; and political science studies the processes, principles, and structure of government and of political institutions.

Economics differs from these other social sciences in that none of the others deals specifically with how society uses its limited resources to satisfy its unlimited wants.

Problem 1-7

Why is it important for people to have an understanding of the economy and society?

Requirement and Clue: *Stress the importance of the economy and society to our lives.*

Solution:

An understanding of the economy and society enables us to improve the performance of the economy and make our society better. We will then be in a better position to deal with many of the problems that we encounter in life. The economy is such an important part of society that it is virtually impossible to understand society without a basic knowledge of economics. Our relationships with one another, our environment, the manner in which our collective wealth is distributed, the types of work we do, our ability to develop and maintain a viable health care system, and the amount of money we earn are all related to our economy. Our lives are shaped by the myriad economic decisions that have been made in the past by others and that are being made by us today. A decision to put more resources into the production of warplanes instead of using them to provide more educational and health facilities will affect our society not only today but also for a long time in the future. The better our understanding of our economy and our society, the better will be the control that we are likely to have over our own destiny.

Problem 1-8

What do professional economists do?

Requirement and Clue: *The solution to this problem requires a statement about occupations for economists. Think of employment situations that require decisions about the use of scarce resources.*

Solution:

Economists are engaged in a wide variety of activities. Some teach in high schools, colleges and universities. Large corporations like Wal-Mart, Ford Motor Company, Imperial Oil, or a public utilities company, might hire economists to estimate the demand for their products or services or to figure out the economic impact of price changes, or to increase the efficiency of their operations. A bank might employ economists to forecast interest rates or the demand for loans. A government might hire economists to determine the effects of certain taxes on its revenue and on the level of economic activity. A union might employ economists to study matters relating to wages and employment. Professional economists serve as presidents, vice-presidents, general managers, and executives of a wide variety of organizations. They also sit on the boards of many companies directing their affairs. Many economists work on their own as independent consultants.

Problem 1-9

What are resources and how can they be classified?

Requirement and Clue: *This is a two-part problem. Answer each part in order. Briefly define each category.*

Solution:

Resources are the things that are used to produce the goods and services that the society requires. They are productive agents such as trees, waterways, roads, oil, factories, air, buildings, tools, and human effort. They are also referred to as *factors of production.*

Economists usually classify them into four categories as follows:

Land: all natural resources such as minerals, rivers, lakes, wildlife, forests, and oil.

Labour: the physical and mental efforts that people contribute to the production process.

Capital: any manufactured item that can be used to produce goods and services. They include buildings, highways, equipment, and manufacturing plant.

Entrepreneurship: the organization of land, labour, and capital for the purpose of production. Entrepreneurship or entrepreneurial services include managerial skills, risk-taking, organizational skills, innovative skills, leadership, and decision-making skills.

Problem 1-10

Indicate whether each of the following should be classified as land (T), labour (L), capital (C), or entrepreneurial services (E).

a. The oil sands in a country
b. A ferry that takes passengers from point A to point B
c. The services provided by technicians employed by a telephone company
d. Deer in the ABC Public Park
e. Forests in North America and Western Europe
f. Lake Erie
g. A park in Australia
h. The services provided by Mavis Grant in securing funds and establishing her small bread and breakfast business
i. The services provided by your economics professor
j. The cranes used in constructing a multi-level parking facility

Requirement and Clue: *This is a test of your knowledge regarding the classification of resources. Before you answer, think of the meaning of each category.*

Solution:

a. The oil sands in a country (T)
b. A ferry that takes passengers from point A to point B (C)
c. The services provided by technicians employed by a telephone company (L)
d. Deer in the ABC Public Park (T)
e. Forests in North America and Western Europe (T)
f. Lake Erie (T)

g. A park in Australia (T)
h. The services provided by Mavis Grant in securing funds and establishing her small bread and breakfast business (E)
i. The services provided by your economics professor (L)
j. The cranes used in constructing a multi-level parking facility (C)

Problem 1-11

What do economists mean by land?

Requirement and Clue: *Recognize that "land" is an economic jargon with its own peculiar meaning. Provide illustrative examples.*

Solution:

"Land" is one of those economic terms that have a meaning that is different from its meaning in ordinary English language. Ordinarily, when we talk of land, we refer to the solid portion of the earth on which one can erect a building or grow crops. In economics also, land refers to the solid portion of the earth but the concept includes more than that. Any non-human resource that is made available by nature is called land in economic jargon. Thus land includes minerals embedded in the earth; fish in the seas; rivers, and lakes; the vast expanse of oceans; the natural waterfalls; wildlife; oxygen in the air; and even the space within which economic activity takes place. In economics, land is synonymous with "natural resources".

Problem 1-12

What is the economic definition of labour?

Requirement and Clue: *Provide examples in your answer.*

Solution:

Simply stated, labour is human effort. It consists of all human abilities or talents that may be employed in the production of goods and services. This definition includes both physical and mental abilities or talents. Examples of labour are the work of physicians, economic professors, movie actors, sales people, as well as farmers, mechanics, and material handlers.

Economists now generally exclude from the economic definition of labour one particular type of mental ability, that is, entrepreneurial ability which is classified as a separate resource category.

Problem 1-13

Distinguish between real capital and money capital.

Requirement and Clue: *Think of the usage of these terms in economics. Recognize that for most people, capital is money. Provide examples of real capital.*

Solution:

In economics, a distinction is made between real capital and money capital or financial capital. Real capital refers to any produced factor of production that can be used to produce other capital goods or consumer goods. Some examples of real capital are machines, tools, equipment, buildings, railroad tracks and highways. Money capital or financial capital, on the other hand, is defined as funds available to purchase real capital. Since money itself is not used as a factor of production until it is exchanged for real capital, economists focus on real capital and generally do not include money in their definition of capital.

Problem 1-14

What particular types of income are generated by the factors of production?

Requirement and Clue: *Recall that each category of resource generates a particular type of income. Be careful with capital and entrepreneurial services.*

Solution:

Land, labour, capital, and entrepreneurial services generate incomes for their owners. Owners of land receive *rent*, and owners of capital receive *interest and dividend* income. Those who provide labour services receive *wages and salaries*, and individuals who provide entrepreneurial services earn *profits*.

Problem 1-15

In the following table, the left-hand column shows factors of production while the middle column shows earning/income types that are incorrectly matched with the factors of production. In the right-hand column enter the correct income categories that match the factors of production.

Factors of production and their earnings

Factors of production	Earning/Income	Corrected income category
Land	Interest and dividends	
Labour	Rent	
Capital	Profits	
Entrepreneurial services	Wages and salaries	

Requirement and Clue: *You are required to demonstrate that you know which income type is associated with each resource category. Again, be careful with capital and entrepreneurial services.*

Solution:

Factors of production	Earning/Income	Corrected income category
Land	Interest and dividends	*Rent*
Labour	Rent	*Wages and salaries*
Capital	Profits	*Interest and dividends*
Entrepreneurial services	Wages and salaries	*Profits*

Problem 1-16

Indicate whether each of the following types of income would be classified technically as rent (R), wages and salaries (W), interest and dividends (i), or profit (π).

a. *The income that executive officers receive for their services*
b. *The money Mr. Jenkins (a landlord) collects each month from his tenants*
c. *The income that a student receives from a college as payment for her part-time tutoring services*
d. *The annual amount that Bell Canada Enterprises (BCE) pays out to its shareholders for their investment in the company*
e. *The income received by parking assistants for their services*
f. *The net earnings of Mr. Edwards, the proprietor of a parking lot business*
g. *The income that Mr. Peters receives monthly from Mr. Edwards for the use of his parking lot*
h. *The net revenue received by an inventor for developing and marketing a space-saving device*

Requirement and Clue: *You need to figure out which resource category generates the income indicated and then assign the appropriate income type.*

Solution:

a. The income that executive officers receive for their services (W)
b. The money Mr. Jenkins (a landlord) collects each month from tenants in his building (i)
c. The income that a student receives from a college as payment for her part-time tutoring services (W)
d. The annual amount that Bell Canada Enterprises (BCE) pays out to its shareholders for their investment in the company (i)
e. The income received by parking lot assistants for their services (W)
f. The net earnings of Mr. Edwards, the proprietor of a parking lot business (π)
g. The income that Mr. Peters receives monthly from Mr. Edwards for the use of his parking lot (R)
h. The net revenue received by an inventor for developing and marketing a space-saving device (π)

Problem 1-17

In what sense can economics claim to be a science?

Requirement and Clue: *Ask yourself, "What does science mean in this context?" You are expected to show that economics follows the scientific approach and thus qualifies as a science.*

Solution:

To qualify as a science, a discipline must follow certain procedures. Scientists, in attempting to explain certain phenomena, construct theories or models. In so doing, they must carefully define words and phrases so as to avoid confusion. They make certain assumptions that describe the conditions under which the theory is meant to apply. Then they specify the relationships that exist between the variables under consideration, i.e. they make certain hypotheses. Scientists also proceed to test their theories to see how well they predict or explain events. Scientists must relate their theories to empirical evidence. This is the scientific procedure. Any discipline that follows this method of enquiry earns the right to be called a science.

The discipline of economics follows the procedure outlined above, so economics can claim legitimately to be a science. It must be pointed out however, that economics is not an *exact* science like physics, or chemistry, for example. What distinguishes economics and other social sciences from the so-called exact or hard sciences is the difficulty that social scientists face in conducting experiments. Physicists, for example, can enter their laboratories and create the ideal condition for their experiments. Economists, on the other hand, cannot conduct any such controlled experiments. Their laboratory is the real world and their subjects of investigation are people. The variables with which the economist works are constantly changing so exact measurement is often not possible.

Problem 1-18

How has the use of mathematical tools and econometrics affected the scientific element in economics?

Requirement and Clue: *Think of the precision of mathematical tools and of the importance of measurement in science.*

Solution:

The increasing use of mathematical tools in economics has helped economists to be more scientific in that economists are forced to specify clearly and concisely their assumptions and the relationships among the variables with which they are working. The development of econometrics has also helped economists in testing their theories, and in encouraging economic theorists to formulate their theories in a testable manner.

Problem 1-19

Economics has been categorized as a social science. What is science?

Requirement and Clue: *The emphasis here is on the meaning of science. Briefly discuss this.*

Solution:

Science refers to a particular method of acquiring knowledge that includes observation, measurement, and testing. Science can be defined as a branch of study, especially one concerned with facts, principles, and methods. Science refers not only to a method of acquiring knowledge but also to the knowledge produced by the approach. Science, as in the scientific approach is the systematic investigation and observation of phenomena and the formulation of general laws and tendencies there from, after testing and verifying hypotheses.

Problem 1-20

What is a hypothesis?

Requirement and Clue: *Provide a clear definition of "hypothesis" and give an example that clarifies the meaning of the concept.*

Solution:

The process of observation often leads to ideas, hunches, or guesses about relationships among the variables observed. A hypothesis is a statement of suspected relationships among two or more variables. It does not state some fact that is already known but something to be tested. For example, consider the following two statements:

> A: *The average weight of economics professors in North America is 175 pounds.*
>
> B: *Students who have a strong mathematical background get better grades in economics than those without a strong background in mathematics.*

Statement **A** is not a hypothesis; it merely expresses a fact that is already known, perhaps from a previous study. Statement **B,** however, is a hypothesis because the statement expresses a relationship between students' grades in economics and their mathematical backgrounds. Hypotheses should be stated in a verifiable manner so that they can be confirmed or rejected on the basis of test results.

Problem 1-21

Does economics follow the scientific approach?

Requirement and Clue: *Briefly outline the scientific approach and then show that the methods of economics are scientific.*

Solution:

The scientific approach involves observation and measurement, the formulation of hypotheses, and verification through testing of hypotheses. Economics deals with human behaviour and therefore cannot conduct experiments in traditional laboratories. No laboratory instruments can measure human behaviour with any degree of precision. Nevertheless, economics follows the scientific procedure as faithfully as do the natural sciences such as physics, chemistry and biology. In attempting to explain economic phenomena, economists follow the scientific approach. They gather information, analyze it, and select what they consider to be the most relevant facts. They formulate and test hypotheses and thus arrive at general statements or laws concerning economic phenomena.

Problem 1-22

Describe the methodology used by economists in studying economic phenomena.

Requirement and Clue: *The focus here is on model building. Define a model and discuss its ingredients.*

Solution:

The factors involved in studying real-world economic events are often quite complex. The economist comes to grips with these complexities by constructing economic models. An economic model is a simplification of the real economy or some aspect of it, and it consists only of the factors that appear to pertain most to what is being studied. Details that do not pertain directly to the question or problem being studied are simply stripped away in the model.

In constructing economic models, economists use definitions, assumptions, hypotheses and predictions. Definitions serve to identify the variables in the model so that measurement can be facilitated; assumptions state the conditions under which the model is supposed to work and greatly reduce the complexities of the real economy; hypotheses are statements about how the variables are related. They are usually cause-effect statements such as, "if people earn more money, they will buy more goods and services." Predictions are the outcome of testing hypotheses. If a certain relationship is suspected to exist between two variables and a test confirms the suspicion, then the economist can make prediction. For example, if it is confirmed that people buy more goods and services when their incomes rise, then economists can predict that an increase in income will cause an increase in spending.

Problem 1-23

How does economic methodology differ from that of natural sciences? Does the economist have any advantage over the natural scientists in studying phenomena?

Requirement and Clue: *This is a two-part problem. In your solution, address each part in order. Briefly state what makes it necessary for economists to construct models. Explain why economists might have an advantage over natural scientists.*

Solution:

Economic methodology differs from that of the natural sciences mainly in that the economist cannot generally conduct controlled experiments, whereas the natural scientist usually can. Economics is concerned with the behavior of human beings engaged in various types of economic activities. These activities are influenced by a variety of factors over which the economist has little or no control, and these uncontrollable factors often do exert considerable influence on the variable(s) that might be of interest to the economist. This difficulty forces the economist to construct models in which restrictions can be placed on some variables. By contrast, natural scientists are usually able to isolate the phenomena they are studying under laboratory conditions in which all extraneous factors have been excluded or held at some controlled level.

The economist does have an advantage over the natural scientist in that the natural scientist cannot place himself or herself in the place of the object that is being studied. He or she cannot meaningfully ask the question: "What would I do if I were platinum being examined?" Economists, on the other hand, can make generalizations about human actions from introspection since they can put themselves in the place of their subjects and ask, "What would I do if I were given a Christmas bonus of $1500.00?" Economists can do this because they have approximately the same makeup, motives, and abilities as the subjects of their inquiry.

Problem 1-24

What are some of the dangers of using models in economics?

Requirement and Clue: *Recognize that models are simplifications of reality and as such, there are short comings. Point out these.*

Solution:

Although models are extremely useful in studying economics, there are some dangers associated with their use. First, there is the danger that in determining which facts are most relevant, the economist might strip away too many of the relevant facts, thus severely limiting the applicability of the model. For example, in studying demand and supply of oranges during a particularly good harvest year, the economist might neglect to include the weather as a variable in his or her model. In this case, the model will work well as long as the weather is favourable for orange production. It will not work well in a drought year.

Another danger of using models is that it becomes very easy to forget that they are simplifications of reality and so people may rely too heavily on them. Referring to the example above about the demand and supply of oranges, fifteen successive years of weather that is favourable to orange production could lull economists into forgetting that they have excluded the weather from their model, so that when unfavourable weather does occur, they may be unable to account for changes in the orange market.

Finally, in using economic models, economists must keep in mind that they are purely *positive* as opposed to *normative*. They state simply what is, not what ought to be.

Problem 1-25

"Economic theories are abstractions from reality. That makes them practically useless in real life." Is this statement true or false? Defend your answer.

Requirement and Clue: *Recall that if any part of a statement is false, then the entire statement is false. In your solution, stress the advantages of models.*

Solution:

The statement is false. Economists are confronted with a massive volume of facts when studying the economy. In formulating useful theories of the behavior of the economy, they must extract the most relevant facts, and eliminate the less relevant ones. If nothing were stripped away, then the theory would prove to be too unwieldy for practical use. It would accurately describe the reality of a particular situation, but it would be so encumbered by the enumerable details of the situation that it would be useless if any of the details changed. Prediction with such a theory would be practically impossible and one would not learn much about the economy using such a theory.

By weeding out the less relevant data, and focusing on the most relevant facts, economists formulate theories that are more useful in explaining/predicting economic phenomena. The basis of a good theory is its foundation in facts. A theory that ignores the facts is worse than one that tries to include too many irrelevant facts.

Problem 1-26

How is the "goodness" of an economic model determined?

Requirement and Clue: *Focus on the purpose of an economic model and the extent to which it (the model) accomplishes its purpose.*

Solution:

The whole purpose of an economic model is to use it to explain some aspect of economic reality or to predict certain economic outcomes. An economic model that does this well is a good model. If model A explains and predicts economic phenomena better than the competing model B, then model A is judged to be better than model B. If an economic model fails to explain what we observe in the real world, then it may be rejected. The "goodness" of a model should be based primarily on its ability to explain or predict reality.

Problem 1-27

What is the role of assumptions in economic models?

Requirement and Clue: *First define assumptions and then state their roles. Provide examples.*

Solution:

Assumptions are statements of the conditions under which a particular economic model is expected to work. Basically, economists make two types of assumptions. One type relates to what motivates economic behavior. For example, economists assume that consumers are motivated by the desire to maximize their satisfaction, whereas businesses are motivated by the desire to maximize their profits. The other type of assumption that economists make is aimed at simplifying the complexities of the actual economy so that the task of the economist is made much easier. For example, if economists are not currently concerned with how government spending and taxes affect the economy, they may simplify their analyses by *assuming* that the government neither spends nor taxes. Such abstractions are necessary because of the complexities of the actual economy. Admittedly, economic assumptions are sometimes quite unrealistic, but often what is lost in realism is more than compensated for in understanding.

Problem 1-28

What is the importance of the "ceteris paribus" assumption in economic analysis?

Requirement and Clue: *Define the "ceteris paribus" assumption and discuss its importance by stating how economists use it.*

Solution:

"*Ceteris paribus*" is a Latin phrase meaning "other things being equal." This assumption allows economists to investigate the effects of one variable while assuming that others remain constant. Suppose we are interested in finding out the effect of a fall in the price of smart phones on the quantity of smart phones that university students will buy. Some of the factors, in addition to the price of smart phones that will affect the quantity of smart phones that students will buy include their incomes, their preference for smart phones over ordinary cell phones, and the prices of textbooks. We can hypothesize that if the price of smart phones falls, students will buy more of them. If we observe that a fall in the price of smart phones is accompanied by an increase in the quantity purchased, can we then conclude that the increase in quantity purchased results from a fall in price? It is possible that the increase in quantity purchased results from an increase in income or from a fall in the prices of textbooks that leaves students with more money to spend on smart phones, or from an increase in the prices of ordinary cell phones or some other reason.

To determine how a change in one factor affects other factors, economists must find some way of isolating the effects of other factors. In the above example, economists must isolate students' income, preference, the prices of textbooks, and other factors other than the price of smart phones that can affect the quantity of smart phones that students will purchase. Economists accomplish this task by using the *ceteris paribus* assumption. This assumption allows them to keep other factors constant while they examine the effects of the variable that currently interests them. Thus they can investigate how a change in price affects the quantity purchased by assuming that income, preference, and all other factors except the price of smart phones remain unchanged.

Problem 1-29

Differentiate between positive statements and normative statements. Give one example of each.

Requirement and Clue: *It's a good idea to define positive statements and normative statements. Recognize that positive statements are not necessarily true. Don't forget the examples.*

Solution:

Positive statements are expressions about what is, was, or will be. They are statements about facts and can be verified. Positive statements may be true or false. *Normative statements*, on the other hand, are expressions about what ought to be. They are statements about opinions and value-judgments and cannot be empirically verified.

An example of a positive statement is, "The price of oil is $100 a barrel." An example of a normative statement is, "The price of oil should be lowered."

Problem 1-30

Categorize each of the following as either a positive (P) or a normative (N) statement:

a. *One way of increasing the number of units of air conditioners sold is to reduce their prices.*
b. *If the prices of air conditioners rise, people will buy more of them.*
c. *The government should control the prices of essential items such as electricity and gasoline and basic foodstuff.*
d. *Cigarettes and alcohol should be banned.*
e. *Lower interest rates on credit cards will encourage people to spend more.*
f. *The current interest charges on credit cards are much too high.*
g. *Lower interest rates across the board will have a positive impact on job creation.*
h. *Higher interest rates on loans will result in more consumption and more investment spending.*

Requirement and Clue: *Does it talk about what is, was, or will be or does it talk about what ought to be? It is important to remember that positive statements may be true or false.*

Solution:

a. One way of increasing the number of units of air conditioners sold is to reduce their prices. (P)
b. If the prices of air conditioners rise, people will buy more of them. (P)
c. The government should control the prices of essential items such as electricity and gasoline and basic foodstuff. (N)
d. Cigarettes and alcohol should be banned. (N)
e. Lower interest rates on credit cards will encourage people to spend more. (P)
f. The current interest charges on credit cards are much too high. (N)
g. Lower interest rates across the board will have a positive impact on job creation. (P)
h. Higher interest rates on loans will result in more consumption and more investment spending. (P)

Problem 1-31

If economics is a science, why do economists disagree?

Requirement and Clue: *Science is not determined by the amount of agreement or disagreement. State that natural scientists sometimes disagree. Then discuss reasons for disagreement among economists.*

Solution:

Disagreement among economists has nothing to do with whether or not economics is a science. Physics and chemistry are sciences yet physicists disagree, and chemists disagree. Economists disagree for different reasons. First, economists have different values, and they judge economic situations and events differently. When economists are asked to express their opinions about some economic action, they may try to be objective, but their objectivity might be coloured by their own moral sentiments. One economist might argue that wearing a seat belt prevents injuries in a collision, and therefore severe fines should be levied on people caught without wearing seatbelts in their cars. Another economist might take the position that the compulsory use of seatbelts is an unnecessary infringement of people's rights, and it's entirely their business if they don't want to wear seatbelts. Therefore the government has no business levying fines on people who do not wear seatbelts.

But it is not only on such normative issues that economists disagree. They disagree also on positive issues. Different explanations exist as to how the economy actually operates, and it is not always clear which explanation is best. That is, economists may disagree over the appropriate model of the economy, and the available data might not be such as to allow for definitive conclusions so the disagreement persists.

Economists may disagree even though they use the same economic model. They may agree on the qualitative aspects but disagree on the quantitative aspects. For example, two economists might agree that a fall in interest rates will result in an increase in the level of investment. They might disagree, however, over the magnitude of the increase, one claiming that the increase will be negligible, and the other claiming that the increase will be significant. This type of disagreement can be prolonged because of the inadequacy of relevant data.

Problem 1-32

What is the difference between an endogenous variable and an exogenous variable?

Requirement and Clue: *Recall that "en" means inside or within and the "ex" means outside. Give grief definitions of the concepts with examples.*

Solution:

An endogenous variable is one whose value is determined within a model, while an exogenous variable is one whose value is determined outside a model. The difference can be illustrated by the following example. Suppose we are trying to determine the quantity of gasoline that people will buy in a week. We could say that the quantity of gasoline depends on the price of gasoline, suggesting that the lower the price of gasoline, the more of it people will buy. In this case, the quantity of gasoline and the price of gasoline are endogenous variables. We know, however, that the quantity of gasoline that people will buy also depends on their income. In this case, income will be an exogenous variable.

Problem 1-33

Distinguish between stocks and flows. Give an example of each.

Requirement and Clue: *Notice that this is a two-part problem. Address each part in order. Define each concept. Remember to use the time dimension as a distinguishing feature.*

Solution:

A stock (or stock variable) is the amount of anything existing *at a particular time* while a flow (or flow variable) is the change in a stock *during a period of time.* A noticeable feature of these concepts is that a stock does not need a time dimension (per day, per hour, per year) but a flow does. Examples of stocks are the quantity of books in your school and the amount of money you have in your purse or wallet. Examples of flows are the amount of gasoline you purchase each week and the amount of money you earn each month.

Problem 1-34

Indicate whether each of the following variables is a stock (S) or a flow (F).

A. *The current balance on your credit card*
B. *The amount you spend each semester on books*
C. *The number of students in your economics class*
D. *The amount invested to start a business*
E. *The amount allocated each year to maintain a company's plant and equipment*
F. *The estimated amount of oil in an oil well*
G. *The amount of oil extracted from an oil well each month*
H. *The total amount of taxes collected by the government each year*
I. *The total amount of taxes collected by the government on April 30, 2013*
J. *The amount of money a family spends on groceries each month*
K. *The number of a particular type of car produced by General Motors on October 7*
L. *The number of CDs you currently own*

Requirement and Clue: *Check for the existence of a time dimension.*

Solution:

A. The current balance on your credit card (S)
B. The amount you spend each semester on books (F)
C. The number of students in your economics class (S)
D. The amount invested to start a business (S)
E. The amount allocated each year to maintain a company's plant and equipment (F)
F. The estimated amount of oil in an oil well (S)
G. The amount of oil extracted from an oil well each month (F)
H. The total amount of taxes collected by the government each year (F)
I. The total amount of taxes collected by the government on April 30, 2013 (S)
J. The amount of money a family spends on groceries each month (F)
K. The number of a particular type of car produced by General Motors on October 7 (S)
L. The number of CDs you currently own (S)

Problem 1-35

A seller of a particular type of computers wanted to know how a change in the price of her computers would affect the quantity of computers sold. So she lowered her price slightly and noticed that the quantity sold increased. On the basis of the result of this experiment, can she conclude that the increase in the quantity sold was due to the lower price?

Requirement and Clue: *This could be a "Post Hoc" fallacy. Recognize that the increase in quantity sold could be the result of a change in some factor other than the lower price.*

Solution:

This question is related to the "Post Hoc" fallacy. The fallacy lies in thinking that because event A precedes event, then event B must have been caused by event A. In the case of the computer seller, it could very well be that the increase in the quantity of computers sold had more to do with an increase in income, an increase in the prices of competing types of computers, or an increase in people's interests in computers resulting from a successful advertising campaign than with a fall in the price of this particular type of computers.

Problem 1-36

Define and distinguish between macroeconomics and microeconomics.

Requirement and Clue: *It is clear from the problem that it is not enough simply to define both concepts. You must also highlight the difference between them. Examples of microeconomic and macroeconomic problems would be helpful in showing the difference.*

Solution:

Macroeconomics is the study of broad economic aggregates (totals) such as inflation, unemployment in the economy as a whole, total production, and economic growth. The focus of macroeconomics is the economy as a whole. For example, one concept with which macroeconomics deals is gross domestic product (GDP) which is an aggregation or summing up of the total output of goods and services produced by all economic units and treating it as a single whole. A typical macroeconomic problem would be to determine the effect of a tax change on the overall level of activity within an entire economy.

In contrast to macroeconomics, microeconomics is the study of the behavior of the individual components of the economy, such as firms and households, and the economic relationship among them. Basic to the study of microeconomics is the efficiency with which scarce resources are allocated among various uses. Microeconomics focuses upon individual, rather than aggregate economic data. A typical microeconomic problem would be to determine the price that a firm should charge in order to maximize its profits.

Problem 1-37

Indicate whether each of the following falls under microeconomics (Micro) or macroeconomics (Macro):

a. *A study of the major causes of the 2007-2009 recession*
b. *A theory explaining why the prices of personal computers has declined over the years*
c. *A model explaining the effect of an increase in wages on the overall level of employment*
d. *An explanation of how a tax on cigarettes affects the price of cigarettes*
e. *A theory that explains the economic role of banks in a society*
f. *A theory explaining the price that firms should charge in order to maximum their profits*
g. *An explanation of how consumers should spend their income in order to maximize their satisfaction*
h. *A study of how an economy allocates its scarce resources among competing ends*
i. *A model showing that when interest rates fall, total consumer and investment spending both increase*
j. *A theory that explains how minimum wage legislation affects employment in an economy*

Requirement and Clue: *This problem is designed to test your understanding of the difference between micro and macro issues. It's macro if it deals with the whole economy; otherwise, it's micro.*

Solution:

a. A study of the major causes of the 2007-2009 recession (Macro)
b. A theory explaining why the prices of personal computers has declined over the years (Micro)
c. A model explaining the effect of an increase in wages on the overall level of employment (Macro)
d. An explanation of how a tax on cigarettes affects the price of cigarettes (Micro)
e. A theory that explains the economic role of banks in a society (Macro)
f. A theory explaining the price that firms should charge in order to maximum their profits (Micro)
g. An explanation of how consumers should spend their income in order to maximize their satisfaction (Micro)
h. A study of how an economy allocates its scarce resources among competing ends (Micro)
i. A model showing that when interest rates fall, total consumer and investment spending both increase (Macro)
j. A theory that explains how minimum wage legislation affects employment in an economy (Macro)

Multiple-Choice

In each case, circle the letter that corresponds with the correct answer.

1. Having an understanding of economics is important because:

a. it guarantees a good job with a good salary
b. it insulates you against any type of unemployment
c. it helps you to think logically
d. everyone agrees that it is by far the most important subject to study

Answer: c

Reason: Economics is analytical and it develops a particular way of thinking and making decisions. Economics helps to develop the science and art of logical thinking.

2. One of the main disadvantages of understanding economics is that:

a. it gives one a false view of world affairs
b. although it helps one to understand the economy, it does not help one to understand society

c. it is an extremely difficult subject and studying it does tend to reduce personal satisfaction

d. none of the above

Answer: d

Reason: One would be hard pressed to find a single disadvantage of understanding economics. That's why it is compulsory in many college and university programs.

3. A knowledge of economics is important because:

a. it guarantees perpetual employment

b. it helps us to understand many of the issues that affect our lives directly and indirectly

c. it ensures that we will always make decisions that are in our own self interest

d. all of the above

Answer: b

Reason: Many of the issues facing us today are of an "economic" nature.

4. Economists are employed:

a. only in profit-seeking companies

b. only by the government

c. only in international organizations, such as the United Nations and the World Bank

d. in all of the above

Answer: d

Reason: Economists are employed in a vast number of private and public organizations, both domestic and international.

5. Scarcity gives rise to:

a. Unnecessary waste

b. Inefficient methods of production

c. the necessity to choose

d. full employment of resources

Answer: c

Reason: Because of scarcity, society cannot have all the goods and services that it would like to have. Society is therefore forced to choose.

6. Choice is a direct result of:

a. pride b. extravagance

c. scarcity d. all of the above

Answer: c

Reason: Had it not been for scarcity, society would not have to choose.

7. By scarcity economists mean:

a. low stocks of goods

b. limited availability in the face of unlimited wants

c. limited wants in the face of unlimited resources

d. limited resources as well as limited wants

Answer: b

Reason: Economic or relative scarcity relates the amount available to the amount required. It exists when resources are insufficient to produce all the goods and services required to satisfy human wants.

8. Which of the following statements is true?

a. Scarcity would not exist if society were more efficient in its production of goods and services

b. Scarcity would not exist if society as a whole were more efficient in its use of available resources

c. Scarcity is totally unrelated to a society's resources

d. Scarcity would exist even if society used its available resources as efficiently as possible

Answer: d

Reason: The efficient use of resources would not make resources sufficient to produce all the goods and services that people want.

9. Scarcity exists:

a. Even in relatively rich countries like Canada and the United States

b. Only in underdeveloped countries like Haiti and Afghanistan

c. Only in countries ruled by dictators

d. Only in countries with limited resources

Answer: a

Reason: Even in Canada and the United States, people's wants far outstrip the economy's ability to produce enough goods and services.

10. Which of the following statements is correct?

a. Canada and the United States do not have to worry about scarcity because their citizens enjoy high standards of living

b. Democracy and the Rule of Law prevent Canada, the United States, and the United Kingdom from experiencing scarcity

c. As long as citizens of a country have limited resources and unlimited wants, they will experience scarcity

d. None of the above

Answer: c

Reason: This is the very essence of scarcity.

11. Because of scarcity:

a. individuals, not society, are forced to choose

b. society, not individuals, has to choose

c. neither society nor individuals have to choose

d. both society and individuals have to choose

Answer: d

Reason: The existence of limited resources coupled with unlimited wants (scarcity) is an individual and collective problem, forcing all to choose.

12. Economics is a social science because:

a. its variables are all measureable

b. economists like to socialize

c. ultimately, it all boils down to economics

d. it deals with human behaviour

Answer: d

Reason: Any discipline that studies human behaviour is a social science. Economics does this.

13. Which of the following is *not* a social science?

a. Chemistry b. Psychology

c. Political science d. Sociology

Answer: a

Reason: Chemistry does not study human behavior.

14. Which of the following disciplines studies the origin and development of humans as social beings?

a. Biology b. Anthropology

c. Economics d. All of the above

Answer: b

Reason: That is the definition of anthropology.

15. Economics deals with:

a. how people make decisions about the use of scarce resources to satisfy their wants

b. the mental characteristics associated with a particular kind of behavior

c. the nature and functions of the state and the way we are governed

d. the study of human social behavior, society and its institutions

Answer: a

Reason: Choices b, c, and d define psychology, political science, and sociology respectively. Choice "a" defines the subject matter of economics.

16. Which of the following definitions of economics is preferable?

a. The study of buyers and sellers in markets exchanging goods and services

b. The study of how a government organizes production activities

c. The study of how people use scarce resources to satisfy their wants

d. The study of all the factors that contribute to human happiness

Answer: c

Reason: No "preferred" definition of economics can omit the use of scarce resources to satisfy wants. This is the heart of economics.

17. A social science is:

a. any discipline that is socially acceptable

b. any discipline that studies human behavior

c. any discipline that avoids the use of mathematics

d. none of the above

Answer: b

Reason: Social science is the study of human behavior.

18. The government owns a quarry. It hires workers with pickaxes, shovels, and electric drills to extract stones from the quarry. The stones are loaded on to trucks and taken to a site where a road is being built. In this case:

a. the quarry, the shovels, the pickaxes, and the drills are all examples of capital

b. the quarry is land, the stones in it are capital, and the quarry workers are labour

c. the quarry and the stones in it are land, and the shovels, pickaxes, and drills are capital

d. the trucks are capital but the workers and the shovels, pickaxes, and drills represent labour

Answer: c

Reason: All natural resources (the quarry and the stones) are classified as land. Any human-made resources (shovels, pickaxes, and drills) are classified as capital.

19. Factors of production are:

a. the costs involved in using resources to produce goods and services

b. all the factors that must be considered when producing resources

c. things that can be used to produce goods and services

d. things like sunlight and air that we cannot produce

Answer: c

Reason: They are the resources (land, labour, capital, and entrepreneurial services) used to produce goods and services.

20. Alcohol and cigarettes are:

a. bads because they are harmful

b. bads because society frowns on their use

c. goods because they satisfy wants

d. goods because their sale is not illegal

Answer: c

Reason: Goods are tangible things that give satisfaction.

21. Illegal substances and chemicals, and items smuggled into a country, are classified as:

a. bads because taxes are not paid on them

b. bads because they are illegal

c. goods because someone wants them

d. goods because they are produced

Answer: c

Reason: They give satisfaction; therefore they are defined as goods.

22. The difference between a good and a service is that:

a. a good is tangible while a service is not

b. a service is tangible while a good is not

c. a good gives satisfaction while a service does not

d. a service gives satisfaction while a good does not

Answer: a

Reason: Both goods and services give satisfaction. Goods have physical substance. They can be touched. Services have no physical substance. They cannot be touched.

23. Bads are:

a. things like garbage and pollution that are unwanted and give no satisfaction

b. things like cigarettes, alcohol and guns that hurt people

c. items whose use is declared to be illegal

d. all of the above

Answer: a

Reason: Bads are undesirable. People are willing to pay money to get rid of bads.

24. An economy produces:

a. goods but not bads

b. both goods and bads

c. bads always as a result of people's wants for them

d. none of the above

Answer: b

Reason: An economy does not make a point of producing bads; but in the process of producing goods, some bads are also produced.

25. Which of the following statements about resources is true?

a. All resources are scarce

b. Some resources such as air and sunlight in most circumstances are not scarce

c. All resources command a price in the market

d. None of the above

Answer: b

Reason: All economic resources are scarce in an economic sense. Some resources, however, such as sea water in the ocean, are not scarce.

26. Resources are also referred to as:

a. consumer goods and services

b. goods generating agents

c. factors of production

d. all of the above

Answer: c

Reason: Resources are the factors used to produce things, hence the name.

27. The various types of resources can be grouped into the following four categories:

a. Goods, services, natural, and manufactured

b. Capital, human, scarce, and desired

c. Land, labour, capital, and entrepreneurship

d. Land, natural resources, capital, and man-made resources

Answer: c

Reason: This is the four-way classification normally used by economists.

28. In economics, land refers to:

a. real estate

b. the solid portion of the earth only

c. the solid portion of the earth and water only

d. all natural resources

Answer: d

Reason: Economists group all "gifts of nature" into this category called land.

29. In economics, forests, lakes, oil, and minerals are classified as a resource category called:

a. land b. wealth producers

b. capital d. none of the above

Answer: a

Reason: These are all examples of natural resources that economists categorize as land.

30. Which of the following is an example of labour?

a. The work produced by a machine to replace human effort

b. The services provided by a stand-up comedian

c. A plow that prepares a field for planting

d. None of the above

Answer: b

Reason: Labour is human resources.

31. In economics, capital refers to:

a. any produced means of production

b. anything that can be used to produce goods and services

c. items such as land, coal mines, and crops that can be sold for money

d. the income that people earn for their labour services

Answer: a

Reason: Capital is any manufactured factor of production.

32. Entrepreneurship is:

a. any act of production for money

b. the organization of land, labour, and capital into the production process

c. is just another name for marketing services which involves bringing goods and services from producers to consumers

d. the use of the most sophisticated method of production

Answer: b

Reason: Entrepreneurship includes the functions of managing, coordinating, leading, and risk-taking necessary for the production of goods and services.

33. Entrepreneurial skills include:

a. innovative skills

b. risk-taking

c. leadership skills

d. all of the above

Answer: d

Reason: The skills listed are all required to perform the entrepreneurial function.

34. The income generated by natural resources is called:

a. land b. natural money

c. rent d. profit

Answer: c

Reason: Land (or natural resources) earns rent.

35. Capital generates a type of income called:

a. profit income

b. rental income

c. wages and salaries

d. interest and dividends

Answer: d

Reason: Interest and dividends are earned by capital.

36. For their services, entrepreneurs earn a type of income called:

a. salaries b. profit

c. interest income d. rent

Answer: b

Reason: The reward for entrepreneurial services is called profits.

37. If someone is paid wages or salaries at the end of a certain period, we know that he or she provided:

a. entrepreneurial services
b. labour services
c. real capital
d. natural resources

Answer: b

Reason: *Wages and salaries are the reward for labour services.*

38. The sum of wages and salaries, rent, interest and dividends, and profit can be correctly called:

a. total income
b. total factor earnings
c. both a and b
d. neither a nor b

Answer: c

Reason: *The items listed constitute the total earnings from the factors of production.*

39. The main elements of the scientific approach include:

a. argumentation, realistic assumptions, and mathematics
b. mathematics, estimation, and statistics
c. educated guesses, estimation, and judgement
d. observation and measurement, hypotheses, and verification

Answer: d

Reason: *The scientific procedure involves data collection and observation, measurement, the formation of hypotheses, and finally testing for the purpose of verifying or rejecting the hypothesis.*

40. A hypothesis is:

a. a statement of known facts
b. a statement of suspected relationships among variables
c. an assumption that simplifies a complicated relationship
d. a conclusion that is drawn from facts that cannot be observed

Answer: b

Reason: *It is an "if...then..." statement relating cause and effect. It states how variables are believed to be related until refuted or verified by testing.*

41. An economic model is:

a. an exact replication of an economy with all its features intact
b. a simplification of a real economy with irrelevant details stripped away
c. is a vivid portrayal of what an economy ought to look like
d. none of the above

Answer: b

Reason: *An economic model or theory is a simplified representation of a real economy or of some part of it.*

42. Which of the following statements is correct?

a. An economic model can be expressed verbally, mathematically, or graphically
b. Only models expressed mathematically can be used to explain economic reality
c. Economic models that are expressed verbally should always be chosen in preference to those expressed graphically
d. An economic model cannot be expressed verbally

Answer: a

Reason: *Those are the various forms that can be used to present economic models. Usually, more than one form is used to present the same model.*

43. The components of an economic model are:

a. definitions, assumptions, hypotheses and predictions
b. equations, questions and answers, and solutions
c. ceteris paribus and normative statements
d. positive statements and ceteris paribus

Answer: a

Reason: *The elements listed in choice "a" are the constituent parts of an economic model.*

44. *Ceteris paribus* means:

a. all is well
b. nothing else matters
c. other things being equal
d. certain to occur

Answer: c

Reason: *This is the Latin phrase used to hold all other influences on a variable constant in order to examine the effect of a single variable on some other.*

45. Statements of the conditions under which a model is supposed to work are called:

a. hypotheses
b. predictions
c. assumptions
d. definitions

Answer: c

Reason: *Assumptions specify the "rules of the game" so to speak. The model is expected to work well provided that certain conditions are fulfilled.*

46. Statements about suspected cause-effect relations among variables are called:

a. assumptions
b. hypotheses
c. definitions
d. ceteris paribus

Answer: b

Reason: *A hypothesis is a statement about cause and effect.*

47. Positive statements:

a. are statements about facts
b. can be verified
c. can be true or false
d. all of the above

Answer: d

Reason: *Positive statements are statements about what is, was, or will be. They can be true or false and can be verified or falsified by referring to the facts.*

48. Normative statements:

a. are statements about facts
b. are statements of opinions

c. can be easily verified

d. generate the best hypotheses

Answer: b

Reason: Normative statements are subjective statements about what ought to be. They are value judgments and opinions.

49. Economists may disagree because:

a. they have different values

b. they use different models of the economy

c. neither a nor b

d. both a and b

Answer: d

Reason: Major reasons for disagreement among economists are differences in values, the use of different models, and differences about the severity of the impact of one variable on another.

50. A variable whose value is determined within a model is called:

a. an endogenous variable

b. an exogenous variable

c. a stock variable

d. a flow variable

Answer: a

Reason: The prefix "en" means within or inside. An endogenous variable is one whose value is determined inside a model.

51. The branch of economics that studies the behavior of individual economic units and focuses on resources allocation is called:

a. independent economics

b. econometrics.

c. microeconomics

d. macroeconomics

Answer: c

Reason: Microeconomics deals with the study of the individual units that make up the economy and focuses on the allocation of resources.

52. Macroeconomics studies:

a. the allocation of scarce resources among competing ends and is also called price theory

b. the economy as a whole and analyzes such topics as inflation, unemployment, and economic growth

c. group behavior and institutions in a social setting

d. all of the above

Answer: b

Reason: Macroeconomics studies the behavior of broad economics aggregates such as the topics mentioned in choice b.

True or False

Determine whether each of the following statements is true or false.

1. As important as economics may be, economic analysis sheds no light on the more serious issues that face society today.

Answer: False

Explanation: Some of society's most pressing issues are "economic" in nature.

2. One of the most important reasons for studying economics is that it develops a particular way of thinking and making decisions.

Answer: True

3. Economists find employment everywhere except as government employees.

Answer: False

Explanation: Economists are employed at all levels of government.

4. Scarcity is the situation that exists when resources are inadequate to produce all the goods and services that people want.

Answer: True

5. The means available to satisfy all society's wants are severely limited.

Answer: True

6. Advanced countries such as Canada, the United States, Sweden, and the United States are lands of plenty, well endowed with resources, so they do not have the problem of scarcity.

Answer: False

Explanation: With all their resources, these countries still cannot produce all the goods and services that would be required to satisfy all human wants.

7. Scarcity and the necessity to choose are both facts of life, but the two are unrelated.

Answer: False

Explanation: The necessity to choose is a direct result of scarcity.

8. Particular individuals in a society may be confronted with scarcity but society as a whole does not face scarcity.

Answer: False

Explanation: Because society's resources are limited (scarce), the society cannot produce all the goods and services required to satisfy everyone's wants.

9. Economics is a social science by virtue of the fact that economists are social beings.

Answer: False

Explanation: Economics is a social science because it studies human behavior, not because of any characteristics that economists may possess.

10. Resources are the things that are needed to produce the items needed to satisfy our wants.

Answer: True

11. In economics, resources are referred to as factors of production.

Answer: True

12. The essential difference between goods and services is that goods are intangible while services are tangible.

Answer: False

Explanation: Goods are tangible while services are intangible.

13. Our society is now so sophisticated and cares so much about human well-being that the economy no longer produces bads.

Answer: False

Explanation: Although serious efforts may be made to reduce the production of bads, the economy cannot avoid producing bads.

14. One of the fundamental teachings of economics is that all resources are scarce.

Answer: False

Explanation: Some resources such as sunlight and air are not scarce.

15. Economists generally classify resources into land, labour, capital and entrepreneurial services.

Answer: True

16. In economics, land includes only the solid portion of the earth.

Answer: False

Explanation: Land includes all natural resources, including the solid portion of the earth.

17. In economics, land includes minerals embedded in the earth, fish in the seas, oxygen in the air, and lakes.

Answer: True

18. In our modern society, the only capital of importance is money.

Answer: False

Explanation: Although money is important and may be considered to be capital by some people, we cannot underestimate the importance of real capital: highways, buildings, machinery, etc.

19. Human capital is the total amount of money owned by human beings and is also referred to as human wealth.

Answer: False

Explanation: Human capital does not include money. It refers to education, training, skills and health possessed by humans.

20. Human capital refers to the education, training, skills, health, and so on, that improve the quality of labour.

Answer: True

21. Entrepreneurial skills include managerial skills, organizational skills, decision-making skills, innovative skills, leadership skills, and risk-taking.

Answer: True

22. Capital generates a type of income known as profit.

Answer: False

Explanation: Capital generates interest and dividends; entrepreneurship generates profits.

23. Interest and dividends are a type of income earned by entrepreneurs.

Answer: False

Explanation: Entrepreneurs earn profits; capital earns interest and dividends.

24. Wages and salaries are the compensation for labour services.

Answer: True

25. Economics is not a science; therefore the scientific approach cannot be applied to it.

Answer: False

Explanation: In their study of the economy and economic phenomena, economists do follow the scientific procedure.

26. The scientific approach involves observation and measurement, the formulation of hypotheses, and verification.

Answer: True

27. An example of a hypothesis in economics is: "By the end of the year, the rate of unemployment will fall to 5%.

Answer: False

Explanation: A hypothesis expresses a cause-effect relationship among variables. The statement given is a forecast.

28. An economic model is a presentation of an economy at its best—an economy that is worthy of imitating.

Answer: False

Explanation: An economic model is just a simplified economy with many details omitted.

29. The ceteris paribus assumption allows economists to ensure that all the factors that can affect a given situation are allowed to change.

Answer: False

Explanation: On the contrary, the ceteris paribus assumption ensures that only the factor being considered is allowed to change. All other factors are assumed to remain constant.

30. An economic prediction and an economic forecast are one and the same thing.

Answer: False

Explanation: An economic prediction is an "if...then..." statement. A forecast simply assigns a future value to a variable.

31. The following is an example of an economic prediction: "If interest rates rise, people will tend to save more."

Answer: True

32. The following is an example of an economic prediction: "In the next six months, the price of gasoline will be no more than $1.33/litre.

Answer: False

Explanation: The statement is an example of an economic forecast.

33. The goodness of a model can only be judged by the realism of its assumptions.

Answer: False

Explanation: *The goodness of a model should be judged primarily by its predictive ability.*

34. A statement cannot be positive unless it is true.

Answer: False

Explanation: *A positive statement may be true or false.*

35. Normative statements are value judgments or statements of opinions about what ought to be.

Answer: True

36. Economists can never disagree because economics is a science.

Answer: False

Explanation: *The scientific nature of any discipline is unrelated to agreement among its practitioners. Scientists do disagree.*

37. An exogenous variable can never become an endogenous variable, and an endogenous variable can never become an exogenous variable.

Answer: False

Explanation: *Any variable can be endogenous or exogenous. It all depends on the particular model.*

38. Stocks and flows are both variables.

Answer: True

A stock is a constant while a flow is a variable.

Answer: False

Explanation: *Stocks and flows are both variables.*

39. A significant difference between a stock and a flow is that a flow needs a time dimension while a stock does not.

Answer: True

40. A stock needs a time dimension while a flow does not.

Answer: False

Explanation: *A flow needs a time dimension, not a stock.*

41. If A increases when B decreases, we know that the increase in A is caused by the decrease in B.

Answer: False

Explanation: *Not necessarily. This could be a case of the post hoc fallacy.*

42. The *post hoc fallacy* is another name for *ceteris paribus*.

Answer: False

Explanation: *They are distinct concepts.*

43. The sequential fallacy is the erroneous conclusion that one event causes another simply because it precedes the other.

Answer: True

44. Microeconomics studies the behavior of individual economic units and focuses on the allocation of resources.

Answer: True

45. Microeconomics is concerned with what determines the composition of total output and analyzes such topics as the behavior of consumers and firms, the determination of relative prices, and the distribution of the economy's output among various groups.

Answer: True

46. Macroeconomics studies individual economic units rather than the economy as a whole.

Answer: False

Explanation: *The statement would be true with respect to microeconomics.*

47. A thorough understanding of the operation of the economic system requires only a good understanding of microeconomics.

Answer: False

Explanation: *Much of the operation of an economic system has to do with macroeconomics.*

48. A thorough understanding of the operation of the economic system requires only a good understanding of macroeconomics

Answer: False

Explanation: *Microeconomics is also important for understanding the operation of the economic system.*

49. A thorough understanding of the operation of the economic system requires knowledge of both microeconomics and macroeconomics.

Answer: True

Completion

Fill in the blanks

Use each word or combination of words from the list exactly once.
*(**Hint**: Proceed by elimination)*

Word list

Assumptions - Bads - Bads - Capital - Ceteris Paribus - Dividends - Econometrics - Economic Model - Economic Prediction - Endogenous - Exogenous - Entrepreneurial Services - Goods - Services - Human Capital - Hypotheses - Interest - Labour - Labour - Land - Land - Macroeconomics - Microeconomics - Positive - Post Hoc - Profit - Real - Salaries - Scarcity - Social Science - Social - Scarce - Stock - Flow - Stock - Wages

Questions

1. Economics is the ____________ science that studies how people use ____________ resources to satisfy their unlimited wants.

2. ____________ is the situation that exists when resources are inadequate to produce all the goods and services that people want.

3. A ____________ is any discipline that studies human behavior.

4. ____________ are tangible things that satisfy wants; ____________ are intangible things that satisfy wants.

5. ____________ are things that are unwanted and do not give any satisfaction. Toxic waste and environmental pollution are examples of____________.

6. Economists classify the various types of resources into ____________, ____________, ____________, and ____________ ____________.

7. ____________ ____________ refers to the education, training, skills, health, and so on, that improve the quality of labour.

8. The services rendered by sales representatives, lawyers, teachers, doctors, musicians, and actors are all classified under the category of____________.

9. ____________ capital includes power tools, equipment, buildings, and machinery.

10. Labour earns ____________ and ____________; capital earns ____________ and ____________; ____________ earns rent; and entrepreneurial services earn ____________.

11. An ____________ ____________ is a simplification of the real economy or some aspect of it, and it consists only of the factors that appear to pertain most to what is being studied.

12. ____________ are statements of the conditions under which a model is supposed to work.

13. The assumption by which an economist isolates the effect of an economic variable in a situation is the ____________ ____________ assumption.

14. Statements of suspected relationships among variables are referred to as ____________.

15. An ____________ ____________ is a statement about the general direction of an economic variable resulting from the fulfilment of certain conditions.

16. The branch of economics that deals with the use of statistical methods to test economic hypotheses is called ____________.

17. ____________ economics explains or describes how the economy actually works and the behaviour of economic units. It attempts to explain what will happen under certain conditions, but it does not explain what the economic situation ought to be.

18. An____________variable is one whose value is determined within a model while an ____________ variable is one whose value is determined by factors outside the model.

19. A ____________ variable is the quantity of anything existing at a particular time, while a ____________ variable is a measure of the change in the ____________ over time.

20. A severe drought destroys the pumpkin crop in a country one year. The seeds that farmer McDonald intends to plant the following spring are affected, without his knowledge, by radiation that causes each plant to produce twice as many pumpkins. Upon seeing his bumper crop the following fall, farmer McDonald concludes that a drought one year will cause a bumper crop the next. This is an example of the ____________ ____________ fallacy.

21. ____________ studies the behaviour of individual economic units such as households and firms and focuses on the allocation of resources.

22. ____________ studies the behaviour of broad economic aggregates such as total income and overall unemployment.

Solutions

1. Social, Scarce
2. Scarcity
3. Social, Science
4. Goods, Services
5. Bads, Bads
6. Land, Labour, Capital, and Entrepreneurial Services—In Any Order
7. Human Capital
8. Labour
9. Real
10. Wages, Salaries; Interest, Dividends; Land; Profit
11. Economic Model
12. Assumptions
13. Ceteris Paribus
14. Hypotheses
15. Economic Prediction
16. Econometrics
17. Positive
18. Endogenous, Exogenous
19. Stock, Flow, Stock
20. Post Hoc
21. Microeconomics
22. Macroeconomics

2 FUNCTIONS, GRAPHS & SLOPES

SYNOPSIS

To a large extent, the study of economics involves the study of relationships among variables. The *functional notation* is a very convenient way of expressing relationships among variables. For example, the notion that consumption depends on income and on the rate of interest may be conveniently expressed by the functional notation as:

$$C = C(Y,r)$$

Where C represents consumption, Y income, and r t he rate of interest. In this expression, consumption is the **dependent** variable while income and the rate of interest are **independent** variables.

Graphs are also used extensively in economics to show relationships among variables. An upward-sloping curve illustrates a **direct** relationship while a downward-sloping curve illustrates an inverse relationship. It is difficult to use graphs in cases where more than two variables are involved.

The **slope** of a line is the vertical distance divided by the horizontal distance. A declining line has a negative slope while a rising line has a positive slope. A 45-degree line through the origin has a slope of 1. The slope of a non-linear curve at a point on the curve is the slope of the line drawn tangent to the curve at the particular point.

LEARNING OBJECTIVES

In connection with this module, you should be able to:

1. use symbols and the functional notation to express relationships among variables
2. distinguish between dependent and independent variables
3. use graphs to represent certain relationships
4. explain and calculate slopes

DEFINITIONS & CONCEPTS

You should be able to define the following terms and concepts:

functional notation
function
dependent variable
independent (explanatory) variable
graphs
direct relation
inverse relation
slope
negative slope
positive slope
slope of a non-linear curve

2

FUNCTIONS, GRAPHS & SLOPES

Concepts, Definitions & Problems

Problem 2-1

What is the functional notation and what is its main use in economics?

Requirement and Clue: *This is a two-part problem. Answer each part in order and do so as directly as possible. Think of occasions when you can use the functional notation in economics.*

Solution:

The functional notation is a way of expressing relationships among variables. A large part of economics is concerned with examining relationships among variables. The main use of the functional notation in economics is to express these relationships in a very compact way. For example, we can express the idea that an individual's income depends on his or her level of education. If we use the letter y to represent income and the letter e to denote the level of education, we can express the idea as follows:

$$y = f(e) \text{ or } y = y(e)$$

which means simply that income depends on (or is a function of) the level of education.

Problem 2-2

Use the functional notation to express each of the following statements:

a. *If the level of income (Y) changes, spending on consumer goods and services (C) will also change.*

b. *Changes in interest rates (r) cause changes in the amount of saving (S).*

c. *The quantity of cell phones purchased (Q) depends on the price (P) of cell phones.*

d. *Attendance at the movies (A) is a function of the price of movie tickets (P).*

e. *Attendance at the movies (A) is a function of the price of movie tickets (P) and the weather (W).*

f. *Changes in interest rates (r) and the level of income (Y) affect the quantity of automobiles purchased (Q).*

g. *The amount of vacation (V) that people take depends on their income (Y) and the price of gasoline (P)*

h. *If the price of gasoline (P) changes, people will tend to change the number of automobile trips (T) taken.*

Requirement and Clue: *For this solution you must carefully determine which variable is dependent and which is independent.*

Solution:

C= C(Y)	e. A = A(P,W)
S = S(r)	f. Q = Q(r,Y)
Q = Q(P)	g. V = V(Y,P)
A = A(P)	h. T = T(P)

Problem 2-3

What is the difference between a dependent variable and an independent variable?

Requirement and Clue: *You are required to define each concept. Provide examples to illustrate the difference between them.*

Solution:

In a relationship among variables, the dependent variable is the variable that we are trying to explain, while the independent variable is the one that provides the explanation. An example will help to illustrate the difference. Consider the statement: "A family's grocery bill depends on the size of the family and on the family income." In this case, the family's grocery bill (what we are trying to explain) is the dependent variable, while the size of the family and family income (the variables that do the explaining) are independent variables.

Problem 2-4

What is the purpose of graphs in economics?

Requirement and Clue: *Think of graphs as illustrative pictures. Focus on relationships among variables.*

Solution:

For the most part, economics discusses relationships among variables, such as the relationship between income and consumption; interest rates and investment; saving and income; investment and economic growth, etc. Graphs are an effective way of showing relationships among variables, and since economics consists of so many of these relationships, economists find it useful to use graphs. Graphs add clarity to ideas that we try to express—they can actually *show* the changes that take place. For example, we can use graphs to show the growth in total production of goods and services within a country during a period of time. This type of graphic, visual presentation brings economic concepts to life. No wonder that graphs are used so pervasively in economics!

Problem 2-5

What methods or tools do economists use to express economic relationships? Give examples.

Requirement and Clue: *Graphs and tables will probably come to mind. Remember that words are tools also. Don't forget to give examples.*

Solution:

Economists use four methods of expressing economic relationships: verbal expressions (words), equations (functions), tables, and graphs. For example, the concept of total expenditure may be viewed in various ways. First, total expenditure may be expressed verbally as:

"Total expenditure equals price times quantity purchased."

We can also state that: "Total expenditure is a function of quantity purchased."

Second, we can express the idea using an equation:

TE = f(Q) where TE is total expenditure and Q denotes quantity purchased. This equation is saying that if quantity changes, total expenditure will change.

Third, the relationship can be expressed using a table. For example, if we know that the price of the item is $3.00, we can show the relationship in a table as follows:

Quantity	Total Expenditure
10	30
20	60
30	90
40	120

The fourth method of expressing the relationship is the graph shown below.

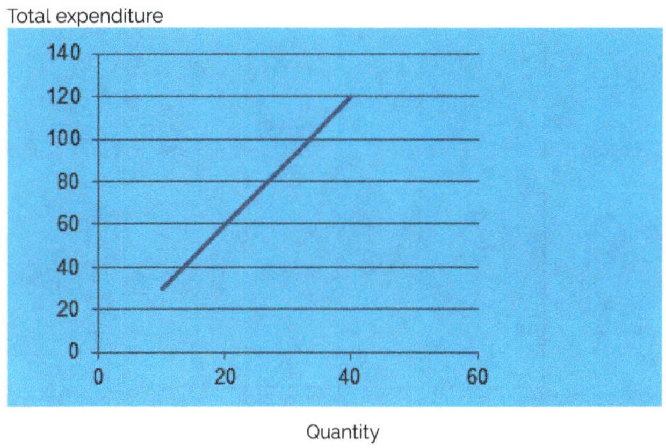

This graph shows the value of total expenditure for all possible quantities purchased. The graph makes certain information immediately apparent. For example, because the graph is upward-sloping, it is obvious that the relationship between quantity bought and total expenditure is positive.

Problem 2-6

Below are four graphs showing relationships between X and Y.

a. *In which of these graphs is the quantity of Y unrelated to the quantity of X?*

b. *In which of these graphs is the quantity of Y directly related to the quantity of X?*

c. *In which of these graphs are Y and X inversely related?*

d. *In which of these graphs is the quantity of X unrelated to the quantity of Y?*

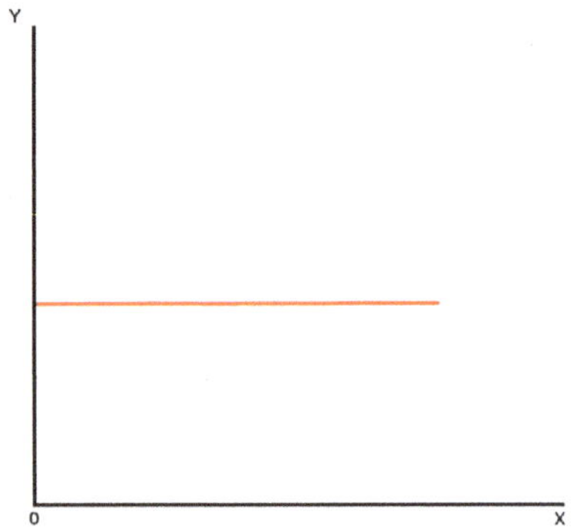

DIAGRAM 1

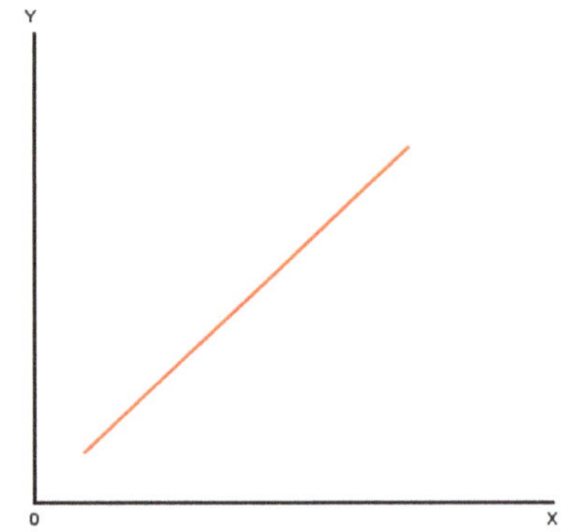

DIAGRAM 2

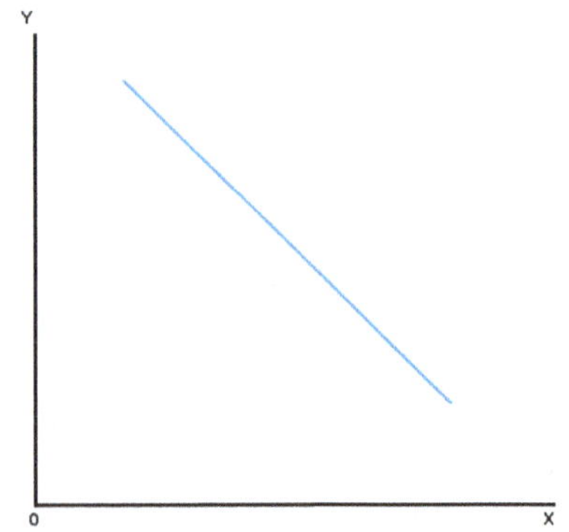

DIAGRAM 3

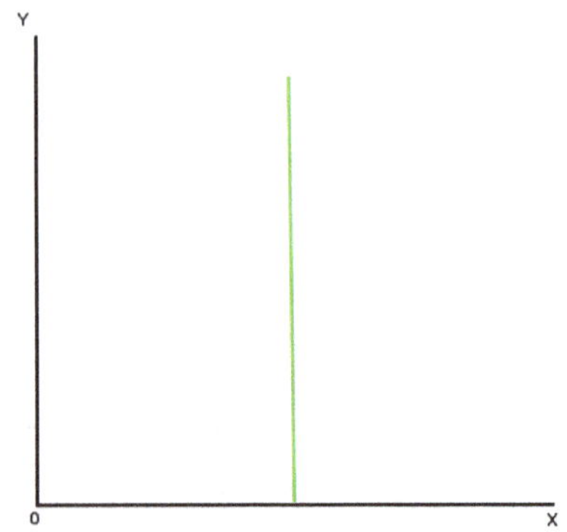

DIAGRAM 4

Requirement and Clue: *Think of direct and inverse relationships and how graphs can depict such relationships.*

Solution:

The quantity of Y is unrelated to the quantity of X in Diagram 1. No matter what value X takes, Y will remain the same.

a. The quantity of Y is directly related to the quantity X in Diagram 2. As X increases, Y also increases, and as X decreases, Y also decreases. These two variables move together in the same direction.

b. The quantity of Y is inversely related to the quantity of X in Diagram 3. As X increases, Y decreases. The two variables move in opposite directions.

c. The quantity of X is unrelated to the quantity of Y in Diagram 4. Here, X remains the same regardless of changes in Y.

Problem 2-7

Use words to express the idea contained in the following functional notations:

a. *C = C(Y,r,t) where C is consumption, Y is the level of income, r is the rate of interest, and t is time.*

b. *QMd = f(Y,r) where QMd is the quantity of money demanded, Y is the level of income, and r is the rate of interest.*

Requirement and Clue: *Recognize that the functional notation is nothing more than an idea expressed in the form of a mathematical function. You will need to identify the dependent and independent variables when using words.*

Solution:

a. *C = C(Y, r,t)* is read: Consumption is a function of the level of income, the rate of interest, and time, and it means that if either the level of income, the rate of interest, or time changes, consumption will also change.

b. *QMd = f(Y,r)* is read: The quantity of money demanded is a function of the level of income and the rate of interest, and it means that changes in the level of income or the rate of interest will cause changes in the quantity of money demanded.

Problem 2-8

In each of the following statements, identify the dependent and independent variables:

a. *The level of saving (S) depends on the level of income (Y).*

b. *If the level of income (Y) changes, the demand for money (Md) will change.*

c. *If the money supply (Ms) changes, the rate of interest (r) will also change.*

d. *Changes in the demand for money (Md) will cause the rate of interest (r) to change.*

e. *Changes in income (y) and the rate of interest (r) will cause the level of investment (I) to change.*

Requirement and Clue: *Recall that the dependent variable is the one* *we are trying to explain and the independent is the one that is doing the explaining.*

Solution:

a. *S* is the dependent variable and *Y* is the independent variable.
b. *Md* is the dependent variable and *Y* is the independent variable.
c. *r* is the dependent variable and *Ms* is the independent variable.
d. *r* is the dependent variable and *Md* is the independent variable.
e. *I* is the dependent variable and *y* and *r* are the independent variables.

Problem 2-9

Assume that the price of an item is $5.00.

a. *Construct a table to show total revenue (i.e. price times quantity) for quantities 1, 2, 3, 4, 5, 6 units sold.*
b. *Plot the information from your table on a graph with quantity on the horizontal axis and total revenue (TR) on the vertical axis.*

Requirement and Clue: *You require a two-column table: quantity for one and total revenue for the other. Your total revenue curve should be an upward-sloping straight line.*

Solution:

a.

Quantity	Total Revenue ($)
1	5
2	10
3	15
4	20
5	25
6	30

b.

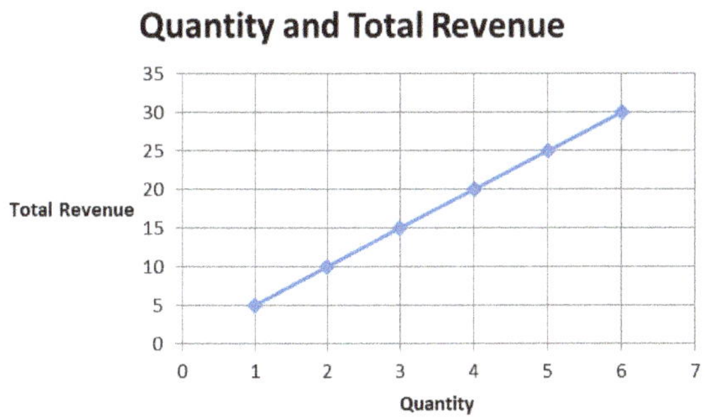

Problem 2-10

Draw graphs to illustrate the relationship you would expect to find between the following pairs of variables, and indicate whether the relationship is direct or inverse.

a. *The price of apples and the quantity of apples bought in a month.*
b. *The level of income and the frequency of eating out in restaurants.*
c. *The rate of interest and the frequency of credit card use.*
d. *The price of gasoline and the frequency of automobile trips.*
e. *The number of students and government spending on education.*

Requirement and Clue: Consider whether the variables move together in the same direction (direct—upward sloping graph) or in opposite directions (inverse—downward sloping graph).

Solution:

a. The higher the price of apples, other things being equal, the smaller the quantity that will be bought. This inverse relationship is shown by a downward-sloping curve as shown in Diagram A.

DIAGRAM A

b. It is reasonable to expect that the higher the level of income, the more frequently people will tend to eat at restaurants. This direct relationship is shown by the upward sloping curve in Diagram B.

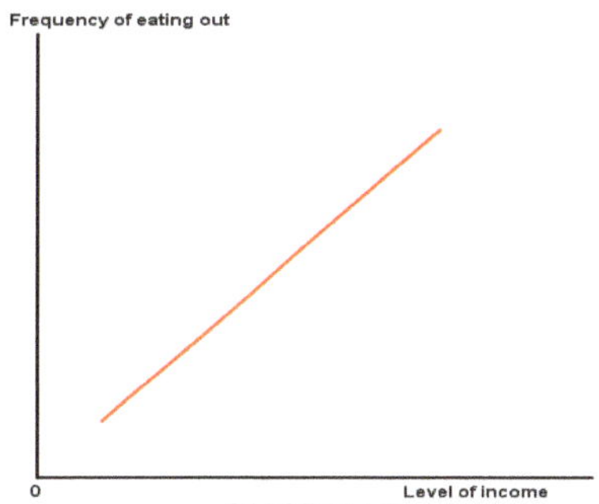

DIAGRAM B

c. Lower interest rates will tend to encourage credit card use, while high interest rates will tend to deter credit card use. This inverse relationship is shown by the downward sloping curve in Diagram C.

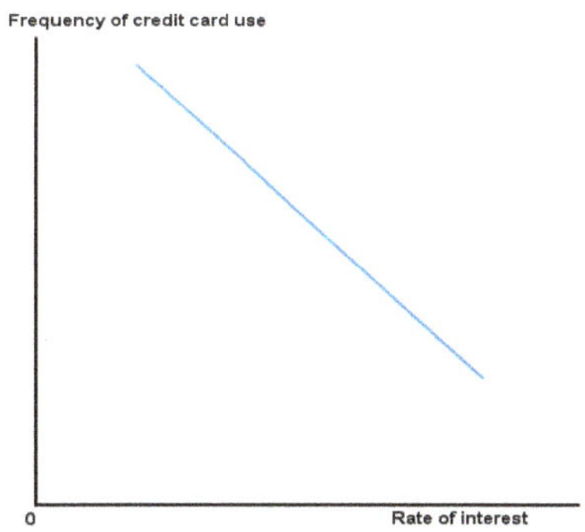

DIAGRAM C

d. People will tend to reduce the number of automobile trips when gasoline prices rise and to increase automobile trips when gasoline prices fall. This inverse relationship is shown by the downward sloping graph in Diagram D.

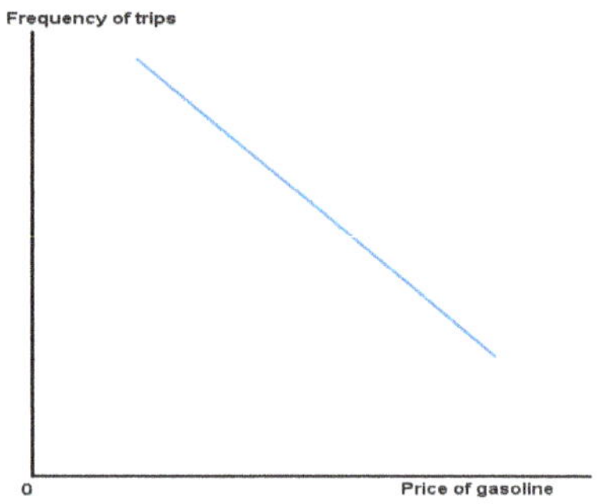

DIAGRAM D

e. Other things being equal, the greater the number of students, the more money the government will spend on education and vice versa. This direct relationship is shown by the upward sloping curve in Diagram E.

f.

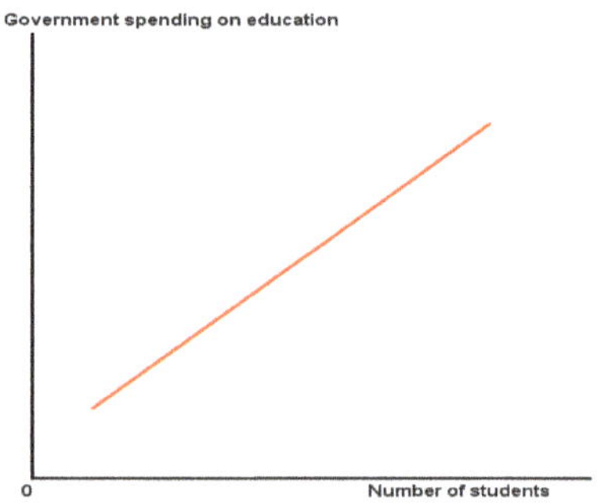

DIAGRAM E

Problem 2-11

What is the difference between a concave and a convex curve?

Requirement and Clue: *Illustrate with diagrams.*

Solution:

Concave and convex curves are used frequently in economics to illustrate behaviour of certain variables. A concave curve is bowed outward, as shown in Diagram A. A convex curve, on the other hand, is bowed toward the origin, as shown in Diagram B.

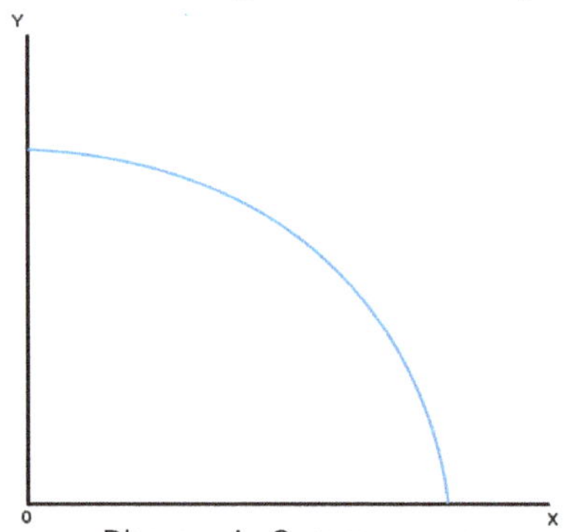

Diagram A: Concave curve

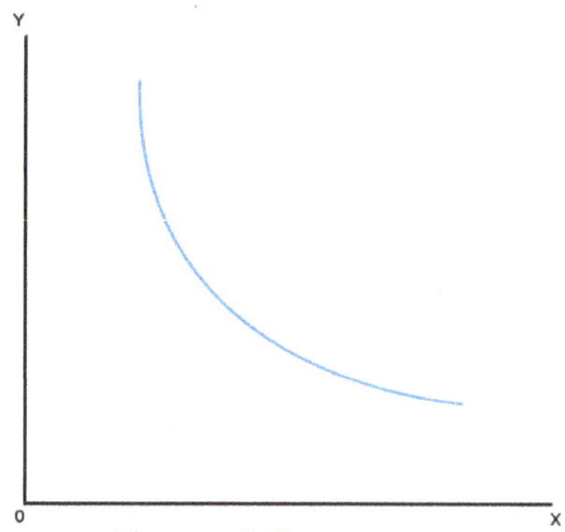

Diagram B: Convex curve

Problem 2-12

What kind of graph would you use to illustrate each of the following?

a. *The monthly sales for a company in 2013*
b. *The distribution of earnings among five banks*
c. *The growth in population over a 10-year period*
d. *The rates of inflation in 12 countries in 2012*
e. *The percentage of total sales attributable to five different products sold by a company*

Requirement and Clue: *Your choices are line graph, pie chart, bar chart. It's a good idea to justify your choice.*

Solution:

a. The monthly sales for a company in 2013 could be illustrated well using a bar chart. This chart makes it easy to compare one month's sale with another month's sale.

b. Since there are only five banks, a pie chart could be used effectively to illustrate the distribution of earnings among them. It would facilitate comparison of the earnings of one bank with that of any other bank.

c. A line graph would be appropriate to illustrate the growth in population since growth is continuous over the period.

d. The rates of inflation in 12 countries could be illustrated using a bar chart. The difference among the rates of inflation in the various countries would be seen at a glance.

e. Since there are only five products, a pie chart would be appropriate here for effective illustration.

Problem 2-13

What are the limitations to the use of graphs in economics?

Requirement and Clue: *Think, for example, of the difficulty of drawing and using graphs of more than two dimensions.*

Solution:

Although graphs are very useful in economics, some limitations exist. First, the use of graphs is limited to cases where there are only few variables. As the number of variables increases, one's ability to graph relations among them decreases rapidly. How would one graph the idea that the quantity of smart phones that people will buy varies with current income, the rate of interest, and buyers' expectations? Second, many students have been "turned off" graphs before they begin their study of economics. Thus, the use of graphs may be intimidating for some students.

Problem 2-14

Why is the concept of slope important in economics?

Requirement and Clue: *Relate your solution to rates of change.*

Solution:

The slope of a curve refers to its steepness or flatness. Economists are interested not only in changes in certain variables, but also in the rate of change of these variables. For example, it is important to know that income is rising or falling, but it may be even more important to know how fast it is rising or falling. The *slope* of a curve provides this information.

Problem 2-15

The following table contains information on combinations of As and Bs that can be bought for a given sum of money.

Quantity of A	Quantity of B
0	12
1	10
2	8
3	6
4	4
5	2
6	0

a. With A on the horizontal axis and B on the vertical axis, draw a graph showing the various combinations of A and B that can be bought.

b. Calculate the slope of your graph.

Requirement and Clue: *Recall that the slope is the change in the value on the vertical axis divided by the change in the value on the horizontal axis.*

Solution:

a.

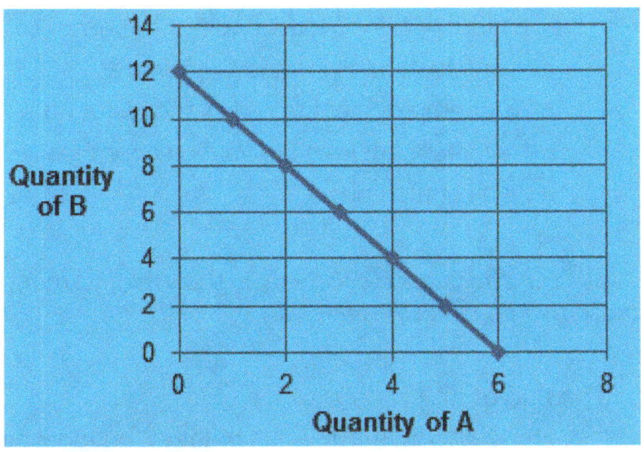

b. The slope is (Vertical distance) / (Horizontal distance) and so applying the formula we have,

(Vertical distance) / (Horizontal distance) = (–2) / 1 = – 2

Multiple-Choice

In each case, circle the letter that corresponds with the correct answer.

1. A mathematical function:

a. is an expression of the kind of work that a particular variable is designed to perform

b. expresses a relationship among two or more variables

c. is designed to prevent the use of sophisticated mathematics in economics

d. must be presented graphically to be meaningful

Answer: b

Reason: A mathematical function is an equation that expresses a relationship among variables. It deals with how a change in one variable affects some other variable or variables.

2. The functional notation:

a. is a mathematical tool for expressing relations among variables

b. is very useful in mathematics but not in economics

c. is very useful in economics but not in mathematics

d. can be used only by those who have significant mathematical training

Answer: a

Reason: The functional notation is the use of mathematical symbols to express how variables are related.

3. Relationships among variables can be expressed:

a. only verbally

b. only by using the functional notation

c. by using words, graphs, tables, or functions

d. by using graphs but not tables

Answer: c

Reason: The various forms given in choice c can be used to express relationships among variables.

4. The first step in using the functional notation is:

a. to eliminate all symbols that may be contained in the statement

b. to identify the work performed by each exogenous variable and then ignore the endogenous variable

c. discard all traces of mathematics

d. use symbols instead of words

Answer: d

Reason: The functional notation is a symbolic expression of a concept.

5. The idea that when hotel rates (r) change, the number of people taking vacations (V) in foreign countries also changes can be expressed as:

a. r = V
b. r = r(V)
c. V = V times r
d. V =V(r)

Answer: d

Reason: The dependent variable is the number of people taking vacations in foreign countries while the independent variable is hotel rates.

6. If I denotes investment, y denotes income, and r denotes the rate of interest, then the expression $I = I(y,r)$ means that:

a. investment is the product of income and the rate of interest
b. income and the rate of interest are constant but investment varies
c. investment will change if either income or the rate of interest changes
d. changes in income and the rate of interest are due to changes in investment

Answer: c

Reason: Investment is a function of income and the rate of interest. Changes in the independent variables (income and the rate of interest) will cause the dependent variable (investment) to change.

7. In the expression c = c(y,i):

a. c is the dependent variable while y and i are independent variables
b. c is the independent variable while y and i are dependent variables
c. the value of c can be determined by multiplying y and i
d. dependent and independent variables cannot be determined unless the variables are defined

Answer: a

Reason: The expression can be read as c depends on y and i. Therefore c is dependent while y and I are independent.

8. Which of the following statements is correct?

a. The dependent variable is the variable that we are trying to explain while the independent variable is the variable that provides the explanation
b. The dependent variable is the variable that provides the explanation while the independent variable is the variable that we are trying to explain
c. Dependent and independent variables can be interchanged without changing the relationship among variables
d. The dependent variables is the variable whose value is known while the independent variable is the variable whose value is unknown

Answer: a

Reason: The independent variable or the explanatory variable is the variable that is used in a relationship to explain or predict changes in some other (dependent) variable.

9. Graphs are useful in economics because:

a. most students these days are comfortable with graphs
b. they are effective in illustrating relationships among variables
c. they elevate economics to the status of science
d. all of the above

Answer: b

Reason: Economics deals a great deal with relationships among variables and graphs do this well.

10. A graph showing a direct relationship between two variables is:

a. horizontal   c. upward sloping
b. vertical   d. downward sloping

Answer: c

Reason: A graph with a positive slope shows a direct relationship.

11. A graph showing an inverse relationship between two variables is:

a. horizontal   c. upward sloping
b. vertical   d. downward sloping

Answer: d

Reason: If two variables are inversely related, the graph will be negatively sloped.

12. Which of the following statements is correct?

a. Concave curves are used in economics, but not convex
b. Convex curves are used in economics but not concave
c. Both concave and convex curves are used in economics
d. Neither concave nor convex curves are used in economics

Answer: c

Reason: Economics deals with a wide variety of relationships among variables; thus curves of all shapes are used, including concave and convex curves.

13. Which of the following statements is correct?

a. A concave curve is bowed outward while a convex curve is bowed toward the origin
b. A concave curve is bowed toward the origin while a convex curve is bowed outward
c. Concave and convex curves are both bowed toward the origin
d. Concave and convex curves are both bowed outward

Answer: a

Reason: Choice "a" correctly describes the shapes of concave and convex curves.

14. A bar chart can be effectively used to show:

a. inflation rates in various countries
b. unemployment rates in various countries
c. investment levels in various countries
d. all of the above

Answer: d

Reason: Bar charts are a good way to show relative magnitudes, such as those mentioned in the choices.

15. The use of graphs is:

a. ineffective in illustrating relationships among variables in economics
b. ineffective in showing changes in variables
c. limited to cases with few variables
d. more effective as the number of variables increases

Answer: c

Reason: The ability to use graphs decreases as the number of variables increases.

16. If a change in one variable has no effect on another variable, a graph showing the relationship between them will be:

a. impossible to draw
b. a straight line through the origin though not necessarily at 45 degrees
c. drawn cutting both axes
d. either vertical or horizontal

Answer: d

Reason: If the variables are x and y with x on the horizontal axis and y on the vertical axis, a change in x that has no effect on y will be a horizontal straight line; a change in y that has no effect on x will be a vertical straight line.

17. Graphs enable us to show:

a. inverse relations but not direct relations
b. direct relations but not inverse relations
c. both direct and inverse relations
d. dependent but not independent variables

Answer: c

Reason: An upward sloping curve shows a direct relationship between two variables, while a downward sloping curve shows an inverse relationship.

18. The concept of slope helps economists to:

a. understand the rate at which a variable changes
b. work with curves but not straight lines
c. work with straight lines but not curves
d. none of the above

Answer: a

Reason: Slope gives information about the rate of change.

19. A downward sloping curve means that the variables are:

a. inversely related   b. directly related
c. not closely related   d. none of the above

Answer: a

Reason: A curve showing an inverse relationship between two variables has a negative slope.

20. When income rises, people consume more goods and services. This relationship between consumption and income would be shown on a graph as:

a. an upward sloping curve
b. a downward sloping curve
c. a vertical line
d. a horizontal line

Answer: a

Reason: A direct relationship exists between variables that move in the same direction. This direct relationship is shown by an upward sloping curve.

21. The slope of a straight line can be measured by:

a. the ratio of the horizontal distance to the vertical distance
b. the ratio of the vertical distance to the horizontal distance
c. taking the sum of the vertical and horizontal distances
d. the horizontal distance minus the vertical distance

Answer: b

Reason: The slope is the change in the y coordinate divided by the change in the x coordinate.

22. A curve with a negative slope is:

a. upward sloping   c. downward sloping
b. vertical   d. horizontal

Answer: c

Reason: A downward sloping curve has a negative slope.

23. A curve with a positive slope is:

a. upward sloping   c. downward sloping
b. vertical   d. horizontal

Answer: a

Reason: An upward sloping curve has a positive slope.

24. The slope of a non-linear curve at a particular point:

a. cannot be determined because slopes exist only for straight lines
b. cannot be determined because there are various slopes at any particular point
c. is the slope of any straight line drawn through the origin
d. is the slope of the straight line drawn tangent to the curve at that particular point

Answer: d

Reason: At the point of tangency, slopes are equal.

True or False

Determine whether each of the following statements is true or false.

1. Even the most elementary course in economics requires a relatively high level of mathematics.

Answer: False

Explanation: *Although mathematics is important in economics, a high level is not required in most introductory courses.*

2. The functional notation is used only when a complicated mathematical operation is to be performed.

Answer: False

Explanation: *The functional notation is just a way of expressing relations among variables.*

3. A mathematical function describes in detail the work that a variable is expected to perform.

Answer: False

Explanation: *It is only an expression of relationship among variables.*

4. The functional notation is a useful tool in economics because economics deals substantially with relations among variables.

Answer: True

5. The expression R = R(P,S), means that P and S will change only when R changes.

Answer: False

Explanation: *It means that changes in P or S will cause R to change.*

6. The expression R = R(P,S) means that R will change if P or S changes.

Answer: True

7. In the expression R = R(P,S), R is the dependent variable while P and S are independent variables.

Answer: True

8. The dependent variable is the variable that we are trying to explain and the independent variable is the variable that does the explaining.

Answer: True

9. It is quite impossible to draw graphs from data contained in tables. That's why economists use both graphs and tables.

Answer: False

Explanation: *It is often quite possible and even easy to draw graphs from data contained in tables.*

10. When variables move up and down together, we say that there is a direct relation between them.

Answer: True

11. When variable *A* rises we observe that variable *B* falls. We can therefore conclude that *A* and *B* are directly related.

Answer: False

Explanation: *Variables that move in opposite directions like A and B in the statement are inversely related.*

12. If an inverse relationship is established between the price of gasoline and the number of miles travelled by automobiles, we know that if the price of gasoline rises, the number of miles travelled by automobiles will fall.

Answer: True

13. Because graphs are often difficult to understand, only straight line graphs are used in economics.

Answer: False

14. A concave curve is bowed outward while a convex curve is bowed toward the origin.

Answer: True

15. A bar graph is a vertical or horizontal graph with categories on one axis and the value assigned to each category measured along the other axis.

Answer: True

16. A pie chart is a circular graph whose pieces add to 100%.

Answer: True

17. As the number of variables increases, our ability to graph relations among them also increases.

Answer: False

Explanation: *It becomes more difficult, not easier.*

18. The slope of a line is the change in the x value divided by the change in the y value when y is on the vertical axis and x is on the horizontal axis.

Answer: False

Explanation: *It's the change in the y value divided by the change in the x value.*

19. A downward sloping curve has a negative slope while an upward sloping curve has a positive slope.

Answer: True

20. The slope of a non-linear curve at a particular point is the slope of the straight line drawn tangent to the curve at that particular point.

Answer: True

Completion

Fill in the blanks

Use each word or combination of words from the list exactly once.
*(**Hint**: Proceed by elimination)*

Word list

Direct x 2 — Upward — Bar — Chart — Concave — Convex — Dependent x 2 — Negative— Positive — Q = QP — Downward — Function x 2 — Function — Graph — Graphs — Horizontal — Independent x 2 — Independent — Inverse x 2 — Pie — Tables — Vertical

Questions

1. If changes in income affect the level of consumption, we can say that consumption is a ____________ of income. In this case, consumption is the ____________ variable while income is the ____________ variable.
2. The idea that the quantity (Q) of grapes bought depends on the price (P) of grapes can be expressed by the ____________. (Q = Q(P)
3. In the equation P = P(t,m), t and m are the ____________ variables while P is the ____________ variable.
4. Economists use the concept of a ____________ to express relationships among variables.
5. Relations among variables can be expressed using words, ____________, ____________, and equations or functions.
6. Two variables move together in the same direction if there is a(n) ____________ relationship between them. Two variables move in opposite directions if there is a(n) ____________ relationship between them.
7. A graph showing a direct relationship between two variables is ____________ sloping, while a graph showing an inverse relationship is ____________ sloping.
8. A downward-sloping curve has a ____________ slope, while an upward-sloping curve has a ______________ slope.
9. A ____________ curve is bowed outward, while a(n) ____________ curve is bowed toward the origin.
10. A ____________ ____________ is a vertical or horizontal graph with categories on one axis and the value assigned to each category measured along the other axis.
11. A ____________ ____________ is a circular graph whose pieces add up to 100%.
12. The slope of a straight line is measured by the ____________ distance divided by the ____________ distance.
13. If two variables have a(n) ____________ relation, the slope of the curve showing that relationship will be negative.
14. If two variables have a(n) ____________ relation, the slope of the curve showing that relationship will be positive.

Solution

1. (function, dependent, independent)
2. (Q = Q(P)
3. (independent, dependent)
4. (function)
5. (tables, graphs)
6. (direct, inverse)
7. (upward, downward)
8. (negative, positive)
9. (concave, convex)
10. (bar graph)
11. (pie chart)
12. (vertical, horizontal)
13. (inverse)
14. (direct)

3 THE ECONOMIC PROBLEM: SCARCITY & CHOICE

SYNOPSIS

Because resources are limited and human wants are unlimited, society cannot produce all the goods and services that its members want. It must therefore choose. When a choice is made, something has to be given up or sacrificed. Opportunity cost is the term used to describe the alternative that is sacrificed.

Production possibility schedules and production possibility curves are used to show various combinations of goods and/or services that an economy can produce if it uses all its resources, assuming that technology is constant. A linear production possibility curve illustrates constant opportunity cost, while a concave production possibility curve illustrates increasing opportunity cost.

A point below the production possibility curve represents unemployment of resources. A point on the curve represents full employment, while a point above the curve represents a combination of goods/ services that is unattainable. A change in technology or a change in the quantity or quality of resources will shift the production possibility curve.

LEARNING OBJECTIVES

In connection with this module, you should be able to:

1. establish a relationship between scarcity, choice and opportunity cost.
2. explain the concept of opportunity cost.
3. explain the usefulness of the concept of opportunity in decision making.
4. explain and use the concepts of production possibility schedules and production possibility curves.
5. discuss the factors that can cause the production possibility curve to shift.

DEFINITIONS & CONCEPTS

You should be able to define the following terms and concepts:

scarcity and choice
opportunity cost (alternative cost)
production possibility schedule
production possibility curve
economic growth

3

THE ECONOMIC PROBLEM: SCARCITY & CHOICE

Concepts, Definitions & Problems

Problem 3-1

"Every act of choosing involves a sacrifice." Discuss this statement.

Requirement and Clue: *View choice as giving up something rather than as taking something. Illustrate with examples.*

Solution:

The statement is true. Because of scarcity, we are forced to choose. In exercising choice, we must give up or sacrifice something. More steaks might mean fewer movies; an extra car might mean fewer vacations; and a new ipad might mean giving up the printer that I was planning to purchase. If nothing was sacrificed, then choice was not exercised. If I have the means to acquire both A and B and took them both, then I did not choose. One cannot choose without giving up something.

Problem 3-2

What do economists mean by opportunity cost and how can it be measured?

Requirement and Clue: *This is a two-part problem. Solve each part in order. Define opportunity cost and give examples. Say how it can be measured.*

Solution:

Opportunity cost can be defined as the next best alternative that is sacrificed when a choice is made. In a situation of economic scarcity, a decision to produce one good or service involves an opportunity cost represented by the good or service that might have been produced instead. The idea behind the concept of opportunity cost is that when we use funds to purchase goods and services, we are also deciding not to purchase some other goods or services. Similarly, when an economy uses resources to produce certain goods and services, it is also making a decision not to produce some other goods and services. What we decide not to purchase is the opportunity cost of what we do purchase; and what we decide not to produce is the opportunity cost of what we do produce. Suppose a manufacturer has material suitable for producing computer cases or briefcases. If he or she produces computer cases, the opportunity cost of the computer cases is the briefcases that could have been produced instead.

The discussion in the previous paragraph leads to the conclusion that the opportunity cost of what we get is equal to what we give it. If an economy gives up 2 units of apples for 1 unit of butter, then the opportunity cost of the unit of butter is the 2 units of apples given up. Opportunity cost, then, can be measured by the ratio of what is given up to what is obtained.

Problem 3-3

Establish a relationship among scarcity, choice and opportunity cost.

Requirement and Clue: *The basic idea is that we choose because of scarcity and choosing involves a sacrifice—a cost.*

Solution:

Scarcity means that society does not have sufficient resources to enable it to produce all the goods and services wanted, thus, society must choose. If scarcity did not exist, everyone would have as much of everything as he or she wants. Choice then, is a direct result of scarcity. Whenever a choice is made, something has to be given up. Whatever is given up or sacrificed is the opportunity cost of what was chosen. The following relationship has been established among scarcity, choice, and opportunity cost: scarcity forces us to choose, and choice results in opportunity cost.

Problem 3-4

Briefly define the coast-benefit approach to decision-making.

Requirement and Clue: *A clear and precise definition is required.*

Solution:

In any decision, there are benefits and costs. The cost benefit approach to decision-making is the comparison of the costs and benefits associated with a decision. If the benefits of taking a certain course of action outweigh the cost, then take the action; otherwise, don't.

Problem 3-5

For each of the following, name a possible opportunity cost.

a. *You decided to take a summer job.*
b. *You attended a concert on the night before a major test.*
c. *You took a couple of courses in summer school.*
d. *You decided to treat your friend to a restaurant meal.*
e. *Your family went on a one-week cruise to Alaska.*

Requirement and Clue: *Your solution to this problem will determine the extent to which you understand the concept of opportunity cost. Focus on the alternative that was sacrificed.*

Solution:

Opportunity cost is whatever is given up when a choice is made.

a. The opportunity cost of taking a summer job could be a summer course that you could have taken instead or a summer vacation in Mexico.
b. A possible opportunity cost of attending a concert on the night before a major test could be studying and getting a higher grade on the test.
c. The opportunity cost of these courses could be a summer job that you could have taken instead
d. A possible opportunity cost of treating your friend to a restaurant meal is a DVD that you could have bought instead.
e. The opportunity cost of the cruise to Alaska could be the repairs that could have been done on the house or the entertainment set that could have been purchased instead.

Problem 3-6

The following table contains information about an economy that produces only cups and hand bags with its available resources.

Combinations	Cups x (1000)	Handbags x (1000)
A	0	10
B	1	9
C	2	7
D	3	4
E	4	0

a. *If the economy is producing only handbags and then decides to produce 1,000 cups, what is the opportunity cost of the 1,000 cups in terms of handbags?*
b. *On the basis of the data contained in the table, draw the economy's production-possibility (p-p) curve.*
c. *On your diagram, indicate a point of productive inefficiency with the letter I.*
d. *Indicate a point of full employment with the letter E.*
e. *Indicate an unattainable combination of cups and handbags with the letter U.*

Requirement and Clue: *Note that opportunity cost is whatever is given up. Recall that a point of inefficiency would lie below the curve. A point of full employment would be on the curve, and an unattainable combination would be beyond (above) the curve.*

Solution:

a. In order to produce 1,000 cups, the economy would have to divert resources from the production of handbags and use them to produce cups. The output of handbags would fall from 10,000 to 9,000. The economy would thus give up 1,000 handbags for 1,000 cups. Therefore, the opportunity cost of 1,000 cups would be 1,000 handbags.

b. (See below)

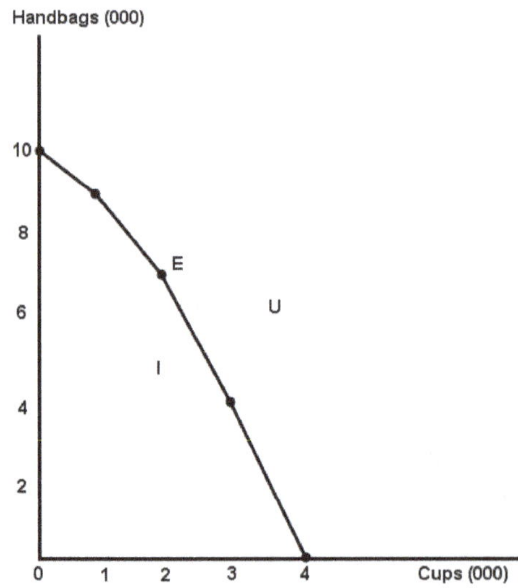

c. A point of productive inefficiency would lie below the production-possibility curve. See *I* on the graph above.

d. A point of full employment would lie on the production-possibility curve as shown by *E* on the graph above.

e. An unattainable combination of cups and handbags would lie above (beyond) the production-possibility curve as shown by *U* in the graph above.

Problem 3-7

The city of Courtland (a factitious city) hires 10 previously unemployed workers and pays them $500 per week each. What is the opportunity cost to Courtland of the extra output produced by the 10 new workers? If the 10 workers were employed elsewhere in Courtland, what would be the opportunity cost to the city of hiring them under the same payment conditions?

Requirement and Clue: *Recognize that there is no opportunity cost associated with unemployed resources. There is a cost associated with transferring workers, that is, the loss of output from where they were previously employed.*

Solution:

The opportunity cost would be the loss of output in Courtland caused by hiring the new workers. Since the 10 workers were unemployed, there is no loss of output associated with hiring them. Therefore the opportunity cost to Courtland is zero. If the 10 workers were employed elsewhere in Courtland, the opportunity cost of the extra output they produce for the city would be the loss of output that they were previously producing.

Problem 3-8

The following table shows production possibilities for a hypothetical economy producing only two goods: lap top computers and telephones.

# lap top computers x (1000)	# of telephones x (1000)
0	15
1	14
2	12
3	9
4	5
5	0

a. *What is the table called?*

b. *With telephones on the vertical axis and lap top computers on the horizontal axis, draw a graph from the data contained in the table. What is the graph called?*

c. *From your graph, determine whether the economy faces constant opportunity cost or increasing opportunity cost.*

Requirement and Clue: *Think of production possibility schedule and production possibility curve. Consider the meaning/significance of concave and linear production possibility curves.*

Solution:

a. The table is a production-possibility schedule or production-possibility table.

b. See graph below. The graph is a production-possibility curve. It is also called a production-possibility frontier or production-possibility boundary.

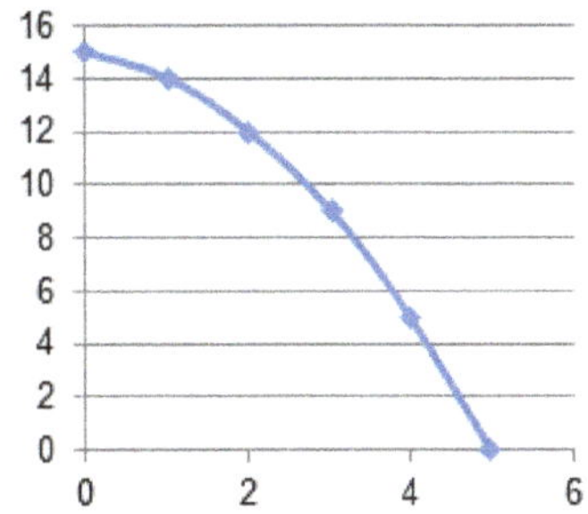

c. Because the production-possibility curve is concave, we can conclude that the economy faces increasing opportunity cost.

Problem 3-9

Use production-possibility graphs to show the immediate effect of each of the following events on a country's production-possibility curve.

a. *A significant number of people immigrate into the country.*

b. *The country embarks on a successful training program for all workers.*

c. *The country discovers a new and more efficient method of using its resources, but decides to delay the use of the new method for a year*

d. *The economy hires workers who were previously unemployed.*

Requirement and Clue: *Ask whether or not the event suggests a change in the quantity or quality of resources, or a change in technology.*

Solution:

If a significant number of immigrants enter the country, it will experience an increase in its human resources and its ability to produce goods and services will immediately increase. This means that its production-possibility (p-p) curve will shift to the right as shown in the following diagram.

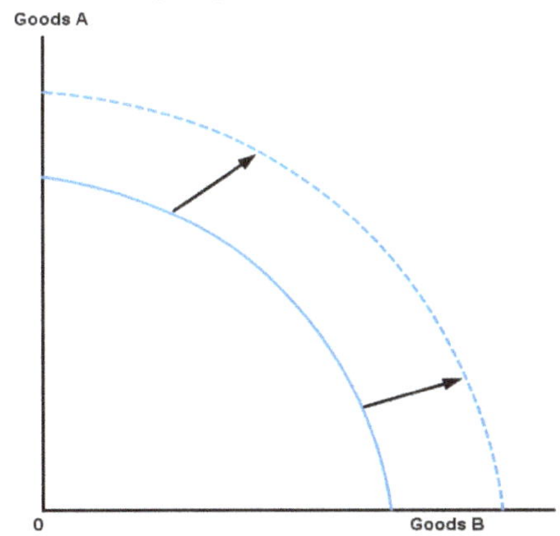

a. A successful training program for all workers will improve the quality of the country's human resources and will increase its productive capacity. Its p-p curve will shift outward to the right as shown in the following diagram.

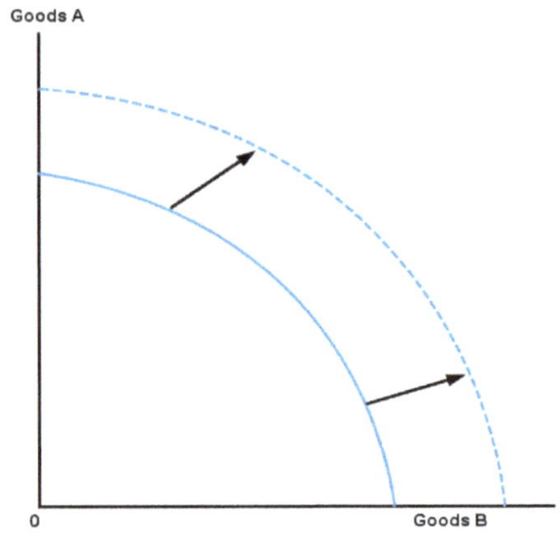

b. A new and more efficient method of using resources represents an improvement in technology. This will increase the country's ability to produce goods and services and will shift its p-p curve outward to the right as shown in the following diagram.

Note that although there is a delay in the use of the new method, its existence immediately increases the economy's potential to produce goods and services, so the curve shifts to the right.

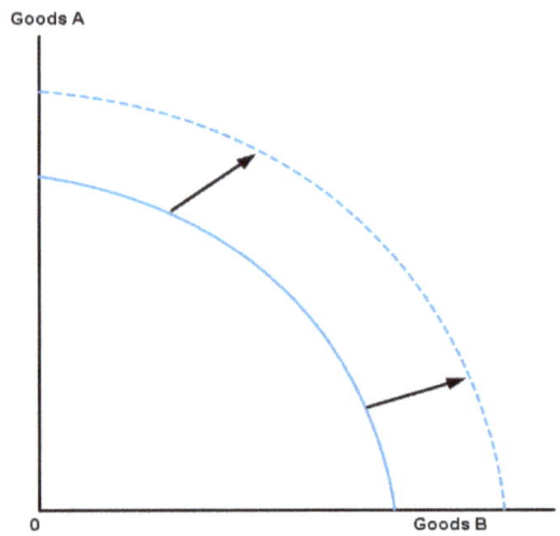

c. If the economy hires workers who were previously unemployed, there is no change in the quantity of human resources because they were already there. There is no change in the country's ability to produce goods and services so the p-p curve remains unchanged as shown in the following diagram.

Problem 3-10

It is observed that classes scheduled for 8:00 a.m. are less crowded than those scheduled for 11:30 a.m. Can the concept of opportunity cost be used as a possible explanation for this phenomenon?

Requirement and Clue: *Compare the opportunity cost of attending an 8:00 a.m. class with that of attending an 11:30 a.m. class.*

Solution:

Opportunity cost is the alternative that is given up when a choice is made. Some of the costs of attending an 8:00 a.m. class may include contending with rush-hour traffic, missing breakfast, and extra sleep. These costs may not be associated with attending an 11:30 a.m. class. It is possible that because of the lower opportunity cost involved in attending the 11:30 scheduled class, more students opt for this option.

Problem 3-11

Give a practical example of the use of the concept of opportunity cost in real life.

Requirement and Clue: *Numerous examples should come to mind. Almost every decision involves a choice and choosing involves giving up something.*

Solution:

Our daily lives are filled with decisions. Should I buy a car and drive to school or should I take public transportation? Should I live on campus while attending university or should I commute? Should we buy a new car or should we carry out extensive renovations on our home? Should I attend the concert tonight or should I use the time to study for my economics test? These are typical decisions that people make all the time. Some are major while others are minor. The concept of opportunity cost is used regularly in real life. Suppose Jane has arrived at school this morning. She is deciding whether or not she should attend her economics class. She attends classes because she believes that she will derive certain benefits from doing so. But attending class also has costs associated with it. These may include spending time with friends, visiting a mall, or doing some work on a psychology paper that is due in a couple of days. These are what Jane will give up by attending the class. They are the opportunity cost of going to the class.

To make the decision, Jane weighs the benefits against the costs. If, in her own subjective evaluation, the benefits of going to the class outweigh the costs, then she will decide to attend the class. If not, she will decide not to attend class. The costs referred to here are opportunity costs.

Problem 3-12

John Green has just graduated from a junior college where he earned his college diploma. He has been offered a job for $25,000 a year. He would like to go to university to obtain his bachelor's degree in business. This is a two-year program since he already holds a diploma from the junior college. Tuition, books, transportation, supplies and other things directly *related to his university education will cost $35,000 for the two-year period.*

a. *On the basis of this information, what is the full cost to John of a degree?*

b. *How should John decide whether or not to go for the degree?*

Requirement and Clue: *This is another two-part problem. Answer each part in order. Be careful not to omit opportunity cost. John could base his decision on a comparison of costs and benefits.*

Solution:

a. If John bases his decision only on the $35,000, he would severely underestimate his cost. The full cost of his degree must include the $25,000 a year (or $50,000 for the two-year period) that he could have received as salary from his employment. That is the opportunity cost. Thus the full cost of the degree is ($35,000 + $50,000) = $85,000.

b. To decide whether or not to go for the degree, John must consider the benefits of having the degree. These may include a higher-paying job, better working conditions, greater job security, and the prestige of having a university degree. If these benefits outweigh the $85,000 cost, then John would sacrifice the job and attend university. Otherwise, he would take the job for $25,000 a year.

Problem 3-13

What is the difference between a production-possibility schedule and a production-possibility curve?

Requirement and Clue: *The technical difference between the two concepts must be noted. An example of each would be helpful.*

Solution:

Although the terms "production-possibility schedule" and "production-possibility curve" are sometimes used interchangeably, there is a technical difference between them. A production-possibility schedule is a table showing *various* combinations of goods and services that can be produced with full utilization of all resources and a given state of technology. A production-possibility curve, on the other hand, is a graph showing *all* combinations. The following table is a production-possibility schedule showing various combinations of x and y that can be produced. When the information shown in the table is plotted on a graph and the points are connected as in the following graph, the result is a production-possibility curve.

Production-possibility schedule

Combinations	Quantity of y	Quantity of x
A	12	0
B	10	1
C	8	2
D	6	3
E	4	4
F	2	5
E	0	6

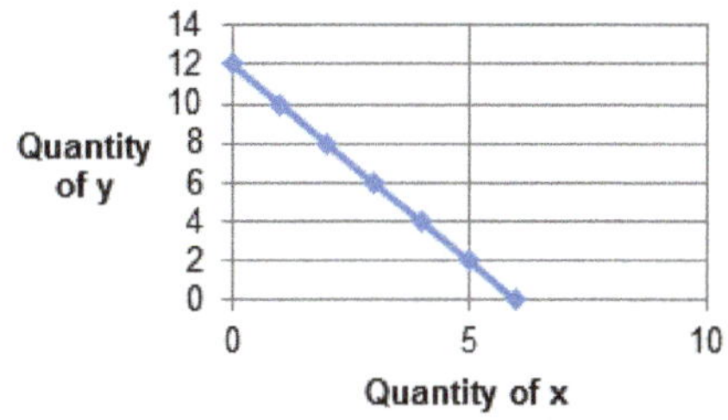

Production-possibility curve

Problem 3-14

Answer the following questions:

(a) *What is the production possibility curve?*

(b) *What can you conclude about an economy that is operating at a point on its production-possibility curve?*

(c) *What can you conclude about an economy that is operating at a point below its production-possibility curve?*

Requirement and Clue: *This is a three-part problem. Answer each part in order. Consider the significance of a point on the curve and a point below the curve.*

Solution:

(a) The production-possibility curve is a graph that shows all combinations of goods and services that an economy can produce with a given technology, using all its resources. Since it defines the limits of what an economy can produce, it is also referred to as the production-possibility boundary or production-possibility frontier. The following diagram shows a production-possibility curve.

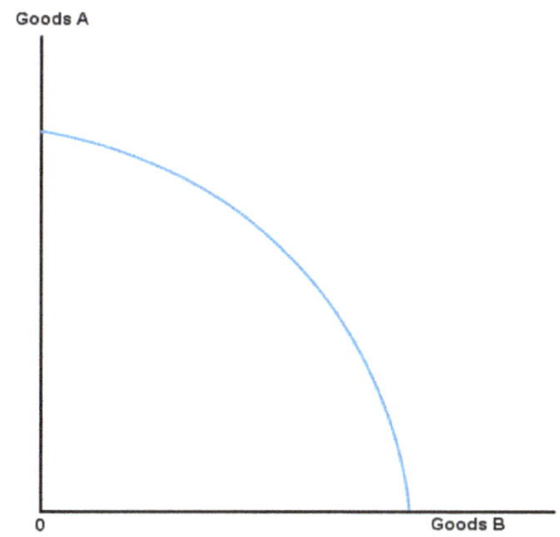

The economy cannot produce any combination of goods and services that lies above this curve.

(b) If an economy is operating at a point on its production-possibility curve, it means that the economy is using all its resources efficiently. In such a situation, the economy cannot produce more of one good without producing less of some other good. Thus, a point on the production-possibility curve represents efficient production. The following diagram illustrates the point.

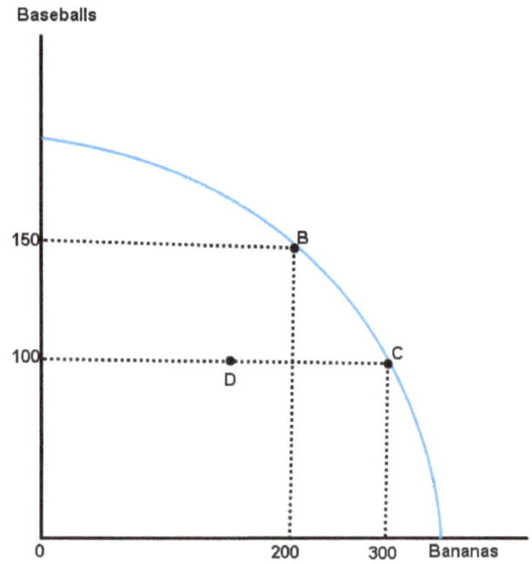

If the economy is operating at point B, producing 150 baseballs and 200 bananas, it can move to point C, producing 300 bananas only by producing 100 baseballs instead of 150, thus sacrificing 50 baseballs.

(c) If an economy is operating at a point below its production-possibility curve, such as point D in the diagram, it means that the economy is not using all its resources or is not using them efficiently. This economy can produce more baseballs by moving vertically from D toward the curve, without sacrificing the production of any bananas, or more bananas by moving horizontally from D toward C, without sacrificing the production of any of baseballs. It can produce more baseballs and more bananas by moving diagonally from D towards a point on the curve such as B.

Problem 3-15

Are production-possibility (p-p) curves likely to be linear or concave?

Requirement and Clue: *Explore the conditions for linear and concave p-p curves.*

Solution:

A straight line (linear) p-p curve means that opportunity cost is constant. This would be the case only if all resources were equally efficient in all uses. A concave p-p curve means that opportunity cost is increasing. This would be the case if resources were not all equally efficient in all uses. In reality, however, some resources are more suitable for some uses than for others. For example, some human resources are better equipped to be teachers than mechanics, and some natural resources are better suited for building sites than for cultivation. Moreover, land, labour, and capital are certainly not substitutable. We can conclude, therefore, that p-p curves are more likely to be concave than linear.

Problem 3-16

How can a production-possibility curve be used to show economic scarcity?

Requirement and Clue: *Say what economic scarcity is and consider why an economy cannot operate at a point beyond its production possibility curve.*

Solution:

Economic scarcity exists when available resources are insufficient to produce all the goods and services required to satisfy human wants. The existence of economic scarcity can be well illustrated by the production-possibility curve which shows all the choices available to society in terms of the combinations of goods and services that it is capable of producing, using all its resources with given technology. Consider the following graph.

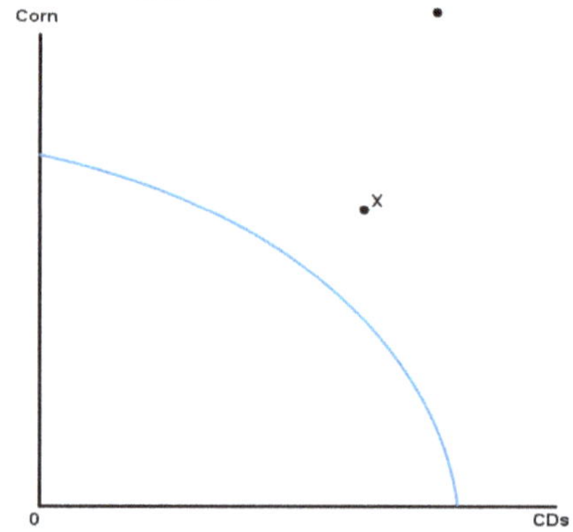

Each point on the production-possibility curve represents some maximum output of any two goods, corn and compact discs (CDs), for example. Society must choose which combination it desires; more corn means fewer CDs and more CDs means less corn. The fact that society cannot have more corn *and* more CDs at the same time means that scarcity exists. Moreover, consider point X. Society would like to have a combination of corn and CDs represented by this point; but this is not possible. Why? Because the resources and technology available do not permit that combination of goods. That is economic scarcity.

Problem 3-17

An economy produces only two goods, computers and cellular telephones. Like all economies, its economic resources are limited, so in order to produce more computers it must divert resources from cell phone production. Therefore, in order to produce more of one good, it must produce less of the other. The following table shows maximum quantities of computers and cell phones that the economy can produce.

Prod. Possibilities	Cell phones	Computers
A	100	0
B	90	10
C	70	20
D	40	30
E	0	40

Use the data in the table to construct a production-possibility curve for this economy.

Requirement and Clue: *This is just a matter of plotting the points and connecting them to get the production possibility curve.*

Solution:

With the quantity of computers on the vertical axis and the quantity of cell phones on the horizontal axis, we can plot the points as shown in the graph.

Problem 3-18

In the production-possibility diagram below, which points indicate full employment and which points indicate underemployment?

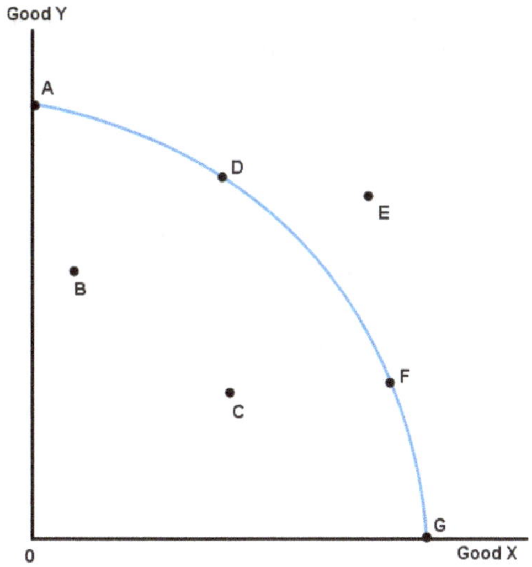

Requirement and Clue: *Consider the significance of points on the p-p curve and points below it.*

Solution:

Any point on the production-possibility curve represents full employment; therefore points A, D, F and G indicate full employment. Any point below the production-possibility curve represents underemployment or unemployment. Therefore points B and C indicate underemployment.

Problem 3-19

The following is the production-possibility curve for a hypothetical economy that produces books and bread.

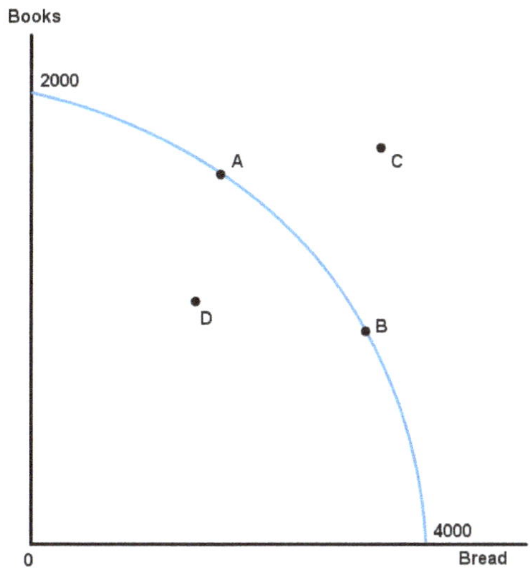

(a) *What is the maximum number books that this economy can produce?*

(b) *What is the maximum amount of bread that this economy can produce?*

(c) *Which points represent maximum use of resources?*

(d) *Which point represents unemployment?*

(e) *Which point is impossible to attain?*

Requirement and Clue: *This requires familiarity with the production possibility curve and the significance of points below, on, and above the curve.*

Solution:

(a) If this economy uses all its resources in the production of books, it will be able to produce a maximum of 2,000 books.

(b) If the economy produces no books but uses all its resources to produce only bread, it will be able to produce a maximum of 4,000 loaves of bread.

(c) Maximum use of resources is represented by points on the production-possibility curve. In this case, points A and B represent maximum use of resources.

(d) Any point below the production-possibility curve represents unemployment. Point D is such a point.

(e) The production-possibility curve defines the limit of what an economy can produce. Point C represents a combination of bread and books that this economy cannot attain.

Problem 3-20

Describe two ways by which an economy's production-possibility curve can be made to shift outward.

Requirement and Clue: *Focus on changes in resources and technology. Use a diagram to illustrate.*

Solution:

An outward shift of an economy's production-possibility curve occurs when the economy's productive capacity increases. This increase in productive capacity can occur if (a) there is an increase in the quantity and/or quality of resources available to the economy and (b) there is an improvement in technology. Either or both of these occurrences can shift the production-possibility curve outward.

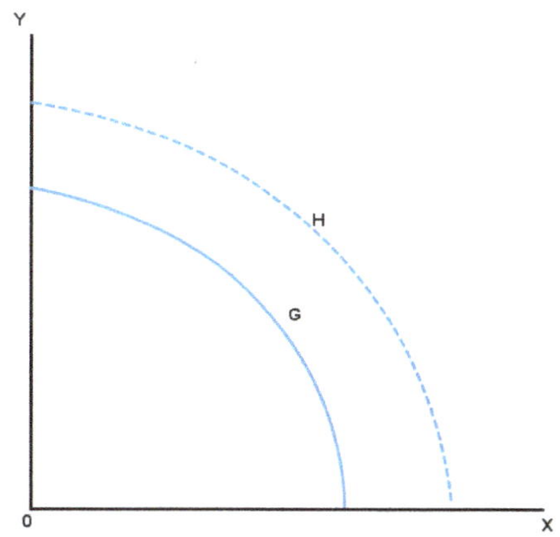

In the diagram above, *G* is the original production-possibility curve.

An increase in the quantity of human resources through immigration or an improvement in labour quality through education and training will cause the production-possibility curve to shift outward from production-possibility curve *G* to production-possibility curve *H* as shown in the diagram. An increase in the quantity or quality of any other factor of production will have a similar effect.

An improvement in technology means that a given quantity of resources can now produce more goods and services than before, or that fewer resources can now produce the same quantity of goods and services as before. For example, the discovery of a more efficient method of producing automobiles or airplanes will shift the production-possibility curve outward.

Problem 3-21

The economy of Wadidla (a fictitious country) produces only two goods: potatoes and wooden carvings. Over a two-year period, technological advance occurred in the wood carving industry but not in potato production. Show how Wadidla's production-possibility curve would be affected by the technological advance.

Requirement and Clue: *You are required to use a production possibility diagram to show the effects of technological advance in one industry but not in the other.*

Solution:

This particular technological advance positively affects the economy's potential to produce wooden carvings, but its impact on the ability to produce potatoes is nil. In the following graph, the old technology is shown. The new p-p curve resulting from technological advance in the wooden carving industry only would look like the p-p curve labeled new technology.

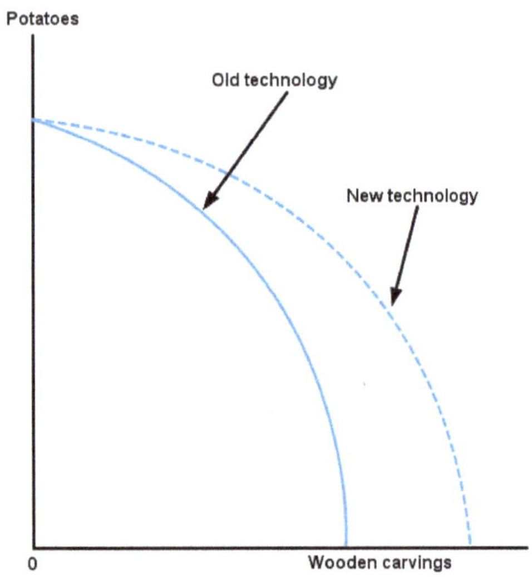

Problem 3-22

Briefly discuss the fundamental questions of microeconomics.

Requirement and Clue: *You should demonstrate that you are familiar with the fundamental questions of microeconomics: What, How and for whom.*

Solution:

The fundamental questions of microeconomics are usually stated as What?, How?, and For whom?

"What?" refers to what goods and services will the economy produce and in what quantities. Because of scarcity, society cannot have all the goods and services that are needed. It has to decide what will be produced and what will be sacrificed, knowing that more of one good or service means less of some other good or service.

"How?" refers to how the goods and services will be produced—the method of production. It's a question about the technology that will be used to produce the goods and services that society decides will be produced. The society must decide how the factors of production will be combined to produce its output of goods and services.

"For whom?" refers to who gets the goods and services that the economy produces. This is a question about the distribution of the economy's output of goods and services. Society must decide on the mechanism that will be used to distribute goods and services to its members.

Problem 3-23

What is the relationship between the fundamental microeconomic question, "What to produce?" and economic scarcity?

Requirement and Clue: *The central point here is that scarcity prevents the economy from producing all the goods and services necessary to satisfy human wants. A decision therefore has to be made with regard to what will be produced.*

Solution:

Had it not been for the existence of economic scarcity, society would simply produce all the goods and services necessary to satisfy all human wants. But economic scarcity is a fact of life and every economy must decide whether to produce more of A and less of B. Producing more automobiles might mean producing fewer miles of highway; producing more classrooms might mean producing fewer hospital beds; and producing more entertainment sets might mean producing fewer tons of wheat. Since economic scarcity limits society's ability to produce goods and services, society must decide what goods and services it will produce and in what quantities. What to produce and economic scarcity are integrally related.

Problem 3-24

"The fundamental microeconomic questions, What?, How? and For whom are essentially questions of allocation." Discuss.

Requirement and Clue: *The following points should be noted. Resources have to be allocated to whatever the economy decides to produce. The method of production involves allocating resources. The distribution of the output deals with allocating the output.*

Solution:

The fundamental microeconomic questions refer to what goods and services the economy will produce and in what quantities, what method of production will the economy use to produce its output of goods and services, and how the economy's output of goods and services will be distributed among the members of society. The question of what to produce is an allocation problem in the sense that resources have to be allocated to whatever goods and services the society decides it will produce. The question of how to produce is also an allocation question. If a decision is made to produce wheat, for example, will the production be done using a labour-intensive method or a capital-intensive method? In other words, how will resources be allocated to the production of wheat? Finally, the question of for whom to produce is also an allocation problem. Whereas the questions of what to produce and how to produce involve the allocation of resources or inputs, the question of for whom to produce is a question of the allocation of output. The question refers to how the society's output of goods and services will be allocated among the members of society. Thus we see that the fundamental microeconomic questions are really questions of allocation.

Multiple-Choice

In each case, circle the letter that corresponds with the correct answer.

1. When we choose:

a. we necessarily give up something
b. we don't necessarily give up something but we must take something
c. there is no cost involved unless the choice costs us money
d. we always incur a monetary cost

Answer: a

Reason: *Choice always involves giving up something.*

2. Choice is:

a. always without a cost because we have freedom of choice
b. always associated with a cost
c. a problem that is faced only by poor people
d. identical to taking

Answer: b

Reason: *Choice involves giving up something, and whatever is given up is a cost.*

3. The term used for the next best alternative that is sacrificed when a choice is made is:

a. sacrificial cost
b. next-best cost
c. opportunity cost
d. all of the above

Answer: c

Reason: *Opportunity cost is whatever is given up when a choice is made.*

4. Opportunity cost of an item is:

a. the monetary price of an item
b. the monetary cost of producing the item
c. the monetary cost of an opportunity that is missed
d. whatever is given up in order to obtain the item

Answer: d

Reason: *Opportunity cost is whatever is sacrificed when a choice is made.*

5. Opportunity cost can be measured by:

a. what we get when we give up something
b. what we give up divided by what we get
c. what we give up minus what we get
d. what we get minus what we give up

Answer: b

Reason: *A measure of opportunity cost is the ratio of what we give up to what we get.*

6. In order to get 5 more bananas, you have to give up 10 erasers. From this we can conclude that the opportunity cost of bananas is:

a. 2 erasers
b. 50 erasers
c. 5 erasers
d. none of the above

Answer: a

Reason: *You give up 10 erasers and you get 5 bananas. Opportunity cost is what you give up (10 erasers) divided by what you get (5 bananas): 10/5 = 2*

7. The cost-benefit approach:

a. is useful only in making business decisions
b. involves comparing costs and benefits
c. is a method of minimizing production costs
d. is a sure way of eliminating costs

Answer: b

Reason: *A rule of thumb in decision making is to compare benefits and costs.*

8. The cost-benefit approach is applicable:

a. only when costs can be measured in monetary terms
b. only when benefits can be measured in monetary terms
c. only when both costs and benefits can be measured in monetary terms
d. none of the above

Answer: d

Reason: *The cost-benefit approach is applicable whether or not cost and benefits can be measured in monetary terms.*

9. Cost-benefit analysis can be used:

a. to determine whether or not to take a vacation in France
b. to decide whether or not to attend a particular class
c. to choose between going to university or taking a full-time job
d. all of the above

Answer: d

Reason: Coast-benefit analysis can be used in all the circumstances listed in the choices.

10. A production-possibility schedule is:

a. a graph that shows possible combinations of goods that are available to consumers

b. a curve that separates the possible from the impossible

c. a table that shows various combinations of goods and services that can be produced under certain conditions

d. all of the above

Answer: c

Reason: Unlike the p-p curve that is a graph, the p-p schedule is a table that shows production possibilities, given the quantity and quality of resources and the state of technology.

11. A production possibility curve is:

a. A graph that shows all combinations of goods and services that an economy can produce under certain conditions

b. drawn on the assumption that resources and technology are constantly changing

c. applicable only small countries with underdeveloped economies

d. always upward-sloping because of increasing opportunity cost

Answer: a

Reason: Unlike the p-p schedule that is a table, the p-p curve is a graph that shows all production possibilities, given the quantity and quality of resources and the state of technology.

12. A linear (straight line) production possibility curve for an economy means that:

a. a constant amount of goods and services can be produced with given resources

b. all resources must always be used at a constant rate in the economy

c. the economy faces constant opportunity cost

d. all resources are not equally efficient in all uses

Answer: c

Reason: A situation of constant opportunity cost is represented by a downward sloping linear p-p curve.

13. If an economy is facing increasing opportunity cost, then we know that its production-possibility (p-p) curve will be:

a. upward sloping
b. horizontal
c. downward sloping but linear
d. concave

Answer: d

Reason: A situation of increasing opportunity cost is represented by a concave p-p curve.

14. Production-possibility curves are usually drawn concave because:

a. of the law of scarcity and resource use

b. all resources are limited

c. not all resources can be used equally efficiently in all uses

d. of an agreement among economists to use concave curves

Answer: c

Reason: Increasing opportunity cost occurs because resources are not all equally efficient in all uses. Concave p-p curves illustrate increasing opportunity cost.

15. The production-possibility curve illustrates the fundamental fact that:

a. an economy's productive capacity increases with the passage of time

b. if an economy is using all its resources and technology is given, it can produce more of one good only by producing less of some other good

c. an economy will always operate at the highest level of efficiency

d. the quantities of goods and services that an economy can produce are limited only by people's imagination

Answer: b

Reason: This is the scarcity issue. Because of limited resources, we can produce more of one thing only by producing less of something else.

16. A point below a production-possibility curve means that:

a. the economy is deliberately and consciously saving resources for future use

b. the economy is not using all its resources or is not using them efficiently

c. the economy is operating at more than full employment

d. the economy is using all its resources in an efficient manner

Answer: b

Reason: A point on the curve means that the economy is using all its resources. A point below (inside) the curve means that it is not using all its resources.

17. The following diagram is the production-possibility curve for Betterland (a fictitious country). With reference to the diagram, which of the following is true?

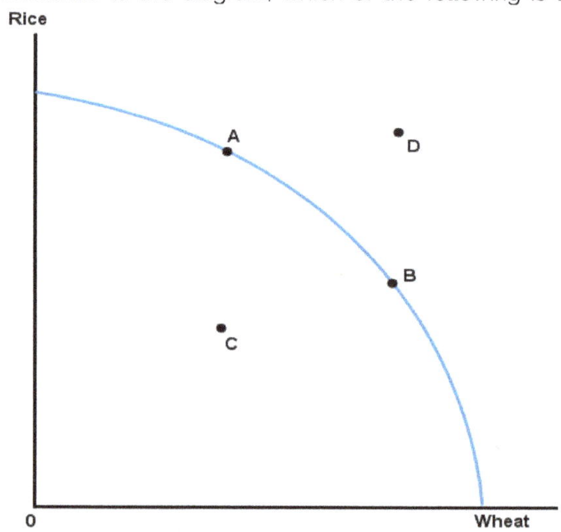

a. Betterland cannot move from point A to point B without an increase in available resources or an improvement in technology.

b. Betterland can move from point C to point B with no increase in the quantity of resources available or in its technology.

c. Betterland can move from point D to point A if it

ceases to produce rice.

d. At point C, Betterland can produce either more rice or more wheat, but not more of both.

Answer: b

Reason: *At point C, Betterland has idle resources that it can employ to move to point B.*

18. Which of the following will cause an economy's p-p curve to shift outward, other things being equal?

a. An increase in demand for all goods and services
b. A more intensive use of available resources
c. The acquisition of more resources or better technology
d. All of the above

Answer: c

Reason: *An increase in the quantity or quality of resources or an improvement in technology will enhance the economy's productive capacity.*

19. Which of the following is not illustrated in a production-possibility curve?

a. Opportunity cost b. Choice
c. Economic scarcity d. Price

Answer: d

Reason: *The p-p curve tells us nothing about price.*

20. A *free lunch*:

a. refers to the additional output produced by an economy without sacrificing the production of some other good or service
b. can occur if an economy is operating below its production-possibility curve
c. is possible if an economy is not using all its resources
d. all of the above

Answer: d

Reason: *The concept of a free lunch is getting something for nothing. If the economy has idle resources, it can use them to produce goods and services. This use of idle inputs does not result in a loss of output elsewhere in the economy.*

21. An outward shift of the production-possibility curve is often referred to as:

a. economic growth b. a production shift
c. graph expansion d. all of the above

Answer: a

Reason: *Economic growth can be defined as an increase in the economy's ability to produce more goods and services. This is represented by an outward shift in the p-p curve.*

22. An outward shift of an economy's production-possibility curve means that:

a. the economy is actually producing more goods and services
b. the economy is capable of producing more goods and services
c. the economy is using its resources efficiently
d. all of the above

Answer: b

Reason: *An economy's p-p curve gives information about what the economy is capable of producing. It speaks to the economy's potential in terms of production.*

23. The following diagram shows the production-possibility (p-p) curve for a hypothetical economy.

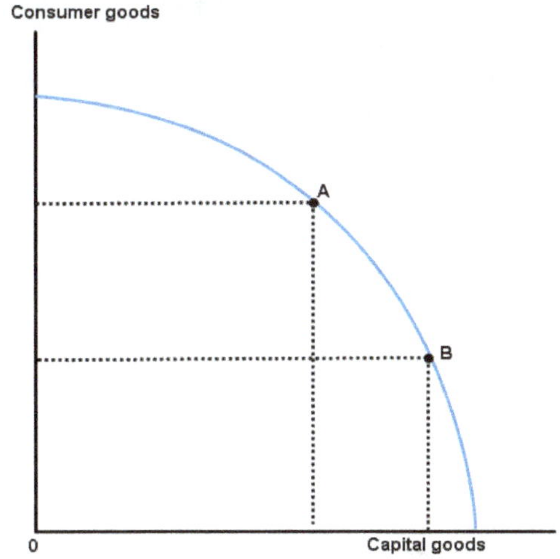

If the economy shifts production from point A to point B:

a. it will have no effect on the p-p curve in the future
b. it will cause the p-p curve to shift towards the origin
c. it will cause the p-p curve to shift outward in the future
d. none of the above

Answer: c

Reason: *By shifting production from A to B, the economy would increase its production of capital goods, which will enable it to produce more capital and more consumer goods in the future.*

24. The fundamental microeconomic questions are:

a. What to produce, how to produce it, and who gets what is produced
b. How large the population should be and what kind of economic system is best
c. Why are resources limited and how can the quantity be increased
d. How can unemployment and inflation be controlled

Answer: a

Reason: *Because of scarcity, every economy has to decide what goods and services it will produce, the method of production that it will use, and how to distribute the output that is produced.*

25. The fundamental microeconomic questions must be addressed by:

a. only developing economies
b. only economies in transition
c. only advanced economies
d. all economies

Answer: d

Reason: *No matter how the economy is organized, it has to decide what, how, and for whom.*

True or False

Determine whether each of the following statements is true or false.

1. One cannot choose without giving up something.

Answer: True

2. If economic scarcity did not exist, one would not have to choose.

Answer: True

3. Opportunity cost is the name given to the monetary cost of production.

Answer: False

Explanation: *It is an alternative that is sacrificed and may have nothing to do with production cost.*

4. The opportunity cost to a farmer of producing more wheat is the corn that he or she could have produced instead.

Answer: True

5. Opportunity cost can be defined as the next best alternative that is sacrificed when a choice is made.

Answer: True

6. Opportunity cost can be measured by what we give up divided by what we get in its place.

Answer: True

7. If you have to give up 8 CDs in order to get 4 more Blu-ray movies, then the opportunity cost of a Blu-ray movie is 2 CDs.

Answer: True

8. Economic scarcity forces us to choose, but we can choose without incurring any opportunity cost.

Answer: False

Explanation: *Choosing always involves a cost in terms of what is given up.*

9. A production possibility curve is a graph that shows all combinations of goods and/or services that an economy is currently producing with all its resources, using the available technology.

Answer: False

Explanation: *The graph shows what the economy is capable of producing, not necessarily what it is producing.*

10. Other names for the production possibility curve are the transformation curve, the production possibility boundary, and the production possibility frontier.

Answer: True

11. If the production possibility curve for an economy is linear and downward sloping, we know that the economy is facing decreasing opportunity cost.

Answer: False

Explanation: *This would be a case of constant opportunity cost.*

12. If the production possibility curve for an economy is linear, we know that the economy is facing constant opportunity cost.

Answer: True

13. An economy that is facing increasing opportunity cost will have an upward sloping production possibility curve.

Answer: False

Explanation: *Upward sloping p-p curves don't make any economic sense. If the economy is facing increasing opportunity cost, its p-p curve will be concave.*

14. A country's production possibility curve will be linear (i.e. a straight line) if all its resources are equally efficient in all uses.

Answer: True

15. Production possibility curves are likely to be concave because of the law of increasing opportunity cost.

Answer: True

16. Because resources are not all equally efficient in all uses, production possibility curves are likely to be concave.

Answer: True

17. A point below a production possibility curve indicates unemployment; a point on the curve indicates full employment; and a point above the curve indicates an unattainable combination of output.

Answer: True

18. An economy can never be in a situation where it can produce more of one good without producing less of some other good.

Answer: False

Explanation: *It can if it has unemployed resources. By using unemployed resources, it can produce more of one good without producing less of some other good. Recall the case of a "free lunch."*

19. A production possibility curve shows the maximum output that an economy can produce; therefore the curve can never shift to the right.

Answer: false

Explanation: *The curve can shift to the right if the economy obtains more or better resources or if technology improves.*

20. A greater quantity and better quality of resources or an improvement in technology will shift the production possibility curve to the right.

Answer: True

21. In a modern economy that is well organized, a production possibility curve cannot shift downward to the left.

Answer: False

Explanation: *A p-p curve can shift to the left if the economy loses resources through a flood or forest fires, for example.*

22. The production possibility curve will shift to the right if the country uses idle resources that were previously unemployed.

Answer: False

Explanation: Using resources that the economy already has will not affect its capacity to produce and will therefore not shift the curve.

23. The production possibility curve gives information about what the economy is actually producing, not what it is capable of producing.

Answer: False

Explanation: The p-p curve is about the economy's productive capacity.

24. A decision to reduce current consumption by investing in capital goods will shift the production possibility curve to the right in the future.

Answer: True

25. Referring to the fundamental microeconomic questions, What and How are essentially questions of allocation of resources while the question of For whom is a question of the allocation of output.

Answer: True

Completion

(Fill in the blanks)

Use each word or combination of words from the list exactly once.
*(**Hint**: Proceed by elimination)*

Word list

Concave x 2 — Constant — Cost x 2 — Cost-Benefit — Economic — For Whom — Free — Graph — Growth — How — Increasing — Linear — Lunch — Opportunity x 2 — Produce — Resources — Right —Technology x 2 — Underemployment — Unemployment — What

Questions

1. Choice involves giving up something, and whatever is given up is ____________ ____________ .
2. The ____________ approach to decision making involves comparing benefits and costs.
3. The next best alternative that is sacrificed when a choice is made is referred to as ____________ ____________. (opportunity cost)
4. A country's production possibility curve is a ____________ that shows all combinations of goods and services that the country can____________ if it uses all its resources and if technology is constant.
5. A production possibility curve represents the maximum amount of goods and services than an economy can produce with a given level of ____________ and ____________.
6. A linear production possibility curve indicates ____________ opportunity cost, while a concave production possibility curve indicates ____________ opportunity cost.
7. The production possibility curve for a country facing increasing opportunity cost will be ____________.
8. Because resources are not all equally efficient in all uses, production possibility curves are more likely to be ____________ than ____________.
9. The additional output produced without sacrificing the production of any other good or service is called a ____________ ____________.
10. An outward shift of a country's production possibility curve is sometimes referred to as ____________ ____________.
11. A country's production possibility curve will shift to the right if it acquires more or better resources or if its ____________ improves.
12. A country's production possibility curve will shift to the ____________ in the future if it reduces current consumption and invests in capital goods.
13. The fundamental microeconomic questions are ____________ to produce, ____________ to produce it, and ____________ to produce.
14. A point below the production possibility curve means that the economy is experiencing either ____________ or ____________.

Solutions

1. (opportunity cost)
2. (cost-benefit)
3. (opportunity cost)
4. (graph, produce)
5. (resources, technology)
6. (constant, increasing)
7. (concave)
8. (concave, linear)
9. (free lunch)
10. (economic growth)
11. (technology)
12. (right)
13. (what, how, for whom)
14. (unemployment, underemployment)

4 A MARKET-ORIENTED ECONOMIC SYSTEM

SYNOPSIS

An economic system comprises households, firms, and government authorities who make decisions about the use of the economy's resources. Economic systems may be classified loosely as free enterprise and socialist economic systems. In a free enterprise economic system, most economic decisions are made by households and firms responding to the market forces of demand and supply. Consequently, free enterprise economies are often called **market-oriented economies**. In a socialist economic system, the state dominates most economic decisions. Consequently, socialist economic systems are often called **command economies**. In practice, all economies are mixed economies where decisions are made by households, firms, and government.

Every economic system, no matter how it is organized, must deal with the fundamental economic problem of scarcity. It must decide *what* goods and services will be produced, how they will be produced, and *for whom* they will be produced. In addition, an economic system is expected to provide economic stability, economic security, and economic growth.

The role of government in a market economy includes the protection of individual freedom, the protection of property rights and the enforcement of contracts, the prevention of the abuse of monopoly power, the promotion of economic stability and an equitable distribution of income.

The three basic sectors of the economy are the consumer sector (households), the business sector (producers or firms), and the government sector. Consumers provide resources to firms, and they purchase a large part of the output of the economy. The business sector purchases resources mainly from households and other firms, and produces goods and services. The government engages in production, and in a number of regulatory activities.

LEARNING OBJECTIVES

In connection with this module, you should be able to:

1. describe economic systems and their functions
2. explain the role of households in a market economy
3. explain the role of firms in a market economy
4. explain the role of government in a market economy
5. construct a simple circular flow model of a market-oriented economy

DEFINITIONS & CONCEPTS

You should be able to define the following terms and concepts:

economic systems
command economy
free enterprise system
mixed economy
market mechanism
consumer sovereignty
household sector
business sector
government sector
factor market
product market

4

A MARKET-ORIENTED ECONOMIC SYSTEM

Concepts, Definitions & Problems

Problem 4-1

What is a market-oriented economic system?

Requirement and Clue: *What is required here is demonstration of your knowledge of what a market-oriented economy is. You are not required to write a thesis on a market-oriented economic system. Just say what it is and provide an example, if you can.*

Solution:

A market-oriented economic system is one in which the fundamental economic questions of what, how and for whom are made by private individuals and groups through the market forces of demand and supply. In such an economic system, most of the economy's resources are owned and controlled privately rather than by the government. Consumers are free to maximize their satisfaction and firms are free to maximize their profits by working through markets. Such an economic system is often referred to as a *free enterprise* economic system. Examples of countries with a market-oriented economic system are Canada, the United Kingdom, and the United States.

Problem 4-2

What are the main advantages of a market-oriented economic system?

Requirement and Clue: *Although it may be tempting to discuss the disadvantages as well as the advantages or benefits, and to compare a market-oriented economic system with some alternative, the question requires only that you state the main advantages of a market-oriented economic system. You may briefly define the system and then state its main advantages.*

Solution:

A market-oriented economic system is one in which most economic decisions are made by individuals and firms acting through free markets to achieve their economic objectives.

One of the most important advantages of a market-oriented economic system is the freedom of choice that individuals enjoy. Because individuals and groups are free to use their resources to advance their own interests, a market-oriented economic system provides initiative and incentive for people to pursue their economic objectives and improve their economic well-being. Under a market-oriented economic system, every individual has an opportunity to use his or her talents and resources for his or her own benefit.

Another major advantage of a market-oriented economic system is that the goods and services that consumers want are produced without any deliberate coordinated decision-making. The system works automatically for the most part and is therefore relatively efficient. There is no need to make any special arrangement with a grocery store to provide you with milk today. If you wanted to, you could go to the grocery store and buy milk. Under this system, you don't have to make any arrangements with the college cafeteria for breakfast on any particular morning, yet you are quite confident that you will be able to obtain breakfast any morning. The system works in such a way that it does not require a great deal of coordination for a market-oriented economy to produce the goods and services that consumers want.

Problem 4-3

Does a market-oriented economy have any weaknesses? If so, what are they?

Requirement and Clue: *The question is designed to determine whether or not you are familiar with the weaknesses of a market-oriented economy. The solution requires that you focus on the weaknesses. Notice that the problem has two parts. You are expected to address both.*

Solution:

Despite major advantages, a market-oriented economic system does have some notable weaknesses. If left to itself, it often produces results that are quite socially unacceptable; and that's why the government often intervenes so that the system gives results that are more acceptable.

First, a market-oriented economic system does not automatically generate full employment. There are many people who genuinely want to work but are unable to find jobs. After you have completed your studies, there is a good chance that you will find a job where you can use the training and skills that you have developed, but the system does not guarantee it. Associated with the problem of unemployment is the problem of economic instability. A market-oriented economic system is susceptible to wide fluctuations in economic activity, sometimes with serious economic consequences.

Second, under a market-oriented economic system, certain goods and services may not be produced at all, or may be produced only in vastly inadequate quantities. A market-oriented economic system tends to produce goods and services that are wanted by those members of the society who can pay for them. Some goods and services, such as sanitation and defence, which benefit the entire society, may not be produced by private businesses since it is difficult for private firms to exact a payment from all members of the society. Such goods, known as public goods, are better provided collectively through the government.

Third, a market-oriented economic system, with its emphasis on private property, may not provide adequate protection to the environment. Resources such as rivers, lakes, and the air are common property, owned by everyone but by no one in particular. Often, no price is charged for the use of common property with the result that the environment becomes a dumping ground for all types of pollutants. This is a serious weakness of a market-oriented economic system.

Fourth, the promotion of self-interest, a feature of a market-oriented economic system, may result in a very inequitable distribution of income, which may be socially unacceptable. Critics of the market-oriented economic system charge that under this system, the rich get richer and the poor get poorer. When this occurs, government intervention may be necessary to deal with the problem.

Finally, a market-oriented economic system does not guarantee the competition that is necessary to ensure the efficient allocation of resources. Under a market-oriented economic system, the production of certain goods may be controlled by one seller or a few sellers who may take advantage of the opportunity to exploit other members of the society.

Problem 4-4

What is the main identifying feature of a free enterprise economic system?

Requirement and Clue: *Simply defining a free enterprise economic system will not be adequate for a solution to this problem. Although it would do no harm to briefly define a free enterprise economic system, the emphasis should be placed on indicating its main identifying feature.*

Solution:

A free enterprise economic system is one in which economic decisions are made by individuals and firms responding to a system of prices and markets—the system in which prices are used to allocate resources and goods and services.

The main identifying feature of a free enterprise economic system is the right of private persons and private groups to own property—a concept known as the institution of private property. In this type of economic system, people are free, not only to own resources, but also to use them in whatever way they choose, subject to certain legal limitations designed to safeguard society. In this kind of economic system, individuals enjoy freedom of choice. Consumers are free, within certain legal and social constraints, to use their income to purchase the goods and services that they want to maximize their satisfaction. They are also free to use the resources at their disposal to maximize their income. Businesses also have freedom of choice. They are free to use their resources in such a way as to maximize their profits.

Problem 4-5

Discuss the role of government in a market-oriented economy.

Requirement and Clue: *The problem recognizes that government plays a role in a market-oriented economy. Your job is to discuss that role.*

Solution:

In a market-oriented economy, most economic decisions are left to private individuals acting in response to the market forces of demand and supply. However, the market system does not perform some tasks satisfactorily and the government therefore enters the market to assist the system to produce results that are in accordance with the goals of society.

The government plays an important role in a market-oriented economy. First, government intervention in a market-oriented economy is often necessary to protect individual freedom, to protect the institution of private property, to enforce contracts, and to regulate economic activity. Thus, laws and regulations and public policies exist to ensure that these objectives are net.

Second, government intervention is often necessary to ensure that social problems do not arise from a socially unjust distribution of income. For example, under a market-oriented economy, individuals who own large quantities of valuable resources and who use them where they make sizeable contributions to the economy's output will likely receive huge incomes, while those individuals who happen to be in less fortunate circumstances may hardly be able to afford the bare necessities of life. In this case, government may intervene to achieve what is considered to be social justice.

Finally, government may intervene in a market-oriented economy to ensure that the environment is protected from abuse that will harm society. The enacting and enforcement of a law forbidding the dumping of waste into the environment is an example of the role of government intervention into a market-oriented economy.

Problem 4-6

In many countries, government provides free elementary and secondary education. How can such use of public funds be justified?

Requirement and Clue: *What is required here is an argument that society benefits from a more educated population.*

Solution:

Education provides benefits not only to the recipient directly, but also to society as a whole. A better educated population implies a better educated labour force and generally a more productive economy. It can also be argued that a more educated population benefits society by creating better informed and socially involved citizens. Since the entire society benefits from education, then public expenditure on education is justified.

Problem 4-7

How does a free enterprise economy system answer the question, "What to produce"?

Requirement and Clue: *You are required to explain how the workings of a free enterprise economic system result in a decision regarding what goods and services will be produced and in what quantities. A brief definition of a free enterprise economic system may be included, but it is not necessary. It is expected that you show some awareness of the meaning of the question, "What to produce"?*

Solution:

A free enterprise economic system is one in which most economic decisions are made by private individuals and firms interacting in a system of markets and prices to achieve their economic objectives. What to produce refers to what goods and services will the economy produce and in what quantities.

Firms in a free enterprise economic system engage in production because they hope to make a profit by selling the product at a price that exceeds the cost of production. It follows then, that firms will produce what consumers want to buy. Consumers express their wants by their behaviour in the market. Firms respond by producing those goods and services that receive the highest number of dollar votes. Suppose a manufacturing company decides to produce a certain product called *asitis*, and then find out that consumers are unwilling to spend their money on that particular product. The firm will soon discover that the production of *asitis* is not profitable and would put its resources into some other venture. By their decision not to purchase *asitis,* consumers have communicated effectively to the manufacturing company that they do not want *asitis* produced.

Problem 4-8

What is meant by consumer sovereignty?

Requirement and Clue: *This is a definitional problem. There is no need to write all you know about the concept of consumer sovereignty. You are not even required to explain how it works. All that is required is a clear statement of the meaning of the term.*

Solution:

Consumer sovereignty refers to the role of consumers in determining what goods and services will be produced in an economy and in what quantities. It refers to the idea that consumers, by their buying behaviour, that is, by their dollar votes, have the power to determine ultimately what is produced.

Problem 4-9

How does a free enterprise economic system determine how goods and services are produced?

Requirement and Clue: *Your task here is to explain how the decision regarding the method of production to be used is made in a free enterprise economic system.*

Solution:

The economic system must have a way of organizing its productive resources in order to provide the members of the society with appropriate quantities of goods and services. A mechanism must exist for shifting resources away from uses that contribute less to consumers' satisfaction and toward uses that contribute more to consumers' satisfaction.

In a free enterprise economic system, individual producers decide on the methods of production (that is, the technology to be used) but their decisions are guided by the system of prices and markets. If the goal of a producer is to earn as large a profit as possible, then the producer will use the method of production with the lowest cost; that is, the producer will use an efficient method of production.

Problem 4-10

How does a free enterprise economic system answer the question of the distribution of output among members of the society?

Requirement and Clue: *This question tests your understanding of the "For whom" question in microeconomics and your knowledge of how the free enterprise system addresses the problem. People's ability to buy depends on their income. How is income determined in a free enterprise economic system? Here is where your focus should lie.*

Solution:

In a free enterprise economic system, the task of distributing the economy's output among members of the society is accomplished mainly through the market system. The share of the total output that individuals receive depends mainly on their abilities to purchase goods and services. The ability of any individual to purchase goods and services depends on the individual's income, which in turn depends on the quantity and quality of human and physical resources over which that individual has control. If the market places a high value on particular resources, their owners will receive large payments for their use and will be able to obtain a large share of the total output of goods and services. Individuals who own very few resources that are poorly employed will receive low incomes and consequently, only small portions of the total output. Thus, the distribution of the economy's total output in a free enterprise economic system depends largely on the distribution of income, which in turn depends on the distribution of resources among the members of society.

Problem 4-11

How does a free enterprise economic system answer the three basic questions of microeconomics?

Requirement and Clue: *Before you can answer this question, you need to know what a free enterprise economic system is and the three basic microeconomic questions. Having settled that in your head, you must now consider how these three questions are solved through the workings of a free enterprise economic system.*

Solution:

A free enterprise economic system is one in which most economic decisions are made by private individuals and firms interacting in a system of markets and prices to achieve their economic objectives. The three basic questions of microeconomics are: (1) what goods and services will be produced and in what quantities, (2) how the economy's inputs (resources) will be used to produce those goods and services, and (3) who will get the goods and services that the economy produces.

What to Produce

Firms in a free enterprise economic system engage in production because they hope to make a profit by selling the product at a price that exceeds the cost of production. It follows then, that firms will produce what consumers want to buy. Consumers express their wants by their behaviour in the market. Firms respond by producing those goods and services that receive the highest number of dollar votes.

How to produce

In a free enterprise economic system, individual producers decide on the methods of production (that is, the technology to be used) but their decisions are guided by the system of prices and markets. If the goal of a producer is to earn as large a profit as possible, then the producer will use the method of production with the lowest cost; that is, the producer will use an efficient method of production.

For whom to produce

The free enterprise system solves the question of the distribution of the economy's output by determining, in markets, the value of resources and the incomes that they generate. . If the market places a high value on particular resources, their owners will receive large payments for their use and will be able to obtain a large share of the total output of goods and services. Individuals who own very few resources that are poorly employed will receive low incomes and consequently, only small portions of the total output. Thus, the distribution of the economy's total output in a free enterprise economic system depends largely on the distribution of income, which in turn depends on the distribution of resources among the members of society.

Problem 4-12

In most countries, there are no laws forcing authors to write books; yet, when you register for your courses, you are confident that there will be textbooks in the bookstores for your courses. Why?

Requirement and Clue: *This is an application problem. By carefully examining it, you will see that it is referring to the problem of what to produce. Essentially, you are required to explain how a market-oriented economy decides to produce textbooks for students.*

Solution:

Authors know that students are willing to purchase textbooks, so in a free enterprise economic system, they write them in the hope of finding publishers who are willing to publish them and pay royalties to the authors. The publishers, on the other hand, publish the books in the hope of making a profit in the process. Although there is no direct command to authors or publishers to produce books, they respond to market signals, which indicate to them that writing and publishing textbooks can be a profitable undertaking.

Problem 4-13

What is meant by a "mixed economy"?

Requirement and Ckue: *This is a definitional problem. There is no need for you to write a term paper on mixed economies. That would be far beyond the requirements of this question. Simply define a mixed economy and give examples. A brief mention of a completely free market economy and a command economy for comparison may be helpful but not absolutely necessary.*

Solution:

In contrast to an entirely free market enterprise economy where private individuals and firms exercise total control over the economy's resources, and a totally planned economy where all resources and owned and controlled by the government, a mixed economy is one where public and privately owned enterprises exist. The *mixture* is one of government and private enterprises.

In the real world, all economies are "mixed" to some extent. But the economies of the United States, Canada, the United Kingdom and Germany are examples of major mixed economies.

Problem 4-14

__Briefly__ define the circular flow model.

Requirement and Clue: *The word "briefly" is underlined for emphasis. You cannot ignore it. All that you are required to do here is to provide a clear definition of the circular flow model.*

Solution:

The circular flow model is an economic model—a simplification of a real economy—showing the flow of resources, goods and services, expenditures, and income between sectors of the economy.

Problem 4-15

Define each of the following terms:

a. *Market*
b. *Product market*
c. *Factor market*
d. *Real flows*

Requirement and Clue: *You are required just to state what each of the terms is, giving examples if you can. You are not asked to write an essay on the terms or concepts.*

Solution:

a. A market is a mechanism that facilitates the buying and selling of goods and services and resources.
b. A product market is a market in which goods and services are bought and sold. An example of a product market is the market for shoes.
c. A factor market is the market in which factor of production or resources are bought and sold. An example of a factor market is the market for steel.
d. Real flows are flows of physical goods and services and of resources. An example of a real flow is the flow of goods and services from firms to households.

Problem 4-16

What is meant by real flows and money flows in a simple circular flow model?

Requirement and Clue: *What is required here is the identification of real and money flows in a simple circular model.*

Solution:

Real flows are flows of resources and goods and services. In a simple circular flow model, resources such as land, labour, and capital flow from households to firms, and finished goods and services flow from firms to households. These are the real flows.

Money flows are the flows of money that result from purchasing resources and finished goods and services. Payments made by firms to households for resources, and payments made by households to firms for finished goods and service are examples of money flows in the circular flow model.

Problem 4-17

Clearly describe the two types of markets in the simple circular flow model.

Requirement and Clue: *Before you can describe the markets in question, you must know what they are. Think of the simple circular model and identify the two markets in your head and then provide the solution. Note that the solution involves a little more than simply defining the markets.*

Solution:

The two types of markets in the simple circular flow model are the product market and the factor market. The product market is the market in which firms sell finished goods and services to households. Money is used to effect the transfer of goods and services from firms to households. The market for ipods is an example of a product market. In this market, the buyers are the households while the sellers are the firms.

The factor market (also called the resource market) is the market in which households sell resources (land, labour, capital, and entrepreneurial services) to firms. Money is used to effect the transfer of resources (factors of production) from households to firms. The market for labour services is an example of a factor market. In this market, the buyers are the firms while the sellers are the households.

Problem 4-18

Use a simple circular flow diagram to illustrate the flows of resources, goods and services, and money in an economy.

Requirement and Clue: *Essentially, you are to draw and explain a simple circular flow diagram.*

Solution:

Below is a simple circular flow diagram. It shows households and businesses, product and resource markets, and flows of resources, finished goods and services, and money.

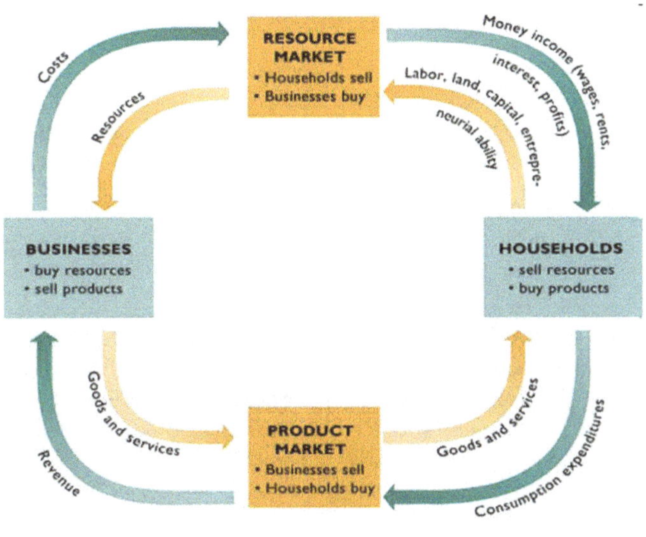

There is a flow of resources from the households to the resource market and a flow of money/costs from the business sector to the resource market. Households sell and businesses buy resources in the resource market. After the transaction, there is a flow of resources from the resource market to the businesses and a flow of money (income) from the resource market to the households. Firms/businesses use the resources to produce goods and services which are sold in the product market. Thus there is a flow of goods and services from the firms to the product market. Households buy and firms sell goods and services in the product market. Thus, there is a flow of money from households to the product market. After the transaction, there is a flow of goods and services from the resource market to the households and a flow on money from the product market to the firms.

Problem 4-19

In the simple circular flow model, the roles of households and firms are reversed in the factor and product markets. Explain.

Requirement and Clue: *This problem is designed to test your understanding of the roles of the key actors in the circular flow model. The solution calls for a statement of the roles of households and firms in the factor and product markets.*

Solution:

Most people probably think of households as buyers of goods and services and firms as sellers of goods and services. That, of course, is true of the product market. Firms sell their output of goods and services in that market and households buy finished goods and services in that market. But in the factor market, the roles of households and firms are reversed. In this market, firms are buyers while households are sellers. Firms buy resources and households sell resources in this market. Thus we see that households and firms are both buyers and sellers.

Problem 4-20

How is labour accounted for in the circular flow model?

Requirement and Clue: *The solution requires you to determine where labour fits into the circular flow model. To do this you must know whether labour is a factor of production or a finished product. Having decided that labour is a resource, then it will be accounted for in the factor market.*

Solution:

Labour is a factor of production—a resource that is used along with other factors of production to produce finished goods and services and other resources. In the circular flow model, households provide labour by selling labour services in the factor market to firms. Firms then use the labour services to produce finished goods and services to be sold in the product market to households.

Problem 4-21

What set of transactions that normally occur in a real economy are omitted from the simple circular flow model?

Requirement and Clue: *The problem is testing your familiarity with transactions in a real economy and with the limitations of the simple circular flow model. You are expected to identify transactions that are, for simplicity, omitted from the circular flow model, even though they are normal in a real economy.*

Solution:

One of the limitations of the simple circular flow model is its exclusion of transactions between firms and between individuals. In a real economy, firms do buy goods and services from other firms, and consumers do carry our transactions between each other. However, these types of transactions are not captured in the simple circular flow model. The simple circular flow model also assumes no economic role for the government. In reality however, there are transactions between firms and the government and between individuals and the government. For example, private firms provide aircrafts and road construction services to the government, and the government engages the services of households in a wide range of employment activities.

Problem 4-22

Indicate whether each of the following is true or false as it relates to the simple circular flow model with only households and firms:

a. *Households sell resources to the firms.*
b. *Firms purchase finished goods from the households.*
c. *Households' income includes wages, rent, and interest.*
d. *Firms sell their products in the factor market.*
e. *Households buy resources in the factor market and sell goods and services in the product market.*
f. *Households operate only in the product market, buying goods and services.*
g. *Households and firms operate in both product and factor markets.*
h. *Firms earn dividends for their entrepreneurial services.*

Requirement and Clue: *You should read each statement carefully and then determine whether it is true or false. Remember to consider the solution as it relates to the simple circular flow model.*

Solution:

a. True
b. False
c. True
d. False
e. False
f. False
g. True
h. False

Multiple-Choice

In each case, circle the letter that corresponds with the correct answer.

1. An economic system is:

a. the same as a political system
b. not necessary for production and distribution of goods and services
c. a set of laws, institutions and customs whereby a society accomplishes the task of producing goods and service
d. a mechanism for ensuring economic freedom, equitable distribution of wealth, fair competition, and social justice

Answer: c

Reason: *It is the function of an economic system to produce and distribute goods and services to satisfy consumers' wants.*

2. A market-oriented economy is one where:

a. money is the most important thing for every member of society
b. most economic decisions are made by households and firms responding to market forces
c. the government forces all individuals and firms to comply with the dictates of capitalism
d. there is a tendency for markets to develop but their development is prevented because of the disadvantages of market-determined decisions

Answer: b

Reason: *A market-oriented economy is one in which a system of prices and markets dictates the flow of resources and goods and services.*

3. All modern economies are:

a. mixed economies
c. capitalistic
b. socialistic
d. command economies

Answer: a

Reason: *All real world economies combine private ownership and decision making and public enterprise.*

4. An advantage of a free enterprise economic system is:

a. the ability to generate full employment at all times
b. freedom of choice by consumers
c. government assurance of huge profits for businesses
d. guarantee of an equitable distribution of income

Answer: b

Reason: *One of the greatest advantages of a free enterprise economy is that consumers enjoy freedom of choice.*

5. A major weakness of a market-oriented economy is that:

a. it does not guarantee full employment
b. government intervention tends to be pervasive
c. choices of individuals and firms are severely limited
d. it is relatively inefficient

Answer: a

Reason: *Because individuals enjoy freedom of choice regarding the use of their resources in a market-oriented economy, the economy may fail to generate full employment.*

6. Features of a free enterprise economic system include:

a. the right of private individuals and groups to own property
b. freedom of enterprise
c. reliance on the price system
d. all of the above

Answer: d

Reason: *The features listed in choices a, b, and c are all characteristics of a free enterprise economic system.*

7. Which of the following is a distinguishing feature of a free enterprise economic system?

a. Private ownership of economic resources
b. Limited use of money
c. Use of capital as opposed to labour
d. Pervasive government intervention

Answer: a

Reason: *Private ownership and control of resources is a feature of a free enterprise economy.*

8. An example of a market-oriented economic systems:

a. the economy of the United States
b. the Canadian economy
c. the economy of the United Kingdom
d. any of the above

Answer: d

Reason: *The economies listed are all market-oriented economies.*

9. The economies of Cuba and the People's Republic of China are examples of:

a. pure capitalism
b. centrally planned economies
c. market-oriented economies
d. free enterprise economies

Answer: b

Reason: *Cuba and China are classified as centrally planned economies.*

10. Which of the following is a weakness of a free enterprise economic system?

a. It may produce economic instability
b. It may not encourage the production of public goods
c. It may not distribute income equitably
d. All of the above

Answer: d

Reason: *The issues cited in choices a, b, and c all apply to a free enterprise economic system.*

11. A mixed economy is:

a. one that has difficulty deciding what to produce and how to produce it
b. one that is mandated to produce a wide mixture of

goods and services
c. one that allows both private and public ownership and control of the means of production
d. one where the government decides on the mix of output that should be produced

Answer: c

Reason: In a mixed economy, there is a combination (mixture) of private enterprise and public ownership of resources.

12. Which of the following functions the price system does not perform?
a. Informing producers of consumers' wants
b. Determining the most efficient method of production
c. Conserving the use of scarce resources
d. Redistributing income among the owners of the factors of production

Answer: d

Reason: The price system does not redistribute income; public policy may do that.

13. Under a free market economic system, the government does not:
a. set all wages and prices
b. enforce contracts
c. allow the institution of private property
d. play any role in society

Answer: a

Reason: Under a free market economy, the system of prices and markets sets wages and prices.

14. Which of the following statements is true of a market-oriented economy?
a. It solves the problem of what to produce but not how to produce
b. It solves the problem of how to produce but not what to produce
c. It solves the problem of how to produce, what to produce, but not for whom to produce
d. It solves the problem of what to produce, how to produce, and for whom to produce

Answer: d

Reason: In a market-oriented economy, the fundamental economic problems of what, how, and for whom are dealt with by the system of prices and markets.

15. A free enterprise economic system solves the question of what to produce by:
a. conducting monthly surveys of consumer wants and preferences
b. allowing the government to make the decision
c. paying attention to what consumers are buying, that is, consumer sovereignty
d. none of the above

Answer: c

Reason: Wanting to earn a profit, firms in a free enterprise economic system produce the goods and services that consumers indicate willingness and an ability to buy.

16. Consumer sovereignty exists when:
a. consumers can do whatever they want without fear of being prosecuted
b. consumers ultimately determine what goods are produced by their dollar votes in markets
c. consumers are forced to abandon their preferences and purchase whatever firms produce and offer for sale
d. none of the above

Answer: b

Reason: Consumer sovereignty is the concept that firms produce what consumers indicate by their buying behaviour they want firms to produce.

17. The flow of resources, goods and services, expenditures, and income between households and firms is called:
a. the circular flow
b. producers' circle
c. consumer sovereignty
d. none of the above

Answer: a

Reason: The circular flow describes the flow of resources, income, goods and services, and expenditures between households and firms.

18. Which of the following is a true statement?
a. The product market is the market in which firms sell resources
b. The factor market is the market in which firms buy goods and services
c. The product market is the market in which households buy resources
d. The factor market is the market in which firms buy resources

Answer: d

Reason: Firms buy factors of production (resources) in the factor market from households. They use these resources to produce goods and services.

19. Flows of income and expenditures are:
a. real flows
b. money flows
c. normative flows
d. none of the above

Answer: b

Reason: Income and expenditures are in monetary terms, as opposed to resources and goods and services that are in real terms.

20. In the simple circular flow model, the flow of income from the factor market to households:
a. consists of wages, rent, interest & dividends, and profit
b. represents payment for factors of production
c. is a money flow as opposed to a real flow
d. all of the above

Answer: d

Reason: Choices a and b amount to the same thing, and the flow of income is in monetary terms.

True or False

Determine whether each of the following statements is true or false.

1. An economic system is characterized by a set of laws, institutions, and customs by means of which a society is governed.

Answer: False

Explanation: *The statement describes a political system, not an economic system.*

2. An economic system is a set of mechanisms—laws, institutions, and customs—by means of which the society accomplishes the task of producing goods and services.

Answer: True

3. Economic decision makers can be classified into households or consumers, firms or producers, and government authorities.

Answer: True

4. In all free enterprise economic systems, most of the economy's resources are privately owned.

Answer: True

5. Examples of market-oriented economies are the United States, Canada, the United Kingdom and Germany.

Answer: True

6. The economies of the People's Republic of China and Cuba are examples of market-oriented economies.

Answer: False

Explanation: *The economies listed are centrally planned economies.*

7. The economies of the People's Republic of China and Cuba are examples of centrally planned economies.

Answer: True

8. The basis of a free enterprise economic system is the institution of private property.

Answer: True

9. In a free enterprise economic system, consumers are free, within certain legal and social constraints, to use their income to purchase the goods and services that maximize their satisfaction.

Answer: True

10. In a free enterprise economic system, the government intervenes to ensure that all members of society get an equal share of the economy's output of goods and services.

Answer: False

Explanation: *In a free enterprise economic system, there is little or no government intervention, and certainly not to ensure equal distribution of output.*

11. The freedom of choice that is characteristic of the free enterprise economic system more often than not results in chaos.

Answer: False

Explanation: *Order and not chaos results from freedom of choice.*

12. The free enterprise economic system ensures that the goods and services that consumers want are those that are produced.

Answer: True

13. One advantage of a free enterprise economic system is that the goods and services that consumers want are produced without any deliberate coordinated decision-making.

Answer: True

14. One of the advantages of a free enterprise economic system is that it guarantees the production of public goods such as education and general sanitation.

Answer: False

Explanation: *A disadvantage is that it may not produce sufficient public goods.*

15. A major weakness of a free enterprise economic system is that it has no way of dealing with the fundamental economic questions of what, how and for whom.

Answer: False

Explanation: *It's a strength that the free enterprise economic system deals with the questions in a relatively efficient manner.*

16. A mixed economy is one in which the government forces producers to produce a good blend of public and private goods.

Answer: False

Explanation: A mixed economy is one in which there is a mixture of private and public ownership of resources.

17. In practice, all economies are mixed economies with varying degrees of government intervention.

Answer: True

18. The free enterprise economic system distributes more goods and services to those individuals and groups with more dollar votes.

Answer: True

19. Government intervention is never warranted and cannot be justified in a market-oriented economic system.

Answer: False

Explanation: *Government intervention is justified in some cases.*

20. In a simple circular flow model, households exchange factors of production for income, and firms exchange goods and services for revenue.

Answer: True

21. The circular flow model shows flows of resources and flows of goods and services but not flows of money.

Answer: false

Explanation: It does show money flows as well.

22. The factor market is the market in which goods and services are traded while the product market is the market in which resources are traded.

Answer: False

Explanation: Goods and services are sold in a product market while resources are bought and sold in the factor market.

23. In the simple circular flow model with money as the means of exchange, only money flows are shown.

Answer: False

Explanation: Real as well as money flows are shown.

24. In the circular flow model, money flows represent the monetary values of the real flows.

Answer: True

25. One of the advantages of the simple circular flow model is that it shows clearly how the prices of individual goods and services are determined.

Answer: False

Explanation: One of the disadvantages of the simple circular flow model is that it does not show how prices are determined.

Completion
(Fill in the blanks)

Use each word or combination of words from the list exactly once.
*(**Hint**: Proceed by elimination)*

Word list

Consumer — Economic — Economy — Factor / Resource x 2 — Free — Free Enterprise / Market-Oriented x 2 — Government — Interest and Dividends — Market — Mixed — Money — Price System — Private — Product — Profit — Property — Public or Government — Real — Rent — Resources — Resources / Factors Of Production — Show / Does Not Show x 2 — Sovereignty — System — Wages

Questions

1. A(n) ____________ ____________ is a set of mechanisms by means of which a society accomplishes the task of producing goods and services.
2. In a(n) ____________ enterprise economic system, most of the factors of production are owned privately. (free)
3. The economies of the United States, Canada, and Great Britain are examples of ____________ ____________ economies.
4. The basis of a ____________ ____________ economic system is the right of private persons and private groups to own property.
5. The right of private individuals and private groups to own property is referred to as the institution of ____________ ____________
6. A free enterprise economic system is essentially a(n) ____________ ____________ because a system of prices and markets coordinates the allocation of resources.
7. In practice, all economies are ____________ economies.
8. In a market-oriented economic system, consumers ultimately determine what to produce. This idea is known as ____________ ____________.
9. In a free enterprise economic system, consumers and firms play major roles in determining the allocation of scarce resource, while the ____________ plays a minor role.
10. A mixed economy is one in which both private and ____________ ownership of resources exists.
11. In a free enterprise economic system, the incentive to coordinate the use of resources in production and consumption is facilitated by the ____________ ____________.
12. The circular flow model shows the flows of income, expenditures, goods and services, and ____________.
13. In the circular flow model, households sell ____________ in the ____________ market.
14. In the circular flow model, firms buy resources in the ____________ market and sell finished goods and services in the ____________ market.
15. The flow of income from the factor market to households consists of ____________, ____________, ____________, and ____________.
16. In the circular flow model, the flows of resources and goods and services are ____________ flows, while the flows of income and expenditures are ____________ flows.
17. The simple circular flow model without a government sector ____________ (shows, does not show) transactions between firms.
18. The circular flow model ____________ (shows, does not show) how the prices of goods and services are determined.

Solution

1. (economic system)
2. (free)
3. (free enterprise / market-oriented)
4. (free enterprise / market-oriented)
5. (private property)
6. (market economy)
7. (mixed)
8. (consumer sovereignty)
9. (government)
10. (public or government)
11. (price system)
12. (resources)
13. (resources or factors of production, factor or resource)
14. (factor or resource, product)
15. (wages, rent, interest and dividends, and profit [in any order])
16. (real, money)
17. (does not show)
18. (does not show)

5

DEMAND & SUPPLY

SYNOPSIS

Demand and supply play important roles in a market-oriented economy. **Demand** is the term used to refer to the various quantities of a good or service that people will be willing and able to purchase at various price during a period of time. Demand may be represented by a **demand schedule,** a **demand curve,** or a **demand function.**

The **law of demand** states that as the price of a product falls, other things being equal, the quantity demanded increases; and as the price of a product rises, other things being equal, the quantity demanded decreases. This inverse relationship between price and quantity demanded exists because as the price falls, (1) more people are drawn into the market, (2) the real income or purchasing power of the buyers rises, and (3) people will substitute the cheaper product for a more expensive product.

Factors affecting quantity demanded include:

- the price of the product
- the incomes of buyers
- prices of complements and substitutes
- tastes and preferences
- the number of buyers
- expectations

A change in the price of a product will cause a change in quantity demanded (i.e., a movement along the demand curve). A change in a determinant other than the price of the product will cause a change in demand (i.e., s shift of the demand curve).

Supply refers to the various quantities of a good or service that sellers will be willing and able to offer for sale at various prices during a period of time. The **law of supply** states that as the price of a product falls, other things being equal, the quantity offered for sale decreases; and as the price of a product rises, other things being equal, the quantity offered for sale increases.

Factors other than price that affect the quantity offered for sale include:

- the number of sellers
- prices of related goods (production complements and substitutes)
- technology
- production costs
- expectations

A change in the price of a product causes a movement along the supply curve while a change in a non-price determinant causes a shift of the supply curve.

Equilibrium price and **equilibrium quantity** occur at the point of intersection of the demand and supply curves. When the market is in equilibrium, neither a **shortage** nor a **surplus** exists. An increase in demand, other things being equal, will raise equilibrium price and equilibrium quantity. A fall in demand, other things being equal, will lower equilibrium price and equilibrium quantity. An increase in supply, other things being equal, will lower equilibrium price and increase equilibrium quantity. A fall in supply, other things being equal, will raise equilibrium price and reduce equilibrium quantity.

A **price floor** will generally result in a surplus while a **price ceiling** will generally result in a shortage. A price ceiling may also result in a **black market**.

LEARNING OBJECTIVES

In connection with this module, you should be able to:

1. define demand
2. distinguish between demand and quantity demanded
3. identify the factors affecting quantity demanded
4. define supply
5. distinguish between supply and quantity supplied
6. identify the factors affecting quantity supplied
7. explain market price determination
8. use demand-supply analysis to solve simple economic problems

DEFINITIONS & CONCEPTS

You should be able to define the following terms and concepts:

demand schedule
law of demand
market-size effect
income effect
substitution effect
demand curve
normal good
inferior good
independent good
demand shifters
supply schedule
law of supply
supply curve
substitutes
complements
joint products
supply shifters
surplus
shortage
equilibrium price
equilibrium quantity
price floor
price ceiling
black market

5

DEMAND & SUPPLY

Concepts, Definitions & Problems

Problem 5-1

What do economists mean by a market? What are the requirements for a market to exist?

Requirement and Clue: *The problem has two parts, both of which must be answered. The solution requires that you understand and can demonstrate what a market is, as understood by economists. You are then required to state the elements without which there can be no market.*

Solution:

Economists think of a market as a mechanism or institution that facilitates exchange by bringing buyers and sellers together. Although it may be a specific geographical area, the spatial condition is not necessary for a market to exist. To economists, a market exists as long as buyers and sellers are in contact to do business.

The existence of a market requires four things. First, there must be at least one *buyer*. Buying and selling are the fundamental activities in markets. There can be no buying unless there is at least one buyer. Second, there must be at least one *seller*. Exchange—a market fundamental—suggests the existence of at least one seller. Third, there must be something to buy or sell, something to trade. That "something" is a good, service, or resource, or even a idea. It is a *product* without which, there can be no market. Finally, buying and selling (trading) requires a *price* at which exchange takes place. Price is often a deciding factor in whether or not exchange does take place.

Problem 5-2

Briefly define the market process.

Requirement and Clue: *Your task is to state clearly what the market process is. You must resist the temptation to write reams about the market. A simple straightforward definition is sufficient. Be careful not to confuse the market process with a market. Do not ignore the request for brevity.*

Solution:

Buyers and sellers are the players in the market. The buying and selling decisions of the players are reflected in their behaviour in the marketplace. The market process is the process by which buyers and sellers exchange goods and services. In this process, prices play a crucial role in determining the flow of goods and services between market players.

Problem 5-3

Give a brief definition of the concept of demand.

Requirement and Clue: *Although many people may have different ideas of what constitutes demand, you are expected to define demand as used in economics.*

Solution:

Demand refers to the various quantities of a good or service that people will be willing and able to buy at various possible prices during a period of time.

Problem 5-4

What methods do economists use to illustrate demand?

Requirement and Clue: *This problem is designed to test your knowledge of the tools used to show demand. Think of all the ways that demand may be represented.*

Solution:

Economists use a variety of methods/tools to depict concepts. They use words (a verbal statement of the concept), demand schedules (tables that show the relationship between price and quantity), demand curves (graphs that show the relationship between price and quantity) and demand functions (equations that express the relationship between price and quantity).

Problem 5-5

Distinguish between demand and quantity demanded.

Requirement and Clue: *Think of an effective way to illustrate the difference between these two concepts.*

Solution:

The difference between demand and quantity demanded is not just a matter of semantics. There is, in fact, a real difference. Demand is a *relationship* between price and quantity demanded. It refers to a whole range of prices with the various quantities associated with them. Quantity demanded, on the other hand, is just one quantity that will be bought *at some specific price.*

A demand schedule can be used to illustrate the difference. Consider the following table showing a relationship between the price of an item and the quantity demanded.

Price	Quantity demanded
10	60
9	70
8	80
7	90
6	100

The entire table, a demand schedule, represents demand. But quantity demanded is represented by any of the numbers in the right hand column. For example, 70 is the quantity that will be demanded at a price of $9, and 100 is the quantity that will be demanded at a price of $6.

A demand curve can also be used to illustrate the difference between demand and quantity demanded. Consider the following diagram.

The entire curve represents demand whereas quantity demanded is represented by a point such as A on the demand curve.

Problem 5-6

What do economists mean by "demand" and what is a demand curve?

Requirement and Clue: *This is a two-part problem and each part must be addressed. You must provide a clear statement of the meaning of demand and then proceed to describe a demand curve.*

Solution:

Demand refers to the various quantities of a good or service that people are willing and able to buy at various prices during a period of time. The desire for a good does not by itself constitute demand for that good. The ability to buy it must also be present.

A demand curve is a graphical representation of the various quantities of a good or service that people will be willing and able to buy at various prices during a period of time. The demand curve is drawn on the assumption that influences other than the price of the item being considered—factors such as income, prices of related goods, number of buyers, etc.)—remain constant.

The curve below labelled DD, illustrates a demand curve.

Note that the curve is downward sloping depicting the inverse relationship between price and quantity demanded.

Problem 5-7

Explain what economists mean by "demand" and give an example to illustrate the concept.

Requirement and Clue: *You must know that demand has a specific meaning in economics. You are required to demonstrate that knowledge. You are also required to give an example to support your knowledge of the concept.*

Solution:

Demand refers to the various quantities of a good or service that people are willing and able to buy at various prices during a period of time. The desire for a good does not by itself constitute demand for that good. The ability to buy it must also be present.

For example, perhaps people are willing and able to buy 1,000 smart phones per week when the price per smart phone is $400 each; 1,050 when the price is $350; 1,100 when the price is $300; 1,150 when the price is $250; 1,200 when the price is $200; and 1,250 when the price is $150. This information is shown in the following table which is called a demand schedule, representing the demand for smart phones.

Price ($)	Quantity demanded per week
400	1,000
350	1,050
300	1,100
250	1,150
200	1,200
150	1,250

This same information can be plotted on a graph known as a demand curve (shown below) which is also a way of illustrating demand.

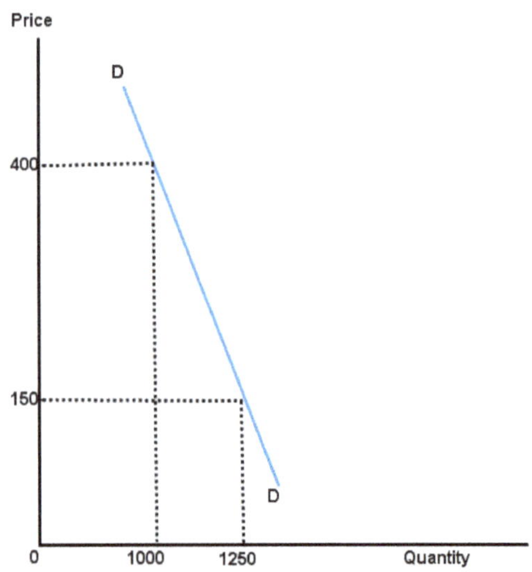

Problem 5-8

The following table represents the demand schedule for cornflakes for a one-week period. Construct the demand curve for cornflakes.

Price ($)	Quantity of boxes demanded per week
5.50	70,000
5.00	80,000
4.50	90,000
4.00	100,000
3.50	110,000
3.00	120,000
2.50	130,000
2.00	140,000

Requirement and Clue: *This problem is straightforward. With price on the vertical axis and quantity of the horizontal axis, you are to plot the data from the table on a graph. This graph will be the demand curve for cornflakes.*

Solution:

See graph below.

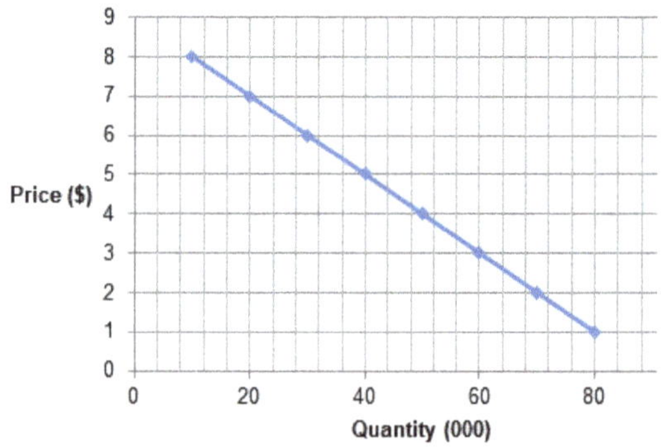

Problem 5-9

The following demand curve is given for novels for a particular period of time.

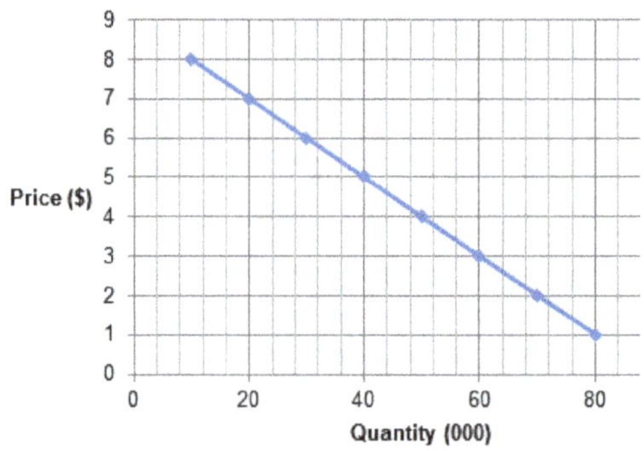

(a) *If the price of a novel was $4, how many novels would people buy?*

(b) *Why wouldn't they buy 60,000 at a price of $4?*

(c) *Given that people bought 70,000 novels, what was the price?*

(d) *Why wouldn't the price have been $3 when they bought 70,000?*

Requirement and Clue: *This problem is associated with one's ability to read graphs. For each price, there is a unique quantity that is associated with it, and for each quantity demanded, there is a unique price associated with it. Your task is to use the graph to locate any unique given price-quantity pair.*

Solution:

(a) According to the graph, the quantity that is associated with a price of $4 is 50,000. Thus we know that people will buy 50,000 novels when the price is $4.

(b) The point representing a quantity of 60,000 and a price of $4 lies off this demand curve and is therefore not a valid combination. The price that is associated with 60,000 novels is $3. Therefore the price would have to be $3 for 60,000 novels to be bought.

(c) The graph shows that the only price associated with a quantity of 70,000 is $2.

(d) The point representing a quantity of 70,000 and a price of $3 is not on this demand curve. If the price were $3, only 60,000 novels would have been bought.

Problem 5-10

Carefully state the law of demand.

Requirement and Clue: *What is required here is a clear statement of the relationship between price and quantity demanded. Remember to include the "ceteris paribus" assumption.*

Solution:

The law of demand states that as the price of a good or service falls, other things being equal, the quantity demanded increases; as the price of a good or services rises, other things being equal, the quantity demanded decreases. In other words, an inverse relationship exists between the price of an item and the quantity of that item demanded.

It is important to note that the law does not say that if the price of an item falls, the quantity demanded will rise, and vice versa. It says that if the price falls and nothing else changes (other things being equal), then the quantity demanded will rise. So if the price of an item falls, and consumers' incomes also fall, the quantity demanded may not increase. This would not be a violation or negation of the law of demand, because other things did not remain constant.

Problem 5-11

What explanation can you give for the observation that people tend to buy more of an item when its price falls and less of it when its price rises?

Requirement and Clue: *Basically, you are being asked to explain the law of demand, that is, the inverse relationship between price and quantity demanded.*

Solution:

There are three explanations for the inverse relationship between price and quantity demanded: (1) the market –size effect, (2) the real income effect, and (3) the substitution effect.

As the price of an item falls, more and more people are drawn into the market. In other words, as the price falls, the size of the market increases, thus the quantity demanded increases. More people buy the item *as its price falls.* This is the market-size effect.

When the price of an item falls, other things being equal, the people who buy that item experience an increase in purchasing power or real income even if there is no change in their money income, so they buy more—they buy more as the price falls. This is the real income effect.

When the price of an item falls, some people will switch from other items that they were previously purchasing but that have now become relatively more expensive. That is, some people will substitute the cheaper item for a more expensive substitute. This is the substitution effect.

Problem 5-12

What are the major determinants of demand?

Requirement and Clue: *You are to discuss important factors that affect the demand for a good or service. It is crucial not to include the price of the good or service as a determinant of demand. The price of the good or service will affect the quantity demanded, not the demand. Think of factors other than the price of the item that will exert significant influence of the quantity demanded. In other words, think of factors that will shift the demand curve.*

Solution:

Some of the important determinants of demand are consumers' income, prices of related goods, consumers' tastes and preferences, consumer expectations of future prices and future incomes, and population.

Consumers' income: If consumers' incomes increase, they will tend to buy more goods and services because they will be able to afford to buy more, other things being equal. If their incomes decrease, they will tend to buy fewer goods and services. This will be the case for normal goods. For inferior goods, they will buy less as their incomes increase.

Prices of related goods: If the price of a substitute for a certain good increases, the demand for the good will increase as some people will switch from the substitute to the now relatively cheaper good. If the price of a substitute for a good or service decreases, the demand for the good will tend to decrease as some people will switch from the good to the relatively cheaper substitute. For example, if people consider limes and lemons to be substitutes and the price of lemons rises, they will tend to buy more limes, thus the demand for limes will increase.

If the price of a complement for a certain good rises, the demand for the good will decrease. Since they will buy less of the complement, they will also buy less of the good. If the price of a complement for a certain good falls, the demand for the good will increase. Since they will buy more of the complement, they will also buy more of the good. For example, if people consider french-fries and ketchup to be complements and the price of french-fries falls, they will buy more french-fries *and* more ketchup, thus the demand for ketchup will increase.

Tastes and preferences: People will tend to buy more of something for which they have a liking. If people's preference or taste for vegetarian food increases, their demand for vegetarian food will increase. If their liking decreases, their demand for vegetarian food will fall.

Expectations: People's expectations regarding the course of future prices will affect present demand for goods and services. If people expect the price of an item to rise, they are likely to increase their purchases of that item now to avoid paying the expected higher price in the future. On the other hand, if they expect the price of an item to fall, they will attempt to delay their purchases of that item now to take advantage of the lower future price.

People's expectations about future changes in their incomes will also influence the present demand for goods and services. If people expect substantial raises in their salaries sometime in the near future, they are likely to buy more goods and services even before the increase in income materializes. If people expect decreases in their incomes, they are likely to buy fewer goods and services. Thus, the demand for an item will tend to increase if future income is expected to rise and fall if future income is expected to fall.

Population: The more buyers there are to buy any item, the greater the demand for that item will be. The greater the population, the greater the number of potential buyers will be. Other things being equal, the demand for vegetables in a city with a population of 2,000,000 people will be greater than the demand for vegetables in a city with only 100,000 people. If the number of potential buyers increases, the demand for an item will likely increase.

Problem 5-13

What is the difference between:

(a) *normal goods and inferior goods?*

(b) *Substitutes and complements?*

Requirement and Clue: *First, you must know the meaning of these terms. Then you must state how normal goods differ from inferior goods and how substitutes differ from complements.*

Solution:

(a) Normal goods and inferior goods refer to people's responses to goods as their incomes change. If people buy more of a good when their incomes rise, and less when their incomes fall, then the good is a normal good. If they buy less of a good when their incomes rise then the good is an inferior good. These terms are not necessarily descriptions of the goods, but they provide information about people's responses to them as their incomes change. People tend to buy more of most goods when their incomes increase. This seems normal, hence the term "normal goods". If people's income rise, they tend to buy more new cars, more new furniture, more steaks, and more movie tickets. Such goods are normal goods. On the other hand, if people's incomes rise, they tend to buy fewer used furniture, fewer used clothing, fewer Kraft dinners, and fewer reconditioned (re-treaded) tires. Goods in this latter category are inferior goods.

(b) Substitutes are goods that can replace each other in use. For many purposes, lemons and limes, tea and coffee, pens and pencils, and milk and cream are substitutes. Complements, on the other hand, are goods that can be used together. If you buy more of one, you are likely to buy more of the other. Examples of complements are coffee and cream, cars and gasoline, computers and flash drives, and pillows and pillow cases.

Problem 5-14

What is the difference between a change in demand and a change in quantity demanded?

Requirement and Clue: *This problem is not just dealing with semantics. The two concepts are totally different and you are required to state that difference as clearly as possible.*

Solution:

A change in demand means that a different quantity is bought *at any given price* because of a change in a determinant of demand such as income, price of related good, expectations, population, etc. Note that a change in the price of the item being considered will not change the demand for the item.

A change in quantity demanded means that a different quantity of an item is demanded as the price of the item changes.

Graphically, a change in demand is illustrated by a shift of the entire demand curve, either to the right for an increase in demand as shown in the following diagram, from DD to D1D1, or to the left.

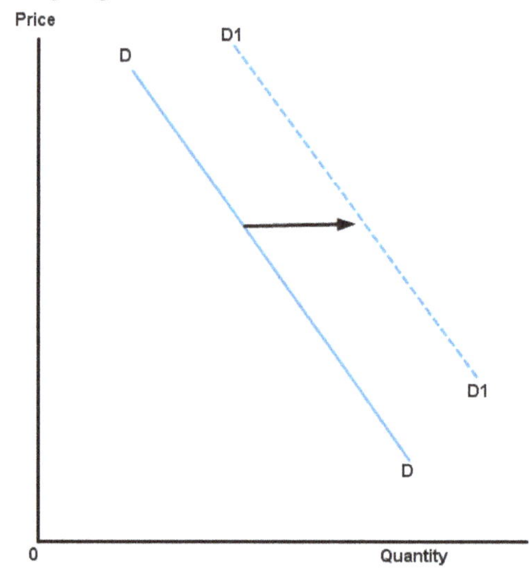

A change in quantity demanded is illustrated graphically by a movement along a given demand curve as shown as a movement from point A to point B on demand curve DD in the diagram below.

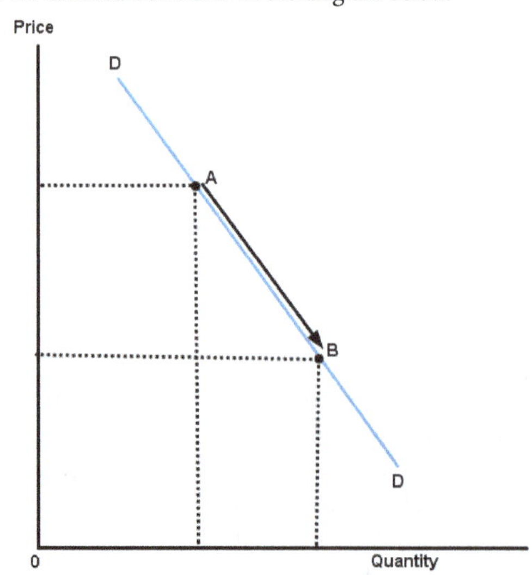

Problem 5-15

Determine whether each of the following represents a change in demand or a change in quantity demanded. In each case, indicate whether there is a shift in the demand curve or a movement along the demand curve.

a. *The price of eggs rises by 10 cents per dozen and consumers purchase fewer eggs.*
b. *The price of lap top computers falls and as a result, people buy more flash drives.*
c. *The price of electricity for heating purposes rises. As a result, homeowners turn down their thermostats to lower temperatures.*
d. *Households, on a whole, get income tax refunds and consequently take more frequent and longer vacations.*

Requirement and Clue: *This problem is designed to test your understanding of factors that change demand and those that change quantity demanded. The key is to determine whether the change is due to a change in the price of the item or to a change in one or more of the determinants of demand. If it's a price-induced change, then it's a change in quantity demanded represented by a movement along the demand curve. If it's a change in a determinant of demand, then it's a change in demand represented by a shift in the demand curve.*

Solution:

a. The increase in the quantity of eggs purchased is in response to a change in the price of eggs. Therefore, this is a change in quantity demanded. There will be a movement from one point on the demand curve to another.
b. The increase in the quantity of flash drives bought is due to a fall in the price of lap top computers. Since the change is not in response to a change in the price of flash drives, then this is a change in demand. The demand for flash drives increases so the demand curve shifts to the right.
c. In this case, homeowners are responding to an increase in the price if electricity. They purchase less (lower the thermostats) as the price rises. This is a change in quantity demanded which would be indicated by a movement along the demand curve.
d. Here, households are responding to a change in a variable other than the price of vacations. They buy more vacations because of an increase in their incomes caused by income tax refunds. This is an increase in demand which would be incicated by a shift in the demand curve.

Problem 5-16

One Tuesday afternoon you went to the grocery store to buy some oranges. Upon arriving at the store, you noticed that oranges were on sale at 20% below the regular price. Therefore, you bought more oranges than you intended to buy.

Did your demand for oranges increase?

Requirement and Clue: *Here, you must be careful not to confuse a change in demand with a change in quantity demanded. Yes, you bought more oranges, but that does not necessarily mean that your demand for oranges had increased. You must consider whether you bought more oranges because of the lower price or because of a change in a determinant of demand.*

Solution:

There is no indication here that income, tastes and preferences, prices of substitutes or complements, your expectations or any other determinant of demand had changed. Therefore, your demand for oranges did not change. What did change, however, is the quantity of oranges demanded in response to the change in the price of oranges. Expressed graphically, your demand curve did not shift, but there was a movement down the demand curve.

Problem 5-17

One week a grocer charged $2.99 for Sunkist oranges and sold 5,000 oranges. The next week, he brought in a stock of Navel oranges, raised the price to $3.99 and sold 6,000 oranges. Apparently, he sold more oranges when he raised the price. Is this a contradiction of the law of demand?

Requirement and Clue: *This solution requires that you pay careful attention to the law of demand. Did people buy more Sunkist oranges at a higher price? No. Did they buy more Navel oranges at a higher price? No. Did they buy more oranges at a higher price? This is what you need to explain.*

Solution:

According to the law of demand, as the price of <u>an item</u> rises, other things being equal, the quantity demanded will fall, and vice versa. In this problem, there are two items: Sunkist oranges and Navel oranges. On the surface, it may seem as if a greater quantity of the item (oranges) was bought as the price rose; but on closer examination, there are really two items being considered here: Sunkist oranges and Navel oranges. What is happening here is that there are two demand curves—one for Sunkist oranges and the other for Navel oranges. There is little doubt that if the price of Sunkist oranges had risen, other things being equal, the quantity demanded would have fallen; and if the price of Navel oranges had risen, the quantity demanded would have fallen, according to the law of demand. The law of demand remains intact.

Problem 5-18

Music Mack raised the price of a set of guitar strings from $10.99 to $12.99, informing his customers that guitar strings were in short supply. Expecting the price to rise even higher, Music Mack's customers bought more guitar strings at $12.99 than they bought at $10.99.

Is this a sign of an upward-sloping demand curve? Explain.

Requirement and Clue: *The question you need to ask is this: Did people buy guitar strings because Music Mack raised the price or because of the expectation of a higher price in the future? Clearly, the latter is the case. Your task then is to explain how an expected higher price led to an increase in demand for guitar strings.*

Solution:

People bought more guitar string not because of a rise in the price of guitar strings but because of the *expectation* of a higher price in the future. Their reasoning may have been along these lines. Since the price is expected to be higher in the future, it makes good sense to stock up on guitar strings now (they are not perishable) to avoid paying the future higher price. What we have here is a shift of a downward-sloping demand curve, not an upward-sloping demand curve.

Problem 5-19

What do economists mean by supply?

Requirement and Clue: *Although "supply" may be used in ordinary language to mean many different things, the term has a very definite meaning in economics. Your job is to provide the specific meaning of "supply" as used by economists.*

Solution:

As used by economists, supply refers to the various quantities of a good or service that sellers will be willing and able to sell at various prices during a period of time. It is an entire schedule of prices and their associated quantities. Supply must be distinguished from the quantity that will be offered for sale at some particular price, which is referred to as *quantity supplied.*

Problem 5-20

Define supply. What is a supply schedule?

Requirement and Clue: *This is another two-part problem. First, you must state precisely what supply is. Having done that, you proceed to a definition of a supply schedule. An example would be helpful here.*

Solution:

Supply refers to the various quantities of an item that sellers will be willing and able to offer for sale at various prices during a period of time.

A supply schedule is a tabular representation of the various quantities of an item that sellers will be willing and able to sell at various possible prices during a period of time. The following table is an example of a supply schedule.

Price *($)*	Quantity supplied per week *(000)*
10	60
15	80
20	100
25	120
30	140
35	160
40	180

The schedule shows that at a price of $10, the quantity supplied per week is 60,000. At a price of $15, the quantity supplied is 80,000; at a price of $20, the quantity supplied is 100,000, and so on.

Problem 5-21

What methods do economists use to illustrate supply?

Requirement and Clue: *This problem is designed to test your knowledge of the tools used to show supply. Think of all the ways that supply may be represented.*

Solution:

Economists use a variety of methods/tools to depict concepts. In the case of supply, they use words (a verbal statement of the concept), supply schedules (tables that show the relationship between price and quantity supplied), supply curves (graphs that show the relationship between price and quantity supplied) and supply functions (equations that express the relationship between price and quantity supplied).

Problem 5-22

What is the difference, if any, between supply and quantity supplied?

Requirement and Clue: *Think of an effective way to illustrate the difference between these two concepts.*

Solution:

There is an important difference between supply and quantity supplied. It is not just a matter of semantics. Supply is a *relationship* between price and quantity supplied. It refers to a whole range of prices with the various quantities associated with them. Quantity supplied, on the other hand, is just one quantity that will be offered for sale *at some specific price.*

A supply schedule can be used to illustrate the difference. Consider the table below showing a relationship between the price of an item and the quantity supplied.

The entire table, *a supply schedule*, represents supply. But *quantity supplied* is represented by any of the numbers in the right hand column. For example, 70 is the quantity that will be demanded at a price of $7, and 100 is the quantity that will be demanded at a price of $10.

Price	Quantity supplied
10	100
9	90
8	80
7	70
6	60
5	50
4	40
3	30

A supply curve can also be used to illustrate the difference between supply and quantity supplied. Consider the following diagram.

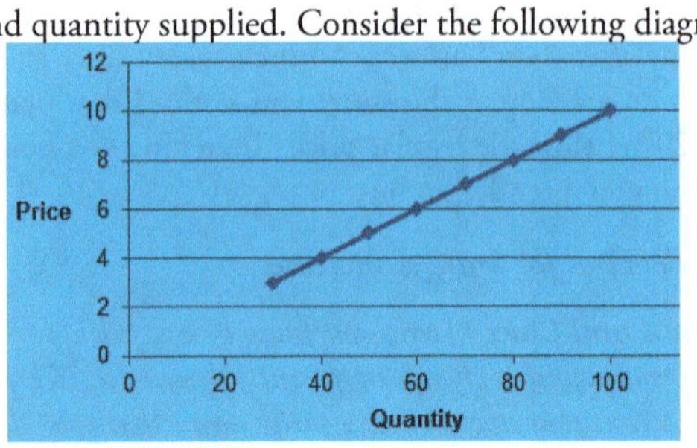

The entire curve represents supply whereas quantity supplied is represented by any point on the supply curve shown in the diagram.

Problem 5-23

Carefully state the law of supply.

Requirement and Clue: *The word "carefully" in the problem should not be ignored. It might just be a subtle reminder not to forget the ceteris paribus assumption.*

Solution:

According to the law of supply, a direct relationship exists between the price of an item and the quantity supplied. The law states that as the price of an item falls, *other things being equal*, the quantity offered for sale decreases; or alternatively, as the price of an item rises, *other things being equal*, the quantity offered for sale increases. Stated differently, the law says that sellers are motivated to offer more for sale at higher prices.

Problem 5-24

The following schedule represents the supply of a particular type of pen. Use the information to construct the supply curve for that kind of pen.

Price ($)	Quantity supplied (000)
0.40	100
0.50	120
0.60	140
0.70	160
0.80	180
0.90	200
1.00	220
1.10	240

Requirement and Clue: *Plotting the points in the supply schedule on a graph will give the supply curve. That's what you are required to do.*

Solution:

See graph below

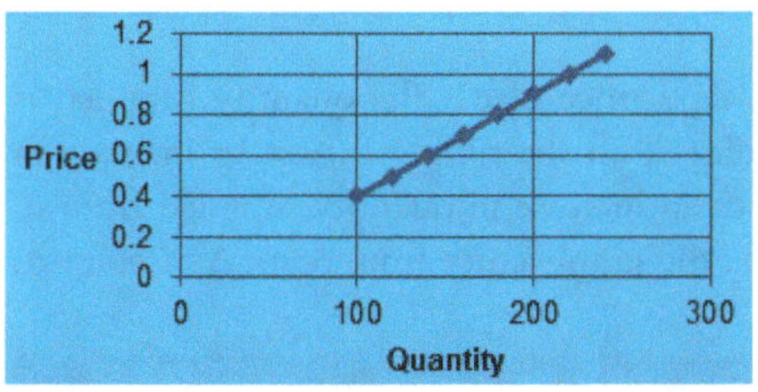

Problem 5-24

The following diagram shows the supply curve for CDs.

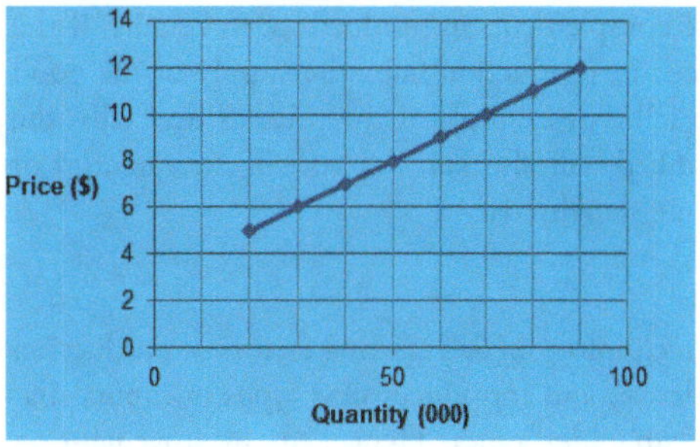

Use the graph to construct the supply schedule for CDs.

Requirement and Clue: *This problem is designed to test your ability to read information from a supply curve. Select each point on the graph and read its associated price and quantity. Record them on the supply schedule.*

Solution:

The table below is the resulting supply schedule.

Price ($)	Quantity supplied (000)
5	20
6	30
7	40
8	50
9	60
10	70
11	80
12	90

Problem 5-25

What are the major determinants of supply?

Requirement and Clue: *You are to discuss important factors that affect the supply of a good or service. It is crucial not to include the price of the good or service as a determinant of supply. The price of the good or service will affect the quantity supplied, not the supply. Think of factors other than the price of the item that will exert significant influence of the quantity offered for sale. In other words, think of factors that will shift the supply curve.*

Solution:

Some of the important determinants of supply are the number of producers/sellers, prices of related goods, technology, sellers' expectations of future prices, and prices of inputs.

Number of sellers:

As the number of sellers of an item increases, others things being equal, the greater the quantity that will be offered for sale at any given price; and as the number of sellers decreases, the quantity will also decrease.

Prices of related goods:

Consider lettuce and tomatoes which can be considered substitutes in production. If the price of lettuce increases, other things being equal, the supply of tomatoes will decrease as producers shift from tomato production to lettuce production. In general, if the price of a substitutable product increases, sellers will tend to reduce the supply of the substitute in question.

For goods that are complements in production, in general, if the price of a complement in production falls, the supply of the good in question will also fall. For example, if the price of beef falls, the quantity of beef supplied will also fall, but so will the quantity of hides as fewer cattle are slaughtered.

Technology:

An improvement in technology makes existing factors of production (inputs) more productive, and introduces new types of inputs that are more efficient than older types. Hence, an improvement in technology causes an increase in supply.

Expectations:

If producers expect prices to rise in the future, they might begin now to expand their productive capacity and thus increase their present output levels. If they expect prices to fall, they will likely switch resources into the production of items that have a more promising outlook, thus expectations of price decreases will tend to reduce supply.

Prices of inputs:

The costs of production reflect the prices of inputs. An increase in the prices of inputs (production costs) will result in a reduction in the supply of a product. A reduction in input prices will cause the supply to increase.

Problem 5-26

How will an increase in wages in the electronic components industry affect the supply of electronic components?

Requirement and Clue: *Think if there is any relationship between wages and any of the determinants of supply. It is easy to establish a relationship between wages and production costs. Once you've made that connection, the solution is clear.*

Solution:

An increase in wages in the electronic components industry will result in an increase in the cost of producing electronic components, other things being equal. This increase in cost will reduce produces ability to produce these components and therefore reduce supply of electronic components.

Problem 5-27

What is the difference between an increase in supply and an increase in quantity supplied? Illustrate graphically.

Requirement and Clue: *Here is another two-part problem. What does an increase in supply mean and what does an increase in quantity supplied mean? You are asked to demonstrate your knowledge of the difference verbally and then graphically.*

Solution:

An increase in supply means that at any given price, a greater quantity is supplied. If at a price of $5.00 sellers were placing 2,000 cups on the market for sale, and because of lower production costs, for example, they are willing and able to offer 2,200 cups for sale at the same price of $5, then supply has increased. If the price rises from $5 to $6 and as a result, sellers are willing and able to offer 2,300 cups for sale, then that's an increase in quantity supplied.

Graphically, an increase in supply is shown by a shift in the supply curve to the right as shown in the diagram below.

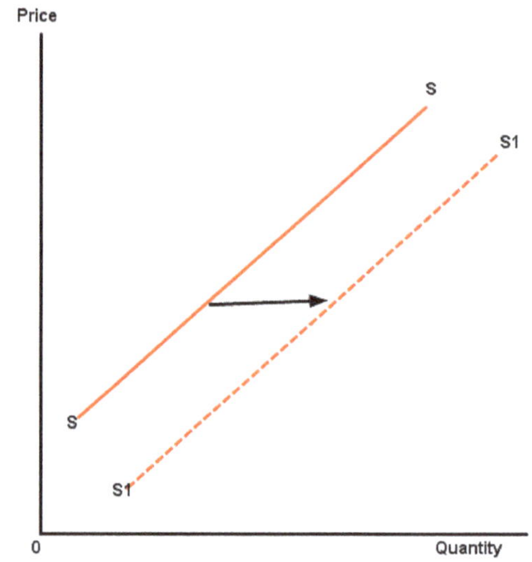

The initial supply is SS. With an increase in supply, the entire supply curve shifts from SS to S1S1.

An increase in quantity supplied is illustrated in the diagram below.

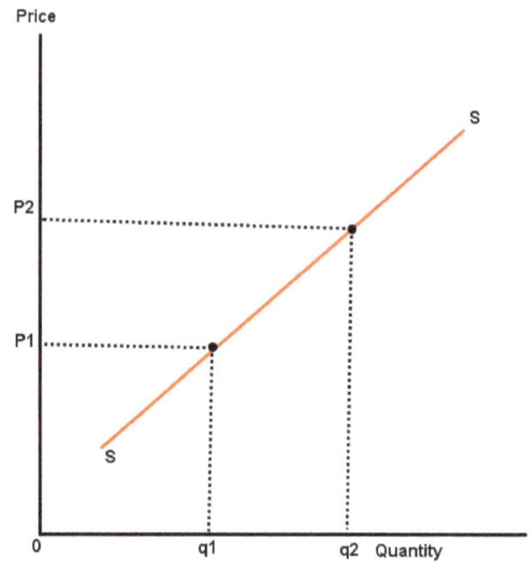

The supply curve is SS. At a price of p1, the quantity supplied is q1, corresponding to point A on the supply curve. An increase in price from p_1 to p_2 causes an increase in quantity supplied from q_1 to q_2—a movement along the supply curve from point A to point B.

Problem 5-28

Determine whether each of the following represents a change in supply or a change in quantity supplied. In each case, indicate whether there is a shift in the supply curve or a movement along the supply curve.

a. *The price of eggs rises by 10 cents per dozen and sellers offer more eggs for sale.*

b. *The price of lap top computers falls and as a result, sellers produce more flash drives.*

c. *The price of electricity for heating purposes rises. As a result, electricity providers increase their output of electricity.*

d. *Firms, on a whole, get tax incentives and consequently increase the production levels.*

Requirement and Clue: *This problem is designed to test your understanding of factors that change supply and those that change quantity supplied. The key is to determine whether the change is due to a change in the price of the item or to a change in one or more of the determinants of supply. If it's a price-induced change, then it's a change in quantity supplied represented by a movement along the supply curve. If it's a change in a determinant of supply, then it's a change in supply represented by a shift in the supply curve.*

Solution:

a. The increase in the quantity of eggs sold is in response to a change in the price of eggs. Therefore, this is a change in quantity supplied. There will be a movement from one point on the supply curve to another.

b. The increase in the quantity of flash drives produced is due to a fall in the price of lap top computers. Since the change is not in response to a change in the price of flash drives, then this is a change in supply. The supply of flash drives increases so the supply curve shifts to the right.

c. In this case, providers of electricity are responding to an increase in the price if electricity. They produce more as the price rises. This is a change in quantity supplied which would be indicated by a movement along the supply curve.

d. Here, firms are responding to a change in a variable other than the price of any item. They produce more goods and services because of the incentive provided by the tax. This is an increase in supply which would be indicated by a shift in the supply curve.

Problem 5-29

Use a supply schedule to illustrate the difference between supply and quantity supplied.

Requirement and Clue: *You need to know what a supply schedule is and how to construct one. Then you are required to construct a supply schedule and by referring to it, demonstrate your understanding of the difference between supply and quantity supplied.*

Solution:

A supply schedule is a table that shows the direct relationship between price and quantity supplied. The following is a supply schedule.

Price ($)	Quantity supplied (000)
14	140
12	120
10	100
8	80
6	60
4	40
2	20

Supply refers to the entire schedule—all the quantities with their associated prices. Quantity supplied, on the other hand, refers to a specific quantity that sellers will be willing and able to sell at a specific price. Thus, 100,000 is the quantity supplied at a price of $10; and 40 is the quantity supplied at a price of $4.

Problem 5-30

When the price of coffee falls from $1.10 per pound to $1.00 per pound, it is observed that coffee growers produce 25% less coffee. Does this signal a decrease in the supply of coffee?

Requirement and Clue: *This problem is designed to test your understanding of the difference between a change in supply and a change in quantity supplied. A decrease in the supply of coffee would occur only if a determinant of supply changed. Recall that the price of coffee is not a determinant of the supply of coffee.*

Solution:

The problem establishes a direct relationship between price and quantity supplied. When the price of coffee falls, coffee growers produce less coffee. The change in the quantity of coffee supplied is a direct result of the fall in coffee prices, all other influences on the quantity of coffee supplied being held constant. This is an example of movement along the supply curve rather than a shift in the supply curve. There is no change in the supply of coffee, only a change in quantity supplied.

Problem 5-31

Explain how each of the following is likely to affect the supply curve.

a. *The costs of production*

b. *Technology*

c. *The number of sellers*

d. *Taxes and subsidies*

Requirement and Clue: *Each of these is a non-price determinant of supply and will therefore shift the supply curve. Once you realize this, you have to state for each, whether it will shift the curve to the right or to the left.*

Solution:

a. *The costs of production:* A lowering of the costs of production will tend to increase supply. Lower production costs make it more profitable for firms to offer a larger quantity at each possible price. This will shift the supply curve to the right. An increase in the costs of production will reduce supply. This will shift the supply curve to the left.

b. *Technology:* An improvement in technology suggests a more efficient method of producing goods and services. With a better technology, producers are able to produce more with given resources. This will shift the supply curve to the right.

c. The number of sellers: Other things being equal, the larger the number of sellers, the greater will be the supply; and the smaller the number of sellers, the less will be the supply. A larger number of sellers will cause the supply curve to shift to the right while a smaller number of sellers will shift the supply curve to the left.

d. *Taxes and subsidies:* The imposition of taxes tends to increase the cost of production and thus reduce supply, causing the supply curve to shift to the left. Lower taxes tend to reduce the cost of production and this increase supply, causing the supply curve to shift to the right. Subsidies tend to reduce cost and thus increase supply, causing the supply curve to shift to the right. The elimination of reduction in subsidies tends to increase cost and thus reduce supply, causing the supply curve to shift to the left.

Problem 5-32

The following demand and supply schedules are given for apples.

Price ($)	Quantity demanded (000)	Quantity supplied (000)
12	40	120
11	50	110
10	60	100
9	70	90
8	80	80
7	90	70
6	100	60
5	110	50
4	120	40

On the basis of these schedules:

a. *What is the equilibrium price?*

b. *What is the equilibrium quantity?*

c. *If the government sets the price at $9, will there be a surplus or a shortage?*

d. *What action will the government have to take in order to maintain the price of $9?*

Requirement and Clue: *You must be familiar with the equilibrium condition and also with surpluses and shortages when price is fixed.*

Solution:

a. Equilibrium occurs when quantity demanded and quantity supplied are equal. The price that equates quantity demanded and quantity supplied as indicated in the schedule is $8. This is the equilibrium price.

b. The equilibrium quantity is the quantity that is traded (bought and sold) at the equilibrium price. In the schedule, this quantity is 80,000.

c. At a price of $9, the quantity supplied will be 90,000 while the quantity demanded will be 70,000. At $9 therefore, there will be a surplus of 20,000.

d. To maintain the price at $9, the government will have to purchase 20,000 at a price of $9.

Problem 5-33

Define each of the following terms and use demand and supply schedules to illustrate each.

a. *Equilibrium price*

b. *Surplus*

c. *Shortage*

Requirement and Clue: *This is another two-part problem. You must remember to answer both parts. You are required to state precisely what each term is. Then you should construct a table with demand and supply schedules and use it to illustrate each term.*

Solution:

a. Equilibrium price is the price at which quantity demanded equals quantity supplied.

b. A surplus is the amount by which quantity supplied exceeds quantity demanded at some particular price.

c. A shortage is the amount by which quantity demanded exceeds quantity supplied at some particular price.

Consider the following table.

Price ($)	Quantity demanded	Quantity supplied
10	60	100
9	70	90
8	80	80
7	90	70
6	100	60

The equilibrium price is $8 because at that price, the quantity demanded equals the quantity supplied.

At a price of $9, a surplus exists because the quantity supplied (90) exceeds the quantity demanded (70)

At a price of $7, a shortage exists because the quantity demanded (90) exceeds the quantity supplied (70).

Problem 5-34

Explain how the equilibrium price of a commodity is determined in a purely competitive market.

Requirement and Clue: *You must first demonstrate that you know what is meant by a purely competitive market. Then you must explain how the forces of demand and supply determine equilibrium price.*

Solution:

A purely competitive market is characterized by a large number of firms producing a homogeneous product. The output of each firm is such a small proportion of the total industry output that variations in the output of any firm will have no effect on the price at which the product is sold. Each producer can sell his entire stock at the existing price.

In this type of market, the price of a commodity is determined by the forces of demand and supply. We assume that as the price of a commodity rises, other things being equal, consumers will purchase less of that commodity, and as the price falls, they will purchase more of it. This gives the negatively (downward) sloping demand curve DD shown in the diagram below. We assume also that as the price of a commodity falls, sellers will want to offer less for sale, and as the price rises, they will want to offer more for sale. This gives the positively (upward) sloping supply curve SS shown in the diagram. The two curves intersect to give the equilibrium price of $2.

If the price were $3, sellers would wish to sell a larger quantity than that which consumers would wish to buy at that price: there would be a surplus in the market and price would be forced down.

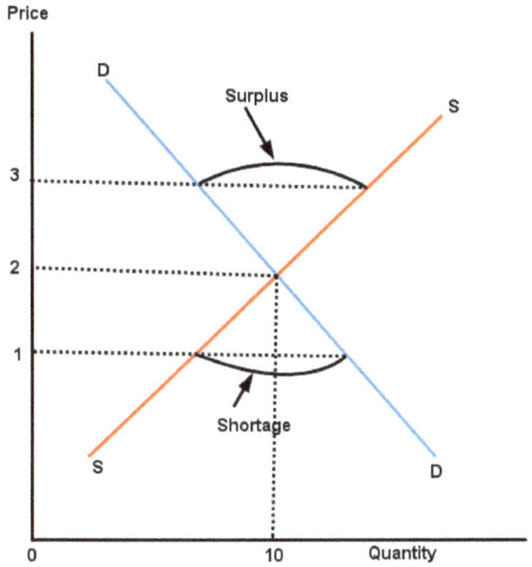

Also, if the price were $1, sellers would wish to sell a smaller quantity than that which consumers would be willing to buy at that price: there would be a shortage in the market and price would be forced up. The only price at which buyers and sellers are willing to trade the same quantity is $2. This is known as the equilibrium price. This price will be maintained unless some force disturbs the balance between quantity demanded and quantity supplied.

Problem 5-35

The first three columns of the following table show demand and supply for belts. Complete the last two columns. The first row is completed as an example.

Price ($)	Quantity Demanded (000)	Quantity supplied (000)	Market condition	Effect on price
12	60	140		
11	70	130		
10	80	120		
9	90	110		
8	100	100		
7	110	90		
6	120	80		
5	130	70		

Requirement and Clue: *The last two columns are the "Market conditions" and "Effect on price" columns. In the "Market conditions" column you are to indicate whether there is a shortage, surplus, or equilibrium in the market at each price. In the last column you are expected to indicate whether price will rise, fall, or whether there will be no effect.*

Solution:

Price ($)	Quantity Demanded (000)	Quantity supplied (000)	Market condition	Effect on price
12	60	140	*Surplus*	*Fall*
11	70	130	*Surplus*	*Fall*
10	80	120	*Surplus*	*Fall*
9	90	110	*Surplus*	*Fall*
8	100	100	*Equilibrium*	*None*
7	110	90	*Shortage*	*Rise*
6	120	80	*Shortage*	*Rise*
5	130	70	*Shortage*	*Rise*

Problem 5-36

Use a demand/supply graph to show the effect of an increase in demand on equilibrium price and quantity, other things being equal.

Requirement and Clue: *You are required to show the initial equilibrium price and quantity on a graph and then show the new equilibrium price and quantity following the increase in demand.*

Solution:

In the following diagram, DD and SS represent the initial demand and supply curves respectively.

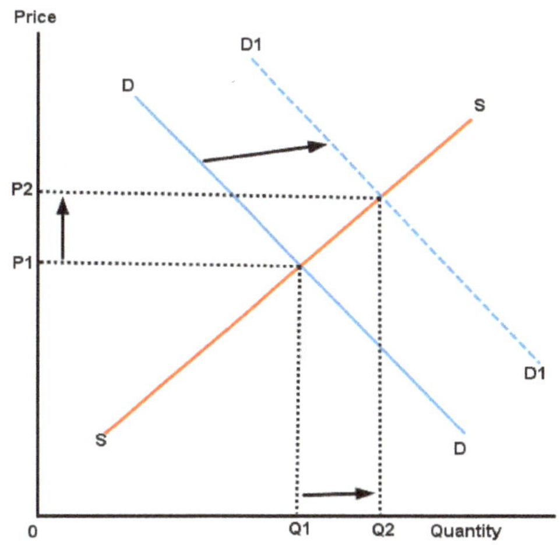

The equilibrium price is P1 and the equilibrium quantity is Q1. An increase in demand, other things being equal, shifts the demand curve from DD to D1D1. The new equilibrium price rises from P1 to P2 and the new equilibrium quantity rises from Q1 to Q2.

Problem 5-37

When the price of a corn is 35 cents, people will buy 50 but Pete the Grocer wants to sell 450. For every 5 cents fall in the price of corn, people want to buy 100 more while Pete wants to offer 100 less corn. What will be the equilibrium price of corn?

Requirement and Clue: *From the data given, you must try to construct a table showing demand and supply schedules for corn. From the table, you can then see the price that equates quantity demanded and quantity supplied.*

Solution:

The following demand/supply schedules can be constructed from the data provided in the problem.

Price ($)	Quantity Demanded	Quantity supplied
0.35	50	450
0.30	150	350
0.25	250	250
0.20	350	50

As can be seen from the table, at a price of $0.25, consumers are willing and able to buy 250, while Pete is willing and able to offer 250 for sale. Thus, the equilibrium price is $0.25.

Problem 5-38

Use graphs to show the effect of each of the following changes on the market for wheat, other things being equal.

a. *The demand for wheat increases*

b. *Bad weather results in a poor wheat harvest*

c. *The price of corn falls (consider corn and wheat to be substitutes)*

d. *Farmers expect wheat prices to rise*

e. *A group of agricultural scientists declare that wheat is beneficial to health*

Requirement and Clue: *Determine whether the change will affect demand or supply and how. Then show the result graphically. You are to state what will happen to the price and quantity of wheat in each case.*

Solution:

a. In the diagram below, DD and SS are the initial demand and supply curves for wheat. The equilibrium price is P1 and the equilibrium quantity is Q1.

As the demand for wheat increases, the demand curve shifts to the right from DD to D1D1 as shown in the graph above. This results in an increase in the equilibrium price from P1 to P2 and an increase in the equilibrium quantity from Q1 to Q2.

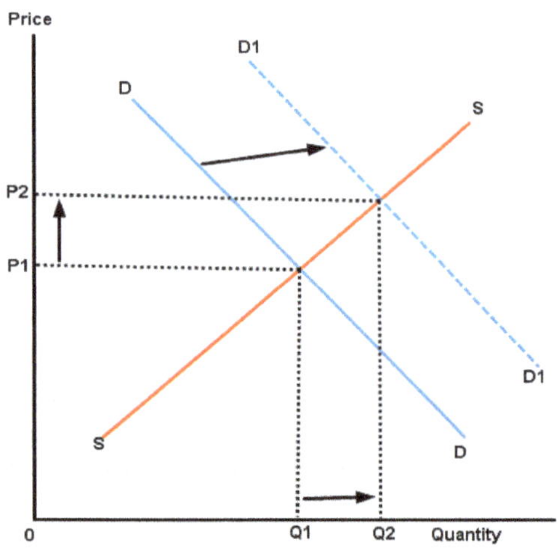

b. Initially, the demand and supply curves for wheat are DD and SS as shown in the following graph, and the initial equilibrium price and quantity are P and Q respectively.

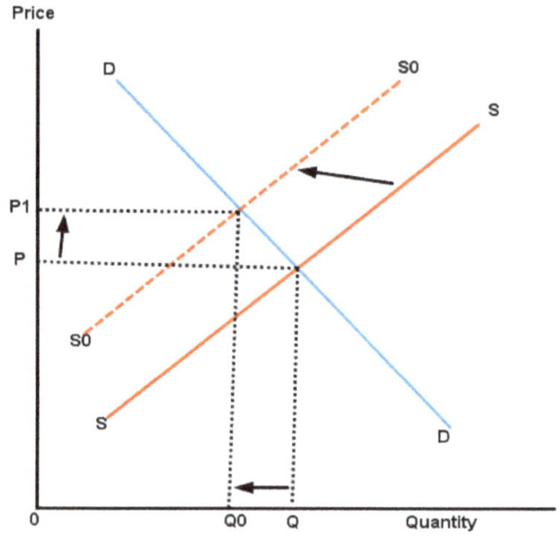

The poor wheat harvest means a reduction in the supply of wheat, so the supply curve shifts to the left from SS to S0S0.As a result, the equilibrium price rises from P to P1 and the quantity falls from Q to Q0.

c. The initial demand and supply curves for wheat are shown as DD and SS respectively in the diagram below. The equilibrium price and quantity are P and Q respectively.

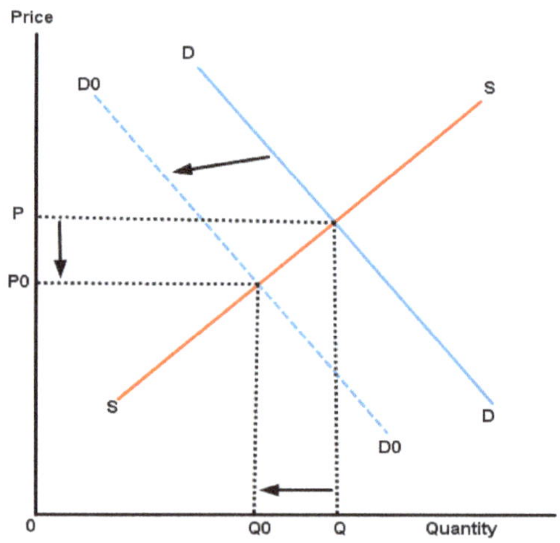

Since wheat and corn are substitutes, a fall in the price of corn will cause some consumers to switch from wheat to corn, thus reducing the demand for wheat. Consequently, the demand curve shifts to the left from DD to D0D0 as shown in the diagram, causing equilibrium price to fall from P to P0, and equilibrium quantity to fall from Q to Q0.

Alternatively, we can look at the problem from the producers' perspective. The diagram below shows the initial demand curve DD and the initial supply curve SS. The equilibrium price and quantity are P and Q respectively. A fall in the price of corn will cause growers to grow less corn and more wheat. Accordingly, the supply curve for wheat will shift to the right, lowering the price from P to P0, and increasing the quantity from Q to Q1.

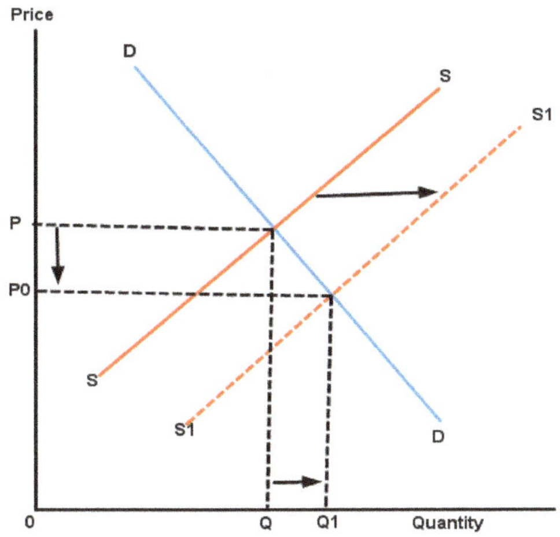

d. If farmers expect wheat prices to rise, other things being equal, they will produce more wheat. The following diagram illustrates the market for wheat. The initial demand and supply curves are DD and SS respectively, and the equilibrium price and quantity are P and Q.

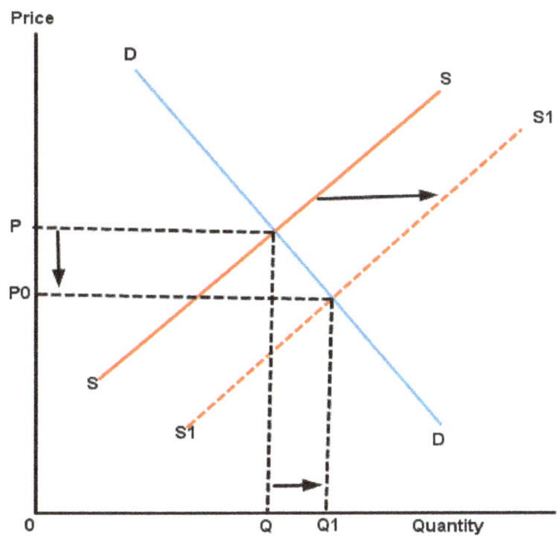

The production of more wheat by farmers shifts the supply curve from SS to S1S1 as shown in the graph. This causes a fall in price from P to P0, and an increase in quantity from Q to Q1.

e. The declaration by scientists that wheat is beneficial to health will increase the demand for wheat as more people try to take advantage of the health benefits. The following diagram shows the market for wheat.

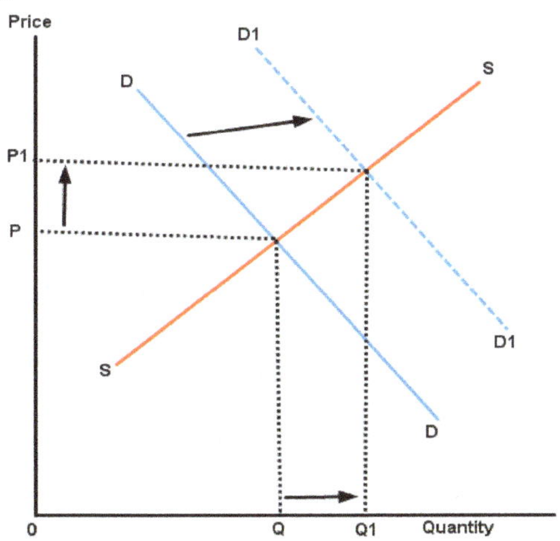

The initial demand and supply curves for wheat are DD and SS respectively. The initial equilibrium price and quantity are P and Q respectively. The demand curve shifts to the right from DD to D1D1 following the declaration; and the equilibrium price rises from P to P1, while the equilibrium quantity also rises from Q to Q1.

Problem 5-39

Parker runs a small hot dog stand. If a new amusement park opens up across the street from him, use demand/supply graphs to show what is likely to happen to the price that Parker can charge for his hotdogs?

Requirement and Clue: *You need to figure out how the opening of the amusement park will likely affect demand for Parker's hotdogs. An amusement park attracts people, and Parker will likely benefit from the greater traffic. You must graphically show the effect of the change in demand on price.*

Solution:

The following diagram shows the initial demand (DD) and supply (SS) for Parker's hotdogs. The equilibrium price and quantity are P and Q respectively. The opening up of the new amusement park across the street from Parker's hot dog stand will most likely increase the demand for Parker's hotdogs. The demand curve will shift to the right from DD to D1D1. This increase in demand will raise the equilibrium price from P to P_1.

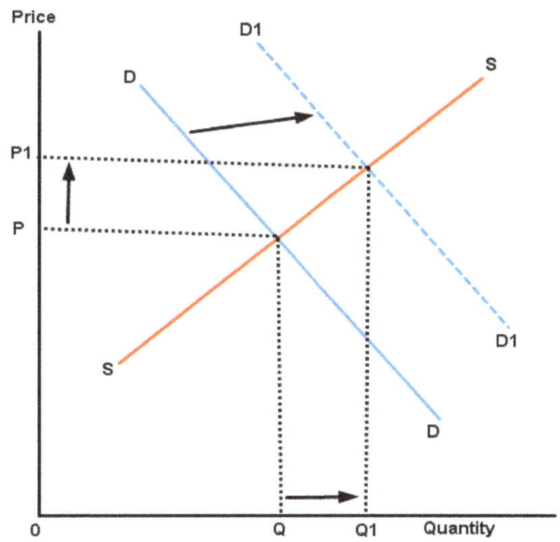

Problem 5-40

The development of a new technology increases the efficiency of ipad production. Show graphically how this development will affect the market for ipads.

Requirement and Clue: *This is clearly a supply-side shock. You are required to state the effect of this supply-side shock on the equilibrium price and equilibrium quantity of ipads.*

Solution:

The initial demand and supply curves for iPads are DD and SS in the following figure. The initial equilibrium price and equilibrium quantity are P and Q respectively.

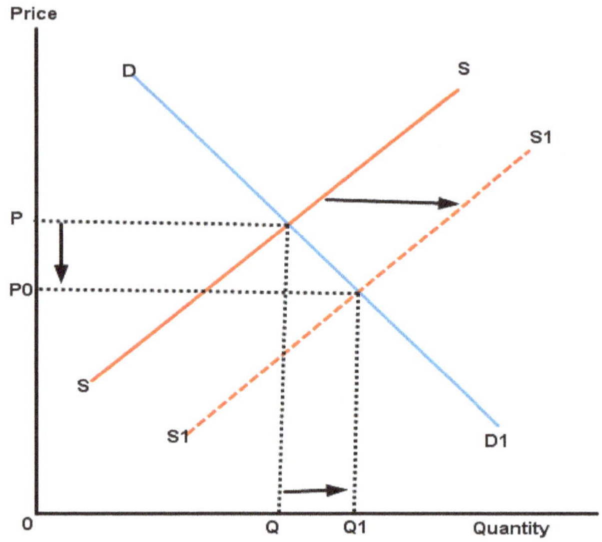

The new technology enables a greater quantity of iPads to be produced at every price. In other words, the new technology increases the supply of iPads. The increase in supply is shown by shifting the supply curve to the right from SS to S1S1. This results in a fall in the equilibrium price of iPads from P to P0 and an increase in the equilibrium quantity from Q to Q1.

Problem 5-41

It is observed that apples are inexpensive in the fall and that Christmas trees are quite cheap on December 26. Use demand and supply graphs to explain why this is so.

Requirement and Clue: *Think about the quantity of apples available in the fall as opposed to other seasons of the year. Thank also of the change in demand for Christmas trees between the day before Christmas and the day after Christmas. Use this information to analyse the markets for apples and Christmas trees at the times indicated.*

Solution:

First, let us consider the market for apples. In the diagram below, the demand and supply curves for apples are DD and SS respectively, and the equilibrium price and equilibrium quantity are P and Q respectively.

The fall is the usual harvest time for apples so their supply increases. The supply curve shifts from SS to S1S1 as shown in the diagram. This increase in the supply of apples causes a surplus of apples at the initial price which reduces the equilibrium price from P to P0.

Let us now consider the market for Christmas trees. In the diagram below, the demand and supply curves for Christmas trees are DD and SS respectively, and the equilibrium price and equilibrium quantity are P and Q respectively. Between December 25 and December 26, the demand for Christmas trees falls significantly.

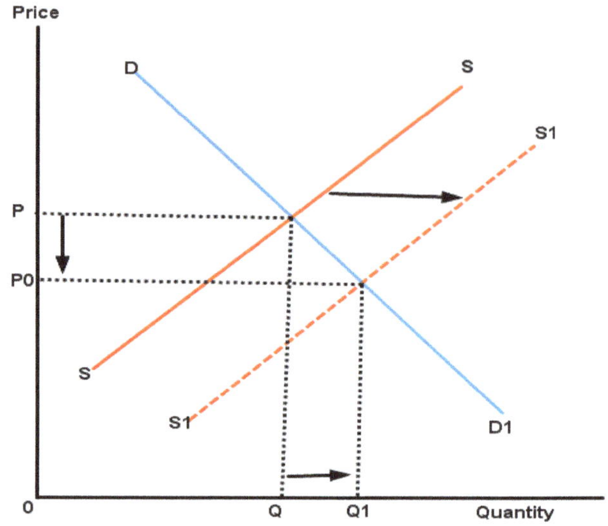

Very few people will be buying Christmas trees on Boxing Day. This drastic drop in the demand for Christmas trees is shown by shifting the demand curve to the left as shown in the diagram below. The price falls from P to P0.

Apples are inexpensive in the fall because the supply of apples increases during that time. Christmas trees are quite cheap on December 26 because of the drastic fall in demand for Christmas trees on December 26.

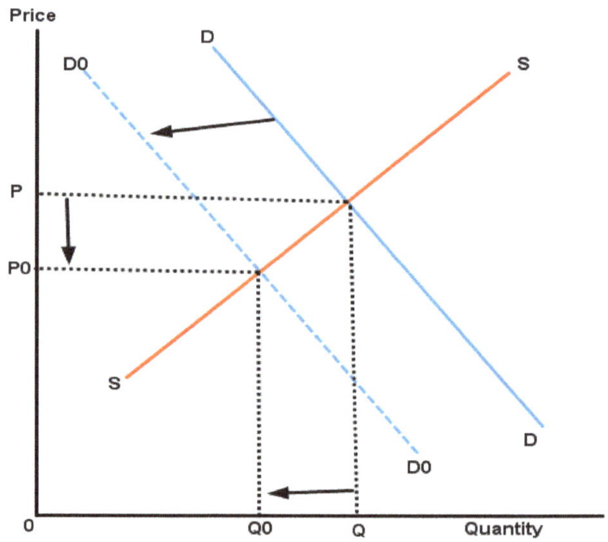

Problem 5-42

Explain with the help of demand/supply diagrams, the effect of a good banana crop on the price of apples, assuming that apples and bananas are substitutes in consumption.

Requirement and Clue: *There are two markets to consider here: the market for bananas and the market for apples. However, the problem requires you to state how the price of apples will be affected.*

Solution:

A good banana crop will increase the supply of bananas. Other things being equal, this will cause the price of bananas to fall as shown in Figure 1 below.

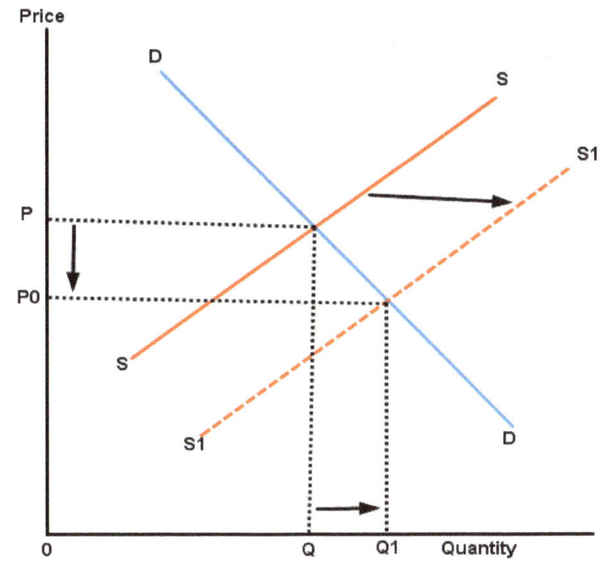

Figure 1

The original demand and supply curves for bananas are shown by DD and SS. The equilibrium price of bananas is P. The increase in supply caused by the good banana crop is shown by a shift in the supply curve from SS to S1S1, and the price is forced down from P to P0.

It is given that apples and bananas are substitutes, so as the price of bananas falls, consumers will switch from apples which are now relatively more expensive. This means that the demand for apples will fall and, other things being equal, this fall in demand will cause the price of apples to fall as shown in Figure 2. The original demand and supply curves for apples are DD and SS, and the price established by the market is P. The fall in demand is represented by a shift in the demand curve from DD to D0D0 in Figure 2.

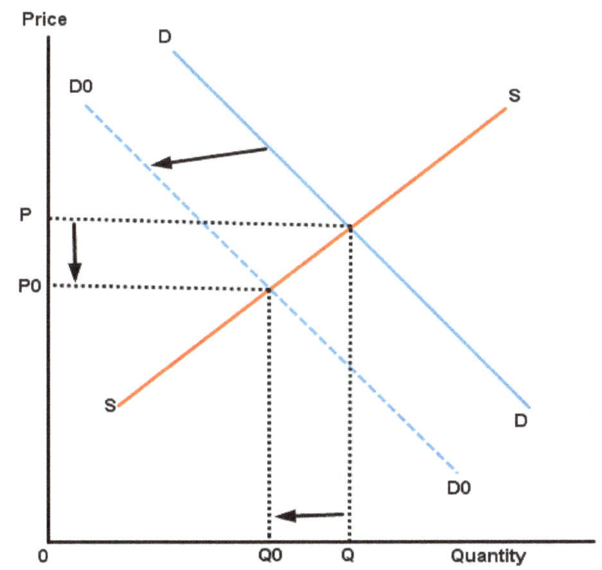

Figure 2

The decrease in demand causes the price to fall from P to P0. Thus, the good banana crop will cause the price of bananas to fall and this in turn will lower the price of apples. As a general rule, a fall in the price of a good will lower the price of a substitute.

Problem 5-43

Use demand and supply graphs to show that minimum wage legislation can cause unemployment.

Requirement and Clue: *This problem is an application of demand/supply analysis to the market for labour services. The problem requires an analysis of the effects of minimum wage legislation on the quantity of labour demand and on the quantity supplied.*

Solution:

The following graph shows the market for labour services. Weq is the equilibrium wage rate where the quantity of labour demanded equals the quantity supplied. The equilibrium quantity of labour (number of workers) is Neq.

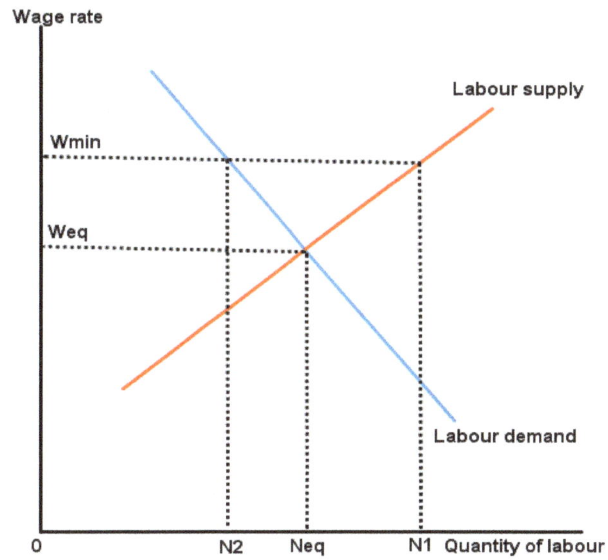

If the minimum wage is set below the equilibrium wage rate, it will have no effect. The equilibrium wage rate will prevail. However, if the minimum wage is set above the equilibrium wage rate (Wmin for example), the number of workers demanded by firms will be N2, while the number of workers offering to work will be N1. Thus, the number of workers who will not be hired is (N1 – N2). This represents unemployment that is due to the minimum wage legislation. Minimum wage legislation is an example of a price floor.

Problem 5-44

Explain, with the use of graphs, the effect of a price ceiling. Give an example of a price ceiling.

Requirement and Clue: *You should recognize the problem as an application of demand/supply analysis. You are expected to show your understanding of the concept of a price ceiling and your ability to use graphs in this particular case. Don't forget to give an example of a price ceiling.*

Solution:

A price ceiling is a point beyond which a price is not allowed to rise. Consider the diagram below. The demand and supply curves are DD and SS respectively, and the equilibrium price and quantity are $500 and 5,000 respectively. Suppose a price ceiling of $300 is established. Sellers may not charge more than $300. At this price, sellers are willing and able to offer only 3,000 for sale as can be seen from the supply curve, while consumers are willing to purchase 7,000 as can be seen from the demand curve. Thus, a price of $300 results in a shortage of 4,000. Quite often, a black market, in which the item is sold at a price above that prescribed by law, is the result of a price ceiling. A popular example of a price ceiling is rent control.

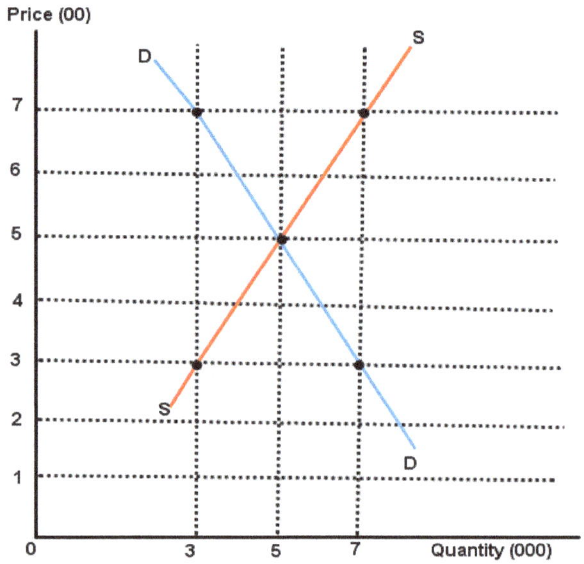

Problem 5-45

When the price of gold rises considerably, the price of silver also tends to rise. How might this occurrence be explained?

Requirement and Clue: *The problem suggests that a relationship exists between silver and gold. Silver and gold can be considered substitutes in consumption, perhaps as jewelry. Apply demand/supply analysis to the effect of a change in the price of a substitute.*

Solution:

A plausible explanation could be as follows. Gold and silver are substitutes. As the price of gold rises, people will tend to buy less gold, turning instead to silver, a relatively cheaper substitute. They may also substitute silver for gold in their investment portfolios. This increase in demand for silver results in an increase in the price of gold. This situation can be analyzed with the help of the diagram below.

The original demand and supply curves for silver intersect to determine an equilibrium price of P and an equilibrium quantity of Q for silver. When the price of gold increases significantly, people will switch from gold to a cheaper substitute such as silver. Therefore the demand for silver will rise. The demand curve shifts from DD to D1D1 as shown in the diagram. This increase in the demand for silver raises the price from P to P1 as shown in the diagram.

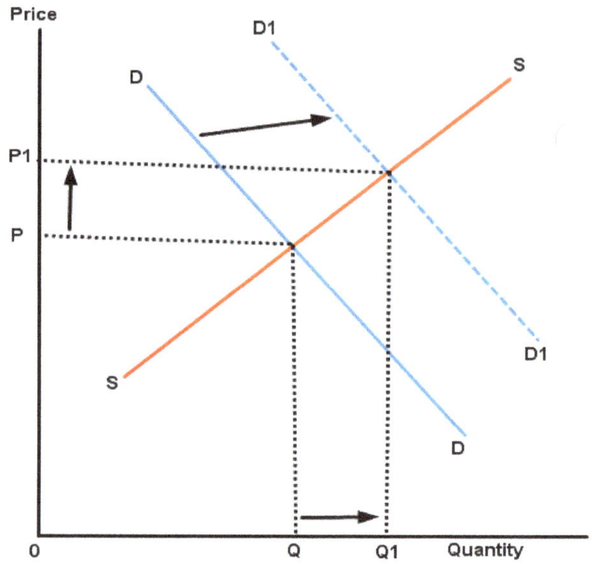

Problem 5-46

Use demand and supply graphs to analyze the effect of an excise tax on:

(a) *the price of the taxed item*
(b) *the quantity traded*
(c) *the consumers' share of the tax*
(d) *the producers' share of the tax*
(e) *the government's revenue from the tax*

Requirement and Clue: *Here is an example of the application of demand and supply analysis to a popular tax problem. You are expected to know what an excise tax is and to show (by graphs) how such a tax affects the indicated variables. You need to know how an excise tax affects the supply of the taxed item.*

Solution:

An excise tax is a tax levied on a domestically produced good or service. Let us assume, for this solution, that the government imposes a tax of $1.00 on each gallon of gasoline sold. The following graph shows the demand curve DD and the supply curve SS before the imposition of the tax.

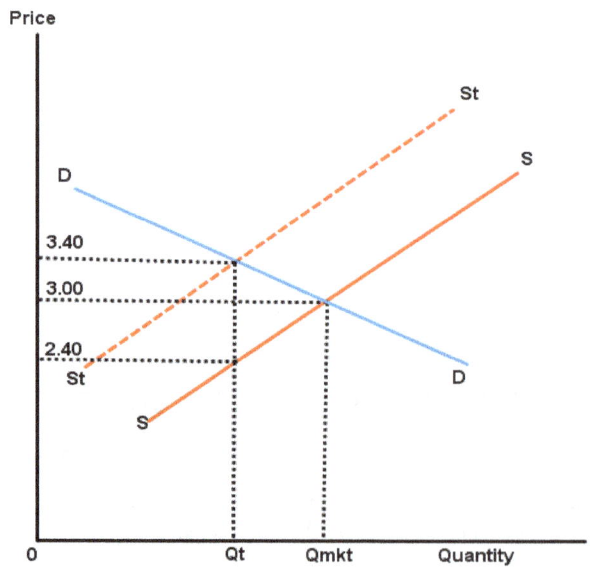

The equilibrium price of gasoline is \$3 and the quantity traded at that price is Qmkt which we assume to be 14,000 gallons. The tax causes production costs to rise by \$1.00 per gallon and this reduces supply. The supply curve shifts up by the amount of the tax, as shown by St, so the vertical distance between SS and StSt represents the tax. The new equilibrium price is now \$3.40 and consumers now buy Qt, which we assume to be 12,000 gallons at that price.

(a) The price of the taxed item (gasoline in this example), has increased

(b) The quantity traded has fallen from 14,000 bottles to 12,000 gallons

(c) Consumers were paying \$3.00 before the tax. After the tax they are paying \$3.40 Therefore, their share of the tax is \$0.40

(d) The producers' share of the tax is \$0.60

(e) Since 12,000 gallons are sold and the tax is \$1 per gallon, the government's revenue from the tax is (12,000 × \$1) = \$12,000

Problem 5-47

Consider the demand and supply equations:

$$Q_d = 50 - 4P$$
$$Q_s = -10 + 8P$$

Find the equilibrium price and the equilibrium quantity.

Requirement and Clue: *We know that in equilibrium, Q_d and Q_s are equal. You are required to solve the equations for P and Q.*

Solution:

$$50 - 4P = -10 + 8P$$
$$12P = 60, \text{ so } P = 5$$

By substituting P = 5 in either the demand or the supply equation, we obtain Q = 30.

The equilibrium price is **\$5** and the equilibrium quantity is **30**.

Problem 5-48

You are given the following demand and supply equations:

$$Q_d = 130 - 3P$$
$$Q_s = -20 + 12P$$

Complete the following demand and supply schedules

Price	Quantity Demanded	Quantity supplied
5	130 – 3(5) = 115	–20 + 12(5) = 40
10	130 – 3(10) = 100	–20 + 12(10) = 100
15	130 – 3(15) = 85	–20 + 12(15) = 160
20	130 – 3(20) = 70	–20 + 12(20) = 220

(a) *From the schedules, determine the equilibrium price and equilibrium quantity*

(b) *Solve the demand and supply equations for P and Q and compare your answer with the answer obtained in part (b).*

Requirement and Clue: *Try to solve the problem in order suggested by the problem. To obtain the demand schedule, you need to plug each price into the demand equation; and to obtain the supply schedule, you need to plug each price into the supply equation. Once you have the demand and supply schedules, the equilibrium price and quantity can be easily determined by observing the price at which quantity demanded equals quantity supplied. Equating Q_d with Q_s you can solve for P and Q.*

Solution:

Price	Quantity Demanded	Quantity supplied
5	130 – 3(5) = 115	–20 + 12(5) = 40
10	130 – 3(10) = 100	–20 + 12(10) = 100
15	130 – 3(15) = 85	–20 + 12(15) = 160
20	130 – 3(20) = 70	–20 + 12(20) = 220

(a) At a price of 10, the quantity demanded (100) equals the quantity supplied (100). Therefore, the equilibrium price is **10** and the equilibrium quantity is **100.**

$$130 - 3P = -20 + 12P$$
$$15P = 150$$
$$\mathbf{P = 10}$$
$$Q = 130 - 3(10) = \mathbf{100}$$

The answer is the same as that obtained in part (b).

Problem 5-49

The market demand and supply equations are given as:

$$Qd = 18 - 2P$$
$$Qs = 3 + 5P$$

(a) *By selecting prices ranging from \$1 to \$6, construct the demand and supply schedules.*

(b) *Solve the equations for the equilibrium price and the equilibrium quantity.*

Requirement and Clue: *The demand and supply schedules can be constructed by plugging prices from \$1 to \$6 into each equation.*

Solution:

Price	Quantity Demanded	Quantity supplied
1	18 – 2(1) = 16	3 + 5(1) = 8
2	18 – 2(2) = 14	3 + 5(2) = 13
3	18 – 2(3) = 12	3 + 5(3) = 18
4	18 – 2(4) = 10	3 + 5(4) = 23
5	18 – 2(5) = 8	3 + 5(5) = 28
6	18 – 2(6) = 6	3 + 5(6) = 33

$$18 - 2P = 3 + 5P$$
$$7P = 15$$
$$P = 15/7 = \mathbf{2.14}$$
$$Q = 18 - 2(2.14)$$
$$Q = 18 - 4.28 = \mathbf{13.72}$$

Problem 5-50

The demand and supply equations are given as

$$Q_d = 28 - 2P$$
$$Q_s = 5P$$

What are the equilibrium price and quantity?

Requirement and Clue: You are required to solve the equations for P and Q. Remember that in equilibrium, $Q_d = Q_s$.

Solution:

$$28 - 2P = 5P$$
$$7P = 28$$
$$\mathbf{P = 4}$$
$$Q = 28 - 2(4) = \mathbf{20}$$

The equilibrium price is 4 and the equilibrium quantity is 20.

Multiple-Choice

In each case, circle the letter that corresponds with the correct answer.

1. The market process refers to:

a. the methods used my merchants to take their products to market
b. the various laws and regulations governing behaviour in markets
c. the means by which a government sets the price of an item in the market
d. the process by which buyers and sellers exchange goods and services.

Answer: d

Reason: A market exists for the buying and selling of goods and services. This process of buying and selling is the market process.

2. The existence of a market requires:

a. at least one buyer
b. a good or service
c. at least one seller
d. all of the above.

Answer: d

Reason: A market cannot exist without buyers, sellers, a product, and a price.

3. Which of the following is not necessary for a market to exist?

a. A specific geographical location
b. A price at which the product is sold
c. A specific good or service
d. At least one buyer and one seller.

Answer: a

Reason: A market is more of a mechanism that facilitates exchange than a particular place.

4. A market is:

a. a point of contact between buyers and sellers
b. a mechanism that facilitates exchange
c. both a and b
d. neither a nor b.

Answer: c

Reason: A market exists as long as buyers and sellers are in contact to exchange goods and services.

5. Demand refers to:

a. the quantity that will be bought at a particular price
b. the quantity that sellers place on the market for sale as a result of buyers' wants
c. consumers wants and needs
d. the various quantities that buyers will be willing and able to buy at various prices.

Answer: d

Reason: A set of prices with the associated quantities that people will be willing and able to buy constitutes demand. It is not a specific quantity that will be purchased at some stipulated price.

6. To the economist, demand refers to:

a. the actual quantity purchased at a particular price
b. the buyers' need for a product
c. people's ability to buy a product
d. none of the above.

Answer: d

Reason: Demand refers to the various quantities of an item that buyers will be willing and able to buy at various prices during a period of time.

7. A demand schedule is:

a. a table that shows various quantities of an item that buyers will be willing and able to buy at various prices
b. a downward sloping curve that shows various quantities of an item that will be bought at various prices
c. a graph that shows the direct relationship between the price of an item and the various quantities that people will purchase
d. a table that shows price increasing as demand increases.

Answer: a

Reason: Choice "a" defines a demand schedule. It differs from a demand curve in that the curve is a graph while the schedule is a table.

8. In a demand schedule, a price of $6 is associated with a quantity of 100 units. This tells us that:

a. the demand is 100 units
b. the demand is $6
c. the product will be sold for $6 per unit
d. none of the above.

Answer: d

Reason: *The quantity of 100 units associated with a price of $6 is referred to as the quantity demanded at $6.*

9. Demand can be illustrated:

a. only by a demand curve
b. only by a demand schedule
c. only by a demand schedule or a demand curve
d. none of the above.

Answer: d

Reason: *Demand can be illustrated by a demand schedule, a demand curve, or a demand function.*

10. Demand is:

a. a stock concept
b. a flow concept
c. a combination of a stock and a flow
d. none of the above.

Answer: d

Reason: *Demand occurs "during a period of time". This time dimension makes demand a flow concept.*

11. If the demand curve for an item is downward sloping and its price falls from $5 to $4.75:

a. the demand will fall
b. the demand will rise
c. the quantity demanded will fall
d. the quantity demanded will rise.

Answer: d

Reason: *A fall in the price of an item does not affect the demand for the item. It affects the quantity demanded. It will be reflected in a movement along the demand curve.*

12. According to the law of demand:

a. demand and price are directly related
b. demand and price are inversely related
c. an inverse relationship exists between price and quantity demanded
d. if the price falls, quantity demanded with rise.

Answer: c

Reason: *The law of demand states that, other things being equal, an increase in price will cause a decrease in quantity demanded and vice versa. The relationship between price and quantity demanded is inverse.*

13. The law of demand states that:

a. price will fall as demand rises
b. price will rise as demand falls
c. quantity demanded will fall as price rises, other things being equal
d. people should buy only what they can afford.

Answer: c

Reason: *The law of demand stipulates an inverse relationship between price and quantity demanded.*

14. According to the law of demand:

a. the demand curve slopes downward
b. people will buy more of an item as its price falls, other things being equal
c. the variables in the demand schedule move in opposite directions
d. all of the above.

Answer: d

Reason: *Choices a, b, and c are just different ways of saying the same thing.*

15. The demand for a product is represented graphically by:

a. a point on the demand curve
b. the entire demand curve
c. the intersection of the demand curve and the price of the item
d. all of the above.

Answer: b

Reason: *The entire curve represents demand while a point on the curve represents quantity demanded.*

16. A downward sloping demand curve implies that:

a. demand will increase as price falls
b. a greater quantity will be bought as price falls
c. price and quantity demanded are positively (directly) related
d. a smaller quantity will be bought at any price.

Answer: b

Reason: *A downward sloping curve illustrates an inverse relationship. Price and quantity demanded move in opposite directions.*

17. Which of the following is likely to have the least effect on the quantity of a product that consumers will be willing and able to buy?

a. An increase in population
b. A decrease in the price of the product
c. A fall in consumers' total income
d. The state of technology.

Answer: d

Reason: *All of the choices affect quantity demanded except technology.*

18. Which is the following is unlikely to cause a change in the demand for steak?

a. An increase in the price of steak
b. Farmers launch a successful campaign extolling the benefit of steak
c. An announcement by scientists that beef consumption is injurious to health
d. A significant fall in the price of hamburgers.

Answer: a

Reason: *The price of an item does not affect the demand for the item; it affects quantity demanded.*

19. Which of the following explains the inverse relationship between price and quantity demanded?

a. the income effect
b. the substitution effect
c. both a and b
d. neither a nor b.

Answer: c

Reason: *The income effect, the market-size effect, and the substitution effect all explain the inverse relationship between price and quantity demanded.*

20. When the price of an item falls, more buyers are attracted to the market, so the quantity demanded rises. This phenomenon is known as:

a. the attraction effect
b. the falling price syndrome
c. the "quantity demanded" phenomenon
d. the market size effect.

Answer: d

Reason: *Note that the market-size is an explanation for the law of demand. It is related to a movement along the demand curve, not a shift of the curve.*

21. The demand curve shows:

a. the inverse relationship between price and income
b. the direct relationship between income and demand
c. the inverse relationship between income and demand
d. none of the above.

Answer: d

Reason: *The demand curve shows an inverse relationship between price and quantity demanded.*

22. The market demand curve is:

a. upward sloping
b. vertical in most cases
c. downward sloping
d. horizontal in most cases.

Answer: c

Reason: *The market demand curve is downward sloping signifying that as price moves in one direction, quantity demanded moves in the other direction.*

23. Which of the following is likely to increase the demand for a product?

a. A fall in the price of the product
b. An increase in total income
c. Expectations of a fall in the price of the product in the future
d. All of the above.

Answer: b

Reason: *An increase in income will cause people to buy more at any given price.*

24. Tide and Cheer are substitutes as laundry detergents. If the price of Cheer rises from \$8 to \$9.50, other things being equal:

a. the quantity of Cheer demanded will fall
b. the demand for Cheer will not be affected
c. the demand for Tide will increase
d. all of the above.

Answer: d

Reason: *An increase in the price of Cheer causes the quantity demanded to fall. A change in the price of Cheer will affect the quantity demanded, not the demand. As the price of Cheer rises, people will switch to a substitute, Tide; thus increasing the demand for Tide.*

25. In general, the market supply curve will be:

a. upward sloping
b. downward sloping
c. vertical
d. horizontal.

Answer: a

Reason: *There is an inverse relationship between price and quantity supplied, giving rise to an upward sloping supply curve.*

26. In economics, supply:

a. is everything that producers place on the market for sale
b. is the various quantities that sellers will be willing and able to offer for sale at various possible prices
c. refers to a specific quantity that sellers will actually sell at some specific price during a given period of time
d. all of the above.

Answer: b

Reason: Supply is a relationship between price and quantity supplied. That is implied in choice "b".

27. An increase in the price of steel is likely to:

a. increase the demand for cars
b. increase the supply of cars
c. decrease the supply of cars
d. have no effect on the market for cars.

Answer: c

Reason: *Steel is an input in the production of cars. An increase in the price of steel increases the cost of producing cars, which decreases the supply of cars.*

28. Which of the following is not a supply shifter?

a. The price of the item being considered
b. Technology
c. The prices of inputs used to produce the item
d. The number of producers of the item under consideration.

Answer: a

Reason: *A change in the price of an item causes a movement along the supply curve. It does not shift the curve.*

29. An increase in supply is shown graphically by:

a. a movement down the supply curve
b. a movement up the supply curve
c. an upward shift (to the left) in the supply curve
d. a downward shift (to the right) in the supply curve.

Answer: d

Reason: *An increase in supply means that a greater quantity is supplied at each price. This implies a rightward shift of the entire supply curve.*

30. Which of the following is likely to affect the supply of a product?

a. The cost of resources
b. Technology
c. Weather conditions
d. All of the above.

Answer: d

Reason: *Supply shifters include the number of producers, prices of related products, technology, expectations of future price changes, and production costs.*

31. All of the following will cause the supply curve for peaches to shift except:

a. an increase in workers' wages by 15%
b. a fall in the price of a complement
c. an increase in the market price of peaches from \$1.05

to $1.15 per pound

d. a bountiful peach harvest

Answer: c

Reason: *An increase in the price of peaches will cause a movement along the supply curve, but the curve will not shift.*

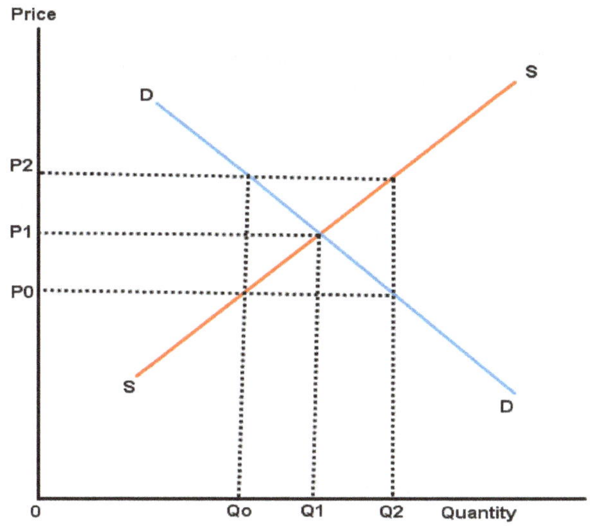

Diagram for questions 32-34

Questions 32, 33 and 34 refer to the preceeding diagram displaying the demand and supply curves for peanuts.

32. The equilibrium price and equilibrium quantity are:

a. P2 and Q2 because they are the highest

b. Po and Qo because consumers pay the least at that price

c. P1 and Q1 because at the price there is no shortage or surplus

d. Po and Q2 because at that price and quantity, buyers and sellers are doing their best

Answer: c

Reason: *Equilibrium occurs when the quantity demanded and the quantity supplied are equal. At that price, there is neither a shortage nor a surplus.*

33. We can notice that:

a. a shortage exists at Po

b. the equilibrium price is P2

c. a surplus exists at P1

d. the equilibrium quantity is Q2

Answer: a

Reason: *At Po, the quantity demanded exceeds the quantity supplied. A shortage exists.*

34. A surplus exists at:

a. P2

b. P1

c. Po

d. Q2

Answer: a

Reason: *At P2, the quantity supplied exceeds the quantity demanded. A surplus exists.*

35. If demand increases, other things being equal, we predict:

a. an increase in price and a decrease in quantity

b. an increase in price and an increase in quantity

c. a decrease in price and an increase in quantity

d. a decrease in price and a decrease in quantity.

Answer: b

Reason: *An increase in demand, other things being equal, shifts the demand curve to the right and causes a shortage which raises the price. The equilibrium quantity also increases.*

36. Assume that tea and coffee are substitutes. An increase in the price of tea is likely to have which of the following effects on the price of coffee?

a. An increase in the price of coffee

b. A fall in the price of coffee

c. No effect on the price of coffee

d. It is impossible to tell

Answer: a

Reason: *When the price of tea increases, some people will switch from tea to coffee, causing the demand for coffee to increase. This increase in the demand for coffee raises the price of coffee.*

37. A price floor will be effective:

a. if the minimum price is set below the market equilibrium price

b. if the minimum price is set above the market equilibrium price

c. regardless of the level at which the minimum price is set

d. only if the minimum price coincides with the equilibrium price.

Answer: b

Reason: *If the minimum price is set below the equilibrium price, it will be ineffective because the equilibrium price will prevail. To be effective, it must be set above the market equilibrium price.*

38. A price ceiling will most likely benefit:

a. consumers of the product

b. producers and sellers of the product

c. both producers and consumers

d. neither producers nor consumers

Answer: a

Reason: *In the absence of the price ceiling, consumers would pay a higher price.*

39. A black market is:

a. a market dominated by black people

b. a market in which stolen items are sold

c. often the result of price ceilings

d. none of the above.

Answer: c

Reason: *Price ceilings often result in black markets because some buyers are willing to pay the higher market equilibrium price.*

40. If the demand and supply equations are

Q_d = 900 −20P and Q_s = −100 + 30P, then the equilibrium price and quantity are:

a. P = 50 and Q = 10
b. P = 20 and Q = 500
c. P = 100 and Q = 40
d. P = 500 and Q = 20

Answer: b

Reason: *Equating quantity demanded and quantity supplied and solving for P and Q give P = 20 and Q = 500.*

True or False

Determine whether each of the following statements is true or false.

1. Demand refers to how much of an item consumers will buy at some specific price and can be represented by a demand schedule.

Answer: False

Explanation: *Demand can be represented by a demand curve, but the concept defined in the statement is quantity demanded, nit demand.*

2. Demand is defined as the various quantities of an item that consumers will be willing and able to buy at various prices during a period of time.

Answer: True

3. There is absolutely no difference between a demand schedule and a demand curve. They are just different names for the same thing.

Answer: False

Explanation: *They both represent demand, but the demand schedule is a table while the demand curve is a graph.*

4. A demand schedule is a table that shows the inverse relationship between price and quantity demanded, while a demand curve is a graph that shows the inverse relationship between price and quantity demanded.

Answer: True

5. A demand curve shows the inverse relationship between price and demand.

Answer: False

Explanation: *The relationship is between price and quantity demanded.*

6. The law of demand states that as the price of an item falls, the demand for it will rise.

Answer: False

Explanation: *First, a change in price affects the quantity demanded, not the demand. Second, the "other things being equal" condition must be included.*

7. According to the law of demand, as the price of an item falls, other things being equal, the quantity demanded will rise.

Answer: True

8. The market size effect, the substitution effect, and the income effect explain why people buy more of an item as its price falls.

Answer: True

9. The market size effect refers to the change in quantity demanded as the number of buyers changes in response to a change in price.

Answer: True

10. The market demand curve is downward sloping indicating that a greater quantity will be demanded as the price falls.

Answer: True

11. The demand curve will shift to the right when the price falls because a greater quantity will be bought.

Answer: False

Explanation: A greater quantity will be bought when the price falls, but this will be shown as a movement along the demand curve, not as a shift in the curve.

12. The market demand curve will shift to the right if the number of buyers increases or if buyers' incomes increase.

Answer: True

13. Changes in income, prices of related goods, the price of the item under consideration, population, and expectations will shift the demand curve and are therefore called demand shifters.

Answer: False

Explanation: *All of the variables listed in the statement, except the price of the item, will shift the demand curve. The price of the item being considered is not a demand shifter.*

14. Demand shifters include income, prices of related goods, population, tastes and preferences, and expectations.

Answer: True

15. All goods are normal goods because people buy more of all goods and services when their incomes increase.

Answer: False

Explanation: *People buy less inferior goods and their incomes increase.*

16. A good is said to be an inferior good if a smaller quantity of the good is bought as income increases.

Answer: True

17. A change in demand is shown by shifting the demand curve while a change in quantity demanded is shown by a movement along a demand curve.

Answer: True

18. Supply is expected to rise if the price of the item rises.

Answer: False

Explanation: If the price of an item rises, quantity supplied is expected to rise.

19. A supply schedule is an upward sloping graph that shows the direct relationship between price and supply.

Answer: False

Explanation: The relationship is between price and quantity supplied.

20. A supply schedule is a table that shows the direct relationship between price and quantity supplied.

Answer: True

21. The law of supply states that as the price of an item rises, the quantity supplied will also rise.

Answer: False

Explanation: The "other things being equal" condition is required to make the statement true.

22. According to the law of supply, as the price of an item falls, other things being equal, the quantity supplied will also fall.

Answer: True

23. The supply curve is an upward sloping curve showing the direct relationship between price and quantity supplied.

Answer: True

24. Factors that will shift the supply curve include a change in the price of the good or service and a change in the number of producers.

Answer: False

Explanation: A change in the price of the good or service will cause a movement along the supply curve. It will not shift it.

25. Factors affecting supply include the number of producers, technology, prices of inputs, prices of related products, and expectations.

Answer: True

26. A supply curve shifting to the left means that producers will offer a smaller quantity for sale at each price.

Answer: True

27. The equilibrium price is the highest price at which an item can be sold.

Answer: False

Explanation: The equilibrium price is the price that equates quantity demanded and quantity supplied.

28. Whenever a surplus exists, it will exert downward pressure on the price; and whenever a shortage exists, it will exert an upward pressure on the price.

Answer: True

29. An increase in the demand for product *A* will always raise the price of *A*.

Answer: False

Explanation: This will be true only if all other things remain equal.

30. Other things being equal, an increase in supply will cause a shortage that forces the price down.

Answer: False

Explanation: The increase in supply will cause a surplus, not a shortage.

31. A tax imposed on a product will tend to raise the price of the product by the full amount of the tax.

Answer: False

Explanation: The tax will increase the price but generally not by the full amount of the tax.

32. If demand and supply both increase, we know that the equilibrium quantity will increase, but we cannot be certain about the effect on the equilibrium price.

Answer: True

33. A price ceiling that is set above the equilibrium price is likely to be ineffective.

Answer: True

34. If carpets and vacuum cleaners are considered to be complementary goods, then an increase in the price of carpets will lead to a decrease in the demand for vacuum cleaners.

Answer: True

35. An increase in the minimum wage is likely to result in an increase in jobs for low-skilled workers.

Answer: False

Explanation: An increase in the minimum wage will make it more expensive for firms to hire low-skilled workers. Hence, a decrease in the number of jobs will likely result.

Completion

(Fill in the blanks)

Use each word or combination of words from the list exactly once.

*(**Hint**: Proceed by elimination)*

Word list

six — seven — five x 2 — Above — Below — Curve — Demand x 3 — Downward — Equilibrium x 2 — Expectations — Fall — Greater — Horizontal — Income x 2 — Increase x 2 — Left — Lower — Normal — Population — Prices Of Related Goods — Quantity Demanded x 2— Raise — Right — Schedule — Shortage x 3 — Substitutes/Complements — Substitution — Supply — Surplus x 2 — Tastes and Preferences

Questions

1. The various quantities that consumers will be willing and able to buy at various prices during a period of time constitute ______________. The quantity that will be bought at a specific price is referred to as ______________ ______________.

2. A(n) ______________ ______________ is a table showing various quantities that people will be willing and able to buy at various prices.

3. The increase in quantity demanded resulting from an increase in the buyers' real income as the price falls is known as the ______________ effect. The change in quantity demanded resulting from substituting one good for another when the price of a good changes is called the ______________ effect.

4. The law of demand states that if the price of an item rises, other things being equal, the quantity demanded will ______________.

5. On a demand/supply graph, economists usually place price on the ______________ axis and quantity on the ______________ axis.

6. A change in ______________ is shown by a shift in the demand curve; a change in ______________ is shown by a movement along the demand curve.

7. The major determinants of demand are ______________, ______________, ______________, ______________, and ______________.

8. The market demand curve slopes ______________, indicating that a ______________ quantity will be demanded as the price falls.

9. Electric guitars and guitar amplifiers would be considered to be ______________.

10. An increase in income, other things being equal, will cause the demand curve to shift to the ______________. A decrease in income will cause it to shift to the ______________.

11. Good *A* is a(n) ______________ good if people buy more of it as their incomes rise.

12. A graph showing the direct relationship between price and quantity offered for sale is called a(n)______________ ______________.

13. The intersection of the demand and supply curves determines the ______________ price and the ______________ quantity.

14. A(n)______________ exists when quantity demanded exceeds quantity supplied t some specific price; and a(n)______________ exists when quantity demanded is less than quantity supplied at some specific price.

15. A surplus will tend to ______________ the price while a shortage will tend to ______________ it.

Questions 16-19 refer to the following diagram.

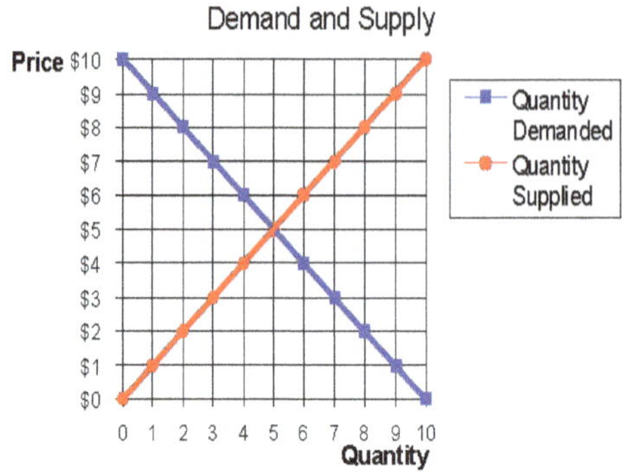

16. If the price is $8, there will be a surplus of ______________ units.

17. If the price is $2, there will be a(n) ______________ of 6 units.

18. The highest price that buyers will be willing and able to pay for 3 units of this product is $ ______________.

19. The equilibrium price and quantity as reflected in this diagram are $ ______________ and ______________ units.

20. Any price below the equilibrium price will result in a(n)______________ of the product. Any price above the equilibrium price will result in a(n)______________ of the product.

21. If demand increases, other things being equal, we predict a(n)______________ in price and a(n)______________ in quantity traded.

22. To be effective, a price ceiling must be set ______________ the equilibrium price. To be effective, a price floor must be set ______________ the equilibrium price.

Solution

1. (demand, quantity demanded)
2. (demand schedule)
3. (income, substitution)
4. (fall)
5. (vertical, horizontal)
6. (demand, quantity demanded)
7. (income, tastes and preferences, population, prices of related goods, expectations—in any order)
8. (downward, greater)
9. (complements)
10. (right, left)
11. (normal).
12. (supply curve)
13. (equilibrium, equilibrium)
14. (shortage, surplus)
15. (lower, raise)
16. (6)
17. (shortage)
18. (7)
19. (5, 5)
20. (shortage, surplus)
21. (increase, increase)
22. (below, above)

6 ELASTICITY & ITS USES

SYNOPSIS

Changes in price cause consumers to purchase different quantities of a good or service. It is important to be able to measure consumers' responses to changes in price. Price elasticity of demand measures the extent to which quantity demanded changes as the price of a product changes. Price elasticity of demand may be measured either by the point formula or by the arc or average formula.

If a small change in the price of a product causes an infinitely large change in the quantity demanded, then demand is **perfectly elastic**. If a given change in the price of a product causes a more than proportional change in the quantity demanded, then demand is **elastic**. If a given change in price produces a proportional change in quantity demanded, then demand is **unitary elastic.** If a given change in the price of a product leads to a less than proportional change in the quantity demanded of that product, then demand is **inelastic**. If a given change in the price of a product causes no change in quantity demanded, then demand is **perfectly inelastic**.

If the demand for a product is elastic, a fall in its price will increase total revenue, while an increase in its price will reduce total revenue. If the demand for a product is unitary elastic, a change in its price will leave total revenue unchanged. If the demand for a product is inelastic, a fall in its price will reduce total revenue, while a rise in its price will increase total revenue.

Among the factors affecting elasticity of demand are: the number of available substitutes for the product, the number of uses the product has, the share of the product in the buyers' total budget, and whether the product is a luxury or a necessity.

Cross elasticity of demand is a measure of the effect of a change in the price of one good on the quantity demanded of another good. Substitute goods have positive cross elasticities of demand while complementary goods have negative cross elasticities of demand. **Income elasticity of demand** is a measure of the effect of a change in income on the quantity of a product demanded.

Elasticity of supply measures the degree to which quantity offered for sale responds to changes in price. The time period is an extremely important factor in determining the elasticity of supply for a product.

LEARNING OBJECTIVES

In connection with this module, you should be able to:

1. explain the concept of elasticity.
2. interpret the elasticity coefficient.
3. explain the relationship between elasticity of demand an total revenue.
4. identify the factors that affect price elasticity of demand
5. discuss cross elasticity and income elasticity.
6. explain elasticity of supply.
7. identify the determinants of price elasticity of supply.
8. discuss the uses of the elasticity concept.

DEFINITIONS & CONCEPTS

You should be able to define the following terms and concepts:

elasticity	elasticity of demand
coefficient of elasticity	point elasticity
arc elasticity	elastic demand
inelastic demand	unitary elastic demand
cross elasticity of demand	income elasticity of demand
elasticity of supply	normal and inferior goods
very short (market) period	reservation price

6

ELASTICITY & ITS USES

Concepts, Definitions & Problems

Problem 6-1

Define price elasticity of demand. How is it measured?

Requirement and Clue: *This is a two-part problem. Be sure to answer each part in order. Just give a precise definition of the concept. You are not required to write all you know about elasticity. State briefly how elasticity is measured.*

Solution:

Price elasticity of demand is a measure of the degree to which quantity demanded responds to a change in price.

Price elasticity of demand can be measured as follows:

$$PE = \frac{\text{Percentage change in quantity demanded}}{\text{Percentage change in price}}$$

$$PE = \frac{\text{\% change in Qd}}{\text{\% change in P}}$$

where PE is price elasticity of demand, P is price, and Qd is quantity demanded.

Alternatively, the measure for price elasticity of demand can be expressed as:

$$PE = \frac{\Delta Qd}{Qd} \div \frac{\Delta P}{P}$$

where ΔQd is the change in quantity demanded and ΔP is the change in the price of the product. For example, if the price of an item falls by 10% and as a result, quantity demanded rises by 15%, then the price elasticity of demand can be calculated as

$$PE = \frac{\text{\% change in quantity demanded}}{\text{\% change in price}} = \frac{15}{10} = 1.5$$

Problem 6-2

What is the coefficient of price elasticity of demand and why does it have a negative sign?

Requirement and Clue: *This problem has two parts. You should address each part in order. You are required simply to define the coefficient of price elasticity of demand and then explain why it has a negative sign.*

Solution:

The coefficient of price elasticity of demand is a number that is used to determine the degree of elasticity of demand. By looking at the number, one can determine whether demand is elastic or inelastic.

We know that there is an inverse relationship between price and quantity demanded. If the change in price is positive, the change in quantity will be negative; and if the change in price is negative, the change in quantity will be positive. That means that in the price elasticity formula, either the numerator or the denominator will be negative, which means that the quotient will always be negative.

Problem 6-3

What is one advantage of the arc formula for price elasticity of demand over the point formula? What is one advantage of the point formula over the arc formula?

Requirement and Clue: *A brief statement of the difference between the arc formula and the point formula would be in order, but your main task is to point out one advantage of each over the other.*

Solution:

One advantage of the arc formula over the point formula is that the arc formula gives a unique value for the price elasticity coefficient regardless of the direction of the price change. On the other hand, the point formula gives two different measures of the coefficient of elasticity: one for a price increase, and another for a price decrease.

One advantage of the point formula over the arc formula is that the point formula is simpler and easier to use than the arc formula.

Problem 6-4

Carefully describe and illustrate the five degrees of price elasticity of demand.

Requirement and Clue: *This question is referring to the range or categories of elasticity of demand, from perfectly inelastic to perfectly elastic. Graphical illustration of each is required.*

Solution:

The demand for a product can be perfectly inelastic, inelastic, unitary elastic, elastic, or perfectly elastic. If a change in the price of an item has no impact at all on the quantity demanded, then the demand for the item is said to be perfectly inelastic.

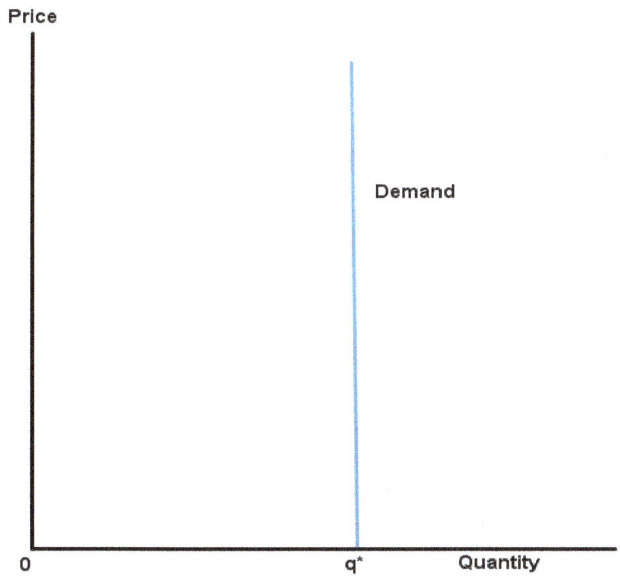

Figure 1

Perfectly inelastic demand is shown by a vertical demand curve as shown in Figure 1 below. A change from one price to another leaves the quantity demanded unchanged at q*.

Usually, when the price of an item changes, the quantity demanded of it also changes. If a 10% change in price causes the quantity demanded to change by less than 10%, then the demand for the product is inelastic. In this case, the change in quantity demanded is less than proportional to the change in the price that caused it. Inelastic demand is illustrated in Figure 2 below. An increase in price from P1 to P2 results in a relatively small decrease in quantity from Q2 to Q1.

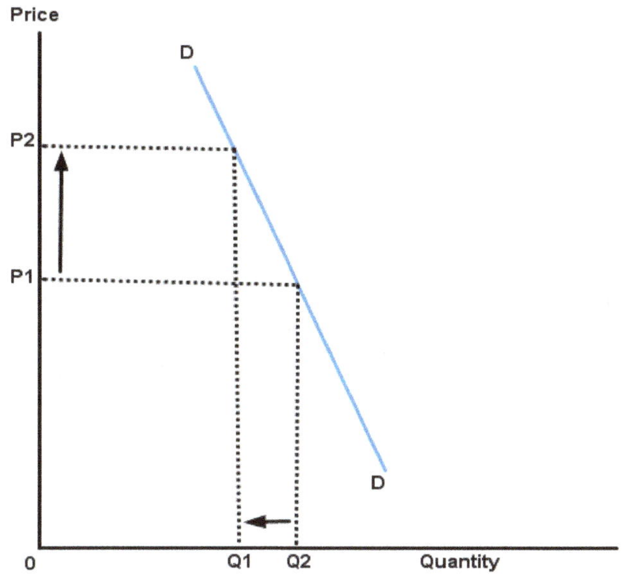

Figure 2

If a 10% change in the price of an item results in a 10% change in the quantity demanded, the demand for the product is said to be unitary elastic. Figure 3 below illustrates the case of unitary elastic demand. A change in price from P2 to P1 causes a proportional change in quantity demanded from Q1 to Q2.

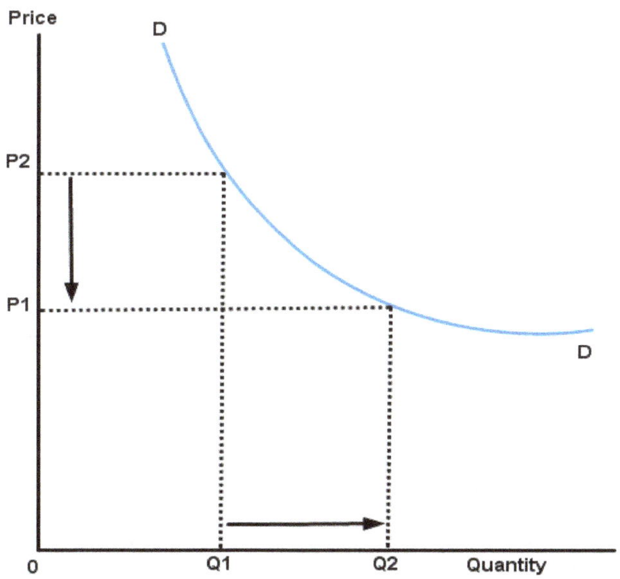

Figure 3

Demand is said to be elastic if a 10% change in the price of the item results in a more than 10% change in quantity demanded. In this case the change in quantity demanded is more than proportional to the change in price that caused it. Figure 4 below illustrates elastic demand. A fall in price from P2 to P1 results in a relatively large increase in quantity demanded from Q1 to Q2.

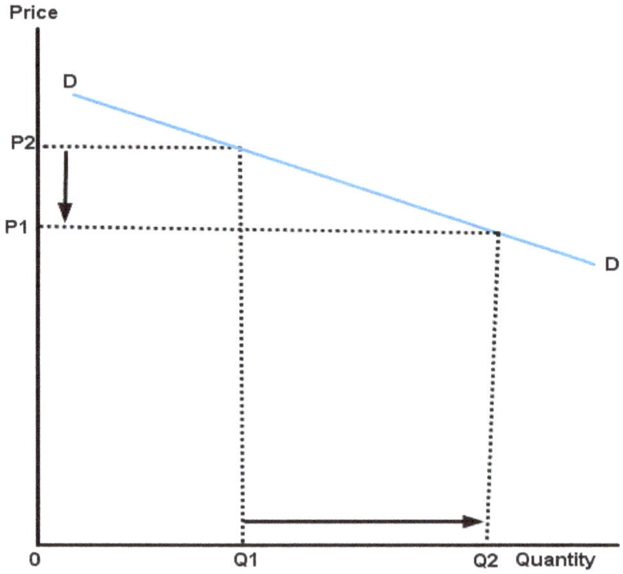

Figure 4

Finally, we have the case of perfectly elastic demand. In this case, a small change in price results in an infinitely large change in quantity demanded. Perfectly elastic demand is illustrated in Figure 5 below by a horizontal demand curve.

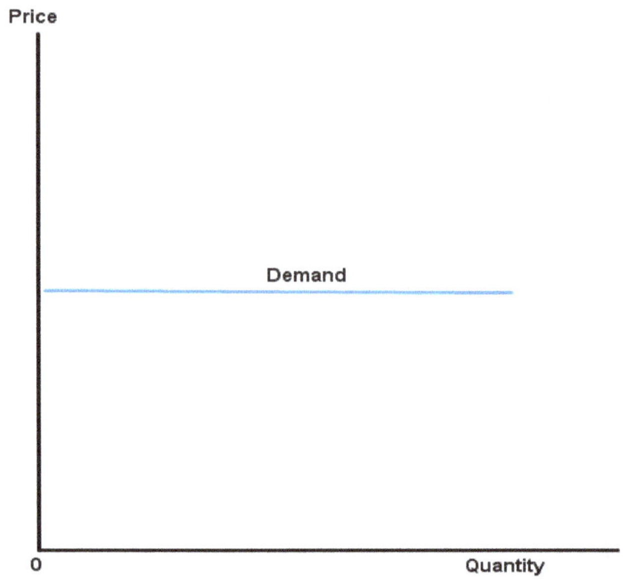

Figure 5

Problem 6-5

How would you interpret a price elasticity of demand coefficient of 1.7?

Requirement and Clue: *Think in terms of degrees of elasticity and numerical impact of a price change.*

Solution:

A price elasticity coefficient of 1.7 means that the demand for the product is elastic. Specifically, it tells us that a 10% change in price will cause a 17% (10 × 1.7) change in quantity demanded in the opposite direction.

Problem 6-6

You operate a store that specializes in men's ties. You have been informed by an economist that the price elasticity of demand for your ties at current prices is 2.7. What effect will a price reduction of 15% have on the quantity of ties that you sell?

Requirement and Clue: *Consider the meaning of a price elasticity of demand of 2.7. Since you have the actual elasticity coefficient, you can be specific about the numerical impact of a reduction in price.*

Solution:

A price elasticity of demand of 2.7 means that a given percentage fall in price will cause quantity demanded to increase by 2.7 times the percentage decrease in price. Since the reduction in price is 15%, then the quantity demanded will increase by 2.7 × 15 = 40.5%.

Problem 6-7

The following diagram shows the demand curve for sandwiches per week. What does it tell us about the demand for sandwiches?

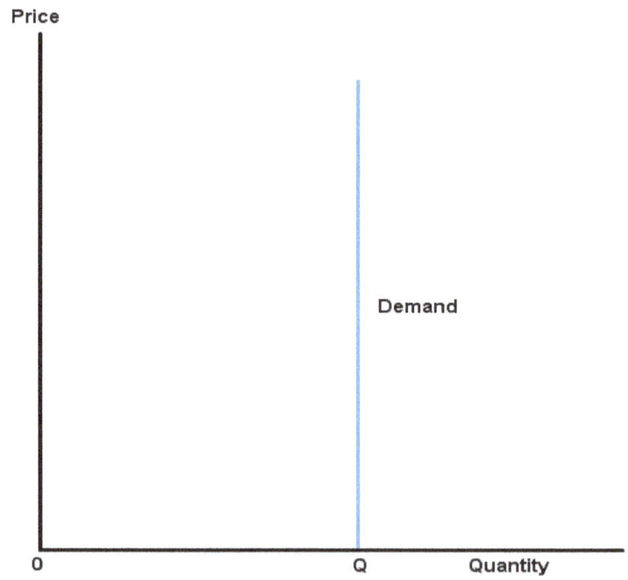

Requirement and Clue: *You are required to recognize the significance of a vertical demand curve and relate it to the elasticity concept.*

Solution:

A demand curve shows the various quantities of an item that buyers will buy at various prices during a period of time. A vertical demand curve like that shown in the diagram, means that the demand for sandwiches is perfectly inelastic. In this case, a change in the price of sandwiches has absolutely no effect on the quantity demanded.

A quantity of Q sandwiches per week will be bought regardless of the price. Even if sandwiches were free, only a quantity of Q will be demanded.

Problem 6-8

When Rosalie raised the price of her roses from \$20 to \$25 per bouquet, she observed that her sales dropped from 300 to 250 bouquets. What is the state of demand (elastic, inelastic) for Rosalie's roses?

Requirement and Clue: *You can use a formula to calculate the coefficient of elasticity of demand and then use the value of the coefficient to determine whether the demand is elastic or inelastic.*

Solution:

From the information given in the problem, we can deduce that P = 20, ΔP = 5, Q = 300, ΔQ = 50 (ignoring the signs). The elasticity formula is:

$$E_d = \frac{\Delta Q}{Q} \div \frac{\Delta P}{P} \quad \text{where } E_d = \text{elasticity of demand}$$

$$= \frac{50}{300} \div \frac{5}{20} = 0.67$$

Since the price elasticity coefficient is less than 1, we can conclude that the demand for roses is inelastic.

Problem 6-9

The demand for an item is known to be highly inelastic at the current price. What effect will a price increase have on total revenue?

Requirement and Clue: *Bear in mind what it means when we say that demand is highly inelastic. Say what total revenue is and then figure out what will happen to total revenue if a price increase has little impact on quantity bought.*

Solution:

We know from the stated problem that the demand for the item is highly inelastic. This tells us that a change in the price of the item will have no appreciable impact on the quantity demanded. Total revenue is price times quantity sold:

TR = P × Q where TR is total revenue, P is price, and Q is quantity

A price increase will cause quantity demanded to decrease, but the decrease in quantity will be relatively small compared with the increase in price. Therefore an increase in price will raise total revenue.

Problem 6-10

The demand for an item is known to be highly elastic at the current price. What effect will a price increase have on total revenue?

Requirement and Clue: *Bear in mind what it means when we say that demand is highly elastic. Say what total revenue is and then figure out what will happen to total revenue if a price increase has tremendous impact on quantity bought.*

Solution:

We know from the stated problem that the demand for the item is highly elastic. This tells us that a change in the price of the item will have a significant impact on the quantity demanded. Total revenue is price times quantity sold:

TR = P × Q, where TR is total revenue, P is price, and Q is quantity

A price increase will cause quantity demanded to decrease, but the decrease in quantity will be relatively large compared with the increase in price. Therefore an increase in price will lower total revenue.

Problem 6-11

A store keeper is contemplating raising her prices in order to raise her total revenue. Under what condition will the contemplated price increase achieve its objective?

Requirement and Clue: *Recognize that an increase in price will reduce quantity demanded, other things being equal. The question is, how large will be the reduction in quantity demanded? This, of course, depends on the price elasticity of demand. Comparison of the relative increase in price with the relative decrease in quantity demanded will determine the effect on total revenue.*

Solution:

The store keeper's objective is to increase total revenue. Total revenue is price times quantity. The store keeper will achieve her objective of raising revenue if the increase in price results in a relatively small decrease in quantity demanded. In other words, total revenue will increase if the demand for the store keeper's product is inelastic.

Problem 6-12

Egg producers raise the price of their eggs from \$1.50 to \$2.00 a dozen. Consequently, their total sales dropped from 200,000 to 100,000 dozen a week. What is the effect of this price increase on the egg producer's total revenue? On the basis of the change in total revenue, determine whether the demand for eggs is elastic or inelastic.

Requirement and Clue: *This is a two-part problem. Address each part in order. Consider total revenue prior to the price increase and total revenue after the price increase. The change in total revenue following a price change can determine whether demand is elastic or inelastic.*

Solution:

At a price of \$1.50, the quantity sold is 200,000. Total revenue is (\$1.50 × 200,000) = \$300,000.

At a price of \$2.00, the quantity sold is 100,000. Total revenue is (\$2.00 × 100,000) = \$200,000

Since an increase in price leads to a reduction in total revenue, we can conclude that the demand for eggs is elastic.

Problem 6-13

When chocolate bars are sold at \$1.25 each, a total of 500,000 bars per week are sold. When the price falls to \$1.00, the weekly sales increase to 550,000.

What can you deduce from this information about the demand for chocolate bars? (Is it elastic or inelastic?)

Requirement and Clue: *You can consider the effect of the price decrease on total revenue and from that determine whether the demand is elastic or inelastic. Alternatively, you could use a price elasticity formula to calculate the elasticity coefficient and thence determine whether demand is elastic or inelastic.*

Solution:

At a price of \$1.25, quantity sold is 500,000. Total revenue is (\$1.25 × 500,000) = \$625,000

At a price of \$1.00, quantity sold is 550,000. Total revenue is (\$1.00 × 550,000) = \$550,000

Thus the fall in price reduces total revenue. This happens when the demand for the product is inelastic. We can conclude that the demand for eggs is inelastic.

Alternatively, we get the following information from the problem:

P = 1.25, ΔP = \$0.25, Q = 500,000, ΔQ = 50,000 (ignoring signs), where P = price, Q = quantity, and E_d = elasticity of demand

$$Ed = \frac{\Delta Q}{Q} \div \frac{\Delta P}{P} = \frac{50{,}0000.25}{500{,}000} \div \frac{}{1.25} = 0.5$$

Since E_d is less than 1, we know that the demand for eggs is inelastic.

Problem 6-14

There is a gigantic sale on CDs and you have decided that regardless of the price of CDs, you will spend exactly \$20. What can you say about your demand curve for CDs?

Requirement and Clue: *Clearly, you will adjust the quantity of CDs you buy according to the price so that the price × quantity always equals \$20. Consider the state of elasticity of demand for which total expenditure remains the same no matter what the price is.*

Solution:

If the price of CDs is \$10, you will buy 2 CDs. If the price is \$4, you will buy 5 CDs; and if the price is \$5, you will buy 4 CDs. So total expenditure (TE) = P × Q = \$20. This is the case when the demand is unitary elastic.

Problem 6-15

What are the main factors that affect the degree of price elasticity of demand?

Requirement and Clue: *What is required here is a discussion of the main factors that determine whether demand is elastic or inelastic. Think whether buyers will respond slightly or significantly to a change in the price of the item.*

Solution:

Main factors that will affect the price elasticity of demand include the number and types of substitutes, the number of uses the product has, the importance of the item in the budget, the nature of the product, and time.

If an item has a large number of close substitutes, then an increase in its price will cause some buyers to switch to some of the many close substitutes that have now become relatively less expensive. If there are hardly any close substitutes, then an increase in the price of the item will probably not have a significant impact on the quantity demanded. Consider the case of non-alcoholic beverages where there are numerous substitutes. If the price of one rises, consumers can easily switch to a substitute. Now consider the case of electricity for lighting. If electricity rates go up, the quantity demanded will fall, but not by much, because consumers don't have many good alternatives. We can conclude that in general, if an item has many close substitutes, its demand is likely to be elastic.

In general, the greater the number of uses an item has, the more elastic the demand for that item is likely to be. Eggs have a variety of uses. If the price of eggs falls, people will buy more to allocate to different uses. On the other hand, a hand-calculator does not have many uses. It is unlikely that a fall in the price of hand calculators will cause a significant increase in the quantity demanded.

The fraction of the spending budget allocated to the item will exert some influence on the elasticity of demand. If the item accounts for only a tiny fraction of the spending budget, then its demand is likely to be inelastic. Table salt is relatively inexpensive and therefore does not account for any appreciable share of the budget. A 10% change in the price of table salt will not likely cause any significant change in quantity demanded. Thus, the demand for table salt is likely to be inelastic. On the other hand, consider an item such as an ipad. It is a relatively expensive device. If the price changes, consumer will likely respond significantly to the change in price. The demand for such as item is likely to be elastic.

Whether the item is considered to be a necessity or a luxury will affect its price elasticity of demand. Medication prescribed by a physician will be viewed by most people to be a necessity. A change in price will not appreciably affect the quantity demanded. Its demand is likely to be highly inelastic. On the other hand, a vacation package to an exotic destination may be considered to be a luxury. If the price rises, it will significantly affect the quantity demanded; hence the demand will be elastic. In general, the demand for luxury items is likely to be elastic.

The time period being considered will also have some effect on the elasticity of demand for a product. In general, the longer the time period being considered, the more elastic the demand is likely to be. This is due mainly to the fact that it takes time for people to adjust to new situations.

Problem 6-16

State whether you expect demand for each of the following to be elastic or inelastic. Give reasons for your choice.

1. The services of medical doctors
2. Toilet paper
3. Diamond necklaces
4. Telephone services

Requirement and Clue: *This is a two-part problem. Address each part in order. This problem is based on the factors affecting price elasticity of demand. Consider them when solving the problem.*

Solution:

1. *The services of medical doctors:* When people are ill, medical attention becomes a necessity. Therefore, the demand for the services of medical doctors is likely to be inelastic.
2. *Toilet paper:* The demand for toilet paper is likely to be inelastic for two main reasons. First, this product has no close substitutes. Second, the fraction of the budget spent on it is relatively small.
3. *Diamond necklaces:* There are many substitutes for diamond necklaces. Moreover, many people would consider them to be luxuries. Therefore, the demand for diamond necklaces is likely to be elastic.
4. *Telephone services:* Telephone services are essential. A small change in price is unlikely to cause any significant change in quantity demanded. Therefore, the demand is likely to be inelastic.

Problem 6-17

What does each of the following situations indicate about the elasticity of demand for the product?

(a) *The price of gasoline rises from $1.27 to $1.49 per litre and you buy just about the same amount.*

(b) *At $50 per ticket for a concert you would buy two tickets. At $70, you stay at home and watch a movie on TV.*

(c) *The price of potato chips rises from $0.79 to $1.49, but you buy the same amount as before.*

Requirement and Clue: *The question to consider is what kind of response does the change in price evoke from the buyer?*

Solution:

(a) The increase in the price of gas does not significantly affect the amount that you buy. The response is minimal; hence the demand for gasoline at the given prices is highly inelastic.

(b) Your response to the increase in price from $50 to $70 is quite significant. You buy none. Therefore, your demand for concert tickets at the indicated prices is elastic.

(c) The increase in the price of potato chips from $0.79 to $1.49 has absolutely no impact on the quantity demanded. You buy the same amount; therefore, the demand is perfectly inelastic.

Problem 6-18

Explain briefly why an increase in the price of farm products may lead to larger incomes for farmers.

Requirement and Clue: *"Briefly" suggests that a long drawn out explanation is not required. Focus on the likely impact of an increase in the price of farm products on the quantity demanded. Elasticity should readily come to mind.*

Solution:

Farm products are essentially food. The demand for food, in general, is highly inelastic. A change in the price of food will not usually cause a large change in quantity demanded. If price increases, people will not eat a great deal less food, and if price falls, they will not eat considerably more food. If the price of food increases, and the demand for food is inelastic, then the increase in price will raise total revenue, which is the income of farmers.

Problem 6-19

Is it possible for the demand for a product to be elastic at a price of zero?

Requirement and Clue: *This problem requires a good understanding of the relationship between elasticity and total revenue. Think about total revenue when the price is zero and then tie this to elasticity.*

Solution:

At a price of zero, total revenue is zero. Before the price reached zero, total revenue was positive. So as the price fell to zero, total revenue decreased. If demand were elastic, then a fall in price would increase total revenue. But the fall in price to zero actually reduced total revenue. This leads to the conclusion that it is impossible for the demand to be elastic at a price of zero.

Problem 6-20

What do economists mean by cross elasticity of demand and how is it measured? What is the significance of the sign of the coefficient of cross elasticity of demand?

Requirement and Clue: *Note that this is a three-part problem. Answer each part in order. Give a clear definition of the concept and carefully explain how it is measured. You are expected to state how one can determine complements and substitutes by looking at the sign of the coefficient of cross elasticity of demand.*

Solution:

Cross elasticity of demand is a measure of the degree to which the quantity demanded of one item responds to a change in the price of another item. Cross elasticity of demand for product *A* is measured by the relative change in the quantity of *A* demanded divided by the relative change in the price of product *B*.

Symbolically, the cross elasticity of demand between *A* and *B* ($E_{A,B}$) can be expressed as follows:

$$E_{A,B} = \frac{\%\Delta Q_A}{\%\Delta P_B} = \frac{\Delta Q_A}{Q_A} \div \frac{\Delta P_B}{P_B}$$

Where Q_A is the quantity of *A*, Q_B is the quantity of *B*, P_A is the price of *A*, and P_B is the price of *B*.

The sign of the coefficient of cross elasticity of demand is significant because from it we can determine the nature of the relationship between the two goods—whether they are substitutes, complements, or independent. If the coefficient of the cross elasticity of demand between *A* and *B* is positive, then *A* and *B* are substitutes. If it is negative, then *A* and *B* are complements; and if it is zero, then *A* and *B* are not related.

Problem 6-21

You operate a small coffee shop. The cross elasticity of demand between coffee and tea is estimated to be 2.5. If the price of tea rises by 6%, what change should you expect in the demand for coffee?

Requirement and Clue: *Focus on the cross elasticity of 2.5. What does it mean in terms of a change in the price of one on the demand for the other?*

Solution:

Tea and coffee are substitutes, so we know that an increase in the price of tea leads to an increase in the demand for coffee, other things being equal. Some buyers of tea will respond to the increase in the price of tea by switching to coffee. Since the cross elasticity of demand between coffee and tea is 2.5 as stated in the problem, then a 6% increase in the price of tea causes the demand for coffee to increase by (6 × 2.5) = 15%. You should expect a 15% increase in demand for coffee.

Problem 6-22

Define income elasticity of demand. How is it measured?

Requirement and Clue: *This is a two-part problem. Answer each part in order. You are not required to write a term paper on income elasticity of demand. What is required is a clear statement of the meaning of the concept and how it is measured.*

Solution:

Income elasticity of demand is a measure of the degree to which quantity demanded responds to a change in income.

Income elasticity of demand is measured by the percentage change in income divided by the percentage change in income. Symbolically, if E_y denotes income elasticity of demand, Q denotes quantity demanded, and Y denotes income, then income elasticity of demand (E_y) can be measured as follows:

$$E_y = \frac{\%\Delta Q}{\%\Delta Y} = \frac{\Delta Q}{Q} \div \frac{\Delta Y}{Y}$$

Problem 6-23

Does the sign of the coefficient of the income elasticity of demand have any significance?

Requirement and Clue: *The problem is hinting at normal and inferior goods. Relate the sign of the income coefficient to normal and inferior goods.*

Solution:

For most goods, as income rises, the quantity demanded also rises. These are normal goods. The income elasticity of demand for normal goods will be positive. There are instances, however, when smaller quantities of certain goods are demanded as income rises. Such goods are inferior goods. The income elasticity of demand for inferior goods will be negative. In sum, if the coefficient of income elasticity of demand is positive, the good is a normal. If it is negative, the good is an inferior good.

Problem 6-24

What is the difference between normal goods and inferior goods? Give an example of each.

Requirement and Clue: *This problem has two parts. Answer each part in order. Think of normal and inferior goods as consumers' reaction to them as their incomes rise. Don't forget the second part of the problem.*

Solution:

The characteristic feature of normal goods is that a greater quantity of them is bought as income rises. When consumers' incomes rise, other things being equal, they will likely buy more vacations, more kitchen appliances, more suits, and more restaurant meals. All these items are examples of normal goods.

On the other hand, there are instances when consumers buy less of certain items as their incomes rise. Inferior goods are those goods whose quantity demanded falls as income rises. Items such as used clothing, used furniture, and imitation leather are examples of inferior goods.

Problem 6-25

How can the coefficient of income elasticity of demand be used to determine whether an item is a normal good or an inferior good?

Requirement and Clue: *The purpose of this question is to test your knowledge of the relationship between the income elasticity coefficient and normal and inferior goods. You should define normal and inferior goods and make the connection.*

Solution:

A normal good is defined as one of which a greater quantity is bought as income rises. An inferior good is defined as one of which a smaller quantity is bought as income rises. The coefficient of income elasticity of demand tells the extent to which quantity demanded responds to a change in income. If consumers buy more of a good as their incomes increase, the income coefficient will have a positive sign and the good will be a normal good. If consumers buy less of a good as their incomes increase, the income coefficient will have a negative sign and the good will be an inferior good.

Problem 6-26

Farmers have been informed that the income elasticity of demand for beef is 2.2. If the price of beef is fixed, and on average, people's incomes are expected to increase by 10%, what change should beef farmers make in their production of beef?

Requirement and Clue: *The problem requires that you figure out the effect of a 10% increase in income on the quantity of beef demanded. Consider using the income elasticity formula.*

Solution:

The formula for the income elasticity of demand is

$$E_y = \frac{\%\Delta Q}{\%\Delta Y},$$

where E_y is income elasticity, Q is quantity demanded and Y is in income.

The problem provides information that $E_y = 2.2$, and $\%\Delta Y = 10$. From the formula we can write:

$\%\Delta Q = E_y \times \%\Delta Y$. Substituting we obtain

$\%\Delta Q = (2.2 \times 10) = 22\%$

Beef farmers should therefore increase their production of beef by 22%.

Problem 6-27

When income in a certain community increases from $500,000 to $600,000, consumers increase their purchases of personal computers from 100 units to 120 units. On the basis of this information, calculate the coefficient of the income elasticity of demand. On the basis of your answer, how would you describe the income elasticity of demand for personal computers?

Requirement and Clue: *This problem has two parts. Answer each part in turn. Just plug the figures provided by the problem into the income elasticity formula.*

Solution:

The formula for the coefficient of income elasticity of demand is

$$E_y = \frac{\Delta Q}{Q} \div \frac{\Delta Y}{Y}$$

where E_y is income elasticity, Q is quantity demanded, and Y is income.

From the problem, we note that Q = 100, ΔQ = 20, Y = $500,000, and ΔY = 100,000. Substituting, we obtain:

$$E_y = \frac{20}{100} \div \frac{100,000}{500,000} = 1$$

Alternatively, from the problem, we see that the change in income is 20% and the change in quantity demanded is also 20%. Using the formula,

$$Ey = \frac{\%\Delta Q}{\%\Delta Y}$$

gives 20/20 = 1.

Since the coefficient of income elasticity of demand is 1, the income elasticity of demand for personal computers can be described as being unitary elastic.

Problem 6-28

Define price elasticity of supply. How is it measured?

Requirement and Clue: *This is a two-part problem. Be sure to answer each part in order. Just give a precise definition of the concept. You are not required to write all you know about elasticity. State briefly how elasticity of supply is measured.*

Solution

Price elasticity of supply is a measure of the degree to which quantity supplied responds to a change in price.

Price elasticity of supply can be measured as follows:

$$E_s = \frac{\text{Percentage change in quantity supplied}}{\text{Percentage change in price}}$$

$$E_s = \frac{\text{\% change in Q}}{\text{\% change in P}}$$

where E_s is price elasticity of supply, P is price, and Q is quantity supplied.

Alternatively, the measure for price elasticity of supply can be expressed as:

$$E_s = \frac{\Delta Q}{Q} \div \frac{\Delta P}{P}$$

where ΔQ is the change in quantity supplied and ΔP is the change in the price of the product. For example, if the price of an item rises by 10% and as a result, quantity supplied rises by 15%, then the price elasticity of supply can be calculated as

$$E_s = \frac{\text{\% change in quantity supplied}}{\text{29\% change in price}} = \frac{15}{10} = 1.5$$

Problem 6-29

Draw five graphs to show the various degrees of price elasticity of supply. .

Requirement and Clue: *The problem is straight forward. It is designed to test your knowledge of the graphs for the various categories of elasticity of supply.*

Solution:

See graphs below.

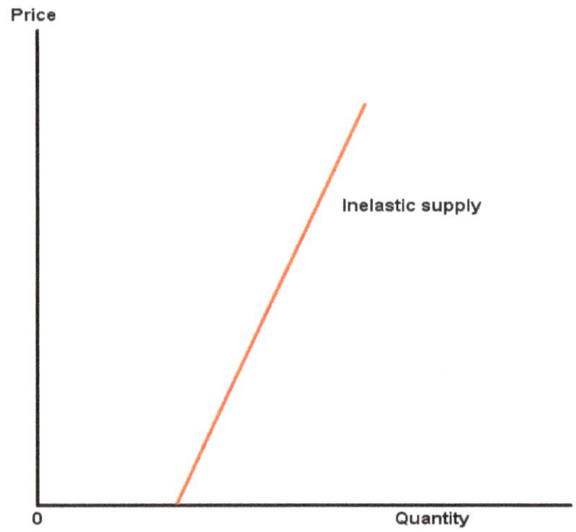

Figure 1

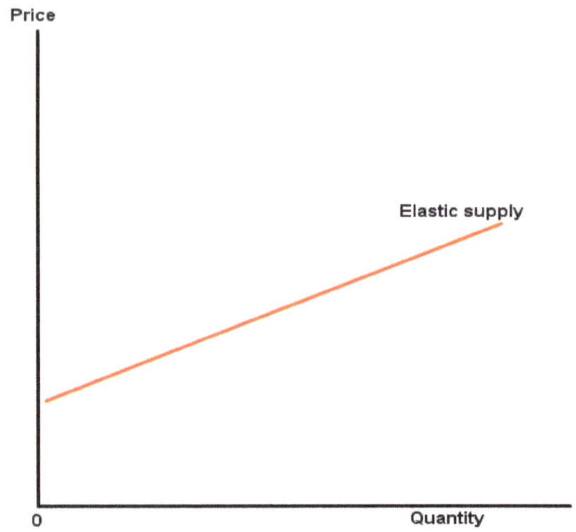

Figure 2

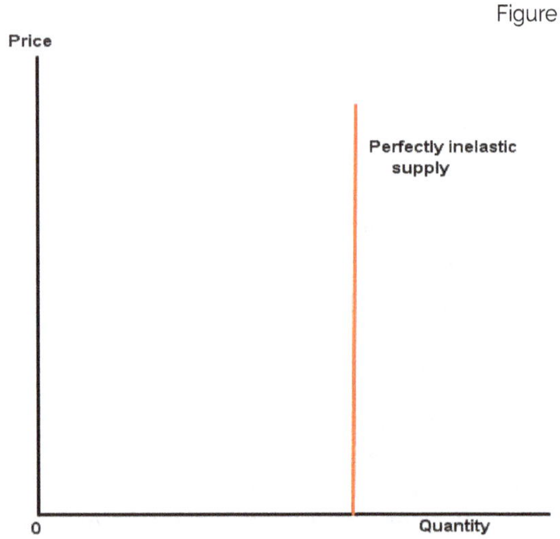

Figure 3

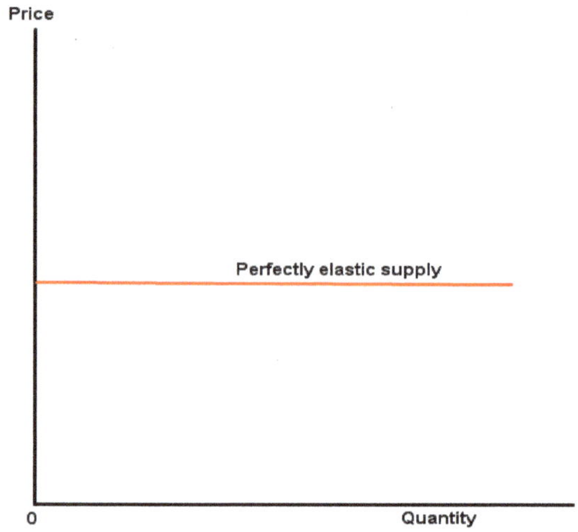

Figure 4

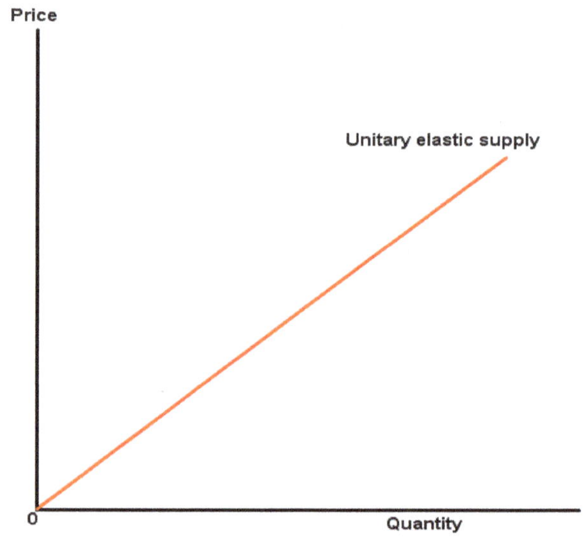

Figure 5

Figure 1 shows inelastic supply. In this case, a 10% change in price will cause a less than 10% change in quantity supplied. In such a case, the supply curve cuts the quantity axis. Figure 2 shows the case of elastic supply. Any given percentage change in price will cause a larger percentage change in quantity supplied. In this case, the supply curve cuts the price axis. Figure 3 represents perfectly inelastic supply. The same quantity will be offered for sale regardless of the price. The supply curve is thus vertical. Figure 4 shows perfectly elastic supply. The curve is a horizontal straight line. It signifies that any change in price will result in an infinitely large change in quantity supplied. Finally, Figure 5 is the case of unitary elastic supply. A 10% change in price will cause a 10% change in quantity supplied. The supply curve comes out of the origin.

Problem 6-30

What are the main factors that affect price elasticity of supply?

Requirement and Clue: *What is required here is a discussion of the* *main factors that determine whether supply is elastic or inelastic. Think whether sellers/producers will respond slightly or significantly to a change in the price of the item.*

Solution:

The main factors that affect price elasticity of supply are time, storage cost, production substitutes and complements, and the cost of increasing output.

Time:
If the time period is very short, an increase in price does not significantly affect the quantity supplied. A longer time period allows producers to adjust to the change in price. Therefore, the longer the time period being considered, the more elastic will be the supply.

Storage cost:
The elasticity of supply for goods that are not perishable and that can be stored at a relatively low cost tends to be greater than the elasticity of supply for perishables and goods with high storage cost.

Production substitutes and complements:
If a product has a large number of substitutes in production, its supply is likely to be elastic. If the price of such a product falls, producers can shift resources into the production of any of the many substitutes. The supply of a relatively minor joint product is likely to be inelastic. Consider the case of beef and hides. A small increase in the price of hides is unlikely to induce farmers to butcher their cattle. Moreover, once cattle are slaughtered for beef, the hides will be sold at whatever the price may be. Therefore the supply of hides is likely to be inelastic.

The cost of increasing output:
To increase the quantity supplied requires an increase in production, which increases the cost of production. If the cost of increasing output is relatively small, then producers will be willing and able to increase output. Therefore, if the cost of increasing output is low, the supply of the item is likely to be elastic. If the cost is high, the supply is likely to be inelastic.

Problem 6-31

The cost of producing Hollywood sunglasses is $10 each. Ken has a fixed supply of these sunglasses, which he will not sell unless he can make a profit of at least 10%. There are no storage costs and the product (sunglasses) is durable. What will Ken do (sell or not sell) if the market price is (a) $20, (b) $15, (c) $12, or (d) $10?

Requirement and Clue: *Focus on Ken's reservation price. At what price will Ken withdraw his sunglasses from the market?*

Solution:

Ken has incurred a cost of $10 on each unit produced. His minimum acceptable profit is 10%. His reservation price is therefore $11. He will withdraw his sunglasses from the market unless the price is at least $11. For (a), (b) and (c), the market price is above his reservation price, so he will sell. But a market price of $10 is below his reservation price, so he will withdraw his product from the market.

Problem 6-32

Define each of the following terms.

(a) *Market period*

(b) *Reservation price*

Requirement and Clue: *You can probably write a full essay on each of the concepts listed. However, your task here is simply to provide a clear and concise meaning of the terms.*

Solution:

(a) The market period is a situation in which the supply is perfectly inelastic. A higher or lower price will not affect the quantity supplied. It is also referred to as the very short period.

(b) Reservation price is the price below which suppliers will withdraw the product from the market. It is the lowest price that sellers will accept for an item.

Problem 6-33

With the help of an appropriate diagram, explain why rare paintings are so expensive.

Requirement and Clue: *Consider what is peculiar about rare paintings. Any connection here with elasticity of supply? An appropriate diagram would be a demand/supply graph.*

Solution:

One explanation for the high price of rare paintings is that the demand for them is high. But that is only a part of the explanation. The supply of these rare paintings must also be considered. The supply is perfectly inelastic. A higher price will not cause another painting to be produced. In such a case, the supply curve will be vertical as shown in the diagram below.

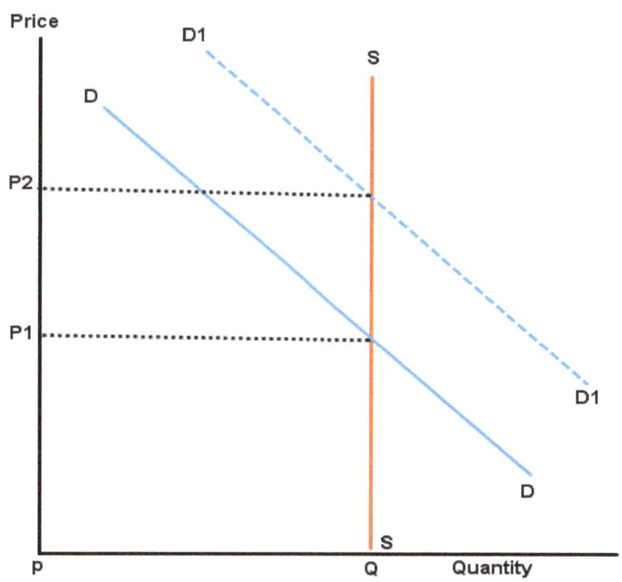

The initial demand and supply curves are DD and SS respectively;

and the equilibrium price and quantity are P_1 and Q respectively. An increase in demand from DD to D1D1 is reflected fully in an increase in price from P1 to P2 since there can be no increase in quantity supplied to absorb or dampen the effect of the increase in demand.

Problem 6-34

Show that if the supply of a product is perfectly price inelastic, the burden of a tax imposed on each unit produced (sold) will be borne entirely by the producers (sellers).

Requirement and Clue: *"Show" suggests the use of graphs. Consider the shape of a supply curve illustrating perfectly inelastic supply. Consider also the effect of the tax on the supply curve. Compare the price before the tax with the price after the tax.*

Solution:

Consider the following diagram.

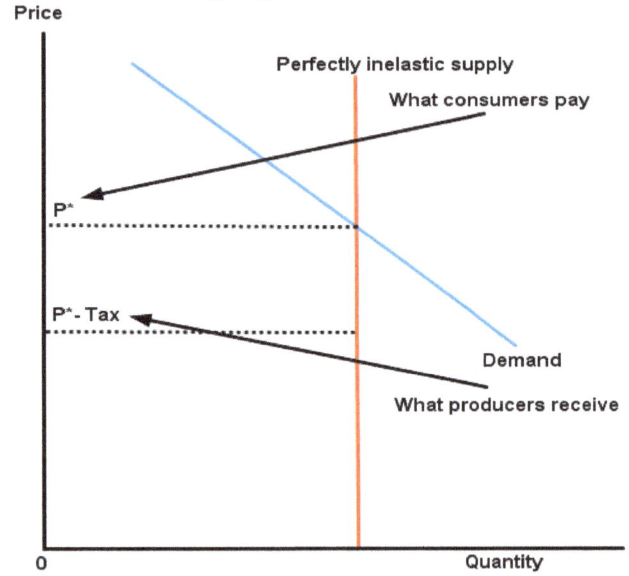

The supply curve is vertical because the supply is perfectly inelastic. The initial equilibrium price is P*. The tax is the vertical distance between P* and P* – Tax. The producer gets a price of P* – Tax instead of P* because of the tax. The tax has no effect on the supply curve in this case, so the producer pays the full amount of the tax.

Multiple-Choice

In each case, circle the letter that corresponds with the correct answer.

1. To the economist, elasticity refers to:

a. items such as rubber bands and elastic strips that can be stretched
b. goods that are distributed over a wide market area
c. the degree to which one variable responds to changes in another variable
d. items that are kept together by elastic bands

Answer: c

Reason: A change in one variable may cause a change in another variable. The extent of the change caused is what economists refer to as elasticity.

2. Which of the following is true of elasticity?

a. It is an important concept that can actually be measured
b. It is an important concept but it cannot be measured
c. It is measureable but it is not very important
d. It cannot be measured but it is not very important

Answer: a

Reason: The elasticity concept has a variety of uses and it can be measured by the percentage change in quantity demanded divided by the percentage change in price.

3. The elasticity concept is:

a. purely theoretical, but not practical
b. entirely practical with no foundation in theory
c. theoretical but it has practical applications
d. much too technical to be of any practical value

Answer: c

Reason: The elasticity concept has a theoretical framework and it has a number of practical uses.

4. Price elasticity of demand measures:

a. the highest price that consumers are willing and able to pay for a good or service
b. how much more consumers will buy as their incomes rise
c. the effect of a change in price on the amount that consumers will be willing to buy
d. the percentage change in price resulting from a given change in quantity

Answer: c

Reason: Price elasticity of demand is the percentage change in quantity demanded divided by the percentage change in price.

5. The point elasticity formula is:

a. the change in price divided by the change in quantity
b. the change in quantity divided by the change in price

c. the percentage change in price divided by the percentage change in quantity

d. the percentage change in quantity divided by the percentage change in price

Answer: d

Reason: The price elasticity formula is given by the percentage change in quantity demanded divided by the percentage change in price.

6. If P represents price and Q represents quantity demanded, the formula for the price elasticity of demand can be written as:

a. ΔP/ΔQ c. %ΔP/%ΔQ

b. ΔQ/ΔP d. %ΔQ/%ΔP

Answer: d

Reason: Price elasticity of demand is the percentage change in quantity demanded divided by the percentage change in price.

7. The number derived from the calculation of the elasticity measure is referred to as:

a. the coefficient of elasticity

b. the argument with respect to elasticity

c. the elasticity derivative

d. none of the above

Answer: a

Reason: The coefficient of price elasticity is a number that measures the effect of a change in price on quantity demanded.

8. Since price and quantity demanded are inversely related, the sign of the coefficient of elasticity of demand will be:

a. negative c. positive

b. either positive or negative d. irrelevant

Answer: a

Reason: A negative sign implies an inverse relationship.

9. All of the following statements about the price elasticity of demand are true except:

a. It is a pure number like 2.0 or 4.6

b. It always has a negative sign because of the inverse relationship between price and quantity demanded

c. It is measured by the percentage change in price divided by the percentage change in quantity demanded

d. It tells the extent to which quantity demanded will respond to changes in price.

Answer: c

Reason: The price elasticity of demand is measured by the percentage change in quantity divided by the percentage change in price.

10. If the coefficient of price elasticity of demand is 0.79, then:

a. demand is inelastic at the given prices

b. demand is elastic because the coefficient is less than 1

c. demand is unitary elastic

d. demand is perfectly inelastic

Answer: a

Reason: A price elasticity coefficient of less than 1 means that the demand for the item is inelastic.

11. If price falls by 2% and, as a result, quantity demanded rises by 3%, then demand is:

a. inelastic c. 2/3 inelastic

b. elastic d. 1.5 times the coefficient

Answer: b

Reason: Since the percentage change in quantity demanded is greater than the percentage change in price, demand is elastic.

12. The arc elasticity formula is also called the:

a. mid-point formula

b. average formula

c. both a and b

d. neither a nor b

Answer: c

13. If a reduction in the price of an item from \$10 to \$8 causes quantity demanded to increase from 1200 units to 1800 units, we know that the coefficient of elasticity of demand for the item is:

a. 2.5 c. 5.0

b. 0.25 d. 0.4

Answer: a

Reason: Applying the price elasticity formula gives an answer of 2.5 for the coefficient of elasticity.

14. One advantage of the arc formula over the point formula is that the arc formula:

a. is easier to use

b. gives the same value for the coefficient regardless of the direction of the price change

c. both a and b

d. neither a nor b

Answer: b

Reason: The arc formula is a bit more complicated but it avoids the confusion of different values for the coefficient depending on the direction of the price change.

15. A fall in the price of good A from \$80 to \$75 results in an increase in quantity demanded from 1600 to 2000. This implies that the demand for A is:

a. inelastic c. elastic

b. unitary elastic d. perfectly elastic

Answer: c

Reason: The value obtained for the coefficient is 4; hence demand is elastic.

16. The coefficient of elasticity of demand for video games is calculated to be 2.1. If the price of video games increases by 10%, the quantity demanded will fall by:

a. 12.1% c. 5%

b. 7.9% d. 21%

Answer: d

Reason: The percentage change in quantity demanded is the coefficient multiplied by the percentage change in price. That is (2.1 × 10%) = 21%

17. The coefficient of price elasticity of demand for a certain item X is calculated to be 1.46. If the price of X falls slightly, then the total revenue realized from the sale of X will:

a. increase c. remain constant
b. decrease d. it is impossible to tell

Answer: a

Reason: Since demand is elastic, then a fall in price will increase total revenue.

18. If Joan increases the price of her hand bags in order to increase her revenue, this suggests that she believes that the demand for her hand bags is:

a. elastic c. unitary elastic
b. inelastic d. declining

Answer: b

Reason: If demand is inelastic, an increase in price will raise total revenue.

19. Determinants of elasticity of demand include:

a. the availability of substitutes
b. the number of uses of the item
c. the percentage of income spent on the item
d. all of the above

Answer: d

Reason: The choices given in a, b, and c will all affect the price elasticity of demand.

20. Because table salt is relatively cheap, its demand is likely to be:

a. inelastic c. elastic
b. perfectly elastic d. unitary elastic

Answer: a

Reason: Items like table salt that use up only a small fraction of the budget, tend to have inelastic demands.

21. If the cross elasticity of demand between goods A and B is -3.5, then A and B are:

a. substitutes
b. independent as indicated by the sign complements
c. none of the above

Answer: c

Reason: Complements have negative cross elasticity coefficients.

22. An increase in the price of beef from $1.00 per lb. to $1.20 causes the quantity of chicken bought to increase from 1500 lbs. to 2500 lbs. This implies that the cross elasticity of demand between chicken and beef is:

a. elastic c. unitary elastic
b. inelastic d. unknown

Answer: a

Reason: The value of the cross elasticity coefficient is 3.3, which means that the cross elasticity of demand is elastic.

23. The cross elasticity of demand between A and B is known to be positive. From this we can infer that:

a. A and B are substitutes
b. A and B are complements
c. c. A is an inferior good
d. B is an inferior good

Answer: a

Reason: Substitutes have a positive cross elasticity of demand.

24. Which of the following are complementary goods?

a. Transistor radios and batteries
b. Computers and USB flash drives
c. Baseballs and baseball bats
d. All of the above

Answer: d

Reason: Complementary goods are goods that are used together, like the examples given in choices a, b, and c.

25. The income elasticity of demand is:

a. the relative change in quantity demanded multiplied by the income
b. the relative change in quantity demanded divided by the relative change in income
c. the relative change in income divided by the relative change in quantity demanded
d. how much income can be stretched to purchase as many goods as possible.

Answer: b

Reason: The income elasticity of demand refers to the extent to which quantity demanded changes as a result of a change in income. Choice b defines the concept.

26. When we calculate the income elasticity of demand for a good or service:

a. We assume that the price of the good or service changes
b. We measure the extent of the movement from one point on the demand curve to another
c. We measure the extent to which the demand curve shifts as a result of the change in income
d. None of the above

Answer: c

Reason: For income elasticity of demand, the variable that is causing the change in quantity demanded is income. A change in income shifts the demand curve.

27. Which of the following is likely to have the highest income elasticity coefficient?

a. Matches c. Vacation cruises
b. Food d. Cigarettes

Answer: c

Reason: Income is likely to affect the demand for vacation cruises more than any of the other choices.

28. An increase in income from $7500 to $9000 causes an increase in purchases of a good from 3000 to 3500 units. The income elasticity of demand for that good must therefore be:

a. 1.20 c. 3.60
b. 0.83 d. 0.61

Answer: b

Reason: Using the income elasticity formula gives an answer of 0.83.

29. If the income elasticity of demand for a product is negative, then we know that the product is:

a. a normal good c. an inferior good
b. relatively scarce d. free

Answer: c

Reason: An inferior good is such that as income rises, a smaller quantity is demanded. This will give a negative income elasticity of demand.

30. If the income elasticity of demand for a product is positive, then we know that the product is:

a. a normal good c. an inferior good
b. an independent good d. abundant

Answer: a

Reason: A good is said to be normal if people buy more of it as their incomes increase. In this case, the income elasticity of demand will be positive.

31. Price elasticity of supply is:

a. the percentage change in quantity supplied divided by the percentage change in price
b. the percentage change in price divided by the percentage change in quantity supplied
c. the change in supply caused by a change in technology
d. a measure of the effect of a change in supply on the price of an item

Answer: a

Reason: Choice "a" defines the price elasticity of supply.

32. We would expect the sign of the coefficient for the price elasticity of supply to be:

a. infinitely large because suppliers want to make money
b. infinitely small because of the high cost of producing more
c. negative at higher prices
d. positive because price and quantity supplied move in the same direction

Answer: d

Reason: A direct relationship exists between price and quantity supplied, so the price elasticity of supply will be positive.

33. The supply curve for an item with a unitary elastic supply is:

a. downward sloping and cuts the vertical axis
b. upward sloping and passes through the origin
c. downward and cuts the horizontal axis
d. vertical

Answer: b

Reason: Unitary elastic supply is illustrated by an upward sloping straight line through the origin.

34. The supply curve for a product with a perfectly inelastic supply is:

a. horizontal c. upward sloping
b. vertical d. downward sloping

Answer: b

Reason: Perfectly inelastic supply means that a change in price has no effect on the quantity supplied. In this case, the supply curve will be vertical.

35. A vertical supply curve for product A:

a. shows that producers will not sell any of A regardless of the price
b. shows that producers (sellers) will not vary the quantity supplied regardless of the price of A
c. means that the supply of A is perfectly elastic
d. none of the above

Answer: b

Reason: If supply is perfectly inelastic, the supply curve will be vertical.

36. In the very short (market) period, supply is:

a. perfectly elastic c. perfectly inelastic
b. unitary elastic d. none of the above

Answer: c

Reason: *The very short period is so short that sellers cannot adjust their output in response to changes in price. In such a case, the supply curve is vertical.*

37. Important determinants of elasticity of supply include:

a. the time period under consideration
b. storage cost
c. the availability of production substitutes and complements
d. all of the above.

Answer: d

Reason: The choices given in a, b, and c all affect the elasticity of supply.

38. Which of the following is likely to yield the highest tax revenue?

a. A tax on a product with an elastic demand
b. A tax on a product with an inelastic demand
c. A tax on a luxury item
d. A tax on a product with a unitary elastic demand

Answer: b

Reason: If the demand is inelastic, buyers will not react significantly to the tax. They will not purchase significantly less so revenue from the tax will be substantial.

True or False

Determine whether each of the following statements is true or false.

36. Price elasticity of demand refers to the change in price resulting from a change in demand.

Answer: False

Explanation: It refers to the extent to which quantity demanded will change as a result of a change in price.

1. Price elasticity of demand can be measured by the percentage change in quantity demanded divided by the percentage change in price.

   Answer: True

2. The coefficient of price elasticity of demand measures the responsiveness of price to a change in quantity demanded.

   Answer: False

   Explanation: The coefficient of price elasticity of demand measures the responsiveness of quantity demanded to changes in price.

3. Price elasticity of demand depends mostly on the size of the market as reflected in the number of buyers.

   Answer: False

   Explanation: Price elasticity of demand has nothing to do with the size of the market.

4. If a 10% increase in the price of gasoline leads to a 7% reduction in the quantity bought, then the demand for gasoline is inelastic.

   Answer: True

5. The formula for the point elasticity of demand is exactly the slope of the demand curve.

   Answer: False

   Explanation: With price (P) on the vertical axis and quantity (Q) on the horizontal axis, the slope of the demand curve is $\Delta P/\Delta Q$. The point elasticity formula is $P/Q\ (\Delta Q/\Delta P)$.

6. The point elasticity formula gives the same value for the elasticity coefficient regardless of the direction of the price change.

   Answer: False

   Explanation: The point formula gives different values depending on whether there is a price increase or a price decrease. The arc formula gives the same value.

7. A vertical demand curve means that the elasticity of demand is zero.

   Answer: True

8. If a demand curve is horizontal, then the demand for the product is zero.

   Answer: False

   Explanation: A horizontal demand curve means that the demand for the product is perfectly elastic.

9. If the demand for airline tickets is elastic, a reduction in the price of airline tickets will increase total revenue on airline travel.

   Answer: True

10. If the demand for toilet paper is inelastic, an increase in the price of toilet paper will reduce total revenue.

    Answer: False

    Explanation: With inelastic demand, an increase in price will cause less than a proportional decrease in quantity demanded; therefore total revenue will rise.

11. Time is not an important determinant of price elasticity of demand.

    Answer: False

    Explanation: Time is an important determinant of elasticity of demand. Time allows buyers to adjust more fully to price changes.

12. Complementary goods normally have a positive cross elasticity of demand.

    Answer: False

    Explanation: Complementary goods have a negative cross elasticity of demand.

13. If two goods are substitutes, their cross elasticity coefficient will have a positive sign.

    Answer: True

14. The income elasticity of demand is the extent to which quantity demanded will change as income changes.

    Answer: True

15. The coefficient of income elasticity of demand is the percentage change in income divided by the percentage change in quantity.

    Answer: False

    Explanation: It is the percentage change in quantity demanded divided by the percentage change in income.

16. If the coefficient of income elasticity of demand for a product is positive, the product is a normal good.

    Answer: True

17. The coefficient of income elasticity of demand for an inferior good is positive.

    Answer: False

    Explanation: For an inferior good, the coefficient of income elasticity is negative.

18. The concept of elasticity applies only to demand; it cannot be applied to supply because supply cannot be predicted.

    Answer: False

    Explanation: The elasticity concept applies to demand as well as to supply. Elasticity is unrelated to predictability.

19. The elasticity of supply is the extent to which a change in supply affects price.

Answer: False

Explanation: It is the extent to which quantity supplied is affected by a change in price.

20. Like the price elasticity of demand, the price elasticity of supply will always be negative.

Answer: False

Explanation: The price elasticity of supply will be positive because price and quantity supplied move in the same direction.

21. The sign of the coefficient of price elasticity of supply is unrelated to the law of supply.

Answer: False

Explanation: It is because of the law of supply that the sign of the coefficient of elasticity of supply is positive.

22. The elasticity of supply for goods that are not perishable and can be stored at a relatively low cost tends to be greater than the elasticity of supply for perishables and goods with high storage costs.

Answer: True

23. A reservation price is a priced reserved for the best customers of a seller.

Answer: False

Explanation: It is a price below which the seller will not sell the product, but would prefer to withdraw it from the market.

24. In the market period, the supply curve is vertical.

Answer: True

25. Storage cost is an important determinant of the elasticity of supply.

Answer: True

26. In the very short period, the elasticity of supply is zero.

Answer: True

27. The price below which producers refuse to sell their products is known as the elimination price.

Answer: False

Explanation: It is called the reservation price.

28. A tax imposed on an item will always raise the price by the full amount of the tax.

Answer: False

Explanation: The price will rise by the full amount of the tax if the demand for the product is perfectly inelastic, but if the demand curve is downward sloping, the price will rise by less than the full amount of the tax.

29. The concept of elasticity helps to explain why the prices of items such as rare paintings and rare books are so high.

Answer: True

Completion

(Fill in the blanks)

Use each word or combination of words from the list exactly once.
*(**Hint**: Proceed by elimination)*

Word list

9 — Elastic — Substitutes — Budget — Coefficient — Complements

Demanded x 2 — Elastic x 10 — Income — Increase x 2 — Increases/ Decreases x 2 — Inelastic x 8 — Inferior — Joint — Negative — Normal — Perfectly x 3 — Perfectly x 2 — Positive — Price x 4 — Quantity x 2 — Raise/ Lower — Substitutes — Supply

Time — Unitary x 2 — Vertical x 3

Questions

1. Price elasticity of demand is measured by the percentage change in ______________ ______________ divided by the percentage change in ______________.
2. The degree of responsiveness of quantity demanded to a change in price is the ______________ of elasticity.
3. The sign of the coefficient of price elasticity of demand is ______________.
4. The various degrees of elasticity of demand from the most elastic to the least elastic are ______________ ______________, ______________, ______________ ______________, ______________, and ______________ ______________.
5. If the coefficient of elasticity of demand is 1.8, then demand is known to be ______________. In this case, a 5% fall in price will lead to a ______________% ______________ in Quantity demanded.
6. Demand is said to be ______________ if the elasticity coefficient is greater than 1 but less than infinity, and ______________ if the coefficient lies between zero and 1. If the coefficient is exactly equal to 1, then the demand is ______________ ______________.
7. If the price elasticity of demand is zero, then the demand is ______________ ______________. This would appear on a graph as a(n) ______________ line.
8. If the demand for a product is perfectly price inelastic, the shape of the demand curve is ______________.
9. The price elasticity of demand ______________ [increases, decreases] as the price falls.
10. A firm can increase its total revenue by raising its price if the demand for its product is ______________. It can increase its total revenue by lowering its price if the demand for its product is ______________.
11. If the demand for an item is inelastic, an increase in price over the relevant range will ______________ [increase, decrease]

total revenue.

12. If the demand for an item is elastic, a fall in its price will ______________ [raise, lower] total revenue.

13. Cross elasticity of demand between goods A and B is the percentage change in the ______________ ______________ of good A, holding its ______________ constant, divided by the percentage change in the ______________ of good B.

14. If two goods have a positive cross elasticity of demand, we can conclude that they are ______________. If they have a negative cross elasticity of demand, we can conclude that they are ______________.

15. The demand for goods with a wide variety of uses is likely to be ______________. If the good has many close substitutes, its demand is likely to be ______________, and if it is considered a necessity, its demand will be ______________.

16. Factors affecting price elasticity of demand include the availability of close ______________, the number of uses the product has, ______________, and the importance of the item in the ______________.

17. The ______________ elasticity of demand is measured by the percentage change in quantity demanded divided by the percentage change in income.

18. If the coefficient of income elasticity of demand for a good is positive, the good is a ______________ good; if the coefficient of income elasticity of demand for a good is negative, the good is a(n) ______________ good.

19. The price elasticity of supply is the percentage change in quantity supplied divided by the percentage change in ______________.

20. The sign of the coefficient of price elasticity of supply is ______________ because of the law of ______________.

21. If the supply of an item is perfectly price inelastic, then the supply curve is ______________.

22. If a product has a large number of substitutes in production, its supply is likely to be ______________.

23. Production complements are also called ______________ products.

24. In the short run, supply is likely to be ______________. In the long run, supply will tend to be more ______________.

25. If the sales tax on basic necessities were increased, the total revenue from the tax would ______________ because the demand for necessities is ______________.

Solution

1. (quantity demanded, price)
2. (coefficient)
3. (negative)
4. (perfectly elastic, elastic, unitary elastic, inelastic, perfectly inelastic)
5. (elastic, 9, increase)
6. (elastic, inelastic, unitary elastic)
7. (perfectly inelastic, vertical)
8. (vertical)
9. (decreases)
10. (inelastic, elastic)
11. increase, decrease] (increase)
12. (raise)
13. (quantity demanded, price, price)
14. (substitutes, complements)
15. (elastic, elastic, inelastic)
16. (substitutes, time, budget)
17. (income)
18. (normal, inferior)
19. (price)
20. (positive, supply)
21. (vertical)
22. (elastic)
23. (joint)
24. (inelastic, elastic)
25. (increase, inelastic)

7 CONSUMER BEHAVIOUR

SYNOPSIS

Utility refers to the satisfaction a consumer derives from consuming a good or service. The extra satisfaction derived from consuming an additional unit is the **marginal utility**. The law of diminishing marginal utility states that marginal utility declines as more of a good or service is consumed.

In economic theory, it is assumed that the objective of the consumer is to maximize his or her satisfaction. This objective is achieved when consumers have arranged their purchases in such a way that the last dollar spent on each commodity yields the same satisfaction. The consumer will be in equilibrium when

$$\frac{MUa}{Pa} = \frac{MUb}{Pb}$$

Where MUa is the marginal utility of good A, Pa is the price of good A, MUb is the marginal utility of good B, and Pb is the price of good B. Alternatively, the above equation can be stated as

$$\frac{MUa}{MUb} = \frac{Pa}{Pb}$$

The paradox of value is the apparent contradiction in the observation that water that is so essential to life has a lower price than diamonds without which we can live.

Indifference curves are downward sloping, convex, and non-intersecting. They can be used to show preference or indifference on the part of the consumer. All points on an indifference curve indicate the same level of satisfaction. Higher indifference curves represent higher levels of satisfaction.

In terms of indifference curves and budget lines, the consumer will maximize his or her satisfaction when the budget line is tangent to an indifference curve. Changes in income will shift the budget line outward or inward; changes in relative prices will change the slope of the budget line.

LEARNING OBJECTIVES

In connection with this module, you should be able to:

1. explain the concept of utility.
2. state the principle of utility maximization.
3. explain the water-diamond paradox.
4. discuss the relationship between utility and demand.
5. derive the market demand curve.
6. explain the concept and significance of consumer surplus.
7. outline the properties of indifference curves.
8. explain the budget line.
9. use indifference analysis to illustrate the consumer's equilibrium.
10. show how changes in income and changes in prices affect the consumer's equilibrium
11. use indifference curve analysis to derive the consumer's demand curve.

DEFINITIONS & CONCEPTS

You should be able to define the following terms and concepts:

utility
marginal utility
utility maximization
paradox of value
indifference curve
budget line
indifference map
Engel curve
Giffen good

7

CONSUMER BEHAVIOUR

A. Utility Theory

Concepts, Definitions & Problems

Problem 7-1

According to economists, what is the objective of consumers?

Requirement and Clue: *Objectives motivate people. Focus on what it is that economists assume that consumers are trying to achieve?*

Solution:

According to economists, the objective of consumers is to spend their income in purchasing goods and services in such a way as to maximize their satisfaction.

Problem 7-2

Briefly discuss the view that the satisfaction of wants is at the heart of economic activity.

Requirement and Clue: *Consider what constitutes economic activity and its real purpose. Don't ignore the word "briefly."*

Solution:

In a very real sense, the satisfaction of wants is at the core of economic activity. Production, consumption, and exchange are all carried out with the ultimate objective of satisfying wants. Firms produce goods and services with the expectation of selling them to earn income to satisfy their wants. Consumers sell their resources with the expectation of obtaining income with which they can purchase goods and services to satisfy their wants. Trading (exchange) between the members of a community enables them to obtain exactly what they want to maximize their satisfaction.

Problem 7-3

Define utility.

Requirement and Clue: *This is a definitional problem and it is not designed to elicit an essay on utility. Just state as clearly as possible what economists mean by utility.*

Solution:

Utility is the term used to refer to the satisfaction derived from the consumption of goods and services.

Problem 7-4

What is the difference between total utility and marginal utility?

Requirement and Clue: *Clearly, a relationship exists between total utility and marginal utility; but there is a significant difference. Your task is to point out that difference. Examples can be helpful.*

Solution:

The difference between total utility and marginal utility is important. Total utility is the total satisfaction derived from the consumption of a good or service. For example, if you are really fond of ice cream crackers, the more you consume per week, the greater will be your total utility. Marginal utility is the extra or additional satisfaction derived from the consumption of additional units of a good or service. The difference between total utility and marginal utility can be emphasized by looking at the formula for marginal utility,

$$MU = \frac{\Delta TU}{\Delta Q}$$

where MU is marginal utility, TU is total utility, and Q is quantity.

Problem 7-5

Use hypothetical schedules of total and marginal utility to illustrate the relationship between the two concepts. What can you conclude about the sum of the marginal utility values?

Requirement and Clue: *This is a two-part problem. Answer each part in order. Construct a table with three columns: quantity, total utility, and marginal utility. Fill in the quantity and total utility columns. From the total utility numbers, calculate the marginal utility and complete the third column. Don't forget the second part of the problem.*

Solution:

In the following table, Column 1 contains quantity of milk shakes per week, Column 2 contains total utility, and Column 3 contains marginal utility.

Quantity of milk shakes	Total utility	Marginal utility
0	0	40
1	40	30
2	70	25
3	95	20
4	115	10
5	125	5
6	130	3
7	133	1
8	134	0
9	134	-2
10	132	-4
11	128	-7
12	121	

The sum of the marginal utility values is equal to the total utility.

Problem 7-6

State the law of diminishing marginal utility and illustrate with an example.

Requirement and Clue: *Much can be said about diminishing marginal utility, but here, your task is to state the law of diminishing marginal utility. Although it may be tempting to comment, it is not required. An illustrative example is obligatory.*

Solution:

The law of diminishing marginal utility can be stated as follows:

As a consumer consumes more of a commodity, the utility or satisfaction derived from each additional unit diminishes.

For example, on a hot summer afternoon, you would probably really appreciate a cold can of ice tea. You might appreciate a second can, though perhaps to a lesser extent than the first. You would likely enjoy a third can even less than you enjoyed the second, and a fourth less than you enjoyed the third, and so on. Even though your total enjoyment increased, each can of ice tea would give you less and less satisfaction. In other words, the marginal utility would diminish.

Problem 7-7

Assume that you have been given a case of orange juice, and you must decide how much of it to consume within a given period of time. If, according to your subjective evaluation, the total utility derived after you have consumed the third bottle of orange juice is 16 utils, and the marginal utility is positive but decreasing, should you consume more orange juice?

Requirement and Clue: *This problem is an application of the utility concept and a test of your understand of the relationship between total utility and marginal utility.*

Solution:

Provided that the marginal utility is positive, additional orange juice consumption will increase your total satisfaction. This is so whether the marginal utility is increasing or decreasing. Since the marginal utility is positive after the third bottle or orange juice is consumed, you should continue to drink orange juice.

Problem 7-8

Under what condition can consumers be said to be in equilibrium?

Requirement and Clue: *Consider the objective of consumers and focus on the meaning and implication of the concept of equilibrium.*

Solution:

We assume that the objective of consumers is to maximize their total satisfaction. Consumers act in such a way as to ensure that they obtain maximum satisfaction from their purchases of goods and services. When this happens, consumers have achieved their objectives, and can be said to be in equilibrium. Consumers in equilibrium have no desire to re-arrange their purchases of goods and services, since any rearrangement will only result in a lower level of satisfaction.

Problem 7-9

Explain, using the concept of marginal utility, how Ethlyn, a consumer, can decide on how to allocate a given budget between apples and beans in order to maximize her satisfaction.

Requirement and Clue: *The solution requires demonstration of an understanding of the utility maximization rule. A careful explanation of the process is required.*

Solution:

Suppose Ethlyn has spent her budget in such a way that the Last dollar spent on apples gives more satisfaction than the last dollar spent on beans. For simplicity, let us assume that the utility derived from the last dollar spent on apples is 15, while the utility derived from the last dollar spent on beans is 10. Obviously, since an extra dollar spent on apples gives greater satisfaction than an extra dollar spent on beans, Ethlyn can increase her total satisfaction by buying more apples and fewer beans. If the utility of the last dollar spent on beans were greater than the utility of the last dollar spent on apples, then Ethlyn could increase her satisfaction by buying more beans and fewer apples. As long as the utility of the last dollar spent on apples is different from the utility of the last dollar spent on beans, Ethlyn can increase her satisfaction by rearranging her purchases. It is only when the utility of the last dollar spent on each commodity is equal that the consumer will be maximizing her satisfaction.

When the utility derived from the last dollar spent on apples is 15 and that derived from the last dollar spent on beans is 10, Ethlyn will buy more apples and fewer beans. As she does so, the marginal utility of apples will fall, while the marginal utility of beans will increase. If the utility of the last dollar spent on apples falls to 12 while the utility of the last dollar spent on beans increases to 12, Ethlyn will maximize her satisfaction and will therefore have no desire to rearrange her purchases.

Ethlyn's equilibrium position can be restated in terms of marginal utility and price. The marginal utility per dollar of apples is the marginal utility of apples divided by the price of apples. Similarly, the marginal utility per dollar of beans is the marginal utility of beans divided by the price of beans. Thus, the condition to be met for Ethlyn to be in equilibrium can be formulated as follows:

> For a consumer purchasing two goods, A and B, to maximize satisfaction, the marginal utility of A divided by the price of A must equal the marginal utility of B divided by the price of B.

This utility maximization rule can be expressed as:

$$\frac{MU_A}{P_A} = \frac{MU_B}{P_B}$$

where MU_A is the marginal utility of A, MU_B is the marginal utility of B, P_A is the price of A, and P_B is the price of B.

Problem 7-10

The following table represents the utility schedules for Constance for two commodities A and B. If Constance has a budget of $11 to spend on A and B, how should she allocate her budget between A and B in order to maximize her satisfaction?

$ worth of A	MU_A	$ worth of B	MU_B
1	80	1	58
2	70	2	56
3	60	3	52
4	50	4	48
5	40	5	44
6	30	6	40
7	20	7	35
8	10	8	30
9	5	9	25
10	1	10	20

Requirement and Clue: *The solution requires that the marginal utility per dollar of A must be equal to the marginal utility per dollar of B. Be careful to ensure that the total amount spent is $11.*

Solution:

At $5 worth of A and $6 worth of B, the marginal utility per dollar of A equals the marginal utility per dollar of B. Each is 40, and the budget is $11, which is the solution to the problem.

(Note that at $7 worth of A and $10 worth of B, the marginal utility per dollar of A equals the marginal utility per dollar of B. Each is 20, but that combination costs $17, not $11. Also at $6 of A and $8 of B, the marginal utility per dollar of A equals the marginal utility per dollar of B. Each is 30, but that combination costs $14, not $11.)

Problem 7-11

Given the data shown in the following table on the utilities of A and B, and given that the price of A is $2 and the price of B is $3:

Quantity of A	MU_A	MU_A/P_A	Quantity of B	MU_B	MU_B/P_B
1	16	1	21		
2	18	2	24		
3	16	3	18		
4	14	4	15		
5	10	5	12		
6	6	6	6		
7	2	7	3		

(a) *Fill in the MU_A/P_A and the MU_B/P_B columns.*

(b) *How should a consumer allocate a budget of $12 between A and B?*

(c) *What change should be made in the consumer's purchases if his or her budget increases to $22?*

Requirement and Clue: The required columns can be filled in easily, knowing that P_A = $2 and P_B = 3. Remember that the utility maximizing condition is $MU_A/P_A = MU_B/P_B$ and that the cost of the combination of A and B purchased should be equal to the budget.

Solution: (a)

Quantity of A	MU_A	Quantity MU_A/P_A	of B	MU_B	MU_B/P_B
1	16	16/2 = 8	1	21	21/3 = 7
2	18	18/2 = 9	2	24	24/3 = 8
3	16	16/2 = 8	3	18	18/3 = 6
4	14	14/2 = 7	4	15	15/3 = 5
5	10	10/2 = 5	5	12	12/3 = 4
6	6	6/2 = 3	6	6	6/3 = 2
7	2	2/2 = 1	7	3	3/3 = 1

(b) With $12, the consumer should buy 3 units of A for $6, and 2 units of B for $6. ($MU_A/P_A = MU_B/P_B = 8$)

(c) What a budget of $22, the consumer should buy 5 units of A for $10 and 4 units of B for $12. ($MU_A/P_A = MU_B/P_B = 5$)

Problem 7-12

State the water-diamond paradox. How can the paradox be explained?

Requirement and Clue: *This is a two-part problem. Address each part in order. Recall that the water-diamond paradox is the paradox of value. Relate your explanation to marginal utility.*

Solution:

The water-diamond paradox is this: "Why is water so much cheaper than diamonds when water is so much more useful than diamonds?" One solution to the paradox is that diamonds are relatively scarce while water is relatively abundant. In price determination, marginal utility—not total utility—is the relevant concept. Water is useful but its marginal utility is low, while the marginal utility of diamonds is high. Since price is proportional to marginal utility, the price of diamonds is higher than the price of water.

Problem 7-13

Is there any relationship between marginal utility and the consumer's demand curve? Explain.

Requirement and Clue: *The request for an explanation suggests that a yes or no answer will not suffice. Focus on the fact that consumer demand reflects marginal utility.*

Solution:

There is a close relationship between marginal utility and the consumer's demand curve. Consider the demand curve shown in the following diagram for Denise for oranges for a certain period of time.

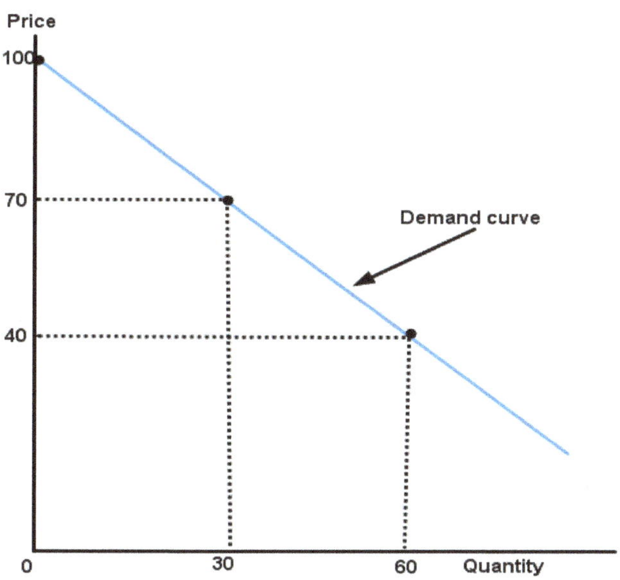

Figure 7.1

We can interpret demand curve (see figure 7.1 above) as follows: For a quantity of 30 bags of oranges, the maximum price that Denise is willing to pay is $2,100. If the price were higher than $70 per bag, she would not purchase the 30th bag of oranges. This is so because according to her evaluation of the extra satisfaction derived from the 30th bag (that is, its marginal utility), it is worth just $70 and no more. Likewise, she will not buy the 60th bag for more than $40 because that is her evaluation of the marginal utility derived from the 60th bag. The more oranges Denise consumes, less satisfaction she derives from each additional orange, and hence, the less she is willing to pay for extra bags of oranges. This analysis clearly brings out the relation between marginal utility and demand.

Problem 7-14

What is the relationship between individual demand and market demand for a product? Use the demand schedules for Marcia, Eddy and Josie given below to derive the market demand for the product. The time period is one week.

Marcia's demand		Eddy's demand		Josie's demand		Market demand	
P	Q	P	Q	P	Q	P	Q
8	2	8	0	8	3		
6	3	6	2	6	5		
4	4	4	4	4	7		

Requirement and Clue: *This is a two-part problem. Solve each part in order. Once you know the demand curves for the individual buyers, it should be easy to derive the market demand. Focus on what constitutes the total number of buyers in the market.*

Solution:

Market demand is obtained by adding the demand for each buyer of the product.

At a price of $8, Marcia will buy 2 units a week, Eddy will buy none, and Josie will buy 3 units a week. The total quantity demanded at $8 is therefore (2 + 3) = 5 units. This is shown on the market demand schedule shown below.

Marcia's demand		Eddy's demand		Josie's demand		Market demand	
P	Q	P	Q	P	Q	P	Q
8	2	8	0	8	3	8	5
6	3	6	2	6	5	6	10
4	4	4	4	4	7	4	15

At a price of $6, Marcia will buy 3 units a week; Eddy will now enter the market and buy 2 units, while Josie will buy 5 units. The total quantity demanded at a price of $6 is thus (3 + 2 + 5) = 10 units, as shown in the market demand schedule. At a price of $4, Marcia will buy 4 units, Eddy will buy 4, and Josie will buy 7; so together they will buy a total of (4 + 4 + 7) = 15 units at a price of $4. The market demand is the sum of the demands of the individual consumers in the market.

Problem 7-15

What is consumer surplus? Use a demand/supply graph to show consumer surplus.

Requirement and Clue: *Note that this is a two-part problem. Make sure you answer each part in order. Your solution requires a clear definition of the concept of consumer surplus. An example will be helpful. Think of consumer surplus as some sort of benefit that accrues to the consumer.*

Solution:

Consumer surplus is the difference between what consumers are willing to pay for a product and what they actually pay. Suppose apples are sold at $0.50 per kilogram. Consumers might be willing to pay $3 for the first kilogram, but they pay only 50 cents because this is the market price. They get a consumer surplus of $2.50. They might be willing to pay $2 for the second kilogram, but they still pay only 50 cents. That means that they would be willing to pay $5 for 2 kilograms, but they only pay $1.00, getting a consumer surplus of $4.00. See the table below.

Apples (kg)	Total amount the consumer would have paid	Total amount actually paid	Consumer surplus
1	$3.00	$0.50	$2.50
2	$5.00	$1.00	$4.00

The diagram below illustrates consumer surplus.

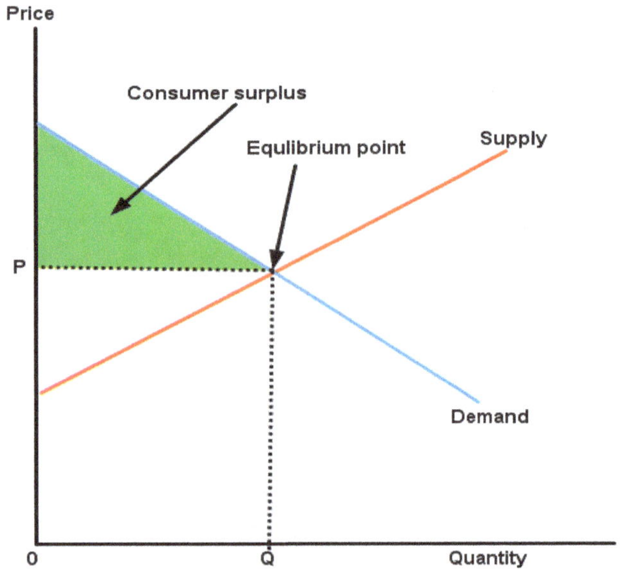

The equilibrium price and the equilibrium quantity established by the market for this good or service are P which we assume to be $0.50 and Q which we assume to be 5 kg respectively. Many buyers would have been willing to pay a higher price than $0.50 to obtain this product. But because they are required to pay only $0.50, they actually receive a surplus or gain, which is the consumer surplus.

Problem 7-16

The following table shows the demand schedule for beef for Sabrina. Plot Sabrina's demand curve. If the market price of beef is $4 per kilogram, show Sabrina's total consumer surplus on your graph and calculate its value.

Price ($)	Quantity demanded per week (kg)
8	0
7	1
6	2
5	3
4	4
3	5
2	6
1	7
0	8

Requirement and Clue: You are required to do three things: (1) Plot Sabrina's demand curve, (2) show her consumer's surplus on a graph, and (3) calculate the value of the consumer's surplus.

Solution:

The diagram below indicates Sabrina's demand curve.

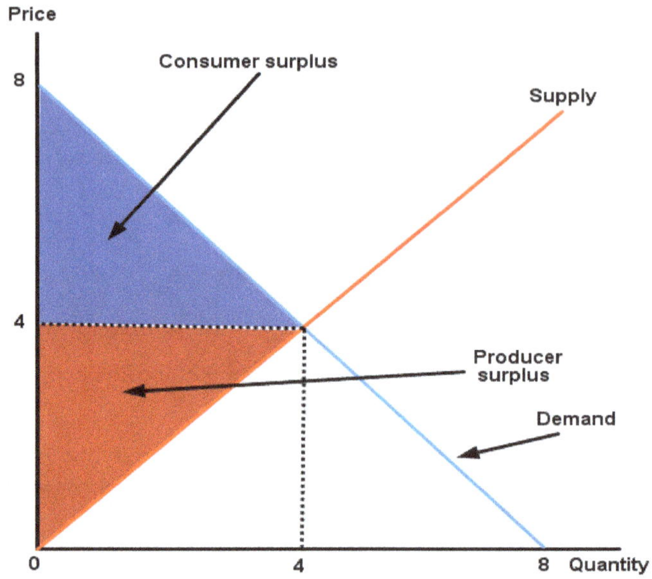

Sabrina's total consumer's surplus is shown by the shaded blue triangle.

The value of the consumer's surplus is (4 × 4 ÷ 2) = 8.

B. Indifference Curve Analysis

Problem 7-17

Define indifference schedule and construct a hypothetical indifference schedule between apples and pears.

Requirement and Clue: *This problem has two parts. Answer each part in turn. Be careful not to confuse an indifference schedule with an indifference curve. Your definition should state exactly what the concept is. In your solution to the second part of the problem, consider the combinations in your indifference schedule.*

Solution:

An indifference schedule is a table that shows various combinations of commodities that give a consumer the same level of satisfaction. The consumer is indifferent between one combination and another, hence the term "indifference" schedule.

The following table shows a hypothetical indifference schedule for apples and pears. The total satisfaction derived from each combination is S.

Combination	Apples	Pears	Total utility
A	40	29	S
B	32	30	S
C	26	31	S
D	23	34	S
E	21	39	S
F	20	46	S

Combination A, consisting of 40 apples and 29 pears, gives the same level of satisfaction as combination F that contains 20 apples and 46 pears.

Problem 7-18

What does it mean to say that the consumer's preferences are transitive?

Requirement and Clue: *The solution requires an explanation of the axiom of transitivity.*

Solution:

In economics, we assume that consumers order or rank their preferences in a consistent manner. The axiom of transitivity states that if choice *A* is preferred to choice *B*, and choice *B* is preferred to choice *C*, then it must be that choice *A* is preferred to choice *C*. To say that the consumer's preferences are transitive means that the consumer does not violate the axiom of transitivity. There is logical consistency in the consumer's choices.

Problem 7-19

Point out the difference between an indifference schedule and an indifference curve.

Requirement and Clue: *You must be able to demonstrate that you know the difference between the two concepts. Focus on what is different about them.*

Solution:

An indifference schedule is a table that shows various combinations of goods and services that give the consumer the same level of satisfaction. An indifference curve, on the other hand, is a graph that shows all combinations of goods and services that give the consumer the same level of satisfaction. Two points of difference need to be emphasized. One is that an indifference schedule is a ***table*** whereas an indifference curve is a ***graph***. The other point is that an indifference schedule shows ***various*** combinations of goods and services whereas an indifference curve shows all combinations of goods and services from which the consumer derives equal satisfaction.

Problem 7-20

Discuss the properties of indifference curves.

Requirement and Clue: "Discuss" suggests that simply listing or mentioning the properties will not suffice.

Solution:

Indifference curves have three properties: (1) they are downward sloping; (2) they are convex, and (3) they are non-intersecting.

Downward sloping: Each point on an indifference curve gives the consumer the same level of satisfaction as any other point on the curve. If the consumer loses some quantity of one commodity, he or she would require additional quantities of some other commodity in order to maintain the same level of satisfaction. This implies a trade-off which suggests a downward sloping indifference curve.

Convexity: The convexity of indifference curves arises from an assumption that consumers prefer middling combinations of goods and services as opposed to extreme combinations. Consider a consumer with a large quantity of bananas, but only a small quantity of pineapples. Such a consumer is likely to be willing to give up (trade-off) some bananas for a given quantity of pineapples. As the quantity of bananas diminishes, however, the consumer is likely to give up a smaller and smaller quantity of bananas for the same quantity of pineapples. Similarly, starting with any quantity of pineapples, a consumer is likely to give up an increasingly smaller quantity of pineapples for bananas as the quantity of pineapples decreases. The point being made is this: The more you have of something, the more willing you will be to trade for something of which you have only a small amount. This implies that indifference curves are convex to the origin as shown in the following diagram.

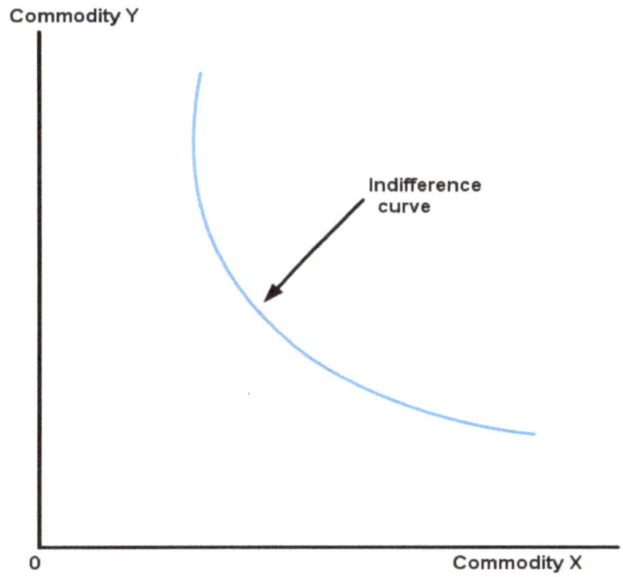

Non-intersecting: Indifference curves for the same individual do not intersect. Let us assume that indifference curves do interest as shown in the following diagram.

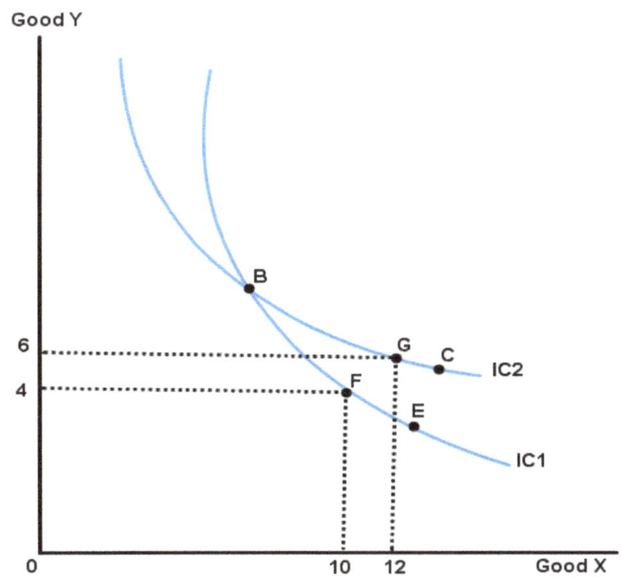

Combinations B and F are on the same indifference curve, i.e., indifference curve 1 (IC1), and therefore give the same level of satisfaction. Combinations B and G lie on the same indifference curve, i.e., indifference curve 2 (IC2), and therefore give the same level of satisfaction. It follows then that combinations F and G yield the same level of satisfaction, and must therefore lie on the same indifference curve. But it can be clearly seen that F and G are on different indifference curves. In fact, G contains more of both X and Y than does F. This leads us to conclude that indifference curves do not intersect.

Problem 7-21

State the law of diminishing marginal rate of substitution.

Requirement and Clue: *All that is required here is a clear statement of the law.*

Solution:

The marginal rate of substitution is the rate at which a consumer is willing to trade off units of one commodity for units of another commodity so as to keep his or her level of satisfaction unchanged. The law of diminishing marginal rate of substitution states that the rate at which the consumer is willing to trade off one commodity for another diminishes. In graphical terms, as the consumer moves down an indifference curve, the rate of trade off diminishes.

Problem 7-22

What is an indifference map? What is it used for?

Requirement and Clue: *This is a two-part problem. Address each part in order. Say what an indifference map is and explain what it is used for.*

Solution:

An indifference map is a collection of indifference curves.

An indifference map is used to describe a consumer's tastes and preferences. For example, an indifference curve that is higher on an indifference map represents a higher level of satisfaction. Any point on a higher indifference curve is preferred to any point on a lower indifference curve.

Problem 7-23

Carefully define a budget line.

Requirement and Clue: *All is required is a clear statement of what a budget line is. Remember that examples are always helpful.*

Solution:

A budget line is a graphical representation of all possible combinations of two commodities that a consumer can purchase for the same amount of money. For example, suppose Michael has $20 to be used to purchase pens and pencils. The price of pens is $2.00 each and the price of pencils is $1.00 each. If Michael buys only pens, he can buy 10 of them. If he buys only pencils, he can buy 20. The following table shows combinations of pens and pencils that Michael can afford, given his budget of $20.

Quantity of Pens	Quantity of Rice	Amount ($)
10	0	20.00
8	4	20.00
6	8	20.00
4	12	20.00
2	16	20.00
0	20	20.00

If the data contained in the above table were plotted on a graph, the result would be a budget line shown in the following diagram.

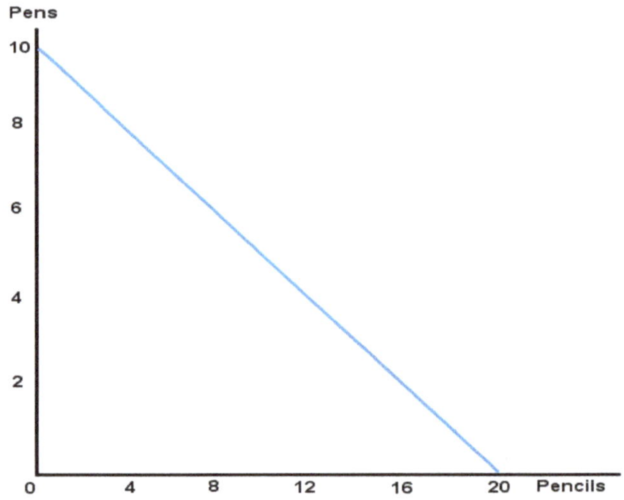

Problem 7-24

Show the effect of an increase in the consumer's income, other things being equal, on the budget line.

Requirement and Clue: *"Show" suggests the use of graphs. To show the effect of an increase in income, you need to show the budget line <u>before</u> the income change and the budget <u>after</u> the income change.*

Solution:

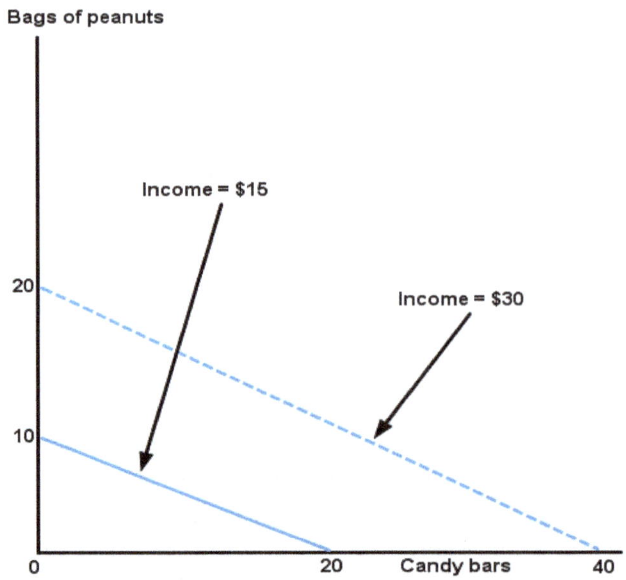

Suppose the prices of peanuts and candy bars are $1.50 per bag and $0.75 each respectively and that the consumer has a budget of $15.00. If the consumer spends all her income on peanuts, she will be able to buy 10 bags. If she spends all her budget on candy bars, she will be able to buy 20. Under these conditions, the initial budget line is as shown in the figure above for an income of $15.

If the consumer's budget increases from $15 to $30, other things being equal, she will now be able to purchase 20 bags of peanuts or 40 candy bars. The new budget line will be as shown in the above figure for an income of $30. We can conclude that other things being equal, an increase in the consumer's income will shift the budget line outward as shown in the figure. The new budget line will be parallel to the initial one.

Problem 7-25

Show and explain the effect of a change in price on the budget line.

Requirement and Clue: *You are required to draw a budget line and then explain how a chance in price will affect the budget line. Comparing the initial budget line with the budget line after the price change will show the effect of the price change.*

Solution:

Suppose the consumer has a budget of $24 to spend on A and B, and suppose the price of A is $3, and the price of B is also $3. The consumer will be able to buy 8 units of A if he or she buys none of B. If the entire budget is spent only on B, he or she will be able to buy 8 of B. The initial budget line will be as shown in the inner line on the diagram below.

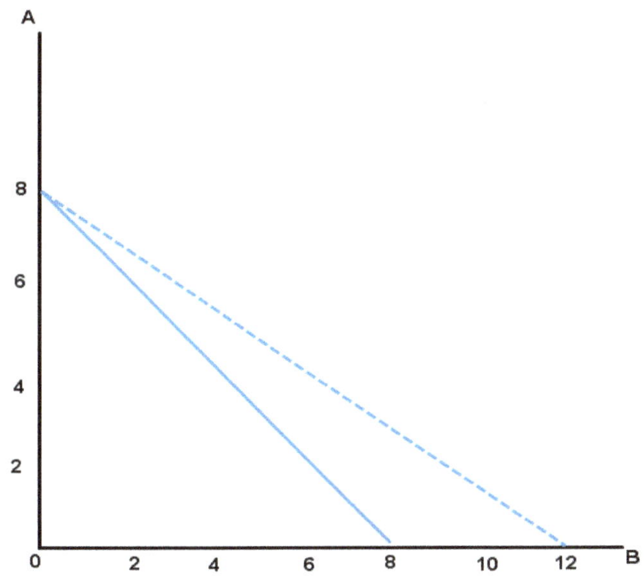

Suppose the price of B now falls from $3 to $2, the consumer will now be able to purchase 12 of B if he or she buys none of A. This new budget line is shown in the diagram above to the right of the initial budget line. The fall in price causes the budget line to rotate, thus changing its slope as shown in the diagram. We can conclude that other things being equal, a change in the price of one of the commodities that the consumer buys causes the slope of the budget line to change.

Problem 7-26

Use an appropriate diagram to illustrate how a consumer would allocate a budget between two goods in order to maximize his or her satisfaction.

Requirement and Clue: *The "appropriate" diagram expected here is an indifference curve graph showing the equilibrium of the consumer. A careful explanation is required.*

Solution:

Let us refer to the consumer as Susan Meade. In the diagram below, we show her indifference curves and budget line. She uses her budget to purchase olives (B) and figs (A).

Susan can choose any combination of olives and figs that lies on or below the budget line, and she wants to be on the highest attainable indifference curve. Susan is going to spend her entire budget, so she can choose between any combination such as X, E, or Z that lies on the budget line. Points X, Y, and Z are on a lower indifference curve than point E; hence each yields a lower level of satisfaction than point E does. Susan achieves maximum satisfaction at point E where the budget line is just tangent to an indifference curve. Any move from this position will diminish Susan's satisfaction. Susan is in equilibrium at point E, purchasing 6 units of figs and 4 units of olives. To summarize, a consumer maximizes his or her satisfaction by moving along the budget line to the highest indifference curve attainable. This occurs when the budget line is tangent to the indifference curve.

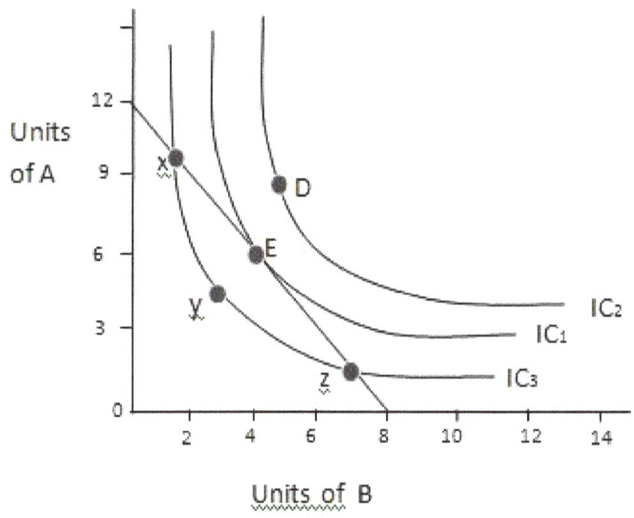

Problem 7-27

Use indifference curve analysis to show that consumer Cora Greene can be made better off by increasing her income.

Requirement and Clue: *In terms of indifference curve analysis, being better off means being on a higher indifference curve. You are expected to show that an increase in the consumer's income, other things being equal, places him or her on a higher indifference curve.*

Solution:

The following diagram shows that Cora Greene is in equilibrium on indifference curve 11, consuming X1 of Good X and Y1 of Good Y. An increase in Cora's income will cause the budget constraint to shift out in a parallel manner from BC1 to BC2 as shown in the diagram. The new budget line will be tangent to a higher indifference curve such as indifference curve 12. Cora is now in equilibrium on indifference curve 12, consuming X2 of Good X and Y2 of Good Y. A further increase in income shifts to budget constraint from BC2 to BC3. Budget constraint, BC3, is now tangent to indifference curve 13, and Cora is in equilibrium consuming X3 of Good X and Y3 of Good Y.

As Cora's income increases, she attains a higher level of satisfaction. Another way of saying it is that she is better off with more income.

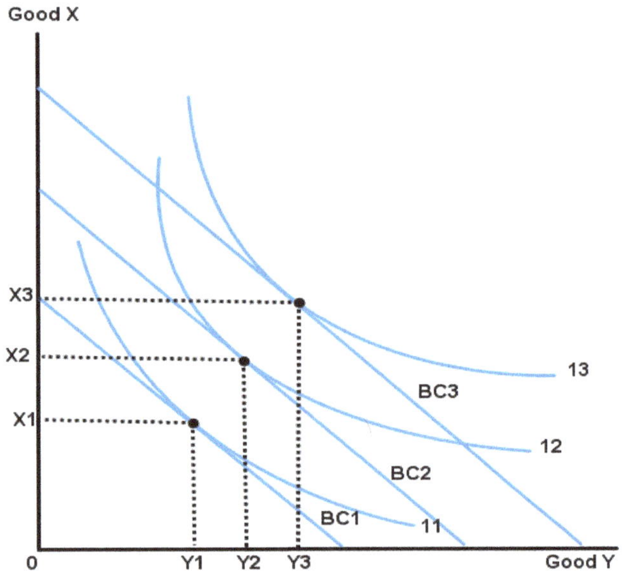

Problem 7-28

What is an income consumption curve?

Requirement and Clue: *Here you are expected to describe an income consumption curve. A diagram of an income consumption curve will be helpful.*

Solution:

An income consumption curve is a line joining the points of tangency between budget lines and indifference curves as the consumer's income changes. It shows how the consumer responds to changes in income in terms of buying goods and services.

The following diagram shows an income consumption curve.

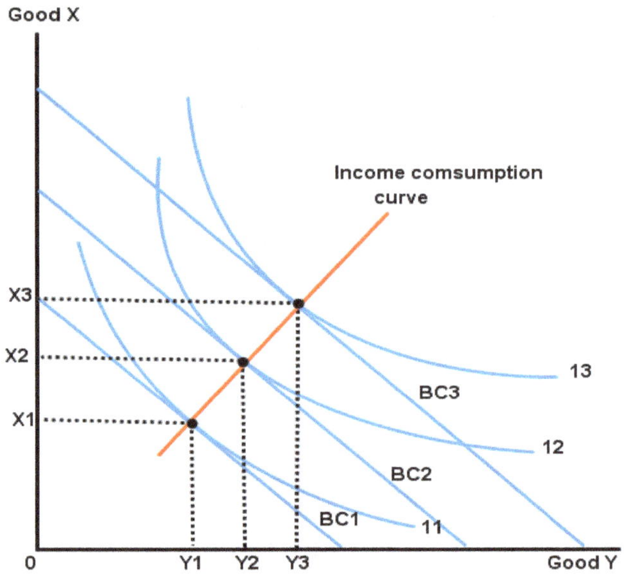

Problem 7-29

What are Engel curves? For what can they be used? Draw an Engel curve for a normal good and one for an inferior good.

Requirement and Clue: *This is a three-part problem. Address each part in order. You are expected to give a clear definition of Engel curves. You are also expected to demonstrate your knowledge of normal and inferior goods and you ability to use Engel curves to show normal and inferior goods.*

Solution:

Engel curves show graphically the relationship between income and quantity demanded.

Engel curves can be used to illustrate how a consumer responds to changes in income. Also from the shape of an Engel curve, one can determine whether the good or service in question is a normal good or an inferior good.

Diagram A

A normal good is a good of which more is bought as income rises. An inferior good in one of which less is bought as income rises. Diagram A below shows an Engel curve for a normal good, while Diagram B shows the Engel curve in which a section is for a normal good and a section for an inferior good.

Diagram A shows that as income rises from $10 to $30, the quantity of food demanded increases from 4 units to 16 units. Diagram B shows that as income rises from $20 to $30, the quantity of food demanded falls from 15 units to 10 units.

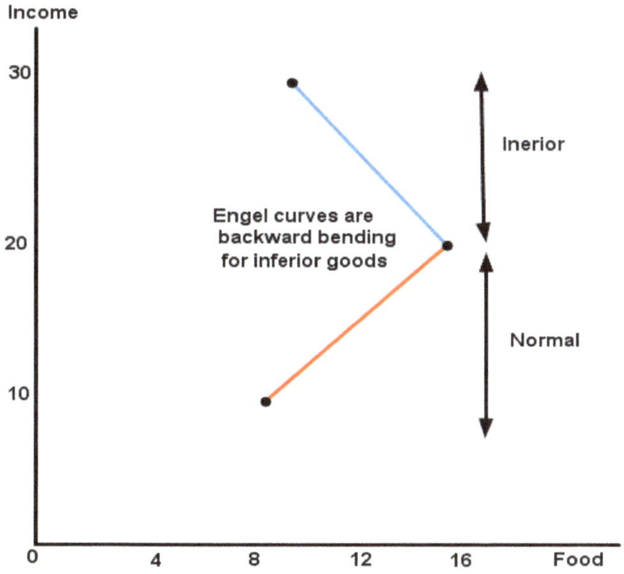

Diagram B

Problem 7-30

What is the difference between an inferior good and a Giffen good?

Requirement and Clue: *This problem is straightforward. You should state what an inferior good is and what a Giffen good is, and point out the difference.*

Solution:

An inferior good is a good such that as income increases, a greater quantity of the good is demanded. A Giffen good is a good such that as price increases, a greater quantity is demanded. The difference can be seen from these definitions. In the case of an inferior good, it is income that I causing the change in quantity demanded. In the case of a Giffen good, it is price that is causing the change in quantity demanded. Both concepts seem to contradict the ordinary. An inferior good gives rise to a downward sloping Engel curve. A Giffen good gives rise to an upward sloping demand curve.

Problem 7-31

Briefly explain the case of a Giffen Good.

Requirement and Clue: *Don't be one of the people who confuse a Giffen good with an inferior good. Focus on this: Why might a consumer buy less of an item as the price of the item falls?*

Solution:

Ordinarily, a demand curve is downward sloping, depicting an inverse relationship between price and quantity demanded. But a Victorian economist by the name of Robert Giffen explored the possibility of an upward sloping demand curve. Consider a relatively inexpensive product such as potatoes. If the price of potatoes falls, other things being equal, the law of demand states that the quantity of potatoes demanded will rise. But when the price of potatoes falls, consumers' real income rises, so instead of buying more potatoes, consumers may substitute another product such as steak for potatoes. In this case, the quantity of potatoes demanded falls as the price of potatoes falls. This is the case of a Giffen good.

Problem 7-32

The prices of clothing and food are $6 and $15 respectively. Dawn has a budget of $240. The following diagram shows that Dawn will be in equilibrium when she buys 20 units of clothing and 8 units of food. If Dawn's budget and the prices of clothing and food all double, how many of each item will Dawn now buy in order to maximize her satisfaction?

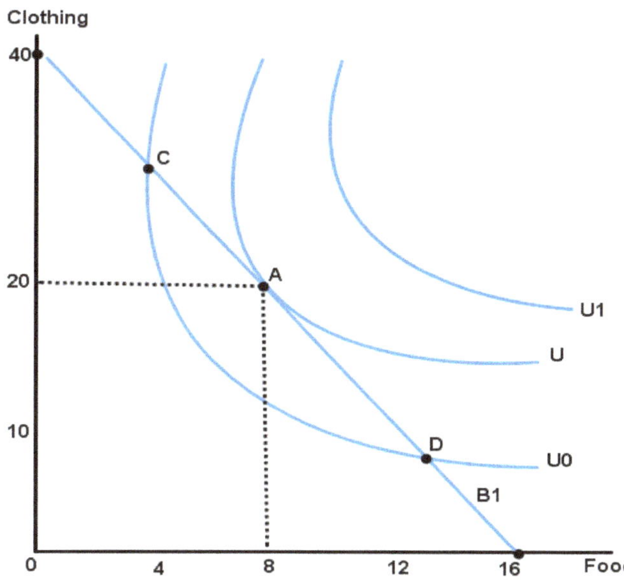

Requirement and Clue: *Focus on the combined effect of a doubling of prices and income on Dawn's budget line.*

Solution:

A doubling of the prices of clothing and food reduces Dawn's real income. Now she can only afford 20 units of clothing or 8 units of food, instead of the previous 40 units of clothing or the 16 units of food. Consequently, her budget line shifts to the left. But the doubling of Dawn's income forces the budget line back into its original position, leaving her equilibrium position unchanged. Dawn will still buy 20 units of clothing and 8 units of food.

Multiple-Choice

In each case, circle the letter that corresponds with the correct answer.

I. Utility Theory

1. In economics, the term utility refers to:

a. satisfaction derived from consumption
b. services provided by utility companies such as electricity and telephone
c. the usefulness of an item
d. a penknife

Answer: a

Reason: Utility refers to the amount of satisfaction that a consumer derives from consuming goods and services.

2. Economists refer to a unit of satisfaction as:

a. a satisfice
b. a unisat
c. a util
d. none of the above

Answer: c

Reason: In the same way that distance can be measured in miles and weight can be measured in kilograms, satisfaction is measured in units called utils.

3. In consumer theory, utility refers to:

a. the usefulness of a good
b. the satisfaction derived from a good or service
c. large business enterprises producing public services
d. all of the above

Answer: b

Reason: Utility is the satisfaction that a consumer derives from consuming goods and services.

4. A formula for marginal utility (MU) where TU is total utility and Q is quantity is:

a. $MU = TU/Q$
b. $MU = \Delta Q/Q$
c. $MU = \Delta TU/Q$
d. $MU = \Delta TU/\Delta Q$

Answer: d

Reason: Marginal utility is the extra satisfaction derived from consuming an additional unit of a good or service. That is stated in choice d.

5. Marginal utility is:

a. the minimum use obtained from a good or service
b. the minimum satisfaction derived from consuming a good or a service
c. the additional satisfaction derived from consuming one more unit of a good or service
d. always zero

Answer: c

Reason: Choice c precisely defines the concept.

6. Marginal utility:

a. is always positive
b. can be positive or negative
c. can assume any value except zero
d. must always be negative because goods and services are being used up

Answer: b

Reason: Marginal utility is the extra satisfaction derived from consuming additional units of goods and services. This value can be positive, zero, or negative.

7. If marginal utility is positive, then total utility is:

a. negative
b. increasing
c. zero
d. decreasing

Answer: b

Reason: A positive marginal utility means that a positive value is added to total utility. This will increase total utility.

8. When total utility is at its maximum, we know that marginal utility is:

a. zero
b. positive
c. negative
d. equal to total utility

Answer: a

Reason: Total utility is at its maximum if it is neither rising nor falling. This means the marginal utility is zero.

9. If total utility is rising, we know that marginal utility is:

a. falling
b. negative
c. rising
d. positive

Answer: d

Reason: A rising total utility means that some positive value is being added to it. This positive value is marginal utility.

10. The idea that after a point, a consumer gets less satisfaction from additional units of a good or service consumed is called:

a. the minimax principle
b. the minimizing postulate of consumer behavior
c. the law of diminishing total utility
d. the law of diminishing marginal utility

Answer: d

Reason: The law of diminishing marginal utility states that as a consumer consumes more of a commodity, the satisfaction derived from each additional unit diminishes.

11. In economics, it is assumed that:

a. consumers try to buy as much of a good as they can afford
b. consumers spend an equal amount of money on all goods and services
c. consumers try to buy the largest quantities of the most expensive items to satisfy the equimarginal principle
d. consumers try to maximize their satisfaction

Answer: d

Reason: Consumers spend their income in such a way as to get the highest level of satisfaction from the goods and services that they purchase.

12. To say that a consumer is in equilibrium means that:
   a. the value of the consumer's purchases equals the consumer's income
   b. the consumer has succeeded in getting the maximum amount of goods and services for as little money as possible
   c. the consume buys just as much goods and services as sellers want to sell
   d. the consumer is maximizing his or her satisfaction

Answer: d

Reason: The objective of the consumer is to maximize his or her satisfaction. In that utility maximizing position, the consumer would not want to rearrange his or her purchases of goods and services. Because no change is desired from that position, the consumer can be said to be in equilibrium.

13. The law of diminishing marginal utility states that:
   a. as additional units of a good or service are consumed, eventually, the marginal utility will diminish
   b. total utility will always increase, while marginal utility will always diminish
   c. as more and more of a good or service is consumed, the total utility will diminish
   d. as additional units of a good or service are consumed, after a while, people will spend more for less.

Answer: a

Reason: Choice "a" echoes the law of diminishing marginal utility.

14. The equimarginal principle states that:
   a. marginal utility must always be equal to total utility for the consumer to be in equilibrium
   b. an equal amount of money spent on two goods yields equal utility
   c. if you spend the same amount of money on two goods, then it can be concluded that they are equally useful
   d. satisfaction is maximized when the last dollar spent on any good yields the same satisfaction as the last dollar spent on any other good.

Answer: d

Reason: Choice d is the correct statement of the equimarginal principle.

15. If the utility derived from the last dollar spent on A is greater than that derived from the last dollar spent on B, the consumer can increase total utility by:
   a. buying more of A and less of B
   b. buying more of B and less of A
   c. making sure that the same amount of money is spent on A and B
   d. none of the above

Answer: a

Reason: If a dollar spent on A gives more satisfaction that a dollar spent on B, then a rational consumer would spend the dollar on A.

16. If MU_A is the marginal utility of A, MU_B is the marginal utility of B, P_A is the price of A and P_B is the price of B, Which of the following expresses the utility maximization rule?
   a. $MU_A/P_A = MU_B/P_B$
   b. $MU_A = MU_B$
   c. $MU_A - MU_B = P_A - P_B$
   d. $P_A \times P_B = MU_A \times MU_B$

Answer: a

Reason: For utility maximization, the marginal utility of A per dollar of A must equal the marginal utility of B per dollar of B. This is expressed by choice a.

17. Which of the following statements about utility is <u>incorrect</u>?
   a. If a good is wanted, it yields utility
   b. Total utility is the relevant concept in price determination
   c. Utility is subjective
   d. Utility is a measure of satisfaction

Answer: b

Reason: In price determination, marginal utility, not total utility is the relevant concept.

18. If $MU_A/P_A > MU_B/P_B$
   a. the consumer is maximizing his or her satisfaction
   b. the consumer would purchase more of good A
   c. the consumer would purchase more of good B
   d. we cannot predict what the consumer would do

Answer: b

Reason: The consumer would spend the dollar where it gives more satisfaction.

19. The consumption of a free god will continue until:
   a. the marginal utility becomes positive
   b. the total utility is rising
   c. the total utility is falling
   d. the marginal utility is zero

Answer: d

Reason: It is at that point that total satisfaction would be maximized.

20. Which of the following is **<u>least</u>** important in deciding whether or not to buy an additional unit of good X?
   a. The price of X
   b. The marginal utility of X
   c. The consumer's income
   d. The total utility of X

Answer: d

Reason: The additional unit of X will affect the total utility of X, but total utility is not very important in determining whether or not to buy one more unit.

21. The paradox of value is also called:
   a. the money paradox
   b. the value optimization paradox
   c. the water-diamond paradox
   d. the paradigm of non-existent value

Answer: c

Reason: The paradox of value is related to a comparison of the value of water with the value of diamonds.

22. The paradox of value:
   a. deals with the importance of paradoxes
   b. relates to the apparent contradiction in the fact that

some useful items such as water have relatively low prices, while some less useful items such as diamonds have relatively high prices

c. is unrelated to total and marginal utilities

d. is none of the above

Answer: b

Reason: Choice b accurately summarizes the paradox of value.

23. The market demand curve is:

a. identical to the consumer demand curve

b. unrelated to the individual consumers' demand curves

c. the sum of all the demand curves of all the consumers in the market

d. none of the above

Answer: c

Reason: The market demand curve is the horizontal summation of all the individual demand curves.

24. Which of the following is likely to yield the greatest consumer surplus?

a. a car c. ice cream

b. bread d. water

Answer: d

Reason: Water is critically important to life yet it is relatively inexpensive. Most people would be willing to pay a much higher price for water than they do now. Hence the consumer surplus is enormous.

II. Indifference Curve Analysis

25. If a consumer says that she prefers A to B and B to C, then we expect her to say that she prefers A to C because we assume that her preferences are:

a. linear c. contingent

b. transitive d. sequential

Answer: b

Reason: The consumer is expected to demonstrate logical consistency in his or her choices. That is the meaning of transitive preferences.

26. A table showing various combinations of goods and services that give the consumer the same level of satisfaction is called a(n):

a. indifference schedule c. marginal utility table

b. indifference map d. indifference curve

Answer: a

Reason: An indifference schedule is the term given to the table described in the question. If the presentation were graphical, it would be called an indifference curve.

27. An indifference curve is:

a. a table showing various combinations of goods that give the same level of satisfaction

b. an upward sloping graph showing preference and indifference

c. a graph showing various combinations of goods that give the same level of satisfaction

d. a total utility curve because each point on the curve represents total utility

Answer: c

Reason: Choice c defines an indifference curve.

28. Which of the following are properties of indifference curves?

a. They are downward sloping

b. They are convex to the origin

c. They do not intersect

d. All of the above

Answer: d

Reason: Choices a, b, and c are the properties of indifference curves.

29. The marginal rate of substitution is:

a. the rate at which a consumer buys substitute goods and services

b. the rate at which the consumer makes marginal purchases

c. the rate at which the consumer is willing to trade one good for another while maintaining the same level of satisfaction

d. the rate at which the consumer is willing to trade off one commodity for another while at the same time moving to a higher indifference curve

Answer: c

Reason: The marginal rate of substitution is the slope of the indifference curve which shows the rate of trading off one good for another along the same indifference curve. Choice c is consistent with this definition.

30. An indifference curve that is convex to the origin means that:

a. a consumer will not be able to maximize his or her satisfaction

b. the marginal rate of substitution increases as the consumer moves along the indifference curve

c. any point on the indifference curve represents utility maximization

d. the marginal rate of substitution diminishes as the consumer moves down the indifference curve

Answer: d

Reason: The marginal rate of substitution is the slope of the indifference curve. That slope diminishes as the consumer moves down the indifference curve.

31. Intersecting indifference curves means:

a. inconsistent preferences

b. utility maximization

c. consumer rationality

d. none of the above

Answer: a

Reason: Intersecting indifference curves violate the axiom of transitivity. This means that the consumer has inconsistent preferences.

32. An indifference map is:

a. a consumer shopping guide

b. a map that indicates where consumers can find items to which they are indifferent

c. a collection of indifference curves

d. none of the above

Answer: c

Reason: Choice c accurately defines an indifference map.

33. The following diagram shows a set of indifference curves. Which of the following is **incorrect**?

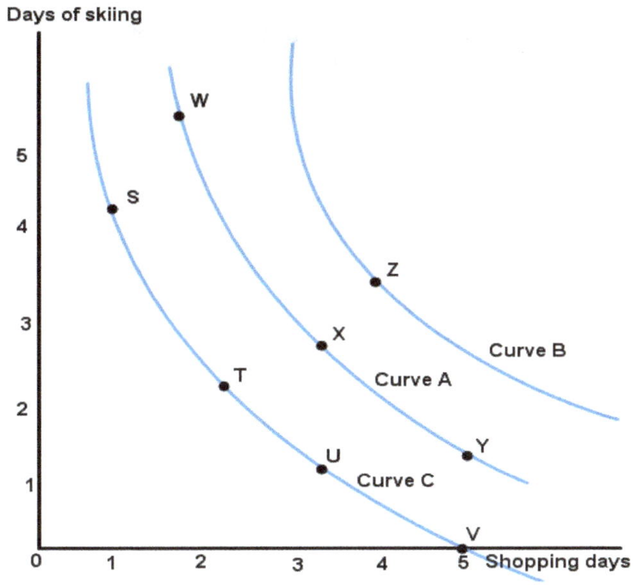

a. S and T give the same level of satisfaction

b. W gives a higher level of satisfaction than does Y because W is higher up the curve

c. Z is preferred to Y

d. X and Y give a higher level of satisfaction than does U

Answer: b

Reason: W and Y are on the same indifference curve and therefore give the same level of satisfaction.

34. A graphical representation of all possible combinations of two commodities that a consumer can purchase with a given amount of money is called a(n):

a. budget line

b. demand curve

c. indifference curve

d. none of the above

Answer: a

Reason: All points on a budget line represent combinations of two commodities that cost the same amount of money.

35. If a consumer's income increases, other things being equal:

a. the slope of the budget line will change

b. the indifference curve will shift out to the right but will remain convex

c. the budget line will shift out to the right but will be parallel to the initial budget line

d. the indifference curve will shift out to the right and remain parallel to the initial indifference curve

Answer: c

Reason: As the consumer's income rises with the prices remaining unchanged, the consumer will be able to buy more of both commodities. This is shown by an outward shift of the budget line as described in choice c.

36. A change in relative prices is shown by:

a. a parallel shift in the budget line

b. a rotation of the indifference curve

c. a parallel shift of the indifference curve

d. a rotation of the budget line

Answer: d

Reason: When relative prices change, the slope of the budget line changes. This is equivalent to a rotation of the budget line.

37. The consumer is in equilibrium when:

a. the budget line is tangent to an indifference curve

b. two indifference curves intersect

c. the budget line intersects the highest indifference curve

d. none of the above

Answer: a

Reason: the point of tangency between the budget line and an indifference curve is the highest indifference curve attainable, given the budget.

38. An Engel curve shows a relationship between:

a. price and income

b. price and quantity demanded

c. price and supply

d. income and quantity demanded

Answer: d

Reason: When the relationship between income and quantity demanded is shown on a graph, the graph is called an Engel curve.

39. The Engel curve for an inferior good is:

a. upward sloping   c. vertical

b. downward sloping   d. horizontal

Answer: b

Reason: For an inferior good, as income rises, the quantity demanded decreases. This inverse relationship is shown by a downward sloping Engel curve.

40. When the price of an item rises, people buy more, and when its price falls, they buy less. From this we know that the item is a(n):

a. inferior good   c. normal good

b. Giffen good   d. none of the above

Answer: b

Reason: A Giffen good is a good such that as its price rises, the quantity of it demanded also rises, and as its price falls, the quantity demanded also falls.

True or False

Determine whether each of the following statements is true or false.

I. Utility Theory

1. Economists use the term utility to refer to the satisfaction derived from the consumption of goods and services.

Answer: True

2. A unit of satisfaction is referred to as a metrifaction.

Answer: False

Explanation: A unit of satisfaction is referred to as a util.

3. Total utility is the amount of usage consumers get out of a product.

Answer: False

Explanation: Total utility is the total satisfaction derived from the consumption of a good or service.

4. Marginal utility is the extra satisfaction derived from the consumption of additional units of a good or service.

Answer: True

5. If MU is marginal utility, TU is total utility, and Q is quantity, then the formula for marginal utility can be written as $MU = \Delta Q/\Delta TU$.

Answer: False

Explanation: $MU = \Delta TU/\Delta Q$

6. If total utility is rising, marginal utility must be positive.

Answer: True

7. If marginal utility is positive, then total utility must be rising

Answer: True

8. If marginal utility is falling, then total utility must also be falling.

Answer: False

Explanation: If marginal utility is falling but is positive, then total utility will rise.

9. The law of diminishing marginal utility states that as a consumer consumes more and more of a commodity, after a while, the total utility will rise at an increasing rate.

Answer: False

Explanation: The law states that as a consumer consumes more of a commodity, the satisfaction or utility derived from each additional unit diminishes.

10. The greater the price of the product, the less the consumer will buy and hence the less the marginal utility.

Answer: False

Explanation: The first part of the statement is true but the conclusion is false. Because of diminishing marginal utility, when the consumer buys less, the marginal utility increases.

11. For a consumer purchasing two goods, A and B, to maximize satisfaction, the marginal utility of A divided by the price of A must equal the marginal utility of B divided by the price of B.

Answer: True

12. A consumer will consume additional units of a free good until the total utility reaches zero.

Answer: False

Explanation: Consumption of a free good will be carried to the point where the marginal utility is zero. At that point, total satisfaction is maximized.

13. If a consumer is buying two goods, A and B, he or she will be in equilibrium (maximizing satisfaction) when the utility of the last dollar spent on A equals the utility of the last dollar spent on B.

Answer: True

14. The problem posed by the water-diamond paradox was, "Why was water so much more plentiful than diamonds when people obviously needed more diamond?"

Answer: False

Explanation: The paradox was this: "Why was water so much cheaper than diamonds when water was so much more useful than diamonds?

15. The paradox of value can be solved by recognizing that price is proportional to total utility.

Answer: False

Explanation: Price is proportional to marginal, not total, utility.

16. The consumer's demand curve is unrelated to the equimarginal principle.

Answer: False

Explanation: The consumer's demand curve can be derived from the consumer's attempt to maintain the equimarginal relation following a change in price.

17. Consumer surplus is the difference between what consumers are willing to pay for an item and what they actually pay.

Answer: True

18. The existence of consumer surplus means that consumers most often derive much less satisfaction from a good or service than is suggested by the price of the good or service.

Answer: False

Explanation: Consume often derive more satisfaction from a good or service than is suggested by the price.

II. Indifference Curve Analysis

19. The numbers on an indifference curve have cardinal significance.

Answer: False

Explanation: The numbers represent a ranking only. They have only ordinal significance.

20. Indifference curves show various combinations of goods that give the same level of satisfaction.

Answer: True

21. Indifference curves intersect at the point of equilibrium.

Answer: False

Explanation: The assumption that the consumer is consistent in his or her choices rules out intersecting indifference curves.

22. Indifference curves are vertical because the consumer is always trying to get more goods and services.

Answer: False

Explanation: The consumer is always trying to maximize satisfaction subject to a budget constraint, but indifference curves are downward sloping.

23. Any combination of goods chosen must lie on an indifference curve.

Answer: True

24. The marginal rate of substitution remains constant as the consumer moves down along an indifference curve.

Answer: False

Explanation: The marginal rate of substitution diminishes. That's why indifference curves are convex to the origin.

25. The marginal rate of substitution is the rate at which the consumer is willing to trade off one good for another while maintaining the same level of satisfaction.

Answer: True

26. A budget line and an indifference curve cannot have the same slope.

Answer: False

Explanation: If the budget line is tangent to the indifference curve, they have the same slope at the point of tangency.

27. The budget line shows various bundles of goods that yield most satisfaction to the consumer.

Answer: False

Explanation: The budget line shows various combinations of goods that the consumer can buy for the same amount of money.

28. If the price of both commodities that a consumer buys doubles and the consumer's income also doubles, the budget line will be unchanged.

Answer: True

29. The slope of the budget line will change if the relative prices of the items that the consumer buys change.

Answer: True

30. An inferior good is a good of which less is purchased as the consumer's income rises.

Answer: True

31. In order to maximize satisfaction, the consumer must purchase a combination of goods such that the marginal rate o substitution equals the ratio of the prices.

Answer: True

32. Changes in relative prices will not affect the slope of the budget line.

Answer: False

Explanation: Changes in relative prices cause the slope of the budget line to change. It will rotate.

33. The price consumption curve is a line joining the points of tangency between budget lines and indifference curve as the price of one of the items changes.

Answer: True

34. The consumer's demand curve can be derived from the income consumption curve.

Answer: False

Explanation: The consumer's demand curve can be derived from the price consumption curve, not from the income consumption curve.

35. The demand curve for X will be upward sloping if X is a Giffen good.

Answer: True

Completion

(Fill in the blanks)

Use each word or combination of words from the list exactly once.
*(**Hint**: Proceed by elimination)*

Word list

Budget x 2 — Constraint — Consumption x 2 — Curve x 6 — Decrease — Demand — Diminishing — Giffen x 2 — Good — Income x 2 — Income / Budget — Increase — Indifference x 5 — Indifference Map / Preference Map — Inferior — Line — Marginal x 2 — Maximum — Normal x 2 — Prices — Rate — Rotate / Change Its Slope — Schedule — Shift — Slope — Substitution — Tangent — Util — Utility x 2

Questions

I. Utility Theory

1. Economists use the term ______________ to refer to the satisfaction derived from consuming goods and services.
2. A ______________ is a measure for a unit of satisfaction.

3. ________________ ________________ is the extra or additional satisfaction derived from the consumption of additional units a good or service.

4. If marginal utility is positive, then total utility will ________________. If marginal utility is negative, then total utility will ________________. If marginal utility is zero, then total utility will be at its ________________.

5. A fundamental hypothesis of the theory of consumer behavior that as a consumer consumes more of a commodity, the satisfaction derived from each additional unit diminishes is called the law of ________________ ________________ ________________.

6. It is assumed that the consumer tries to maximize satisfaction subject to a ________________ ________________.

7. The consumer will be in equilibrium when the ratio of the marginal utilities equals the ratio of the ________________.

8. The market ________________ ________________ is the horizontal summation of the individual demand curves.

II. Indifference Curve Analysis

9. The ordinal approach to consumer behavior is also referred to as ________________ ________________ analysis.

10. The ________________ ________________ is a graphical representation of all possible combinations of two commodities that a consumer can purchase for the same amount of money.

11. The ________________ of the budget line is the same as the ratio of the prices of the two items, but with a negative sign.

12. Other things being equal, an increase in the consumer's ________________ results in a parallel right to the right in the budget line.

13. A table showing various combinations of commodities that give a consumer the same level of satisfaction is called a(n) ________________ ________________. A graph that shows all combinations of two commodities that yield the same level of satisfaction is called a(n) ________________ ________________.

14. If A and B yield the same level of satisfaction, then they lie on the same ________________ ________________.

15. The rate at which a consumer is willing to trade off units of one commodity for units of another commodity so as to keep his or her level of satisfaction unchanged is called the ________________ ________________ of ________________.

16. The marginal rate of substitution is the slope of the ________________ ________________.

17. A collection of indifference curves is referred to as a(n) ________________.

18. The consumer is in equilibrium when the budget line is ________________ to an indifference curve.

19. As income increases, a consumer buys more of good A and less of good B. This means that good A to this consumer is a(n) ________________ good, while good B is a(n) ________________ good.

20. A change in income causes the budget line to ________________. A change in relative prices causes the budget line to ________________.

21. The ________________ ________________ ________________ is the line joining the points of tangency between budget lines and indifference curves as the consumer's income changes.

22. Engel curves show the relationship between ________________ and ________________.

23. A(n) ________________ ________________ is a good whose quantity demanded rises as its price rises and falls as its price falls, other things being equal.

24. The demand curve for a ________________ good is upward sloping.

25. An Engel curve for a ________________ good is upward sloping.

Solutions

1. (utility)
2. (util)
3. (Marginal utility)
4. (increase, decrease, maximum)
5. (diminishing marginal utility)
6. (budget constraint)
7. (prices)
8. (demand curve)
9. (indifference curve)
10. (budget line)
11. (slope)
12. (income / budget)
13. (indifference schedule, indifference curve)
14. (indifference curve)
15. (marginal rate substitution)
16. (indifference curve)
17. (indifference map / preference map)
18. (tangent)
19. (normal, inferior)
20. (shift, rotate / change its slope)
21. (income consumption curve)
22. (income, consumption)
23. (Giffen good)
24. (Giffen)
25. (normal)

8 BUSINESS ORGANIZATION

SYNOPSIS

The major forms of business organization are the **single proprietorship, the partnership, the corporation,** and the **cooperative.**

The advantages of the single proprietorship are (1) independence of the owner, (2) incentive to be efficient, (3) ability to make quick decisions, (4) incentive to promote goodwill, and (5) earnings are taxed only once. The disadvantages include: (1) inability to raise huge sums of money, (2) uncertainty of the life of the business, and (3) no protection by limited liability.

The advantages of a partnership include: (1) the ability to raise more money than can a single proprietorship, (2) income is taxed only once, (3) discussion among partners may lead to better decisions, and (4) greater pool of talent and skills. The disadvantages include: (1) lack of continuity, (2) capital may be limited, and (3) no protection by limited liability.

The advantages of the corporation are: (1) ability to raise huge amounts of capital, (2) the firm has continuity, (3) ability to hire the services of experts, and (4) owners are protected by limited liability. The disadvantages are: (1) earnings are taxed twice, (2) owners may have no significant control over policies, and (3)no close relationship between the firm and its customers.

The advantages of the cooperative are: (1)it can benefit from economies of scale, and (2) there is significant cooperation between managers and customers for the success of the enterprise. The disadvantages are: (1) it may not look beyond its membership for expert management, and (2) inability to raise huge capital.

A corporation has four main ways of raising capital: retained earnings, bond issue, bank credit, and selling shares. The capital raised by bank credit and issuing bonds is called **debt capital**. The capital raised by selling shares is called **equity capital.**

Specialization has a number of advantages. Each peon performs the task ay which he or she is most proficient. Specialization saves time, maximizes the use of tools and equipment, and develops skills. The main disadvantages of specialization are that it limits the individual's competence to one or two areas, it may lead to boredom, and it may inhibit creativity.

LEARNING OBJECTIVES

In connection with this module, you should be able to:

1. discuss various forms of business organization.
2. state the advantages and disadvantages of each form of business organization.
3. discuss business financing.
4. discuss the advantages and disadvantages of specialization.

DEFINITIONS & CONCEPTS

You should be able to define the following terms and concepts:

single proprietorship	partnership
limited partnership	corporation
cooperative	limited liability
specialization	shareholder (stockholder)
dividends	undistributed profits (retained earnings)
bond	equity capital
debt capital	prime (lending) rate

8
BUSINESS ORGANIZATION

Concepts, Definitions & Problems

Problem 8-1

What are the major forms of business organization? Briefly describe each.

Requirement and Clue: *This is a two-part problem. Address each part in order. After listing the major forms of business organization, you should mention the main features of each. Do not ignore the word "briefly".*

Solution:

The major forms of business organization are:

1. Sole proprietorship
2. Partnership
3. Corporation
4. Cooperative

Sole proprietorship The sole or single proprietorship is a form of business that is owned and managed by a single individual who is solely responsible for all aspects of the business. He or she earns off the profits and suffers all the losses. The single proprietorship does not have limited liability.

Partnership A partnership is a business owned by two or more people. Each partnership is personally responsible for all the debts of the partnership. They earn the profits and suffer the losses. The partnership does not have limited liability.

Corporation A corporation is a business organization in which the owners are not personally responsible for decisions made in the name of the business. The corporation exists as a legal entity apart from its owners (shareholders). The corporation enjoys limited liability.

Cooperative A cooperative is a business owned, financed, and controlled by its members, who share in the profits and risks in proportion to their patronage of the business.

Problem 8-2

What are the advantages of the single proprietorship?

Requirement and Clue: *Focus on benefits that the single proprietor may derive. Think of benefits to employees, and customers also. Of course, you are expected to know what a single proprietorship is.*

Solution:

A single proprietorship is a business that is owned, financed, and managed by a single owner. The single proprietorship enjoys certain advantages:

1. The single proprietor derives a certain amount of satisfaction, pride, and independence from owning his or her own business.

2. The single proprietor is likely to make special effort to run his or her business efficiently, knowing that he or she can lose all his or her possessions if the business fails. Single proprietorship provides a motive for efficiency.
3. In situations demanding swift action, the single proprietorship enjoys a considerable advantage over other forms of business organization, since the single proprietor does not need to consult with or seek the agreement of anyone.
4. The single proprietor is likely to be more concerned about developing good working relationships with the few employees he or she may have, and with securing the goodwill of his or her customers.
5. The single proprietor may enjoy tax benefits. The earnings of the single proprietor are subject to tax once only.

Problem 8-3

What are the disadvantages of the single proprietorship?

Requirement and Clue: *You are expected to know what a single proprietorship is. Think of anything that places the single proprietorship at a disadvantage.*

Solution:

A single proprietorship is a business that is owned, financed, and managed by a single owner. The single proprietorship faces the following disadvantages:

1. The biggest disadvantage that the single proprietorship faces is unlimited liability. If the business fails, the single proprietor is fully liable and stands to lose personal assets such as cars, furniture or even his or her home.
2. In situation requiring huge capital outlays, the single proprietor is at a distinct disadvantage. In most cases, single proprietors are unable to raise huge sums of money.
3. The single proprietorship suffers from the uncertainty about the continuation of the business in the event of the death or retirement of the owner.

Problem 8-4

List some of the characteristics of a sole proprietorship.

Requirement and Clue: *Pay attention to the word "list". Four or five features should suffice.*

Solution:

The following are some characteristics of a sole proprietorship.

1. The business is financed by the single owner
2. All business decisions are made by the owner
3. The owner manages and controls the business
4. The single owner is personally fully liable for all debts incurred by his or her business
5. The single owner earns all profits and suffers all losses.

Problem 8-5

What is a partnership? State the advantages and disadvantages of a partnership.

Requirement and Clue: *This sounds like a two-part problem but, in effect, it has three parts. First you are required to define a partnership; second, you are to state its advantages, and third, its disadvantages. Answer in order.*

Solution:

A partnership is a form of business organization in which two or more individuals agree to own and operate a business.

Advantages

The following are the main advantages of a partnership.

1. The partnership has the ability to raise more capital than the sole proprietorship is able to raise.
2. The partnership is not subject to tax.
3. Decisions are likely to be good because of the likelihood of discussions among partners before decisions are made.
4. The partnership may benefit from the variety of special talents and skills possessed by the partners.

Disadvantages

The following are the main disadvantages of a partnership.

1. The partnership does not have limited liability. Each partner is fully liable to the extent of his or her personal possessions for any debts incurred by the business.
2. The partnership lacks continuity. If one partner dies or if agreement cannot be reached among the partners, the partnership may have to be dissolved.
3. Although the partnership may be able to raise more capital than the single proprietorship, it is still severely limited in the amount of funds it can raise.

Problem 8-6

List some of the characteristics of a partnership.

Requirement and Clue: *Notice the word "list" in the problem. Four or five characteristics should be sufficient.*

Solution:

1. In a partnership, the partners are bound by a contract
2. Decisions are made by majority vote
3. Each partner is fully liable for the debts of the partnership. There is no limited liability
4. The partners share profits according to the partnership agreement
5. The partnership is dissolved upon the death, or retirement of any partner, thus the partnership lacks continuity.

Problem 8-7

Why is a partnership the ideal form of business organization for a law firm, from the viewpoint of the client?

Requirement and Clue: *What is it about a partnership that provides an incentive for good decision-making? How can clients benefit from this?*

Solution:

In a partnership, each partner is fully liable, not only for debts resulting from his or her own actions, but also for those resulting from the actions of the other partners. If one lawyer in the firm bungles a case, it exposes the other lawyers as well to any unfavourable consequences. This is a sort of safety net that ensures that each lawyer in the firm will do his or her best to see that the best decisions are made. It provides an incentive for consultation among the lawyers, which is definitely a great advantage to the firm's clients.

Problem 8-8

What is a corporation? What are its advantages and disadvantages?

Requirement and Clue: *This is a three-part problem. First, you are required to define a corporation; second, you are asked to state its advantages, and third, you are expected to state its disadvantages.*

Solution:

A corporation is a form of business organization in which a group of persons agree to engage in business in which they have limited liability. Legally, the corporation is an entity that exists apart from its shareholders. It can sue or be sued, enter into contracts, and be taxed lust like an individual.

Advantages of the corporation include the following:

1. It has a tremendous ability to raise huge amounts of money by selling shares.
2. The corporation has continuity. If one of its owners dies, the corporation continues to exist.
3. Each owner (shareholder) is liable only to the extent of his or her investment in the business. That is, the owners have limited liability.
4. The corporation can usually afford to hire the services of experts in various aspects of business management. Policy decisions are, therefore, likely to be sound.

Disadvantages of the corporation include the following:

1. The earnings of the corporation are subject to double taxation. The corporation pays a tax before its profits are distributed, and the shareholders also pay a tax on their dividends.
2. The size of the corporation often forces a wedge between labour and management, and also destroys the close personal relationship between owner and customer that is typical of the single proprietorship.
3. The owners of the corporation may have little or no control over its operation, and those who make the day-to-day decisions of the corporation may not have the same incentives as the owners.

Problem 8-9

A profitable partnership finds that it could earn even larger profits if it expanded its operation. Potential partners are unwilling to join the partnership because of unlimited liability. What course of action might the firm take to overcome this difficulty?

Requirement and Clue: *The problem facing the partnership is lack of funds and unlimited liability. Focus on a form of business organization that can raise huge amounts of capital and avoid the problem of unlimited liability.*

Solution:

The most effective form of business organization, from the capital-raising perspective, is the corporation. The corporation provides limited liability to its shareholders. Potential investors who are unwilling to invest in an enterprise that does not have limited liability can safely do so in a corporation. Should the business go bankrupt, the personal assets of the investors are protected. Therefore, the partnership might be able to raise sufficient capital to expand its operation if the partners were to form a corporation.

Problem 8-10

What is a cooperative? How does a cooperative differ from a corporation?

Requirement and Clue: *This is a two-part problem. Address each part in order. You should point out differences between a cooperative and a corporation.*

Solution:

A cooperative is a form of business organization that is owned, financed, and controlled by its member-patrons, who share the risks and benefits in proportion to their patronage.

A cooperative is similar to a corporation in many respects. In fact, it is a modified version of the corporation. Unlike the corporation, however, in which a shareholder is entitled to one vote for each share he or she owns, each member of the cooperative has only one vote no matter how many shares he or she controls. Hence a true cooperative exhibits democratic control. Also, dividends are distributed not in proportion to the number of shares held, as in the case of a corporation, but in proportion to the amount of business that each member conducts with the cooperative.

Problem 8-11

Describe:

(a) *A consumer cooperative*

(b) *A producer cooperative*

Requirement and Clue: *In solving this problem, take care to point* *out any specific identifying features of the concepts. If possible, provide examples.*

Solution:

(a) A consumer cooperative is a business formed by a group of consumers who join together to operate a business that provides consumer goods and services. Since dividends are distributed among the members in proportion to the volume of business that each member transacts with the cooperative (that is, according to patronage), the members find it advantageous to do as much business as possible with the cooperative.

(b) A producer cooperative is a business formed by a group of producers who believe that by banding together they can better serve their interests. A group of dairy farmers or fruit growers, for example, may form a cooperative for the purpose of increasing efficiency through joint action.

Problem 8-12

What are the advantages and disadvantages of a cooperative?

Requirement and Clue: *Of course, you must know what a cooperative is in order to solve this problem. State the advantages and disadvantages in order. Think of benefits and limitations.*

Solution:

A cooperative is a form of business organization that is owned, financed, and controlled by its member-patrons, who share the risks and benefits in proportion to their patronage.

Advantages

1. The cooperative can take advantage of the benefits of large-scale operation.
2. The managers and customers of a cooperative are likely to work together towards the success of the business.

Disadvantages

1. The cooperative may fail to look beyond its own membership for expert management.
2. The cooperative may be limited by its inability to raise huge amounts of capital for two reasons. First, only those individuals who intend to conduct a large volume of business with the cooperative are likely to purchase its shares. Second, its members are unlikely to contribute additional funds since dividends are distributed not in proportion to funds invested, but by patronage.

Problem 8-13

You have come up with an idea for a good or service that you believe will be successful on the market, and you would like to experiment with this idea. It does not require a great deal of money to get it started. What form of business organization would you choose to establish your business?

Requirement and Clue: *Carefully consider the information provided in the problem. Quickly think of the characteristics of the main forms of business organization and determine the best one under the situation. A brief explanation for your choice should be given.*

Solution:

Under the circumstances outlined in the problem, it appears that a sole proprietorship is the most appropriate form of business organization for this proposed business. The organization of a sole proprietorship entails ni legal red tape and is relatively inexpensive. Once the experimental stage is over and the idea proves to be good, then some other form of business organization could be considered.

Problem 8-14

Complete the following table by indicating the form of business organization you would suggest for each type of business.

	Type of business	*Suggested form of business organization*
a.	*A small coffee shop*	______________
b.	*A chain restaurant*	______________
c.	*A law practice with two lawyers*	______________
d.	*A large trucking company*	______________
e.	*A small boutique*	______________

Requirement and Clue: *The purpose of this problem is to test your understanding of the characteristics of the various forms of business organization. Focus on these features as you match the type of business with a suitable form of business organization.*

Solution:

	Type of business	Suggested form of business organization
a.	A small coffee shop:	Single proprietorship or partnership
b.	A chain restaurant:	Corporation
c.	A law practice with two lawyers:	Partnership
d.	A large trucking company:	Corporation
e.	A small boutique:	Single proprietorship or partnership

Problem 8-15

A corporation can raise funds through bonds, through credit, and through shares. Describe each method of financing.

Requirement and Clue: *You are to explain how the corporation can raise funds through these methods.*

Solution:

Bonds: The corporation that issues bonds is actually borrowing from the purchasers of the bonds, with a promise to pay a certain amount of money as interest payment periodically. If you buy a $1000 bond from a corporation that promises to pay $100 every year for a period of five years, the corporation is actually borrowing $1000 from you. You will earn $100 every year for five years; and you will receive the principal of $1000 at the end of the five-year period on the maturity date of the bond.

Bank credit: A corporation may negotiate a loan with a bank of other financial institution. The corporation and the lending institution negotiate the terms of the loan. The rate of interest that the corporation pays depends largely on the lending institution's evaluation of the degree of risk associated with the corporation.

Shares: A corporation may issue shares. When you buy shares or stocks in a company, you are actually buying part ownership in the corporation. As a part owner, you are entitled to a share of the profits, but you must also suffer any losses that may occur.

Problem 8-16

What are retained earnings? How important are retained earnings as a source of investment funds?

Requirement and Clue: *This is a two-part problem. Answer each part in order. Provide a clear definition of retained earnings. You are not required to write an essay on the concept. For the second part of the problem, think of the extent to which corporations depend on retained earnings to finance investment.*

Solution:

Retained earnings are a portion of the corporation's profits that are kept back by the firm instead of being distributed to the corporation's shareholders. Retained earnings are also referred to as undistributed profits.

Retained earnings are extremely important to the firm as a source of investment funds. In fact, they provide the main source of funds for total investment.

Problem 8-17

What is the nature of the double taxation faced by corporations? How might this double taxation be avoided?

Requirement and Clue: *This is a two-part problem. You should answer each part in order. Focus on the sense in which double taxation exists. Think of a means whereby a corporation may avoid double taxation.*

Solution:

Double taxation arises because the corporation's income is taxed, and when dividends are made out to shareholders, those shareholders are also taxed.

Double taxation may be avoided by not distributing dividends to shareholders. Since only dividends that are paid out are subject to personal income tax, then dividends left within the firm escape taxation.

Problem 8-18

Briefly state the difference between debt capital and equity capital.

Requirement and Clue: *Emphasis should be directed at the difference between the two concepts.*

Solution:

Debt capital is capital raised through issuing bonds and by using bank credit. Equity capital is money raised from selling shares. The difference between the two concepts is that debt capital is essentially a loan that has to be repaid out of normal business operations whereas equity capital does not have to be repaid out of the corporation's business operations. Shareholders are part owners, not lenders like bondholders and bank creditors.

Problem 8-19

Large corporations facilitate specialization. What are some of the advantages of specialization?

Requirement and Clue: *Do not be fooled into thinking that this is a two-part Problem. The first sentence in the problem merely provides information. Three or four advantages should suffice.*

Solution:

Specialization is concentration on a particular occupation or task. Advantages of specialization include the following:

1. Specialization allows people to choose the jobs for which they are best suited. It results is greater output than if specialization did not take place.
2. Specialization saves time. It takes a great amount of time for a worker to acquire the skills for a new job. It also takes a certain amount of time to change from one set of tools to another. Specialization eliminates this changeover time.
3. Specialization maximizes the use of machines. In the absence of specialization, tools and equipment would lie idle for considerable length of time, and this would significantly reduce the output of goods and services.
4. The repeated performance of a specific task causes performers to develop skills to increase their efficiency. Also, their general knowledge of their jobs is likely to increase with the length of time spent at the job.

Problem 8-20

What are the disadvantages of specialization?

Requirement and Clue: *Focus on the negative effects of specialization on those who specialize.*

Solution:

The disadvantages of specialization include:

1. Specialization restricts the sphere of competence of workers who specialize. Workers develop the skills necessary for the performance of their particular tasks or jobs, but have little or no competence in other areas.
2. Specialization my cause boredom. Workers who are performing the same tasks day after day become bored. There is little scope for creativity, since after a while, jobs lose their challenge. Complaints from assembly-line

workers that they are hardly more than machines are common.

3. Specialization implies a certain degree of interdependence. For example, those who specialize in fishing must depend on bakers for bread, and those who specialize in baking bread must depend on fishermen for fish. Specialization results in the loss of some measure of independence.

Multiple-Choice

In each case, circle the letter that corresponds with the correct answer.

1. Which of the following is a major form of business organization?

a. Corporation c. Single proprietorship
b. Partnership d. All of the above

Answer: d

Reason: The corporation, the partnership, and the single proprietorship are all major forms of business organizations.

2. In a single proprietorship:

a. all partners must share equally in the profits of the business

b. all shares issued to shareholders must have the same market price

c. a single owner takes the risks, enjoys the profits, or suffers the losses

d. the firm has a naturally continuous existence.

Answer: c

Reason: There are no partners in a single proprietorship, only corporations can issue shares, and the continuation of a single proprietorship is uncertain. Choice c is characteristic of the single proprietorship.

3. Which of the following is an advantage of a sole proprietorship?

a. Ability to raise funds
b. Unlimited liability
c. Limited liability
d. Control over business decisions

Answer: d

Reason: A single proprietorship has total control over all decisions made by the business.

4. Which of the following is protected by limited liability?

a. The corporation c. The single proprietorship
b. The partnership d. All of the above

Answer: c

Reason: Only the corporation is protected by limited liability.

5. One of the great advantages of the partnership is that:

a. it enjoys limited liability
b. its ability to raise capital is unlimited
c. it is not subject to income tax
d. all of the above.

Answer: c

Reason: The partnership, like the single proprietorship, is not subject to income tax.

6. Partners in business:

a. never draw up a contract
b. always draw up a partnership agreement
c. may or may not draw up a partnership agreement
d. never comply with any agreement.

Answer: c

Reason: It is advisable for partners to draw up a partnership agreement but they may or may not do so.

7. Which of the following is true of a partnership?

a. It has limited liability
b. It's continuity is assured
c. Partners are not liable for mistakes made by other partners
d. It may benefit from skills possessed by individual partners.

Answer: d

Reason: Partners may have expertise in various areas of business from which the partnership may benefit.

8. Which of the following statements is correct?

a. If partners in a partnership cannot agree, the partnership may have to be dissolved
b. It is impossible for partners not to agree because a partnership agreement exists
c. Disagreement among partners in a partnership can be easily settled by the shareholders
d. None of the above

Answer: a

*Reason: Choice **a** describes one of the weaknesses of a partnership.*

9. One of the advantages of a corporation is that:

a. it does not have to distribute any profits at any time
b. it has so many owners that it does not have to borrow to raise capital
c. it has limited liability
d. it pays taxes only on dividends declared.

Answer: c

Reason: The corporation is the only form of business organization that has limited liability.

10. Which of the following is not true of a corporation?

a. It has unlimited liability
b. It can obtain funds relatively easily

c. It may enjoy economies of scale (lower cost because of size)

d. It has greater opportunity for specialization.

Answer: a

Reason: A corporation has limited liability.

11. When we say that a corporation is a legal person we mean that:

a. shareholders cannot be held liable for illegal acts committed in the name of the corporation

b. the corporation can sue or be sued just like a person

c. it exists as a legal entity only because its shareholders are legal persons

d. none of the above

Answer: b

Reason: The corporation`s status as a legal person means that it can enter into contracts on its own behalf, it pays income taxes like a real person does, it can take legal action on its own behalf, and it can be sued in a court of law.

12. In a cooperative:

a. profits are distributed to shareholders in proportion to the amount of shares help

b. profits are never distributed, they are simply re-invested in the business

c. each shareholder is entitled to one vote for each share held

d. benefits are distributed according to patronage.

Answer: d

Reason: Choice d describes one of the features of a cooperative.

13. Which is the least popular (least numerous) form of business organization in North America?

a. The sole proprietorship

b. The partnership

c. The corporation

d. The cooperative

Answer: d

Reason: The other forms of business organization are more popular in North America than the cooperative.

14. Which of the following is the simplest form of business to start?

a. The sole proprietorship

b. The partnership

c. The corporation

d. The cooperative

Answer: a

Reason: To establish a business as a sole proprietorship, the owner simple has to "open" for business. It is a simple matter to "register" the business.

15. One of the advantages of a partnership over a single proprietorship is:

a. the partnership has limited liability while the single proprietorship does not

b. the partnership affords greater opportunity to specialize

c. the establishment of a partnership has less red tape

d. the partnership has unlimited liability while the single proprietorship has limited liability

Answer: b

Reason: The partners may have different business skills and so be able to specialize to the benefit of the partnership.

16. In which of the following forms of business organization does one become an owner by buying shares?

a. a single proprietorship c. a partnership

b. a corporation d. all of the above

Answer: b

Reason: Only corporations sell shares.

17. Double taxation means:

a. corporate profit tax rates are twice as high as personal income tax rates

b. the corporation's profits are taxed first as corporation's income as then as personal income when paid out as dividends

c. corporate income tax rate is double the income tax rate on single proprietorships and partnerships

d. corporate income is taxed first by the federal government, then the local government taxes the income again.

Answer: b

Reason: Choice b accurately describes "double taxation".

18. In which of the following forms of business organization is there separation of ownership and control?

a. The partnership c. The corporation

b. The sole proprietorship d. All of the above

Answer: c

Reason: The sole proprietorship and the partnership are managed and controlled by their owners. The corporation is managed by hired managers who may or may not be shareholders.

19. To become an owner of a corporation, the investor must:

a. sign a partnership agreement

b. become an executive director

c. become a shareholder by buying the corporation's common shares

d. be elected to the board of directors of the corporation and must serve for at least two years.

Answer: c

Reason: The corporation's common shareholders are its owners.

20. Which of the following is a method of financing a corporation?

a. The selling of shares

b. Using bank credit

c. Using retained earnings

d. All of the above

Answer: d

Reason: Choices a, b, and c are ways of financing a corporation.

21. Capital acquired by bank credit is called:

a. share capital c. debt capital

b. equity capital d. none of the above

Answer: c.

Reason: By borrowing from a bank, the corporation establishes a debt with the bank.

22. Capital acquired by selling shares is called:

a. equity capital
b. debt capital
c. maturity capital
d. retained capital

Answer: a

Reason: Choice a correctly defines equity capital.

23. Which of the following provides the main source of funds for corporations?

a. equity capital
b. retained earnings
c. bank credit
d. partnership funds

Answer: b

Reason: Firms keep back a part of their profits to be re-invested in the business. This is typically the main source of investment funds for a corporation.

24. Specialization permits all of the following except:

a. increases in production
b. more efficient use of tools and equipment
c. more efficient use of time
d. proficiency in a wide variety of jobs.

Answer: d

Reason: Specialization involves concentration on one or two areas. It does not permit skill development and proficiency in many jobs.

True or False

Determine whether each of the following statements is true or false.

1. Popular forms of business organization include the single proprietorship, the partnership, and the corporation.

Answer: True

2. The forms of business organization represent, among other things, the financial arrangements under which they operate.

Answer: True

3. Owners of single proprietorships are liable for the debts of the business only to the extent of their investment in the business.

Answer: False

Explanation: Single proprietors are fully liable for all debts of the business. Their personal assets are at stake.

4. Single proprietorships can raise funds easily by selling shares in their business.

Answer: False

Explanation: Single proprietorships cannot sell shares in their business. Only corporations can do so.

5. The single proprietorship form of business organization is found mainly in small businesses such as confectionaries and in certain professions such as accounting, and independent management consulting.

Answer: True

6. Knowing that they can lose all of their possessions if their businesses fail, single proprietors are likely to make special efforts to run their businesses efficiently.

Answer: True

7. An advantage of the single proprietorship form of business organization is that its profits are taxed only once.

Answer: True

8. Limited liability is an advantage enjoyed by all partners in a business.

Answer: False

Explanation: Only corporations and limited partners in a limited partnership have limited liability.

9. The biggest advantage enjoyed by sole proprietorships is limited liability. That is the only form of business organization that has such a feature.

Answer: False

Explanation: The sole proprietorship has unlimited liability.

10. Because of its size, the single proprietorship is certain of continuity.

Answer: False

Explanation: The uncertainty of continuity of a single proprietorship is one of the disadvantages of that form of business organization.

11. The single proprietorship is subject to double taxation.

Answer: False

Explanation: The single proprietorship itself pays no income tax, but the owner pays income tax.

12. A general partnership has limited liability.

Answer: False

Explanation: A general partnership, like the sole proprietorship, has unlimited liability.

13. A partnership can be established only if two or more single proprietorships decide to merge.

Answer: False

Explanation: A partnership does not need to be the result of a merger of single proprietorships. Two or more people can decide to form a partnership.

14. A partnership has a greater ability to raise money than does a corporation.

Answer: False

Explanation: The corporation has the greatest potential to raise capital because it can sell shares.

15. In a limited partnership, certain partners have limited liability, and those partners with limited liability cannot manage the partnership.

Answer: True

16. A partnership, like a corporation, has continuity as one of its advantages.

Answer: False

Explanation: A corporation has continuity but a partnership does not. If a partner leaves the partnership for whatever reason, the partnership must be dissolved.

17. In a corporation, ownership can be identified simply by looking at management personnel.

Answer: False

Explanation: In a corporation, management and ownership may be completely separated.

18. A corporation is subject to double taxation.

Answer: True

19. Limited liability of a corporation means that the shareholders in a corporation are liable only to the extent of their investment in the corporation.

Answer: True

20. Profits in a cooperative are distributed according to the number of shares held by the shareholders.

Answer: False

Explanation: The profits of a cooperative are distributed according to patronage.

21. Types of cooperatives include consumer cooperatives, producer cooperatives, and purchasing cooperatives.

Answer: True

22. The main objective of a purchasing cooperative is to take advantage of economies of scale in purchasing.

Answer: True

23. Retained earnings are portions of profits that the firm does not distribute to shareholders as dividends. They constitute the main source of investment funds.

Answer: True

24. Single proprietorships and partnerships can raise capital by selling shares, but corporations do not have this means of raising funds.

Answer: False

Explanation: Corporations can raise capital by selling shares, but single proprietorships and partnerships cannot.

25. The capital raised by issuing bonds and by using bank credit is referred to as debt capital. The capital raised from selling shares is called equity capital.

Answer: True

26. Equity capital is obtained by selling shares.

Answer: True

27. Debt capital is obtained by contracting bank credit or by issuing bonds.

Answer: True

28. Specialization by occupation occurs when an individual specializes in a particular trade, occupation, or profession, instead of engaging in a number of separate occupations.

Answer: True

29. Specialization has the disadvantage of leaving tools and equipment grossly underutilized.

Answer: False

Explanation: On the contrary, specialization maximizes the use of tools and equipment, and this is an advantage, not a disadvantage.

Completion

(Fill in the blanks)

Use each word or combination of words from the list exactly once.
*(**Hint**: Proceed by elimination)*

Word list

Cooperatives — Cooperative x 2 — Corporation x 3 — Corporations — Debt — Earnings x 2 — Equity — Limited x 2 — Occupation x 2 — Partnership x 4 — Partnerships — Prime — Rate — Retained x 2 — Shareholders — Shares x 2 — Single Proprietorship x 3 — Single/ Sole Proprietors — Single/Sole Proprietorships — Task

Questions

1. The easiest form of business organization to establish is the ______________.
2. ______________ ______________ own their own businesses, finance them themselves, and make all of the decisions regarding the operation of their businesses.
3. The main forms of business organization are ______________, ______________, ______________, and the ______________.
4. In a ______________, swift action can be taken because there is no need to discuss matters with anyone.
5. A ______________ is a form of business organization in which two or more individuals decide to own and operate a business.
6. In a ______________ ______________, certain partners have limited liability.
7. The greatest disadvantage of the ______________ and the ______________ is that they are not protected by limited liability.
8. In a ______________ partnership, certain partners may have limited liability.
9. In a ______________, shareholders have limited liability.
10. The ______________ is able to raise more capital than any other form of business organization. It can sell ______________ to the public, and purchasers of these ______________ become the owners of the business.
11. A corporation is owned by its ______________.
12. Portions of the profits of a corporation that are kept back to be re-invested in the firm are known as ______________ ______________.
13. The form of business organization with the highest chance of continuity is the ______________.
14. In a ______________, dividends are distributed according to patronage.
15. A ______________ is formed by a group of consumers who join together to operate a business that provides consumer goods and services.
16. ______________ ______________ provide the main source of funds for total investment.
17. The ______________ ______________ is the rate of interest that banks charge their most credit- worthy corporate borrowers.
18. Specialization by ______________ occurs when an individual specializes in a particular trade, occupation or profession.
19. The capital raised by issuing bonds and by using bank credit is referred to as ______________ capital. The capital obtained by selling shares is called ______________ capital.
20. The two main types of specialization are specialization by ______________ and specialization by ______________.

Solutions

1. (single proprietorship)
2. (Single or Sole proprietors)
3. (single/sole proprietorships, partnerships, corporations, cooperatives)
4. ('single/sole proprietorship)
5. (partnership)
6. (limited partnership)
7. (single proprietorship' partnership)
8. (limited)
9. (corporation)
10. (corporation, shares, shares)
11. (shareholders)
12. (retained earnings)
13. (corporation)
14. (cooperative)
15. cooperative
16. (Retained earnings)
17. (prime rate)
18. (occupation)
19. (debt, equity)
20. (task, occupation)

9 THEORY OF PRODUCTION

SYNOPSIS

Production of goods and services takes place in economic units called **firms**. In economic theory, we assume that the objective of the firm is to maximize profits. Profits are defined as the difference between total revenue (TR) and total cost (TC). The firm will choose the method of production that is economically most efficient.

The short run is defined as a situation in which the firm has at least one **fixed factor** of production. The firm cannot vary all its factors of production in the short run. The **long run** is a situation in which the firm is able to vary all its factors of production. In the long run, all is variable. The relation between a firm's output and its inputs is referred to as the **production function**.

The **total product** is the total output of goods and services produced over a period of time. **Average product** is total product divided by the number of units of the variable factor. **Marginal product** is the addition to total product caused by one more unit of the variable factor.

The law of diminishing (marginal) productivity (returns) states that when successive increments of a variable factor are added to a fixed factor, after a while, the increase in the total product (that is, the marginal product) will diminish.

A firm purchasing capital and labour will minimize its cost when the ratio of the marginal product of capital to the marginal product of labour equals the ratio of the price of capital to the price of labour.

LEARNING OBJECTIVES

In connection with this module, you should be able to:

1. explain the objectives if the firm.
2. differentiate between economic efficiency and economic efficiency.
3. explain production runs or periods.
4. describe the production function.
5. explain the relationship between total, marginal, and average product.
6. explain the law of diminishing marginal returns.
7. discuss the principle of substitution.

DEFINITIONS & CONCEPTS

You should be able to define the following terms and concepts:

firm
entrepreneur
technological (technical) efficiency
economic efficiency
economic efficiency ratio
fixed factor
variable factor
principle of substitution
short run
long run
production function
total product
marginal product
average product
law of diminishing returns

9

THEORY OF PRODUCTION

Concepts, Definitions & Problems

Problem 9-1

Briefly define a firm. What do economists assume to be the objective of a firm?

Requirement and Clue: *This is a two-part problem; answer each part in order. Don't disregard the word "briefly" in the problem. Different assumptions are made regarding the objective of the firm. What do economists assume?*

Solution:

A firm is the business unit or enterprise that acquires and assembles resources and produces goods and services for sale at a profit. Examples of firms are Walmart, General Motors, or your favourite restaurant in town.

Although different assumptions have been proposed as the objective of the firm, economists assume that the objective of the firm is to maximize profits.

Problem 9-2

Which of the following would you consider to be a firm and why?

(a) *A commercial farmer*

(b) *A privately operated auto driving school*

(c) *A small private radio station*

(d) *A college teachers' union*

Requirement and Clue: *Start by defining a firm as a backdrop to your solution. Focus on what distinguishes a firm from other entities.*

Solution:

A firm is the economic unit that acquires inputs (factors of production) and uses them to produce goods and services for sale at a profit.

(a) A commercial farmer is a firm because he or she acquires land, seeds, farm equipment, labour services, fertilizers, animals, etc. and uses these resources to produce farm output such as eggs, wheat, meat, vegetables, fruit, milk, etc. for sale to consumers.

(b) A privately operated auto driving school acquires cars, gasoline, driving instructors, instructional equipment and materials, office space, desks and chairs, etc. and uses these inputs to provide theoretical and practical instruction to students at a profit. Hence, a driving school qualifies as a firm.

(c) A small private radio station uses office space, broadcasting equipment, reporters, program hosts, announcers, secretarial services, technicians, sales people, etc. to provide information and entertainment. Although the radio audience may not pay for the information and entertainment they receive, sponsors and advertisers do pay so that the radio station can make a profit. It is a firm.

(d) A college teachers' union collects union dues from its members. It uses these monies to pay for the resources it uses to provide a variety of services to its members. Because the union is not really a profit-seeking entity, it does not qualify as a firm.

Problem 9-3

Economic theory assumes that the objective of the firm is to maximize its profits. How are profits calculated? What criticisms have been made about the profit-maximizing assumption?

Requirement and Clue: *This is a two-part problem. Answer each part in order. The calculation of profits is implied by its definition. A simple arithmetic example will help to illustrate the calculation. Focus on objectives other than profit maximization that a firm might pursue.*

Solution:

Profits are defined as the difference between a firm's total revenue and its total cost. To calculate profits, sum up the firm's revenues, sum up its cost, and then subtract its total cost from its total revenue. For example, if a firm's total revenues amount to \$200,000 and its total costs are \$180,000, then its profits are \$200,000 - \$180,000 = \$20,000.

Critics of the profit-maximizing assumption claim that firms pursue objectives other than profit maximization. The agree, in general, that the firm will attempt to make a certain level of profits, but once this level is reached, the firm pursues other objectives including maximizing sales, creating a certain public image, satisfying customers, maintaining or increasing market share, and pursuing the managers' personal well-being.

Problem 9-4

What are some objectives other than profit maximization that firms might pursue? Why do economists continue to rely on the profit maximization assumption?

Requirement and Clue: *This is a two-part problem. You should answer each part in order. Profit maximization may not be the only objective that firms pursue. You should think of other possible objectives. Is there any justification for economists to rely on the profit maximization assumption? Focus.*

Solution:

Critics of the profit maximization assumption advanced by economists have made alternative assumptions. Some other objectives advanced are: (1) sales maximization, (2) creating and maintaining a certain public image, (3) the growth of the firm, (4) the satisfaction and general welfare of the firm's customers. Economists see these suggested alternative objectives as avenues through which the firm may maximize its profits in the long run. Economists continue to rely on the profit maximization assumption because it has enabled them to analyze and predict the behavior of firms with a great degree of success.

Problem 9-5

If the only objective of a firm is to maximize its profits, will it discriminate against workers on the basis of sex or race in its hiring practices?

Requirement and Clue: Focus on the effects of discriminatory practices on the firm's profits.

Solution:

A firm seeking to maximize its profits will be cost conscious. It will tend to hire workers on the basis of their ability to contribute to the output of the firm, and not on the basis of sex or race. In fact, to the extent that workers of a certain sex or race (for example women and blacks) are skilled and relatively inexpensive, the profit motive dictates that they will be hired in preference to more expensive groups. Discrimination in hiring will not be in the best interest of the firm seeking to maximize its profits.

Problem 9-6

How are profits defined?

Requirement and Clue: *This is a definitional problem. Provide a clear and precise definition of the concept. An example will be helpful.*

Solution:

Profits may be defined as the difference between the firm's total revenue (that is, its receipts from the sale of its goods and services) and its costs. Symbolically,

$$\pi = TR - TC$$

where π is profit, TR is total; revenue, and TC is total cost.

For example, if the firm's total revenue amounts to \$2,500 and its total cost is \$2,000, then its profit is (\$2,500 – \$2,000) = \$500.

Problem 9-7

When is a production method technically efficient? When is it economically efficient?

Requirement and Clue: *This is a two-part problem. Answer each part in order. Your solution should demonstrate that you know the difference between technical efficiency and economic efficiency.*

Solution:

A production method is deemed to be technically efficient if it uses fewer inputs than some other method to produce a given volume of output. Consider the following example.

Method	Capital	Labour	Output
A	100	500	10,000
B	180	900	10,000

Method A uses 100 units of capital and 500 units of labour to produce 10,000 units of output. On the other hand, method B uses 180 units of capital and 900 units of labour to produce the same volume of output. In this case, method A is technically efficient while method B is technically inefficient.

A production method is said to be economically efficient if it produces a given volume of output at the lowest cost. Consider the following example.

Method	Capital	Labour	Output
A	100	500	10,000
B	50	800	10,000

Method A uses more capital but less labour than does method B. We need to know which method has the lower cost.

Suppose the prices of capital and labour are \$40 and \$5 respectively. We can calculate the cost of using each method as follows:

For method A, 100 units of capital and 500 units of labour cost (100 × \$40) + (500 × \$5)

= \$4,000 + \$2,500 = \$6,500

For method B, 50 units of capital and 800 units of labour cost (50 × \$40) + (800 × \$5)

= \$2,000 + \$4,000 = \$6,000

Therefore, it can be concluded that method B is economically efficient.

Problem 9-8

You are contemplating going into business to produce pen-holders. You are faced with the methods of producing pen-holders shown in the following table. The prices of capital and labour are \$5 and \$6 respectively, and the market price of pen-holders is \$10. Which method should you choose?

Method	Capital	Labour	Output
1	10	6	24
2	15	2	25

Requirement and Clue: *Your choice should be based on economic efficiency. Since the output varies with each method, you need to consider the economic efficiency ratios of the two methods.*

Solution:

The choice between methods 1 and 2 will be made on the basis of their relative economic efficiency. Using method 1, the value of the inputs is (10 × \$5) + (6 × \$6) = \$86. The value of the output is (24 × \$10) = \$240. The economic efficiency ratio (EER) is the value of the output divided by the cost of the inputs. For method 1,

$$\text{EER} = \frac{240}{86} = \mathbf{2.79}$$

Using method 2, the cost of the inputs is (15 × \$5) + (12 × \$6) = \$87. The value of the output is (25 × \$10) = \$250. Therefore for method 2,

$$\text{EER} = \frac{250}{87} = \mathbf{2.87}$$

Method 2 should be chosen since it is more efficient—it has a higher EER.

Problem 9-9

The following table shows units of labour and capital required to produce 500 units of output. Labour costs \$8 per unit and capital \$5 per unit.

Combination	Labour	Capital
A	10	18
B	15	24
C	7	20

(a) *Which of these methods is technically inefficient and why?*

(b) *Which method is economically most efficient?*

(c) *If the price of labour falls to \$5 per unit, while the price of capital doubles, which method will be economically most efficient?*

(d) *From the results obtained for the answers to parts (b) and (c) about the impact of input prices on the choice of the method of production?*

Requirement and Clue: *Focus on the meanings of technical efficiency and economic efficiency. Although you are not asked to define these concepts, you must know them in order to solve this problem.*

Solution:

(a) Just by sight, method B is technically inefficient because it uses more labour and more capital than any of the other methods. (This method will be eliminated from considerations of economic efficiency).

(b) The cost, using method A, is (10 × \$8) + (18 × \$5) = \$170. The cost, using method C, is (7 × \$8) + (20 × \$5) = \$156. Hence, method C is economically most efficient because it has the lowest cost.

(c) With the new factor prices, the cost, using method A, is (10 × \$5) + (18 × \$10) =\$230, while the cost, using method C, is (7 × \$5) + (20 × \$10) = \$235. Method A is now economically most efficient because it has the lowest cost.

(d) From the results obtained for parts (b) and (c), we can conclude that the prices of inputs affects the choice of the method of production.

Problem 9-10

Distinguish between fixed factors and variable factors.

Requirement and Clue: *Your solution should demonstrate that you understand the difference between these two concepts.*

Solution:

The firm's inputs can be classified as fixed factors and variable factors. The fixed factors are those whose quantities cannot be varied within the period under consideration. For example, if the period being considered is one year, and the firm cannot vary its plant within a year, then its plant would be a fixed factor. Variable factors, on the other hand, are those whose quantities can be varied within the period being considered. A firm can usually reduce or increase its labour force within a short period of time. Labour would be an example of a variable factor.

Problem 9-11

What is (a) the short run and (b) the long run? Why should these "runs" not be considered periods of calendar time?

Requirement and Clue: *This problem has three parts. Address each part in order. You are required to clearly define the two concepts. Focus on how it may be misleading to interpret these concepts as periods of calendar time.*

Solution:

(a) The *short run* is a situation in which the firm has at least one fixed factor of production. The short run is such that the firm does not have sufficient time to vary all of its inputs.

(b) The long run is a situation in which the firm is able to vary all of its factors of production. In the long run, there are no fixed factors.

The short run and the long run should not be considered as periods of calendar time since they do not correspond to any such periods. In some industries, the short run may be quite long, while in other industries, the long run may be quite short. For example, the long run may be only a few hours for a shoe shine business, but it may be several years for a business such as a public utility. Equating the short run and the long run with specific time horizons can lead to erroneous conclusions and misunderstanding.

Problem 9-12

Define production function.

Requirement and Clue: *What is required is a clear statement of what a production function is. Resist the temptation to write an essay on the production. An illustrative example will be helpful.*

Solution:

A production function is a technical or engineering relation between the firm's inputs and its output of goods and services. If the firm's output is denoted by Q, and its inputs are capital (K) and labour (L), the production function may be expressed as:

$$Q = Q(K,T)$$

This equation says that the firm's output depends on its capital and labour inputs.

Problem 9-13

Sketch a short-run total product curve and show the effect of an increase in technology on the total product curve.

Requirement and Clue: *This is a two-part problem. Address each part in order. You are expected to demonstrate familiarity with the shape of the total product curve. Focus on the effect of technology on the efficiency of inputs.*

Solution:

The graph of short-run total product curves is presented below.

We can see here that technology increases the efficiency of inputs. A given quantity of a variable factor will produce a greater quantity of output than before the technological improvement. In the above diagram, the red curve represents the initial total product curve. An increase in technology pushes the total product curve upward to the green total product curve. A further improvement in technology pushes the total product curve even further to the mauve total product curve.

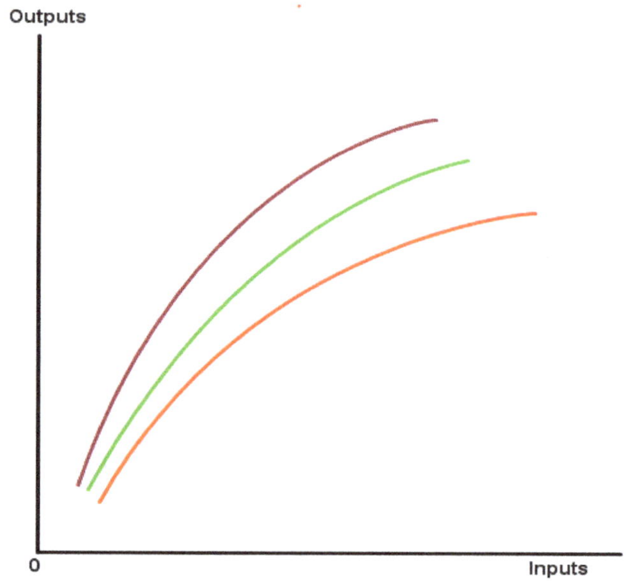

Problem 9-14

(a) Given the following short-run production schedule, complete the marginal product column.

(b) Does this production schedule depict diminishing returns?

Units of variable factor	Total product	Marginal product
0	0	-----------
1	30	-----------
2	65	-----------
3	95	-----------
4	120	-----------
5	135	

Requirement and Clue: *Recall the definition of marginal product. Remember the placement of the marginal product values. Focus on the meaning of diminishing returns and answer on the basis of the marginal* *product column.*

Solution:

Units of variable factor	Total product	Marginal product
0	0	30
1	30	35
2	65	30
3	95	25
4	120	15
5	135	

(a) The marginal product diminishes after the second unit of the variable factor is employed. Thus, the production schedule exhibits diminishing returns.

Problem 9-15

Describe the behavior of total product when marginal product is:

(a) *positive*
(b) *negative*
(c) *positive but falling*

Requirement and Clue: *The solution to this problem requires a demonstration of a thorough understanding of the relationship between marginal product and total product. Focus on what happens to total product when marginal product is as described in (a), (b), and (c) of the problem.*

Solution:

(a) When marginal product is positive, something positive is added to total product so total product increases.

(b) When marginal product is negative, something is being subtracted from total product, so total product falls

(c) When marginal product is positive but falling, total product will continue to rise but at a diminishing rate.

Problem 9-16

Describe the behavior of average product when marginal product is:

(a) *greater than average product*
(b) *equal to average product*
(c) *less than average product*
(d) *falling*

Requirement and Clue: *You are required to demonstrate that you understand the relationship between average product and marginal product. Concentrate on what happens to average product when marginal product is as described in (a), (b), and (c) of the problem.*

Solution:

(a) When marginal product is greater than average product, marginal product will pull average product up, causing it to rise.

(b) When marginal product is equal to average product, it exerts no influence on average product. Average product will be at its maximum.

(c) When marginal product is less than average product, marginal product will pull average product down, causing it to fall.

(d) When marginal product is falling, average product could be rising or falling or be at its maximum depending on its position with regard to average product. If marginal product is above average product but falling, average product will rise. If marginal product is below average product and falling, average product will fall. If marginal product is falling but is equal to average product, then average product will be maximized.

Problem 9-17

Define marginal product and average product.

Requirement and Clue: *Here you have two tasks: (1) to say what marginal product is, and (2) to say what average product is. You are not required to write a paper on marginal product and average product.*

Solution:

Marginal Product: Marginal product is the change in total product resulting from using an additional unit of the variable factor. If MP represents marginal product and TP represents total product while VF represents the quantity of the variable factor, then marginal product can be expressed symbolically as:

$$MP = \frac{\Delta TP}{\Delta VF}$$

For example, if the total product increases from 30 to 37 when an extra worker is hired, the marginal product of that extra worker is 7.

Average Product: Average product is total product divided by the number of units of the variable factor. Average product is simply then total output per unit of the variable factor. If AP represents average product and TP represents total product while VF represents the quantity of the variable factor, then average product can be expressed symbolically as:

$$AP = \frac{TP}{VF}$$

For example, if the total product is 30 when 10 workers are employed, then the average product is 30/10 = 3.

Problem 9-18

Draw a graph to show the relationship between marginal product and average product. Explain your graph.

Requirement and Clue: *This is a two-part problem. Answer each part in order. The problem is a test of your knowledge of the relationship between marginal product and average product.*

Solution:

The following graph shows the relationship between marginal product and average product.

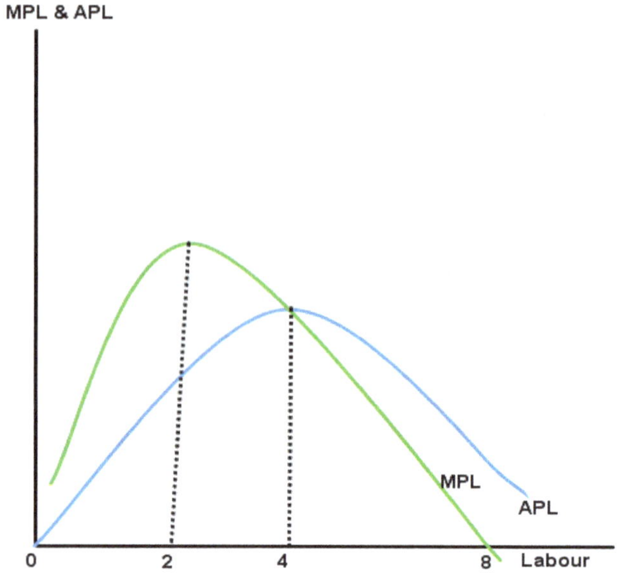

On the graph, APL and MPL are the average product of labour and the marginal product of labour respectively. The graph shows the following:

1. When marginal product is greater than average product, average product will rise. This is the case up to the employment of 4 units of the variable factor—labour in this case.
2. When marginal product is less than average product, average product will fall. This is the case after 4 units of labour are used.
3. When marginal product is equal to average product, average product is at its maximum. This is the case when 4 units of labour are employed.

Problem 9-19

State the law of diminishing returns. Is this a long-term or short-term phenomenon? Under what conditions will this law hold?

Requirement and Clue: *This is a three-part problem. Deal with each part in order. Much can be written about the law of diminishing returns, but your task is mainly to state the law. Give a reason for your answer to the second part of the problem. A careful consideration of the law should give a hint regarding the solution to the third part of the problem.*

Solution:

The law of diminishing returns states that as additional quantities of a variable factor are added to a given quantity of fixed factors, after a point the marginal product will diminish.

This is a short–term phenomenon because the law talks about fixed factors which are applicable only to the short run.

The law will hold under the following conditions:

(1) There must be at least one fixed factor

(2) The factors of production must not be perfectly substitutable

(3) Technology must remain constant.

Problem 9-20

The following table shows the marginal product of capital and the marginal product of labour at various levels of capital and labour usage for a firm. The price of capital is \$3 and the price of labour is \$5.

Level of usage of inputs	Marginal product of capital	Marginal product of labour
1	36	95
2	39	85
3	36	75
4	33	70
5	30	55
6	24	45

On the basis of this information, what is the optimum input mix for this firm?

Requirement and Clue: *You must be aware of the condition that must be satisfied for the attainment of the optimum input combination.*

Solution:

Level of usage of inputs	Marginal product of capital	Marginal product of labour	MP_K/P_K	MP_L/P_L
1	36	95	12	19
2	39	85	13	17
3	36	75	12	15
4	33	70	11	14
5	30	55	10	11
6	24	45	8	9

The optimum input mix occurs when the following condition holds:

$$\frac{MP_K}{P_K} = \frac{MP_L}{P_L}$$

Where MP_K denotes the marginal product of capital, P_K is the price of capital, MP_L is the marginal product of labour, and P_L denotes the price of labour.

By constructing the last two columns of the above table, we can more easily see when the required condition is met. The condition is met when the firm uses 4 units of capital and 5 units of labour.

Problem 9-21

Identify the error in the following statement:

"The law of diminishing returns is an important economic concept. It helps to remind us that we can increase output up to a point, in

the short run, by varying the quantity of a variable factor. Once diminishing returns become operative, then total output will, according the law of diminishing returns, begin to decline. It makes sense to use an input only if its marginal product is rising because only then will it contribute positively to total output."

Requirement and Clue: *Clearly, you must understand the law of diminishing returns. Examine the statement carefully and look for errors and carefully point them out.*

Solution:

In the quoted passage, the concept of diminishing returns is correctly identified as a short-run phenomenon. However, there is a serious misunderstanding and misapplication of the law of diminishing returns. When diminishing returns set in, total output will continue to increase as long as marginal product is positive. Marginal product will contribute positively to total product not only when marginal product is rising. If marginal product is positive, it will contribute to total product, regardless whether marginal product is rising or falling.

Problem 9-22

Describe an isoquant and list its features.

Requirement and Clue: *This is a two-part problem. Answer each part in order. You are required to state clearly what an isoquant is. A long drawn out essay is not required. Recall the features of an indifference curve; it might help you here.*

Solution:

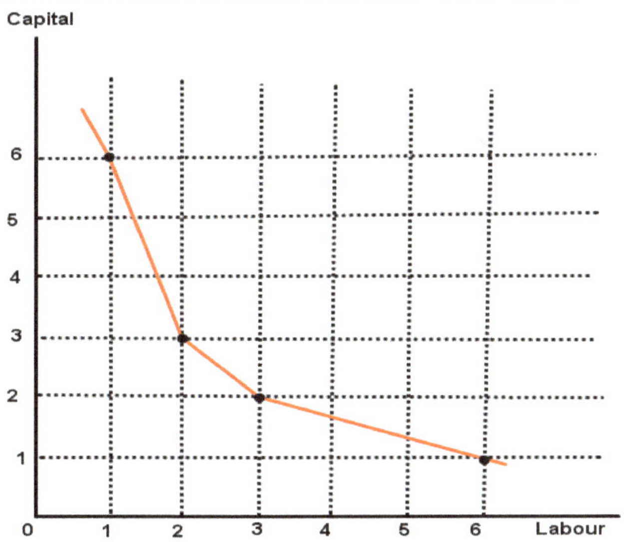

An isoquant is a graph that shows the various combinations of two inputs that yield the same level of output. The diagram above shows an isoquant. The inputs are capital (K) and labour (L).

Three units of capital and 2 units of labour produce the same level of output as 6 units of capital and 1 unit of labour.

An isoquant has the following features:

1. It slopes downward to the right
2. It is convex to the origin
3. It does not intersect another isoquant.

Problem 9-23

Define each of the following concepts without sketching:

(a) *Marginal rate of technical substitution (MRTS)*

(b) *Isoquant map*

Requirement and Clue: *Note that the problem states specifically not to sketch the concepts. You must rely solely on words. This problem is definitional. A brief statement of what each concept means is all that is required.*

Solution:

(a) The *marginal rate of technical substitution (MRTS)* is the rate at which one input can be traded off for another without changing the level of output. It is the slope of the isoquant.

(a) An *isoquant map* is a collection of isoquants, each one representing a different level of output.

Problem 9-24

What is an isocost line? What is the effect of an increase in the firm's budget on its isocost line? How does a change in the price of one of the inputs affect the isocost line?

Requirement and Clue: *This is three-part problem. Answer each part in order. Graphs can be used here to effectively support your solutions.*

Solution:

An isocost line is a line showing combinations of two inputs that can be bought for the same amount of money. Diagram 1 below shows isocost lines. The lowest isocost line shows that 4 units of capital and 1 unit of labour cost the same as 2 units of capital and 3 units of labour, i.e. $5.

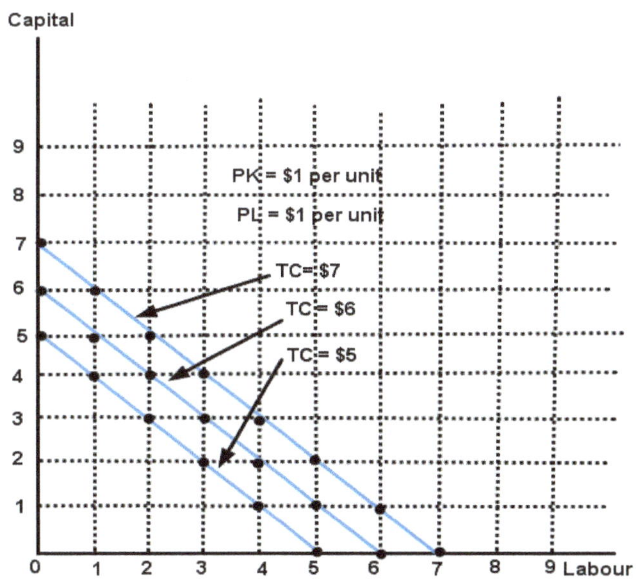

Diagram 1

An increase in the firm's budget from $5 to $6 causes the isocost line to shift to the right as shown in the diagram, but does not change its slope. A further increase in the budget to $7 shifts the isocost line even further to the right as shown. The isocost lines remain parallel.

If the price of one of the inputs changes, then the slope of the isocost line will change. Consider Diagram 2 below.

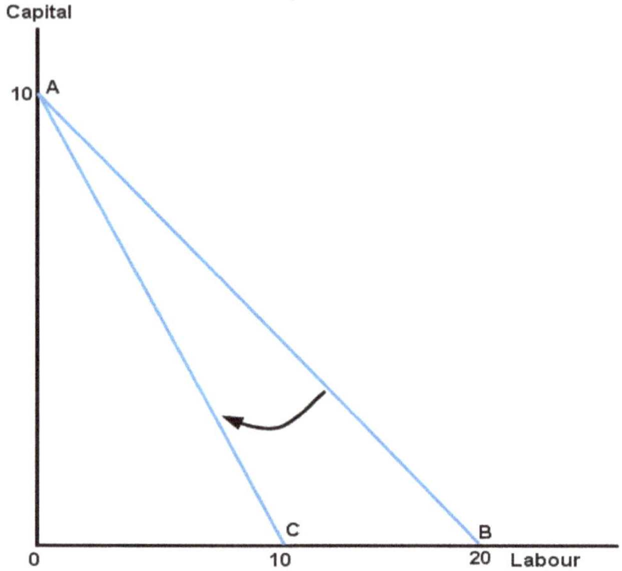

Diagram 2

The initial isocost line is isocost line AB. If the price of labour doubles, other things being equal, the firm will be able to purchase only 10 units of labour instead of the original 20. An increase in the price of labour causes the slope of the isocost line to change as shown in isocost line AC. The isocost line rotates inward from AB to AC.

Problem 9-25

The following table shows combinations of capital and labour that can be used to produce a given level of output.

Units of capital	Units of labour
1	15
2	10
3	7
4	5
5	4

On a graph, draw the isoquant.

Requirement and Clue: *It is helpful to use quad paper for a problem such as this. Plotting the data provided in the table will give the isoquant.*

Solution:

See the graph below for the isoquant.

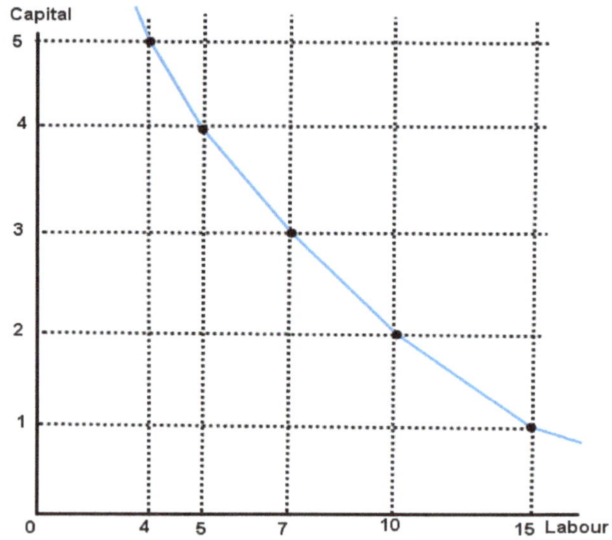

Problem 9-26

A firm uses two variable inputs, labour and capital. The price of labour is $10 per unit and the price of capital is $10 per unit. The firm has a monthly budget of $150 to purchase labour and capital.

(a) *Plot the isocost line for this firm*

(b) *The firm's monthly capital and labour budget now falls to $100. On the same graph, plot the new isocost line.*

Requirement and Clue: *Recall what an isocost line is. Remember to identify the initial and new isocost lines. Solve each part of the problem in order.*

Solution:

(a) See graph below.

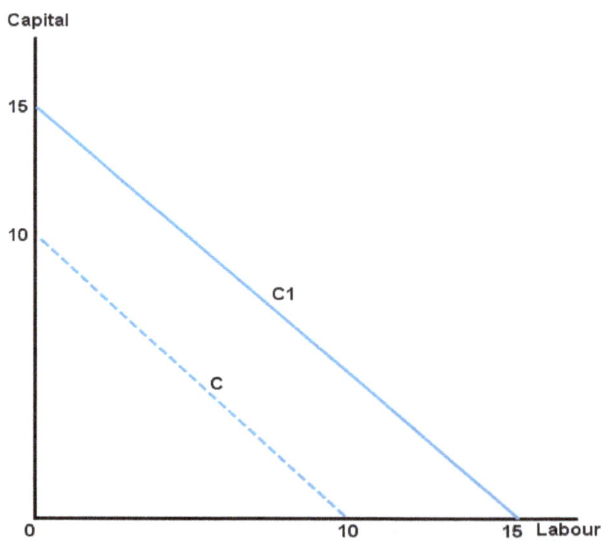

(b) See graph above. With a budget of $100, this firm can buy either 10 units of capital or 10 units of labour.

Problem 9-27

Answer the following questions based on the graph below.

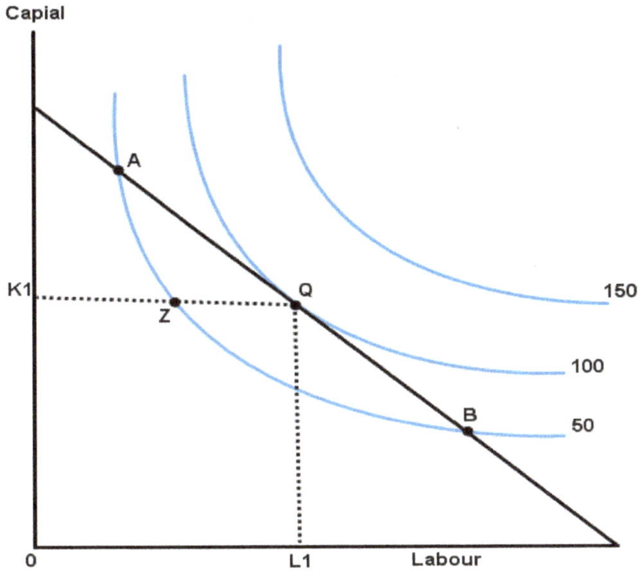

a. *Which combination of capital and labour will produce the same level of output?*

b. *What happens to the ratio of labour to capital if the firm moves from point A to point Z?*

c. *What happens to output as the firm moves from point Z to point B? From point Z to point Q?*

d. *What determines the intersection of the isocost line and the vertical axis?*

e. *What can you say about combination Q if the firm's output is 100?*

Requirement and Clue: *This is a multiple-part problem. Answer each part in order. This problem is a good test of your knowledge of isoquant/isocost analysis. Remember the properties of isoquants.*

Solution:

a. Combinations A, Z, and B are on the same isoquant so they will produce the same level of output, namely, 50.

b. If the firm moves from point A to point Z, it reduces its use of capital and increases its use of labour; therefore the ratio of labour to capital increases.

c. As the firm moves from point Z to point B, output remains the same because points Z and B are on the same isoquant. As it moves from point Z to point Q, output increases because point Q is on a higher isoquant than point Z.

d. The intersection of the isocost line and the vertical axis is determined by the firm's budget and the price of capital. Specifically, the quantity of capital that the firm can buy is determined by the budget divided by the price of capital.

e. Combination Q is the point of tangency between an isoquant and the isocost line. This represents the least-cost combination of inputs for an output of 100.

Multiple-Choice

In each case, circle the letter that corresponds with the correct answer.

1. A firm is any organization that:

a. provides goods and services to the public
b. uses resources to produce goods and services for sale at a profit
c. hires workers
d. buys inputs to produce goods and services

Answer: b

Reason: *Many organizations use resources to produce goods and services, but unless their motive is to make a profit, they are not considered to be firms.*

2. Which of the following would be considered a firm?

a. A small grocery store   c. Ford Motor Company
b. A cinema   d. All of the above

Answer: d

Reason: *Choices a, b, and c produce goods and services for sale at a profit.*

3. In economic theory, we assume that the main objective of the firm is to:

a. maximize sales   c. maximize profits
b. satisfy customers   d. all of the above

Answer: c

Reason: *Firms may pursue other objectives, but economists embrace profit maximization as the firm's primary objective.*

4. Objectives other than profit maximizations that a firm may pursue include:

a. sales maximization
b. the personal interests of managers
c. increase in market share
d. all of the above

Answer: d

Reason: *Firms may pursue the objectives listed in choices a, b, and c.*

5. Economists maintain the assumption of profit maximization because:

a. it most often leads to correct predictions about the firm's behavior
b. they cannot think of any other factor that motivates firms
c. all managers endorse the profit maximization assumption
d. a firm cannot exist unless it maximizes its profits.

Answer: a

Reason: *Using the assumption of profit maximization, economists have had great success in explaining much of the firm's behavior.*

6. The profit maximization assumption is that:

a. firms always maximized their profits

b. firms know that it is impossible to maximize profits so they do not aim at profit maximization

c. firms try to maximize their profits

d. governments regulate prices in order that firms may Maximize their profits.

Answer: c

Reason: *Economists assume that the firm's objective is to maximize its profits.*

7. A firm's profits are defined as:

a. its total cost minus is total revenue

b. its total revenue

c. receipts from sale less taxes

d. the difference between its total revenue and its total cost

Answer: d

Reason: Choice d accurately defines the firm's profits.

8. A firm receives $250,000 from selling its product. Its total cost of production is $200,000. From this we can conclude that the firm's profit is:

a. $250,000 c. $200,000

b. $ 50,000 d. none of the above

Answer: b

Reason: *Profit is total revenue minus total cost: $250,000 $200,000 = $50,000.*

9. A firm's yearly revenues amounted to $160,000. It profits were $14,500. We can conclude that the firm's yearly cost was:

a. $174,500 c. $29,000

b. $145,500 d. none of the above

Answer: b

Reason: *Total cost is total revenue minus profit.*

10. Economic efficiency exists when the firm:

a. uses many factor inputs

b. maximizes input cost

c. minimizes input cost

d. earns a profit

Answer: c

Reason: *The method that is economically most efficient is the one that has the lowest cost.*

11. A method of production is technically efficient if:

a. it uses more capital than labour

b. it uses more labour than capital

c. it uses equal amounts of capital and labour

d. none of the above

Answer: d

Reason: *A method of production is technically efficient if it uses fewer inputs than some other method.*

12. Which of the following statements is correct?

a. Product ion methods are always efficient in a technical sense

b. A production method that is technical efficient must also be economically efficient

c. A production method that is economically efficient must also be technically efficient

d. Technical efficiency depends on input prices

Answer: c

Reason: *An economically efficient method is a technically efficient that has a lower cost than some other method.*

13. If EER denotes economic efficiency ratio, then EER equals:

a. value of output divided by cost of inputs

b. value of output minus cost of inputs

c. cost of inputs minus value of output

d. none of the above

Answer: a

Reason: *Choice a accurately defines the economic efficiency ratio*

14. Economic efficiency ratios measure:

a. the profitability of a certain project

b. the degree of technical efficiency associated with a production method

c. the economic efficiency associated with a production method

d. all of the above

Answer: c

Reason: *Economic efficiency ratios are used to compare the economic efficiencies of different production methods.*

15. Fixes factors are:

a. immovable factors of production

b. inputs that are available only in limited quantities

c. resources whose quantities cannot be varied within the period under consideration

d. all of the above

Answer: c

Reason: *Quantities of fixed factors cannot be varied during the period being considered.*

16. In economics, the short run refers to:

a. a time period not exceeding one year

b. a situation in which the firm has at least one fixed factor

c. a period less than three months

d. none of the above

Answer: b

Reason: *The short run does not refer to any period of calendar time. It's a situation in which the firm is unable to vary all its inputs.*

17. In the short run, the firm has:

a. only fixed factors

b. only variable factors

c. neither fixed nor variable factors because the time is too short for either

d. both fixed and variable factors

Answer: d

Reason: *The short run is defined is a situation in which the firm cannot vary all its factors. It has at least one fixed factor.*

18. In economics, the long run refers to:

a. a situation in which the firm can vary all its inputs
b. a period of time longer than one year
c. a period of time longer than five years
d. none of the above

Answer: a

Reason: In the long run, the firm has no fixed factors.

19. Which of the following statements is correct?

a. In the short run, all factors are fixed
b. In the short run, all factors are variable
c. In the long run, both fixed and variable factors exist
d. In the short run, there are both fixed and variable factors

Answer d

Reason: *In the short run, the firm can vary some, but not all of its factors of production. It has at least one fixed factor.*

20. The production function:

a. describes the functions performed by a firm's output
b. states the various uses of a firm's output
c. describes the various uses of a firm's inputs
d. states the relationship between a firm's inputs and its output

Answer: d

Reason: *A function expresses a relationship among variables. In the case of the production function, the relationship is between the firm's inputs and its output.*

21. A production function:

a. details the types of work to be performed by all the factors of production
b. expresses an engineering relationship between inputs and output
c. concerns only fixed factors of production
d. details the lowest cost associated with producing a given level of output

Answer: b

Reason: *Choice b accurately defines a production function.*

22. If Q represents the quantity of output, L represents the quantity of labour, and K represents the quantity of capital, which of the following is a correct way of writing the production function?

a. Q = Q(L,K)   c. Q = L + K
b. Q = L × K   d. Q = QL + QK

Answer: a

Reason: *The functional relationship between output, labour and capital is written as indicated in choice a.*

23. Marginal product is:

a. the last unit produced in a production run
b. a good whose production will be discontinued because of marginal sales
c. total product divided by the quantity of the variable factor
d. the extra output produced by using one more unit of the variable factor.

Answer: d

Reason: *Marginal product is the change in the total product resulting from additional unit of the variable factor. This is captured by choice d.*

24. If total product is rising, then:

a. average product must be falling
b. average product must be at its maximum
c. marginal product must be positive
d. marginal product must be rising

Answer: c

Reason: *If marginal product is positive, it means that a positive number is added to the total. This will cause the total to rise.*

25. Total product will be at its maximum when:

a. marginal product is at its maximum
b. marginal product is zero
c. average product is zero
d. none of the above

Answer: b

Reason: *When marginal product is zero, total product will stop rising and will not fall. It will be at its maximum.*

26. If average product is rising, then:

a. average product must be greater than marginal product
b. marginal product must be positive and rising
c. marginal product must be at its maximum
d. marginal product must be greater than average product

Answer: d

Reason: *If marginal product is above average product, it will pull the average product up.*

27. The law of diminishing returns states that, as increasing quantities of a variable factor are added to a fixed factor:

a. the increase in total product will eventually diminish
b. the total product will diminish
c. the total product will never reach its maximum
d. none of the above

Answer: a

Reason: *The law states that, eventually marginal product (i.e. the increase in total product) will diminish, if increasing quantities of a variable factor are added to a fixed factor, as stated in choice a.*

28. For a firm using two variable factors of production, capital and labour, its optimum input mix occurs when:

a. labour and capital are used in equal amounts
b. the ratio of the marginal product of capital to the marginal product of labour equals the ratio of the price of capital to the price of labour
c. the prices of capital and labour begin to rise and the marginal products of capital and labour begin to fall
d. none of the above

Answer: b

Reason: *Choice b describes the cost minimization condition. That gives the optimum input mix.*

29. An isoquant shows:

a. various combinations of inputs needed to produce a given level of output
b. various combinations of output that can be produced with given inputs
c. various combinations of inputs that have the same total cost
d. the relation between price and quantity of inputs bought

Answer: a

Reason: *An isoquant shows various combinations of inputs that produce the same quantity of output as defined in choice a.*

30. Isoquants are sometimes called:

a. isoproduct curves
b. production indifference curves
c. both a and b
d. neither a nor b

Answer: c

Reason: *Isoquants are also called isoproduct curves or production indifference curves.*

31. Which of the following is true of isoquants?

a. They slope downward
b. They do not intersect
c. They are convex to the origin
d. All of the above

Answer: d

Reason: *Choices a, b, and c describe the properties of isoquants.*

32. The marginal rate of technical substitution (MRTS) is:

a. the rate at which one input can be traded off for another without changing the level of output
b. the rate at which technological advance causes new products to be introduced into the market
c. the rate at which products with limited demand are phased out of the market
d. none of the above

Answer: a

Reason: *The marginal rate of technical substitution is the slope of the isoquant. This measures the rate of trade off between two inputs while leaving the level of output unchanged.*

33. The slope of an isoquant is:

a. constant
b. positive
c. the sum of the price ratios
d. the marginal rate of technical substitution

Answer: d

Reason: *The slope of an isoquant measures the rate at which the firm can trade off one input for another while maintaining the same level of output. This is the marginal rate of technical substitution.*

34. An isoquant map:

a. provides instructions about how to locate isoquants
b. traces out the path to different input markets
c. is a collection of isoquants
d. all of the above

Answer: c

Reason: *A collection of isoquants is called an isoquant map.*

35. An isocost line shows:

a. various combinations of output that can be produced with the same amount of inputs
b. various combinations of output that would yield the same total revenue
c. various combinations of inputs that can produce a given level of output
d. none of the above

Answer: d

Reason: *An isocost line shows various combinations of inputs that cost the same amount of money.*

36. An increase in the firm's budget will:

a. shift the isoquant to the right
b. shift the isoquant to the left
c. shift the isocost line to the right
d. shift the isocost line to the left

Answer: c

Reason: *With a larger budget, the firm can buy more of both inputs as long as the input prices remain unchanged. The isocost line shifts to the right.*

37. A line showing various combinations of inputs that can be purchased for the same total cost is called:

a. a total cost curve
b. an isocost line
c. a least-cost combination set
d. none of the above

Answer: b

Reason: *Choice b accurately defines an isocost line.*

38. If the firm spends its entire budget in buyinh two inputs, it will choose an input combination that lies:

a. below the isocost line
b. on the isocost line
c. above the isocost line
d. anywhere in input space

Answer: b

Reason: *Points along the isocost line represent combinations of inputs that exhaust the budget.*

39. If two inputs, labour (L) and capital (K) are employed by a firm and their prices are P_L and P_K respectively, at the point of tangency between an isocost line and an isoquant:

a. the slopes of the two curves are equal
b. the marginal product of labour $(MP_L)/P_L = MP_K/P_K$
c. a least-cost combination of inputs is being used
d. all of the above

Answer: d

Reason: *At the point of tangency, choices a, b, and c apply.*

40. A least-cost combination of inputs means that the firm is:

a. producing a given output at the least possible cost
b. maximizing its profits
c. producing the maximum output for a given expenditure outlay
d. both a and c

Answer: d

Reason: A least-cost combination of inputs occurs where the isocost line is tangent to an isoquant. At this point, both a and c hold.

True or False

Determine whether each of the following statements is true or false.

1. The firm is an economic entity that transforms inputs into output for sale at a profit.

Answer: True

2. An example of a firm would be a government department that provides services to the public.

Answer: False

Explanation: *A government department would not be considered a firm because it does not really sell its services for profit. Citizens pay for government services collectively through taxation.*

3. Economic theory assumes that the main objective of the firm is to produce as much output as possible.

Answer: False

Explanation: *The main objective of the firm is assumed to be profit maximization.*

4. Firms might pursue objectives such as company growth, increasing market share, satisfying customers, and maximizing profits.

Answer: True

5. The profit maximizing assumption has been abandoned by economists because it leads to misleading predictions of the firm's behavior.

Answer: False

Explanation: *Economists retain the profit maximizing assumption because it enables then to predict very well the behavior of firms.*

6. The profit maximization assumption has led to successful predictions and explanations about the behavior of firms.

Answer: True

7. A technically efficient method of production is one that uses more resources than some other method.

Answer: False

Explanation: *A technically efficient method of production is one that uses fewer inputs (resources) than some other method.*

8. An economically efficient method of production is one that has a lower cost than some other method.

Answer: True

9. Any production method that is technically inefficient must also be economically inefficient.

Answer: True

10. Variables factors are those factors of production that the firm can mix in a variety of ways.

Answer: False

Explanation: *Variable factors are those inputs that the firm can vary during the period being considered.*

11. Fixed factors are those factors of production whose quantities cannot be varied during the period under consideration.

Answer: True

12. A production function expresses a relationship between the firm's inputs and its output.

Answer: True

13. In economics, the short run is a period of calendar time that is less than one year.

Answer: False

Explanation: *The short run is a situation in which the firm cannot vary all its inputs.*

14. A short-run production function has no fixed inputs.

Answer: False

Explanation: *A short-run production function has both fixed and variable inputs.*

15. In the short run, a firm has only fixed factors, and in the long run, it has only variable factors.

Answer: False

Explanation: *In the short run, a firm has both fixed and variable factors. In the long run, it has only variable factors.*

16. The production function tells the firm's managers exactly how much to spend on each input used in the production process.

Answer: False

Explanation: The production function tells about the relationship that exists between the firm's inputs and its output.

17. If 5 units of a variable factor generate 74 tons of output and 6 units of the variable factor generate 81 tons, the marginal product of the variable factor is 74 tons of output.

Answer: False

Explanation: Marginal product is the additional output produced by an extra unit of the variable factor. In this case, it is 81 - 64 = 7.

18. If marginal product is falling, total product must be declining.

Answer: False

Explanation: If marginal product is negative, total; product must be declining. Total product will rise even if marginal product is falling, provided that marginal product is positive.

19. The law of diminishing returns states that if all inputs are increased simultaneously, the firm's output will increase at a diminishing rate.

Answer: False

Explanation: The law assumes that at least one factor is held constant.

20. The point after which diminishing average productivity sets in is the point where marginal and average products are equal.

Answer: True

21. The law of diminishing returns refers to the short run where the firm has at least one fixed factor.

Answer: True

22. The law of diminishing marginal productivity is a long run concept because diminishing returns set in only after a while.

Answer: False

Explanation: The law of diminishing returns is a short run concept because it deals with a situation in which the firm has at least one fixed factor.

23. The least-cost combination of inputs is achieved when the ratio of the marginal products equals the ratio of the input prices.

Answer: True

24. In the long run, substitution of factor inputs is less difficult than in the short run.

Answer: True

25. The isoquant-isocost analysis is in many ways similar to indifference curve analysis.

Answer: True

26. Isoquants are sometimes called isoproduct curves.

Answer: True

27. An isoquant is a curve that shows various combinations of two inputs that cost the same amount of money.

Answer: False

Explanation: An isoquant is a curve that shows various combinations of inputs that produce the same level o output.

28. Unlike indifference curves, isoquants intersect because of technological changes.

Answer: False

Explanation: Like indifference curves, isoquants do not intersect.

29. The marginal rate of technical substitution is the rate at which one input can be traded off for another without changing the level of output.

Answer: True

30. The marginal rate of technical substitution is constant because it is the slope of the isocost line.

Answer: False

Explanation: The marginal rate of technical substitution (MRTS) is the slope of an isoquant.

31. An isoquant that is convex to the origin implies that the marginal rate of technical substitution diminishes.

Answer: True

32. An isoquant map enables the firm to locate markets where inputs are sold at relatively low prices.

Answer: False

Explanation: An isoquant map is a collection of isoquants.

33. An isocost line shows various combinations of inputs that can be bought for the same total cost.

Answer: True

34. The input combination that yields the maximum output is where the isocost line is tangent to an isoquant.

Answer: True

Completion
(Fill in the blanks)

Use each word or combination of words from the list exactly once.
*(**Hint**: Proceed by elimination)*

Word list

Isocost — greater — negatively — rotate — shift — Average x 2 — Convex — Cost x 2 — Fewer — Fixed x 2 — Function — Greater — Inputs — Isocost — Isoquant x 4 — Line x 2 — Long x 2 — Map — Marginal — Maximum — Output — Principle — Product x 3 — Production — Profits — Revenue — Run x 2 — Short x 3 — Substitution — Tangent — Than — Variable

Questions

1. A firm is an economic unit that buys ______________ and transforms them into ______________ for sale at a profit.
2. A firm's profits are defined as its total ______________ minus its total ______________.
3. In economic theory, we assume that the main objective of the firm is to maximize its ______________.
4. ______________ factors are those that the firm cannot vary during the time being considered. ______________ factors are those whose quantities can be changed within the time period under consideration.
5. The ______________ ______________ is a situation in which the firm cannot vary all its factor inputs. In the ______________ ______________, the firm can vary all of its factor inputs.
6. The method of production that is economically most efficient is the one that has the lowest ______________.
7. A production method is technically efficient if it uses ______________ inputs than some other method.
8. If a firm has at least one fixed factor of production, then it is operating in the ______________ run. If it can vary all its inputs, then it is in the ______________ run.
9. The ______________ ______________ defines the relationship between a firm's inputs and its output.
10. The change in total product resulting from using an additional unit of a variable factor is called the ______________ ______________.
11. ______________ ______________ is total product divided by the quantity of the variable factor.
12. If average product is rising, we know that marginal product is ______________ ______________ average product.
13. When marginal product is zero, total product is at its ______________.
14. Marginal product and average product are equal when ______________ ______________ is at its maximum.
15. The law of diminishing returns assumes that the firm has at least one ______________ factor of production. The law is therefore a ______________ run concept.
16. The tendency for a firm to substitute a cheaper factor for a more expensive factor is known as the ______________ of ______________.
17. The indifference curve in consumer theory is similar to the ______________ in production theory. The ______________ ______________ of the firm is similar to the budget line of the consumer.
18. A curve showing the various combinations of inputs that yield the same level of output is called a(n) ______________.
19. The marginal rate of technical substitution is the slope of an ______________.
20. Because the marginal rate of technical substitution diminishes, isoquants are ______________ to the origin.
21. A collection of isoquants is called a(n) ______________ ______________.
22. The higher the isoquant, the ______________ [greater, lesser] the level of output that it represents.
23. A(n) ______________ ______________ shows various combinations of inputs that can be bought for the same amount of money. It is ______________ [positively, negatively] sloped.
24. A change in the price of one of two inputs causes the isocost line to ______________ [rotate, shift]. A change in the firm's budget causes it to ______________ [rotate, shift].
25. The least-cost input combination occurs when the isocost line is ______________ to an isoquant.

Solutions

1. (inputs, output)
2. (revenue, cost)
3. (profits)
4. (Fixed, Variable)
5. (short run, long run)
6. (cost)
7. (fewer)
8. (short, long)
9. (production function)
10. (marginal product)
11. (Average product)
12. (greater than)
13. (maximum)
14. (average product)
15. (fixed, short)
16. (principle, substitution)
17. (isoquant, isocost line)
18. (isoquant)
19. (isoquant)
20. (convex)
21. (isoquant map)
22. [greater, lesser] (greater)
23. [positively, negatively] (isocost line, negatively)
24. [rotate, shift]. [rotate, shift]. (rotate, shift)
25. (tangent)

10 COST ANALYSIS

SYNOPSIS

Costs are payments for the factors of production that the firm purchases. **Explicit costs** are direct payments for factor inputs, while **implicit costs** are the indirect costs of using resources that the firm already owns.

The firm's total cost consists of **fixed costs** and **variable costs.** The relationship between the firm's short-run costs can be expressed as:

$$TC = TFC + TVC$$

In the short run, the firm has both fixed and variable costs.

Average total cost (ATC) is total cost divided by the number of units produced.

Average fixed cost (AFC) is total fixed cost divided by the number of units produced.

Average variable cost (AVC) is total variable cost divided by the number of units produced.

Marginal cost (MC) is the extra cost incurred by increasing total output by one unit.

In the long run, the firm has only variable costs. The firm's long-run average cost is the lowest cost per unit at which the firm can produce a given level of output. The firm's long-run average cost curve is sometimes called the **envelope curve.**

When the firm increases its entire scale of operation, it may experience increasing returns to scale, constant returns to scale, or diminishing returns to scale. Increasing returns to scale are associated with decreasing costs, constant returns to scale with constant costs, and decreasing returns to scale with increasing costs.

Increasing returns to scale may result from greater specialization, and the ability to take advantage of quantity discounts. Decreasing returns to scale result primarily from inefficiency in management as the scale of operation expands.

LEARNING OBJECTIVES

In connection with this module, you should be able to:

1. analyze costs in the short run.
2. describe the relations between marginal cost and marginal product, and between average variable cost and average product.
3. analyze costs in the long run.
4. explain returns to scale
5. explain economies of scope

DEFINITIONS & CONCEPTS

You should be able to define the following terms and concepts:

cost function
explicit (direct) cost
implicit (imputed) cost
total cost (TC)
total fixed cost (TFC)
total variable cost (TVC)
average fixed cost (AFC)
average variable cost (AVC)
minimum efficient scale
average total cost (ATC)
marginal cost (MC)
long-run cost
increasing returns to scale
constant returns to scale
decreasing returns to scale
economies of scale
diseconomies of scale
economies of scope

10 COST ANALYSIS

Concepts, Definitions & Problems

Problem 10-1

Define cost and cost function

Requirement and Clue: *This is a definitional problem. Remember to define a concept does not mean to write a long essay on it. You are required to state the meanings of the two concepts clearly, giving examples, if possible.*

Solution:

Cost is the value of the inputs used to produce goods and services. They include wages and salaries, rent for land and buildings, and expenditures for raw materials, fuel, transportation, electricity, and taxes.

A cost function is a mathematical expression of the relationship between the firm's cost and its output of goods and services. If C denotes cost, and Q represents the quantity of output, the cost function can be expressed as:

$$C = (Q)$$

which says that C depends on the quantity of output produced.

Problem 10-2

What is the difference between explicit costs and implicit costs?

Requirement and Clue: *Your solution should clearly state the difference between these two cost concepts. Illustrative examples will be helpful.*

Solution:

Explicit Costs : Explicit costs are direct payments made to someone outside the firm for the factors of production used in producing goods and services. Explicit costs, also known as accounting costs, include expenses such as wages and salaries, electricity bills, expenditures on supplies, interest charges on loans, etc.

Implicit Costs: In addition to the usual business money outlays that the firm incurs, it can also use resources that it already owns to produce goods and services. The costs of resources that the firm already owns are called implicit costs. They are costs that do not involve any direct monetary payments to anyone outside the firm. They are, in fact, opportunity costs.

The following example will further illustrate the difference between explicit costs and implicit costs. An accountant sets up her office in her basement from which she serves her clients. Her explicit costs may include a computer system, filing cabinet, accounting software, telephone, etc. But by using her basement as an office, she incurs another kind of cost. This cost can be estimated by using the concept of opportunity cost. In this case, the opportunity cost would be the best possible alternative use to which the accountant could put her basement. Suppose she could have rented the basement for \$350 a month. Then her implicit cost would be \$350 a month.

Problem 10-3

Do accountants and economists look at costs the same way?

Requirement and Clue: *Here you are required to discuss the accountants' and the economists' concepts of cost.*

Solution:

Economists and accountants view cost differently. To the accountant, costs are entirely explicit costs. They are direct expenditures on the firm's resources. They exclude the costs of resources that the firm already owns and uses in production. To the economist, costs are both explicit and implicit. Costs to the economist include direct money outlays to someone outside the firm for resources that the firm uses plus the cost of resources that the firm owns and uses in production. The difference between the two cost concepts can be seen by looking at the following equation:

Economic costs = Accounting costs + implicit costs

Problem 10-4

You decide to go into house painting for the summer months. You spend $50 to place an advertisement in one of the local newspapers. You use your own car to transport your tools. You spend $550 for paint, brushes, rollers, and other materials. At the end of the summer, your total receipts from your painting business amount to $2000. Did you make a profit?

Requirement and Clue: *This problem tests your understanding of economic cost. In your solution, focus on the economist's concept of cost.*

Solution:

The total revenue from my painting business is $2000. My expenses are $50 for the advertisement plus $550 for paint, brushes, etc. These add up to $600. When I take my expenses from my total revenue I am left with ($2000 - $600) = $1400. Is this all profit? I must remember I used my own car to get from one job to the next, so I must deduct something for gas, oil, wear and tear—let's say $200. This still leaves me with $1200. To determine whether or not I have made a profit, I must estimate the opportunity cost of my time. If I could have earned more than $1200 elsewhere, I have actually incurred a loss. If I could have earned only $800 elsewhere, then I have made a profit of $400.

Problem 10-5

What are sunk costs? Give an example of a sunk cost.

Requirement and Clue: *This is a two-part problem. You should answer each part in order. First give a clear statement of sunk cost; then provide an example to clarify the concept.*

Solution:

Sunk costs are costs that have already been incurred and cannot be recaptured. For decision-making purposes, they are irrelevant.

The following is an example of a sunk cost: You buy a tape recorder for $250 to tape your economics notes in class. At the end of the course, you want to sell the tape recorder. The fact that you paid $250 for it has nothing to do with whether you keep it or sell it. It is sunk cost.

Problem 10-6

Distinguish between fixed costs and variable costs.

Requirement and Clue: *Although examples are not specifically requested, they will be helpful.*

Solution:

Fixed costs are those costs that do not vary with the volume of output. The firm continues to incur fixed costs even if it closes down temporarily. For example, rent for the firm's office space has nothing to do with the quantity of goods and services produced. The rent remains the same whether the firm produces 1,000 units or zero units of output. Rent is an example of fixed cost.

Variable costs, on the other hand, are those costs that vary with the volume of output. As output increases, the firm's variable costs also increase. For example, wages increase as more workers are hired to produce a greater quantity of output. Wages are variable costs.

Problem 10-7

Under what condition will depreciation on machinery be considered (a) a fixed cost, (b) a variable cost?

Requirement and Clue: *This is a two-part problem. Answer each part in order. This problem is a test of your understanding of the concepts of fixed costs and variable costs. Focus on what distinguishes these concepts from each other.*

Solution:

Fixed costs are those costs that do not vary with the quantity of output. The firm incurs fixed costs even if it closes down temporarily. If the depreciation on machinery is not related to the quantity of output produced, but rather to time, then such depreciation is a fixed cost. This depreciation will occur whether the firm produces nothing or a lot.

(a) Variable costs are those costs that vary with the quantity of output produced. The firm incurs variable costs only when it produces some positive quantity of output. If the depreciation on machinery is attributable to the volume of output produced and not mainly to time, then depreciation is a variable cost.

Problem 10-8

What relationship exists between total cost, total fixed costs, and total variable costs?

Requirement and Clue: *Simply defining these concepts does not state the relationship that exists between them. You must state specifically how the concepts are related.*

Solution:

Total cost is the sum of all costs that the firm incurs in producing its output of goods and services. They include wages and salaries, cost of raw material, equipment cost, rent, interest payments on borrowed money, utilities, etc.

Total fixed costs are all those costs that do not vary with the quantity of goods and services that the firm produces. They may include rent, certain salaries, interest payment, insurance premiums, electricity, and other costs that are not directly associated with the volume of output produced. When these are added together the result is total fixed costs.

Total variable costs are all those costs that vary with then quantity of goods and services produced by the firm. They may include wages, bills for raw materials, electricity and fuel, and certain taxes, and other cost items directly associated with the volume of output produced by the firm. The sum of these costs is total variable costs.

The relationship that exists between total cost, total fixed cost, and total variable cost can be shown in the following equation:

$$TC = TFC + TVC$$

Where TC is total cost, TFC is total fixed costs, and TVC is total variable costs.

Problem 10-9

Define average total cost, average fixed cost, and average variable cost. How are they related?

Requirement and Clue: *Your definitions must be precise and clear. Don't forget to state specifically how the concepts are related.*

Solution:

Average total cost (ATC) is total cost divided by the quantity produced. In other words, it is total cost per unit of output. If TC denotes total cost and Q denotes the quantity produced, then

$$ATC = TC/Q$$

Average fixed cost (AFC) is total fixed cost (TFC) divided by the quantity produced (Q). It is total fixed cost per unit of output. Symbolically,

$$AFC = TFC/Q$$

Average variable cost (AVC) is total variable cost (TVC) divided by the quantity produced (Q). It is total variable cost per unit of output. Symbolically,

$$AVC = TVC/Q$$

These cost concepts are related as shown by the following equation:

$$ATC = AFC + AVC$$

Problem 10-10

Define marginal cost.

Requirement and Clue: *This is a definitional problem. Be careful not to write a dissertation on marginal cost. It is not required. Give a clear meaning of the concept and clarify with an example.*

Solution:

Marginal cost (MC) is the extra cost incurred by increasing output by one additional unit. If TC denotes total cost and Q denotes the quantity of output, then marginal cost (MC) can be expressed as follows:

$$MC = \frac{\Delta TC}{\Delta Q}$$

For example, if the total cost of producing 8 units of output is \$200, and the total cost of producing 9 units is \$230, then the marginal cost of increasing output to 9 units (that is, the extra cost of producing one more unit—the 9th unit) is (\$230 - \$200) = \$30.

Problem 10-11

The following table shows total fixed cost and total cot schedules. From the data given in the table, construct the total variable cost at each level of output.

Quantity	Total fixed cost	Total cost
1	\$1,000	\$1,500
2	1,000	1,950
3	1,000	2,350
4	1,000	2,700
5	1,000	3,000
6	1,000	3,300
7	1,000	3,650
8	1,000	4,000
9	1,000	4,400
10	1,000	4,900

Requirement and Clue: *This problem requires you to know the relationship between total fixed cost, total cost, and total variable cost. Once you have this information, use it to construct the required total variable cost schedule.*

Solution:

The total cost consists of total fixed costs and total variable costs. The table provides data on total cost and total fixed cost at each level of output. Total variable cost is total cost minus total fixed cost. Thus, for output level 1, total variable cost is \$1,500 - \$1,000 = \$500. Total variable cost can be determined in the same way for each level of output. The information is contained in the total variable cost column of the following table.

Quantity	Total cost($)	Total fixed cost($)	Total variable cost ($)
1	1500	1000	500
2	1950	1000	950
3	2350	1000	1350
4	2700	1000	1700
5	3000	1000	2000
6	3300	1000	2300
7	3650	1000	2650
8	4000	1000	3000
9	4400	1000	3400
10	4900	1000	3900

Problem 10-12

With an output level of 10,000, the average fixed cost is $0.5. If production is expanded to an output level of 12,500, what would be the average fixed cost?

Requirement and Clue: *The solution requires a bit of elementary mathematics and knowledge of the relationship between total fixed cost and average fixed cost.*

Solution:

From the problem, we know that at an output level of 10,000, the average fixed cost is $0.5. The total fixed cost is therefore $(10,000 × 0.5) = $5,000. This total fixed cost remains the same at each level of output. Therefore at an output level of 12,500 and fixed cost of $5,000, the average fixed cost is total fixed cost divided by quantity.

Average fixed cost = $5,000/12,500 = $0.4

Problem 10-13

Briefly describe the shape of each of the following cost curves and sketch them on a graph. Assume that the curves are linear.

(a) *The total fixed cost (TFC) curve*

(b) *The total variable cost (TVC) curve*

(c) *The total cost (TC) curve*

Requirement and Clue: *Do not confuse this problem with a definitional problem. Your task here is not to define the concepts but to state briefly what the curves look like. Describe the shape of each curve in order. You are required to draw the three curves on a graph.*

Solution:

The total fixed cost (TFC) curve is a horizontal straight line, indicating that total fixed cost does not vary with the volume of output.

The total variable cost (TVC) curve starts at the origin and rises continuously as output increases.

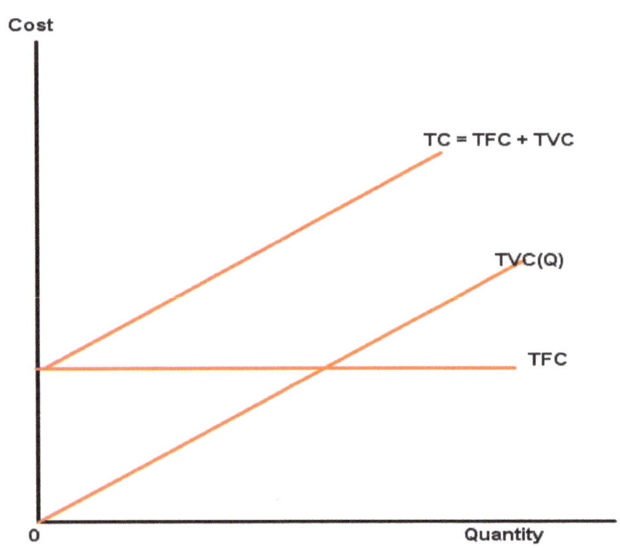

Since the total cost (TC) curve is obtained by adding the TFC and TVC curves, and since the TFC curve is horizontal, then the TC curve will have the same shape at the TVC curve (the two curves will be parallel), and the distance between them will be the total fixed cost.

The diagram above shows the TFC, TVC, and TC curves.

Problem 10-14

On the basis of the information contained in the following table, compute each of the following:

(a) *Marginal cost*

(b) *Total variable cost*

(c) *Average total cost*

(d) *Average variable cost*

Output	Total cost
0	90
1	95
2	100
3	105
4	110
5	115
6	126
7	146
8	186

Requirement and Clue: *In order to solve this problem, you must be familiar with the various concepts mentioned in the problem. It's a good idea to indicate how each concept is calculated and to construct marginal cost, total variable cost, average total cost, and average variable cost columns.*

Solution:

(a) Marginal cost is the change in total cost divided by the change in quantity. The third column in the table below shows marginal cost. For example, for a change in output from zero to 1, total cost changes from 90 to 95; hence the marginal cost is 5.

Output	Total cost	Marginal cost
0	90	5
1	95	5
2	100	5
3	105	5
4	110	5
5	115	11
6	126	20
7	146	40
8	186	

(b) Total variable cost (TVC) is TC – TFC. But when output is zero, total cost is 90, hence total fixed cost (TFC) is 90, hence total variable cost is 0. When output is 4, for example, total cost is 110, total fixed cost is 90, hence total variable cost is 110-90 = 20. Total variable cost is calculated in column 4 of the following table.

Output	Total cost	TFC	TVC	ATC	AVC	MC
(1)	(2)	(3)	(4)	(5)	(6)	(7)
0	90	90	0	---	---	5
1	95	90	5	95	5	5
2	100	90	10	50	5	5
3	105	90	15	35	5	5
4	110	90	20	27.5	5	5
5	115	90	25	23	5	11
6	126	90	36	21	6	20
7	146	90	56	20.85	8	40
8	186	90	96	23.25	12	

(c) Average total cost (ATC) is total cost (TC) divided by quantity. Total cost is 100 for 2 units of output. The ATC then would be 100 ÷ 2 = 50. ATC at zero output is not defined because division by zero is undefined. Average total cost is contained in column 5 in the table above.

(d) Average variable cost (AVC) is TVC/Q. At an output of 5, TVC is 25, therefore AVC would be 25 ÷ 5 = 5. AVC is contained in column 6 in the table above.

Problem 10-15

What can you say about average variable cost (AVC) when:

(a) *marginal cost (MC) is less than AVC?*

(b) *marginal cost (MC) is greater than AVC?*

(c) *marginal cost (MC) equals AVC?*

Requirement and Clue: *This problem is a test of your understanding of the relationship between marginal cost and average variable cost. State precisely what happens to AVC in each of the situations listed in the problem.*

Solution:

(a) When marginal cost is less than average variable cost, marginal cost will pull the average variable cost down. Thus average variable cost will fall.

(b) When marginal cost is greater than average variable cost, average variable cost will rise because the marginal cost will pull the average variable cost up.

(c) When marginal cost equals average variable cost, average variable cost will neither rise nor fall; it will be at its minimum.

Problem 10-16

What can you say about average total cost (ATC) when:

(a) *marginal cost (MC) is less than ATC?*

(b) *marginal cost (MC) is greater than ATC?*

(c) *marginal cost (MC) equals ATC?*

Requirement and Clue: *This problem is a test of your understanding of the relationship between marginal cost and average total cost. State precisely what happens to ATC in each of the situations listed in the problem.*

Solution:

(a) When marginal cost (MC) is less than average total cost (ATC), average total cost will fall because MC will pull ATC down.

(b) When marginal cost (MC) is greater than average total cost (ATC), average total cost will rise because MC will pull ATC up.

(c) When marginal cost (MC) equals average total cost (ATC), average total cost will be at its minimum. It will neither rise nor fall.

Problem 10-17

Why does the average fixed cost curve decline continuously while the average variable cost curve is u-shaped?

Requirement and Clue: *Think of the theory behind these curves. Focus on how average fixed cost is derived. For a curve to be u-shaped, it must fall first and eventually rise. Explain why average variable cost might fall and why it might rise.*

Solution:

Average fixed cost (AFC) is total fixed cost (TFC) divided by quantity produced (Q).

AFC = TFC/Q

Total fixed cost remains constant as quantity increases. The numerator (TFC) is fixed while the denominator (Q) increases. That means TFC/Q gets increasingly smaller.

The average fixed cost curve declines continuously because as output expands, the fixed cost is spread over more and more units of output. The following table illustrates the point.

Quantity	Total fixed cost ($)	Average fixed cost
1	100	100/1 = 100
2	100	100/2 = 50
3	100	100/3 = 33.3
4	100	100/4 = 25

The average variable cost (AVC) curve slopes downward initially for this reason: The total product curve increases rapidly at first because of increasing marginal productivity. Under conditions of increasing marginal productivity, increasingly fewer variable inputs are needed to increase output by an additional unit. This implies decreasing average variable cost and hence a downward-sloping average variable cost initially. Diminishing marginal returns eventually set in. This implies that increasingly larger quantities of inputs are required for additional unit increases in output. Consequently, average variable cost rises, so the AVC curve slopes upward. Thus, the average variable cost curve initially slopes downward then eventually slopes upward, making it u-shaped.

Problem 10-18

Complete each of the following statements.

(a) *When marginal product rises, marginal cost _______.*

(b) *When marginal product falls, marginal cost ________.*

(c) *When marginal product is at its maximum, marginal cost is at its ________.*

(d) *When average product rises, average variable cost ________.*

(e) *When average product falls, average variable cost ________.*

(f) *When average product is at its maximum, average variable cost is at its________.*

Requirement and Clue: *This problem is a test of your understanding of the relations between marginal cost and marginal product, and between average variable cost and average product. Focus on these relations.*

Solution:

(a) When marginal product rises, marginal cost *falls*.

(b) When marginal product falls, marginal cost *rises*.

(c) When marginal product is at its maximum, marginal cost is at its *minimum*.

(d) When average product rises, average variable cost *falls*.

(e) When average product falls, average variable cost *rises*.

(f) When average product is at its maximum, average variable cost is at its *minimum*.

Problem 10-19

Why could the following diagram not depict average fixed cost?

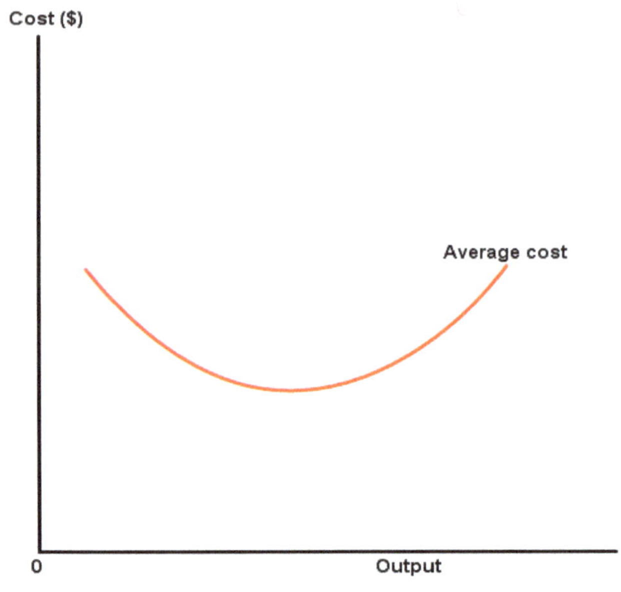

Requirement and Clue: *Think of the shape of the average fixed cost curve and the reason for its shape. Focus on the unique feature of average fixed cost.*

Solution:

Average fixed cost (AFC) is total fixed cost (TFC) divided by the quantity produced. In other words, average fixed cost is total fixed cost per unit of output. As the quantity of output increases, the total fixed cost, which is constant, is divided among increasingly larger quantities of output, thus total cost per unit of output decreases continuously. This can be seen more clearly as:

AFC = TFC/Q, so as quantity increases 1,2,3,4,5... AFC = TFC/1, TFC/2, TFC/3, TFC/4, etc.

Hence AFC gets smaller and smaller. It has no minimum as the diagram suggests, and it never rises. Average fixed cost can never be depicted by the diagram presented.

Problem 10-20

Indicate what is wrong (if anything) with the set of statements about short-run cost curves:

(a) *At low levels of output, the average variable cost (AVC) curve and the average total cost (ATC) curve are relatively close, but as output increases, the two curves get further and further apart.*

(b) *The minimum points of the ATC and AVC curves occur at the same level of output.*

(c) *The marginal cost (MC) curve passes through the minimum points of the ATC and the average fixed cost (AFC) curves, but it cuts the AVC curve while the AVC curve is yet falling.*

Requirement and Clue: *You are required to examine the statements regarding the relationships between cost and quantity and to point out any inaccuracies.*

Solution:

The following list indicates what is wrong with the diagram presented.

(a) The vertical distance between average variable cost (AVC) and average total cost (ATC) is average fixed cost (AFC). Since AFC declines as output expands, the ATC and AVC curves should get closer and closer together as quantity increases.

(b) The minimum point of the AVC curve is supposed to occur at a lower output than that of the ATC curve. The statement is contrary to this fact.

(c) The marginal cost (MC) curve is supposed to pass through the minimum points of the AVC and ATC curves. Therefore, it does not cut the AVC curve while it is falling. The MC curve cannot pass through the minimum point of the AFC curve because the AFC curve has no minimum point. It declines continuously.

Problem 10-21

It is given that TC = TFC + TVC. Use this information to prove that ATC = AFC + AVC.

Requirement and Clue: *Focus on the relationship between total and average.*

Solution:

If all the elements of the total cost equation are divided by quantity (Q), we obtain:

$$\frac{TC}{Q} = \frac{TFC}{Q} + \frac{TVC}{Q}$$

But by definition, TC/Q = ATC, TFC/Q = AFC, and TVC/Q = AVC

Therefore, ATC = AFC + AVC

Problem 10-22

Why is it necessary to analyse costs in the long run?

Requirement and Clue: *Think of the definition of the long run and consider the firm in that situation. Remember you are to justify analysing costs in the long run.*

Solution:

Long-run cost analysis is necessary because in the long run, the firm is in a different situation from in the short run. The environment within which it makes its decisions is not the same as in the short run. In the long-run situation, the firm has no fixed factors of production and, hence, no fixed costs. In the long run, the firm can make any adjustment to the size of its plant and to its scale of operation that it deems necessary.

Problem 10-23

Carefully explain how the firm chooses the size of its plant in the long run.

Requirement and Clue: *Focus on the fact that the firm will try to produce any given output level at minimum average cost. The word "carefully" in the problem suggests that details are required in your solution.*

Solution:

For simplicity, let us assume that the firm has a choice of four plants of different sizes: Plant *a* is the smallest of the four plants; plant *b* is larger than plant *a* but smaller than plant *c*. Plant *d* is the largest of the four plants. The following diagram will help with the explanation.

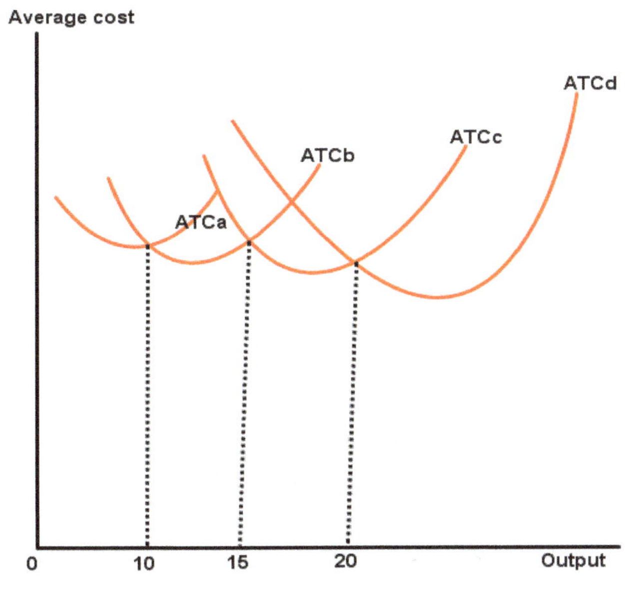

The diagram shows the short-run average total cost (ATC) curves for the four plants and allows us to compare the average cost of producing any given level of output in each of the four plants.

ATCa is the short-run average cost for plant *a*, ATCb is the short-run average cost curve for plant *b*, ATCc is the short-run average cost curve for plant *c*, and ATCd is the short-run average cost curve for plant *d*. If the firm contemplates a level of output less than 10 units, it will choose plant *a*. This is so because plant *a* has the lowest average cost at that output level. If the firm contemplates an output level between 10 and 15 units, it will choose plant *b*. For an output level between 15 and 20 units, the firm will choose plant *c*. For any level of output beyond 20, the firm will choose plant *d* which evidently has the lowest cost at that level of output. It can be concluded then, that for any desired level of output, the firm will choose the plant size for which the average cost is lowest.

Problem 10-24

Define long-run average cost, and describe the shape of the long-run average cost (LRAC) curve.

Requirement and Clue: *This is a two-part problem. Address each part in order. Remember that a definition is not an essay. Just state the meaning of the concept. Be careful to be exact in your description of the shape of the LRAC curve.*

Solution:

The long-run average cost (LRAC) is the minimum cost per unit at which a firm can produce each level of output when its inputs are all variable.

The long-run average cost (LRAC) curve declines initially, reaches a minimum, and then rises eventually. It is u-shaped. The following diagram illustrates a long-run average cost curve.

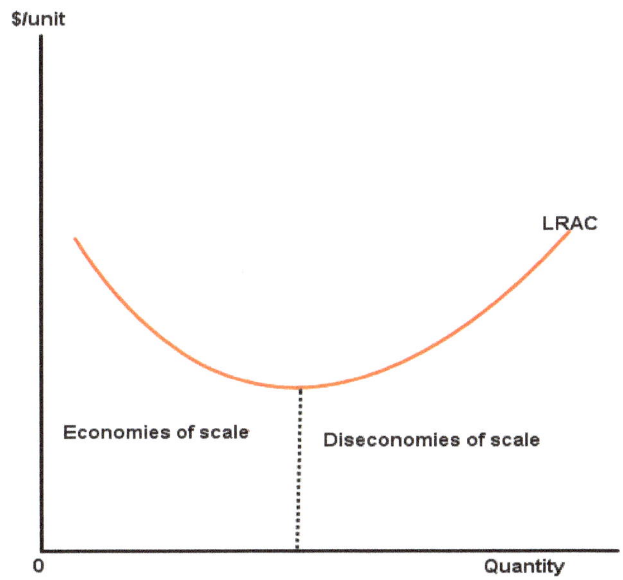

Problem 10-25

"Long-run cost analysis is unnecessary if we really understand short-run cost analysis." Discuss briefly.

Requirement and Clue: *The discussion should center on whether or not you agree with the statement in the problem and giving a reason for your decision.*

Solution:

Both short-run and long-run cost analyses are necessary in order to understand the behaviour of the firm. The fact is, the firm makes decisions when it has at least one fixed factor and also when all its factors can be varied. For example, without long-run cost analysis, how can the firm decide on its choice of plant size or on adjustments to its scale of operation? Short-run and long-run cost analyses are both necessary.

Problem 10-26

Define the concept of returns to scale.

Requirement and Clue: *This is a definitional problem. A clear statement of the meaning o the concept is all that is required.*

Solution:

Returns to scale describe how the firm's total output responds to changes in all the firm's inputs, that is, to its scale of operation.

Problem 10-27

What is the difference between diminishing returns and diminishing returns to scale?

Requirement and Clue: *This problem is a test of your understanding of the two concepts. The solution requires that you focus on the difference between them.*

Solution:

Diminishing returns refer to returns to a factor input when at least one factor of production is fixed. When at least one factor of production is fixed and increasing quantities of a variable factor are added to that fixed factor, after a while, the marginal product will diminish. That is the phenomenon of diminishing returns. Since at least one fixed factor exists, the concept refers to the short run.

Diminishing returns to scale, on the other hand, refer to the condition that exists when a firm increases all its inputs by a certain proportion and, as a result, its output increases by a smaller proportion. Since diminishing returns to scale concern a situation in which there are no fixed factors, it is a long-run concept.

Problem 10-28

What reasons can you give for the existence of increasing returns to scale?

Requirement and Clue: *You must demonstrate that you are familiar with the concept of increasing returns to scale. Two or three reasons should suffice.*

Solution:

Increasing returns to scale occur when a firm increases all its inputs by a certain proportion and, consequently, its output increases by a greater proportion. Under increasing returns to scale, if the firm doubles all its inputs, its output will more than double.

Increasing returns to scale may occur because of <u>specialization.</u> A large-scale operation has more opportunities to take advantage of specialization which will tend to increase total output.

Increasing returns to scale may also result from <u>quantity discounts</u> that may be given because the firm may be able to order large quantities of inputs. Larger firms might be able to qualify for quantity discounts for which smaller orders may not qualify.

Finally, increasing returns may result from <u>capacity</u> related to dimensions. Suppose that a wooden storage room for a certain raw material has dimensions of 3m by 3m by 3 m which gives a storage capacity of 27 cu. m. Doubling the dimensions of the room to 6 m by 6 m by 6 m may double the building materials used, and thus the cost, but it will more than double the capacity. The capacity will increase from 27 cu. m. to 216 (6 x 6 x 6). Under these circumstances, the percentage increase in raw materials would be less than the percentage increase in the volume (storage capacity) of the room.

Problem 10-29

Define decreasing returns to scale. Why do decreasing returns to scale occur?

Requirement and Clue: *This is a two-part problem: a definitional part and an explanation part. You should state clearly the meaning of decreasing returns to scale. Focus on any reason that might cause output to increase by less than a proportional increase in all inputs.*

Solution:

Decreasing returns to scale refer to the condition that exits when an increase in all the firm's inputs results in a less-than-proportional increase in its output. Thus, under decreasing returns to scale, if the firm increases its inputs by 50%, its output will increase by less than 50%.

The main reason for decreasing returns to scale is inefficiency in management. As the size of the operation grows, management becomes increasingly complex and the decision-making process becomes bogged down with red tape.

Problem 10-30

What are economies of scope? How does the concept differ from economies of scale? What phenomenon do economies of scope help to explain?

Requirement and Clue: *This is a three-part problem. Make sure you* *answer each part in order. You are required to demonstrate a thorough understanding of the concepts. The definition of economies of scope should point to the phenomenon that it explains.*

Solution:

Economies of scope define the situation that exists when the costs of producing different goods together are less than they would be if the goods were produced separately.

This concept differs from economies of scale which describe a situation in which the firm's long-run average cost falls as output expands when all the firm's inputs increase.

Economies of scope help to explain why we find certain firms producing several different but closely related products at the same time. Because of economies of scope, it should not be surprising to find the same firm producing refrigerators, washers, dryers, air-conditioning units, dishwashers, ovens, and even vacuum cleaners.

Problem 10-31

Sony produces TV sets, telephone systems, cameras, DVD and Blu-ray players, laptop and desktop computers, security systems, projectors, sound (entertainment) systems, eReaders, clock radios, etc. What economic concept can explain Sony's product offering?

Requirement and Clue: *Focus on an economic concept that allows a firm to produce different products together at a lower cost than otherwise.*

Solution:

Sony's product offering is truly extensive. However, the products listed in the problem are all related to electronics. Sony's history might have some impact on its product offering, but it is certain that economies of scope can likely fully explain Sony's product offering.

Multiple-Choice

In each case, circle the letter that corresponds with the correct answer.

1. Cost, in economics, refers to:

a. any money outlays for inputs
b. payment for goods and services bought by consumers
c. direct or indirect payments for inputs used in production
d. all of the above

Answer: c

Reason: *Economic cost includes expenditures on inputs as well as the cost of resources already owned by the firm.*

2. Which of the following would be included in economic cost?

a. Wages and salaries
b. Cost of raw materials
c. Opportunity cost of office space owned and used by the firm
d. All of the above

Answer: d

Reason: *Economic cost includes the items listed in choices a, b, and c.*

3. A cost function expresses a relationship between:

a. price and the firm's inputs
b. price and the firm's output of goods and services
c. the firm's inputs and its output
d. the firm's cost and its output of goods and services

Answer: d

Reason: *Choice d accurately defines the cost function.*

4. A firm's cost function states the relationship between:

a. inputs and output
b. price and cost
c. cost and output
d. none of the above

Answer: c

Reason: *The cost function expresses a relationship between the firm's cost and its output.*

5. Which of the following is a correct way of writing the cost function where C represents cost and Q represents quantity of output?

a. Q = Q(C) c. Q = Q × C
b. C = C(Q) d. None of the above

Answer: b

Reason: *Choice b says that cost is a function of quantity—an expression of the cost function.*

6. An implicit cost is:

a. the cost of any input used by the firm

b. any cost that can never be estimated
c. the difference between fixed cost and variable cost
d. none of the above

Answer: d

Reason: An implicit cost is a cost of an input owned and used by a firm in production, and therefore does not result in any payment to anyone outside the firm.

7. Costs incurred by using factors of production already owned by the firm are called:

a. uncollectible costs c. implicit costs
b. explicit costs d. marginal costs

Answer: c

Reason: Implicit costs do not result in any direct payment to anyone outside the firm because the firm already owns the resources.

8. Implicit costs are:

a. identical to economic costs
b. the value of productive factors owned and used by the firm
c. identical to sunk costs
d. irrelevant because they do not have to be paid for

Answer: b

Reason: Implicit costs do not involve payment to anyone outside the firm because the firm already owns the resources.

9. Implicit costs are valued at:

a. the expenditures that must be made to acquire the resources
b. the same cost as sunk costs
c. what the resources would earn in their next best use
d. none of the above

Answer: c

Reason: Implicit costs are valued at their opportunity cost.

10. Which of the following is correct?

a. Economic costs = Accounting costs + Implicit costs
b. Accounting costs = Implicit costs + Economic costs
c. Accounting costs = All opportunity costs
d. None of the above

Answer: a

Reason: Economic costs include both implicit costs and explicit (accounting) costs.

11. Which of the following is most likely to be a fixed cost?

a. Wages paid to unskilled workers
b. Payment for raw materials
c. Property taxes
d. None of the above

Answer: c

Reason: Property taxes are unlikely to be related to the firm's output of goods and services.

12. Fixed costs occur because:

a. some inputs are fixed in the short run
b. some inputs are fixed in the long run
c. all inputs are fixed in the short run
d. output is often fixed

Answer: a

Reason: Fixed costs are those costs that do not vary with output. Such costs are associated with the firm's fixed factors of production.

13. If the firm closes down temporarily, its fixed costs will be:

a. positive c. zero
b. negative d. indeterminate

Answer: a

Reason: Fixed costs do not vary with the firm's output, so even it it closes down temporarily, it will continue to incur its fixed costs.

14. Which of the following declines continuously?

a. Average fixed cost (AFC)
b. Marginal cost (MC)
c. Average total cost (ATC)
d. All of the above

Answer: a

Reason: Average fixed cost declines continuously because the fixed cost is spread over increasingly greater quantities.

15. Marginal cost is:

a. total cost divided by the number of units produced
b. the extra cost of producing an additional unit of output
c. the average cost of the last unit produced
d. fixed cost divided by the quantity produced

Answer: b

Reason: Choice b accurately defines marginal cost.

16. If Q is quantity produced, TC is total cost, AVC is average variable cost, TVC is total variable cost, then marginal cost (MC) can be expressed as:

a. MC = TC – TVC c. MC = AVC/Q
b. MC = TVC/Q d. MC = ΔTC/ΔQ

Answer: d

Reason: Marginal cost can be computed by the formula given in choice d.

17. If average variable cost (AVC) is $10 when a firm produces 20 units of output, and $11 when it produces 21 units of output, then we know that the marginal cost (MC) for that output range is:

a. $1 c. $31
b. $11 d. none of the above

Answer: c

Reason: Total variable cost for an output of 20 units is ($10 × 20) = $200. Total variable cost for 21 units is ($11 × 21) = $231. Therefore MC = $231 – $200 = $31.

18. The difference between Total cost (TC) and total fixed cost (TFC) is:

a. average fixed cost (AFC)
b. marginal cost (MC)
c. average variable cost (AVC)
d. total variable cost (TVC)

Answer: d

Reason: *TC – TFC = TVC*

19. Average fixed costs (AFC) can be shown on a diagram as the vertical distance between:

a. the total variable cost (TVC) and the total cost (TC) curves
b. the average total cost (ATC) and the average variable cost (AVC) curves
c. the marginal cost (MC) and the total fixed cost (TFC) curves
d. none of the above

Answer: b

Reason: *AFC = ATC – AVC.*

20. When average total cost (ATC) has reached its minimum, we know that:

a. average total cost (ATC) = Total fixed cost (TFC)
b. marginal cost (MC) = average variable cost (AVC)
c. ATC = MC
d. none of the above

Answer: c

Reason: The marginal cost curve passes through the minimum point of the average total cost curve.

21. If we know total variable cost (TVC) and total fixed cost (TFC) for various levels of output, then we can determine:

a. marginal cost (MC)
b. average fixed cost (AFC)
c. average total cost (ATC)
d. all of the above

Answer: d

Reason: Marginal cost (MC) can be obtained by subtracting the total variable cost (TVC) for the 9th unit, for example, from the TVC for the 10th unit. Average fixed cost (AFC) can be obtained by dividing TFC by quantity, and ATC can be obtained by adding TVC and TFC to obtain total cost (TC) and then dividing TC by quantity.

22. The total cost (TC) of producing 10 units of a product is \$120, and the marginal cost (MC) of the 11th unit is \$34. Thus:

a. average total cost (ATC) of 11 units is \$14
b. total fixed cost (TFC) is \$86
c. ATC of 11 units is \$34
d. We cannot determine ATC from the information given.

Answer: a

Reason: The total cost (TC) of 11 units is \$120 + \$34 = \$154. ATC = TC/Q = \$154 ÷ 11 = \$14

23. If average total cost (ATC) is falling, then:

a. average fixed cost (AFC) must be negative
b. marginal cost (MC) is less than ATC
c. MC > ATC
d. MC must be falling

Answer: b

Reason: When MC is less than ATC, it will pull ATC down.

24. Which of the following is correct?

a. The marginal cost (MC) curve cuts the average total cost (ATC) curve and the average variable cost (AVC) at the same level of output
b. The MC curve always lies above the AVC curve
c. If MC is falling, then the average total cost (ATC) must also be falling
d. The MC curve cuts the ATC curve and the AVC curve at their minimum points

Answer: d

Reason: When the marginal is below the ATC or AVC, it pulls the ATC or AVC down. When marginal is above the ATC or AVC, it pulls the ATC or AVC up. Therefore when the average and the marginal are equal, the average is at its minimum.

25. If marginal cost (MC) is above average total cost (ATC), then:

a. average fixed cost (AFC) will rise
b. average variable cost (AVC) is declining
c. ATC will rise
d. ATC is falling.

Answer: c

Reason: If MC > ATC, MC will pull ATC up.

26. The long run is:

a. a period of time longer than five years
b. a period of time in excess of 10 years
c. a situation in which the firm can vary all its inputs
d. all of the above

Answer: c

Reason: Choice c correctly defines the long run.

27. In the long run:

a. all costs are fixed
b. all costs are variable
c. some costs are fixed while some are variable
d. the firm can operate only at minimum cost

Answer: b

Reason: In the long run, the firm can vary all its inputs. Since all inputs are variable, all costs are variable.

28. The long-run average cost (LRAC) curve represents:

a. the sum of all the firm's short-run cost curves
b. the firm's cost structure for any period in excess of one year
c. the lowest unit cost at which the firm can produce its output when all factors are variable
d. all of the above

Answer: c

Reason: Choice c accurately defines the long-run average cost.

29. A firm is experiencing increasing returns to scale if:

a. output more than doubles when all inputs are doubled
b. long-run average cost (LRAC) increases as the firm expands its scale of operation
c. cost is proportional to output
d. none of the above

Answer: a

Reason: increasing returns to scale exist when a firm increases all its inputs by a certain proportion and, as a result, its output increases by a greater proportion.

30. If the firm's long-run average cost (LRAC) curve is upward sloping, the firm is experiencing:

a. economies of scale
b. constant returns to scale
c. diseconomies of scale
d. none of the above

Answer: c

Reason: When the long-run average cost curve has a positive slope, the firm is experiencing decreasing returns to scale or diseconomies of scale.

31. Decreasing returns to scale can result from:

a. greater specialization of labour and capital
b. large quantity input purchases resulting in quantity discounts
c. the greater efficiency of larger plants
d. inefficiency in management as the operation expands

Answer: d

Reason: Returns to scale can decrease because as the operation expands, managerial decision-making can become bogged down in red bureaucracy.

32. The minimum efficient scale for a firm occurs:

a. at the point where average cost begins to decline
b. when the average fixed cost (AFC) curve begins to rise
c. when marginal cost (MC) is at its minimum
d. none of the above

Answer: d

Reason: The minimum efficient scale occurs where the long-run average cost is at its minimum.

33. The long-run average cost (LRAC) curve is U-shaped because of:

a. the existence of fixed cost
b. the effect of the law of diminishing marginal returns
c. the effect of the declining average fixed cost (AFC) curve
d. increasing, constant, ad decreasing returns to scale.

Answer: d

Reason: The LRAC curve declines first because of increasing returns to scale, then it remains constant, because of constant returns to scale, and then rises because of decreasing returns to scale. This causes it to be U-shaped.

34. Economies of scope exist when:

a. the production of complementary products together rather than separately reduces cost
b. the firm pursues a narrow rather than a broad scope
c. the firm decides to take advantage of the opportunity to produce goods separately rather than together
d. none of the above

Answer: a

Reason: Choice a accurately defines economies of scope.

True or False

Determine whether each of the following statements is true or false.

1. In economics, cost refers only to directly money outlays for resources used in producing goods and services

Answer: False

Explanation: Cost includes direct money outlays as well as the opportunity cost of resources that the firm already owns.

2. The relation between the firm's cost of production and its volume of output is called a cost function.

Answer: True

3. If C = cost and Q = quantity of output produced, then the cost function can be written as C × Q.

Answer: False

Explanation: The cot function can be written as C = C(Q), which means that cost varies with the quantity of output produced.

4. Direct payments to groups outside the firm for inputs are called imputed costs.

Answer: False

Explanation: Imputed costs are costs of resources that the firm owns and uses in production.

5. Implicit costs are also called accounting costs.

Answer: False

Explanation: Accounting costs are called explicit costs.

6. Economic costs are the sum of implicit and explicit costs.

Answer: True

7. Wages and salaries, expenditures on raw materials, transportation costs, and utility bills are likely to be explicitly costs.

Answer: True

8. Depreciation of machines through use over time represents an implicit cost and should be considered as part of the cost of doing business.

Answer: True

9. A firm can significantly reduce its total cost of production by using resources that it already owns instead of purchasing resources from someone outside the firm.

Answer: False

Explanation: There is a cost attached to using resources that the firm already owns. The

concept is referred to as implicit cost.

10. Although sunk costs cannot be recaptured, they should nevertheless be carefully considered in firm's decisions about production costs.

Answer: False

Explanation: Sunk costs are costs that have already been incurred. For decision-making purposes, they are irrelevant.

11. Depreciation of the firm's capital stock is an example of sunk cost.

Answer: False

Explanation: Depreciation of the firm's capital stock is an example of implicit cost.

12. Fixed costs are expenditures that have already been made on the firm's factors of production.

Answer: False

Explanation: Fixed costs are those costs that do not vary with the quantity of output produced by the firm.

13. Variable costs are incurred only in the long run.

Answer: False

Explanation: In the short run, the firm has both fixed and variable costs.

14. Total cost consists of total fixed cost and total variable cost.

Answer: True

15. Variable costs are directly related to the volume out output that the firm produces. They are incurred only if the firm produces some positive level of output.

Answer: True

16. Average total cost is total cost per unit of output and can be obtained by subtracting total fixed cost from total cost.

Answer: False

Explanation: Average total cost is obtained by dividing total cost by the quantity of output. Subtracting total fixed cost from total cost gives total variable cost.

17. Marginal cost can be derived from total fixed cost.

Answer: False

Explanation: Marginal cost refers to a change in total cost. Since total fixed cost does not change, marginal cost is unrelated to it.

18. Marginal cost is the extra cost incurred by producing an additional unit of output.

Answer: True

19. The marginal cost curve cuts the average fixed cost curve at its minimum point.

Answer: False

Explanation: The average fixed cost curve never reaches a minimum.

20. The marginal cost curve cuts the average variable and average total cost curves at their minimum points.

Answer: True

21. The vertical distance between the total cost curve and the total variable cost curve remains constant, but the total cost curve starts at the origin.

Answer: False

Explanation: It is the total variable cost curve that starts at the origin.

22. If marginal cost is rising, then average cost must also be rising.

Answer: False

Explanation: If marginal cost is rising but is below average cost, then average cost will fall.

23. Once we know the total cost column, we can derive the marginal cost column.

Answer: True

24. Given the price of a variable factor, increasing marginal product implies decreasing marginal cost; diminishing marginal product implies increasing marginal cost.

Answer: True

25. Given the price of a variable factor, increasing average product implies increasing average variable cost; diminishing average product implies decreasing average variable cost.

Answer: False

Explanation: If the price of a variable input is fixed, increasing average product implies decreasing average variable cost; diminishing average product implies increasing average variable cost.

26. If we fully understand short-run cost analysis, long-run cost analysis is unnecessary.

Answer: False

Explanation: Long-run cost analysis is necessary in order to understand how the firm makes its decisions when it can vary all its inputs.

27. For any desired level of output, in the long run the firm will choose the plant size for which the average cost is lowest.

Answer: True

28. The long-run average cost is the minimum cost per unit at which a firm can produce each level of output when it has at least one fixed input.

Answer: False

Explanation: In the long run the firm has only variable inputs.

29. Increasing returns to scale refer to the long run and not to the short run.

Answer: True

30. A firm enjoying economies of scale must be operating under conditions of decreasing returns to scale.

Answer: false

Explanation: Such a firm will be experiencing increasing returns to scale.

31. Economies of scale describe a situation in which the firm's long-run average cost falls as output increases.

Answer: True

32. Constant returns to scale refer to the condition that exists when a firm increases all its inputs by a certain percentage and its output remains constant.

Answer: False

Explanation: Constant returns to scale are in effect when the firm increases all its inputs by a certain percentage and, as a result, its output increases by the same percentage.

33. Decreasing returns to scale are reflected in increasing long-run average cost.

Answer: True

34. Diseconomies of scale describe a situation in which the firm's long-run average cost falls as output increases.

Answer: False

Explanation: Diseconomies of scale are reflected in an increase in the firm's long-run average cost as output increases.

35. Economies of scope refer to cost reduction from producing goods and services separately.

Answer: false

Explanation: Economies of scope refer to cost reduction from producing complementary goods together.

36. The minimum efficient scale is the output level at which long-run average costs are minimized.

Answer: True

Completion

(Fill in the blanks)

Use each word or combination of words from the list exactly once.
*(**Hint**: Proceed by elimination)*

Word list

Average x 5 — Constant — Cost x 3 — Decreasing x 2 — Economic — Economies — Explicit — Fixed x 5 — Function — Implicit x 2 — Increasing x 3 — Lowest — Marginal — Rise — Scale x 2 — Scope — Sunk — Total x 2 — Variable x 7

Questions

1. The ______________ ______________ defines the relation between the firm's cost and its volume of output.
2. The cost of all resources used in the production of goods and services is called ______________ cost.
3. Direct outlays of money for factor services are ______________ costs. A cost that does not involve any direct payment to anyone outside the firm is a(n) ______________ cost.
4. Wages, fuel and raw materials are likely to be ______________ costs, while insurance premiums and property taxes are likely to be ______________ costs.
5. The labour services provided by the owner of a butcher shop is an example of an ______________ cost.
6. ______________ costs are those that continue to be incurred even if the firm closes down temporarily.
7. Costs that are incurred regardless of the quantity of goods and services produced are referred to as ______________ costs.
8. Costs that depend on the quantity of output produced are called ______________ costs.
9. Costs that have already been incurred and cannot be recaptured are called ______________ costs.
10. The firm's total cost consists of total ______________ costs and total ______________ costs.
11. ______________ costs are associated with the short run, but not with the long run. ______________ costs are associated with both the short run and the long run.
12. Total cost per unit of output is called ______________ ______________ cost.
13. Total variable cost per unit of output is called ______________ ______________ cost.
14. Total fixed cost per unit of output is called ______________ ______________ cost.
15. ______________ cost is the change in total cost divided by the change in quantity.

16. The marginal cost curve cuts the ______________ ______________ ______________ and the ______________ ______________ ______________ curves at their minimum points.
17. If marginal cost is above average cost, the average cost will ______________.
18. If an increase in all inputs leads to a more than proportional increase in output, the firm is experiencing ______________ returns to ______________. If the increase in output is less than proportional to the increase in inputs, the firm is experiencing ______________ returns to ______________.
19. If a firm increases all its inputs by 15% and its output increases by 15 %, the firm is experiencing ______________ returns to scale.
20. If a firm is experiencing ______________ returns to scale, its long run average cost will fall.
21. The long run average cost curve shows the ______________ per unit cost at which the firm can produce any level of output when it can vary all its inputs.
22. Specialization and quantity discounts help to explain ______________ returns to scale.
23. Inefficiency in management can help to explain ______________ returns to scale.
24. ______________ of ______________ exist when the cost of producing different goods together is less than they would be if the goods were produced separately.

Solution

1. (cost function)
2. (economic)
3. (explicit, implicit)
4. (variable, fixed)
5. (Implicit)
6. (Fixed)
7. (variable)
8. (variable)
9. (sunk)
10. (fixed, variable)
11. (Fixed, variable)
12. (average total)
13. (average variable)
14. (average fixed)
15. (marginal)
16. (average variable cost, average total cost)
17. (rise)
18. (increasing, scale, decreasing, scale.
19. (constant)
20. (increasing)
21. (lowest)
22. (increasing)
23. (decreasing)
24. (Economies (of) scope)

11 PURE COMPETITION

SYNOPSIS

Market structure may be classified as pure or perfect competition, monopoly, monopolistic competition, and oligopoly. The behavior of the firm is influenced by the market structure in which it operates.

In a purely competitive market structure, there is a large number of firms selling identical products. No single firm has any control over the market price of its product, and firms are free to enter or leave the industry. The purely competitive firm is a **price taker** and a **quantity adjuster.**

The demand or average revenue curve of a firm in **pure competition** is a horizontal line. The firm's average revenue and marginal revenue curves coincide. To maximize its profits, the firm chooses the output level at which the difference between total revenue and total cost is greatest; or alternatively, where marginal revenue equals marginal cost.

The **short-run supply curve** of a purely competitive firm is that portion of its marginal cost curve that lies above its average variable cost curve. If price is below average variable cost, the firm should shut down. If price is between average variable cost and average total cost, the firm is incurring losses but should continue to operate in the short run. A firm in that position is **minimizing its losses** provided that it equates its marginal revenue and its marginal cost.

The purely competitive firm is in long-run equilibrium when MR = MC = AC = P. If each firm in the industry is in long-run equilibrium earning zero net profits, there will be no entry or exit of firms, and the industry will be in long-run equilibrium.

In the world of pure competition, resources are efficiently allocated. The firm sells its output at a price that is just equal to the opportunity cost. If all markets are purely competitive, **Pareto optimality** will be attained.

LEARNING OBJECTIVES

In connection with this module, you should be able to:

1. explain market structure
2. explain short-run output decisions in a purely competitive firm
3. discuss the purely competitive firm's short-run supply curve
4. describe the short-run industry supply curve
5. explain long-run equilibrium and adjustment
6. discuss the importance of the purely competitive model

DEFINITIONS & CONCEPTS

You should be able to define the following terms and concepts:

market structure	pure competition
industry	price-taker
monopoly	monopolistic competition
oligopoly	marginal revenue
average revenue	break-even point
short-run shut-down point	profit-maximizing condition
industry equilibrium	Pareto efficiency
constant-cost industry	increasing-cost industry

11

PURE COMPETITION

Concepts, Definitions & Problems

Problem 11-1

Briefly define market structure.

Requirement and Clue: *This is a definitional problem. You are required to state briefly what market structure means. Do not ignore the word "briefly" in the problem.*

Solution:

The term "market structure" describes the environment in which firms make their pricing and output decisions. Market structure emphasizes characteristics such as number of sellers and their ability to influence price.

Problem 11-2

What is the difference between a firm and an industry?

Requirement and Clue: *It is necessary for one to know what a firm is and what an industry is before one can know the difference. In your solution, examples of firms and industries will be helpful.*

Solution:

A firm is an entity that buys factors of production and uses them to produces goods and services for sale at a profit. An industry, on the other hand, is a group of firms that produce similar products. Companies like Ikea and Act II Household Furniture are examples of furniture producing firms, whereas all firms producing furniture constitute the furniture industry. Similarly, Ford, Toyota, and General Motors are examples of firms producing automobiles, whereas, all firms producing automobiles constitute the automobile industry.

Problem 11-3

Briefly describe the different types of market structures.

Requirement and Clue: *A mere listing of the different types of market structures is not enough as a solution to this problem. You are required to identify the main features of each type. The solution requires brevity.*

Solution:

The following are the different types of market structures:

<u>Pure or perfect competition</u>

This is a market structure with a very large number of firms producing identical (homogeneous) products. In this market structure, firms are free to enter or to leave the industry. Because there are so many firms in this industry, each one produces only a tiny fraction of the entire industry output. No single firm can exert any influence over the market price of the product and is therefore a price-taker.

Monopoly

A monopoly is a one-firm industry in which the firm produces a product that has no close substitutes. Being the only firm in the industry, a monopoly exerts significant control over the price it charges for its product. The entry of other firms into the industry is restricted by a variety of entry barriers.

Monopolistic competition

Monopolistic competition is a market structure in which a large number of firms sell differentiated products and exert some slight influence over the market price. Entry into and exit from this market are relatively easy.

Oligopoly

Oligopoly is a market structure in which a few firms sell identical or differentiated products. Because of the fewness of firms in this industry, each firm generally has some control over the price of its output. An important feature of oligopoly is interdependence among the few firms.

Problem 11-4

In the table below, fill in the market structure on the right that matches the description on the left.

Description	Market Structure
The firm and the industry are identical.	a.
The demand curve is horizontal.	b.
The demand curve is relatively flat, products are differentiated, and the number of substitutes is very large.	c.
The demand curve is very steep and very few close substitutes exist.	d.
Collusion is possible and likely.	e.
The firm is a price-taker.	f.

Requirement and Clue: This problem is a test of your familiarity with the characteristics of the different types of market structure. Focus on these characteristics.

Solution:

Description	Market Structure
The firm and the industry are identical.	a. Monopoly
The demand curve is horizontal.	b. Pure competition
The demand curve is relatively flat, products are differentiated, and the number of substitutes is very large.	c. Monopolistic competition
The demand curve is very steep and very few close substitutes exist.	d. Monopoly
Collusion is possible and likely.	e. Oligopoly
The firm is a price-taker.	f. Pure competition

Problem 11-5

List the conditions that are necessary for the existence of pure or perfect competition.

Requirement and Clue: *This problem is a test of your understanding of the concept of pure or perfect competition. Focus on the features of this type of market structure, and don't ignore the word "list".*

Solution:

The following are the conditions that are necessary for pure/perfect competition to exist.

(1) There must be a large number of sellers each selling a tiny fraction of the total industry output.

(2) The product must be homogeneous. Buyers must see the products of each seller as being identical.

(3) Buyers must be aware of the price that each seller charges.

(4) No one seller must be able to influence the market price of the product.

(5) New sellers (firms) must be free to enter or leave the industry.

Problem 11-6

"The purely competitive firm is a price-taker and a quantity adjuster." Explain.

Requirement and Clue: *The problem offers a statement about the purely competitive firm. Your task is to explain the sense in which the statement is true.*

Solution:

The purely competitive market consists of a large number of firms—so many that no single firm has any control over the price of its product. The firm accepts the market price as a given. It is in this sense that the firm is a price-taker. In its profit-maximizing decision, the firm accepts the market price (it has no control over it) and adjusts its output so as to maximize its profits. It is in this sense that the form is a quantity adjuster.

Problem 11-7

What do economists mean by pure or perfect competition? How does this concept differ from the use of the term in everyday usage?

Requirement and Clue: *This is a two-part problem. Answer each part in order. Focus on the meaning of perfect competition in economics and compare that concept with how most people see competition.*

Solution:

To the economist, pure or perfect competition refers to the market structure in which there are so many firms in the industry that the action of any one firm has no effect on the price of the product that is being sold. In this market, firms sell identical or standardized products, and resources move without friction into and out of the industry. Buyers have full knowledge of the price that prevails in the market. In this situation, firms ignore what other firms in the industry are doing. In sharp contrast, the everyday usage of the term competition evokes feelings of rivalry among firms trying to outdo each other. In this context, a marketing specialist might talk about the fierce competition that her product faces in the market.

Problem 11-8

Will a profit-seeking firm in pure competition advertise its product? Explain briefly.

Requirement and Clue: *To answer with a "yes" or "no" answer is not sufficient, the problem requires an explanation. Note that a long drawn out explanation is not required. Focus on the features of pure or perfect competition.*

Solution:

The main purpose of advertising is to increase the demand for the firm's product. In pure competition, the firm can sell as much as it desires at the going price without advertising. Therefore, the firm in pure competition has nothing to gain by advertising its product. The industry might advertise, but not the profit-seeking firm.

Problem 11-9

Provide one or two examples of firms that operate in purely competitive markets.

Requirement and Clue: *The purpose of this problem is to test your understanding of the purely competitive model and its applicability to the real world. Focus on the characteristics of pure or perfect competition.*

Solution:

Agriculture, the stock market, and international money markets are usually cited as close approximations of pure/perfect competition. Actually, it is not easy to find good examples of purely competitive markets in the real world. Even in the case of agriculture, government programs influence the price at which farmers (the firms) sell their products, and marketing boards, for example, give farmers some degree of market power. Pure/perfect competition, therefore, does not really exist in these markets.

Problem 11-10

Pure competition does not exist in the real world. What, therefore, is the use of a theory of pure competition?

Requirement and Clue: *The problem starts by giving you information about the non-existence of pure competition. Accept it and then think of any practical use the theory might have.*

Solution:

Pure competition is a model—an abstraction from reality. There are a few things to note in the purely competitive model. First, the competitive solution occurs where price equals marginal cost. This marginal cost pricing that occurs only in pure competition implies that the firm establishes the equality of price and marginal cost, that is, the firm sells its product at a price just equal to the opportunity cost. Also, long-run competitive equilibrium occurs where price equals minimum average cost. Hence, resources are efficiently employed in the purely competitive model. The purely competitive model therefore has lessons about efficiency that we can learn.

The purely competitive model serves as an ideal by which we can measure other market structures. Moreover, many of the predictions of the purely competitive model hold even in situations where pure competition does not prevail. Many firms operate under conditions that are similar to pure competition—the barber shop or salon, the small restaurant, the florist, and the small ladies' boutique that operate in many large cities. The purely competitive model helps us to be able to analyse and understand the behaviour of such firms.

Problem 11-11

"There can be only one price in a perfectly competitive market." Explain.

Requirement and Clue: *Focus on what will happen if a seller in a purely competitive market tries to charge a price that is different from that charged by other sellers.*

Solution:

A purely competitive market comprises a large number of firms selling a homogeneous product. The number of firms is so large that the action taken by any of them individually has no noticeable effect on the market. Since all firms are selling identical commodities, consumers are indifferent as to the firm with which they carry out their transactions. Also, in this type of market, the buyers know the prices that are being charged by each seller.

Under the above conditions, all transactions will take place at the same price. If a firm raises its price, it would immediately lose all its customers because buyers would not buy its product at that price when they can obtain the identical product at a lower price. On the other hand, a firm would not lower its price because it can sell its entire output at the existing price. If it reduces its price, it will incur a loss that can be measured by the difference between the original price and the lower price. One is therefore likely to observe only one price in a perfectly competitive market.

Problem 11-12

Explain the terms marginal revenue and marginal cost and their significance in the output decisions of a firm in pure competition.

Requirement and Clue: *You are asked to do three things here: (1) explain marginal revenue, (2) explain marginal cost, and (3) explain the significance of these concepts in output determination. Address each part in order.*

Solution:

Marginal revenue may be defined as the additional revenue obtained from selling an extra unit of output. If the total revenue received from selling 100 units of output is \$540, and the revenue obtained from selling 101 units of output is \$545, then the marginal revenue of the 101st unit is ($545 - $540) = $5. In a purely competitive market, where the firm is a trice-taker, the marginal revenue of the firm will be equal to its average revenue, and will be constant. Diagram 1 below shows the marginal revenue curve for a purely competitive firm.

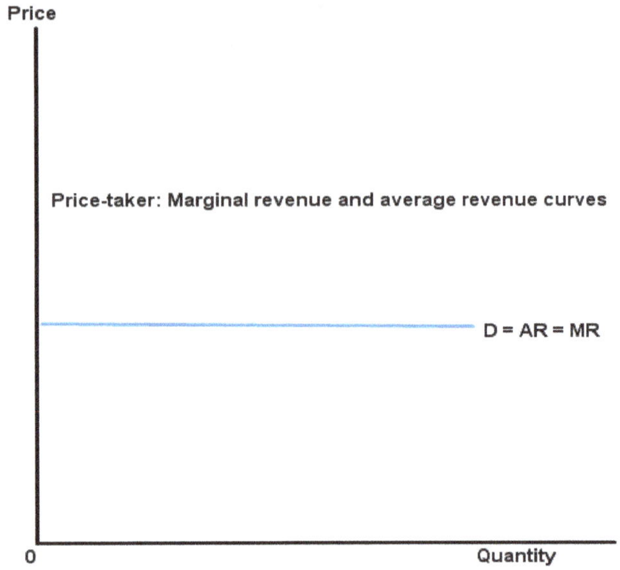

Diagram 1

Marginal cost is the additional cost incurred in producing one more unit of output. If the total cost of producing 10 units of output is $50, and the total cost of producing 11 units is $58, then the marginal cost of producing the 11th unit is ($58 - $50) = $8. Marginal cost falls at first and then rises as shown in Diagram 2 below.

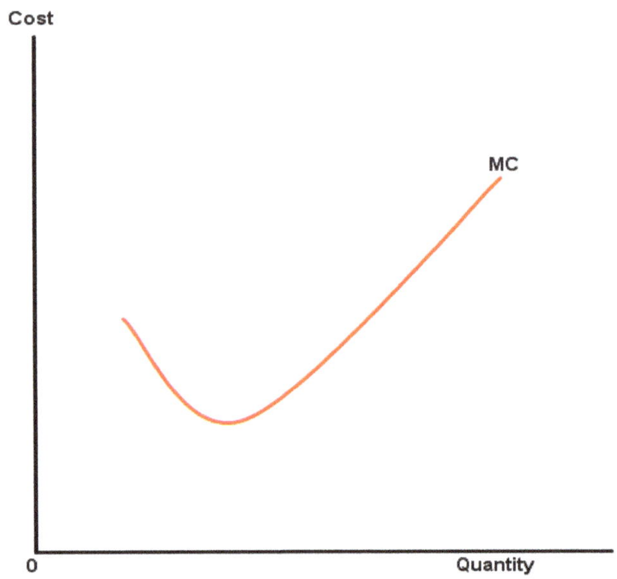

Diagram 2

Marginal revenue and marginal cost are extremely important to the firm. Its profit-maximizing output is that output at which marginal revenue equals marginal cost. If marginal revenue is greater than marginal cost, the firm can increase its profit by increasing its output. If marginal revenue is less than marginal cost, the firm can increase its profit by reducing its output. By comparing marginal revenue and marginal cost, the firm can adjust its output towards the most profitable level.

Problem 11-13

Many people who manage firms know nothing about marginal revenue and marginal cost. Does this mean they can never maximize their profits?

Requirement and Clue: *The problem is hinting at the profit-maximization rule which you are required to know. Focus on whether or not it is necessary for managers of firms to know about these technical concepts and defend your stance.*

Solution:

As long as the firm is maximizing its profits, it must be equating its marginal revenue with its marginal cost. This is the case whether the firm's manager knows the concepts or not. The economist can examine the firm's operations and advise the firm's managers on adjustments that the firm may make in order to increase its profits if they are not being maximized, but if the firm happens to attain the maximum profit position, then its marginal revenue will equal its marginal cost.

Problem 11-14

What is the difference between economic profits and accounting profits? Illustrate with an example.

Requirement and Clue: *This is a two-part problem. You should answer each part in order. It may be helpful to remember the difference between economic costs and accounting costs. An example is required.*

Solution:

An important difference exists between economic profits and accounting profits. Economic profits refer to the difference between the revenues obtained from the sale of goods and services and total costs (explicit and implicit) of producing the goods and services. Accounting profits on the other hand, refer to the difference between the revenues obtained from the sale of goods and services and the expenses incurred (that is the explicit costs) in producing the goods and services. The following example will help to illustrate the difference. The hypothetical revenues and expenses of an entrepreneur are shown in the table below.

Revenue:		
Sales		$50,000
Expenses:		
Rent	$ 2,500	
Utility	600	
Wages	15,000	
Transportation	800	
Materials and supplies	10,000	
Miscellaneous	500	
Total expenses	29,400	
Net income ($50,000 - $29,400)		20,600

The item net income shown in the table above is accounting profit, which is the difference between total revenue and total expenses.

To calculate economic profits, we would need to know not only the expenses incurred by the entrepreneur but also how much he could have earned in the next best alternative job. In other words, we need to know the entrepreneur's opportunity cost. If we assume that the entrepreneur could have earned $20,600 instead of running his own business, then we would have the following situation:

Total revenue.. =$50,000
Total cost = ($29,400 + $20,600)............... = $50,000
Profit ($50,000 – $50,000).............................. = $ 0

In this case, the entrepreneur is earning zero economic profit, or normal profit—returns that just equal the opportunity cost of the resources used. If however, he can earn only $18,000 instead of operating his business, then the situation would change as follows:

Total revenue.. = $50,000
Total cost = ($29,400 + $18,000)............... = $47,400
Profits ($50,000 – $47,400).......................... = $2,600

The entrepreneur would then earn positive economic profits of $2,600.

Problem 11-15

What economic role do profits perform?

Requirement and Clue: *Focus on how things would change if firms were not allowed to earn profits.*

Solution:

Profits perform the following economic functions:

1. They provide an incentive for efficiency
2. They reward the enterprising
3. They serve as a signal to resource owners

Incentive for Efficiency
The desire for profits serves as an incentive for firms to reduce production costs where possible. In the face of competition, high-cost firms will lose their markt shares to low-cost firms. Unless high-cost firms can increase the efficiency, they will ultimately be forced out of the market.

Reward for the Enterprising
Profits serve as a reward for the resourceful, the imaginative, the innovative, and the enterprising. The prospect of earning profits is often the driving force behind the development and maintenance of special resources and talents.

Signal to Resource Owners
The existence of profits in any industry or sector of the economy is a clear signal that price exceeds average cost of production and that resources should be shifted into that industry or sector. Likewise, the existence of losses in an industry is a loud and clear signal that resources should be shifted out of that industry and put to more profitable uses.

Problem 11-16

Use the total cost/total revenue approach to illustrate how the firm in pure competition maximizes its profits in the short run.

Requirement and Clue: *You must show familiarity with the firm's profit situation from the perspective of total revenue and total cost. Graphs are a helpful way to illustrate profit maximization. Remember that the problem specifically refers to the short run.*

Solution:

The following diagram illustrates how the firm in pure competition maximizes its short-run profits. Profit is the difference between the firm's total revenue and its total cost.

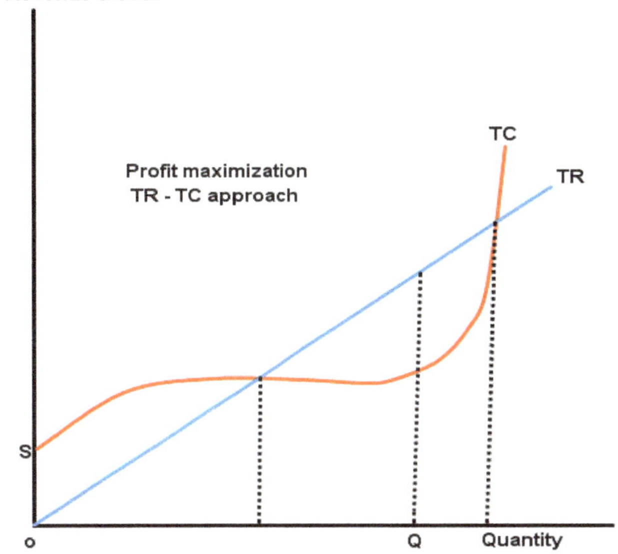

The firm's total revenue (TR) is represented by a straight line through the origin. At zero output, revenue will be zero. As output expands, TR rises in proportion to the increase in output because the price is constant. The total cost of *s* at zero output suggests the existence of fixed costs of *s*. The total cost (TC) rises as output increases. The firm's profit-maximizing output occurs where the difference between TR and TC is greatest. As shown in the diagram, this output level is about Q units.

Problem 11-17

Use the marginal revenue/marginal cost approach to illustrate how the firm in pure competition maximizes its profits in the short run.

Requirement and Clue: *You must show familiarity with the firm's profit situation from the perspective of marginal revenue and marginal cost. Graphs are a helpful way to illustrate profit maximization. Remember that the problem specifically refers to the short run.*

Solution:

Marginal cost (MC) is the extra cost incurred in producing one more unit of output. Marginal revenue (MR) is the extra revenue obtained from selling an additional unit of output. The following diagram illustrates the MR/MC approach to profit maximization.

At a level of output of B units, marginal cost exceeds marginal revenue. Since to produce an extra unit of output, it would cost more than the revenue that unit will bring in, the firm will reduce its output. At a level of output of A units, for example, the marginal revenue exceeds the marginal cost. Since it would be profitable to produce that extra output, the firm would increase its output. At an output level of Q units, the firm cannot increase its profits by changing its quantity of output. Hence an output of Q units is the output level that maximizes the firm's profits.

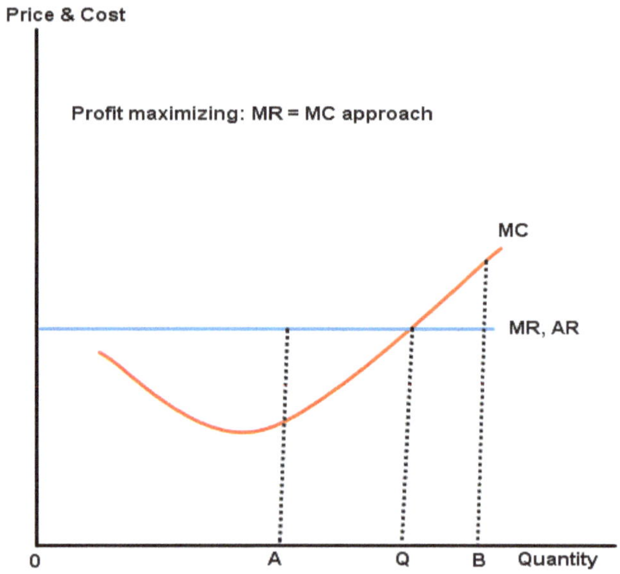

Problem 11-18

Show that average revenue (AR) is the same as price.

Requirement and Clue: *Focus on what average revenue really means and relate it to price.*

Solution:

Average revenue (AR) is the revenue per unit of output sold, or simply total revenue (TR) divided by quantity sold (Q). Average revenue is what the firm receives when it sells one unit of output. But this is exactly the same as price. This can be shown by simple algebra.

TR = P × Q, where P represents price

$$AR = \frac{TR}{Q} = \frac{P \times Q}{Q} = P$$

Therefore, AR = P

Problem 11-19

Draw a graph showing the demand, average revenue, and marginal revenue curves for a firm in pure competition.

Requirement and Clue: *Focus on the definition of each of the concepts referred to in the problem. The problem requires that all curves be shown on one graph. (Draw "a" graph...)*

Solution:

It will be useful to construct a table showing demand (D), average revenue (AR), and marginal revenue (MR) for a purely competitive firm. See the table below. It is assumed that the price of the product (P) is \$7. The following formulas are used to complete the various columns of the table.

$$TR = P \times Q$$
$$AR = TR/Q$$
$$MR = \Delta TR/\Delta Q$$

Quantity	Price (\$)	Total revenue (\$)	Average revenue (\$)	Marginal revenue (\$)
0	7	0	--	7
1	7	7	7	7
2	7	14	7	7
3	7	21	7	7
4	7	28	7	7
5	7	35	7	7
6	7	42	7	

Now the data in the table can be used to graph the demand, average revenue, and marginal revenue curves. The first two columns give the demand curve (the price/quantity relationship), while the average and marginal revenue curves are drawn on the basis of the data contained in the last two columns of the table. See the resulting graph below where P = \$7.

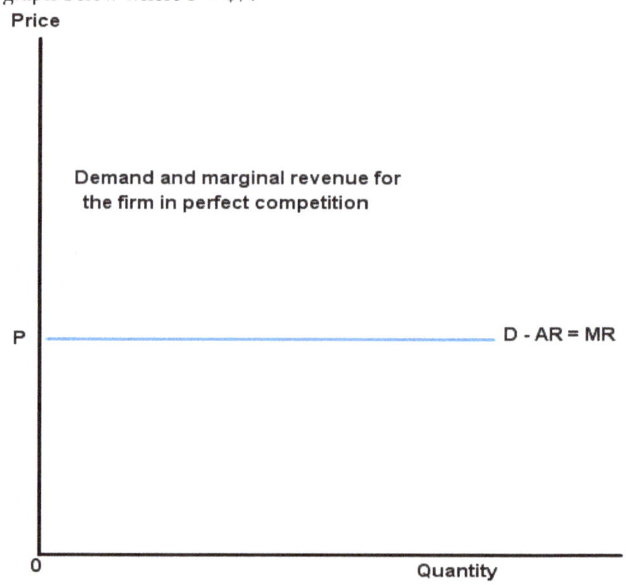

Problem 11-20

Which of the following curves represents the demand curve for a firm in pure competition?

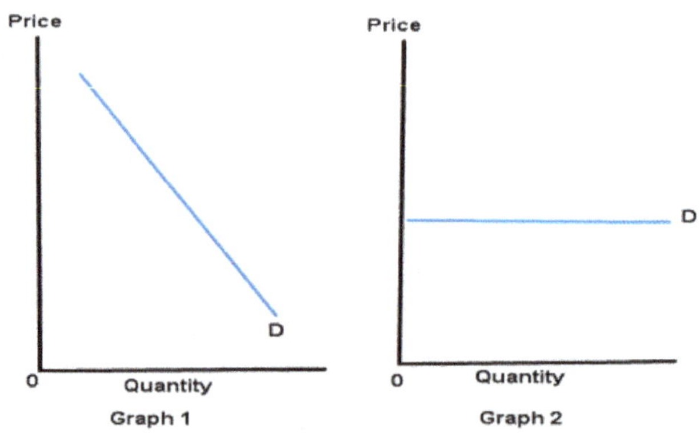

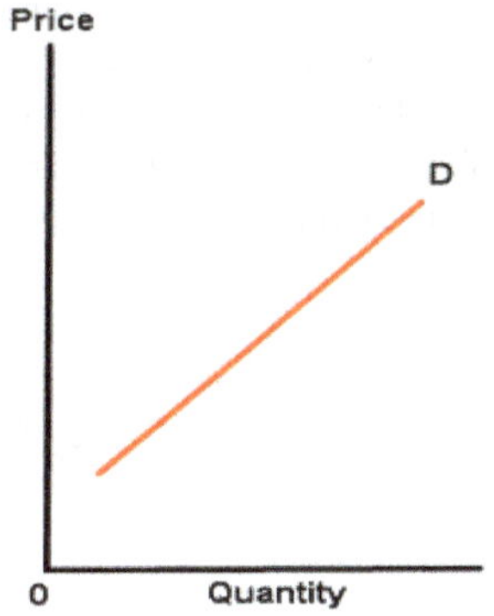

Graph 3

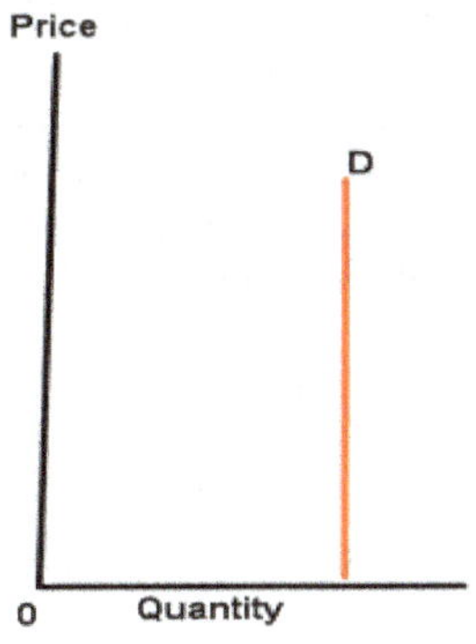

Graph 4

Requirement and Clue: *Consider that in pure competition, the firm faces a fixed price for its product.*

Solution:

A firm in pure competition sells such a tiny fraction of the total market output that it will hardly be noticed if it produces nothing. It has zero influence on the price of its product and can sell its total output at the existing market price. The firm in pure competition faces a fixed price. Since the price remains the same regardless of the quantity the firm sells, its demand curve is a horizontal straight line as shown in Graph 2.

Problem 11-21

The following diagram shows the marginal cost (MC) curve for a price-taking firm. The market price of the firm's product is P. If this firm is a profit maximizer, why would it not produce Q4 or Q8 units of output? What quantity of output would the firm produce?

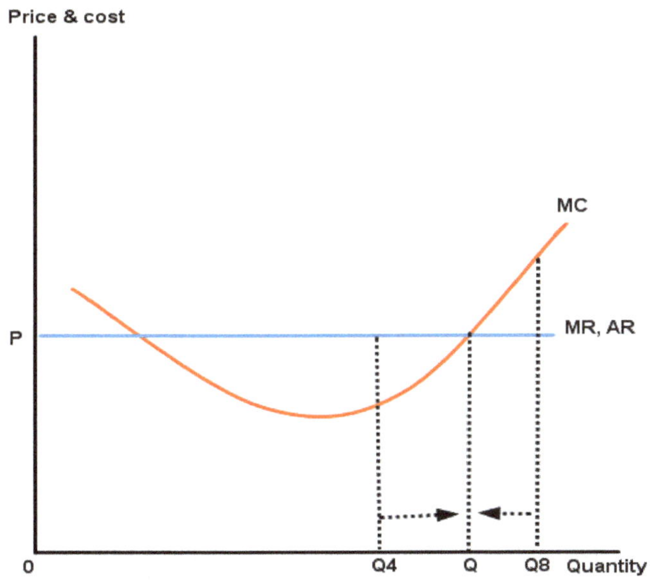

Requirement and Clue: *This is a two-part problem. Answer each part in order. You are expected to realize that a price-taking firm is a purely competitive firm. Essentially, the problem is this: Why should a profit-seeking firm in pure competition not produce an output level at which marginal cost is either greater than or less than the market price? Focus on the profit-maximizing condition for a firm.*

Solution:

A price-taking firm is a firm in pure competition. If P represents price, MR represents marginal revenue, and AR average revenue, we know that for a firm in pure competition, P = AR = MR. At an output level of Q4, MR > MC. An extra unit of output produced will add more to revenue than to cost. The firm will therefore increase its output. It will not produce Q4 units of output. At an output level of Q8, MC > MR. An extra unit of output produced will add more to cost than to revenue. The firm will therefore reduce its output. It will not produce Q8 units of output.

At an output level of Q, MC = MR. If the firm increases its output level beyond Q, the extra cost would be greater than the extra revenue earned by that unit. It would not be worth it. If the firm produces any level of output less than Q, the marginal revenue will be greater than the marginal cost, and the firm would fail to earn extra profits. Any movement away from Q will reduce the firm's profit. Q is the profit-maximizing output.

Problem 11-22

The following diagram shows cost and revenue curves for a firm in pure competition. Describe the firm's position in terms of profitability with respect to each of the four prices shown when its marginal revenue equals its marginal cost (MC).

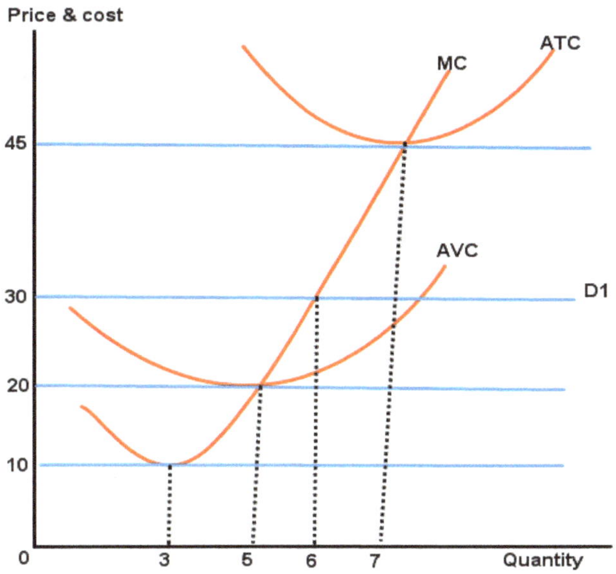

Requirement and Clue: *You are required to be able to interpret the graph to know whether or not the firm is earning profits. You must also realize that in this model, price and marginal revenue are identical.*

Solution:

I will begin with the price of $45. Here, price is just equal to average total cost, so the firm is just breaking even if it produces 7 units of output. It is earning normal profits or zero economic profits. Because MR = MC, the firm is in a profit-maximizing position. Any movement away from this position will place the firm in a worse profit position.

At a price of $30, MR = MC at an output of 6 units. Here, price is below average total cost, so the firm is incurring losses; but it is still doing the best it can because MR = MC. In this position the firm is said to be minimizing its losses. It is better for the firm to continue to operate in the short run than to close down.

At $20, price is equal to average variable cost (AVC). The firm is incurring losses because

P < ATC. The firm is just barely covering its variable cost. This position is referred to as the firm's short-run shut-down point.

At $10, price is below average variable cost, so the firm is incurring losses. In fact, it is not even covering its average variable cost and should therefore shut down, even though MR = MC at an output of 3 units.

Problem 11-23

Describe the short-run shut-down point for a firm in pure competition.

Requirement and Clue: *This problem is a test of your understanding of the concept of short-run shut-down point. A graphical illustration would be helpful.*

Solution:

The short-run shut-down point of a firm in pure competition is the point at which the marginal cost curve cuts the average variable cost curve. This occurs at the minimum point of the average variable cost curve. If the price falls below this level, the firm should shut down. The following diagram will help to describe the firm's short-run shut-down point.

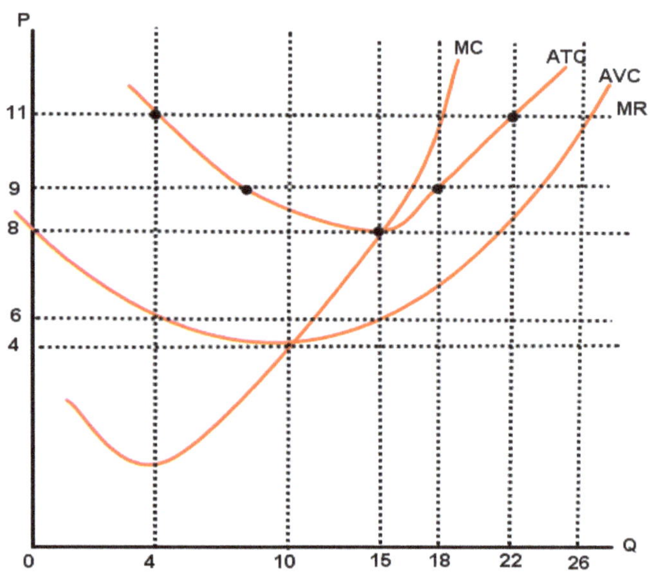

The firm should operate where price equals marginal cost in order to earn maximum profits. At any price above average total cost, say $11.00, the firm is earning positive economic profits and should continue to operate. To maximize profits, it should produce 18 units of output. At a price such as $8, which is just equal to average total cost, the firm is earning normal profits and should continue to operate, producing 15 units of output in order to maximize its profits. If the price is below average total cost but above average variable cost, $6 for example, the firm is incurring losses, but if it produces 12 units of output, it is minimizing its losses. It should continue to operate because it is covering its average variable cost. However, if the price falls below $4, the firm will not even cover its average variable cost and should shut down in the short run. Therefore, $4, the minimum average variable cost, is the firm's short-run shut-down point.

Problem 11-24

The following diagram shows cost and price for a purely competitive firm.

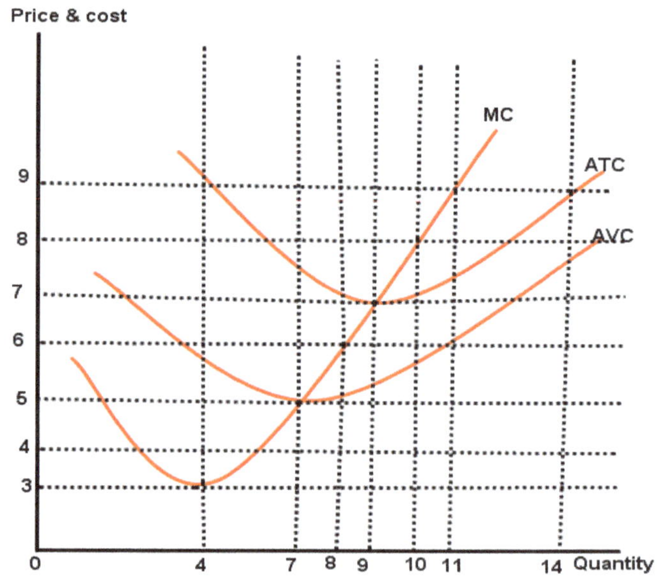

(a) *If the market price is $15, the profit-maximizing output will be _________ units. Total cost will be $________, total revenue will be $________, and total profits will be $_______.*

(b) *If the market price is $13, the equilibrium output will be _____ units. At this output, total revenue will be $_____, total cost will be $_______, and total profit will be $______.*

(c) *If the price is $9, the equilibrium output will be _______ units.*

(d) *This firm should shut down if the price falls below $______.*

Requirement and Clue: *This multiple-part problem is designed to test your ability to read graphs and deduce information from them. Focus on the definitions of the various concepts involved and the theories about the purely competitive firm. Be careful not to make arithmetic errors.*

Solution:

<u>Calculations:</u>

(a) At P = 15, the profit maximizing output is **14**, where P = MC. Total cost will be ATC × Q = $13.50 × 14 = **$189**, total revenue will be P × Q = $15 × 14 = **$210**, total profits will be TR – TC = $(210 – 189) = **$21.**

(b) At P = $13, the equilibrium output will be **12** where P = MC. Total revenue will be P × Q = $13 × 12 = **$156.** Total cost will be ATC × Q = $13 × 12 = **$156.** Total profit will be TR – TC = $(156 – 156) = **$0.**

(c) At P = $9, the equilibrium output will be **8** where P = MC.

(d) The short-run shut down point is $9 where the firm is just barely meeting its variable cost. It should shut down if the price falls below **$9.**

The blanks can now be filled in.

(a) If the market price is $15, the profit-maximizing output will be **14** units. Total cost will be **$189**, total revenue will be **$210**, and total profits will be **$21.**

(b) If the market price is $13, the equilibrium output will be 12 units. At this output, total revenue will be **$156**, total cost will be **$156**, and total profit will be **$0.**

(c) If the price is $9, the equilibrium output will be **8** units.

(d) This firm should shut down if the price falls below **$9.**

Problem 11-25

Elmira's is a small retail outlet that sells ladies' handbags and purses. Elmira's operates in an industry that is as close as possible to pure competition. For all practical purposes, it is a purely competitive firm. Elmira's is a price-taker and a quantity-adjuster. An advertising agency approaches Elmira's and offers to advertise its products at a 40% discount on the regular advertising rate. Should Elmira's accept the agency's offer?

Requirement and Clue: *The problem presents a hypothetical scenario. The task at hand is for you to decide whether the agency's offer will benefit Elmira's and to present an argument to support your position.*

Solution:

Advertising costs money, even if a 40% discount is allowed. Elmira's must weigh the cost of advertising against the benefit derived from the expenditure. Because the outlet is considered to be a purely competitive firm, it can sell as much as it can place on the market at the market price. Therefore, advertising will not benefit Elmira's. Why should the firm incur costs when there are no associated benefits? Elmira's should decline the agency's offer. It is not in the firm's best interest.

Problem 11-26

"Refurbished Chargers" is a firm that is operating with fixed costs. The price of its reconditioned chargers is $10 and it has no control over this price. The firm's average total cost (ATC) is below the given price of $10, thus the firm is earning a profit. Its lowest average variable cost (AVC) is $6. Changes in the market for this firm's product suddenly cause the market price to fall to $8, which is below the firm's ATC. Refurbished Chargers is now incurring losses.

On the basis of the information provided, should Refurbished Chargers close down?

Requirement and Clue: *Focus on the short-run shut-down condition for this firm and its loss minimization position in solving this problem.*

Solution:

The fall in the price results in losses for Refurbished Chargers. But the price of $8 is still higher than the AVC of $6, so the firm is covering its variable costs, with money left over to help to defray some of its fixed costs. If it closes down, it makes no money at all and still has to pay its fixed costs. Clearly, Refurbished Chargers should continue to operate as long as these fixed costs exist.

Problem 11-27

Explain how to derive the short-run supply curve for a firm trying to maximize its profits in pure competition.

Requirement and Clue: *This problem expects you to know what constitutes the short-run supply curve for a firm in pure competition. Focus on how the firm adjusts its output for different prices. A graph will be helpful.*

Solution:

The following diagram shows price and cost for a purely competitive firm. This diagram will help to explain how to derive the short-run supply curve for the firm seeking to maximize its profits.

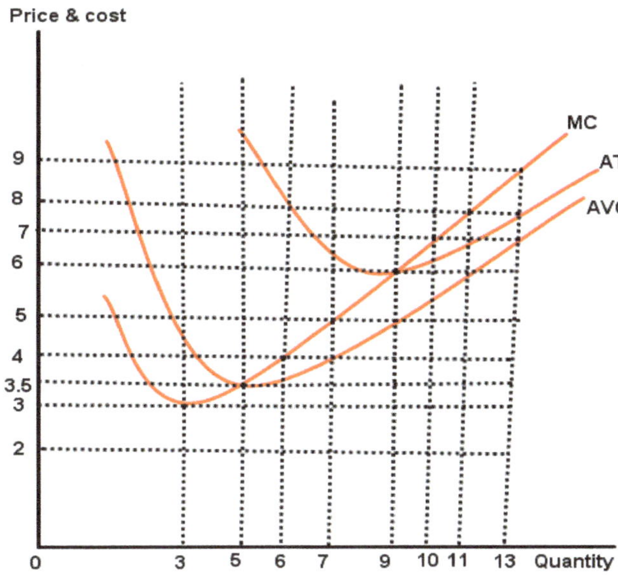

At a price of $9, the firm will produce (supply) 13 units of output. At a price of $8, it will produce 11 units; at a price of $7, it will produce 10 units; at a price of $6, it will produce 9 units; at a price of $5, it will produce 7 units; at a price of $4, it will produce 6 units; and at a price of $3.50, it will produce 5 units. Below $3.50, the firm will shut down.

These price/quantity relations can be put into a schedule as follows:

Price	Quantity supplied
9	13
8	11
7	10
6	9
5	7
4	6
3.50	5

This data can be plotted on a graph to give a supply curve. But this is exactly the marginal cost curve above the average variable cost curve in the diagram. Thus, the short-run supply curve for a firm in pure competition is that portion of its marginal cost curve that lies above its average variable cost curve.

Problem 11-28

Any firm operating at a loss would be better off closing down. Do you agree?

Requirement and Clue: *A decisive yes or no solution to this problem will not suffice. The problem requires a discussion of the issue of closing when the firm is incurring losses.*

Solution:

In certain circumstances, the firm may do better to operate at a loss, in the short run, than to cease operating. This is the case if the firm is in a position where the market price of its product is below its average total cost but above its average variable cost. If the firm suspends its operation temporarily, it still has fixed costs but earns nothing to help to defray these costs. If it continues to operate, any earnings above its average variable costs can be used to help to pay its fixed costs.

Problem 11-29

Describe briefly, without graphs, the long-run equilibrium position of a firm in pure competition.

Requirement and Clue: *Focus on the characteristics of the long-run equilibrium position of the purely competitive firm. The problem requires that no graphs be used. You must therefore rely on words.*

Solution:

In a purely competitive market structure, firms are free to enter or to leave the industry; the market has no entry or exit barriers. If the firms in the competitive industry earn profits in the short run, other firms will enter the industry. The entry of these new firms will increase total industry supply and, assuming no change in demand occurs, the price would tend to fall. New firms will tend to enter the industry provided that positive profits can be made. If firms in the industry are incurring losses, they will leave the industry in the long run. The exit of firms from the industry will cause total industry supply to fall and the price of the product will tend to rise.

This movement of firms in and out of the industry will cease when each firm in the industry is earning zero profit—normal profit and the firm will be in long-run equilibrium.

Problem 11-30

Define the long-run supply curve of a purely competitive industry?

Requirement and Clue: This is a definitional problem. Much can be written about the long run supply curve of a purely competitive industry but you must resist the temptation. You are required only o give a clear and precise meaning of the concept. Be careful not to confuse the firm with the industry.

Solution:

The long-run supply curve of a purely competitive industry is a graph that shows the various quantities of a good or service that all the firms in the industry will be willing and able to supply at various prices when the industry is in long-run equilibrium. Its shape depends on whether the industry is experiencing constant cost, increasing cost, or decreasing cost.

Problem 11-31

What is a constant-cost industry and what is the shape of the long-run supply curve of a constant-cost industry?

Requirement and Clue: *This is a two-part problem. Answer each part in order. You are expected to demonstrate an understanding of the concept and of the shape of the long-run supply curve of a constant-cost industry.*

Solution:

A constant-cost industry is one in which costs remain constant as the industry expands. As new firms enter the industry, the prices of resources remain constant even as the supply of goods and services increases.

When the industry is in long-run equilibrium, the price equals minimum long-run average cost. In a constant-cost industry, the expansion of industry output by the entry of new firms has no effect on cost. The entry and exit of firms cause total industry output to change, but the price of the product always returns to the point at which it is equal to the minimum average cost. Essentially this means that the long-run supply curve of a constant-cost industry is horizontal at the minimum average cost.

Problem 11-32

What is an increasing-cost industry and what is the shape of the long-run supply curve of an increasing-cost industry? Illustrate graphically.

Requirement and Clue: *This is a three-part problem. Answer each part in order. You are expected to demonstrate an understanding of the concept and of the shape of the long-run supply curve of an increasing-cost industry. Don't forget a graphical illustration.*

Solution:

An increasing-cost industry is an industry in which costs increase as the industry expands. As the industry expands, the increase in demand for increasingly scarce resources raises the prices of inputs and thus increases the costs of production.

Consider the diagram below. DD and SS are the initial demand and supply curves for the industry, and the total output for the industry is 150,000. The price is \$100. If the demand for the industry's output increases from DD to D1D1 as shown in the diagram, the price will rise from \$100 to \$120. The existing firms increase their output, and the industry output increases along SS from 150,000 to 180,000. Positive economic profits at a price of $120 induce new firms to enter the industry shifting the supply from SS to S1S1, but the cost rises as the prices of resources rise. Therefore, the increase in supply resulting from the entry of new firms into the industry does not force the price back to its initial level of $100, but only to $110. The long-run supply curve of the industry is obtained by joining the initial equilibrium point and the new equilibrium point as shown in the diagram E. The long-run supply curve of an increasing-cost industry that is purely competitive is upward sloping.

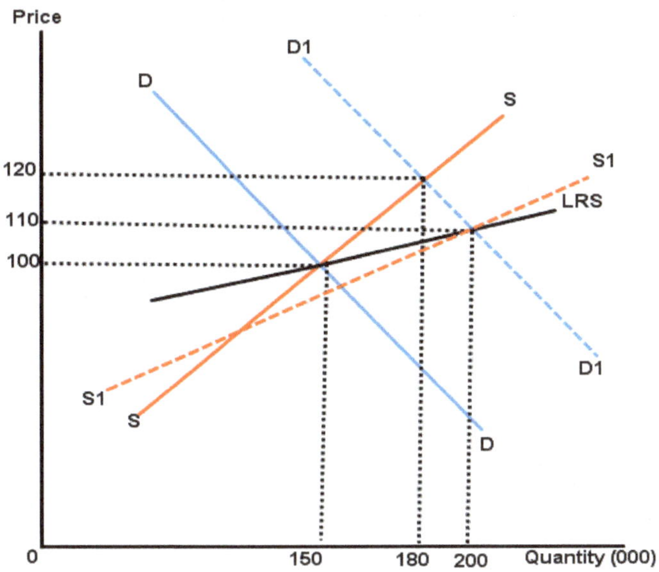

Problem 11-33

What is a decreasing-cost industry and what is the shape of the long-run supply curve of a decreasing-cost industry?

Requirement and Clue: *This is a two-part problem. Answer each part in order. You are expected to demonstrate an understanding of the concept and of the shape of the long-run supply curve of a decreasing-cost industry.*

Solution:

A decreasing-cost industry is an industry in which costs decrease as the industry expands. As new firms enter the industry, improved transportation and communication facilities may occur with industrial expansion, thus reducing cost.

The long-run supply curve of a decreasing-cost industry in pure competition is a downward- sloping curve.

Problem 11-34

In a purely competitive firm, total revenue is $400,000 annually, when it produces 4000 units of output per year.

(a) *What is the price that this firm faces?*

(b) *Find this firm's marginal revenue.*

(c) *If the firm is maximizing its profits, find its marginal cost.*

(d) *If the firm is in long-run equilibrium, find its average total cost.*

Requirement and Clue: *This problem is a test of your understanding of the relationship between various cost and revenue concepts. Focus on theories and conclusions regarding firms in pure competition.*

Solution:

(a) Total revenue is $400,000 and the quantity is 4000. Therefore, average revenue is $400,000 ÷ 4000 = $100. Average revenue and price are identical, so the price is $100.

(b) In pure competition, marginal revenue = average revenue = price. Therefore, this firm's marginal revenue is $100.

(c) If the firm is maximizing its profits, its marginal revenue equals its marginal cost. Therefore, the firm's marginal cost is $100.

(d) In long-run equilibrium, price equals average total cost. Therefore, the firm's average total cost is $100.

Problem 11-35

Would you expect innovation and technological change to flourish in a purely competitive industry?

Requirement and Clue: *A simple "yes" or "no" answer is not sufficient. You are expected to defend your position. In your solution, focus on the purely competitive environment.*

Solution:

Two reasons might prevent firms in a purely competitive environment from engaging in activities that promote innovation and technological change. These are: (a) lack of incentive, and (b) lack of funds.

<u>Lack of incentive</u>: Firms operating in a purely competitive environment earn zero economic profits in the long run. Profits serve as a motive or incentive for undertaking certain economic activities and a reward for risk-taking, innovation, and enterprise. Since profits will be competed away in the long run in pure competition, it is doubtful that firms in that environment will engage in activities that foster technological change and innovation.

<u>Lack of funds</u>: Research and development (R & D) are the main activities that foster technological change in innovation. These activities are very costly. Even if owners of firms in a purely competitive industry are driven by the spirit of risk-taking, innovation and entrepreneurship, they may lack the funds necessary to engage in those activities.

For these two reasons, innovation and technological change are unlikely to flourish in a purely competitive environment.

An alternative solution

The incentive to innovate and to introduce new methods of production (technology) and to be generally efficient is very strong among firms in a purely competitive environment. This is how they may be able to survive in an industry characterized by easy entry and a large number of firms. Moreover, firms in pure competition cn earn positive economic profits in the short run, and will innovate and introduce new technology in order to do so.

Multiple-Choice

In each case, circle the letter that corresponds with the correct answer.

1. Market structure refers to:

a. the manner in which the market deals with shortages and surpluses

b. the market forces that determine whether or not the firm will earn a satisfactory profit

c. certain market characteristics that influence the firm's pricing and output behaviour

d. the manner in which the industry deals with firms that are poorly structured.

Answer: c

Reason: *Market structure refers to characteristics such as number of firms and their ability to control price. This is in accordance with choice c.*

2. The competitive nature of the market environment in which firms make their price and output decisions is called:

a. environmental determinants

b. market structure

c. economic competition

d. competitive statute

Answer: b

Reason: *Market structure refers to market characteristics that determine how firms make their pricing and output decisions.*

3. Which of the following is a category of market structure?

a. Pure competition c. Monopoly

b. Oligopoly d. All of the above

Answer: d

Reason: *The choices are all different types of market structure.*

4. Which of the following is not a characteristic of a purely competitive market?

a. A large number of firms

b. Each firm has some control over the price of its product

c. Firms can enter the industry freely

d. The firms produce homogeneous products.

Answer: b

Reason: *In a purely competitive industry, each firm has no control over the price of its product. The firm is price-taker.*

5. An industry is:

a. a very large company such as McDonalds or General Motors

b. any business that is not owned by the government

c. a group of firms producing similar products or services

d. a group of firms in the same union

Answer: c

Reason: *Choice c correctly defines an industry. All firms producing a particular product or offering a particular service constitute an industry.*

6. Which of the following is not a market structure?

a. Perfect competition c. Monopoly

b. Oligopoly d. Agriculture

Answer: d

Reason: *Agriculture is an economic sector or activity, not a market structure.*

7. The market structure in which the least rivalry among firms exists is:

a. monopoly c. oligopoly

b. monopolistic competition `d. none of the above

Answer: a

Reason: *In a monopoly, there is only one firm in the industry. There is no firm to compete against.*

8. Which of the following is true of pure or perfect competition?

a. Each firm determines the price at which it sells its product

b. A large number of firms engage fiercely in price competition, raising and lowering prices strategically

c. A few firms collude in order to corner the market

d. Each firm is a price-taker and a quantity adjuster.

Answer: d

Reason: *In pure competition, each firm produces such a tiny fraction of total industry output that no single firm has any control over price. In determining its best course of action, it can vary its output, not the market price.*

9. Imperfect competition includes:

a. pure and perfect competition

b. monopoly and pure competition

c. oligopoly and monopoly

d. oligopoly and monopolistic competition

Answer: d

Reason: *In between perfect competition and monopoly are monopolistic competition and oligopoly which together are referred to as imperfect competition.*

10. Which of the following would you expect <u>not</u> to advertise its product?

a. A firm in pure competition

b. A monopoly

c. A monopolistically competitive firm

d. An oligopolist

Answer: a

Reason: *A firm in pure competition can sell its entire output at the existing market price so it has nothing to gain by advertising.*

11. A market structure in which a single firm produces a product that has no close substitutes is a(n):

a. pure competitor c. monopolistic competitor

b. monopoly d. oligopoly

Answer: b

Reason: *In a monopoly, there is only one firm in the industry.*

12. A monopoly is:

a. a market in which a single firm tries to dominate the other firms in the market

b. a situation where a single firm controls more than

50% of the market

c. a market structure with a single firm producing a product with numerous very close substitutes

d. none of the above

Answer: d

Reason: A monopoly is a market structure with one firm producing a product with no close substitute.

13. Which of the following is true of monopolies?

a. They cannot control price because no single firm can do that

b. They cannot exist without government financial support

c. They have significant market power

d. None of the above

Answer: c

Reason: Because a monopoly is the only firm in the industry with a product that has no close substitutes, it wields tremendous market power.

14. A market structure with many firms producing differentiated products is called:

a. pure competition c. oligopoly

b. monopoly d. monopolistic competition

Answer: d

Reason: In monopolistic competition, a large number of firms producing differentiated products constitute the industry.

15. One of the main characteristics of a monopolistically competitive industry is:

a. little or no advertising c. homogeneous products

b. product differentiation d. none of the above

Answer: b

Reason: Production differentiation is prevalent in monopolistic competition.

16. Which of the following is likely to be a firm in monopolistic competition in a large metropolitan area?

a. A furniture retailer c. A clothing retail store

b. A pastry store d. All of the above

Answer: d

Reason: All of the firms listed are likely to be many in a large metropolitan area producing products that are close substitutes.

17. Firms in monopolistic competition advertise in order to:

a. become pure competitors

b. shift their demands curve to the left

c. become monopolies

d. create brand loyalty and increase demand

Answer: d

Reason: Successful advertising shifts the firm's demand curve to the right and creates customer loyalty.

18. Which of the following is likely to engage in collusion?

a. Firms in pure competition

b. Firms in monopolistic competition

c. Firms in oligopoly

d. None of the above

Answer: c

Reason: Because of the fewness of firms in oligopoly markets, collusion is likely.

19. The demand curve for a firm in pure competition is:

a. downward sloping because of the inverse relationship between price and quantity demanded

b. vertical because the firm cannot control the price

c. horizontal because the firm faces a given price

d. undefined because customers demand only a tiny fraction of the firm's output.

Answer: c

Reason: The firm in pure competition has no control over its price. The price is given.

20. Marginal revenue is:

a. the change in total revenue resulting from selling an additional unit of output

b. always equal to marginal cost

c. total revenue divided by the quantity sold

d. none of the above

Answer: a

Reason: Marginal revenue is the extra revenue obtained from selling an additional unit of output as defined in choice a.

21. For a firm in pure competition:

a. price equals total revenue

b. price equals marginal revenue

c. price is greater than average revenue

d. none of the above

Answer: b

Reason: The firm in pure competition has price = marginal revenue = average revenue.

22. The firm's revenue is maximized:

a. when total revenue equals total cost

b. as long as total revenue exceeds total cost

c. when the difference between total revenue and total cost is greatest

d. none of the above

Answer: b

Reason: Profit is the difference between total revenue and total cost. When this difference is greatest, profit is at its maximum.

23. Which of the following is true for a firm in pure competition?

a. The total revenue curve always lies above the total cost curve

b. The total cost curve is always a straight line cutting the vertical axis because of fixed cost

c. The total revenue curve is an upward sloping straight line through the origin

d. The total revenue curve is a horizontal straight line equal to the price because the firm is a price-taker

Answer: c

Reason: At zero output, total revenue is zero. Then because price is fixed, and total revenue is price times quantity, total revenue increases at a constant rate.

24. For a firm in perfect competition, the total profit curve is:

a. N-shaped c. convex to the origin
b. U-shaped d. none of the above

Answer: a

Reason: *The total profit curve first rises, reaches a maximum, and then falls. This makes it N-shaped.*

25. To maximize its profits, a firm in pure competition will:

a. set its price low enough to attract customers
b. produce a level of output at which price equals marginal cost
c. engage in competitive advertising to attract customers
d. raise its price to increase its revenue

Answer: b

Reason: *Profits are maximized when marginal revenue equals marginal cost. In pure competition, marginal revenue equals price. Therefore profits are maximized when price equals marginal cost.*

26. A firm in pure competition will maximize its profits by producing a volume of output where:

a. marginal revenue exceeds average revenue
b. price exceeds marginal cost
c. marginal revenue equals marginal cost
d. price is greater than average revenue

Answer: c

Reason: *Any movement away from the marginal revenue = marginal cost position will reduce the firm's profits.*

27. The short-run supply curve of a purely competitive firm is:

a. the section of its marginal cost (MC) curve that lies above its average variable cost (AVC) curve
b. the section of its AVC curve that lies above its MC curve
c. the same as its average revenue (AR) curve
d. the upward sloping section of its AR curve

Answer: a

Reason: *In the short run, the purely competitive firm will continue to operate as long as it is covering its variable costs and will produce an output at which price equals marginal cost. This produces a short-run supply curve as described in choice a.*

28. A firm maximizes its profits:

a. when it equates marginal cost and average cost
b. at that output level at which cost is zero
c. at that output level at which the difference between total revenue and total cost is greatest
d. when marginal revenue is zero

Answer: c

Reason: *Profit is the difference between total revenue and total cost. When this difference is greatest, profit is at its maximum.*

29. A firm is earning a profit provided that:

a. price exceeds average total cost
b. price equals marginal cost
c. price is less than average variable cost
d. marginal revenue equals marginal cost

Answer: a

Reason: *If price exceeds average total cost, then total revenue exceeds total cost, and this means that the firm is earning a profit.*

30. If marginal revenue is 6 and marginal cost is 4, the purely competitive firm seeking to maximize profits should:

a. increase its output c. raise its price
b. reduce its output d. none of the above

Answer: a

Reason: *Increasing output would add more to revenue than to cost. This would earn extra profits.*

31. A firm must sell its product at the prevailing market price. In order to maximize its profits, this firm should:

a. sell as much as it can produce
b. try to produce that output where average cost is at its minimum
c. operate where its marginal cost is lowest
d. produce and sell an output where marginal revenue equals marginal cost.

Answer: d

Reason: *Any other level of output will reduce the firm's profits.*

32. A purely competitive firm incurring losses should continue to operate in the short run provided that:

a. marginal cost is positive and rising
b. price is above average variable cost
c. average revenue is below average total cost
d. marginal revenue equals marginal cost

Answer: b

Reason: *If price is above average variable cost and the firm operates along its marginal cost curve, it is minimizing its losses and should continue to operate in the short run.*

33. Which of the following is consistent with a firm in pure competition?

a. The firm faces a downward sloping demand curve as all demand curves are downward sloping
b. The firm's marginal cost curve declines continuously
c. The firm faces a perfectly elastic demand curve
d. The firm is usually very large, producing a large share of the total market output

Answer: c

Reason: *The demand curve for a firm in pure competition is horizontal because the firm is a price-taker.*

34. A firm in pure competition will be expected to:

a. advertise its product
b. set its price slightly higher than the market price
c. operate where marginal revenue equals marginal cost
d. all of the above

Answer: c

Reason: *This is where it will maximize its profits or minimize its losses.*

Questions 35-37 are based on the following diagram. The firm faces a fixed price of $20 for its product.

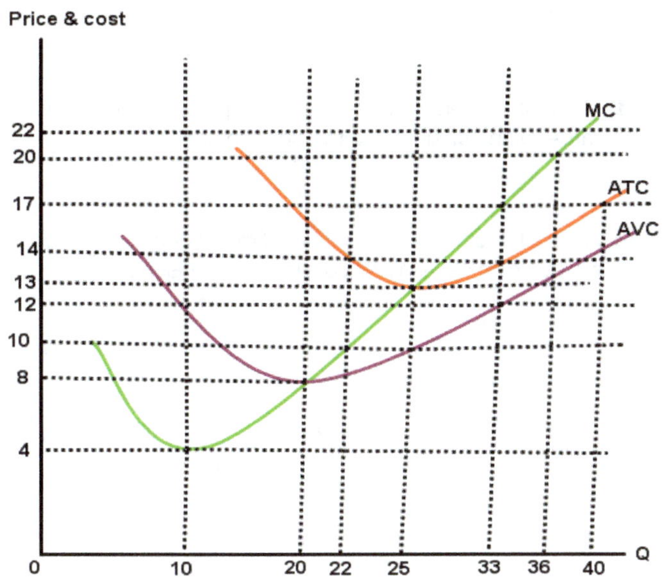

35. To be in short-run equilibrium, the firm should produce an output of:

a. 18 units c. 34 units
b. 54 units d. 43 units

Answer: d

Reason: This is the output level at which MR = MC.

36. At the short-run equilibrium output, the firm is:

a. earning positive net profits
b. earning zero net profits
c. incurring losses
d. producing at minimum cost

Answer: a

Reason: Price exceeds average total cost so the firm is earning positive net profits.

37. The firm should shut down if the price falls below:

a. $14 c. $10
b. $12 d. $8

Answer: d

Reason: The firm should shut down if it is not covering its variable costs.

38. In long-run competitive equilibrium:

a. each firm earns positive economic profits
b. all firms incur slight losses
c. each firm operates where price equals average cost
d. none of the above

Answer: c

Reason: The entry and exit of firms result in the firms earning only zero economic profits.

39. If firms in a purely competitive market structure are earning positive economic profits, then in the long run:

a. firms will leave the industry in search of even larger profits; hence market price will rise
b. firms will enter the industry, increasing total supply and causing price to fall
c. firms will raise their prices to earn even bigger profits
d. each firm will advertise to increase its market share

Answer: b

Reason: Profits serve as a signal for resources to flow into the industry. As total supply increases, the price falls.

40. If firms in a purely competitive market structure are incurring losses, then in the long run:

a. firms will leave the industry, causing the price to rise as industry output falls
b. firms will enter the industry to force out the inefficient ones
c. firms will lower their prices to keep out other firms
d. some firms will advertise to attract more customers

Answer: a

Reason: Losses in an industry will cause firms to shift resources out of the industry in search of more profitable alternatives. This will reduce supply and raise price.

41. The long-run supply curve of a constant-cost industry is:

a. upward sloping c. downward sloping
b. horizontal d. non-existent

Answer: b

Reason: Cost remains constant as industry output expands. Therefore the long-run supply curve is a horizontal straight line.

42. Which of the following is a plausible explanation of an increasing-cost industry?

a. As firms leave the industry, demand for the industry's output falls
b. As new firms enter the industry, the demand for resources causes the prices of factor inputs to rise and thus increases production costs
c. Increases in demand for the industry's output raise the price of the product and increase costs
d. None of the above

Answer: b

Reason: An increasing-cost industry is one in which cost increases as the industry expands. This increase in cost may be due to rising increasing demand for inputs as more firms enter the industry.

43. The long-run supply curve of a decreasing cost industry is:

a. upward sloping c. downward sloping
b. horizontal d. vertical

Answer: c

Reason: Cost decreases as output expands. Therefore the long-run supply curve is downward sloping.

44. Which of the following is true of the purely competitive model?

a. It is a perfect model of the economy
b. It describes every situation in which any firm might find itself
c. Its assumptions perfectly fit any firm in any industry
d. It serves as an ideal by which other market structures can be measured.

Answer: d

Reason: Choice d describes a reason for studying the purely competitive model.

True or False

Determine whether each of the following statements is true or false.

1. When economists talk of pure competition, they are referring to efforts to control price and output.

Answer: False

Explanation: In pure competition, firms have no control over the price of their products.

2. The purely competitive firm is a price adjuster and a quantity taker.

Answer: False

Explanation: The purely competitive firm is a price-taker and a quantity-adjuster.

3. One of the characteristics of a purely competitive industry is freedom of entry and exit of firms.

Answer: True

4. Perfect competition is the most common of all market structures to be observed in the real world.

Answer: False

Explanation: It is extremely difficult, if not impossible, to find perfect examples of pure competition in the real world.

5. The purely competitive firm has no control over the price of its product and is therefore a price-taker.

Answer: True

6. A perfect competitor is one that can sell all it wants to at the prevailing market price.

Answer: True

7. A purely competitive firm will use advertising to gain a competitive edge over its rivals.

Answer: False

Explanation: A purely competitive firm can sell as much as it wants to at the prevailing market price. It has nothing to gain by advertising its product.

8. A market structure characterized by a large number of firms selling differentiated products is called monopolistic competition.

Answer: True

9. A market structure characterized by a few large firms that control the market is called a monopoly.

Answer: False

Explanation: A monopoly is a market structure in which there is a single firm producing a product that has no close substitutes.

10. The demand curve for a firm in pure competition is horizontal.

Answer: True

11. The total revenue curve for a firm in pure competition is an upward-sloping straight line through the origin.

Answer: True

12. A profit-seeking competitive firm should produce an output at which its marginal cost is at its lowest point.

Answer: False

Explanation: The firm should produce at output where marginal revenue equals marginal cost.

13. The marginal cost curve for a firm in pure competition is downward sloping because of the large number of firms.

Answer: False

Explanation: The marginal cost curve is U-shaped.

14. Marginal revenue is the extra revenue obtained by selling an additional unit of output.

Answer: True

15. For a firm in perfect competition, marginal revenue and price are identical.

Answer: True

16. Provided that marginal revenue is greater than marginal cost for a firm in pure competition, the firm must be earning positive economic profits.

Answer: False

Explanation: The marginal revenue could be below average total cost in which case the firm would be incurring losses.

17. A firm in pure competition will be minimizing its losses if it equates marginal revenue and marginal cost when price is between average total cost and average variable cost.

Answer: True

18. A profit-seeking firm in pure competition should always produce at the minimum point of its average total cost curve.

Answer: False

Explanation: The firm should produce where marginal revenue equals marginal cost. In the short run, this may occur above or below the minimum point of the average total cost curve.

19. A competitive firm, seeking to maximize its profits, should produce an output at which the marginal cost curve is at its minimum.

Answer: False

Explanation: The firm should operate where marginal revenue equals marginal cost.

20. A profit maximizing firm should expand its output provided that its marginal revenue is greater than its marginal cost.

Answer: True

21. If a firm's marginal cost exceeds its marginal revenue at its current output level, it can earn maximum profits by decreasing its output.

Answer: True

22. A purely competitive firm's short-run supply curve is its marginal cost curve.

Answer: False

Explanation: *The short-run supply curve is that portion of the marginal cost curve that lies above the average variable cost curve.*

23. It is only in purely competitive firms that price and average revenue are identical.

Answer: False

Explanation: Price and average revenue are identical regardless of the market structure.

24. The short-run shut-down point for a firm in pure competition occurs at the point where marginal cost and average total cost are equal.

Answer: False

Explanation: *The short-run shut-down point occurs where marginal cost and average variable cost are equal.*

25. The short-run industry supply curve in pure competition is the horizontal summation of the short-run supply curves of all the firms in the industry.

Answer: True

26. A firm in pure competition that is earning zero profits will exit the industry.

Answer: False

Explanation: *It will not leave the industry because the resources are earning as much as they can earn in some alternative use.*

27. In the long run, firms in perfect competition earn positive economic profits; otherwise, they leave the industry.

Answer: False

Explanation: *In the long-run, firms in perfect competition earn zero economic profits.*

28. If a purely competitive firm is in long-run equilibrium, its short-run average total cost curve must be tangent to its long-run total cost curve.

Answer: True

29. In a purely competitive industry, output can expand in the long run only if each firm in the industry increases its output.

Answer: False

Explanation: *Industry output can expand by the entry of new firms into the industry.*

30. The existence of positive economic profits in pure competition in the long run will attract new firms into the industry.

Answer: True

31. Pareto efficiency is the condition that exists when it is impossible to make someone better off without making someone else worse off.

Answer: True

32. If the firms in a purely competitive industry are earning positive economic profits, new firms will enter the industry, increasing the supply, lowing price, and reducing profits.

Answer: True

33. If pure competition exists in all markets, Pareto optimality will be attained.

Answer: True

34. The long-run supply curve of an increasing-cost industry is downward sloping.

Answer: False

Explanation: *The long-run supply curve of an increasing-cost industry is upward sloping.*

Completion

(Fill in the blanks)

Use each word or combination of words from the list exactly once.
*(**Hint**: Proceed by elimination)*

Word list

Average x 4 — Barriers — Break — Competition x 2 — Constant Cost x 7 — Entry — Even — Exit — Fall — Horizontal x 2 — Increase — Industry — Marginal x 6 — Market — Maximizing — Minimizing — Monopolistic — Monopolistic Competition — Monopoly x 2 — Normal — Oligopoly x 2 — Output — Pareto — Positive x 3 — Price x 3 — Pure Competition — Pure/Perfect — Revenue x 5 — Structure — Total x 4 — Variable — Zero x 2

Questions

1. ______________ ______________ refers to market characteristics such as number of firms and market power that determine how firms in an industry behave.
2. Market structures include ______________, ______________, ______________ and ______________.
3. A market structure in which a very large number of firms produce identical products and have no control over price is called ______________ ______________.
4. A(n) ______________ is a group of firms producing similar products.

5. A market structure with a single firm producing a product that has no close substitutes is a(n) ______________. (monopoly)

6. Imperfect competition is the term used to describe the market structures referred to as ______________ ______________ and ______________.

7. Firms in a purely competitive market structure can adjust their ______________ [price, output] but not their ______________ [price, output]

8. A purely competitive firm's total revenue is its ______________ ______________ multiplied by the quantity produced.

9. Average revenue is always the same as ______________.

10. The demand curve for a firm in pure competition is a ______________ straight line.

11. The ______________ ______________ curve for a firm in pure competition is an upward sloping straight line through the origin. (total revenue)

12. A firm is earning maximum profits when the difference between its ______________ ______________ and its ______________ ______________ is greatest.

13. The demand curve, average revenue curve, and marginal revenue curve are all represented by a single ______________ straight line.

14. ______________ ______________ is the extra revenue obtained by selling an additional unit of output. ______________ is the money obtained by selling one unit of output.

15. The ______________ - ______________ point is the point at which total revenue equals total cost. (break-even)

16. The break-even point for a firm in pure competition occurs where the price equals the minimum point on the ______________ ______________ ______________ curve.

17. If marginal revenue equals marginal cost, the firm is ______________ its profits or ______________ its losses.

18. The short-run shut-down point for a firm in pure competition occurs at the point where the marginal cost curve cuts the ______________ ______________ cost curve.

19. The short-run supply curve for a firm in pure competition is the section of its ______________ ______________ curve that lies above its average variable cost curve.

20. If marginal revenue exceeds marginal cost, the profit-maximizing firm ______________ [increase, decrease] its output.

21. In order to maximizing its profits using the marginal revenue/marginal cost approach, a firm should choose that level of output at which ______________ ______________ equals ______________ ______________ when ______________ ______________ is rising.

22. For a purely competitive firm, if price is less than average total cost but greater than average variable cost, in the short run, the firm can minimize its losses by choosing that output at which price equals ______________ ______________. If price falls below average variable cost, the firm can minimize its losses by producing an output of ______________.

23. Zero economic profits are also referred to as ______________ profits.

24. Since there are no effective ______________ to entry in a purely competitive industry, the existence of ______________ economic profits will attract new firms into the industry.

25. If a firm were earning zero profits and it subsequently managed to increase its efficiency, it could, conceivably, at the existing price, earn ______________ profits. This could attract new firms thus causing the price to ______________.

26. In long-run competitive equilibrium, the firms in the industry will earn ______________ profits. There will be neither ______________ nor ______________, so industry supply remains constant.

27. Competition forces firms to be efficient in that they produce at the point where price equals long-run minimum ______________ ______________.

28. If all markets are purely competitive, ______________ efficiency will be assured.

29. The long-run supply curve of a(n) ______________ cost industry is horizontal at the minimum average cost.

30. The long-run supply curve of an increasing-cost industry has a ______________ slope.

Solution

1. (market structure)
2. (pure competition, monopoly, monopolistic competition, oligopoly [in any order])
3. (pure or perfect competition)
4. (industry)
5. (monopoly)
6. (monopolistic competition, oligopoly)
7. (output, price)
8. (average revenue)
9. (price)
10. (horizontal)
11. (total revenue)
12. (total revenue, total cost)
13. (horizontal)
14. (Marginal revenue, price)
15. (break-even)
16. (average total cost)
17. maximizing, minimizing)
18. (average variable)
19. (marginal cost)
20. (increase)
21. (marginal revenue, marginal cost, marginal cost)
22. (marginal cost, zero)
23. (normal)
24. (barriers, positive)
25. (positive, fall)
26. (zero, entry, exit)
27. (average cost)
28. (Pareto)
29. (constant)
30. (positive)

12 MONOPOLY

SYNOPSIS

A **monopoly** is a market structure in which there is a single firm producing a product that has no close substitutes. Monopoly exists because of **barriers to entry** such as ownership of essential inputs, patents, franchises, and economies of scale that effectively prevent other firms from entering the industry.

The monopolist is the only producer of the product. Hence in this situation, the firm and the industry are identical. The monopolist faces a downward-sloping demand curve, reflecting the fact that an additional unit of output can be sold only by charging a lower price.

The monopolist maximizes profits when the firm's marginal revenue is equal to its marginal cost. Unlike pure competition, in a monopoly situation, price exceeds marginal cost. The monopolist may produce a given output at a cost that is higher than the minimum for that level of output. Known as **X-inefficiency**, this practice reduces the monopolist's profits.

Monopolists can benefit from **price discrimination** if they can successfully divide their customers into groups on some basis, prevent people from buying in the cheaper market and re-selling the product in the dearer market, and if the demand elasticities in the markets are different. In practicing price discrimination, the monopolist is trying to capture all or a part of the consumer's surplus.

A government regulatory agency may regulate the price charged by a monopolist in order to prevent the monopolist from using its monopoly power in a manner that may be detrimental to the society. Fear of abuse of **monopoly power** is generally the motive for regulation.

LEARNING OBJECTIVES

In connection with this module, you should be able to:

1. discuss barriers to entry
2. describe the demand curve for a firm in monopoly
3. describe the marginal revenue of a monopolist
4. discuss the profit level of the monopolist
5. explain the relation between elasticity and marginal revenue
6. compare monopoly with pure competition
7. explain monopoly regulation
8. discuss price discrimination

DEFINITIONS & CONCEPTS

You should be able to define the following terms and concepts:

monopoly
barriers to entry
patent
franchise
natural monopoly
X-inefficiency
allocative efficiency
monopoly power
regulated monopoly
price discrimination
arbitrage transactions
average-cost pricing

12

MONOPOLY

Concepts, Definitions & Problems

Problem 12-1

Define monopoly.

Requirement and Clue: *This is a definitional problem. There is much to be said about monopolies but your task here is merely to state what a monopoly is.*

Solution:

A monopoly is a market structure consisting of a single firm that produces a product that has no close substitutes. Thus, a monopoly is a single-firm industry. An example of a monopoly might be the public transportation system in a city.

Problem 12-2

A monopoly is defined as an industry with a single firm producing a product that has no close substitutes. What issues are raised by this definition?

Requirement and Clue: *This problem calls for a discussion of the issues arising from the definition of monopoly. Think of the possible difficulties raised by the definition.*

Solution:

The first issue raised by this definition is the notion of "close substitutes". This idea of a close substitute is subjective. While some people might agree that a particular General Motors car is a close substitute for a particular Ford Motors car, others might disagree strongly. Consumers are likely to disagree on the closeness of substitutes such as microwave ovens and convection ovens, electric fans and air conditioners, public transportation and a private car. Two items may be considered close substitutes for one use but not for another. For example, electricity and oil may be considered close substitutes for heating purposes, but very poor substitutes, or not substitutes at all, for lighting purposes. A second issue raised by the definition is the difficulty or impossibility of separating the monopoly from the product that is monopolized. If a firm is described as a monopoly, it must have a monopoly in the production of some particular product.

Problem 12-3

In terms of monopoly, define "barriers to entry." Briefly discuss some barriers to entry.

Requirement and Clue: *This is a two-part problem. Address each part in order. You are required to demonstrate your knowledge of entry barriers. A mere listing of barriers to entry is not sufficient. The problem requires a brief discussion. Do not ignore the word "brief".*

Solution:

"Barriers to entry" are circumstances that make it difficult for new firms to enter a particular market. Without such barriers, monopolies could not exist.

Some barriers to entry include patents, franchises, ownership or control of particular raw materials, economies of scale.

Patents: A patent is an exclusive right that the government grants to a producer to produce a particular product or to render a particular service. Even ideas can be patented. Other firms are not allowed to produce an identical product or offer an identical service, but they can produce a product or offer a service that is similar to the patented product.

Franchises: A franchise is an exclusive right to operate a business in a certain geographical area. A franchise may be granted by a government or by a private franchisor. If you obtain a franchise from McDonald's, you will enjoy a certain degree of protection from competition from other McDonald's restaurants because another one will not be established within the designated boundaries of your business area.

Ownership of essential raw materials: If a firm owns or controls a particular raw material that is necessary for the production of a particular product, and if the firm does not allow any other firm to use that essential material, then the firm will be the only producer of that product.

Economies of scale: It may happen that a single firm can satisfy the entire market demand more cheaply than two or more firms could. This may be the result of substantial economies of scale where the average cost declines as output expands. This is the case of a natural monopoly. In this case, the cost of establishing a firm is enormous, and the average cost will be covered only at a level of output large enough to supply the entire market. One firm will be more efficient than two or more firms.

Problem 12-4

What are natural monopolies? What circumstance might give rise to a natural monopoly?

Requirement and Clue: *This is a two-part problem. Answer each part in order. Simply state what natural monopolies are and give an example of a natural monopoly. Explain how a natural monopoly could emerge.*

Solution:

A natural monopoly is an industry in which a single firm can satisfy the entire market demand more cheaply than two or more firms could. For this reason, competition is impractical or uneconomical.

A natural monopoly could emerge as a result of substantial economies of scale. Consider the diagram below.

ATC is the average cost for the firm, and the demand curve is indicated. Notice the relatively high unit cost at low levels of output; but as output expands, the average cost declines. Suppose the total quantity demanded is 30 billion kilowatt-hours per year. A single firm can produce the total quantity at an average cost of $0.04, while with two firms sharing the same market—each producing 15 billion—the average cost would rise to $0.06. In situations with such economies of scale, it is always cheaper for a single firm to produce the entire industry output.

Typical examples of natural monopolies are telephone companies, gas companies, and electric power companies.

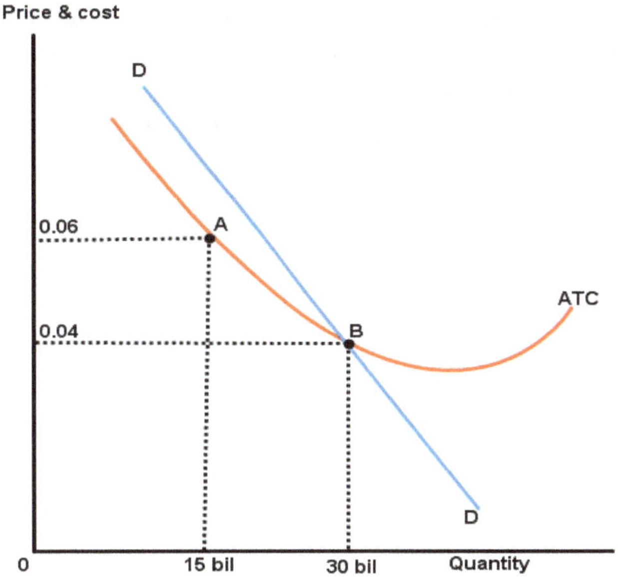

Problem 12-5

Define bilateral monopoly.

Requirement and Clue: *This is a definitional problem. Your task is to state clearly the meaning of the concept without writing a long essay on it.*

Solution:

A bilateral monopoly is a situation in which the industry consists of a single producer (seller) called the monopolist, and a single buyer called the monopsonist. This market situation usually results in bargaining between buyer and seller.

Problem 12-6

"The demand curve for a firm is horizontal. A monopoly has only one firm, therefore the demand curve of a monopoly is horizontal." Discuss this statement.

Requirement and Clue: *You are required to examine the statement carefully to see what is true about it and what is false. The discussion should center on what the examination reveals, pointing out errors (if any) and suggesting corrections.*

Solution:

The opening sentence of the statement is not generally true. It is true only for firms in pure competition where the firms are price-takers. There is only one firm in a monopoly but the demand curve is not horizontal. The demand curve for the monopoly is the same as the demand curve for the industry since the firm and the industry are identical. The monopolist can sell a greater quantity by lowering its price. Hence the demand curve facing the monopolist is downward sloping.

Problem 12-7

The following table represents the demand schedule for a monopoly. Use the information to plot the average revenue curve and the marginal revenue curve for this firm.

Price ($)	Quantity
40	1
36	2
32	3
28	4
24	5
20	6
16	7

Requirement and Clue: *You are expected to be aware of the relationship between demand and average revenue and how to derive marginal revenue, given certain information.*

Solution:

The following two points worth noting: (1) the demand and average revenue curves coincide, and (2) marginal revenue can be obtained from total revenue.

From the information given in the table, a total revenue column can be constructed. Total revenue is price times quantity. From the total revenue column, the marginal revenue can be constructed. Marginal revenue is the change in total revenue divided by the change in quantity. These columns are shown in the table below:

Price ($)	Quantity	Total revenue ($)	Marginal revenue ($)
40	1	40	32
36	2	72	24
32	3	96	16
28	4	112	8
24	5	120	0
20	6	120	-8
16	7	112	

Plotting the information in the first two columns will give the average revenue curve, which is the same as the demand curve. Plotting the information in the second and last columns will give the marginal revenue curve.

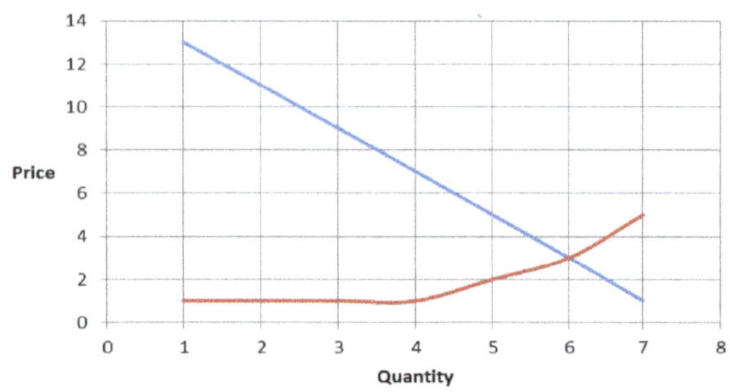

Blue = Demand = Average revenue; Red = Marginal revenue

Problem 12-8

What is the relationship between marginal revenue and price in monopoly?

Requirement and Clue: *Focus on the shape of the demand curve and what you can deduce from it.*

Solution:

In a monopoly, the demand curve or average revenue curve is downward sloping. Average revenue is price. If average revenue is falling, then marginal revenue must be less than average revenue and is pulling average revenue down. We can conclude that in pure competition, marginal revenue is less than price.

Problem 12-9

The following table shows a monopolist's demand and cost data.

Quantity	Price ($)	Total revenue ($)	Marginal revenue ($)	Total cost ($)	Marginal cost ($)
1	15		30		
2	14		31		
3	13		32		
4	12		33		
5	11		34		
6	10		36		
7	9		39		
8	8		42		

(a) *Plot the monopolist's total revenue and total cost curves.*

(b) *Calculate the monopolist's marginal revenue and marginal cost at each output level and complete the relevant columns in the table.*

(c) *Plot the marginal revenue and the marginal cost curves.*

(d) *What is the profit maximizing output?*

(e) *At what price will the firm sell this output?*

Requirement and Clue: *This problem is a test of your knowledge of total revenue, marginal revenue, and marginal cost and how to calculate them from given data. A knowledge of the monopolist's profit-maximizing price and output is also required.*

Solution:

To plot the total revenue and total cost curves, it would be well to calculate total revenue and then complete the total revenue column. Total revenue is price multiplied by quantity. See the table below.

Quantity	Price ($)	Total revenue ($)	Marginal revenue ($)	Total cost ($)	Marginal cost ($)
1	15	15	30	13	1
2	14	28	31	11	1
3	13	39	32	9	1
4	12	48	33	7	1
5	11	55	34	5	2
6	10	60	36	3	3
7	9	63	39	1	3
8	8	64	42		

(a) See graph below.

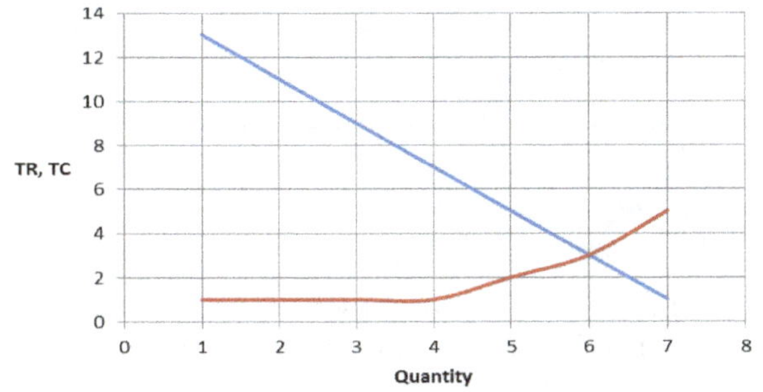

Blue = TR, Red = TC

(b) See table above.

(c) See graph below.

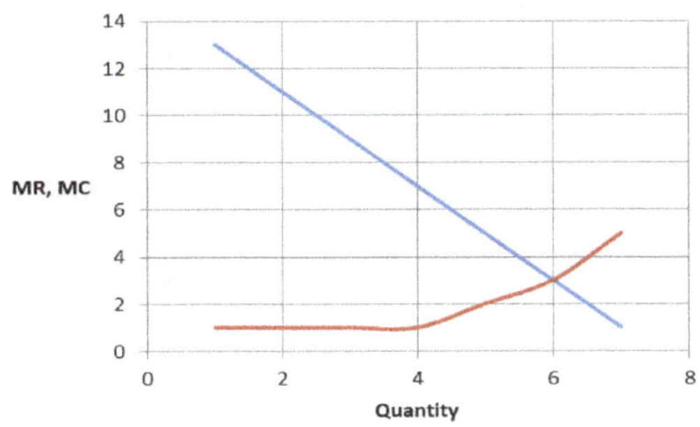

Blue = marginal revenue; red = marginal cost

(d) The profit-maximizing output is 6 units of output where marginal revenue equals marginal cost.

(e) This output will be sold at a price of $9.50.

Problem 12-10

"One of the advantages of being in a monopoly situation is that the monopolist has so much market power that it can at once control both price and quantity. This places all monopolies in an enviable position as far as profit-making is concerned. All the monopolist needs to do to increase profits is to raise its price." Discuss.

Requirement and Clue: *You are required to examine the statement carefully to determine what is right or wrong with it and comment accordingly.*

Solution:

The firm in a monopoly situation may indeed have great market power. However, it cannot control both price and quantity at the same time. It can set the price, and the quantity that it sells at that price would be determined by the demand; or it can decide on the quantity that it will place on the market, and the price would be determined by the demand. The monopolist cannot ignore its demand curve. Raising price does not ensure higher profits. It may lead to a relatively large decrease in quantity demanded, resulting in losses. Consider the theoretical case where the monopolist sets its price so high that hardly anyone buys its product. That certainly would not be a profitable situation.

Problem 12-11

What is X-inefficiency and what can cause it? How does X-inefficiency affect the monopolist's profit level?

Requirement and Clue: *This is a three-part problem. Answer each part in order. The first part is definitional. State clearly the meaning of the concept. The second part of the problem requires a statement of the cause of X-inefficiency, and the third part requires a brief analysis of the impact of X-inefficiency.*

Solution:

The term X-inefficiency is used to describe the condition that exists when a firm fails to use its resources in their most economically efficient way.

X-inefficiency can result from the firm's keeping on unproductive workers perhaps out of loyalty, putting unproductive relatives and friends on the payroll without any economic justification, or padding executives' expense accounts.

X-inefficiency raises the monopolist's cost and thus reduces the firm's profit level. The following diagrams illustrate the point.

Diagram A

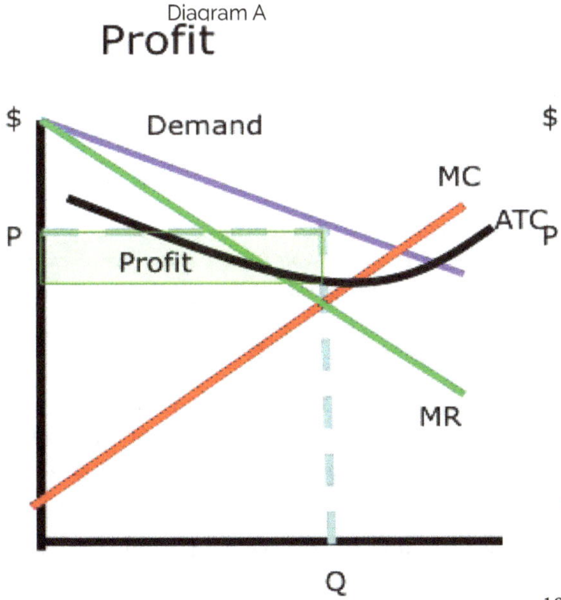

Diagram B

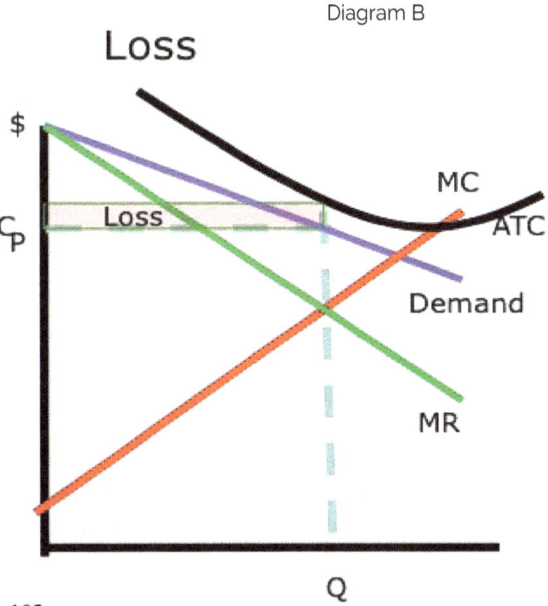

Diagram A illustrates an efficient monopolist, while Diagram B shows an inefficient monopolist. The demand and marginal revenue (MR) curves of both firms are identical. The efficient monopolist produces its output at a much lower average total cost than does the inefficient monopolist. In fact, the inefficient monopolist actually incurs a loss. The profit/loss rectangles are shown as the shaded areas in the diagrams. The inefficient monopolist incurs a loss while the efficient monopolist earns a profit. This is due to X-inefficiency.

Problem 12-12

Is there any relationship among elasticity, total revenue, and marginal revenue of a monopolist?

Requirement and Clue: *The solution to this problem requires more than a simple yes or no answer. If there are relationships among the concepts, you are expected to point them out.*

Solution:

If the demand for a product is elastic, a reduction in price will cause total revenue to increase. But total revenue can increase only if marginal revenue is positive. It follows, therefore, that if marginal revenue is positive, the demand for the product in that range must be elastic.

When the price elasticity of demand for a product is unitary, a reduction in the price of the product will not change total revenue. If total revenue is constant, then marginal revenue most be zero. Therefore, it follows that when marginal revenue is zero, the elasticity of demand for the product at that price must be unitary elastic.

An inelastic demand implies that a reduction in price will cause total revenue to fall. But total revenue can fall only if marginal revenue is negative. Hence, when marginal revenue is negative, the demand for the product must be inelastic.

Problem 12-13

The following diagram shows the demand and marginal cost (MC) curves for a monopolist.

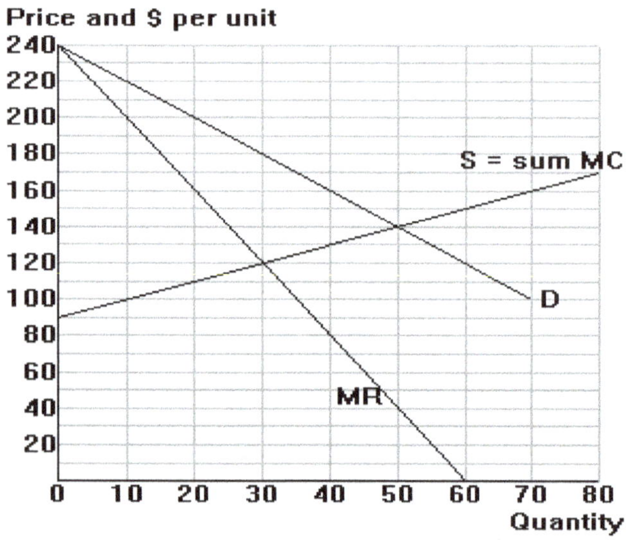

(a) *What is the profit-maximizing level of output for this firm?*

(b) *What is the profit-maximizing price?*

Requirement and Clue: *Focus on the profit-maximizing condition for a monopolist.*

Solution:

(a) The profit-maximizing level of output occurs where marginal revenue equals marginal cost. The marginal revenue curve lies halfway between the demand curve and the vertical axis as shown in the graph.

Marginal revenue equals marginal cot at an output level of 30. This is the profit-maximizing level of output.

(b) The profit-maximizing price occurs where marginal revenue equals marginal cost. Price is read from the demand curve so the profit-maximizing price is $180 as shown in the graph.

Problem 12-14

The following diagram shows cost and revenue curves for a profit-maximizing monopolist.

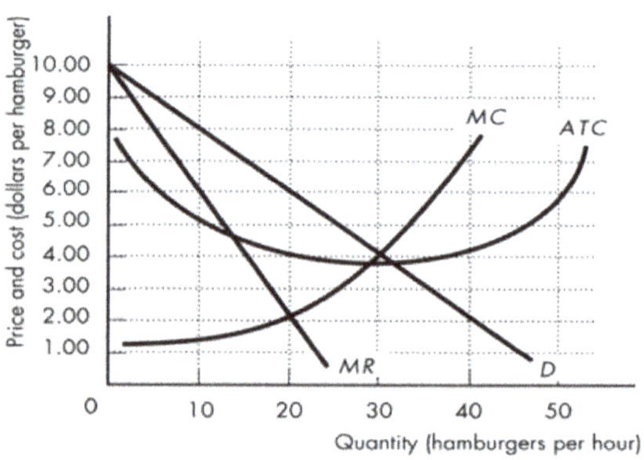

(a) *The firm should produce an output of________ hamburgers and charge a price of $________. Its total revenue will be $________, its total cost will be $________, and its total profit will be $________.*

(b) *If this monopolist is forced to charge a price of $5, it will produce ________ hamburgers. Its total revenue will be $________, its total cost will be $________, and its total profit will be $________.*

Requirement and Clue: *You ability to read graphs as well as your knowledge of certain concepts is being tested here. Focus on the concepts involved and on the relationship among them.*

Solution:

Calculations: (a) Total revenue is price × quantity (6 × 20 = **120**); total cost is average total cost × quantity (4 × 20 = **80**); total profit is total revenue – total cost (120 – 80 = **40**) or profit per unit × quantity (6 – 4) × 20 = 2 × 20 = **40**.

Calculations: (b) Total revenue is price × quantity (5 × 25) = **125**;

total cost is average total cost × quantity (3.75 × 25) = **93.75**); total profit is total revenue – total cost (125 – 93.75 = **31.25**).

(a) The firm should produce an output of 20 units and charge a price of $6.00. Its total revenue will be $120, its total cost will be $80, and its total profit will be $40.

(b) If this monopolist is forced to charge a price of $5, it will produce 25 units. Its total revenue will be $125, its total cost will be $93.75, and its total profit will be $31.25.

Problem 12-15

What is allocative efficiency and what condition is necessary for its existence?

Requirement and Clue: *This is a two-part problem. Answer each part in order. A clear and precise definition of the concept is required as well as a statement of the condition necessary for it to exist.*

Solution:

Allocative efficiency is the term used to refer to the condition that exists when resources are optimally allocated. The resources are employed in their best use. When allocative efficiency is obtained, any change in the distribution of resources will reduce consumers' satisfaction.

Allocative efficiency is achieved when the price of the product is equal to marginal cost. This condition exists when the purely competitive firm is in equilibrium.

Problem 12-16

What do you consider to be the most important economic argument against monopoly?

Requirement and Clue: *What is required here is a strong argument against monopoly. The choice of issue is subjective. Do not ignore the adjective "economic" in the problem. For example, there may be strong political arguments, but you are required to focus on economics.*

Solution:

It is a fundamental economic principle that, given the demand for a product, the greater the supply, the lower will be the price. The monopolist, being the only producer in the industry, is in an ideal position to restrict output. This contrived scarcity ensures a higher price for the product. In a purely competitive market, each firm produces such a small fraction of total output, that no one firm can hope to affect the market price by variation in its output. Only a real scarcity can benefit the competitive firm in terms of a higher industry price.

The monopolist has two main ways of restricting output. First, it may destroy goods already produced. Second, the monopolist may resort to under-utilization of capacity. The restriction of output by these two means represents a real loss to the society in terms of a waste of resources. Consumers get less of the product at a higher price than would be the case under competition. Also, under pure competition, if returns in an industry are relatively high, resources will flow into that industry and output would expand. Barriers to entry prevent this from happening in a monopoly situation, and efficient allocation of resources i not achieved. It seems to me that the most important economic argument against monopoly is the restriction of output and the waste associated with such output restrictions.

Problem 12-17

Do monopolies always earn excessive profits?

Requirement and Clue: *A simple yes or no answer will not be sufficient here. A discussion of the issue of monopoly profits is required.*

Solution:

A commonly held misconception is that monopolies always earn huge profits. In fact, although some monopolies make huge profits, others incur losses. In some cases, excessively high production costs result in losses to the monopolist. If the average total cost curve is so high that it becomes tangent to the average revenue (demand) curve, the monopolist's profit would be zero. The monopolist's profit may therefore be high, low, or may even be zero.

Another issue with the question raised in the problem is the use of the term "excessive". What may be viewed as being excessive by some may be seen as normal or justifiable by others. It is subjective.

Problem 12-18

Why might a monopolist choose not to maximize its profits?

Requirement and Clue: *Focus on the signals that profits may send.*

Solution:

A monopolist might choose not to maximize its profits for several reasons. First, extremely high profits provide incentives for other firms to attempt to break through the entry barriers and end the monopoly. Second, social conscience may prevent those who make the decisions in the monopoly from undertaking measures necessary to maximize profits. Public opinion may enter into such a decision, and the firm may want to appear to be acting in the public interest. In this case, the firm may decide to earn a satisfactory profit instead of trying to earn maximum profits. Third, the monopolist may want to avoid provoking the government to regulate its price and other profit factors.

Problem 12-19

What are the considerations that may deter a monopolist from seeking to maximize profits?

Requirement and Clue: *This problem is similar to the previous one and requires a similar solution.*

Solution:

The monopolist maximizes its profits when it sells its product at a price at which marginal revenue equals marginal cost. But certain circumstances may cause the monopolist to set a price that is different from the profit-maximizing price.

First, a monopolist mat deliberately refrain from earning maximum profits if it feels that there is a chance that such profits may attract other firms into the industry. By keeping price below the profit-maximizing level, the monopolist makes entry into the industry less attractive and more difficult.

Second, fear of government regulation may deter a monopolist from seeking maximum profits. The monopolist may be less noticeable to government regulatory agencies if it charges a price that is below its profit-maximizing level.

Finally, a monopolist may not want to lose favour with the public for charging what the public might perceive as an exorbitant price. This desire to appear reasonable may serve as a deterrent to profit maximization. For all the foregoing reasons, a monopolist may deliberately not take full advantage of its monopoly power in setting the price of its product.

Problem 12-20

Discuss the view that monopoly is beneficial because it eliminates advertisement which is always wasteful.

Requirement and Clue: *You are required to examine the view expressed in the problem. If there are points of disagreement, state them. If not, present arguments to support the statement.*

Solution:

A monopoly exists when a single producer produces a product that has no close substitutes. It is true that such a firm would not need to advertise in an attempt to increase its share of the market, but it may advertise in order to increase the size of the market. Advertising that seeks to increase market share is not the only type of advertising. There is the type of advertising that give consumers greatly needed information about new products, about prices, about events that are to take place, and so on. Although this type of advertising is often costly, it can hardly be said to be wasteful.

The type of advertising that may be justifiably considered wasteful is the type that is prevalent in monopolistic competition. The aim of this type of competitive advertisement is to persuade consumers that one product is different from a close substitute. The firm in monopolistic competition advertises in order to increase preference (and hence demand) for its particular product. If this type of advertisement were eliminated, prices would conceivably be lower.

Problem 12-21

A pharmaceutical company, through substantial research and development activities, has developed a powerful drug that has been tested and proved to be successful in treating migraine headaches. What can this company do to prevent other pharmaceutical companies from duplicating its product?

Requirement and Clue: *This problem requires you to be aware of the means by which a firm can protect itself from competition. Focus on entry barriers erected by the government.*

Solution:

The pharmaceutical company can protect its product from competition by obtaining a patent from the government. A patent is an exclusive right granted by a government to a producer to produce a particular product; it is not extended to any other producer for the duration of the patent. This patent will provide some measure of protection from potential competitors.

Problem 12-22

Can a monopolist always succeed in increasing its profits by raising its price?

Requirement and Clue: *This is a straight forward problem but it requires more than a simple "yes" or "no" solution. A discussion of the question is expected. In your solution, focus on the profit-maximizing condition of the monopolist.*

Solution:

The notion that a monopolist can always increase its profits by raising its price is incorrect. If the monopolist is charging a price that is less than that at which marginal revenue equals marginal cost, then an increase in price will raise its profits. If it is charging a price higher than that at which marginal revenue equals marginal cost, then an increase in price will reduce its profits. If the firm is charging a price that is consistent with the marginal revenue equals marginal cost condition for profit maximization, then any change in its price will result in lower—not higher—profits.

Problem 12-23

Demonstrate that if marginal cost is zero, the monopolist will maximize its profits by producing at that point where the price elasticity of demand is unity.

Requirement and Clue: *The solution to this problem requires an understanding of the relationship between elasticity, total revenue, and marginal revenue, and also the profit-maximizing position of a monopolist.*

Solution:

The monopolistic firm maximizes its profits when it produces a level of output at which marginal revenue equals marginal cost. If marginal cost equals zero, then the profit-maximizing monopolist will produce an output where marginal revenue is zero. But when marginal revenue is zero, total revenue is at its maximum and demand is unitary elastic. Hence, it is shown that if marginal cost equals zero, the monopolist will maximize profits by producing where the price elasticity of demand is one.

Problem 12-24

How does the existence of economies of scale affect the general conclusion that pure competition results in a lower price for the consumer and a larger quantity of output than monopoly does?

Requirement and Clue: *You must be familiar with the concept of economies of scale. Consider whether there are circumstances when the general conclusion does not hold.*

Solution:

Economies of scale are present when long-run average cost declines as output increases. The general conclusion that pure competition results in a lower price and larger quantity than monopoly does is valid, provided that the monopolist faces cost conditions similar to those confronting the purely competitive firm. However, if substantial economies of scale are present, then the general conclusion may no longer hold. A single firm in a purely competitive market may be quite incapable of taking advantage of economies of scale, while the firm in a monopoly may have such a large output that its unit cost may be relatively low. In such a case, the price of the product may be lower in a monopolized market and output may be greater than in a purely competitive market.

Problem 12-25

Complete Electricity, a hypothetical private electricity generating company in a small town, provides all the electricity in the town. Complete Electricity charges a fixed price per day for its electricity. Through thorough economic analysis, Complete Electricity has determined that its profit-maximizing price (rate) is $0.70 per day. Instead of charging $0.70 per day, the company charges $0.65 per day. Is there any rationale in Complete Electricity's pricing policy?

Requirement and Clue: *The question that you have to answer is this: Why would a monopolist deliberately charge a price that is less than its profit-maximizing price?*

Solution:

Complete Electricity's pricing policy might be quite rational. By deliberately charging a price that is less than the profit-maximizing price, Complete Electricity could be acting in a manner that would avoid it being regulated or even nationalized, that is, being taken over by the government. Also, the company could be creating a "caring company" image that could be beneficial and pay dividends in terms of customer loyalty. Moreover, maximizing profits might be seen as an incentive for other firms to enter the industry and end the monopoly reign.

Problem 12-26

How does monopoly affect consumer surplus and producer surplus?

Requirement and Clue: *You must know what consumer surplus and producer surplus are in order to solve this problem. It is well to compare both consumer surplus and producer surplus in the absence of monopoly with consumer surplus and consumer surplus when monopoly exists. Graphs can be used to some advantage here.*

Solution:

Consumer surplus is defined as the difference between the amount that consumers would have paid for a product and the amount that they actually pay. It is a benefit that accrues to the consumers.

Producer surplus is the difference between the amount that producers receive from selling an item and the amount they would have accepted for the item. It is a benefit that accrues to the producers.

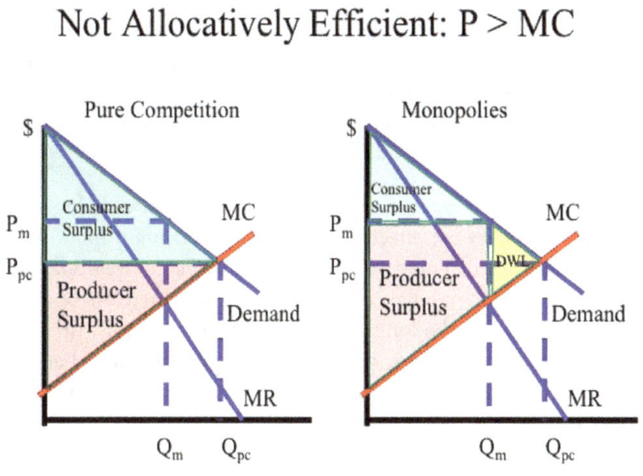

Diagram A Diagram B

In Diagram A, the purely competitive industry produces an output of Q_{pc} at a price of P_{pc}. Consumer surplus is represented by the top green triangle, while producer surplus is represented by the bottom pink triangle. In diagram B, the monopoly produces an output of Q_m at a price of P_m. The green triangle represents consumer surplus while the pink area represents producer surplus. The consumer surplus under monopoly is less than that under pure competition, and the producer surplus under monopoly is greater than that under pure competition. Under monopoly, a deadweight loss also occurs as represented by the small yellow triangle. It can be concluded that monopoly reduces consumer surplus, increases producer surplus, and creates a deadweight loss.

Problem 12-27

How might a government regulatory agency regulate a monopoly?

Requirement and Clue: *Consider guidelines suggested by economic theory. Focus on results from the purely competitive model.*

Solution:

Economic theory suggests some guidelines that government regulators can follow in regulating a monopoly. First, they can force the monopoly to practice allocative efficiency by setting its price equal to marginal cost. This marginal-cost pricing regulation moves the monopoly away from its profit-maximizing position. Marginal-cost pricing prevents the monopolist from restricting output to exact a higher price for the product and may even result in losses.

Second, the regulators can enforce average-cost pricing on the monopolist. Average-cost pricing regulation sets the price of the product equal to average cost. This regulation eliminates any monopoly profits that the monopolist would otherwise have made.

Finally, the regulators can choose to have the monopolist operate at the lowest average cost. If the average cost declines over a large range of output, the minimum average cost could occur at a level of output too large for the market served by the monopolist.

Problem 12-28

What is the significance of entry barriers to monopoly?

Requirement and Clue: *Obviously, you cannot solve this problem without first knowing what entry barriers are. Focus on what would happen in monopoly had it not been for entry barriers.*

Solution:

Entry barriers are obstacles that prevent firms from entering into an industry. If they are effective, they serve to maintain monopoly. Because freedom of entry and exit exist in pure competition (no barriers to entry), purely competitive firms cannot earn positive economic profits in the long run. However, in monopoly, the firm can earn positive economic profits in the long run. Entry barriers prevent new firms from entering into the industry and compete the profits away.

Problem 12-29

Define each of the following terms:

a. *Price discrimination*
b. *Dumping*
c. *Arbitrage transactions*

Requirement and Clue: *This is a definitional problem. Your definitions should be clear and to the point. Rambling is unnecessary.*

Solution:

a. Price discrimination is the practice of selling a product in different markets at different prices for reasons unrelated to cost. An example is the practice of charging different rates for household and commercial users of electricity.
b. Dumping is the practice of selling exports in foreign countries more cheaply than the domestic price. It is a form of price discrimination.
c. Arbitrage transactions refer to the purchase of products in a low-price market and their sale in a higher-price market.

Problem 12-30

What is price discrimination? When is it possible? When is it profitable?

Requirement and Clue: *This is a thee-part problem. You should address each part in order. In solving the first part of the problem, be careful not to be long-winded. Just define the concept clearly and give an example, if possible. The definition of the concept suggests a solution for the second part. For the third part of the problem, focus on demand conditions in the various markets.*

Solution:

Price discrimination is the sale by a firm of a product in different markets at different prices for reasons not associated with cost differentials. An example of price discrimination is a cinema charging different prices to children and seniors for the same movie.

To practice price discrimination, two conditions must be satisfied. First, the firm must be able to group the buyers of its product into different classes, such as rich and poor, adults and children, residential and commercial, or seniors, children under 12, and the rest of the population. Second, the firm must be able to maintain a separation between the markets in which the product is sold so that buyers cannot buy in the low-price market and resell the product in a high-price market.

For price discrimination to be profitable, the price elasticity of demand in each market must be different. The firm will earn a larger profit by charging a higher price in the market with the less elastic (more inelastic) demand.

Problem 12-31

Should price discrimination always be condemned?

Requirement and Clue: *The word "always" in the problem is significant. If one case can be found where price discrimination is beneficial, then the practice should not always be condemned.*

Solution:

Price discrimination exists when a firm charges different prices to different buyers for reasons not associated with cost. It is clear that those who willingly practice price discrimination do so because they benefit from the practice. They will not condemn price discrimination. But there are other benefits that can be derived from price discrimination. Many goods and services might not be produced at all if the firm were not allowed to engage in price discrimination. For example, the only lawyer in a small remote community may find it worthwhile to keep her practice in that community only if she can discriminate by charging her wealthy clients a higher price than she can charge her less affluent clients. Similarly, where airlines and hotels enjoy monopoly power, price discrimination in airfares and hotel accommodation makes it possible for many parents to take their children on vacation. Price discrimination along these lines should probably not be condemned.

Problem 12-32

What arguments can you advance against price discrimination?

Requirement and Clue: *Focus on the possible negative effects of price discrimination. Think of the role of price as a rationing device and as a signal for resource flows.*

Solution:

Price discrimination is the practice of selling the same product at different prices to different customers for reasons unrelated to cost. This practice can be carried to the point where the price is set below marginal cost. For example, price discrimination in water rates could result in such low rates to residential users that they end up wasting water by opening taps and allowing the water to run for extended periods of time without any real justification. When price is set below marginal cost, a misallocation of resources will result. The amount of resources that would flow into the industry is above the social optimum. As another example, consider the case of a public transit system. Price discrimination is usually practised in favour of children and seniors. If price discrimination is carried too far in this case, taxpayers may have to subsidize the transit system. Resources that could be better allocated elsewhere would be diverted into this industry.

Problem 12-33

The government increases the tax on the profits of a monopoly. Should the firm change its price or quantity produced in response to the increase in tax?

Requirement and Clue: *A yes or no answer is not sufficient. You are expected to analyse the situation and arrive at a decision. Focus on the effect of the tax on the firm's profit-maximization position.*

Solution:

Assume that the firm is producing an output and charging a price at which its marginal revenue equals its marginal cost. Here, the firm is maximizing its profits. The increase in the tax on the monopolist's profit is a fixed cost that does not affect the firm's marginal cost. The firm's profit- maximizing position remains the same after the increase in the tax. The increase in the tax on the monopolist's profit does not affect the monopolist's price-output decision. The monopolist should continue to maximize its profits by operating where its marginal revenue and marginal cost are equal and just pay the additional tax out of its profits.

Problem 12-34

"A profit-maximizing monopolist will always set the highest possible price for its product." Is this statement true or false?

Requirement and Clue: *Simply choosing true or false will not suffice as a solution to this problem. You must also defend your position.*

Solution:

The objective of the monopolist is not to set its price as high as possible but to set a price that will result in maximum profits. That price is the one at which its marginal revenue equals its marginal cost. Any other price will result in lower profits for the monopolist.

Multiple-Choice

In each case, circle the letter that corresponds with the correct answer.

1. In economics, a monopoly is:

a. a large firm with many subsidiaries
b. a board game with one or more players
c. a group of firms rivaling each other to gain supremacy of a certain market
d. a single firm that produces a product that has no close substitutes.

Answer: d

Reason: *A monopoly is a one-firm industry.*

2. A monopoly may be defined as:

a. a large number of firms producing the industry's output
b. few firms with significant control over price and output
c. one firm selling a product that has no close substitutes
d. a large number of firms producing differentiated products with many close, though not perfect, substitutes.

Answer: c

Reason: *In a monopoly, there is only one firm in the industry.*

3. Which of the following is true of monopoly?

a. There is no problem with the notion of close substitutes in the definition of monopoly
b. The notion of close substitutes is purely objective
c. The notion of close substitutes is subjective
d. None of the above

Answer: c

Reason: *What constitutes close substitutes will differ from one person to another.*

4. Examples of pure monopoly are:

a. extremely easy to find because they are the dominant form of firms in the real world
b. prevalent in large cities but non-existent in small towns
c. difficult to find in the real world
d. none of the above

Answer: c

Reason: *There are substitutes for most products.*

5. Examples of monopolies are:

a. the central bank
b. the Canadian and U.S. postal service
c. Via Rail (in Canada)
d. all of the above

Answer: d

Reason: *The central bank has a monopoly on the issue of paper currency, the Canadian and U.S. postal services have a monopoly on mail delivery, and Via Rail has a monopoly on rail travel in Canada.*

6. In discussing monopoly, barriers to entry refer to:

a. physical fences erected around certain industries to prevent consumers from crossing the borders
b. security guards placed at the entrance of large companies to prevent theft or forced entry
c. circumstances that restrict the entry of firms into an industry
d. none of the above.

Answer: c

Reason: Anything that serves as a deterrent to the entry of firms into an industry is a barrier to entry.

7. Barriers to entry include:

a. ownership or control of essential resources
b. patents
c. franchises
d. all of the above

Answer: d

Reason: *The choices in a, b, and c can prevent firms from entering into an industry.*

8. Monopolies can be created by:

a. patents and franchises
b. control of essential raw materials
c. substantial economies of scale
d. all of the above

Answer: d

Reason: *All of the choices serve as effective entry barriers that sustain monopolies.*

9. A natural monopoly is:

a. a market in which a single firm can satisfy the entire market demand more cheaply than two or more firms could
b. a monopoly that is formed by acts of nature such as hurricanes, tornadoes, and volcanic action
c. an industry with a single firm selling all natural products
d. a company that is so large that only the government can run it efficiently.

Answer: a

Reason: *Choice a correctly identifies a natural monopoly.*

10. Typical examples of natural monopolies are:

a. telephone companies
b. gas companies
c. electric power companies
d. all of the above

Answer: d

Reason: *It is generally inefficient or impractical to have more than one of the businesses listed operating in the same area at the same time.*

11. The difference between a patent and a franchise is:

a. only a government can grant a franchise but anyone can grant a patent
b. only a government can grant a patent but anyone can grant a franchise
c. a franchise is binding while a patent is not
d. a patent is binding while a franchise is not

Answer: b

Reason: *A patent is an exclusive right granted by a government. Governments and private businesses grant franchises.*

12. Monopolies can exist in the long run because:

a. there are effective barriers to entry into the industry
b. they do not produce at the point where marginal revenue equals marginal cost
c. the long run is defined as a situation in which competition does not exist
d. they minimize cost rather than maximize profits in the long run.

Answer: a

Reason: *It is the existence of effective entry barriers that sustains monopolies. Otherwise, firms would enter the industry and end the monopoly.*

13. The demand curve for a monopolist is:

a. horizontal because it is the only firm in the industry
b. vertical because the monopolist has full control over price and quantity
c. downward sloping because it can sell more by lowering its price
d. upward sloping because its demand curve is its supply curve

Answer: c

Reason: *The monopolist's demand curve is the same as the market demand curve that is negatively sloped.*

14. In monopoly, average revenue is:

a. greater than marginal revenue
b. less than marginal revenue
c. equal to marginal revenue
d. greater or less than marginal revenue depending on demand

Answer: b

Reason: *Average revenue is falling; therefore marginal revenue must be less than average revenue.*

15. In a monopoly:

a. the firm's demand curve is perfectly elastic
b. marginal revenue equals average revenue
c. marginal revenue is less than average revenue
d. marginal revenue is greater than average revenue

Answer: c

Reason: *Average revenue is falling; hence marginal revenue must be less than average revenue.*

16. In order to maximize profits, a monopolist must produce where:

a. marginal revenue equals marginal cost
b. price equals marginal cost
c. price equals average total cost
d. all of the above

Answer: a

Reason: The profit maximizing position for a monopolist is where marginal revenue equals marginal cost.

17. Which of the following is true for a monopolist as well as for a pure competitor?

a. The firm maximizes its profits where its marginal revenue equals its marginal cost
b. The firm has no control over the price of its product
c. The firm should shut down in the short run if its price falls below average total cost
d. The firm always earns positive economic profits in the short run but not in the long run.

Answer: a

Reason: If the firm operates where its marginal revenue and marginal cost are equal, it will maximize its profits regardless of the market structure in which it operates.

18. At its present level of output, a monopolist finds that its marginal revenue is greater than its marginal cost. To maximize profits, the monopolist should:

a. reduce price and leave output unchanged
b. increase price and leave output unchanged
c. continue to operate at current price and output levels
d. reduce price and increase output.

Answer: d

Reason: If marginal revenue is greater than marginal cost, increasing output will reduce marginal revenue to make it equal to marginal cost. But increasing output will reduce price since the demand curve is downward sloping.

19. At an output level of 200 units, a monopolist's marginal cost is $66, its marginal revenue is $70, its average variable cost is $60, and its average total cost is $76. To maximize its profit or minimize its losses, the firm should:

a. increase its output to more than 200 units
b. leave its output at 200 units
c. shut down
d. reduce its output below 200 units

Answer: a

Reason: The firm should try to produce the output at which its marginal revenue equals its marginal cost. Since at 200 units of output the firm's marginal revenue is greater than its marginal cost, the monopolist should increase its output.

20. The monopolist seeking to maximize profits will operate where its demand curve is:

a. inelastic c. elastic
b. unitary elastic d. perfectly elastic

Answer: c

Reason: The monopolist's marginal cost is positive; therefore, when its marginal revenue equals its marginal cost, marginal revenue will be positive, and when marginal revenue is positive, demand is elastic.

21. Which of the following is true for a monopolist?

a. If marginal revenue is positive, demand is elastic
b. If marginal revenue is zero, demand is unitary elastic
c. If marginal revenue is negative, demand is inelastic
d. All of the above

Answer: d

Reason: Choices a, b, and c correctly state the relationship between the marginal revenue of a monopolist and elasticity of demand.

Questions 22-26 refer to the figure below which shows revenue and cost curves for a monopolist.

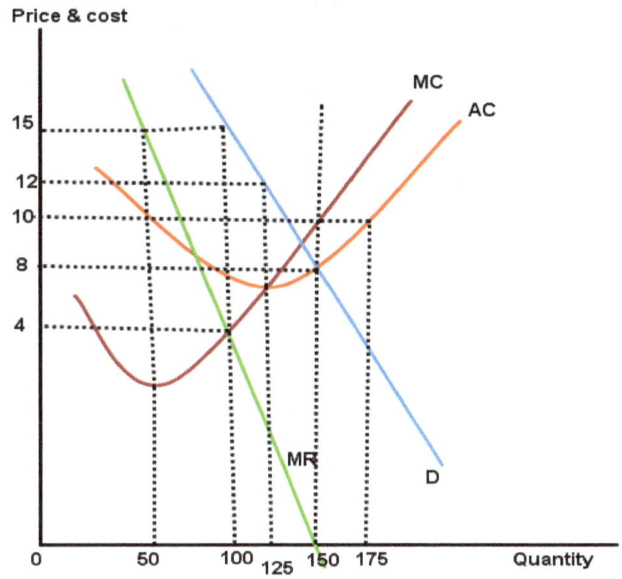

22. In order to maximize its profits, this firm should produce:

a. 100 units of output at a price of $15
b. 150 units of output at a price of $15
c. 125 units of output at a price of $12
d. 100 units of output at a price of $8

Answer: a

Reason: At 100 units of output and a price of $15, the firm's marginal revenue equals its marginal cost, which maximizes its profits.

23. In order to maximize total revenue, the firm should produce:

a. 100 units c. 150 units
b. 125 units d. 175 units

Answer: c

Reason: Total revenue is maximized when marginal revenue is zero. This occurs at an output of 150 units.

24. The optimum price for this firm at the profit-maximizing output is:

a. above $15 c. $10
b. exactly $15 d. $8

Answer: b

Reason: The optimum price is the profit-maximizing price which occurs when marginal revenue equals marginal cost. At this point average revenue or price is $15 (read from the demand curve).

25. When the firm is maximizing its profits, its total revenue is:

a. $1,500 c. $2,625
b. $1,200 d. $1,750

Answer: a

Reason: Total revenue is price multiplied by quantity. The profit-

maximizing price and quantity are $15 and 100 units. Thus total revenue is ($15 × 100) = $1,500.

26. At the profit-maximizing output, the marginal cost is:

a. $10 c. $15
b. $8 d. $4

Answer: d

Reason: The profit-maximizing output is 100 units. At this output, the marginal cost is $4 (read from the marginal cost curve).

27. If in the long run a firm earns positive economic profits, then we know that:

a. the firm is not a profit maximizer
b. the firm is definitely a perfect competitor
c. the industry must have effective barriers to entry
d. price equals long-run average cost.

Answer: c

Reason: Without the existence of effective entry barriers, new firms would enter the industry an the profits would be reduced to normal profits.

28. In the long run, the profit-maximizing monopolist will:

a. maximize short-run profits and ignore long-run profits because they are identical
b. always earn positive economic profits because there are no competitors
c. operate where marginal revenue equals long-run marginal cost
d. none of the above

Answer: c

Reason: When the monopolist has had sufficient time to adjust to the long run, the long-run marginal cost will be the relevant factor to consider.

29. Allocative efficiency occurs when:

a. price is greater than marginal cost
b. marginal revenue is greater than marginal cost
c. marginal revenue is equal to marginal cost
d. price equals marginal cost

Answer: d

Reason: When price equals marginal cost, any re-arrangement of resources will reduce efficiency.

30. Other things being equal, compared with perfect competition, monopoly:

a. produces a larger quantity of output at a higher price
b. produces a larger quantity of output at a lower price
c. produces a smaller quantity of output at a lower price
d. produces a smaller quantity of output at a higher price

Answer: d

Reason: By restricting output, the monopolist creates artificial scarcity and thus sells at a higher price.

31. Monopoly tends to:

a. reduce consumer surplus and increase producer surplus
b. increase consumer surplus and reduce producer surplus
c. reduce both consumer and producer surplus
d. increase both consumer and producer surplus

Answer: a

Reason: Under monopoly, consumers lose because they pay more for less. Producers gain because they exact a higher price for a smaller quantity of output.

32. Which of the following can be used to regulate a monopoly?

a. Marginal-cost pricing
b. Average-cost pricing
c. Minimum average-cost pricing
d. d. All of the above

Answer: d

Reason: Regulators may use any of the choices from a to c to regulate a monopoly.

33. Price discrimination is the practice of:

a. refusing to sell to ethnic minority groups
b. adopting a very conservative approach to pricing
c. setting price above average revenue for certain classes of buyers
d. none of the above

Answer: d

Reason: Price discrimination is the practice of charging different prices to different buyers of a product for reasons not related to cost.

34. The practice of selling the same product in different markets at different prices for reasons not associated with cost is called:

a. product differentiation c. cost allocation
b. price discrimination d. none of the above

Answer: b

Reason: Choice b accurately describes price discrimination.

35. The practice of selling exports in foreign countries more cheaply than the domestic price is referred to as:

a. domestic exploitation c. dumping
b. foreign amelioration d. none of the above

Answer: c

Reason: Choice c accurately describes the practice known as dumping.

36. Arbitrage transactions refer to:

a. the purchase of products in a low-price market and their resale in a high-price market
b. transactions between people in different countries through a third part when the parties to the transactions are strangers
c. the practice of arbitrarily selecting the people with whom transactions will be made
d. none of the above

Answer: a

Reason: Choice a accurately defines arbitrage transactions.

37. A discriminating profit-maximizing monopolist will charge a higher price in the market where:

a. the demand for the product is more elastic or less inelastic

b. the demand for the product is less elastic or more inelastic
c. the customers cannot be separated
d. the output is greater

Answer: b

Reason: Buyers in the market with the less elastic or more inelastic demand will respond less to the higher price.

38. If a sales tax is imposed on each unit of a commodity sold by a profit-maximizing monopolist:

a. the price will rise by an amount less than the tax
b. the price will rise by an amount greater than the tax
c. the marginal cost will not be affected
d. neither the price nor the quantity sold will be affected

Answer: a

Reason: The monopolist will be able to pass on a portion of the tax to buyers, but not the full amount of the tax.

True or False

Determine whether each of the following statements is true or false.

1. Finding perfect examples of pure monopoly in the real world is a very easy matter.

Answer: False

Explanation: Perfect examples of pure monopoly are hard to find because most products have substitutes of one kind or another.

2. Monopolies exist because of effective barriers to entry.

Answer: True

3. Barriers to entry are physical fences erected around large companies to prevent unauthorized persons from entering.

Answer: False

Explanation: Barriers to entry are circumstances that restrict the entry of other firms into a particular industry.

4. Barriers to entry may be created by the government, control of essential resources, and economies of scale.

Answer: True

5. Entry barriers created by the government include patents and franchises.

Answer: True

6. Patents and franchises can be granted only by the government.

Answer: False

Explanation: Only the government can grant patents but the government as well as private businesses can grant franchises.

7. A natural monopoly is a market in which the firms produce and sell only natural products.

Answer: False

Explanation: A natural monopoly is a market in which a single firm can satisfy the entire market demand at a lower cost that two or more firms could.

8. Only monopolies can experience economies of scale.

Answer: False

Explanation: Economies of scale exist when a firm's average cost falls as it increases its scale of operation. Any firm can experience this.

9. A monopolist has so much market power that it can set a price and sell as much as it chooses at that price.

Answer: False

Explanation: The monopolist does not have absolute power over both price and quantity. Its power is restricted by its demand curve.

10. A firm in a monopoly market can sell 9 units of output at a price of \$12 each, and 10 units at a price of \$11 each; therefore the marginal revenue of the 10th unit is \$2.

Answer: True

11. The demand curve of a monopoly is a horizontal straight line because it is the only firm in the industry.

Answer: False

Explanation: The demand curve of a monopolist is downward sloping because it is the industry's demand curve.

12. The monopolist's demand curve is downward sloping but steeper than its marginal revenue curve.

Answer: False

Explanation: The monopolist's demand (average revenue) curve is downward sloping but its marginal revenue curve is steeper than its average revenue curve.

13. The monopolist's total revenue curve starts at the origin, rises, reaches a maximum, and then falls.

Answer: True

14. Whereas in pure competition the firm maximizes its revenue when its marginal revenue equals its marginal cost, in monopoly, the firm must set its marginal revenue above its marginal cost in order to maximize its profit.

Answer: False

Explanation: Whether in pure competition or monopoly, the firm maximizes its profits by operating where its marginal revenue equals its marginal cost.

15. A rational monopolist will always choose to maximize its profits.

Answer: False

Explanation: A monopolist might deliberate choose not to maximize its profits to avoid government regulation or to discourage the entry of new firms.

16. A monopolist maximizes its profits by setting its price equal to its marginal cost.

Answer: False

Explanation: The monopolist maximizes its profits by charging a price at which its marginal revenue and marginal cost are equal. That price will be higher than marginal cost.

17. X-inefficiency means that the firm is operating in an extraordinarily inefficient manner.

Answer: False

Explanation: X-inefficiency means that the firm is not using its resources in the most economically efficient way.

18. If marginal revenue is zero, total revenue is at a maximum, and demand is unitary elastic.

Answer: True

19. A profit-maximizing monopolist will operate only within that range where the demand for its product is elastic.

Answer: True

20. In the long run, the monopolist is likely to operate the same way it does in the short run in terms of setting its price and output levels because it does not need to worry about the entry of new firms in the long run.

Answer: False

Explanation: In the long run, the monopolist maximizes its profits when it equates long-run marginal cost with marginal revenue. This will be different from its short-run profit maximizing position.

21. A profit-maximizing monopolist, in the long run, will always produce an output where price equals long-run average cost.

Answer: False

Explanation: Because of barriers to entry, the monopolist can operate with price above average cost even in the long run.

22. Price discrimination involves setting prices on the basis of cost differentials only.

Answer: False

Explanation: Charging different prices because of differences in cost does not constitute price discrimination. Price discrimination occurs when the monopolist charges different buyers different prices for the same product for reasons not associated with cost.

23. Allocative efficiency is the condition that exists when resources are optimally allocated. This occurs when price equals marginal cost.

Answer: True

24. Compared with pure competition, the price in monopoly is expected to be lower and the quantity to be higher.

Answer: False

Explanation: The monopoly price will generally be higher and the monopoly output lower.

25. Monopoly reduces consumer surplus, increases producer surplus, and creates a deadweight loss.

Answer: True

26. If left to itself, the monopolist will produce that output at which its average cost is at its minimum.

Answer: False

Explanation: It will produce that output at which marginal revenue equals marginal cost.

27. A regulated monopoly will always be forced to produce where marginal revenue equals marginal cost, the extra profits being taxed away.

Answer: False

Explanation: A profit-maximizing monopolist will operate where marginal revenue equals marginal cost in the absence of regulation. Regulation will usually be on some other basis.

28. Price discrimination will be profitable only if the price elasticity of demand is different in each market in which the monopolist sells its product.

Answer: True

29. Arbitrage transactions are transactions that are arbitrarily sanctioned by the government for reasons of national security.

Answer: False

Explanation: Arbitrage transactions refer to the purchase of products in a low-price market and their resale in a high-price market.

30. If a monopolist is maximizing its profits and the tax on its profits increases by 7%, the monopolist should raise its price by 7% to compensate for the loss.

Answer: False

Explanation: If the monopolist raises its price, its profits will be reduced. It should continue to maximize profits and pay the tax.

Completion

(Fill in the blanks)

Use each word or combination of words from the list exactly once.
*(**Hint**: Proceed by elimination)*

Word list

Allocative — Arbitrage — Barriers x 2 — Cost x 2— Discrimination — Does Not — Efficiency — Elastic — Entry x 2 — Franchise — Greater — Higher x 2 — Less Than — Marginal x 4 — Monopolies — Monopoly — Natural — Patent — Price — Revenue x 2— Smaller x 2 — Transactions — X-Inefficiency

Questions

1. Central banks, a city's water supply system, and the Canadian postal service (Canada Post) are examples of ___________.
2. A(n) ___________ is a market structure in which there is only one seller of a product that has no close substitutes.
3. If the situation is such that substantial economies of scale allow one firm to produce the total market output at a lower cost than if there were two or more firms, then the situation is referred to as a(n) ___________ monopoly.
4. Monopolies exist because of various effective ___________ to ___________.
5. A ___________ is an exclusive right granted by the government to a producer to produce a product. A ___________ is an exclusive right to operate a business in a designated area.
6. For a monopoly, marginal revenue is ___________ [greater than, less than] average revenue.
7. In order tom maximize its profits, a monopolist should set a price and produce an output at which ___________ ___________ equals ___________ ___________.
8. ___________ is the condition that exists when a firm fails to use its resources in their most economically efficient way. An example is putting unproductive relatives on the payroll.
9. In terms of elasticity, a profit-maximizing monopolist will operate only within that range where the demand for its product is ___________.
10. ___________ ___________ exists when resources are optimally allocated. This occurs when price equals ___________ ___________.
11. The practice of charging different buyers different prices for the same product for reasons not associated with cost is called ___________ ___________.
12. The purchase of products in a low-price market and their resale in a high-price market, thus making a profit is called ___________ ___________.
13. In the long run, a monopolist may earn positive economic profits because of ___________ to ___________.
14. In the long run, the monopolist maximizes its profits when it equates long-run marginal cost with ___________ ___________.
15. In general, a monopoly produces a ___________ [greater, smaller] quantity and charges a ___________ [higher, lower] price than a purely competitive industry.
16. A discriminating monopolist will produce a ___________ [greater, smaller] output than a non-discriminating monopolist.
17. If an excise tax is imposed on each unit of a commodity sold by a monopolist, the monopolist will produce a ___________ [larger, smaller] quantity and charge a ___________ [lower, higher] price.
18. A tax on the profits of a monopolist ___________ [does, does not] alter the profit- maximizing price or output of the monopolist.

Solution

1. (monopolies)
2. (monopoly)
3. (natural)
4. (barriers, entry)
5. (patent, franchise)
6. (less than)
7. (marginal cost, marginal revenue)
8. (X-inefficiency)
9. (elastic)
10. (allocative efficiency, marginal cost)
11. (price discrimination)
12. (arbitrage transactions)
13. (barriers, entry)
14. (marginal revenue)
15. (smaller, higher)
16. (greater)
17. (smaller, higher)
18. (does not)

13 MONOPOLISTIC COMPETITION & OLIGOPOLY

SYNOPSIS

Imperfect competition exists whenever all the characteristics of pure competition are absent. **Monopolistic competition** is a market structure in which there are many firms selling a similar but differentiated product. Product differentiation is a key feature of monopolistic competition.

The firm in monopolistic competition faces a downward-sloping demand curve. Since there are many substitutes for the products of firms in monopolistic competition, any one firm's demand curve will be relatively elastic.

The monopolistically competitive firm can sell a larger quantity only by lowering its price; therefore, each additional unit sold adds a smaller amount to total revenue. This implies a declining marginal revenue curve.

In order to maximize profits, the firm in monopolistic competition produces an output at which MR = MC. If the monopolistically competitive firm is earning positive economic profits, new firms will enter the industry. In the long run, the firm in monopolistic competition will produce an output where price equals average cost. The output will be less than the competitive output and the price will be higher than the competitive price.

Oligopoly is a market structure in which there are only a few sellers. If there are only two sellers, the situation is defined as **duopoly**. Since the number of firms in oligopoly is so small, interdependent among the firms is recognized.

As in other market structures, the oligopolistic firm maximizes its profits when MR = MC. The **kinked demand curve** model explains price rigidity in oligopoly. Price rigidity can also result from long-term contracts and small menu costs.

In order to discourage other firms from entering the industry, the existing firms may deliberately set a price that is lower than the profit-maximizing price. This practice is known as **limit pricing** or **predatory pricing**.

A **cartel** is formed when the firms in an industry enter into a formal agreement to control price and output in a particular industry. A **perfect cartel** operates like a monopoly. Most actual cartels are imperfect.

Concentration ratios measure the extent to which an industry is dominated by a few firms. As a general rule, the higher the concentration ratio, the less competitive is the industry. The number of firms in an industry is not always a good measure of the degree of competition. A monopolist, for example, might behave more like a pure competitor than like a monopolist is the market is **contestable**.

LEARNING OBJECTIVES

In connection with this module, you should be able to:

1. explain the concept of monopolistic competition
2. describe the demand and marginal revenue of a firm in monopolistic competition
3. explain short-run equilibrium in monopolistic competition
4. discuss the conditions for long-run equilibrium in monopolistic competition
5. discuss the differences and similarities between mobopolistic competition and pure competition
6. explain the effects of advertising
7. explain the behavior of firms in oligopoly
8. explain oligopolistic pricing and output
9. explain the kinked demand curve model
10. discuss alternative pricing strategies
11. discuss cartels and other forms of collusion
12. explain the theory of contestable markets

DEFINITIONS & CONCEPTS

You should be able to define the following terms and concepts:

monopolistic competition	product differentiation
excess capacity theorem	duopoly
oligopoly	differentiated oligopoly
kinked demand curve	limit (predatory) pricing
dominant price leadership	barometric price leadership
cartel	gentlemen's agreements
concentration ratio	workable competition
cost-plus (mark-up) pricing	collusion
contestable market	menu costs

13 MONOPOLISTIC COMPETITION & OLIGOPOLY

Concepts, Definitions & Problems

Problem 13-1

Define imperfect competition.

Requirement and Clue: *This is a definitional problem. You are required only to give a clear statement of the meaning of the concept.*

Solution:

The term "imperfect competition" is often used to refer to a market structure that is neither perfectly competitive nor a pure monopoly. Hence, the term includes both monopolistic competition (many firms producing differentiated products) and oligopoly (a market structure with few firms). Most real world industries are imperfectly competitive.

Problem 13-2

Define monopolistic competition.

Requirement and Clue: *This is a definitional problem. Much can be written about monopolistic competition but you are required only to give a clear statement of the meaning of the concept. Examples will be helpful.*

Solution:

Monopolistic competition, as the name implies, contains elements of monopoly and competition. It is a market structure with a large number of firms producing differentiated products. Freedom into, and exit from, the industry are relatively easy. Examples of monopolistic competition are florists, beauty salons, furniture retail stores, and shoe stores.

Problem 13-3

What are the three main characteristics of monopolistic competition and what is the significance of each characteristic?

Requirement and Clue: *This is a two-part problem. Answer each part in order. You are required to point out the main features of monopolistic competition. Then you are to discuss briefly the implication of each feature.*

Solution:

The main characteristics of monopolistic competition are (1) a large number of firms, (2) differentiated products, and (3) relative freedom of entry into and exit from the market.

Large number of firms

Because of the large number of firms in monopolistic competition, each firm has very little control over market price. Because there are so many firms in this industry, collusion is unlikely to occur. We can expect slight variations in price from one firm to the next.

Differentiated products

This defining feature of monopolistic competition gives each firm a small measure of control over the price of its product. This is the "monopoly" part of monopolistic competition. Product differentiation in fact results in the creation of a large number of close substitutes. Advertising is likely to be vigorous as firms strive to convince customers that their products are "different".

Relative freedom of entry and exit

Relative ease of entry in monopolistic competition prevents firms from earning positive economic profits in the long run. Positive economic profits will attract new firms into the industry since the entry barriers are relatively low, and losses will cause firms to leave the industry in the long run. Relative freedom of entry and exit means that firms in monopolistic competition earn only normal profits in the long run.

Problem 13-4

What are the similarities and differences between pure competition and monopolistic competition?

Requirement and Clue: *The solution to this problem requires that you understand the features of both pure competition and monopolistic competition. Tackle the similarities first and then the differences.*

Solution:

Pure competition and monopolistic competition are similar in two main ways. First, in both market structures, there is a large number of sellers, with each firm producing a small fraction of the total industry output. Second, in each case, there is freedom of entry and exit which means that in both market structures, the firms earn only normal profits in the long run.

Pure competition differs from monopolistic competition in that in pure competition, all firms produce homogeneous products, whereas in monopolistic competition, the products are differentiated. This product differentiation gives firms in monopolistic competition a small amount of control over price. Also, firms in pure competition don't need to advertise their products, whereas firms in monopolistic competition do.

Problem 13-5

How important is product differentiation in monopolistic competition?

Requirement and Clue: *To solve this problem, you must, of course, know what product differentiation is. Focus of the role of product differentiation in monopolistic competition.*

Solution:

Product differentiation is the condition that exists when firms distinguish their products from those of their competitors. Product differentiation is the defining characteristic of monopolistic competition. Without product differentiation, there would hardly be any difference between pure competition and monopolistic competition. The distinction would all but disappear.

Problem 13-6

How can firms differentiate their products from those of other firms?

Requirement and Clue: *Focus on the various techniques firms use to convince customers that their products are different.*

Solution:

Firms can differentiate their products in many ways. First, a firm can achieve product differentiation by highlighting product characteristics such as distinctive designs, packaging, trademarks, colour, durability and branding. Second, a firm can differentiate its product through product image. The idea here is to create a certain image of the product with the hope that it will appeal to certain buyers. For example, a product that has a conservative image will likely appeal to people who have conservative personality traits. Finally, a firm can achieve product differentiation by emphasizing certain of its features, which may include the convenient location, the attention given to customers, and the services provided along with the product. Services such as coffee while you wait, free delivery, and recent issues of magazines may differentiate one firm from others that offer no such service.

Problem 13-7

In which industries is monopolistic competition usually found?

Requirement and Clue: *Focus on the definition of monopolistic competition and typical examples.*

Solution:

Monopolistic competition is prevalent in service industries. The many different beauty salons, barber shops, and restaurants in any large city are good examples of monopolistic competition. Other examples include bakeries, gasoline stations, shoe stores, men's and ladies' clothing stores, automotive garages, stationery stores, and florists.

Problem 13-8

Can monopolistic competition exist in an industry where the firms sell identical products?

Requirement and Clue: *A simple "yes" or "no" answer is not enough here. Focus on ways whereby firms may differentiate otherwise similar products.*

Solution:

The key point in monopolistic competition and product differentiation is not that the products must be different, but that customers *perceive* them to be different. Product differentiation may not necessarily be based on actual, physical product differences, but on other factors. Two dealers of Chevrolet cars sell cars that are essentially similar. However, one can build a reputation on the basis of the service offered to its customers after they purchase the car. Product differentiation on the basis of service rendered is an attempt influence consumers to view the product and the service offered with it as a single item. So although it may be impossible to differentiate the physical characteristics of the product, there can be product differentiation and monopolistic competition even though the products are identical.

Problem 13-9

A seller of coffee beans finds that increasing numbers of coffee retailers have entered the industry. How might the coffee seller set itself apart from other coffee retailers?

Requirement and Clue: *This problem is based on the concept of product differentiation. Think of ways whereby the coffee seller can differentiate itself from its competitors.*

Solution:

The seller of the coffee beans must differentiate its product and publicize its differences from its competitors. It can do this by emphasizing its experience in the coffee business, the fresh nature of its beans, its reliable delivery service, and so on. These measures could set the coffee seller apart from its competitors especially if they were unable to make similar claims.

Problem 13-10

Describe the shapes of the average revenue and marginal revenue curves of a firm in monopolistic competition.

Requirement and Clue: *Perhaps it might be advisable to start with the average revenue curve. Focus on the main characteristic of monopolistic competition and its implication.*

Solution:

The firm in monopolistic competition produces a product that has many substitutes. If the firm raises its price, it will lose some, but not all, of its customers. Customers who have a strong preference for the product in question may remain; brand loyalty will cause them to stay with their preferred brand. If the firm lowers its price, it will attract some customers away from its competitors. Not all customers will be attracted by the small reduction in price. This implies that the demand or average revenue curve for a firm in monopolistic competition is downward-sloping. Because of the availability of so many substitutes, the demand for the product of any one firm in this industry is relatively elastic.

If the average revenue curve is downward-sloping, the marginal revenue curve will also be downward-sloping. Declining average revenue implies that marginal revenue is less than average revenue. The marginal revenue curve lies below the average revenue curve. The following diagram illustrates the shapes of the average revenue and marginal revenue curves for a firm in monopolistic competition.

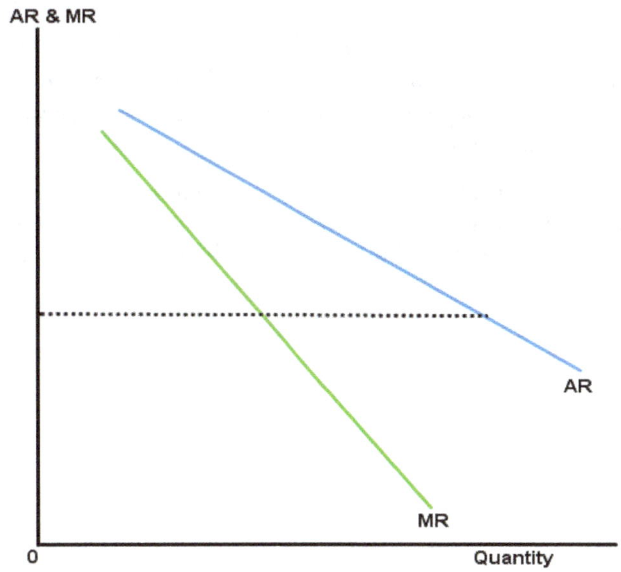

Problem 13-11

You operate a flower shop in your neighbourhood. Will you set your prices significantly above the prices in other flower shops?

Requirement and Clue: *More than a simple "yes" or "no" answer is required. You are required to defend your position. Focus on the market structure in which your flower shop is likely to operate.*

Solution:

A flower shop is a good example of a firm that operates in a monopolistically competitive market structure. Prices could successfully be set slightly above those set by other florists if, by product differentiation, I was able to increase demand for my flowers. However, it would be unwise to charge significantly higher prices. After all, my products may be different, but not that different. And a significantly higher price will result in a significant reduction in my share of the market.

Problem 13-12

Why would you expect the demand curve for a firm in monopolistic competition to be highly elastic?

Requirement and Clue: *Focus on the meaning of highly elastic demand and on the definition of monopolistic competition.*

Solution:

A firm in monopolistic competition produces a product that has many close substitutes. Demand is highly elastic if a small percentage change in price results in a very large percentage change in quantity demanded. If a firm in monopolistic competition raises its price, it will likely lose many customers to its many competitors who are selling products that are similar, though not identical. A 5% increase in price will likely result in a reduction in quantity demanded that is significantly greater than 5%. This means that the demand curve for the firm in monopolistic competition is likely to be quite elastic.

Problem 13-13

Draw graphs to illustrate the difference between the demand curve for a firm in pure competition and the demand curve for a firm in monopolistic competition.

Requirement and Clue: *Essentially you are being asked to demonstrate your understanding of the demand curves for firms in these two market structures. You are expected to give reasons for the difference in shapes.*

Solution:

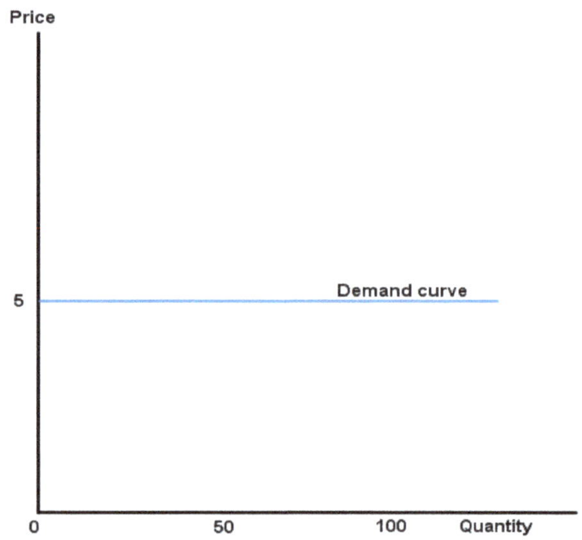

Figure 1

In pure competition, there are numerous small firms producing a tiny fraction of the total industry output. Each firm has no control over the market price, and has to accept it as given. The firm is a price-taker. In such a case, the demand curve for the firm is a horizontal straight line as shown in Figure 1 above.

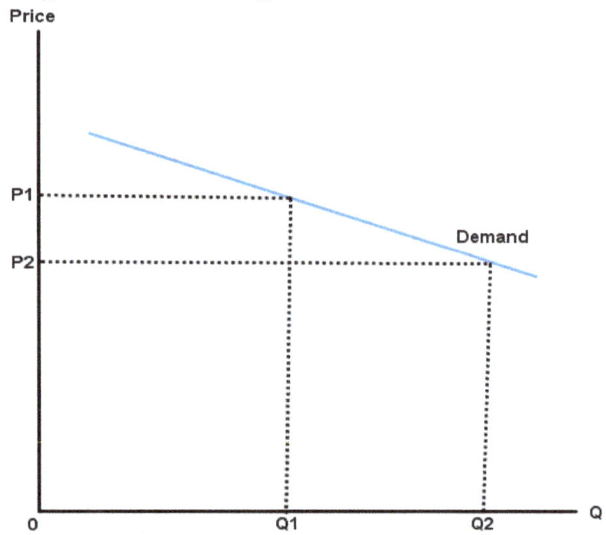

Figure 2

In monopolistic competition, there are many relatively small firms producing products that are close substitutes. Product differentiation gives each firm some slight control over its price. Slight changes in price do not result in infinitely large changes in quantity demanded. The demand curve for a firm in monopolistic competition would be downward sloping as shown in Figure 2 above.

Problem 13-14

Draw a diagram for a firm in monopolistic competition showing marginal cost (MC), average total cost (ATC), marginal revenue (MR), and average revenue (AR). Show what the profit-maximizing price and output will be.

Requirement and Clue: *This problem is a test of your understanding of the cost and revenue curves for a firm in monopolistic competition, and the relationship between them. For the second part of the problem, you should focus on the condition for profit maximization.*

Solution:

See diagram below.

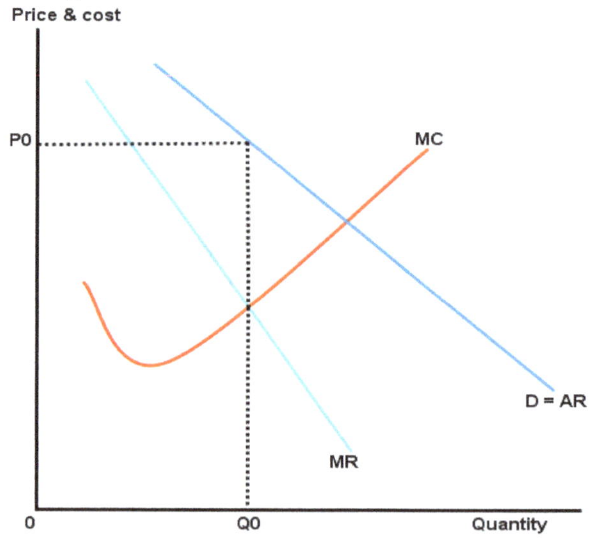

The profit-maximizing price and output for this firm are P0 and Q0 respectively. This is where marginal revenue equals marginal cost.

Problem 13-15

The following diagram shows a monopolistically competitive firm.

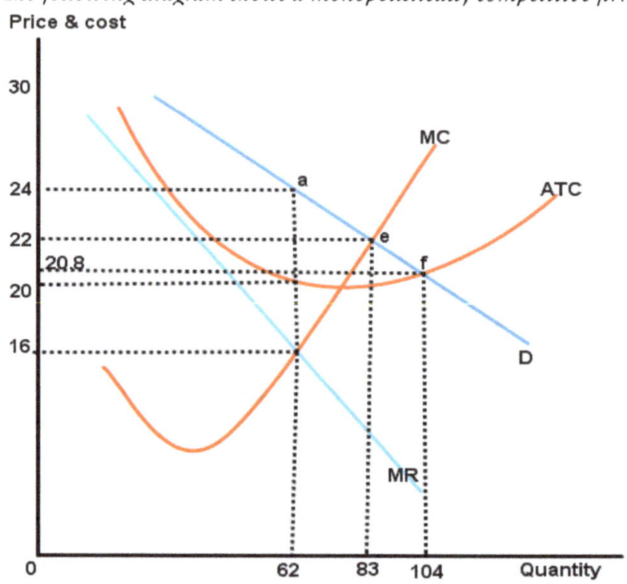

(a) *What level of output should this firm produce to maximize profits?*

(b) *What price should the firm charge for its product?*

(c) *What is the maximum total profit that this firm can earn?*

Requirement and Clue: *This is a test of your ability to understand graphs and certain economic relationships.*

Solution:

(a) The profit-maximizing output occurs where marginal revenue equals marginal cost. In this case it is 62 units.

(b) At this output, the price is $24.

(c) The total revenue is ($24 × 62) = $1488. Total cost is ($20 × 62) = $1240. Total profit is $1488 – $1240 = $248.

Problem 13-16

You manage a café on Main Street. Another café across the street has just installed an air-conditioner. What will you do and why?

Requirement and Clue: *Focus on steps that you might be able to take to entice your customers to remain with you.*

Solution:

The installation of the air-conditioner by the competitor is an example of non-price competition known as quality competition. Other things being equal, patrons will prefer to have coffee in an air-conditioned environment. In order to avoid losing customers to my competitor, and perhaps to attract some of my competitor's customers to my café, I might try installing an air-conditioner in my café, cutting my price, or advertising.

Problem 13-17

Is it possible for a firm in monopolistic competition to operate where marginal revenue equals marginal cost and yet not earn any profits?

Requirement and Clue: *A "yes" or "no" answer is not an adequate solution to this problem. You must explain why this situation is or is not possible. Think of a possible relationship between the firm's average total cost and its average revenue.*

Solution:

It is possible for a firm in monopolistic competition to operate where its marginal revenue and its marginal cost are equal and yet not earn any profits. In such a case, the firm would be minimizing its losses. A firm in monopolistic competition can incur losses in the short run. The firm could be covering its variable costs, but its average revenue could be below its average total cost. The firm would be doing the best in can by operating where its marginal revenue equals its marginal cost.

Problem 13-18

Explain why a firm in monopolistic competition will earn only normal profits in the long run.

Requirement and Clue: *Focus on freedom of entry and exit and their effects on price. You must show some understanding of the concept of normal profits.*

Solution:

In monopolistic competition, there is freedom of entry and exit. If firms in the industry are earning positive economic profits, new firms will enter the industry in the long run. As they do so, total industry supply will increase, causing the price to fall, other things being equal, until all positive economic profits are eliminated. If firms in a monopolistically competitive market structure are incurring losses, some firms will leave the industry in the long run. As they do so, industry output contracts. Other things being equal, the fall in total supply will cause the market price to rise until the firms are no longer incurring losses. Thus, in the long run, because of the entry and exit of firms, a firm in monopolistic competition will operate where price equals average cost. Here, economic profits are zero and the firm is said to earn only normal profits.

Problem 13-19

Is it possible for a firm in monopolistic competition to earn positive economic profits in the long run?

Requirement and Clue: *A simple "yes" or "no" answer will not be sufficient. Note that the question is: "Is it possible?" not "Is it likely?" Focus on possible entry barriers.*

Solution:

Yes, it is possible for a firm in monopolistic competition to earn positive economic profits in the long run. According to theory, if the firms in monopolistic competition are earning above normal profits, new firms will enter the industry in the long run and compete those profits away. But there are two possible reasons why positive economic profits may persist in the long run. First, a firm may be able to differentiate its product to the extent that the products of its competitors are not seen as close substitutes. In this case, a strong monopoly element would be present and the firm could conceivably earn above-normal profits even in the long run.

Second, a firm could be given the exclusive right to do business at a prime location. For example, a private bookstore could be given the exclusive right to operate a bookstore on a university or college campus to sell textbooks and other supplies that students need. Such a firm could earn positive economic profits even in the long run.

Problem 13-20

What is likely to happen to costs in monopolistic competition as new firms enter the industry when there are positive economic profits?

Requirement and Clue: *Focus on resource prices and make the connection with cost.*

Solution:

As new firms enter a monopolistically competitive industry, the demand for scarce resources will tend to rise. This increase in demand will tend to bid the prices of resources up. An increase in resource prices translates into higher costs of production. Moreover, as new firms enter the industry, the established firms are likely to react to the new market situation. They will try to retain their market share perhaps by advertising or by further differentiating their products. These measures will result in higher costs. For these reasons, as new firms enter the industry, costs are likely to increase.

Problem 13-21

Explain the excess capacity theorem?

Requirement and Clue: *Give a clear statement of the theorem and illustrate graphically.*

Solution:

The firm in monopolistic competition is wasteful in the sense that it does not produce at the lowest point of its average total cost curve as the purely competitive firm does. When the firm is in long-run equilibrium, it operates with excess or under-utilized capacity. The excess capacity theorem states that in long-run equilibrium, a firm in monopolistic competition will operate with excess capacity. It will produce an output less than that which minimizes average cost.

The diagram below helps to illustrate the excess capacity theorem. It shows the cost and revenue curves for a firm in monopolistic competition.

To maximize its profits, the firm will produce an output of Qm units and charge a price of Pm, where marginal revenue (MR) equals marginal cost (MC). The firm has capacity to increase its output from Qm to Qo, moving down its average total cost curve, but this would move it away from its profit-maximizing position.

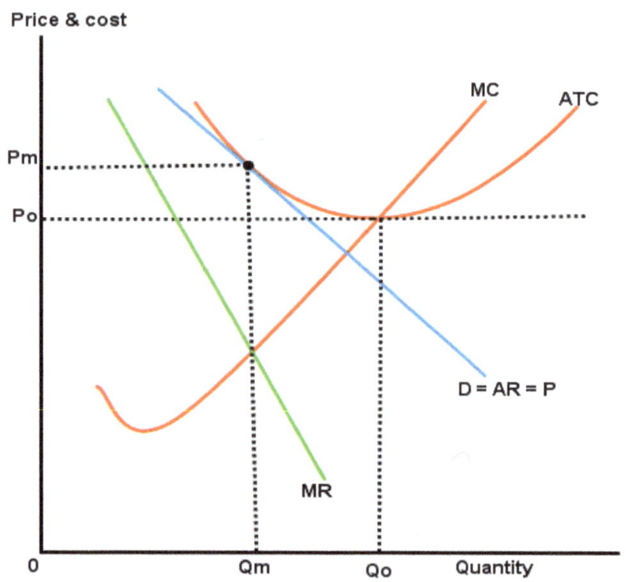

Problem 13-22

How does monopolistic competition compare with pure competition in terms of resource allocation and efficiency?

Requirement and Clue: *Focus on long-run price and output in each market structure, and also on allocative efficiency.*

Solution:

To begin with, in pure competition, the firm operates with a price equal to its marginal cost. In monopolistic competition, price exceeds marginal cost. This means that resources are not optimally allocated in monopolistic competition, while they are in pure competition. An increase in output by the firm in monopolistic competition would benefit society. The firm in monopolistic competition is wasteful in the sense that it does not produce at the lowest point of its average total cost curve as does the purely competitive firm. The purely competitive firm produces a greater output than the firm in monopolistic competition does, and the price charged by the monopolistically competitive firm is higher than the purely competitive price.

Problem 13-23

Is the consumer necessarily better off under pure competition than under monopolistic competition?

Requirement and Clue: *A simple "yes" or "no" solution will not suffice. The word "necessarily" should not be ignored. Focus on the consumers' interests.*

Solution:

It is true that under pure competition consumers pay a lower price, but their choices of products are severely limited. In a purely competitive industry, all of the firms in that industry sell identical (standardized) products. In a monopolistically competitive industry, consumers can choose from a vast array of differentiated products. It can be argued that the higher price under monopolistic competition is offset by the greater choices available to consumers. Whether or not the greater variety of products sufficiently compensates for the higher price is a subjective matter and cannot be answered by economic analysis without additional data. But it can be concluded that consumers are not necessarily better off under pure competition than under monopolistic competition.

Problem 13-24

In recent times, Toyota has issued voluntary safe recalls of several of its vehicles. In many cases the problems were minor but the recalls must have raised some concerns among customers and potential customers.

Knowing that advertising influences people's decisions, what kind of advertising should Toyota have engaged in to attempt to rectify the situation?

Requirement and Clue: *Think of the message that Toyota would want to send to its customers.*

Solution:

Toyota's customers and the public in general must have been a bit concerned about the safety recalls, especially since they have so close. We can even speculate that some customers may have even contemplated switching to some of Toyota's competitors. An informative advertising campaign aimed at educating and convincing customers and prospective customers of the reliability, safety, and high quality of Toyota vehicles could help to rectify the situation and regain or retain many customers.

Problem 13-25

What are some of the arguments in favour of advertising?

Requirement and Clue: *The topic of advertising has been debated for some time now. There is much that can be said for or against it. However, in this problem, you are asked only to present arguments in favour of advertising. Three or four solid points should suffice.*

Solution:

Advertising has been defined as any paid form of non-personal presentation and promotion of ideas, goods and services **through mass media such as newspapers, magazines, television or radio by an identified sponsor".** The following arguments have been used to support advertising.

1. Advertising creates employment and income for people in the advertising business and for people who work in the media. In addition, advertising increases the demand for goods and services, and because the production of goods and services requires the use of resources, including labour, it increases employment in general.
2. Advertising enables firms to take advantage of economies of scale. Successful advertising increases demand. If economies are present, the firm may be able to produce this larger quantity at a lower average cost than it could without advertising. Consumers could benefit by obtaining the product at a lower price than without advertising.
3. Advertising provides consumers with valuable information that enables them to make better decisions in the marketplace. By informing consumers about new products, new locations, and new firms, advertising greatly reduces search cost to consumers.
4. Advertising leads to product improvement and development. When a firm advertises its product, it emphasizes some advantage of its product over the products of its competitors. A firm must therefore improve its product to justify its advertising claims. Moreover, the fact that its competitors are also advertising puts pressure on the firm to improve its product and its services.
5. Advertising increases competition. Advertising makes it easier to successfully launch new products that are close substitutes for existing products. Thus, advertising increases the number of firms in the industry and makes it more competitive.

Problem 13-26

Why might a firm in monopolistic competition advertise its product?

Requirement and Clue: *Focus on the benefits that the firm derives from advertising.*

Solution:

A firm in pure competition need not advertise its product because it can sell as much as it wants to sell at the existing price. It need not advertise any difference between its products and those of other firms because the products are homogeneous. But this is not the case with a firm in monopolistic competition. The defining feature of a firm in monopolistic competition is product differentiation. Advertising is a major tool used by firms to inform customers of the difference between their products and those of their competitors. Advertising in the case of a firm in monopolistic competition can result in an increase in profits. Of course, for advertising to be profitable, it must add more to the firm's total revenue than it does to its total cost. Successful advertising will increase the demand for the firm's product and will also make it less elastic or more inelastic. This will increase the monopolistically competitive firm's market power. For all these reasons, a firm in monopolistic competition will advertise its products.

Problem 13-27

What are some of the arguments against advertising?

Requirement and Clue: *One could conceivably think of numerous arguments against advertising. In this problem, you are asked to discuss some of these arguments. Three or four solid arguments would be adequate.*

Solution:

The following are some of the arguments that have been raised against advertising.

1. Advertising increases monopoly power. Firms in certain industries spend millions of dollars each year on advertising. To break into such industries, potential competitors must be willing to make these massive advertising outlays. This in itself can prove to be an effective barrier to new firms.
2. Advertising is wasteful. Resources that could be productively employed in other industries or even in the same industry to produce goods and services to satisfy wants are wasted in advertising. Why, it is argued, use so much ink and paper in advertising, when those same resources could be used in producing educational books, which would improve society's well-being?
3. Advertising can increase costs and prices. A good portion of advertising simply causes consumers to switch from brand to brand. The output of the industry does not increase as a result of advertising, but costs rise, the market share of each firm hardly changes at all, and consumers end up paying higher prices.
4. Advertising is mainly persuasive, not informational. Many

of the advertisements on radio and television give very little useful information to consumers in terms of helping them make rational choices. Some advertisements, it is claimed, may even give misleading or false information.

5. Advertising imposes indirect costs on society. Unsightly billboards that mar the beauty of the landscape, tons of advertising circulars that must be disposed of, and advertisements that are in bad taste are some examples of the costs imposed on society by advertising.

Problem 13-28

What is oligopoly and what are the main features of oligopoly?

Requirement and Clue: *This is a two-part problem. You must provide a clear statement of the meaning of oligopoly as the solution to the first part of the problem. Then you are required to state its main features.*

Solution:

Oligopoly is a market structure consisting of few firms that recognize their interdependence. The interdependence between the firms is crucial for understanding this market structure.

The main features of oligopoly are:

1. There are few firms in the industry, each producing a relatively large share of the total industry output.
2. There are barriers to the entry of new firms into the industry. A typical entry barrier to this industry is the huge capital investment necessary to establish a firm.
3. Firms in oligopoly recognize their interdependence. Each firm in this industry knows that the actions taken by any one firm have repercussions for the other firms.

Problem 13-29

What do economists mean by market power? How can the extent of market power be determined?

Requirement and Clue: *This is a two-part problem. Address each part in order. Give a clear statement of the concept of market power. For the second part of the problem, focus on the measures used to determine market power.*

Solution:

Market power refers to the amount of influence or control that a firm has over market price and industry output. A monopoly has a great deal of market power while a pure competitor has no market power at all.

The extent of market power can be determined by two measures: concentration ratios and the Herfindahl-Hirschman Index. Concentration ratios show the percentage of total market share accounted for by a few of the largest firms in the industry. The higher the concentration ratio, the greater is the extent of market power. In oligopolies, the concentration ratio will be relatively high. The Herfindahl-Hirschman Index is a measure of the degree of concentration within an industry. It is derived by adding the squares of the market shares of the firms in the industry. If the industry consists of only four firms with market shares of 45%, 30%, 15%, and 10% respectively, then the Herfindahl-Hirschman would be:

$$45^2 + 30^2 + 15^2 + 10^2 = 3250$$

which means that the market is highly concentrated and that there is significant market power.

Problem 13-30

Define each of the following terms:

a. *Duopoly*
b. *Differentiated oligopoly*
c. *Concentration ratio*
d. *Herfindahl-Hirschman Index*

Requirement and Clue: *You are not required to say all you can about each of the concepts. You are expected to give a clear statement of the meaning of each.*

Solution:

a. Duopoly is a special type of oligopoly in which there are only two firms, each recognizing its interdependence with the other. Any move by either of these firms is likely to get a response from the other.
b. Differentiated oligopoly is a situation in which few interdependent firms sell differentiated products. The automobile industry is an example of a differentiated oligopoly.
c. Concentration ratio is the percentage of total market share accounted for by a few of the largest firms in the industry. It is a measure of the degree to which a market is dominated by a few firms.
d. The Herfindahl-Hirschman Index is a measure of industry concentration derived from summing the shares of the market shares of the firms in the industry. The higher this index is, the higher is the concentration of firms in the industry.

Problem 13-31

Suppose you are the manager of a grocery store, and there are only two other grocery stores in the area. Suppose also that you and your competitors are earning satisfactory profits but you know that you could increase your profits if you could increase your sales.

Would you cut your prices in order to woo customers away from your competitors?

Requirement and Clue: *You should not give a simple "yes" or "no" answer to this problem. Think about your market structure in this case and consider the reaction of your competitors to your pricing strategy.*

Solution:

The problem suggests that that market structure is oligopolistic.

My competitors are expected to pay close attention to any moves I may make. On the surface, price cutting may appear to be a good strategy, but it is necessary to analyse the situation. If I cut my prices, my competitors are likely to retaliate with price cuts of their own. They may even undercut my prices. Before you know it, I could be embroiled in a vicious price war. And what are the likely results? They are lower profits, lower prices, and perhaps little or no change in market shares. Price cutting does not therefore appear to be advisable in this case.

Problem 13-32

The following table contains hypothetical information for the textbook publishing industry.

Firm	Value of sales ($million)
A	35
B	30
C	20
D	15
E	12
F	9
G	3

(a) Compute the 4-firm concentration ratio.

(b) Compute the Herfindahl-Hirschman Index.

(c) What do these measures tell us about the degree of concentration in the hypothetical publishing industry?

Requirement and Clue: *Focus on the definitions of the concepts and do the necessary calculations. You are required to interpret the measures.*

Solution:

(a) The 4-firm concentration ratio is the percentage of the total market share accounted for by the four largest firms in the industry. The value of the total market output is the sum of the sales of all the firms. This amounts to \$124 million. The four largest firms account for \$100 million. Therefore, the 4-firm concentration ratio is 100 ÷ 124 × 100 = 80.65%.

(b) The Herfindahl-Hirschman Index is the sum of the squares of the market shares of the firms in the industry. In this case, the index is:

$$35^2 + 30^2 + 20^2 + 15^2 + 12^2 + 9^2 + 3^2$$

$$= 1225 + 900 + 400 + 225 + 144 + 81 + 9 = 2984$$

(c) From the concentration ratio of 80.65% and the Herfindahl-Hirschman Index of 2984, we can conclude that the hypothetical publishing industry is highly concentrated.

Problem 13-33

Answer the following questions on the basis of the following diagram. The firm's marginal cost is MC2.

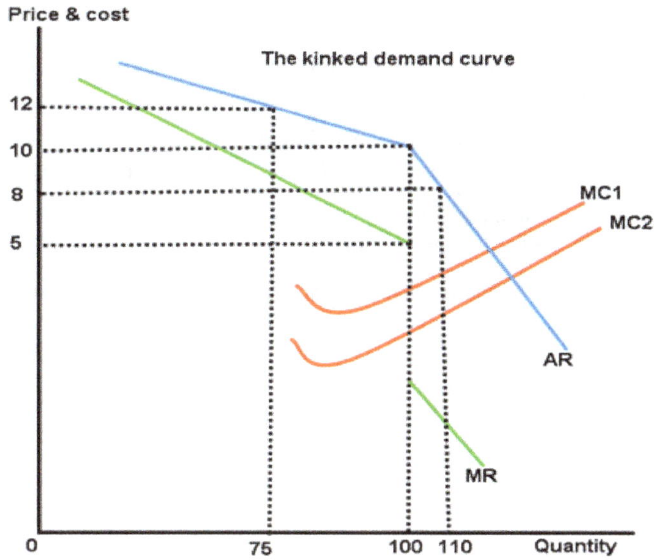

(a) *What output should this firm produce in order to maximize its profits?*

(b) *What price should this firm charge?*

(c) *If the firm's marginal cost rises from MC2 to MC1, what adjustment should the firm make in its pricing and output decisions?*

(d) *At what price range is the firm's average revenue curve elastic?*

Requirement and Clue: *This is a multi-part problem. Answer each part in order. The problem is a test of your ability to read graphs and to do simple arithmetic calculations. You are expected to be familiar with some economics relations.*

Solution:

(a) In order to maximize its profits, this firm should operate where its marginal revenue equals its marginal cost. This output is **100**.

(b) The firm should charge a price of **\$10** (read from the average revenue curve).

(c) Because the new marginal cost curve intersects the marginal revenue curve in the vertical (or broken) section of the marginal revenue curve, MR = MC at the same price and output levels. The firm should not make any adjustment in its pricing and output decisions.

(d) At any price about \$10, the firm's average revenue or demand curve is elastic.

Problem 13-34

What are the basic assumptions underlying the kinked demand curve model? What does this model explain?

Requirement and Clue: *This is a two-part problem. Answer each part in order. Succinctly state the assumptions on which the model is based as the solution for the first part. Every economic model is designed to explain some aspect of the real economy. For the second part of the problem, focus on what the model of the kinked demand curve was designed to explain.*

Solution:

There are two basic assumptions underlying the model of the kinked demand curve:

1. A price increase by one firm in an oligopoly situation will not be matched by similar price increases in other firms.
2. A reduction in price by one firm will be matched by similar reductions in other firms.

It has been observed that in some cases, prices tend to remain relatively stable in oligopoly markets. The kinked demand curve model explains why price may remain constant in oligopoly even when cost increases. This price rigidity is due to a kink in the demand curve that gives rise to a vertical (broken) section of the marginal revenue curve.

Problem 13-35

What is price leadership? What are the advantages and disadvantages of price leadership?

Requirement and Clue: *This is a two-part problem. Address each part in order. For the first part, give a clear meaning of the concept. For the second part of the problem, focus on possible benefits and costs of price leadership to the firms in a price-leadership situation.*

Solution:

Price leadership is the situation in which one firm in an industry takes the lead in changing prices and the other firms follow suit.

The advantages of price leadership are: (1) It can prevent price wars that can be problematic for the firms. (2) Price leadership may benefit some firms to the extent that they do not have to spend money to gather the information that is necessary to formulate a pricing strategy. They can simply adopt the price set by the leader. (3) Price leadership allows for an orderly change from one price to another.

Disadvantages of price leadership include: (1) It causes the followers to depart from their own prices, which may not be in their own interests. (2) Under a situation of price leadership, firms may become complacent and do little or nothing to develop pricing strategies that suit their particular circumstances.

Problem 13-36

What is a cartel? Why do firms in a cartel arrangement have an incentive to cheat?

Requirement and Clue: *This is a two-part problem. Answer each part in order. For the second part of the problem, focus on restrictions that may be imposed on cartel members.*

Solution:

A cartel is a formal agreement among independent firms to act in concert to control price and output in a particular industry. An example of a cartel is the well-known Organization of the Petroleum Exporting Countries (OPEC).

Each member of a cartel is usually given a quota of output to produce. This quota may not be the quantity that maximizes the firm's profits. By producing more than its given quota, the firm could stand to gain from greater profits. For example, suppose the cartel has decided that a particular member firm should produce an output of 500 units per period at the cartel price of \$500. Suppose that particular firm knows that it could produce an extra unit of output at a marginal cost of only \$300. The firm would have a strong incentive to break the cartel rule (that is, cheat) and produce the additional unit of output and sell it for the cartel price of \$500, thereby increasing its profits by \$200.

Problem 13-37

Why are there so many different models of oligopoly behaviour?

Requirement and Clue: *Focus on the nature of oligopoly and the amount of possible reactions to the firms' decisions.*

Solution:

The defining feature of oligopoly is the interdependence of firms in the industry. A price-output decision of one firm will cause a reaction from other firms. What that reaction will be depends to a large extent on the assumptions that one makes; and there are several possible assumptions, each one generating a different model.

Problem 13-38

What is the prisoner's dilemma? How is this applicable to oligopoly?

Requirement and Clue: *This is a two-part problem. Address each part in order. The first part of the problem is definitional. State clearly the meaning of the term without writing an essay on it. Focus on the aspect of the prisoner's dilemma that relates to the behaviour of firms in oligopoly.*

Solution:

The prisoner's dilemma is a situation in which two prisoners, caught in a situation, find it difficult to cooperate even when cooperation is beneficial to both prisoners. It is often used to illustrate the concept of game theory.

In the prisoner's dilemma, each prisoner has to decide on a course of action based on possible courses of action taken by the other prisoner. This situation is similar to oligopoly in which the strategy chosen by one firm is dependent on what the other firms are likely to do. It is this interdependence that makes the prisoner's dilemma so applicable to oligopoly.

Problem 13-39

When is a market contestable? What is the significance of contestable markets?

Requirement and Clue: *This is a two-part problem. Address each part in order. You are required to show familiarity with the concept of* *contestable markets. For the second part of the problem, focus on the behaviour of firms in markets that are contestable.*

Solution:

A market is contestable when entry into the market is so easy that the threat of entry by potential competitors prevents the existing firms from exercising any monopoly power.

The concept of contestable markets suggests that looking at the number of firms in an industry is not enough to determine the extent of market power. The ease of entering the industry must also be considered. The contestability of a particular market will significantly influence the behaviour of firms.

Problem 13-40

What are the undesirable social consequences associated with oligopoly?

Requirement and Clue: *Focus on price and output in oligopoly and on resource allocation.*

Solution:

Oligopoly has some undesirable social consequences. Barriers to the entry of new firms into the industry can result in a price that exceeds average total cost in most firms in oligopoly. Thus, firms in oligopoly are likely to earn excess profits, which may not be socially desirable. Also, the price established in an oligopoly is likely to be above marginal cost. This inequality between price and marginal cost implies a misallocation of resources. Furthermore, firms in oligopoly tend to spend huge amounts of money on advertising in an attempt to maintain or increase their share of the market. Many people consider this enormous advertising outlay to be wasteful.

Multiple-Choice

In each case, circle the letter that corresponds with the correct answer.

1. By imperfect competition, economists mean:

a. a market structure in which buyers and sellers are trying to cheat each other
b. firms compete with one another but do not following the rules of competition
c. markets that are neither purely competitive nor purely monopolistic
d. any market structure other than perfect competition.

Answer: c

Reason: The concept embraces monopolistic competition and oligopoly which are neither purely competitive nor purely monopolistic

2. Which of the following is a characteristic of monopolistic competition?

a. A relatively large number of firms
b. Freedom of entry and exit
c. Differentiated products
d. All of the above

Answer: d

Reason: Choices a, b, and c are all features of monopolistic competition.

3. Which of the following can a firm <u>not</u> use to differentiate its product?

a. Standardization
b. Distinctive designs
c. Product image
d. Emphasizing certain features

Answer: a

Reason: Standardizations aims at making products appear similar, not different.

4. The condition that exists when firms distinguish their products from those of their competitors is called:

a. product competitiveness
b. product differentiation
c. product homogeneity
d. d. product identification

Answer: b

Reason: Firms use product differentiation to make their products appear different from those of their competitors.

5. Which of the following is <u>not</u> an example of a firm in monopolistic competition?

a. A beauty salon in Montreal, Canada
b. A florist in London, England
c. A law firm in New York city
d. Canada Post Corporation

Answer: d

Reason: Canada Post Corporation is an example of a monopoly.

6. Freedom of entry and exit is a characteristic of :

a. monopoly
b. monopolistic competition
c. pure competition
d. b and c

Answer: d

Reason: In pure competition and monopolistic competition, there is freedom of entry and exit.

7. Entry into a monopolistically competitive industry is:

a. harder than entry into a monopoly
b. easier than entry into pure competition
c. harder than entry into oligopoly
d. easier than entry into a monopoly

Answer: d

Reason: Effective barriers to entry make entry into a monopoly extremely difficult.

8. In monopolistic competition, there are:

a. a few competitive firms that have formed a monopoly
b. several monopolies competing for a larger share of the market
c. many purely competitive firms that have agreed not to compete
d. many firms producing differentiated products

Answer: d

Reason: *Choice d captures the definition of monopolistic competition.*

9. The average revenue curve of a firm in monopolistic competition is:

a. identical to its demand curve
b. horizontal because there are many firms with many close substitutes
c. vertical because each firm has a monopoly on its differentiated product
d. none of the above

Answer: a

Reason: *The demand and average revenue curves are the same.*

10. The demand curve for a firm in monopolistic competition is:

a. highly inelastic because of product differentiation
b. highly elastic because of the large number of close substitutes
c. perfectly inelastic because the firm has full control over the price of its differentiated product
d. perfectly elastic because each firm in the industry is a price-taker

Answer: b

Reason: *The large number of firms selling differentiated products gives each firm very slight control over the price of its product. This means that the demand curve is downward sloping and quite elastic.*

11. The marginal revenue curve of a firm in monopolistic competition is:

a. identical to its demand curve
b. a horizontal straight line because marginal revenue and price are identical
c. below its average revenue curve and steeper than the average revenue curve
d. none of the above

Answer: c

Reason: *Because the average revenue curve is downward-sloping, the average revenue curve must be below it.*

12. In the short-run profit-maximizing position, the firm in monopolistic competition operates where:

a. marginal revenue exceeds marginal cost
b. marginal revenue equals marginal cost
c. price equals marginal cost
d. price is less than average total cost

Answer: b

Reason: *This is the profit-maximizing position for any firm.*

13. In the short run, a firm in monopolistic competition can earn:

a. positive economic profits
b. zero economic profits
c. losses
d. all of the above

Answer: a

Reason: *Any of the above is possible for a firm in monopolistic competition.*

14. Which of the following is true for a firm in monopolistic competition operation where marginal revenue equals marginal cost in the short run?

a. The firm must be maximizing its profits
b. The firm could never be incurring losses
c. The firm could be maximizing its profits or minimizing its losses
d. None of the above

Answer: c

Reason: *As long as the firm is operating where marginal revenue equals marginal cost, it is doing the best it can do under the circumstances. It could be maximizing its profits or, if it is incurring losses, it would be minimizing those losses.* Diagram B

15. In the long run, the demand curve of the firm in monopolistic competition becomes:

a. perfectly elastic
b. highly inelastic
c. vertical
d. none of the above

Answer: d

Reason: *In the long run, the demand curve for a firm in monopolistic competition remains highly elastic.*

16. In the long run, firms in equilibrium in monopolistic competition earn:

a. only normal profits
b. above normal profits because of product differentiation
c. negative economic profits because of opportunity cost
d. none of the above

Answer: a

Reason: *The entry and exit of firms in the long run cause the firms in monopolistic competition to earn zero economic profits.*

17. In long-run equilibrium, a monopolistic competitor will have:

a. price equal to marginal cost
b. price equal to average cost
c. price greater than average cost
d. price less than average cost

Answer: b

Reason: *Because of the entry and exit of firms in the long run, the firm in monopolistic competition with earn only normal profit. That is, its price will be equal to its average cost.*

18. In long-run equilibrium, a firm in monopolistic competition will:

a. earn positive economic profits
b. operate at the minimum point of its average cost curve
c. earn zero economic profits
d. operate where marginal cost equals average revenue

Answer: c

Reason: If the firm in monopolistic competition is earning positive economic profits, new firms will enter the industry in the long run and compete those profits away. If it is incurring losses, in the long run firms will leave the industry. Under these circumstances, the firm in monopolistic competition will earn only normal profits, that is, zero economic profits.

19. Compared with the firm in perfect competition, the firm in monopolistic competition in long-run equilibrium:

a. produces a larger output and sells at a higher price
b. produces a smaller output and sells at a lower price
c. produces a smaller output and sells at a higher price
d. produces a larger output and sells at a lower price

Answer: c

Reason: In long-run equilibrium, both the purely competitive firm and the monopolistically competitive firm earn only normal profits, but because the demand curve for the monopolistically competitive firm is downward-sloping whereas that of the purely competitive firm is horizontal, output is less and price is higher in monopolistic competition.

20. The excess capacity theorem is the hypothesis that firms in monopolistic competition will:

a. produce an excess amount of goods and services
b. operate at the minimum point of their long-run average cost in the long run
c. operate with excess capacity, producing an output that is less than the output that can be produced at the lowest point of the average cost curve
d. none of the above

Answer: c

Reason: In long-run equilibrium, the firm in monopolistic competition will not use its full capacity to produce at output at which the average cost is lowest.

21. The excess capacity theorem relates to the fact that a profit-maximizing monopolistic competitor will produce:

a. an output level where long-run average cost equals zero
b. an output level less than the level that minimizes long-run average cost
c. its output with excess capacity no matter what output level is chosen
d. none of the above

Answer: b

Reason: The excess capacity theorem states that in long-run equilibrium, the firm in monopolistic competition will maximize its profits when its output is less than that which minimizes its average cost.

22. Successful advertising by a firm in monopolistic competition will:

a. shift the firm's demand curve to the right
b. shift the firm's demand curve to the left
c. make the firm's demand curve more elastic or less inelastic
d. cause kinks in the marginal revenue curve

Answer: a

Reason: The demand for the firm's product will increase, and this means that the demand curve will shift to the right.

23. Advertising by a firm in monopolistic competition will:

a. always increase the firm's profits
b. always increase the firm's market share, but not its profits
c. always increase the firm's revenue
d. none of the above

Answer: d

Reason: Advertising may not be successful. In fact, it may offend the firm's customers and cause them to turn to the firm's competitors.

24. Arguments in favour of advertising include the following:

a. it creates employment
b. it enables firms to take advantage of economies of scale
c. it leads to product improvement and development
d. all of the above

Answer: d

Reason: Choices a, b, and c are all claims in favour of advertising.

25. Which of the following is an argument against advertising?

a. It wastes resources
b. It increases costs and prices
c. It increases monopoly power
d. All of the above

Answer: d

Reason: Choices a, b, and c are all arguments against advertising.

26. Oligopoly is a market structure with:

a. several independent monopolies
b. several relatively large firms producing identical products
c. several small firms that have decided to control the market by merging
d. few firms producing similar or differentiated products and recognizing their interdependence
e. very few buyers

Answer: c

Reason: In an oligopoly there are a few large firms in the industry and they all recognize their interdependence.

27. One major characteristic of firms in oligopoly is that:

a. they produce identical products
b. they all have kinked demand curves
c. they always collude to control price and output
d. they recognize their interdependence

Answer: d

Reason: Firms in oligopoly recognize that any action taken by one firm will cause other firms to react in one way or another.

28. An industry with only two firms is called:

a. a duo monopoly c. a duopoly

b. a cartel
d. none of the above

Answer: c

Reason: *A duopoly is a two-firm industry.*

29. A differentiated oligopoly is:

a. an oligopoly in which different firms produce similar products
b. an oligopoly in which the firms produce only a few identifiable products
c. an oligopoly in which the firms' products are differentiated
d. none of the above

Answer: c

Reason: *Choice c properly defines a differentiated oligopoly.*

30. Which of the following is used to determine the degree to which a market is dominated by a few firms?

a. Concentration ratios
b. Herfindahl-Hirschman Index
c. Both a and b
d. Neither a nor b

Answer: c

Reason: *Concentration ratios and the Herfindahl-Hirschman Index are used to gauge the extent to which a market is concentrated.*

31. Concentration ratios measure:

a. the extent to which oligopolies produce highly concentrated products
b. the percentage of firms in an oligopoly that produce highly concentrated products
c. both a and b
d. neither a nor b

Answer: d

Reason: *Concentration ratios show the percentage of total market share accounted for by a few of the largest firms in the industry.*

32. A Hirfindahl-Hirschman index of 750 means that:

a. the industry is highly concentrated
b. the industry is moderately concentrated
c. the industry is not at all concentrated
d. the industry is purely competitive

Answer: c

Reason: *A Herfindahl-Hirschman Index of less than 1000 means that the industry is not concentrated.*

33. The model of the kinked demand curve:

a. is based on the assumption that a price increase by one firm will not be matched by similar increases by other firms
b. is based on the assumption that a price reduction by one firm will be matched by similar reductions by other firms
c. explains relative price rigidity in oligopoly
d. all of the above

Answer: d

Reason: *Choices a, b, and c are all true of the kinked demand curve model.*

34. Product prices may remain rigid (inflexible) because of:

a. rivalry among firms
b. the desire to maximize profits
c. long-term contracts
d. all of the above

Answer: c

Reason: *Long-term contracts may enable firms to obtain inputs at pre-arranged prices, thus insulating them against price increases.*

35. Which of the following is least likely to cause price rigidity?

a. A kinked demand curve
c. Long-term contracts
b. Small menu costs
d. Profit maximization

Answer: d

Reason: *Profit maximization has little or nothing to do with price rigidity, but the other choices do.*

36. Which of the following is a possible explanation of rigid prices?

a. A kinked demand curve
c. Long-term contracts
b. Small menu costs
d. All of the above

Answer: d

Reason: *Choices a, b, and c may cause prices to remain unchanged for a relatively long time.*

37. Limit pricing is:

a. a pricing strategy designed to serve as an effective barrier to entry
b. the practice of raising prices to the highest limit
c. a decision by government not to place any limit on prices charged by firms
d. price control by a government agency

Answer: a

Reason: *Firms may deliberately set their prices so low that new entrants will make no profits.*

38. One of the objectives of predatory pricing is:

a. to increase profits in the short run
b. to maintain or increase market share
c. to encourage competition in an industry
d. none of the above

Answer: b

Reason: *Predatory pricing makes it difficult for new firms to enter the industry and take market share from the existing firms.*

39. The price established in oligopolistic industries is likely to be:

a. equal to marginal cost
b. equal to minimum average cost
c. greater than marginal cost
d. less than minimum average cost

Answer: c

Reason: *The firm in oligopoly operates where marginal revenue equals marginal cost in order to maximize its profits. In this situation, price is above marginal cost.*

40. Which of the following is a problem typically faced by a perfect cartel?

a. The tendency for individual members to cheat

b. The problem of deciding how production quotas should be set

c. The problem of deciding how profits should be distributed among members

d. All of the above

Answer: d

Reason: Perfect cartels typically face the problems listed in choices a, b, and c. That's why most cartels are imperfect.

41. Game theory is most applicable to:

a. monopoly c. monopolistic competition

b. oligopoly d. none of the above

Answer: b

Reason: In oligopoly, the action of one firm causes reactions from other firms, just as the "players" in game theory.

42. Oligopoly can be advantageous because it can lead to:

a. perfectly competitive behaviour

b. marginal-cost pricing

c. lower prices resulting from economies of scale

d. all of the above

Answer: c

Reason: Large oligopolistic firms may be able to take advantage of economies of scale and produce at lower average cost, which could result in lower prices.

43. A market is said to be contestable when:

a. it is monopolized

b. the firms in the industry are all oligopolists

c. entry into the industry is easy

d. none of the above

Answer: c

Reason: Choice c accurately defines a contestable market.

44. Workable competition exists when:

a. all the firms in a perfectly competitive industry decide to work together

b. oligopolists decide to collude

c. monopolists allow oligopolists to work with them

d. competition is sufficient to ensure that market power is not excessive

Answer: d

Reason: Choice d captures the essence of the concept of workable competition.

True or False

Determine whether each of the following statements is true or false.

1. Economists use the term imperfect competition to refer to monopolistic competition and oligopoly.

Answer: True

2. Monopolistic competition is a market structure with many monopolies competing for supremacy in the marketplace.

Answer: False

Explanation: Monopolistic competition is a market structure consisting of many firms selling differentiated products.

3. The main features of monopolistic competition are (1) a relatively large number of firms, (2) differentiated products, and (3) freedom of entry and exit.

Answer: True

4. In monopolistic competition, product differentiation makes it relatively easy for firms to collude to control price and output in the market.

Answer: False

Explanation: In monopolistic competition, the number of firms is sufficiently large to make it impractical for them to get together to act jointly to control price and output.

5. Product differentiation is a condition that is most often found in perfect competition since there are so many firms competing for the consumer's money.

Answer: False

Explanation: The products in pure competition are identical. There is no effort to make them appear different.

6. A firm can differentiate its product from those of its competitors by distinctive designs, packaging, product image, and by the service offered to customers.

Answer: True

7. Monopolistic competition is usually prevalent in florists, beauty salons, bakeries, mechanic shops, and shoe stores.

Answer: True

8. A firm in monopolistic competition can exercise some control over the price it charges.

Answer: True

9. Huge advertising costs may prove to be an effective barrier to the entry of new firms into a monopolistically competitive industry.

Answer: True

10. Because of product differentiation, the demand curve of a firm in monopolistic competition is highly inelastic.

Answer: False

Explanation: Because of the large number of close substitutes in monopolistic competition, the demand curve for the firm is highly elastic.

11. The marginal revenue curve of a firm in monopolistic competition lies below the firm's average revenue curve.

Answer: True

12. Because of the benefit of product differentiation, firms in monopolistic competition will charge a price at which marginal revenue exceeds marginal cost in order to earn as much profit as possible.

Answer: False

Explanation: The firm earns maximum profits when it operates where its marginal revenue and its marginal cost are equal.

13. It is impossible for a firm in monopolistic competition to operate where its marginal revenue equals its marginal cost and not earn maximum profits.

Answer: False

Explanation: The firm could be minimizing its losses.

14. Because of the large number of firms in monopolistic competition, the firm's demand curve is horizontal and in its profit-maximizing position, its price will be equal to its marginal cost.

Answer: False

Explanation: The demand curve for a firm in monopolistic competition is downward sloping, and in equilibrium, price will be higher than marginal cost.

15. In long-run equilibrium, a firm in monopolistic competition earns only normal profits.

Answer: True

16. In long-run equilibrium, a firm in monopolistic competition will produce at full capacity, that is, at the lowest point of its average cost curve.

Answer: False

Explanation: In long-run equilibrium, a firm in monopolistic competition will not produce at full capacity. It will operate with excess capacity. It will operate at a lower level of output than that which minimizes its average cost.

17. Consumers are definitely better off under pure competition than under monopolistic competition because of the lower price and greater output with pure competition.

Answer: False

Explanation: Consumers are not necessarily better off with pure competition than with monopolistic competition. The greater variety offered by monopolistic competition may more than compensate for the higher price.

18. Advertising is aimed at increasing the advertiser's share of the market. It may increase the demand for the product and it may make the demand less elastic.

Answer: True

19. Because advertising costs money, it can never result in lower prices to consumers.

Answer: False

Explanation: Advertising may increase demand and enable the firm to take advantages of economies of scale, which may result in reduced price.

20. Firms in oligopoly always sell identical products.

Answer: False

Explanation: They may sell differentiated products.

21. Advertising may impose indirect costs to society in the form of unsightly billboards, advertising circulars scattered all over, and offensive advertising.

Answer: True

22. Oligopoly is a market structure with several monopolies producing differentiated products.

Answer: False

Explanation: Oligopoly is a market structure with a few interdependent firms producing similar or differentiated products.

23. An industry consisting of only two firms is called a duopoly.

Answer: True

24. Since a firm in oligopoly has substantial market power, it can maximize its profits without equating its marginal revenue and its marginal cost.

Answer: False

Explanation: Profits cannot be maximized unless marginal revenue equals marginal cost. This is so regardless of the market structure in which the firm operates.

25. A differentiated oligopoly is a market structure with different oligopolies producing similar products.

Answer: False

Explanation: A differentiated oligopoly is an oligopoly in which the firms' products are differentiated.

26. Concentration ratios show the percentage of total market share accounted for by a few of the largest firms in the industry.

Answer: True

27. In oligopoly, the concentration ratio will be relatively high.

Answer: True

28. The Herfindahl-Hirschman Index is a measure of industry concentration. It is derived by summing the market shares of the firms in the industry.

Answer: False

Explanation: The Herfindahl-Hirschman Index is derived by adding the sum of the squares of the market shares of the firms in the industry.

29. In the kinked demand curve model, the demand curve is relatively flat at higher prices and relatively steep at lower prices. This gives rise to a kink in the demand curve.

Answer: True

30. The kinked demand curve model provides the only explanation for price rigidity in oligopolistic markets.

Answer: False

Explanation: Small menu costs and long-term contracts provide other explanations of price rigidity.

31. The kinked demand curve model assumes that if a firm in oligopoly raises its price, the other firms will raise their prices also; but if a firm lowers its price, the other firms will not lower their prices.

Answer: False

Explanation: The assumption is that if one firm raises its price, the other firms will not raise their prices; but if a firm lowers its price, the other firms will lower their prices also.

32. Long-term contracts and small menu costs are a prime cause of flexible prices in oligopoly markets.

Answer: False

Explanation: On the contrary, they contribute to price rigidity.

33. Limit pricing is a price control mechanism used by the government to limit the price that oligopolists can charge for their products.

Answer: False

Explanation: Limit pricing is a pricing strategy in which firms set their prices so low that new entrants into the market will make no profits.

34. Price leadership exists when one firm in an industry takes the lead in changing prices and the other firms follow the leader.

Answer: True

35. Cost-plus pricing is a pricing is a pricing strategy in which firms determine price by adding a certain percentage mark-up on cost.

Answer: True

36. In practice, most cartels are perfect cartels because they can then act as monopolies and really control price and output.

Answer: False

Explanation: Perfect cartels are rare. Firms have a strong incentive to break the cartel rules.

37. The prisoner's dilemma is a situation in which two prisoners are caught in a situation in which it is difficult to cooperate even when cooperation is beneficial to both prisoners.

Answer: True

38. Nash equilibrium is a term used in game theory to describe a situation in which equilibrium is elusive even though it may seem apparent.

Answer: False

Explanation: Nash equilibrium is a condition that exists when each firm selects the best strategy, given the strategies of the other players.

39. If workable competition exists, oligopoly may not be totally undesirable.

Answer: True

40. A market is contestable if consumers have the legal right to contest those prices that are considered to be too high, especially for products considered to be essential.

Answer: False

Explanation: A contestable market is a market into which entry is so easy that the threat of entry by potential competitors prevents the existing from exercising any monopoly power.

Completion

(Fill in the blanks)

Use each word or combination of words from the list exactly once.
*(**Hint**: Proceed by elimination)*

Word list

Capacity — Cartel — Competition x 2 — Concentration — Contestable — Cost x 2 — Differentiated x 2 — Differentiation x 3 — Duopoly — Entry — Equilibrium — Excess — Fall — Freedom of Entry and Exit — Increase — Interdependence — Kinked — Large Number of Firms — Leadership — Limit — Marginal x 4 — Monopolistic x 2 — Nash — Normal or Zero Economic — Oligopoly x 2 — Price x 2 — Pricing — Product x 3 — Products — Ratios — Revenue x 4 — Rigidity

Questions

1. A market structure in which a large number of firms produce differentiated products is called ____________ ____________.
2. The three main features of monopolistic competition are (1) ____________, (2),____________ and (3) ____________.
3. ____________ ____________ is the condition that exists when firms distinguish their products from those of their competitors. (product differentiation)
4. Brand names, packaging, and trademarks are ways of

achieving ________ ________.

5. The market structure in which barber shops, beauty salons, florists, restaurants, and auto repair shops are typically found is ________ ________.

6. The firm in monopolistic competition faces a demand curve that is very elastic because there are many close substitutes resulting from ________ ________.

7. If the demand curve for a firm is downward sloping, then its ________ ________ curve must also be downward sloping.

8. The profit-maximizing position for a firm in monopolistic competition occurs where its ________ ________ equals is ________ ________.

9. If a firm in monopolistic competition is in equilibrium with price greater than average total cost, there will be a(n) ________ of new firms. Total industry output will ________ and the price will ________.

10. In long-run equilibrium, a firm in monopolistic competition earns only ________ profits.

11. The hypothesis that in long-run equilibrium a firm in monopolistic competition will produce an output less than that at which average cost is lowest is called the ________ ________ theorem.

12. Advertising is profitable only if it adds more to total ________ then to total ________.

13. The petroleum industry, the automobile industry, and the steel industry are examples of ________.

14. An industry consisting of only two firms is called a ________.

15. Because firms in oligopoly are so few, they must recognize their ________.

16. A ________ ________ is an oligopoly in which the firms' products are differentiated. ________ ________ show the percentage of total market share accounted for by a few of the largest firms in the industry.

17. The assumptions that a price increase by one firm will not be matched by similar increases in other firms, and a price decrease by one firm will be matched by similar reductions in other firms lead to a ________ demand curve.

18. The kinked demand curve model provides one explanation of ________ ________.

19. In the kinked demand curve model, the ________ ________ curve has a broken or vertical section because of the kink in the demand curve.

20. The pricing strategy in which firms set their prices so low that new firms entering the market will not make any profits is called ________ ________.

21. ________ ________ is the condition that exists when one firm in an industry takes the initiative in changing prices and the other firms follow suit. (

22. A group of firms that have entered into a formal agreement to control the market for a product is known as a(n) ________.

23. The condition that exists when each player in a game selects the best possible strategy, given the strategies of the other players is referred to as ________ ________.

24. A market into which entry is so easy that the threat of entry by potential competitors prevents the existing firms from exercising any monopoly power is a ________ market.

Solution

1. (Monopolistic Competition)
2. (Large Number Of Firms, Differentiated Products, Freedom of Entry and Exit)
3. (Product Differentiation)
4. (Product Differentiation)
5. (Monopolistic Competition)
6. (Product Differentiation)
7. (Marginal Revenue)
8. (Marginal Revenue, Marginal Cost)
9. (Entry, Increase, Fall)
10. (Normal Or Zero Economic)
11. (Excess Capacity)
12. (Revenue, Cost)
13. (Oligopoly)
14. (Duopoly)
15. (Interdependence)
16. (Differentiated Oligopoly)
17. (Concentration Ratios)
18. (Kinked)
19. (Price Rigidity)
20. (Marginal Revenue)
21. (Limit Pricing)
22. (Price Leadership)
23. (Cartel)
24. (Nash Equilibrium)
25. (Contestable)

14 THE LABOUR MARKET

SYNOPSIS

Labour is a very important input. It is demanded not for its own sake, but for the goods and services it helps to produce. Its demand is therefore a **derived demand**. Labour will be hired up to the point where the value of its marginal physical product equals the wage. The firm's demand curve for labour is the **marginal revenue product** curve.

The **equilibrium wage rat**e in a competitive labour market is determined by the demand for and supply of labour. Increases in the demand for labour will tend to increase the wage rate. Increases in the supply of labour will tend to lower the wage rate.

Wage differentials may be due to difference in education, experience, responsibility, superior ability, union activity, and the degree of danger associated with the job. All these differences may be summed up in one basic cause—the relative scarcity of certain types of labour.

Collective bargaining is the process whereby union and management arrive at an agreement, through negotiations, regarding the terms of employment Labour disputes may be settled through mediation, or through arbitration. A union may use the strike weapon to obtain its demands. The employer may resort to a **lockout** to win a dispute.

In an attempt to secure higher wages, a union may try to shift the demand for labour to the right or shift the supply of labour to the left. The effect of unions on resource allocation is the subject of a lively debate.

LEARNING OBJECTIVES

In connection with this module, you should be able to:

1. explain the demand for and supply of labour
2. explain competitive wage determination
3. explain predictions of the theory of wage determination
4. predict the effects of discrimination in the labour market
5. explain wage differentials
6. discuss unions and collective bargaining
7. identify the main factors in wage negotiations
8. discuss the effects of labour unions in the labour market
9. explain how unions affect resource allocation

DEFINITIONS & CONCEPTS

You should be able to define the following terms and concepts:

derived demand	union shop
marginal revenue product	Rand Formula
craft (trade) union	collective bargaining
industrial union	collective agreement
local union	strike
national union	lockout
international union	mediation (conciliation)
federation	indexation
functional distribution of income	featherbedding
psychic income	COLA
closed shop	escalator clause
open shop	arbitration

14 THE LABOUR MARKET

Concepts, Definitions & Problems

Problem 14-1

What is the difference between direct demand and derived demand?

Requirement and Clue: *You are expected to demonstrate an understanding of the concepts and to focus on the difference between them. Examples will be helpful.*

Solution:

The demand for final goods and services to satisfy wants directly is a direct demand. Consumers buy goods and services because they derive satisfaction directly from such goods and services. The demand for items such as food, clothing, household furniture, and entertainment is a direct demand.

Derived demand, in contrast, is the demand for inputs that is due to the demand for the goods and services produced by the inputs. Labour services, for example, do not satisfy wants directly; but labour services are demanded to produce goods and services that satisfy wants directly. The demand for labour is an example of a derived demand.

Problem 14-2

State the marginal productivity theory of wages.

Requirement and Clue: *Much can be written about the marginal productivity theory of wages, but what is required here is simply a precise statement of the theory.*

Solution:

The marginal productivity theory of wages states that under purely competitive conditions, a profit-maximizing firm will hire labour up to the point at which the wage rate equals the value of the marginal product of labour.

Problem 14-3

What is the relationship between the marginal revenue product of labour curve and the firm's demand curve for labour?

Requirement and Clue: *Carefully examine each of the concepts. By so doing, the relationship between them should be revealed.*

Solution:

The marginal revenue product (MRP) of labour is the additional revenue contributed by the last unit of labour. It is the value of the marginal physical product of labour. As additional units of labour are employed, the marginal product declines. Hence, the marginal revenue product of labour curve is downward sloping as shown in the following diagram.

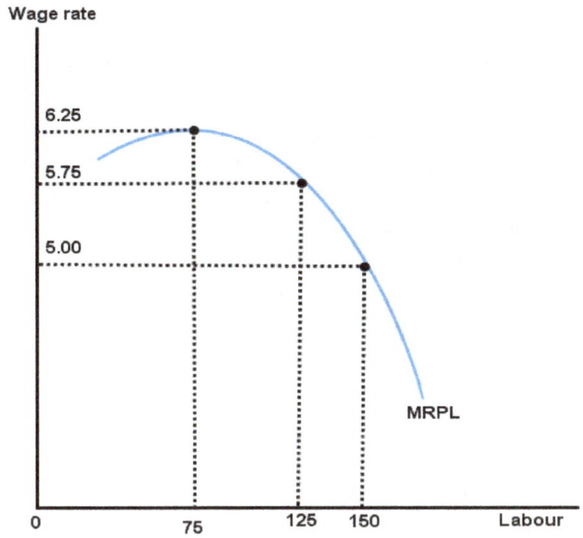

The firm would hire labour up to the point where the wage rate (W) equals the marginal revenue product. If the wage rate were \$6.25, the firm would hire 75 units of labour. If the wage rate were \$5.75, it would hire 125 units of labour, and if the wage rate were \$5.00, the firm would hire 150 units of labour. The marginal revenue product curve shows the various quantities of labour that a firm would hire at various wage rates. But this is exactly the firm's demand curve for labour.

Problem 14-4

What is the supply of labour? What is the shape of the supply curve for labour?

Requirement and Clue: *This is a two-part problem. Answer each part in order. A clear and precise definition of the supply of labour is required. In addition to stating the shape of the supply curve for labour in the second part of the solution, you should provide a rational for your statement. A graph might be helpful.*

Solution:

The supply of labour refers to the various quantities of labour that workers would be willing and able to provide at various wage rates.

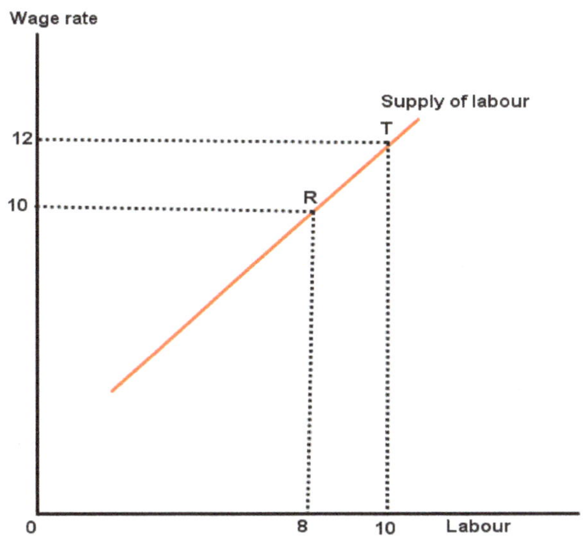

The higher the wage rate, other things being equal, the more willing workers will be to offer their labour services. The lower the wage rate, the less willing workers will be to offer their labour services. This suggests that the supply curve for labour is upward sloping as shown in the diagram above

At a wage rate of \$10, the quantity of labour supplied is 8, and at a wage rate of \$12, the quantity of labour supplied is 10.

Problem 14-5

What are the main factors that affect the quantity of labour supplied in an economy?

Requirement and Clue: *Be careful not to confuse the quantity of labour supplied with the supply of labour.*

Solution:

The quantity of labour supplied is the number of workers offering their labour services at some specific wage rate. Other things being equal, a higher wage rate will cause an increase in the quantity of labour supplied as more workers will be willing to take advantage of the higher wage rate. But the wage rate is not the only factor that influences the quantity of labour supplied. Among the other determinants of the quantity of labour supplied are: (1) the size of the population, (2) opportunities for overtime work, (3) legal and institutional restrictions, (4) non-monetary benefits, and (5) the state of employment in the economy.

<u>Size of the population</u>

The larger the population, other things being equal, the greater will be the number of people willing and able to work at any wage rate. The quantity of labour supplied in an economy with a population of 5,000,000 will tend to be greater than the quantity of labour supplied in an economy with only 1,500,000 people.

<u>Opportunities for overtime work</u>

In general, overtime work earns a higher pay than the regular pay. Thus, the opportunity to work overtime serves as an incentive for workers to offer their labour services at any given wage.

<u>Legal and institutional restrictions</u>

Laws governing the age at which workers can enter the labour market affect the quantity of labour supplied. For example, child labour laws prevent entry into the labour market before a certain age. Institutional restrictions such as retirement age and working hours affect the quantity of labour supplied.

<u>Non-monetary benefits</u>

Non-monetary benefits such as leisure and psychic income influence the quantity of labour supplied. A strong preference for leisure will tend to reduce the quantity of labour supplied, and where psychic income can be derived from employment, there will be a tendency for workers to be willing to offer more labour.

<u>The state of employment</u>

The state of employment in the economy affects the quantity of labour supplied. During periods of significant unemployment, the prospects for employment decline and workers, sensing the difficulty of finding employment, tend to withdraw from the market. On the other hand, when job prospects are bright, workers assess their chances of finding employment as being more positive, so they offer more labour services.

Problem 14-6

How does an increase in the wage rate affect the supply curve for labour?

Requirement and Clue: *In your solution, be careful not to confuse a change in the supply of labour with a change in the quantity of labour supplied.*

Solution:

An increase in the wage rate causes an increase in the quantity of labour supplied, but it does not affect the supply of labour. Graphically, an increase in the wage rate causes a movement up the supply curve for labour but it does not affect the supply curve. The curve remains in its original position.

Problem 14-7

Explain how the equilibrium wage rate is determined in a competitive labour market.

Requirement and Clue: *You are expected to know the meaning of the equilibrium wage rate. You are to explain how the forces of demand and supply determine the equilibrium wage rate.*

Solution:

In a competitive labour market, the wage rate is determined by the market forces of demand and supply. A diagram will be helpful in explaining how the equilibrium wage rate is determined.

Consider the following diagram.

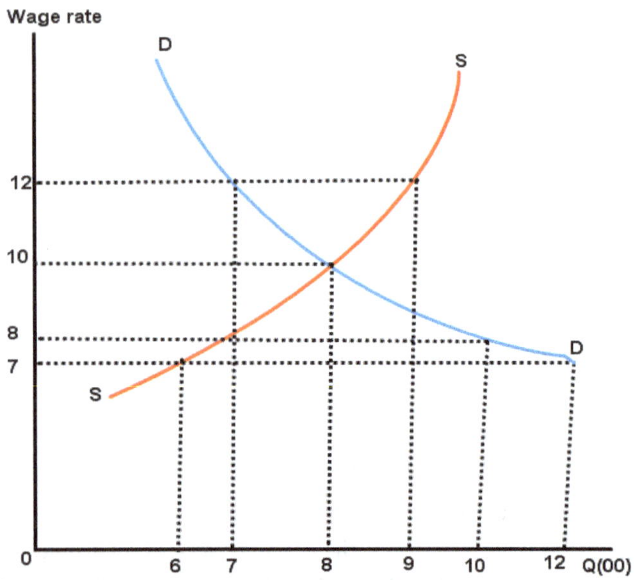

At a wage rate of $12 per hour, the quantity of labour supplied is 900, while the quantity demanded is 700. Therefore, at a wage rate of $12, the quantity of labour supplied is greater than the quantity demanded. There will be a surplus of labour of (900 – 700) = 200. This surplus of labour on the market will tend to force the wage rate down from $12.

At a wage rate of $8 per hour, the quantity of labour demanded is 1000, while the quantity supplied is 700. Therefore at a wage rate of $8, the quantity of labour demanded exceeds the quantity supplied. There will be a shortage of labour of (1000 – 700) = 300. This shortage will force the wage rate up from $8.

At a wage rate of $10, the quantity of labour demanded is 800, and the quantity supplied is also 800. Thus, at a wage rate of $10, there is neither a shortage nor a surplus. The market clears and the wage rate stabilizes. In this way, the equilibrium wage rate is determined by demand and supply for labour.

Problem 14-8

Use a demand/supply diagram to show the effect of an increase in the demand for labour, other things being equal, on the wage rate and on the number of workers hired.

Requirement and Clue: *This problem is a test of you ability to use the tools of demand and supply to explain changes in the labour market. Make sure that your diagram is labelled and that your explanation is clear.*

Solution:

The following diagram represents the market for labour. LD1 is the initial demand curve and L_S is the supply curve. The equilibrium wage rate is W*1 and the number of workers hired at that wage rate is L*1.

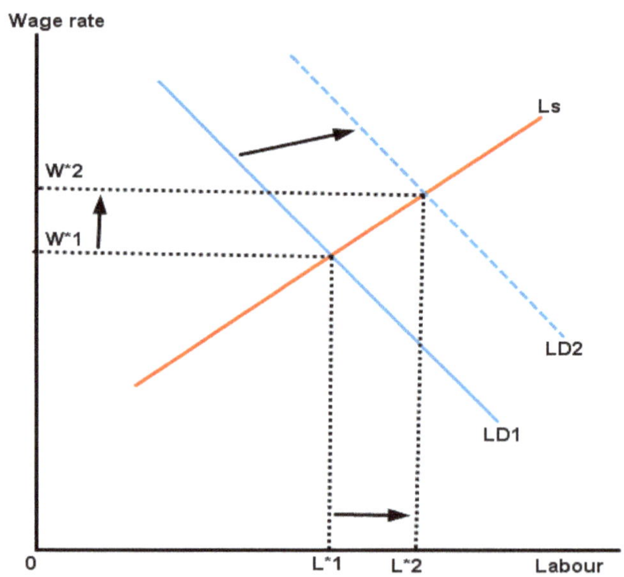

An increase in the demand for labour is shown by the shift in the demand curve from LD1 to LD2. As a result of this increase in demand, the equilibrium wage rate rises from W*1 to W*2 and the number of workers hired increases from L*1 to L*2. An increase in the demand for labour, other things being equal, will raise the wage rate and increase the number of workers hired.

Problem 14-9

What is a labour union? What role do unions play in the labour market?

Requirement and Clue: *This is a two-part problem. Answer each part in order. The first part requires a precise definition of a union. For the second part of the problem, focus on the objectives and activities of unions.*

Solution:

A labour union is an association of workers organized to promote the interests of its members in negotiations with their employees. Unions play an important role in the labour market. Labour unions contribute significantly to the pleasant working conditions that workers enjoy. They fight for and win wage increases for their members, and they secure a certain measure of job security for workers. In addition, unions prevent abuses of human rights, and they lobby for legislation and programs to improve the lives of ordinary workers. Clearly, unions play an important role in the labour market.

Problem 14-10

"The institution of minimum wage legislation contributes to unemployment." Is this assertion valid?

Requirement and Clue: *Consider the effects of minimum wage legislation on the quantity of labour demanded. A diagram is helpful. It is advisable to consider the long-term effect also.*

Solution:

Minimum wage legislation is a law that makes it illegal for employees to pay workers less than a certain wage. So minimum wage legislation acts as a form of wage control. The following diagram will help to analyze the effect of minimum wage legislation on employment.

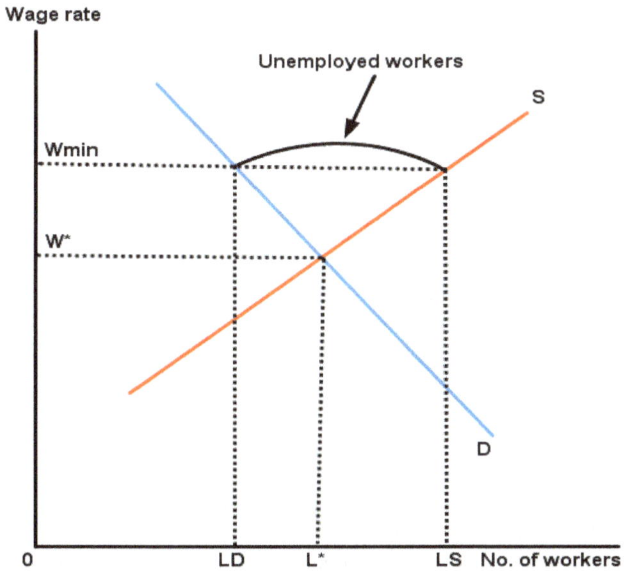

Perfectly Competitive Labour Market

D and S are the demand and supply curves of labour respectively. The equilibrium wage rate is W*, and at that wage rate, the number of workers employed is L*. Now, suppose the government legislates a minimum wage of Wmin. Firms can no longer legally pay workers the market determined wage of W*. The quantity of labour demanded at a wage rate of Wmin has fallen from L* to LD, while the quantity supplied has increased from L* to LS. A surplus of labour (LS – LD) has resulted. Hence the effect of the minimum wage legislation is to increase unemployment.

Up to this point, the assertion that minimum wage legislation contributes to unemployment seems valid. Fewer people are hired though at a higher wage rate. As time progresses, however, those workers who are now earning more money will do more spending. This could provide an incentive for firms to increase their production levels. To do so, they must buy more resources, including labour services. This reduces unemployment. Therefore, the net effect of minimum legislation on unemployment is, in the long run, uncertain.

Problem 14-11

What are the arguments in favour of minimum wage legislation? What are the arguments against it?

Requirement and Clue: *This is a two-part problem. Address each part in order. You are expected to discuss the pros and cons of minimum wage legislation. Focus on the main arguments.*

Solution:

Arguments in favour of minimum wage legislation include the following:

1. Without minimum wage legislation, employers would exploit workers and pay them subsistence wage. Minimum wage legislation ensures a "fair" wage for workers.
2. Minimum wage legislation encourages efficiency. If labour is cheap, employers may tend not to be inefficient (wasteful) in their use of labour services. Minimum wage legislation sets the wage above the market equilibrium wage. At this relatively high wage, employers will tend to more efficient in their use of labour.
3. Minimum wage legislation causes workers' incomes to increase. This increase in income enables them to enjoy better health services, better education, and to become more productive workers.

Arguments against minimum wage legislation include the following:

1. Minimum wage legislation causes employers to hire fewer workers at the higher wage. Thus, minimum wage legislation causes unemployment.
2. Minimum wage legislation makes labour more expensive and this drives up the cost of production. This higher cost of production may even cause some firms to go out of business.

Problem 14-12

What methods do unions use to secure their position?

Requirement and Clue: *Focus on devices used by unions to increase their membership and to encourage unionization of workers.*

Solution:

Unions try to secure their position through the use of closed shops and open shops. The concept of an open shop helps to explain how a closed shop or union shop arrangement helps to secure the union's position. In an open shop workplace, union membership is not a prerequisite for employment. In a closed shop workplace, jobs are given only to union members. Between these two practices is the union shop, in which workers who are not union members can be hired, provided that they become union members within a specified period. It should be obvious that unions are least likely to support open shops. A union is most powerful when all of the workers are unionized.

Problem 14-13

Can an employer benefit from a closed shop?

Requirement and Clue: *The solution requires an understanding of the closed shop concept. Focus on any situation that a closed shop might create that is beneficial to the employer.*

Solution:

A closed shop is a workplace where jobs are given only to members of the union. A closed shop, though obviously beneficial to the union, may also benefit the employer. The closed shop serves as a central employment agency for the employer, from which a pool of workers can be drawn when required. Thus, a closed shop arrangement may reduce the cost to the employer of searching for an employee with the requisite skills. The employer may also benefit from greater industrial peace and harmony resulting from the fact that all of the employees are union members—a fact that will eliminate any conflict between union and non-union workers.

Problem 14-14

Briefly define collective bargaining? What is a collective agreement?

Requirement and Clue: *This is a two-part problem. Answer each part in order. Both parts of the problem are definitional. Do not ignore the word "briefly" in your solution.*

Solution:

Collective bargaining is the entire process by which wages and other working conditions are negotiated between a union, representing workers collectively, and an employer. Instead of each worker negotiating directly with the employer, the union bargains on behalf of all the workers.

The collective bargaining process generally results in a contract between the union and the employer. It is this contract or agreement that is referred to as a collective agreement. The collective agreement specifies the responsibilities of employers and employees concerning wages and salaries, hours of work, vacation, safety on the job, benefits such as maternity leaves and training, job security, and other employment-related issues.

Problem 14-15

Briefly state the difference between a strike and a lockout.

Requirement and Clue: *This problem is basically definitional. You should place emphasis on the difference between the two concepts.*

Solution:

A strike is a temporary work stoppage by a union in an attempt to exert pressure on the employer to grant its demands. A lockout, on the other hand, is a temporary closing of a plant by an employer to win or end a dispute. The fundamental difference between the two concepts is that a strike is action taken by the union while a lockout is action taken by the employer.

Problem 14-16

Discuss the costs of strikes.

Requirement and Clue: *Think of any losses that may result from a strike.*

Solution:

Strikes exact costs from workers as well as from employees. A discussion of the costs of strikes can focus on direct and indirect costs.

Direct costs: The direct costs of a strike can be easily identified. The cost to workers is lost wages. The cost to employers is lost production, lost sales, and lost profits. The cost to the union is lost union dues.

Indirect costs: A strike in one industry affects other industries and the general public. For example, a strike by truck drivers affects grocery stores and other retail outlets, since they cannot obtain supplies during the strike. This is an indirect cost. If workers in the steel industry go on strike, the auto industry may have to shut down because of a shortage of steel, which is an important input in the auto industry. In many cases, strikes cause a great deal of inconvenience to the public—as, for example, when a public transportation company goes on strike.

Problem 14-17

Do strikes necessarily result in a reduction of total output in the economy?

Requirement and Clue: *A direct "yes" or "no" answer will not be enough. Focus on the time horizon.*

Solution:

Many strikes do result in a loss in total output as plants close, but not all strikes do. Consideration must be given to the duration of the strike. A strike in a certain factory at a certain time may mean simply that the factory has to work harder and longer at the end of the strike to compensate for the loss of production during the strike. In this case, the strike results in a shifting of the timing of production rather than in the volume of output. The longer the strike lasts, the more difficult it is to compensate for this loss.

Problem 14-18

A small private school with a staff of five unionized teachers is operated by a husband and wife team of educators. The time for negotiations has arrived. The union claims that wage increases should be based principally on the size of the teacher's family since teachers with large families have greater expenses than teachers with small families. The operators argue that the size of the teacher's family is irrelevant in determining wages increases.

Whose position is valid?

Requirement and Clue: *Focus on the factors that are likely to affect wages.*

Solution:

There is nothing that prevents one from being sympathetic toward workers with large families, but family size has little or nothing to do with a worker's contribution to output. The school operators' position is valid. Wage increases should be based on such factors as the worker's productivity, the profitability of the school, and the cost of living—not on family size.

Problem 14-19

Discuss some of the factors that should be considered in wage negotiations.

Requirement and Clue: *Focus on factors that will justify workers obtaining wage increases.*

Solution:

An important factor in wage negotiations is the cost of living. Workers try to protect their purchasing power against a rising cost of living. The employer cannot easily ignore such a consideration. Unions try to protect their members' purchasing power by escalator clauses, indexation, and cost-of-living adjustments.

Productivity is another factor that is likely to carry some weight in negotiations. Workers will naturally expect to benefit from increases in their productivity. Employers are also less likely to resist demands for wage increases in the face of productivity increases.

A third factor that is likely to feature significantly in wage demands and offers is the profitability of the business. If the firm has had a substantial increase in profits, the union will certainly use that fact as justification for higher wage demands. Conversely, if the firm has undergone a period of declining profits, the employers will likely refuse to agree to higher wages.

Problem 14-20

Define productivity of labour.

Requirement and Clue: *This is a definitional problem. Don't write all you know about this concept. You are required only to state clearly what it is.*

Solution:

The productivity of labour is the average output produced by a unit of labour (e.g. one worker). In other words, it is the average product of labour. For example, if a firm produces 500 units of output with 40 workers, then the productivity of labour is 500 ÷ 40 = 12.5 units of output.

Problem 14-21

Discuss some of the factors that contribute to high labour productivity.

Requirement and Clue: *The solution requires an understanding of the concept of labour productivity. Think of some of the things that make labour more productive.*

Solution:

Labour productivity refers to the average output of goods and services produced by a unit of labour. The following are among the factors that contribute to high labour productivity: the quality of the labour force, capital, technology, natural resources, and labour management.

Quality of the labour force: A highly educated and trained labour force will make labour more productive. Similarly, a healthy, energetic, imaginative, and vigorous labour force will contribute positively to labour productivity.

Capital: Labour works with capital to produce goods and services. The machinery and equipment used in conjunction with labour definitely makes labour more productive. Compare the productivity of a worker preparing a field for planting with a hoe with the productivity of a worker preparing the same field with a tractor.

Technology: Technology can be viewed as a method of production. A high state of technological advance implies that sophisticated methods of production are employed and such methods will generally be more efficient. Efficiency in the use of inputs enhances labour productivity.

Natural resources: As in the case of capital, labour works with natural resources to produce goods and services. In a country that is well-endowed with a large quantity and high-quality of natural resources, labour has more of them to work with, and this contributes to labour productivity.

Labour management: Human resources management is necessary to ensure that labour is properly allocated. When workers are placed in positions where they can make maximum contribution to the production process, their output will be high. When their morale is high, their productivity will also tend to be high.

Problem 14-22

Why is it relatively difficult for unions to increase the demand for labour? How might a union try to increase the demand for labour?

Requirement and Clue: *This is a two-part problem. Answer each part in order. Focus on where the demand for labour originates for the solution to the first part of the solution. For the second part of the solution, recall that the demand for labour is s derived demand.*

Solution:

The demand for labour is a derived demand, depending on the demand for the items that labour is used to produce. The demand for labour therefore originates from producers who use labour to produce goods and services. The demand for labour, then, is in the hands of producers, and not in the hands of the union. That explains why it is relatively difficult for unions to increase the demand for labour.

A union might try to increase the demand for labour by increasing the demand for the products produced with the help of labour. Hence, a union may encourage its members to purchase union-made products.

Problem 14-23

How might some union members be hurt by a successful round of negotiations that result in an increase in wages?

Requirement and Clue: *Consider the effect of higher wages on the market for labour. A diagram will be helpful.*

Solution:

Let us assume that through a successful round of negotiations, a union secures a wage rate for its members—a rate that is higher than the market equilibrium wage. The following diagram will help us to analyze the effects of such a wage rate.

In the diagram below, DD and SS are the demand and supply for labour, respectively. The equilibrium wage rate is W0, and the equilibrium quantity of labour demanded and supplied is E0. Let us assume now that a union enters the picture and succeeds in negotiating a wage rate of W1, which exceeds the market equilibrium wage. At this higher wage rate, the quantity of labour demanded is E1, while the quantity supplied is E2. Thus, the higher wage rate results in a surplus of labour on the labour market, represented by E2 – E1. This surplus of labour is, of course, unemployment. Those who are employed do enjoy the benefits of a higher wage, but unemployment results. The higher wage rate hurts some workers.

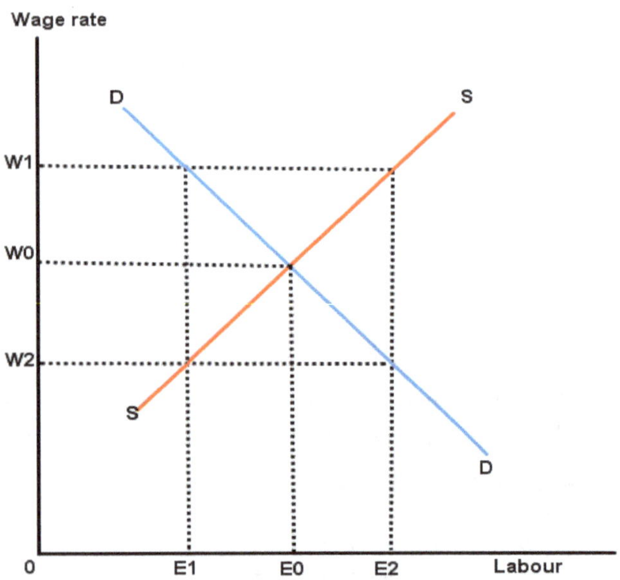

Problem 14-24

If all economists in a certain country had to obtain a licence in order to work as economists, what would happen to the market for economists?

Requirement and Clue: *Focus on which side of the market for economists would be affected. You are required to state the effect of the licence requirement on the salaries and quantity of economics working.*

Solution:

If economists were subjected to a licensing procedure, we could expect some of them to fail the licensing requirements. The total supply of practising economists would therefore decline, shifting the supply curve for economists to the left. Then, assuming no change in the demand for the services of economists, we could expect the average salaries of economists to increase.

Problem 14-25

"Many people are unemployed because the wage rate is too high in many cases. One of the reasons for the high wage rate is the existence of minimum wage legislation. It is very difficult to lower the wage rate on any long-term basis, because when the wage rate falls, the demand for labour will increase (that is, the demand curve for labour will shift to the right). When this happens, it is obvious that wage rates will again increase, and unemployment will increase as firms hire fewer workers."

Can you detect any error in the above statement?

Requirement and Clue: *You should study the statement carefully to see if you can identify any errors. Look out for concepts and their interpretation.*

Solution:

The assertion that unemployment may result from minimum wage legislation is valid, at least in the short run. But the passage contains a common analytical inaccuracy. When the wage rates falls, firms may hire additional workers. This, however, does not represent an increase in demand for labour but an increase in the quantity of labour demanded. The demand curve for labour does not shift because of a fall in the wage rate as the passage states. Instead, there will be a movement along the same demand curve. The analytical inaccuracy has resulted in an erroneous conclusion.

Multiple-Choice

In each case, circle the letter that corresponds with the correct answer.

1. The demand for final goods and services is a:

a. strategic demand c. multiple demand
b. inverse demand d. direct demand

Answer: d

Reason: Final goods and services satisfy consumers' wants directly, thus the demand for them is direct.

2. Derived demand refers to:

a. the demand for inputs that is due to the demand for the goods and services produced by the inputs
b. the demand for final goods and services that is derived from human wants
c. the demand for goods and services created by aggressive advertising
d. the total demand for all goods and services derived from the need to conserve our resources

Answer: a

Reason: Resources (inputs) are not demanded for their own sake, but for the sake of producing goods and services. Their demand is therefore derived from the demand for the goods and services that the inputs produce.

3. The demand for labour is a(n):

a. direct demand c. inverse demand
b. derived demand d. ultimate demand

Answer: b

Reason: It's a derived demand because labour does not satisfy wants directly, but only through the goods and services that it is used to produce.

4. The demand for labour services is derived from:

a. the demand for goods and services to be produced with the use of labour
b. the demand for other factor inputs
c. the satisfaction derived from using labour
d. all of the above

Answer: a

Reason: Labour is used to produce goods and services. So if the demand for goods and services increases, firms will demand more labour.

5. The demand for labour originates from:

a. firms c. households
b. government d. both a and b

Answer: d

Reason: Firms (producers, private employers) and government hire the services of labour to provide goods and services.

6. The marginal physical product of labour is:

a. the quantity of labour required to physically increase output by an additional unit
b. the extra output derived from using a additional unit of labour
c. the exact quantity of labour that would be hired at any particular time
d. the total product of labour divided by the number of workers.

Answer: b

Reason: The marginal product of labour is the change in the total product caused by hiring an extra unit of labour. This corresponds with choice b.

7. If the marginal revenue product exceeds the wage rate, the firm will:

a. hire fewer workers
b. hire additional workers
c. not change the numbers of workers hired
d. be maximizing its profits

Answer: b

Reason: If the marginal revenue product exceeds the wage rate, hiring an extra worker will add more to revenue than to cost.

8. The marginal productivity theory of wages states that:

a. under purely competitive conditions, all firms will hire the same quantity of labour
b. there will be a single wage rate provide that the labour market is competitive
c. under purely competitive conditions, a profit-maximizing firm will hire labour up to the point at which the wage rate equals the value of the marginal product of labour
d. none of the above

Answer: c

Reason: If the value of the marginal product of labour exceeds the wage rate, the firm will benefit by hiring more workers. If the value of the marginal product of labour is less than the wage rate, the firm will benefit by reducing the quantity of labour. But when the value of the marginal product of labour equals the wage rate, the firm has nothing to gain by changing the quantity of labour hired.

9. The marginal productivity theory of wages states that the firm will employ labour up to the point where:

a. the wage rate equals the value of the marginal product of labour
b. the wage rate exceeds the marginal revenue product of labour
c. the wage rate falls below the marginal revenue product of labour
d. productivity decisions cannot be made at the margin

Answer: a

Reason: A divergence of the wage rate from the marginal revenue product of labour will reduce the firm's profits. Choice a is consistent with the marginal productivity theory of wages.

10. The firm's demand curve for labour is:

a. its marginal revenue product curve
b. equal to the marginal cost of labour
c. always greater than its marginal revenue product curve
d. always less than its marginal revenue product curve

Answer: a

Reason: The marginal revenue product curve tells how many workers will be hired at various wage rates. This is exactly the demand curve for labour.

11. Other things being equal, a fall in the wage rate will:

a. increase the demand for labour since firms will hire more workers

b. reduce the demand for labour since firms will hire fewer workers

c. cause the demand for labour curve to shift to the right

d. none of the above

Answer: d

Reason: A fall in the wage rate will increase the quantity of labour demanded, not the demand for labour.

12. An increase in the wage rate, other things being equal, will:

a. shift the demand cure for labour to the right

b. shift the demand curve for labour to the right

c. shift the supply curve of labour to the right

d. none of the above

Answer: d

Reason: An increase in the wage rate will not shift the demand or the supply curve of labour. It will cause a movement along the demand or supply curve.

13. The supply curve for labour is:

a. downward sloping c. upward sloping

b. vertical d. horizontal

Answer: c

Reason: At higher wage rates, workers are more willing to offer their labour services.

14. 14. A change in the wage rate will:

a. change both demand and supply for labour

b. change the demand for labour only

c. change the supply of labour only

d. none of the above

Answer: d

Reason: A change in the wage rate will change the quantity of labour demanded and the quantity supplied.

15. The supply of labour is:

a. the quantity of labour that will be supplied at a particular wage rate

b. the number of people willing and able to work at a particular time

c. the various quantities of labour that will be hired at various wage rates during a period of time

d. the various quantities of labour that will be offered for sale at various wage rates during a period of time

Answer: d

Reason: The supply of labour is a schedule of wage rates and the associated quantities of labour supplied.

16. A backward-bending labour supply curve shows that:

a. at higher wage rates, the supply curve of labour becomes downward sloping

b. workers are inherently lazy and want wages without exerting any effort

c. a higher wage rate attracts more workers into the labour market

d. an increase in the wage rate reduces the demand for labour

Answer: a

Reason: A backward-bending labour supply curve indicates that workers offer fewer labour services as the wage rate rises.

17. The equilibrium wage rate is determined by:

a. the equality of demand and supply

b. the intersection of the demand and supply curves for labour

c. both a and b

d. neither a nor b

Answer: b

Reason: The equilibrium wage rate is the wage rate at which the quantity of labour demanded equals the quantity supplied. This occurs at the intersection of the two curves.

18. Which of the following is likely to increase the demand for labour?

a. An increase in the wage rate

b. A decrease in the wage rate

c. An increase in the demand for goods produced by labour

d. An increase in the number of workers available for work

Answer: c

Reason: Since labour is a derived demand, firms will be willing to hire more workers to produce the additional goods demanded.

19. The supply of labour will tend to increase if:

a. the wage rate rises

b. the wage rate falls

c. a reduced preference for leisure

d. an extremely progressive income tax system

Answer: c

Reason: If workers place a lower value on leisure, they will offer more labour services at each and every wage rate.

20. Other things being equal, an increase in the demand for labour will:

a. result in an increase in the wage rate and an increase in the quantity of labour demanded and supplied

b. cause the wage rate to rise and the quantity of labour demanded and supplied to fall

c. cause the wage rate to fall and the quantity of labour demanded and supplied to fall

d. none of the above

Answer: a

Reason: The demand curve for labour will shift to the right, resulting in a shortage of labour which will force the price of labour up. As the wage rate rises, the quantity of labour supplied rises.

21. An increase in the supply of labour, other things being equal, will:

a. shift the labour supply curve to the right

b. increase the equilibrium quantity of labour

c. reduce the equilibrium wage rate
d. all of the above

Answer: d

Reason: Choices a, b, and c will result from an increase in the supply of labour.

22. An association of workers organized to promote the interests of its members in negotiations with their employers is called:

a. a general assembly of workers
b. a labour union
c. a people's work club
d. all of the above

Answer: b

Choice b defines a trade or labour union.

23. The practice of providing workers with unnecessary work to keep them on the payroll is called:

a. work surfeiting
b. work engineering
c. featherbedding
d. work co-mingling

Answer: c

Reason: Featherbedding is the term used to describe the practice of a labor union of requiring an employer to hire more workers than necessary for a particular task.

24. Which of the following workplace situations gives most security to a union?

a. Open shop
b. Union shop
c. Closed shop
d. None of the above

Answer: c

Reason: In a closed shop workplace, jobs are given only to union members.

25. Wage differentials may be due to:

a. differences in education, experience, and responsibility
b. the existence of unions in some occupations
c. the degree of danger associated with various occupations
d. all of the above

Answer: d

Reason: Any of the choices from a to c could cause differences in wages.

26. Collective bargaining refers to:

a. a legislation ordering striking employees back to work
b. negotiations among employees to determine who should perform certain functions on the job
c. the functional distribution of income for bargaining purpose
d. the process by which labour and management reach a negotiated agreement regarding the terms of employment.

Answer: d

Reason: Collective bargaining is the interaction between a union, representing its members, and an employer, whereby decisions regarding wages, hours of work, and other working conditions are reached. This corresponds with choice d.

27. Which of the following is a procedure for settling disputes between employers and employees?

a. Back to work legislation
b. Voluntary arbitration
c. Mediation
d. All of the above

Answer: d

Reason: The choices given are all procedures used to end strikes and lockouts and to end industrial disputes.

28. A union may shift the equilibrium wage upward by:

a. reducing the demand for goods and services produced by unionized workers
b. restricting the entry of newcomers into certain occupations
c. encouraging the entry of newcomers into certain occupations
d. none of the above

Answer: b

Reason: Restricting the entry of newcomers into certain occupations will shift the labour supply curve to the left and thus raise the wage rate.

29. Which of the following is a cost of a strike?

a. Lost wages
b. Public inconvenience
c. Lost production
d. All of the above

Answer: d

Reason: The choices given are all negative effects (costs) of a strike.

30. Which of the following is a devise for protecting the purchasing power of workers?

a. Escalator clauses
b. Cost-of-living adjustment
c. Indexation
d. All of the above

Answer: d

Reason: As the cost of living rises, workers' real income or purchasing power falls. The choices given protect workers' purchasing power against a rising cost of living.

True-False

Determine whether each of the following statements is true or false.

1. The demand for factor inputs is a direct demand because it comes directly from producers who want the resources to produce goods and services.

Answer: False

Explanation: *The demand for factor inputs is a derived demand because it is due to the demand for goods and services produced by the inputs.*

2. The demand for factors of production comes mainly from firms and government that use the resources to produce goods and services.

Answer: True

3. The marginal physical product (MPP_L) is the marginal revenue product of labour (MRP_L) multiplied by the price of the product.

Answer: False

Explanation: *The marginal revenue product of labour (MRPL) is the marginal physical product of labour (MPPL) multiplied by the price of the product.*

4. The marginal physical product of labour is the extra income earned by selling an additional unit of labour.

Answer: False

Explanation: *The marginal physical product of labour is the extra output derived from using an additional unit of labour.*

5. The marginal physical product of labour is derived by dividing the change in total product by the change in the quantity of labour.

Answer: True

6. If an additional worker will contribute more to total revenue than to total cost, then it will not benefit the firm to hire the extra worker.

Answer: False

Explanation: *Hiring the extra worker when he or she contributes more to revenue than to cost will benefit the firm.*

7. The marginal productivity theory of wages states that the firm should always try to keep wages below the value of the marginal physical product in order to maximize profits.

Answer: False

Explanation: *The theory states that under purely competitive conditions, a profit-maximizing firm will hire labour up to the point where the wage rate equals the value of the marginal product of labour.*

8. The competitive firm will hire more labour if the wage rate equals the marginal revenue product.

Answer: False:

Explanation: *If the wage rate equals the marginal revenue product of labour, the firm will be in equilibrium and will not change the quantity of labour hired.*

9. The marginal revenue product of labour curve is the firm's demand curve for labour.

Answer: True

10. Changes in income, changes in tastes, and changes in market size, which affect the demand for the firm's product, will change the quantity of labour demanded at any given wage rate, and will thus shift the firm's demand curve for labour.

Answer: True

11. The supply of labour refers to the quantity of labour services that will be offered for sale at a particular wage rate.

Answer: False

Explanation: *The supply of labour is not just the quantity that will be offered at a particular wage rate. Instead, it is the various quantities that will be offered at vavious wage rates.*

12. The labour supply curve is upward sloping because the higher the wage rate is, the more willing will workers be to offer their services.

Answer: True

13. If a group of workers works fewer hours when the wage rate increases, then that group has a backward-bending supply curve for labour.

Answer: True

14. Equilibrium in the market for labour services occurs when the demand and supply of labour are equal.

Answer: False

Explanation: *Equilibrium occurs when the quantity of labour demanded equals the quantity supplied.*

15. An increase in the demand for labour will definitely increase the wage rate in a competitive labour market.

Answer: False

Explanation: *An increase in the demand for labour will increase the wage rate if nothing else changes (ceteris paribus).*

16. A fall in the wage rate will increase the demand for labour services, which will raise the wage rate again.

Answer: False

Explanation: *An fall in the wage rate will increase the quantity of labour services demanded; not the demand for labour services.*

17. Wage differentials are due basically to differences in the relative scarcities of different types of labour.

Answer: True

18. A labour union is as association of employees and employers organized to ensure that strikes and lockouts never occur.

Answer: False

Explanation: A labour union is an association of workers organized to promote the interests of its members in negotiations with their employers.

19. An open shop, a closed shop, and a union shop are all arrangements designed to secure a union's position.

Answer: False

Explanation: An open shop arrangement does not secure the union's position. In that arrangement, workers do not have to be union members to be hired.

20. An open shop is an arrangement whereby employees must be union members in order to obtain or keep their jobs.

Answer: False

Explanation: In an open shop arrangement, employees are not required to be union members in order to be employed.

21. Featherbedding benefits no one except the union itself.

Answer: False

Explanation: It benefits some workers because it protects workers who might otherwise experience great difficulty in finding another job.

22. The cost of living, productivity, and profitability are important considerations in wage negotiations.

Answer: True

23. An example of a direct cost of a strike is the inconvenience to the public. An example of an indirect cost is the loss of output during the duration of the strike.

Answer: False

Explanation: Inconvenience to the public is an indirect cost of a strike, while the loss of output is a direct cost.

24. A strike never results in lost profits for the firm because it can always cause its workers to work harder once the strike is over.

Answer: False

Explanation: A strike may cause a firm to lose profits if, for example, some of its clients decide to take their business elsewhere during the strike.

25. Escalator clauses, indexation, and cost-of-living adjustments are devices used to protect the purchasing power of workers.

Answer: True

26. By restricting the entry of newcomers into certain occupations and professions, a union hopes to shift the demand for labour curve to the left.

Answer: False

Explanation: Restriction of entry will shift the supply curve of labour (not the demand curve) to the left.

Completion

Fill in the blanks

Use each word or combination of words from the list exactly once.
(**Hint**: *Proceed by elimination*)

Word list

Agreement — Arbitration —Bargaining — Closed — Collective x 2 — Compulsory —Decrease — Derived — Direct — Equilibrium — Featherbedding — Firms —Government — Households or workers — Increase x 2 — Lockout —Marginal x 3 —Mechanism —Physical — Product x 2 — Productivity —Quantity of labour supplied — Rate — Revenue — Shop x 2 — Strike — Theory — Transfer — Union — Wage x 2 — Wages

Questions

1. The demand for goods and services is a ___________ demand while the demand for productive inputs is a(n) ___________ demand.
2. The demand for labour services comes from ___________ and ___________.
3. The extra output derived from using an additional unit of labour is called the ___________ ___________ ___________ of labour.
4. The firm's demand curve for labour is its ___________ ___________ ___________ curve.
5. The theory that a firm will employ labour up to the point where the wage rate equals the marginal revenue product of labour is called the ___________ ___________ ___________ of wages.
6. The supply of labour comes from ___________.
7. Other things being equal, as the wage rate rises, the ___________ [supply, quantity of labour supplied] also rises.
8. The ___________ ___________ ___________ is determined by the intersection of the demand and supply curves for labour.
9. An increase in the demand for labour, other things being equal, will result in a(n) ___________ [increase, decrease] in the wage rate.
10. An increase in the supply of labour, other things being equal, will result in a(n) ___________ [increase, decrease] in the wage rate.
11. A(n) ___________ ___________ is an arrangement in which membership in a union is compulsory for obtaining employment. A(n) ___________ ___________ is an arrangement whereby an employee may be hired even if that employee is not a union member, but with the condition that the employee becomes a union member within a specified time.
12. The practice of providing workers with unnecessary work to keep them employed is referred to as ___________.

13. ____________ ____________ is the process by which wages and other working conditions are negotiated between a union and an employer.

14. A successful round of negotiations between a union and an employer results in a contract known as a(n) ____________ ____________

15. The obligatory submission of a dispute to a third party whose decision on the matter is binding is called ____________ ____________.

16. A(n) ____________ is a temporary work stoppage by employees, aimed at forcing an employer to grant the union's demands. A(n) ____________ is a temporary closing of a plant by an employer, aimed at winning a dispute between workers and the employer.

17. Unions encourage their members to purchase "union made" products because this will ____________ the demand for labour and lead to an increase in ____________.

18. The process by which changes in wages in one occupation are transmitted to other occupations is referred to as the ____________ ____________ ____________.

Solution

1. (direct, derived)
2. (firms, government)
3. (marginal physical product)
4. (marginal revenue product)
5. (marginal productivity theory)
6. (households or workers)
7. (quantity of labour supplied)
8. (equilibrium wage rate)
9. (increase)
10. (decrease)
11. (closed shop, union shop)
12. (featherbedding)
13. (collective bargaining)
14. (collective agreement)
15. (compulsory arbitration)
16. (strike, lockout)
17. (increase, wages)
18. (wage transfer mechanism)

15 THE PRICING OF LAND & OTHER RESOURCES

SYNOPSIS

Pure economic rent is the earning from a factor of production the supply of which is fixed. If the supply is fixed only in the short run, we use the term quasi rent. The rental value of land is determined the demand for and supply of land.

Changes in the demand for land will cause changes in the rental value of land. Differences in the rental value of land are due to expected yield, resource content, and location.

Transfer earning is the amount that a factor of production can earn in the next best employment alternative. The rental portion of income is calculated by subtracting transfer earnings from total earnings.

Interest is income earned on debt capital.

The **rate of interest** is the ratio of the interest income to the amount of money lent or borrowed, and is determined in the market by the demand for and supply of loanable funds. Differences in interest rates are due to risk, maturity, and the stage of development of financial markets.

The **nominal rate of interest** is the **real rate of interest** plus an adjustment for inflation.

Profits are the returns to an entrepreneur for risk-taking. If the returns are just equal to the opportunity cost of the entrepreneur, then they are called **normal profits**. Profits serve as a signal for resource allocation, a motive for efficiency, and a reward for the enterprising.

LEARNING OBJECTIVES

In connection with this module, you should be able to:

1. explain the meaning of rent
2. explain rent determination
3. explain rent differentials
4. explain interest and interest rate determination
5. discuss profits and its economic significance

DEFINITIONS & CONCEPTS

You should be able to define the following terms and concepts:

rent	quasi rent
transfer earning	interest
interest rate	prime lending rate
maturity	risk premium
real rate of interest	nominal rate of interest
normal profits	income statement

15

THE PRICING OF LAND & OTHER RESOURCES

Concepts, Definitions & Problems

Problem 15-1

How does the economic concept of rent differ from the ordinary usage of the term?

Requirement and Clue: *Examples of the ordinary usage and the technical use of the concept in economics are helpful in providing a solution.*

Solution:

Ordinarily, we use the term rent to refer to the payment made by a tenant to a landlord. A lady may consider renting a car for the week while hers is being repaired. That is the ordinary usage of the term. This usage must be distinguished from the technical usage of the term in economics. In economics, rent refers to the return on a factor of production the supply of which is fixed. Because the supply of land is fixed, the return on land is called rent.

Problem 15-2

Discuss the notion of a fixed quantity of land.

Requirement and Clue: *Focus on the sense in which land may be fixed.*

Solution:

Physically, the quantity of land available to society is fixed. There is just so much land available to society, and offers of higher prices will not induce a greater quantity. The fertility of land, however, can be increased or reduced. Moreover, land can undergo a variety of improvements, such as drainage of swamps. But these improvements do not actually create new land. We can view these improvements to land as increasing capital rather than creating new land. It is important to note also that the quantity of land available for one use can be increased by reducing the quantity available for some other use. For example, farm land can be converted into land for residential purposes.

Problem 15-3

Explain how rent is determined in a competitive market for land.

Requirement and Clue: *Consider rent as the price of land and then explain how that price is determined.*

Solution:

Rent (the price of land) is determined in the market like any other price: by the forces of demand and supply. In the following figure, the demand curve D slopes downward. This downward slope indicates that as the rent decreases, the quantity of land demanded increases.

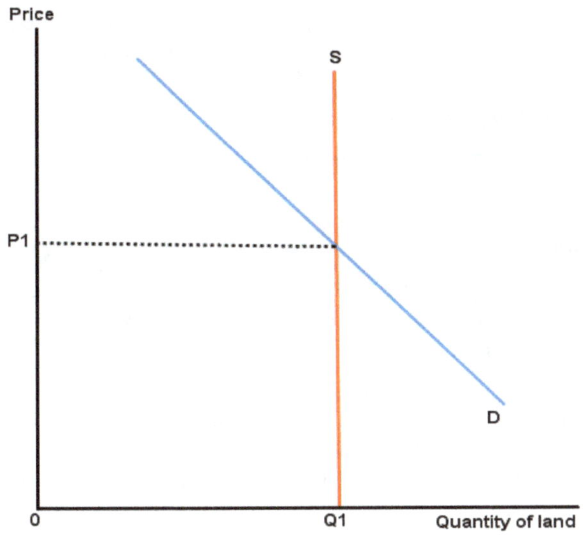

The vertical supply curve S shows that the supply of land is fixed at Q1. The demand and supply curves intersect to give the market-determined rental value of P1.

Problem 15-4

(a) Define economic rent

(b) Show the effect of an increase in demand for land on the equilibrium price and equilibrium quantity of land.

Requirement and Clue: *Part (a) is definitional. You are not required to write a treatise on economic rent. Instead, you are to state clearly the meaning of the concept. The word "show" in part (b) implies that you are required to use graphs.*

Solution:

(a) Economic rent is the income derived from a factor of production whose supply is completely price inelastic. Land is often used as an example of a factor of production whose supply is perfectly inelastic, so the income derived from land is an example of rent.

(b)

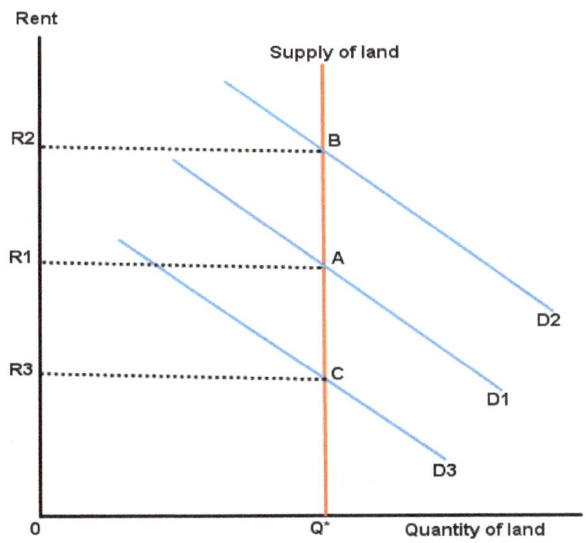

The diagram above shows the initial demand (D3), supply, the equilibrium price of land (R3), and the equilibrium quantity of land Q*. An increase in the demand for land is shown by the new demand curve D1. This increase in demand results in a shortage that forces the equilibrium price up from R3 to R1. The equilibrium quantity remains constant at Q*. A further increase in the demand for land forces the equilibrium price up from R1 to R2. The equilibrium quantity remains at Q*.

Problem 15-5

The following is the demand schedule for a certain type of land. The total quantity available is 500,000 hectares.

Rent per hectare	Quantity demanded	New quantity demanded
$1000	250,000	300,000
900	300,000	
800	350,000	
700	400,000	
600	450,000	
500	500,000	
400	550,000	
300	600,000	
200	650,000	
100	700,000	

(a) *What will be the rent for this land?*

(b) *What quantity of land will be rented?* .

(c) *If the quantity of land bought at each price increases by 50,000 hectares, complete the third column of the table.*

(d) *What will the rent for this land now be?*

(e) *What quantity will be rented at this price?*

Requirement and Clue: *The solution requires reliance on your knowledge of market equilibrium condition.*

Solution:

(a) The rent for this land will be $500 where the quantity demanded and the quantity supplied are equal.

(b) At this price, 500,000 hectares of land will be rented.

(c) See table below.

Rent per hectare	Quantity demanded	New quantity demanded
$1000	250,000	300,000
900	300,000	350,000
800	350,000	400,000
700	400,000	450,000
600	450,000	500,000
500	500,000	550,000
400	550,000	600,000
300	600,000	650,000
200	650,000	700,000
100	700,000	750,000

The rent for this land will now be $600 per hectare where the quantity demanded and the quantity supplied are equal.

(d) At this price, the quantity that will be rented is 500,000 hectares.

Problem 15-6

What are the main determinants of the demand for land?

Requirement and Clue: *Focus on the factors that will shift the demand curve for land. Be careful with the effect of a change in wages.*

Solution:

The following are the main determinants of the demand for land.

1. *Population growth:* Population growth increases the demand for goods and services and, as a result, the demand for land used in the production of goods and services increases.
2. *Resource content:* The existence of mineral deposits in a piece of land will increase the demand for that parcel of land.
3. *Expected yield:* If the expected yield from a piece of land increases, other things being equal, the demand for that piece of land will increase.
4. *Location:* The location of a parcel of land will exert some influence on the demand for it.
5. *Technology:* The introduction of new technology can affect the demand for land. For example, consider a technology that requires the use of land. The introduction of such a technology will increase the demand for land.

Problem 15-7

The downtown area of many cities is cluttered by high-rise buildings. In outlying areas, however, high rises are relatively few. How can this phenomenon be explained?

Requirement and Clue: *In providing a solution, consider the demand for land and the use of scarce resources.*

Solution:

The demand for land in the downtown area of the city is high relative to the demand for land in outlying areas. Consequently, the rental value of land in the downtown area is high relative to the rental value of land in outlying areas. To overcome problems of scarce space and hence high rent, we erect high-rise buildings. In the absence of high-rise buildings, we would have to use a considerable amount of land to obtain the space that is now provided by high-rise buildings. The cost would be astronomical. The abundance of high-rise buildings in the city results largely from the high rental value of land in the city.

Problem 15-8

How can rent differentials be explained?

Requirement and Clue: *Concentrate on the demand for different parcels of land.*

Solution:

Differences in rent are due to differences in demand for different parcels of land. In explaining rent differentials then, we must consider the factors that affect the demand for different parcels of land.

First, let us consider yield per hectare. The demand for a parcel of land depends on the expected yield per hectare from that land. The higher the expected yield per hectare, the greater the demand for the land will be. And the greater the demand, other things being equal, the higher the rent.

Second, the resource content of different parcels of land will cause differences in rent. A parcel of land that is rich in mineral deposits will tend to generate a higher rental value than a parcel with little or no mineral deposits. That is so because the demand for the resource-rich parcel is likely to be higher than the demand for the parcel without deposits.

Third, the location of land will have some effect on its demand and hence on its rental value. The rent for land in the heart of a large city will likely be much higher than the rent for similar land in a remote area.

Problem 15-9

Define transfer earnings and give an example.

Requirement and Clue: *This is a two-part problem. Answer each part in order. The first part is definitional. State clearly what transfer earnings are and then give an appropriate example to indicate that you are familiar with the concept.*

Solution:

The term "transfer earnings" refers to the amount of money that a factor of production can earn in the next best employment alternative. Looked at differently, it is the minimum payment required to attract resources away from other uses. For example, if the best alternative employment opportunity for a football player is $65,000 a year, then his transfer earning is $65,000 a year.

Problem 15-10

Show that the burden of a tax on land falls squarely on the shoulders of the landowner.

Requirement and Clue: *Consider the nature of the supply of land.*

Solution:

The supply of land is perfectly inelastic. This is shown by the vertical supply curve S in the following diagram.

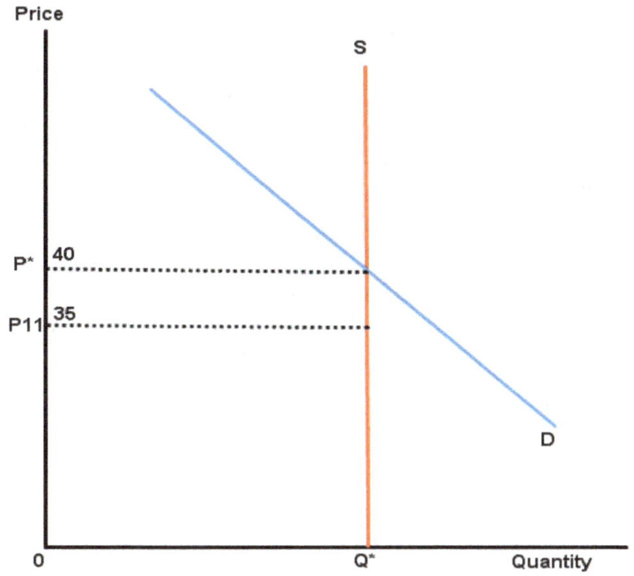

D is the demand curve for land. The equilibrium rent is P* which we assume to be $40 per unit of land. Now, suppose the government imposes a tax of $5 per unit of land. Because the supply of land is fixed, the tax does not affect the supply curve. The quantity of land remains at Q*. The landowner receives $40 per unit of land and pays $5 to the government and he or she is left with $35 ($P_{11}$). The burden of the tax is borne entirely by the landowner.

Problem 15-11

What is the difference between interest and the rate of interest?

Requirement and Clue: *Your solution should highlight the difference between the two concepts.*

Solution:

Interest is the payment for the use of money for a specified period of time. It can also be viewed as the income generated by money capital. Clearly, interest is a sum of money such as $120.00. The rate of interest on the other hand is the price paid for the use of borrowed money and is the ratio of the interest to the principal, expressed as a percentage. For example, if I borrow $1200 for one year and I am required to pay an interest of $120, then the rate of interest is:

$$\frac{120}{1200} \times 100 = 10\%$$

Problem 15-12

What is the loanable funds theory of the rate of interest?

Requirement and Clue: *A clear and accurate statement of the theory is required.*

Solution:

Loanable funds means borrowed money. The loanable funds theory of the rate of interest is a theory that explains how the rate of interest is determined. According to this theory, the rate of interest in determined in the market for funds. The demand for these funds comes from firms that want to borrow money for investment purposes, from households who want to purchase consumer goods and services, and from governments that want to spend more than their revenues. The amount of money demanded by these groups is inversely related to the rate of interest. The higher the rate of interest, the less will be the quantity of loans demanded.

The supply of loanable funds comes from the savings of households, businesses, and governments in surplus positions. Other things being equal, the higher the rate of interest, the more willing these groups will be to offer loanable funds. According to the loanable funds theory, the rate of interest at which the quantity of loans demanded equals the quantity supplied is the equilibrium rate of interest.

Problem 15-13

What would happen to the rate of interest if people decided to reduce their saving?

Requirement and Clue: *Consider the loanable funds theory of the rate of interest and focus on the implication of a greater flow of saving.*

Solution:

If people decided to reduce their saving, a smaller amount of loanable funds would be available at any given rate of interest. The following diagram will help to explain how this would affect the rate of interest.

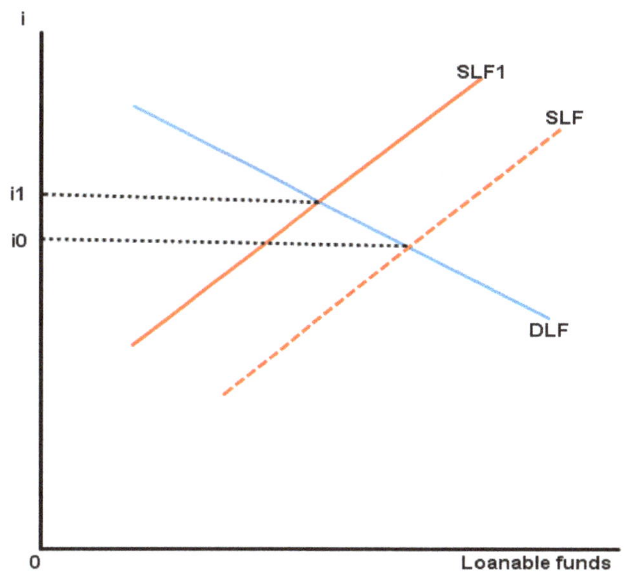

DLF and SLF are the initial demand and supply curves for loanable funds. The initial equilibrium rate of interest is i0. If people decide to reduce their saving, the supply of loanable funds would fall, other things being equal. The supply curve shifts from SLF to SLF1. This results in an increase in the rate of interest from i0 to i1.

Problem 15-14

How can differences in interest rates be explained?

Requirement and Clue: *You are required to discuss the factors that cause differences in interest rates.*

Solution:

Interest rate differentials may be explained by the following factors: First, the degree of risk will influence the rate of interest. The greater the risk of default associated with a given loan, the higher will be the rate of interest. Second, the maturity associated with a given loan will affect the rate of interest. A higher rate of interest might be necessary to induce lenders to lend for longer periods. Finally, if the market for loans is highly developed, the rate of interest is likely to be lower than in markets that are not developed and where the few lenders charge exorbitant rates.

Problem 15-15

Define:

(a) *the real rate of interest*

(b) *the nominal rate of interest*

Requirement and Clue: *This problem does not require you to focus on the difference between the two concepts, although your definitions may reveal the difference. Your task here is simply to state the meaning of each concept in order.*

Solution:

(a) The real rate of interest is the interest rate that a lender would charge if the rate of inflation were zero. The real rate of interest makes no allowance for inflation.

(b) The nominal rate of interest is the rate quoted for a loan or a deposit, which includes a premium for inflation.

Problem 15-16

Is it always less costly to borrow money at a 4% interest rate than at a 17% interest rate?

Requirement and Clue: A simple "yes" or "no" answer will clearly not suffice. You are required to justify your answer. Consider real versus nominal interest rates.

Solution:

On the surface, the answer to his question seems quite obvious. After all, if you borrow $100 for a year at a 4% interest rate, your interest cost is $4, while at an interest rate of 17%, your interest cost is a whopping $17. But we should not be too hasty to jump to any conclusions. Suppose the rate of inflation is only 1% when the rate of interest is 4%. The real interest cost is $3; and if the rate of inflation is 15% when the interest rate is 17%, then the real interest cost is only $2. Clearly, in some circumstances, it is more costly to borrow at 4% than at 17%.

Problem 15-17

Discuss the economic role of profits.

Requirement and Clue: *Consider the role of profits in resource allocation and as a motivator.*

Solution:

Profits perform the following economic functions. First, they serve as a signal to resource owners. The existence of profits in an industry or sector of the economy is a signal that price exceeds average cost of production, and that resources should be shifted from some less profitable use into the profit-earning industry.

Second, profits serve as a motive for efficiency. The desire for profits is an incentive fo producers to cut production costs where possible. In the face of competition, high-cost firms will lose their market shares to lower-cost firms. Unless high-cost firms can increase their efficiency, they will ultimately be forced out of the market.

Third, profits serve as a reward for the resourceful, the imaginative, and the enterprising. The prospect of earning profits is often the driving force behind the development and maintenance of special resources and talents.

Problem 15-18

What are the economic effects of taxation of excess profits?

Requirement and Clue: *Some notion of "excess profits" has to be adopted. Focus on steps that the firm may take to avoid the tax.*

Solution:

The notion of "excess profits" may be subjective and based on some level of profits that is considered to be too high. Maybe the concept of positive economic profits can be substituted for "excess profits". In any event, a tax levied on the excess profits of a firm may cause the firm to forgo certain economic activities that could earn extra profits. The tax may also weaken the incentive to keep cost down. The firm may then engage in certain programs and projects that could not be justified were it not for the excess profits tax. For example, excess profits taxes have resulted in the increased padding of expense accounts.

Problem 15-19

An entrepreneur reports the following data for a month of operation. The entrepreneur has been offered as much as $3800 per month to work for other businesses.

Revenue:

Sale of goods	$5,500.00
Sale of services	2,500.00
TOTAL	$8,000.00

Expenses:

Rent	$1,000.00
Materials	150.00
Telephone	120.00
Utilities	90.00
Wages	2,500.00
Other expenses	75.00
TOTAL	3,935.00

Compute:

(a) *the entrepreneur's profit (in an accounting sense)*

(b) *the entrepreneur's profit (in an economic sense)*

Requirement and Clue: *This two-part problem is designed to test your understanding of the difference between accounting profits and economic profits.*

Solution:

(a) In an accounting sense, the entrepreneur's profit is total revenue minus total expenses. This is:

$(8000 – 3935) = **$4065**

(b) To compute economic profit, we must subtract total cost (including the opportunity cost of $3800 that the entrepreneur could have earned elsewhere) from total revenue.

Total revenue is................................	$8000.00
Total cost is $(3935 + 3800) =	$7735.00
Profit is $(8000 – 7735) =	**$ 265.00**

Problem 15-20

"In this capitalist society, we hear a great deal about profits and wages. This is not at all surprising. After all, the very purpose of firms in a capitalist system is to produce goods and services and sell them at prices that exceed their costs of production, a large part of which is wages. So firms make profits in order to survive and workers earn wages in order to live. But since there is hardly any relationship between profits on the one hand and interest and rent on the other, firms can safely ignore rent and interest in their decision making, and focus mainly on their prime objective of maximizing their profits."

Comment on this statement.

Requirement and Clue: *You are required to examine the passage carefully and see if you detect any error. If there are errors you should point them out and offer a correction.*

Solution:

Indeed, profits are important in a free enterprise economic system. We rely on firms to produce goods and services that satisfy our wants. Firms that do not earn profits will not long survive. The error in the passage lies in the assertion that profits are independent of rent and interest. In the same way that wages constitute a part of the costs of production, so too do rent and interest. Higher rental and interest costs imply greater overall costs, and other things being equal, this translates into reduced profits.

Multiple-Choice

In each case, circle the letter that corresponds with the correct answer.

1. In economics, rent refers to:

a. the monthly payment for living accommodation in a house or apartment

b. the amount paid for the use of a car or other vehicle for a specified period of time

c. the return on a factor of production the supply of which is fixed

d. all of the above

Answer: c

Reason: *Rent is the income derived from land whose supply is fixed.*

2. The demand curve for land is:

a. vertical because there is a fixed amount of land

b. upward sloping because a fall in the price of land increases the demand for land, other things being equal

c. downward sloping because a greater quantity of land will be demanded when the price falls, other things being equal

d. horizontal because it is perfectly elastic at any price.

Answer: c

Reason: *An inverse relationship exists between the price of land and the quantity of land demanded.*

3. Which of the following will not affect the demand for land?

a. Population growth

b. The location of land

c. The resource content of land

d. The price of land

Answer: d

Reason: *The price of land will affect the quantity of land demanded, not the demand for land.*

4. The supply curve for land is:

a. vertical

b. downward sloping

c. upward sloping

d. horizontal

Answer: a

Reason: *The supply of land is perfectly price inelastic. A change in the price of land will not change the quantity supplied.*

5. Rent is determined in the market when:

a. the demand for land equals the supply of land

b. the quantity of land demanded equals the quantity supplied

c. landowners earn the highest rent possible

d. none of the above

Answer: b

Reason: *When the quantity of land demanded equals the quantity supplied, neither a surplus nor a shortage will exist, and rent will be at its equilibrium value.*

6. Other things being equal, an increase in the demand for land will result in:

a. an increase in the equilibrium price of land
b. an increase in the equilibrium quantity of land
c. a fall in the equilibrium price of land
d. a fall in the equilibrium quantity of land

Answer: a

Reason: An increase in the demand for land, other things being equal, will cause a shortage at the initial price. This shortage will force the equilibrium price up.

7. Changes in rent are due to:

a. changes in the supply of land
b. changes in the demand for land
c. changes in both demand and supply of land
d. all of the above

Answer: b

Reason: The supply of land is fixed so changes in rent must be due to changes in the demand for land.

8. The rental value of land is affected by:

a. the expected yield per hectare
b. the resource content of land
c. the location of land
d. all of the above

Answer: d

Reason: Choices a, b, and c affect the demand for land and hence its rental value.

9. The concept of "transfer earnings" refers to:

a. the amount of money transferred from other sources to land
b. the total incomes earned by exceptional people such as movie stars and athletes
c. the amount of tax dollars transferred from wealthy people to low-income people
d. the amount of money that a factor of production can earn in the next best alternative employment

Answer: d

Reason: Transfer earning is the minimum payment required to attract resources away from other uses. This corresponds with choice d.

10. A TV actor earns $1,500,000 annually. The most this actor could earn in an alternative job is $75,000 as a public relations officer for a company. Which of the following is correct?

a. Transfer earnings are $75,000 and the rent portion of the actor's earnings is $1,425,000
b. Transfer earnings are $1,425,000 and the rent portion of the actor's earnings is $75,000
c. Transfer earnings are $1,500,000 and the rent portion of the actor's earnings is $75,000
d. None of the above

Answer: a

Reason: Transfer earnings are the opportunity cost of the actor's services, and the rent portion of the actor's earnings is the difference between the actor's salary and the transfer earnings.

11. A tax on land would be borne:

a. Equally by landowners and people who rent land
b. only by people who rent land
c. only by landowners
d. none of the above

Answer: c

Reason: Because the supply of land is fixed (it is perfectly price inelastic) a tax will have no effect on the supply of land, therefore the landowner bears the full burden of the tax.

12. The payment for the use of money for a specified period of time is called:

a. profit
b. interest
c. neither a nor b
d. both a and b

Answer: b

Reason: Interest is the payment for or income from a loan.

13. If a loan of $5,000.00 carries an annual interest rate of 8.5%, then the annual interest income is:

a. $4,575
b. $ 975
c. $525
d. $425

Answer: d

Reason: 8.5% of $5000 is $425.

14. The demand for loans comes from:

a. firms that want to borrow funds
b. households who want to purchase certain consumer items
c. governments that want to finance certain expenditures
d. all of the above

Answer: d

Reason: All the groups mentioned borrow money, which represents the demand for loans.

15. The theory that states that the rate of interest is determined by the demand for and supply of loanable funds is called the:

a. demand-side theory of interest
b. supply-side theory of interest
c. marketable funds theory of interest
d. none of the above

Answer: d

Reason: The theory is called the loanable funds theory of interest.

16. In the loanable funds theory of the rate of interest, the supply of loanable funds comes from:

a. the savings of households, firms, and government who have money to lend
b. people who are looking for good deals on loans
c. both a and b
d. neither a nor b

Answer: a

Reason: The savings of households, businesses, and government provide the supply of funds for lending purposes.

17. An increase in the rate of interest will:

a. reduce the demand for loans
b. increase the supply of loans
c. both a and b
d. neither a nor b

Answer: d

Reason: An increase in the rate of interest will reduce the quantity of loans demanded and increase the quantity of loans supplied.

18. Interest rate differentials are due to differences in:

a. the level of risk associated with the loan
b. the length of time for which the loan is granted
c. the state of development on financial markets
d. all of the above

Answer: d

Reason: Other things being equal, the greater the risk associated with a loan, the higher the interest rate will be. The longer the term to maturity, the higher the rate of interest; and the more developed the financial market, the lower the rate of interest will be.

19. The interest rate that would be charged if the rate of inflation were zero is called the:

a. real rate of interest
b. the nominal rate of interest
c. the market-influenced rate of interest
d. none of the above

Answer: a

Reason: The real rate of interest is the rate of interest charged without making allowance for inflation.

20. Which of the following is true?

a. The real rate of interest is the nominal rate plus the rate of inflation
b. The nominal rate of interest is the real rate plus the rate of inflation
c. The real rate of interest is always equal to the rate of inflation
d. There is no relationship between inflation and the rate of interest

Answer: b

Reason: The nominal rate of interest is the rate that includes a premium for inflation.

21. Normal profits are:

a. profits that are authorized by the government
b. profits that firms are expected to earn normally
c. profits that allow firms to operate normally
d. none of the above

Answer: d

Reason: Normal profits are returns that just equal the opportunity cost of the resources used.

22. Which of the following functions do profits perform?

a. They serve as a reward for the enterprising
b. They provide an incentive for efficiency
c. They serve as a signal for resource owners regarding where resources should be used
d. All of the above

Answer: d

Reason: Profits perform all of the functions listed.

True-False

Determine whether each of the following statements is true or false.

1. Pure economic rent is rent that has been declared to be legal.

Answer: False

Explanation: Pure economic rent the income derived from a factor of production the supply of which is perfectly price inelastic.

2. Land is often used as the best example of a factor or production that generates pure economic rent because the total quantity of land in existence is fixed.

Answer: True

3. Improvements to land, such as drainage of swamp land, irrigation, and fertilization can be seen as increasing capital rather than creating new land.

Answer: True

4. The demand curve for land is vertical, but the supply curve is upward sloping.

Answer: False

Explanation: The demand curve for land is downward sloping but the supply curve is vertical.

5. Population growth, expected yield per hectare, resource content of land, and the location of land all affect the supply of land.

Answer: False

Explanation: They affect the demand for land. The supply of land is fixed and is not affected by the factors mentioned.

6. A special characteristic of rent is that it is not determined by demand and supply.

Answer: False

Explanation: Rent is determined by the demand for and the supply of land.

7. An increase in the demand for land, other things being equal, will cause an increase in rent.

Answer: True

Explanation: An increase in the demand for land will cause a shortage at the current price. This shortage will force up the price (rent).

8. Differences in rent are due mainly to variations in the supply of land responding to the price of land.

Answer: False

Explanation: Rent differentials are due mainly to differences in demand for various parcels of land.

Questions 9 and 10 refer to the following situation:

A writer earns $250,000 for her writing. She could earn at most $80,000 teaching literature at a college.

9. Her transfer earnings are $170,000.

Answer: False

Explanation: Her transfer earnings are $80,000. That's what she could earn in the next best employment alternative.

10. The rent portion of her income is $170,000.

Answer: True

11. The return on a factor of production whose supply is fixed only in the short run is referred to as short-term returns.

Answer: False

Explanation: It is referred to as quasi-rent.

12. The burden of a tax on land is borne entirely by the landowner.

Answer: True

13. Interest is the payment for the use of money for a specified time.

Answer: True

14. The rate of interest can be computed by the following formula:

$$\text{Rate of interest} = \frac{\text{Principal}}{\text{Interest}} \times 100$$

Answer: False

Explanation: The rate of interest is computed by:

$$\text{Rate of interest} = \frac{\text{Interest}}{\text{Principal}} \times 100$$

15. The loanable funds theory of interest states that the rate of interest is determined solely by the demand for loans because the supply of loans is fixed by banks.

Answer: False

Explanation: The theory states that the rate of interest is determined by the demand and supply of loanable funds.

16. With the rate of interest on the vertical axis and the quantity of loans on the horizontal axis, the supply curve for loans is vertical because the quantity of loans is fixed by the government.

Answer: False

Explanation: The supply curve for loans is upward sloping because higher interest rates will be an incentive for households and firms to save and lend.

17. An increase in the demand for loans will tend to raise interest rates, whereas an increase in the supply of loans will tend to lower interest rates.

Answer: True

18. The degree of risk associated with a loan has nothing to do with the rate of interest charged. Lenders charge the highest rate regardless of the degree of risk.

Answer: False

Explanation: Other things being equal, the higher the risk associated with a loan, the greater will be the rate of interest. A risk premium may be added to compensate for the risk of default.

19. The relationship between interest rates and inflation can be seen in the equation:

NR = RR + e, where NR is the nominal rate, RR is the real rate, and e is the rate of inflation.

Answer: True

20. The nominal rate of interest is the interest rate that would be charged in the absence of inflation.

Answer: False

Explanation: The concept defined here is the real rate of interest.

21. Normal profits are returns that just equal the opportunity cost of the resources used.

Answer: True

22. Accounting profits take the opportunity cost of the resources into consideration.

Answer: False

Explanation: Accounting profits consider only direct outlays (expenses) when measuring cost.

23. Profit is surplus value because it does not perform any economic function.

Answer: False

Explanation: Profit is the reward for entrepreneurial services and risk-taking. It also dictates resources allocation and serves as a motive for efficiency.

24. Profits in an industry will attract investment into that industry while losses will drive investment away from the losing industry.

Answer: True

Completion

(Fill in the blanks)

Use each word or combination of words from the list exactly once.
*(**Hint**: Proceed by elimination)*

Word list

Demand — Earning — Economic — Firms — Government — Households — Income or profit and loss — Interest — Loanable — Maturity — Nominal — Normal — Pure — Rent — Quasi-rent — Raise — Rate — Real — Reduce — Six — Statement — Transfer — Vertical

Questions

1. The income derived from a factor of production whose supply is perfectly price inelastic is referred to as __________ __________ __________. The return on a factor of production whose supply is fixed only in the short run is called __________.
2. Because the quantity of land is fixed, the supply curve for land is __________.
3. Changes in the price of land (rent) are due to changes in the __________ for land.
4. An increase in the demand for land will tend to __________ [raise, lower] the rental value of land.
5. __________ __________ is the term used to describe the amount that a factor of production can earn in the next best employment alternative.
6. __________ __________ is the price paid for the use of money for a period of time.
7. An interest payment of $390 on a principal of $6,500.00 represents an interest rate of __________ per cent.
8. Funds available to lend or wanted to borrow are called __________ funds.
9. The demand for loanable funds comes from __________, __________, and __________.
10. __________ is the term used to indicate the length of time before a loan is supposed to be paid off.
11. The __________ rate of interest is the interest rate that would be charged if the rate of inflation were zero. The __________ rate of interest is the rate quoted for a loan or deposit, which includes a premium for inflation.
12. A(n) __________ __________ is an accounting device for reporting revenues, expenses, and net income.
13. Returns that are just equal to the opportunity cost of the resources used are referred to as __________ profits.
14. The desire for profits will motivate firms to __________ production costs.

Solution

1. (pure economic rent, quasi-rent)
2. (vertical)
3. (demand)
4. (raise)
5. (transfer earning)
6. (interest rate)
7. (6)
8. (loanable)
9. (households, firms, government - in any order)
10. (maturity)
11. (real, nominal)
12. (income statement or profit and loss statement)
13. (normal)
14. (reduce)

16 INCOME DISTRIBUTION

SYNOPSIS

Three views exist on the equitable distribution of income: distribution according to contribution (the contribution standard), distribution according to need (the need standard), and distribution to all equally (the egalitarian standard). Each view has merits and shortcomings.

The **size distribution of income** is the term used when referring to the distribution of income among individuals and households. Income is not distributed exactly equally in the economy, but it is more evenly distributed in some countries than in others.

The **Lorenz curve** is a geometric device used for showing the degree of inequality in the distribution of income. The extent of inequality is measured by the **Gini coefficient**. The larger the Gini coefficient, the greater is the degree of inequality in the distribution of income.

Among the causes of poverty are low productivity, low economic growth, lack of productive resources, physical and mental disabilities, and discrimination. Measures to alleviate poverty include increasing the productivity of workers through education and training, increasing the rate of economic growth, anti-discrimination laws, subsidies to low-income people, and special employment projects for the handicapped.

A negative income tax (NIT) system has been suggested as a solution to the problem of poverty. Under such a system, an individual whose income is below a prescribed level need not pay income tax. Instead, the government pays the individual. The amount of payment varies with the individual's income.

LEARNING OBJECTIVES

In connection with this module, you should be able to:

1. discuss the criteria for income distribution
2. explain the size distribution of income
3. discuss the dimensions of poverty
4. identify the measures used to alleviate poverty
5. discuss aspects of the welfare system
6. explain the negative income tax (NIT)

DEFINITIONS & CONCEPTS

You should be able to define the following terms and concepts:

size distribution of income
Lorenz curve
Gini coefficient
absolute poverty
low-income cut-off
relative poverty
incidence of poverty
economic discrimination
poverty line
negative income tax

16 INCOME DISTRIBUTION

Concepts, Definitions & Problems

Problem 16-1

What is your understanding of an equitable distribution of income? Briefly discuss at least two views about the equitable distribution of income.

Requirement and Clue: *This is a two-part problem. Answer each part in order. Some subjectivity may be allowed.*

Solution:

An equitable distribution of income exists when income is distributed in some manner that is considered to be fair on some basis by the members of society. Granted, what is fair to Jane may be grossly unfair to Sam. Fairness or equity is largely subjective.

The following are some views about the equitable distribution of income and a brief discussion of each. One view states that income should be distributed among members of society according to their contribution to the total output. According to this view, the more productive members of society should receive a greater share of the national output than the less productive. Distribution according to contribution provides incentives for greater productivity.

A second view of an equitable distribution of income is that income should be distributed according to need. There are some problems with applying this criterion. First, how are needs to be determined? Second, if income is distributed according to need (assuming that needs can be correctly assessed), there would be little or no incentive to work.

A third view of an equitable distribution of income is that income should be distributed equally to all regardless of contribution or need. Just divide the total income by the population. This approach does not provide sufficient incentives for people to work hard. Why should Joe exert so much effort only to end up with the same income as Bill?

Problem 16-2

What is the relationship between the Lorenz curve and the Gini coefficient?

Requirement and Clue: *You must demonstrate a clear understanding of the Lorenz curve and the Gini coefficient. A diagram will be helpful.*

Solution:

The Lorenz curve is a graphical device for measuring income inequality. The concept of a Lorenz curve is illustrated in the following diagram.

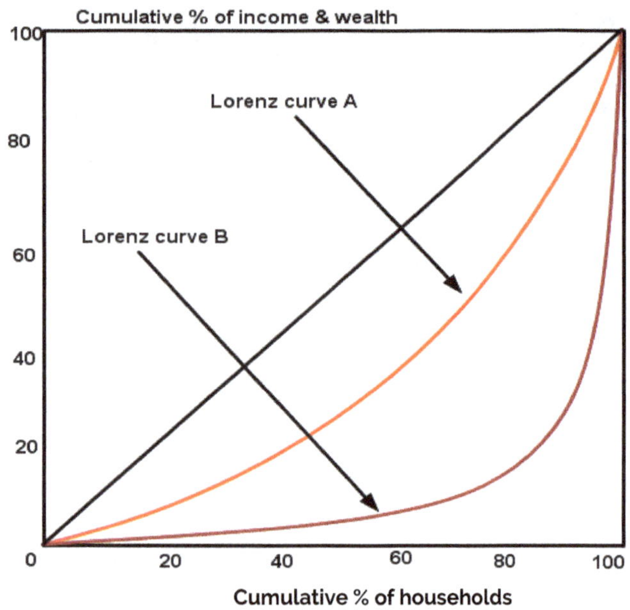

The cumulative percent of income is on the vertical axis, while the cumulative percent of households is on the horizontal axis. The diagonal line from the origin represents perfect equality where 10% of families receive 10% of the income, 40% receive 40% of the income, 60% receive 60% of the income and so on. The curve labelled Lorenz curve A could represent the actual Lorenz curve for a country. Lorenz curve B represents a more unequal distribution of income than either of the two other curves.

The Gini coefficient is the ratio of the area enclosed by an actual Lorenz curve and the line of perfect equality in income distribution expressed as a proportion of the area of triangle enclosed by the horizontal line. Suppose the area enclosed by the horizontal line and Lorenz curve A is 9 and the area of triangle is 31, then the Gini coefficient will be 9/31. The larger the Gini coefficient, the greater is the inequality in the distribution of income.

Problem 16-3

Discuss three main causes of income inequality.

Requirement and Clue: *There are many causes of income inequality. You are asked to discuss three. In your discussion, you are expected to express how inequality in income could result from the factor mentioned.*

Solution:

Three of the main causes of inequality in the distribution of income are education, productivity, and age. Each will be examined in turn.

An individual's level of education often influences his or her income. People with university degrees tend to earn significantly more than people who have completed only high school. The justification for the difference in income is that highly educated people contribute more to their employers than do people with lower levels of education.

More productive workers earn more than less productive workers. This is understandable if workers are paid the value of their marginal physical product. Workers with higher marginal physical productivity will tend to be paid more than workers with lower marginal physical productivity.

Age is closely related to experience and on-the-job training, both of which affect income. Typically, when individuals first enter the workforce, they tend to earn relatively low incomes. As they grow older and gain greater knowledge, their incomes tend to rise until at retirement when their incomes fall.

Problem 16-4

Is there any relationship between social connections and income?

Requirement and Clue: *A simple "yes" or "no" answer will not suffice. You are expected to defend you position.*

Solution:

An individual who is well connected with people of high standing in the society and who is able to network effectively gets opportunities for entry into certain professions and for career advancement. Other things being equal, the individual with good social connections and networking will get the edge over someone without those vital connections and will thus earn a higher income and probably advance more quickly through the ranks.

Problem 16-5

What consequences could be expected from giving everyone the same income?

Requirement and Clue: *Focus on how people might react if everyone were to receive the same income.*

Solution:

If everyone were to receive the same income, regardless of contribution to the total output of goods and services in the economy, certain consequences could be expected. Many people have exerted themselves and have taken risks in the pursuit of an income above the average. If income were distributed equally, then the prospect of earning above average income would disappear. Consequently, the incentive to take risks and to work hard would be greatly reduced. Total output would then fall. Additional reward in the form of income for extra effort is an important motivator for economic activity.

Problem 16-6

Define each of the following terms:

(a) *Absolute poverty*

(b) *Low-income cut-off*

(c) *Relative poverty*

Requirement and Clue: *This is a definitional problem. Clearly state the meaning of each of the concepts. You are not expected to write an essay or a thesis on each.*

Solution:

(a) Absolute poverty is the condition that exists when an

individual or a family lacks the financial resources required for the basic necessities of life. People experiencing absolute poverty cannot afford the goods and services that most people in the society would consider to be just enough to enable them to live in minimum comfort.

(b) The low-income cut-off is an arbitrary level of income below which poverty is said to exist. It is also referred to as the *poverty line.*

(c) Relative poverty is the condition that prevails when an individual or a family has a standard of living that is far below that enjoyed by others in society. According to this concept, an individual with an annual income of $200,000 would be considered to be relatively poor if the vast majority of people in the society have annual incomes exceeding $750,000.

Problem 16-7

Discuss some of the more serious effects of poverty.

Requirement and Clue: *Focus on how poverty may affect the lives of people experiencing it and how the society at large may be affected.*

Solution:

Individuals who are experiencing poverty undergo severe hardships. The poor cannot enjoy the good things in life that many people take for granted. They are deprived of good homes and even good health sometimes, and their children may be deprived of a good education and good social connections. As a result, they may turn to various forms of socially unacceptable behaviours in an attempt to escape the harsh realities of poverty.

In addition to the loss of property that can result from poverty are other economic disadvantages. Because the poor are more likely to have low levels of education and skills, their productivity is likely to be low. This low productivity prevents the economy's output of goods and services from reaching its full potential. Hence, the society as a whole suffers as it must accept a lower standard of living.

Problem 16-8

What is meant by the incidence of poverty? Identify three groups that have a relatively high incidence of poverty.

Requirement and Clue: *This is a two-part problem. Address each part in order. The first part of the problem is definitional. You are to offer a clear and precise statement of the meaning of the concept. The second part of the problem is not asking you to identify groups that are poor, just groups with a high incidence of poverty.*

Solution:

The incidence of poverty refers to the likelihood of being poor. The following three groups have a relative high probability of being poor. First, families with many children have a relatively high incidence of poverty. It is costly to raise young children under the age of 16 when they don't have a job. The cost can be a severe strain on the family budget. Second, families whose heads are 24 years old or younger have a relative high incidence of being poor. One possible reason for the high incidence of poverty among this group is lack of education, lack of valuable marketplace skills, and lack of working experience. Third, senior families have a high incidence of poverty. Heads of families who are 65 years and older may be forced to live only on pension income, making them susceptible to poverty.

Problem 16-9

A relatively large number of unattached individuals living below the poverty line are in the urban areas. Can you account for this fact?

Requirement and Clue: *You are expected to think of reasons that explain the relatively large number of poor, unattached individuals in urban areas.*

Solution:

A good portion of unattached individuals are young people. The prospects of young people finding worthwhile jobs in rural areas are quite limited. Also, for young people, city life is often more inviting and exciting than country life. Entertaining hopes of a more appropriate job and greater excitement, unattached individuals may migrate from the rural areas to the urban areas where they may end up being numbered among those living in poverty.

Problem 16-10

(a) *Define each of the following terms:*

(i) *Employment discrimination*

(ii) *Wage discrimination*

(iii) *Occupational discrimination*

(b) *Explain how discrimination might cause poverty.*

Requirement and Clue: *This is a two-part problem. Answer each part in order. Part (a) is definitional. Clearly and precisely state the meaning of each concept. For part (b), focus on how discrimination may place certain groups at a disadvantage.*

Solution:

(a)

(i) Employment discrimination is a situation in which particular groups are denied employment on the basis of their identification with these groups.

(ii) Wage discrimination is a situation in which particular groups are paid lower wages and salaries than others are paid for similar work.

(iii) Occupational discrimination is a situation in which particular groups are prevented from entering certain occupations.

(b) Discrimination is a major cause of poverty. Because of

discrimination, certain groups can be prevented from taking advantage of opportunities that are open to others. They may be denied access to certain schools, or they may be prevented from entering certain occupations. Visible minorities, for example, may be paid lower wages than others, and women may be paid less than men, not because of any difference in productivity among the groups, but because of prejudice against them. Promotions may be given on the basis of ethnicity and sex rather than on the basis of merit.

Problem 16-11

Poverty is a serious problem. What steps can be taken to alleviate it?

Requirement and Clue: *By focusing on the causes of poverty, you should be able to provide a solution to this problem.*

Solution:

First, poverty can be alleviated by increasing the productivity of the working poor through education and training so that workers can improve their skills. Second, fostering economic growth and adopting policies to promote employment will help to reduce poverty. Third, legislation and the enforcement of legislation against discrimination will help to reduce discriminatory practices and this assist in the alleviation of poverty. Fourth, the provision of certain goods and services at greatly reduced cost to the poor will help to alleviate poverty. Examples of this approach are subsidized housing and food stamps. All of the steps listed above will help to alleviate poverty.

Problem 16-12

In many instances, the depressing statistics on poverty seem to conflict with everyday observations of affluence. Why is this so?

Requirement and Clue: *Focus on reasons why many people may not see the real face of poverty.*

Solution:

Many people do not see poverty to the same extent as the statistics reveal because poverty in many cases, is, to a significant degree, invisible; it is hidden. In many instances, the poor live in city slums, which many people do not see from the highways and the subways. The poor also live in rural areas, which many people do not see. Moreover, many of the poor are elderly and infirm and remain indoors for much of the time. For all these reasons, the statistics on poverty seem more horrific than everyday experiences would suggest.

Problem 16-13

What are the advantages and disadvantages of a negative income tax?

Requirement and Clue: *Of course, you cannot solve this problem without knowing what a negative income tax is. State two or three advantages, and two or three disadvantages.*

Solution:

A negative income tax is a system whereby the government makes payments (gives subsidies) to people whose incomes are below the taxable level. The amount of the subsidy varies with the recipient's income.

Advantages of a negative income tax

1. Individuals are free to spend their income as they see fit. Thus they can exercise freedom of choice.
2. A negative income tax does not eradicate the incentive to work.
3. The administration of a negative income tax would be relatively simple and could be done by the existing income tax administration.

Disadvantages of a negative income tax

1. The cost of a negative income tax would be expensive.
2. A negative income tax could be opposed by people who see the plan as making cash payments to people for staying home and doing nothing.
3. There could be some difficulty in establishing a national low-income cut-off since different regions face difference circumstances.

Problem 16-14

A government guarantees a minimum annual income of $6,000 for each adult citizen, by giving a subsidy. The subsidy is reduced by $0.40 for every extra dollar earned.

(a) *On the basis of this information, complete the following table.*

Earned Income	Government Subsidy (Negative tax)	After-tax Income
$ 0	$6,000	$6,000
1,000		
3,000		
5,000		
7,000		
9,000		
11,000		
13,000		
15,000		
17,000		

(b) *At what level of earned income will an individual neither get a subsidy nor pay a tax?*

Requirement and Clue: *Completing the table is a matter of simple arithmetic. Once the table is completed, the solution to part (b) will be obvious.*

Solution:

(a)

Earned Income	Government Subsidy (Negative tax)	After-tax Income
$ 0	$6,000	$6,000
1,000	5,600	6,600
3,000	4,800	7,800
5,000	4,000	9,000
7,000	3,200	10,200
9,000	2,400	11,400
11,000	1,600	12,600
13,000	800	13,800
15,000	0	15,000
17,000	-800	16,200

(b) As can be seen from the table, at an earned income of **$15,000**, the individual gets no subsidy and pays no tax.

Problem 16-15

"Most people probably consider it an injustice for women to be paid less than men for the same work and unfair for blacks not to be hired because of their colour. But there are cases when discrimination can be justified on economic grounds. The case I want to consider here is discrimination among workers on the basis of their marital and familial circumstances. A person who is married with four children should be paid more than a single person with no children. This can be justified economically on the premise that the married person has a greater financial responsibility than the single person."

Comment on the above statement, pointing out any errors that it may contain.

Requirement and Clue: *You should read the statement very carefully, looking for any errors that it may contain. If errors are found, they should be indicated and corrected.*

Solution:

The case cited by the writer of the statement cannot be justified on economic grounds. The model of a competitive labour market suggests that the wage rate will be equal to the value of the marginal product of labour. Unless the value of the marginal product of the person who is married with four children is higher than that of the single person, then there is no economic justification for wage discrimination.

Multiple-Choice

In each case, circle the letter that corresponds with the correct answer.

1. The sum of earnings from employment and self-employment, investment income, private retirement income, and other incomes, excluding government transfers is called:

a. gross national income
b. independent income
c. total factor income
d. none of the above

Answer: d

Reason: The concept is referred to as market income.

2. The principle of distribution according to contribution means that:

a. income should be distributed as the government sees fit
b. income should be distributed according to productivity
c. income should be distributed according to family size
d. income should be distributed according to the amount needed for survival

Answer: b

Reason: Productivity is used as a measure of one's contribution to total output.

3. Which of the following is a criterion for distributing income?

a. Distribution according to contribution
b. Distribution according to need
c. Distribution to all equally
d. All of the above

Answer: d

Reason: Choices a, b, and c have been suggested as criteria for income distribution.

4. Which of the following criteria for distributing income provides the greatest incentive for productivity?

a. Distribution according to contributions
b. Distribution according to need
c. Equal distribution to all
d. None of the above

Answer: a

Reason: Choices b and c will discourage incentive to be productive. Choice a will motivate people to work harder.

5. The distribution of income among individuals and households is called:

a. the functional distribution of income
b. the factorial distribution of income
c. the size distribution of income
d. the efficient distribution of income

Answer: c

Reason: Choice c correctly defines the size distribution of income.

6. Which of the following is a graphical device used for measuring income inequality?

a. The Lorenz curve
b. The J-curve
c. The transformation curve
d. All of the above

Answer: a

Reason: The Lorenz curve is used for measuring inequality in income distribution.

7. The Lorenz curve is:

a. a curve showing how fast income rises as people become more wealthy
b. always a straight line
c. used to show how evenly income is distributed
d. none of the above

Answer: c

Reason: The Lorenz curve is a graphical device for measuring income inequality.

8. On a Lorenz curve diagram, the closer the Lorenz curve to the horizontal straight line:

a. the more equal is the distribution of income
b. the less equal is the distribution of income
c. there is no relationship between income distribution and the curves
d. none of the above

Answer: a

Reason: The horizontal straight line represents perfect income equality. The closer the Lorenz curve to this line, the more equal is the distribution of income.

9. Income inequality can be measured by:

a. the Lorenz curve
b. the Gini coefficient
c. neither a nor b
d. both a and b

Answer: d

Reason: The Lorenz curve and the Gini coefficient are devices used to measure income inequality.

10. The Gini coefficient of a society with perfect equality in income distribution is:

a. 0
b. 1
c. 0.50
d. 0.10

Answer: a

Reason: If income distribution is perfectly equal, the Gini coefficient will be zero.

11. Differences in income may be due to:

a. differences in educational levels of different people
b. differences in productivity among people
c. discrimination against certain groups
d. all of the above

Answer: d

Reason: Choices a, b, and c can result in income inequality.

12. Absolute poverty exists when:

a. an individual or a family lacks the financial resources required for the basic necessities of life
b. an individual or a family has a standard of living that is far below that enjoyed by others in society
c. both a and b
d. neither a nor b

Answer: a

Reason: Absolute poverty is defined as lack of the minimal requirements necessary to afford minimal standards of food, clothing, health care and shelter. Choice a fits this definition.

13. The poverty line (low-income cut-off):

a. measures relative poverty
b. measures absolute poverty
c. decreases as the society becomes more wealthy
d. is unrelated to the cost of living

Answer: b

Reason: The poverty line is an arbitrary level of income below which poverty is said to exist.

14. The incidence of poverty refers to:

a. the absolute number of people who live in poverty
b. the difficulty of eliminating poverty
c. the likelihood of being poor
d. the percentage of the population living below the poverty line

Answer: c

Reason: The incidence of poverty refers to how likely it is for certain groups or individuals to be poor.

15. Which of the following has a high incidence of poverty?

a. Families with many young children
b. Families whose heads are 24 years old or younger
c. Families headed by individuals who are not in the labour force
d. All of the above

Answer: d

Reason: For a variety of reasons, the groups listed have a relatively high probability of being poor.

16. Which of the following would be considered economic discrimination?

a. Employment discrimination
b. Occupational discrimination
c. Wage discrimination
d. All of the above

Answer: d

Reason: They all represent different treatment of certain groups in the labour market and thus constitute economic discrimination.

17. Measures to alleviate poverty include:

a. increasing the productivity of the working poor
b. pursuing policies that promote economic growth and employment
c. enforcing legislation forbidding discrimination
d. all of the above

Answer: d

Reason: Choices a, b, and c will help to improve the lot of the poor.

18. A negative income tax is a system whereby:

a. all taxes are frowned upon
b. no one pays taxes but the government gives subsidies
c. the government taxes the rich but not the poor
d. none of the above

Answer: d

Reason: A negative income tax is a system whereby the government gives subsidies to people whose incomes are below the taxable level.

True-False

Determine whether each of the following statements is true or false.

1. Market income is the revenue that firms obtain from selling goods and services in the marketplace.

Answer: False

Explanation: Market income consists of employment and self-employment income, investment income, private retirement income, and other incomes, excluding government transfers.

2. There is now general agreement among economists and sociologists on what constitutes fairness or equity in income distribution.

Answer: False

Explanation: There is no general agreement on what constitutes fairness or equity.

3. The distribution of income according to contribution has the advantage that it provides incentives for greater productivity.

Answer: True

4. The distribution of income on the basis of need guarantees maximum incentive for workers.

Answer: False

Explanation: It is unlikely that there will be any incentive to work if income is distributed on the basis of need.

5. If income is distributed equally to all members of the society, it is likely that the level of economic activity will fall, resulting in a decline in income and output.

Answer: True

6. The size distribution of income is a measure that is frequently used to determine how evenly total income is distributed among individuals and households.

Answer: True

7. The Lorenz curve is a graph showing total earnings over an individual's life span. It is also called the "life-cycle earning curve".

Answer: False

Explanation: The Lorenz curve is a graphical device for measuring income inequality.

8. The greater the Gini coefficient, the greater is the inequality in the distribution of income. If income distribution is perfectly equal, the Gini coefficient will be zero.

Answer: True

9. Main causes of income inequality include educational attainment, productivity, and discrimination.

Answer: True

10. Absolute poverty is the condition that exists when an individual or a family has a standard of living that is far below that enjoyed by others in society, regardless of the level of income.

Answer: False

Explanation: The concept of poverty defined here is relative poverty.

11. The low-income cut-off (poverty line) is the same for all families and individuals regardless of their circumstances.

Answer: False

Explanation: The low income cut-off varies with such factors as size of area of residence and size of family unit.

12. Poverty affects only those people living below the poverty line.

Answer: False

Explanation: Other members of the society may be adversely affected by the behaviour of the poor. They may be affected by certain socially unacceptable activities perpetrated by the poor. The population as a whole may be forced to accept lower living standards as a result of the behaviour of the poor.

13. The incidence of poverty refers to the absolute number of poor people living in a community.

Answer: False

Explanation: The incidence of poverty is the likelihood of being poor.

14. Young families 24 years old or younger have a relatively high incidence of poverty largely because of low levels of education and lack of valuable marketplace skills.

Answer: True

15. Types of economic discrimination include employment discrimination, wage discrimination, and occupational discrimination.

Answer: True

16. Wage discrimination occurs when particular groups are paid lower wages and salaries than others for similar work

Answer: True

17. The serious problem with poverty is that nothing can be done to alleviate it.

Answer: False

Explanation: *Steps can be taken to alleviate poverty. These steps include, for example, increasing the productivity of the working poor, enforcing anti-discrimination laws, and granting certain subsidies to the poor.*

18. A negative income tax is a system whereby the government passes legislation making it illegal for any tax payer to claim an amount that makes his or her taxable income negative.

Answer: False

Explanation: *A negative income tax is a system whereby the government grants subsidies to people whose incomes are below the taxable level.*

Completion

(Fill in the blanks)

Use each word or combination of words from the list exactly once.
*(**Hint**: Proceed by elimination)*

Word list

Absolute — Coefficient — Contribution — Economic — Employment — Gini — Incidence — Income x 2 — Line / Cut-Off — Lorenz — Market — Need — Negative — Occupational — Poverty x 2 — Poverty / Low-Income — Productivity / Contributions — Relative — Size — Wage — Zero

Questions

1. ____________ ____________ approximates the sum of earnings from employment and self-employment, investment income, private retirement income, and other incomes, excluding government transfers.
2. According to the ____________ standard of income distribution, income is equitably distributed if it is distributed according to need. The ____________ standard of income distribution calls for distribution in proportion to productivity.
3. The distribution of income according to ____________ provides the greatest incentive to work hard.
4. The ____________ distribution of income is used to measure how evenly total income is distributed among individuals and households.
5. The ____________ curve is a graphical device for measuring income inequality.
6. The ____________ ____________ is the area between the line of perfect income equality and the Lorenz curve expressed as a proportion of the area of the triangle formed by the line of perfect equality.
7. If income distribution is perfectly equal, the Gini coefficient will be ____________.
8. The condition that exists when an individual or a family lacks the financial resources required for the basic necessities of life is called ____________ ____________.
9. The ____________ ____________ is an arbitrary level of income below which poverty is said to exist and below which an individual or a family is unable to maintain a satisfactory standard of living.
10. The condition that exists when an individual or a family has a standard of living that is far below that enjoyed by others in society is called ____________ poverty.
11. The "____________ of ____________" is the term used to refer to the likelihood of being poor.
12. ____________ discrimination occurs when equivalent workers are treated differently in the labour market for reasons other than differences in their productivity.
13. ____________ discrimination is a situation in which particular groups are denied employment on the basis of their identification with those groups. ____________ discrimination is a situation in which particular groups are paid lower wages and salaries than others are paid for similar work. ____________ discrimination is a situation in which particular groups are prevented from entering certain occupations.
14. A ____________ ____________ tax is a system whereby the government gives subsidies to people whose incomes are below the taxable level.

Solution

1. (Market Income)
2. (Need, Contribution)
3. (Productivity or Contributions)
4. (Size)
5. (Lorenz)
6. (Gini Coefficient)
7. (Zero)
8. (Absolute Poverty)
9. (Poverty Line Or Low-Income Cut-Off)
10. (Relative)
11. (Incidence (Of) Poverty)
12. (Economic)
13. (Employment, Wage, Occupational)
14. (Negative Income)

17 ENVIRONMENTAL PROTECTION

SYNOPSIS

In general, the market system works well, but sometimes, malfunctions in the market mechanism (market failure) lead to inefficient outcomes. Sources of market failure include market imperfections, lack of adequate information, the existence of economic externalities, and the existence of public goods.

When **private costs** and social costs diverge, **economic externalities** occur. If the externality results in some benefit, it is called an **external economy** or a **positive externality**. If it results in a cost, it is called an **external diseconomy** or a **negative externality**.

Public goods are goods such that once they are produced, it is virtually impossible to prevent anyone from enjoying the benefits that they provide. Examples of public goods are education, public health services, and police protection.

Merit goods are goods the consumption of which are mandatory because the government has determined that they are good for people.

As an economy experiences economic growth, the amount of pollution tends to increase. Considerable damage has been done to the environment, so environmental protection has become an issue of prime importance. Pollution ruins rivers and lakes, and destroys animal life and vegetation.

Economic analysis provides an answer to the appropriate level of pollution abatement. The optimum level of pollution abatement occurs when the extra costs equal the extra benefits.

Measures to reduce the level of pollution include direct regulation, effluent fees, tax incentives, establishing property rights, and using moral appeal.

Smog is an evidence of air pollution. Many people die prematurely each year from air pollution. Air pollution also affects lakes and crops. Water pollution affects our health and our economy, our ecosystems are under attack, and their ability to maintain environmental balance is weakened. Many countries have made significant progress in dealing with pollution.

LEARNING OBJECTIVES

In connection with this module, you should be able to:

1. discuss the main sources of market failure
2. explain the nature of economic externalities
3. discuss the concept of public good
4. evaluate the role of government in the light of market failure
5. explain how economic analysis can help to arrive at an appropriate level of pollution
6. discuss measures to deal with the problem of pollution

DEFINITIONS & CONCEPTS

You should be able to define the following terms and concepts:

market failure
imperfect competition
public goods
merit goods
effluent charge (fee)
air pollution
water pollution
external diseconomy
product differentiation
private cost
social cost
economic externality
external economy
greenhouse effect

17

ENVIRONMENTAL PROTECTION

Concepts, Definitions & Problems

Problem 17-1

What do economists mean by the term market failure?

Requirement and Clue: *This is a definitional problem. You are to give a clear and precise meaning of the concept as used by economists. There is no need for a long epistle.*

Solution:

Economists use the term market failure to refer to the inability of the market or price system to achieve an efficient allocation of resources. An example of market failure is the restriction of output by a monopolist in order to raise price.

Problem 17-2

Define externalities.

Requirement and Clue: *This is a definitional problem. You are required to state clearly and precisely the meaning of externality in economics. Examples will be helpful.*

Solution:

In economics, externalities refer to costs and benefits related to the production or consumption of goods and services that are not accounted for by the price system. They are sometimes called "spill over effects". An example of an externality would be extra loud music coming from my neighbour's house in the middle of the night that prevents me from sleeping. Another example would be very soothing and entertaining music coming from my neighbour's house in the evening that greatly enhances my enjoyment of the evening.

Problem 17-3

Discuss two sources of market failure.

Requirement and Clue: *You may be able to write about several sources of market failure but the problem requires only two. Let your solution comply with the problem.*

Solution:

Two sources of market failure are market imperfection and the existence of public goods.

Market imperfection: A market is said to be imperfect if individual buyers and sellers have so much power in the market that they can influence the prices of resources and outputs. Market imperfections lead to a misallocation of society's resources or to their unproductive use. In the case of monopoly or oligopoly, barriers to entry prevent firms from entering the industry. Monopolies and oligopolies tend to set the prices of their products in order to earn maximum profits. They may deliberately restrict output in order to keep price above average total cost.

Public goods: Public goods are goods and services that are consumed collectively; no one can be excluded from their consumption once they are produced. Such goods bestow collective benefits on society. Examples of public goods are police protection, national defence, and education. The existence of public goods is a source of market failure. Let us consider the case of national defence. If a private firm were to provide national defence as a service to be sold in the marketplace, every person would benefit from such a service, even if no one bought it. The firm would not be able to enforce payment for the service. Consequently, hardly any firm would be willing to provide public goods. Here the market fails to produce the goods and services that society would want.

Problem 17-4

Carefully define each of the following concepts:

(a) *Public goods*

(b) *Merit goods*

Requirement and Clue: *This is a definitional problem. Lengthy discussions, though possible, are not required. Simply state clearly and precisely the meaning of each concept and provide illustrative examples.*

Solution:

(a) Public goods are goods and services that are consumed collectively; no one can be excluded from their consumption once they are provided. Examples of public goods are police protection, national defence, and public health services.

(b) Merit goods are goods or services that the government has determined to be necessary and therefore mandatory for society, regardless of how people evaluate these goods or services. An example of a merit good is mandatory education at a certain level.

Problem 17-5

Briefly define each of the following concepts:

(a) *private costs*

(b) *social costs*

(c) *economic externality*

(d) *external economy*

(e) *external diseconomy*

Requirement and Clue: *This problem is totally definitional. A clear and precise statement of the meaning of each concept is required. Do not ignore the word "briefly" in the problem.*

Solution:

(a) Private costs are costs borne solely and directly by the individuals or firms making the decision. An example of a private cost is my air fare to the Dominican Republic for a two-week vacation.

(b) Social costs are the total costs to society of decisions made and actions taken by individuals and firms. For example, the social cost of manufacturing a product might be the direct cost to the manufacturer plus the damage that the production of the product might do to the environment.

(c) Economic externality is a cost or a benefit that accrues to persons not directly involved in the actions or decisions made by firms or individuals. An example of an economic externality is the traffic gridlock experienced by a commuter because of road construction. Another example is a billboard posted by an insurance company warning motorists to drive carefully.

(d) An external economy is an economic externality that results in a benefit. It is also referred to as a positive externality. An example of an external economy is the benefit enjoyed by the owner of a gas station when the government decides to build a highway in close proximity to the gas station.

(e) An external diseconomy is an economic externality that results in a cost. An external economy is also called a negative externality. An example of an external diseconomy is the loss of revenue suffered by merchants when the government decides to close a section of the road that passes in front of their places of business.

Problem 17-6

What are economic externalities? How is the concept of economic externality related to environmental pollution?

Requirement and Clue: *This is a two-part problem. Answer each part in order. The first part of the problem is definitional. You are to state clearly and precisely the meaning of economic externalities, giving an example if possible. You are not required to write an essay on economic externalities. For the second part of the problem, focus on the nature of environmental pollution and its association with economic externality.*

Solution:

Economic externalities are benefits or costs that accrue to persons who are not directly involved in the actions or decisions made by firms and individuals. An example of an economic externality is the increased productivity that a firm gets from a well educated labour force. Another example of an economic externality is the lack of attention from an instructor caused by an overcrowded classroom.

Environmental pollution imposes a cost on society. A manufacturing plant dumping pollutants into a river imposes a cost on those who want to use the river for a variety of purposes but cannot because it is polluted by the manufacturer. In this case, the pollution is an economic externality.

Problem 17-7

What is the free-rider problem in economics?

Requirement and Clue: *Clearly state the problem, giving an illustrative example.*

Solution:

A free-rider is someone who enjoys the benefits of a good, service, or resource without paying for it. In economics, the free-rider problem refers to the situation where people benefit from a good or service without having to incur any of the costs of providing that good or service. This is a problem because since payment cannot be exacted for the use of the good or service, which society may find to be beneficial or even necessary, private producers will not find it profitable to produce the good or service.

The example of a lighthouse is often used to illustrate the free-rider problem. Most people would agree that lighthouses are most desirable devices. They prevent ships from running aground and sinking and they save human lives. As important as lighthouses are, few people would pay for the services they provide. Once the lighthouse is in operation, it would benefit all ships, whether they pay for the service or not. It would therefore not pay a private company to erect a lighthouse only for free-riders to reap the benefit.

Problem 17-8

Discuss the view that rapid economic growth is a major cause of environmental problems.

Requirement and Clue: *Focus on the effects of rapid economic growth, including benefits and costs.*

Solution:

There can be little doubt that rapid economic growth is a prime cause of environmental problems. As nations pursue rapid economic growth, they incur a cost in terms of smog, water pollution, acid rain, and greenhouse gases. Ecosystems have become less productive and our health, lifestyles, and economies are all affected adversely by pollution. These facts notwithstanding, it would be a mistake to abandon economic growth altogether. Without economic growth, it is difficult to see how society can meet the many challenges that it faces. The solution lies in balancing economic growth with reasonable protection of the environment.

Problem 17-9

Describe the common-pool problem. Is there a solution to this problem?

Requirement and Clue: *This is a two-part problem. Answer each part in order. Whereas to define a concept is to state what it is clearly and precisely, to describe a concept involves a bit more. To describe is to give some account of the concept, pointing out any features that allow identification. A simple "yes" or "no" answer will not suffice as a solution to the second part of the problem. If there is a solution, you should identify it.*

Solution:

Because of open access resources, that is, resources that are difficult or costly or impractical to exclude individuals from using, the common-pool problem arises. The common pool problem can be defined as the superfluous use of open-access resources that occur because of unrestricted access. An example of the common-pool problem overfishing that depletes the stock of fish. The ocean is considered an open-access resource, and as a result, fishermen, if not restrained or restricted by some means, will fish without regard to any replenishment of the fish stock.

The solution to the common-pool problem is the imposition of restrictions on the use of open-access resources. For example, the authorities may restrict hunting by requiring hunters to have a licence and then issuing licences for a certain time of the year, or they may impose a quota on the size and quantity of fish that can be caught. Such restrictions will ease the common-pool problem.

Problem 17-10

We are a family living upstream of a pharmaceutical company on a certain river. Why should be, as members of society, concern ourselves with the fact that the company is using a part of the river to dispose of wastes. After all, we live upstream and the pollution is occurring downstream.

Requirement and Clue: *Focus on how pollution affects the environment and consider whether upstream dwellers are also affected.*

Solution:

Pollution, in its various forms, imposes a cost on society. In the case of the pollution caused by the pharmaceutical company mentioned in the problem, the society is being robbed of a cleaner environment, of the use of the river for recreational purposes, and of the fish population. All these are costs that we, as members of the society, will be forced to bear whether we live upstream or not. Moreover, any tax dollars that may be used to clean up the river represent additional costs. These costs are sufficient reason for us to concern ourselves about the pollution of the river by the company.

Problem 17-11

From an economic perspective, society should pursue a policy of a zero level of pollution. Discuss.

Requirement and Clue: *Focus on the benefits and costs of achieving a zero level of pollution.*

Solution:

Eliminating pollution altogether might seem to be a laudable objective to pursue, and it would make a great deal of sense if the cost of eliminating pollution were zero. However, the cost of achieving a zero level of pollution would be significantly more than the vast majority of people would be willing to bear. Economic analysis can help us to determine what amount of pollution society should allow. If society considers the level of pollution to be sufficiently serious, then society should be willing to sacrifice some goods and services in order to attain a lower level of pollution. If the benefits derived from further pollution abatement exceed the costs, then additional resources should be allocated to pollution abatement. On the other hand, if the costs of additional pollution abatement exceed the benefits, then the extra costs should not be incurred.

Problem 17-12

With the help of an appropriate diagram, illustrate how the appropriate level of pollution abatement can be determined.

Requirement and Clue: *This is a typical exercise of balancing benefits and costs. The now traditional diagram of marginal cost and marginal benefit can be used in this case.*

Solution:

This is an appropriate problem where the marginal approach to decision making can be applied. If the marginal cost exceeds the marginal benefit, then the cost should not be incurred; if the marginal cost is less than the marginal benefit, then the cost should be incurred. This principle can be applied to pollution abatement.

The following diagram can be used to illustrate how the appropriate level of pollution abatement can be determined.

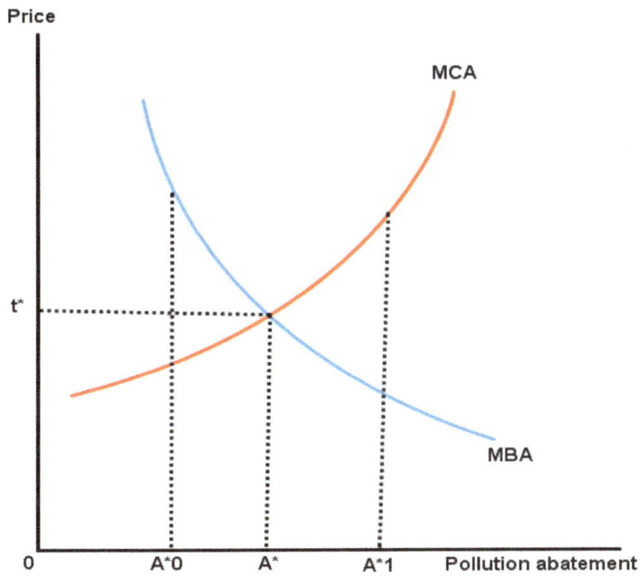

As more and more environmental protection is undertaken, the extra benefit declines. This is shown by the downward sloping marginal benefit curve MBA in the diagram. Conversely, as more pollution abatement is undertaken, the extra cost increases. The upward sloping marginal cost curve MCA depicts this increase. At a pollution abatement level beyond A*, (A*1, for example), the extra benefit is less than the extra cost. Therefore, beyond A*, there is too much pollution abatement. At a pollution abatement level of less than A*, (A*0, for example), additional benefit exceeds the extra cost. Hence, more pollution abatement should be undertaken. At a pollution abatement level of A*, the marginal cost equals the marginal benefit, represented by t*. Hence, A* is considered to be the optimal level of environmental protection.

Problem 17-13

A paper mill emits large quantities of toxic waste into the environment annually. The chair of the board of directors, the president, and the chief financial officer (CFO) meet to discuss the situation. The president is very pro-environmental protection, while the chair and the CFO are more concerned with the company's profit margin. The president argues that the paper mill should aim at reducing its pollution to the bare minimum possible to protect the environment. The chair and the CFO disagree, stating that the company should focus on its operations and just ignore the environment.

Whose position is economically correct as far as protecting the environment is concerned?

Requirement and Clue: *Consider the possibility that both positions may be extreme and focus on the appropriate level of pollution abatement.*

Solution:

This problem involves a decision regarding the appropriate level of environmental protection. Environmental protection has costs as well as benefits. A cost could be the money spent on pollution abatement equipment, while a benefit could be a healthier workforce. The president's position could easily result in too much pollution abatement, while the position of the chair and the CFO could result in too little environmental protection. The appropriate level of environmental protection for the mill is not necessarily the one that results in minimum pollution, but the one that equates the marginal benefit and the marginal cost of environmental protection.

Problem 17-14

Direct regulation preventing the dumping of waste into the environment is one measure that can be taken to protect the environment. Are there any problems with this approach?

Requirement and Clue: *Focus on what is necessary for direct regulation to be effective and point these out.*

Solution:

Examples of direct regulation to protect the environment include forbidding the use of certain chemicals that damage the environment and setting emission standards for automobiles and certain manufacturing plants that pollute the environment.

One problem with direct regulation is the difficulty of enforcing it. For direct regulation to be effective, an effort must be made to detect the offenders; this may involve a substantial cost. The offenders, if caught, must then be prosecuted. This can also be a very costly process. The detection of an offence can be quite difficult. Some polluters, therefore, may find it less expensive to continue to pollute and pay the penalty (if caught) than to install expensive anti-pollution equipment. Many individuals also may continue to dump waste into the environment in spite of the regulation, if the probability of being caught is low.

Another problem with direct regulation is that of determining the permissible level of pollution for each polluter. If the government aims to reduce pollution by say, 20% during a period, should all polluters be required to reduce their pollution levels by 20% regardless of the amount of pollution caused? Or should pollution levels be reduced by more than 20% in some plants and by less than 20% in others. This may not be such an easy decision.

Problem 17-15

Briefly describe three measures that may be taken to reduce the level of pollution.

Requirement and Clue: *You may know of several measures that can be taken to reduce the level of pollution, but you have been asked to describe three. Follow the instruction given in the problem and describe three measures. Do not ignore the word "briefly".*

Solution:

Three measures that may be taken to reduce the level of pollution are the charging of effluent fees, the granting of tax incentives, and moral appeal.

Effluent fees: In this approach, the polluter is charged a fee known as an effluent fee for polluting the environment. This fee forces polluters to consider the social costs rather than just the private costs of their decisions. In other words, effluent fees force polluters to internalize their costs. The fee charged would vary directly with the level of pollution caused by each polluter.

Tax incentives: Anti-pollution devices impose a substantial cost on those why purchase them. If tax relief is given to people who incur the cost of purchasing and installing anti-pollution equipment, the level of pollution is likely to decrease as more and more of these anti-pollution devices are installed.

Moral appeal: An appeal to producers and consumers may help to reduce the level of pollution. Consumers can be persuaded to use public transportation and to organize car pools rather than drive millions of air polluting cars into the city. An appeal to firms to develop cleaner methods of production can also help to win the battle against pollution. Moral appeal is most effective where polluters are convinced that a polluted environment is against their own interests.

Problem 17-16

Discuss the use of property rights as a means of protecting the environment.

Requirement and Clue: *Focus on how ownership might affect the use of the environment or parts of it.*

Solution:

One reason that polluters abuse the environment is that no single individual or firm owns it. For example, no single individual or firm owns the air around us so we can dump all kinds of poisonous gases into it without paying anything. The assignment of private property rights to individuals and firms can lead to a reduction in the overall level of pollution. The following example will illustrate the point. Suppose a lake is owned by no one and a firm uses the lake for waste disposal. In the absence of government regulation forbidding the dumping of waste into the lake, the firm will use the lake for waste disposal. Now suppose that the government offers to sell the lake or to sell exclusive rights to use the lake for any purpose.

If individuals or groups of individuals value the lake for recreational purposes above the value placed on it by the firm for waste disposal, then they will be willing to buy the lake and keep it free from pollution. If the value of the lake to the firm as a place for waste disposal is greater than its value to those people who want to use it for recreation, then the firm will acquire the lake and use it for waste disposal. The firm will purchase the lake for waste disposal only if the cost is lower than the cost of any alternative means of disposing of its waste.

Problem 17-17

Would you expect an individual producer voluntarily to take social costs into account in its production decisions?

Requirement and Clue: *A simple "yes" or "no" solution will not suffice. You are e3xpected to defend your position. Focus on the objective of the producer.*

Solution:

It is unlikely that an individual producer would voluntarily internalize all its costs. The objective of the producer is to maximize profits. In one producer voluntarily takes social costs into consideration when making decisions about production, then that producer voluntarily places itself at a cost disadvantage vis-à-vis other producers. Thus, the producer's profitability relative to that of competitors would decline. An individual producer is unlikely to voluntarily place itself in such an unfavourable position.

Problem 17-18

What is a carbon tax? What are the advantages of a carbon tax?

Requirement and Clue: *This is a two-part problem. Address each part in order. The first part of the problem is definitional. State the meaning of the concept clearly and precisely. Think of the purpose of the tax.*

Solution:

A carbon tax is a tax imposed on fossil fuel such as gasoline and natural gas that emit carbon dioxide.

A carbon tax has the advantage of being effective in reducing pollution because it provides an economic incentive for everyone to reduce the use of the items on which the tax is imposed. The tax raises the price of fossil fuel to users and reduces the quantity used. Another advantage of a carbon tax is that it is considered to be fair in the sense that the tax one pays is proportional to the amount of emission caused.

Problem 17-19

Discuss the cap-and-trade system as a means of reducing the level of pollution.

Requirement and Clue: *A definition of the cap-and-trade system, along with a sketch of its main elements is a good idea. In your discussion, focus on what is good about the system and what is problematic about it.*

Solution:

A cap-and-trade system is a market-oriented approach to pollution control that involves the sale of pollution credits on the open market.

Under this system, the government establishes pollution limits or "caps" on specific sources of pollution such as factories and power plants by giving a certain number of allowances or pollution credits. These allowances set the amounts of pollutants that that facility or organization is allowed to emit. Facilities and organizations that effectively control their pollution, perhaps through implementation of technology, may not use up all their pollution credits. Other polluters may have difficulty operating under the established cap. This creates a market for pollution credits. Polluters that cannot meet their pollution allowances can buy pollution credits from those who have left over credits. In this way, some polluters are able to pollute more without increasing the overall level of pollution because some facilities are polluting less.

The gap-and-trade system is good in that it does result in a reduction in pollution. It also rewards polluters who are successful in coming in under the allowable limit through the use of effective control devices. Additionally, the cap and trade system provides an opportunity for polluters who need a longer adjustment time to buy some adjustment time. It also provides strict environmental accountability without restricting economic growth. One problem with the cap and trade system is that it allows one area to become much more polluted that may be desirable. Regions that purchase pollution credits so that they can support their pollution habits will tend to be more polluted than other regions.

Problem 17-20

An electric generating plant uses coal to propel its turbines. This plant emits large quantities of smoke which pollutes the air. Devise a market-oriented program that will cause this plant to reduce its level of air pollution.

Requirement and Clue: *Focus on how the plant could be forced to internalize its costs.*

Solution:

The plant could be charged an effluent fee. This plan would force the plant to internalize its pollution costs. The plant would reduce the amount of pollution it emits into the air.

Problem 17-21

"One of the great advantages of studying economics is that it helps us to approach certain problems in a rational manner. Consider the problem of pollution. It should be obvious to anyone that society would be better off if our environment was not polluted. Accordingly, society should allocate sufficient funds to ensure that the level of pollution is reduced to zero. This is sound economic logic."

Can you detect any error in the above statement?

Requirement and Clue: *You are required to read the statement carefully and critically. If you detect any error, you should offer a correction.*

Solution:

Surely, society would be better off if there was no pollution. But the achievement of a zero level of pollution involves a cost. Economic reasoning would require an investigation into the cost and benefit of achieving and maintaining a pollution-free society. The optimal level of pollution is that level at which the marginal benefit from pollution reduction equals the marginal cost of pollution reduction; and this level is not zero.

Problem 17-22

"Everyone knows and acknowledges the importance of lighthouses. They have saved ships and lives. Because of the importance of lighthouses, if a company were to operate a chain of lighthouses, it would be assured of huge profits. It is because of their great profitability that the government operates lighthouses instead of allowing private firms to do so."

Can you detect any error in the above statement?

Requirement and Clue: *You should read the statement carefully and identify any error you detect. You should provide a correction.*

Solution:

There can be little doubt about the importance of lighthouses. Their importance, however, does not guarantee that a private firm would earn profits from operating lighthouses. On the contrary, it is more likely that such a business would not be profitable. Once the lighthouse were put into operation, the company would not be able to exclude people from the benefits, whether or not they paid for the service. There would therefore be many free riders who would benefit from the service without having to pay for it. Lighthouses belong to the class of goods known as public goods. They provide benefits to the public but they are unprofitable for private businesses. It is precisely for this reason that public goods are usually provided by the government.

Multiple-Choice

In each case, circle the letter that corresponds with the correct answer.

1. The term market failure refers to:
    a. markets that cease to operate soon after they were established
    b. markets in which buyers and sellers fail to reach agreement after considerable negotiations
    c. the inability of the price system to achieve an efficient allocation of resources
    d. markets taken over by the government because of poor decisions made by firms.

Answer: c

Reason: Choice c offers a correct definition of the concept.

2. Market failure leads to:
    a. socially desirable outcomes
    b. socially undesirable outcomes
    c. outcome that benefit no one
    d. more efficient resource allocation

Answer: b

Reason: *Market failure results in a misallocation of society's resource s. This is socially undesirable.*

3. Market failure may be due to:

a. market imperfection c. inadequate information

b. externalities d. all of the above

Answer: d

Reason: *Choices a, b, and c call all lead to market failure.*

4. A market is imperfect if:

a. the goods and services sold in the market are imperfect

b. the traders in the market are prone to making mistakes

c. the number of buyers far exceeds the number of sellers, or vice versa

d. none of the above

Answer: d

Reason: *A market is imperfect if individual buyers and sellers have so much power in the market that they can influence the prices of inputs and outputs.*

5. Private costs are:

a. costs that are kept a secret by individuals and firms who incur expenses

b. costs that are borne solely and directly by the individuals and firms who make the decisions

c. costs that can be known by accountants only after serious and considerable investigations have been made

d. all costs except those borne by the government

Answer: b

Reason: *Private costs are those costs that are borne directly by individuals and firms in the process of consuming or producing goods and services.*

6. Which of the following is correct?

a. Social costs = Private costs + External costs

b. Private costs = Social costs + External costs

c. External costs = Social costs + Private costs

d. None of the above

Answer: a

Reason: *Social costs are the total costs (private and external) incurred by society of producing or consuming goods and services.*

7. Economic externalities:

a. can be benefits or costs

b. can only be benefits

c. can only be costs

d. cannot really be identified

Answer: a

Reason: *Positive externalities are benefits; negative externalities are costs.*

8. An external diseconomy is:

a. a foreign economy that is diminishing in size

b. any economic system that is outside of the system that is being considered

c. a cost that is incurred by a foreign economy

d. none of the above

Answer: d

Reason: *An external diseconomy is an economic externality that results in a cost.*

9. Goods and services that are consumed collectively, and from which no one can be excluded are called:

a. all inclusive goods c. collective goods

b. consumer collectibles d. none of the above

Answer: d

Reason: *Such goods and called public goods.*

10. Which of the following is an example of a negative externality?

a. The advertising costs of a firm

b. The increased sales resulting from an advertising campaign

c. The dumping of toxic waste near a residential area

d. The money a firm pays out to ship its exports

Answer: c

Reason: *The dumping of toxic waste near a residential area imposes a cost on the residents in the form of reduced property values and possibly reduced health.*

11. Which of the following is a cost of pollution?

a. The amount spent to reduce pollution

b. The destruction of rivers and lakes by pollution

c. The loss of fish and birds because of pollution

d. All of the above

Answer: d

Reason: *All the choices represent costs of pollution.*

12. Public goods are goods:

a. produced by private firms for public consumption

b. that are cherished so much by the public that they are not consumed

c. that bestow collective benefits on society

d. none of the above

Answer: c

Reason: *Public goods are goods and services that are consumed collectively; no one can be excluded from consuming them.*

13. Examples of public goods are:

a. national security c. police protection

b. public health services d. all of the above

Answer: d

Reason: *National security, public health services, and police protection are consumed collectively, and no one can be excluded from consuming them once they are provided. They fit the definition of public goods.*

14. Goods or services that the government has determined to be necessary and therefore mandatory for society are called:

a. societal goods c. mandatory goods

b. merit goods d. government goods and services

Answer: b

Reason: Merit goods and services are deemed to be so important to society that the government declares them to be mandatory.

15. Merit goods are goods that:

a. are good on their own merit
b. have won merits in competitive markets
c. are determined by the government to be good for people
d. none of the above

Answer: c

Reason: Merit goods are goods and services deemed necessary for society and are therefore mandatory.

16. Which of the following is a cost of rapid economic growth?

a. Smog
b. Acid rain
c. Water pollution
d. All of the above

Answer: d

Reason: Smog, acid rain, and water pollution all result from rapid economic growth and are a cost to society in terms of environmental deterioration.

17. Resources such as the sea and the atmosphere which anyone can use freely are called:

a. limitless resources
b. nature's property rights
c. both a and b
d. neither a nor b

Answer: d

Reason: such resources are called open-access resources.

18. Open-access resources are:

a. resources that are sold on the open market
b. resources that are difficult or costly to exclude individuals from using
c. resources to which free access must be given by the government
d. none of the above

Answer: b

Reason: People have free access to open-access resources. It is extremely difficult to prevent anyone from using them.

19. Which of the following is an open-access resource?

a. The sea
b. Wildlife
c. The atmosphere
d. All of the above

Answer: d

Reason: It is difficult or costly to exclude anyone from using the resources listed.

20. The common-pool problem is:

a. the problem caused when too many common people manage resources
b. the problem resulting from people who refuse to join a car pool system
c. the problem that exists in certain areas where there are just too many private swimming pools
d. none of the above

Answer: d

Reason: The common-pool problem is the problem of the overuse of open-access resources.

21. The optimal level of environmental protection is:

a. the maximum amount of pollution that the environment can stand
b. the minimum amount of pollution that is possible
c. nothing but a zero level of pollution because pollution is deadly
d. none of the above

Answer: d

Reason: The optimal level of environmental protection is that level at which the marginal cost of environmental protection is just equal to the marginal benefit of environmental protection.

22. Which of the following is a means of protecting the environment?

a. Direct regulation
b. Effluent fees
c. Property rights
d. All of the above

Answer: d

Reason: All of the choices given will reduce the amount of pollution.

23. An effluent fee is:

a. a fee imposed on the rich but not the poor
b. a special right whereby only the rich can pollute the environment
c. a special pollution charge administered by the rich
d. none of the above

Answer: d

Reason: An effluent fee is a fee imposed on a polluter for polluting the environment.

24. By charging polluters effluent fees, they will:

a. internalize the costs of their polluting activities
b. pollute more, since they own the right to pollute
c. deduct the charge from their direct costs to arrive at total cost
d. none of the above

Answer: a

Reason: Effluent fees force polluters to take account of the cost of polluting the environment.

25. The establishment of property rights will:

a. reduce the level of pollution
b. increase the level of pollution
c. have no effect on the level of pollution
d. make all firms more profitable

Answer: a

Reason: It will cause polluters to have greater regard for the environment. It will also reduce the common-pool problem. Overall, it will reduce the level of pollution.

26. Which of the following is not a method of reducing the level of pollution?

a. Direct regulation
b. Lowering taxes on goods that pollute
c. Establishing property rights
d. Moral suasion

Answer: b

Reason: Lowering taxes on goods that pollute only encourages more pollution.

27. A tax imposed on fossil fuel is referred to as:

a. a carbon tax
b. pollution-induced tax
c. a fuel emission tax
d. none of the above

Answer: a

Reason: A carbon tax is a tax imposed on items that emit carbon dioxide.

28. A carbon tax is effective because:

a. it is taken directly out of income
b. it is a direct tax
c. it is an incentive to protect the environment
d. it is extremely progressive

Answer: c

Reason: It provides an economic incentive for everyone to reduce the use of items on which the tax is imposed.

29. The cap-and-trade system:

a. consistently ignores the market
b. is irrelevant to environmental protection
c. is a foolproof, problem-free system of environmental protection
d. takes the market into consideration

Answer: d

Reason: The cap-and-trade system is a market-oriented approach.

30. Which of the following is a consequence of climate change?

a. The appearance of new infectious diseases
b. Increased health problems from heat stress
c. More frequent forest fires
d. All of the above

Answer: d

Reason: Choices a, b, and c are all associated with climate change.

True-False

Determine whether each of the following statements is true or false.

1. Sometimes the price system fails to achieve an efficient allocation of resources. We refer to this phenomenon as market failure.

Answer: True

2. The inability of the price mechanism to achieve an efficient allocation of resources is referred to as mechanism malfunction.

Answer: False

Explanation: The phenomenon is referred to as market failure.

3. In a free enterprise economic system, markets always produce efficient outcomes.

Answer: False

Explanation: Sometimes markets fail to allocate resources efficiently. This is the situation referred to as market failure.

4. Causes of market failure include inadequate information, the existence of economic externalities, and the existence of public goods.

Answer: True

5. A market is considered to be imperfect if firms have no control at all over the prices they charge for their products.

Answer: False

Explanation: A market is considered to be imperfect if individual buyers and sellers have so much power in the market that they can influence the prices of inputs and outputs.

6. Market imperfections such as monopoly elements are a source of market failure.

Answer: True

7. Product differentiation in some industries ensures that market failure does not occur and that resources are optimally allocated.

Answer: False

Explanation: Product differentiation confers a certain degree of market power on firms and thus promote market imperfection and thus market failure.

8. Lack of adequate information may cause market players to make decisions that do not maximize their profits or their satisfaction.

Answer: True

9. Economic externalities are spillover benefits and costs that have absolutely nothing to do with market failure.

Answer: False

Explanation: *Economic externalities are a major cause of market failure.*

10. Social cost is the sum of all private costs.

Answer: False

Explanation: *Social cost is a cost that is borne by society as a whole. It is the sum of private costs and external costs.*

11. Positive externalities occur when production or consumption by particular firms or consumers results in benefits to other firms or other consumers.

Answer: True

12. An example of an external economy is the increase in private property values because of the development of a resort area by the government.

Answer: True

13. A characteristic of public goods is that every member of society is quite willing to pay for them.

Answer: False

Explanation: *Public goods benefit all, but not everyone is willing to pay for them since they cannot be excluded from the benefits.*

14. Good examples of public goods are education, public health services, police protection, and public transportation.

Answer: False

Explanation: *Public transportation is not a good example of a public good because it is possible for certain individuals not to benefit from it.*

15. Goods such as education and certain health services that the government decides are good for the citizens are called merit goods.

Answer: True

16. Economic growth should be vigorously pursued because it has great benefits without any associated costs.

Answer: False

Explanation: *Economic growth has tremendous benefits but it also has a cost in terms of environmental pollution with all its consequences.*

17. Environmental pollution cannot be considered a cost because it does not involve any monetary payments.

Answer: False

Explanation: *The damage done to the environment is a non-monetary cost.*

18. Because of the serious damage that pollution of the environment causes, society should aim for a zero level of pollution.

Answer: False

Explanation: *This would be true only if the cost of achieving a zero level of pollution were zero.*

19. Because no direct payment is associated with the use of open-access resources, their use will continue up to the point where the average benefit is zero.

Answer: False

Explanation: *The use of open-access resources will be carried to the point at which the marginal (not the average) benefit is zero.*

20. There is absolutely no solution to the common-pool problem.

Answer: False

Explanation: *The common-pool problem can be solved by imposing restrictions on the use of open-access resources.*

21. As more and more pollution abatement is undertaken, the extra benefit of environmental protection decreases.

Answer: True

22. One of the great advantages of direct regulation as a measure to protect the environment is that it is extremely easy to enforce the regulation.

Answer: False

Explanation: *On the contrary, one of the problems with direct regulation is the difficulty of enforcing it.*

23. As long as the marginal benefit of pollution abatement exceeds the marginal cost, more money should be spent on pollution abatement.

Answer: True

24. Effluent fees provide polluters with an economic incentive not to pollute the environment.

Answer: True

25. If the environment were owned by private individuals or firms, there would be a greater incentive to protect the environment from pollution.

Answer: True

26. A carbon tax is a tax imposed on companies that produce carbon paper for use in copying documents.

Answer: False

Explanation: *A carbon tax is a tax imposed on fossil fuel.*

27. Whether a carbon tax is imposed on consumers or producers, its effect is to raise the price and lower the quantity of items that emit carbon dioxide.

Answer: True

28. A cap-and-trade system is a market-oriented approach to pollution control that involves the sale of pollution credits on the open market.

Answer: True

29. The only problem caused by smog is temporary inconvenience.

Answer: False

Explanation: Smog causes temporary or long-term health problems.

30. The Cancun Agreement is an agreement signed by the seven leading industrial nations to meet in Cancun, Mexico annually to celebrate the victory over pollution.

Answer: False

Explanation: It's an agreement signed by more than 190 countries to continue to work towards reducing greenhouse gas emissions.

Completion

(Fill in the blanks)

Use each word or combination of words from the list exactly once.
*(**Hint**: Proceed by elimination)*

Word list

Cap — Access — Carbon — Common — Effluent — Externality — Failure x 2 — Fee — Goods x 2 — Greenhouse — Imperfect — Marginal x 2 — Market x 2 — Merit — Moral — Negative — Negatively — Open — Pool — Positive — Positively — Private — Public — Resources — Smog — Social — Suasion — Tax — Trade

Questions

1. The inability of the price system to achieve an efficient allocation of resources is referred to as ____________ ____________.
2. Market imperfection, inadequate information, economic externality and public goods are all sources of ____________ ____________.
3. A market is said to be ____________ if individual buyers and sellers have so much power in the market that they can influence the prices of inputs and outputs.
4. The cost of my airline ticket and hotel accommodation when I go on a vacation is an example of a(n) ____________ cost. The fact that I cannot fish in a lake because it is polluted is an example of a(n)____________ cost.
5. An economic ____________ is a cost or benefit that accrues to persons not directly involved in the actions or decisions made by firms and individuals.
6. An economic externality that results in benefits is called a(n) ____________ externality. One that results is a cost is called a(n) ____________ externality.
7. Examples of ____________ ____________ are police protection, public health services, and national defence.
8. ____________ ____________ are goods or services that the government has determined to be necessary and therefore mandatory for society.
9. Resources such as the ocean and the atmosphere are called ____________ ____________ ____________ because it is difficult to prevent anyone from using them.
10. Unrestricted access to open-access resources leads to a problem of over-use called the ____________ ____________ problem.
11. The optimal level of environmental protection occurs where the ____________ cost and ____________ benefit of pollution abatement are equal.
12. With cost and benefit on the vertical axis and the amount of environmental protection on the horizontal axis, the marginal benefit curve is ____________ [negatively, positively] sloped, while the marginal cost curve is ____________ [negatively, positively] sloped.
13. A(n) ____________ ____________ is a fee that is imposed on a polluter for polluting the environment.
14. A ____________ ____________ is a tax imposed on fossil fuel such as gasoline, and coal.
15. A(n) ____________ and ____________ system is a market oriented approach to pollution control that involves the sale of pollution credits on the open market.
16. Persuading consumers and producers to voluntarily reduce the level of pollution is called ____________ ____________.
17. The term used to refer to a combination of smoke and fog is ____________.
18. Water vapour, carbon dioxide, methane, ozone, and nitrous are referred to as ____________ gases.

Solution

1. (Market Failure)
2. (Market Failure)
3. (Imperfect)
4. (Private, Social)
5. (Externality)
6. (Positive, Negative)
7. (Public Goods)
8. (Merit Goods)
9. (Open Access Resources)
10. (Common Pool)
11. (Marginal, Marginal)
12. (Negatively, Positively)
13. Effluent Fee)
14. (Carbon Tax)
15. (Cap And Trade)
16. (Moral Suasion)
17. (Smog)
18. (Greenhouse)

18 ECONOMICS OF AGRICULTURE

SYNOPSIS

The agricultural sector in any economy is particularly important because it is the sector that produces food for the population. As an economy develops, the share of agriculture in total output tends to decline. This decline in the share of agriculture is noticeable in many economies.

The prices of farm products and the incomes of farmers fluctuate quite widely. The prices of farm products fluctuate largely because supplies fluctuate. Supplies fluctuate largely because of weather conditions, floods, diseases, insects, etc. Farm incomes fluctuate because farm output fluctuates and because the demand for farm products is inelastic.

According to **Engel's law**, as income increases, the percentage spent on food diminishes. Farm products have a low income elasticity of demand. Thus, income from farm operations does not increase as fast as total income. Farmers are therefore at a disadvantage.

Policies to deal with the economic problems of agriculture include price support, income payments to farmers, market quotas, easy credit to farmers, and fiscal and monetary policies. In addition to these policies, the government supports farmers by offering a variety of services to the agricultural sector through a number of boards and commissions.

LEARNING OBJECTIVES

In connection with this module, you should be able to:

1. discuss the importance of the agricultural sector
2. explain some problems that agriculture faces
3. discuss policies dealing with the problems of agriculture
4. explain the role of government in agriculture

DEFINITIONS & CONCEPTS

You should be able to define the following terms and concepts:

the agricultural (farm) problem
Engel's law
deficiency payments
offers to purchase
market quotas

18

ECONOMICS OF AGRICULTURE

Concepts, Definitions & Problems

Problem 18-1

Briefly discuss the importance of agriculture in an economy.

Requirement and Clue: *Consider what an economy would be like without an agricultural sector. Pay attention to the word "briefly".*

Solution:

There is a good reason that most countries single out agriculture for special treatment. After all, this is the sector that produces food for the population. As the population grows, more food is needed. A country that relies very heavily on imported is obviously in a very vulnerable position. Agriculture is therefore an important economic activity. It provides employment directly to a large number of people, and indirectly to millions more who work in related fields such as transportation, marketing, and the processing of agricultural products.

The importance of agriculture can be appreciated if we consider the effects of floods, insects, hurricanes and other factors that severely limit the economy's agricultural production. Food prices rise drastically, thousands are thrown out of work, and starvation looms in many cases. In many countries, agriculture occupies a significant part of the gross domestic product (GDP), and even in countries where the share of agriculture in GDP is relatively small, the agricultural sector is still important because that's where we get our food.

In some countries, exports of agricultural products earn valuable foreign exchange for the countries. Through trade in agricultural products, such countries can import those items which they cannot themselves produce or which they can produce only with relatively huge amounts of resources. Indeed, agriculture plays an important role in an economy.

Problem 18-2

Briefly describe the agri-food industry.

Requirement and Clue: *You are required to state what the agri-food industry entails, giving examples to illustrate the meaning of agri-food industry.*

Basically, agriculture involves growing food. An industry that is directly and closely related to agriculture has emerged. This is the agri-food industry. The agri-food industry includes, in addition to primary agriculture, such activities as food processing, food services, beverage and proce3ssed exports and imp[orts related to food.

Problem 18-3

Discuss some of the problems that agriculture faces.

Requirement and Clue: *Focus on some peculiarities of agriculture that manufacturing, for example, may not have.*

Solution:

One of the major problems facing agriculture is the wide fluctuation in the prices of farm products and in the incomes of farmers. It is not very difficult to find a reason for the fluctuations in farmers' incomes. A fall in the price of farm products does not cause people to increase their purchases of these products substantially. Similarly, an increase in the price of farm products does not cause people to reduce their purchases of these products substantially. In other words, the demand for farm products is inelastic. Because of this, an increase in the supply of farm products caused perhaps by favourable weather, results in a significant fall in price. And since the lower price does not stimulate a corresponding increase in purchases, farmers' incomes decline.

On the other hand, if supply falls, other things being equal, the price will rise. But because the demand for agricultural products is inelastic, the rise in price is significant. The increase in price does not cause the quantity demanded to fall significantly because the demand is inelastic. This causes the incomes of farmers to increase. The supply of particular farm products is subject to severe fluctuations from year to year because of weather, diseases, insects, floods, and a host of other factors quite beyond the control of the farmer.

Another problem that farmers face is that as total income in the economy increases, the demand for farm products does not increase as fast as the demand for other products. As income increases, a smaller proportion is spent is spent on food—for there is obviously a limit to the amount of food that people can eat! Thus, farmers tend not to benefit as much from economic prosperity.

Problem 18-4

Use an appropriate diagram to show that a large increase in farm productivity may result in reduced incomes of farmers.

Requirement and Clue: *A supply/demand graph will suffice. Focus on the nature of the demand curve for farm products.*

Solution:

The following diagram shows the demand and supply curves for farm products.

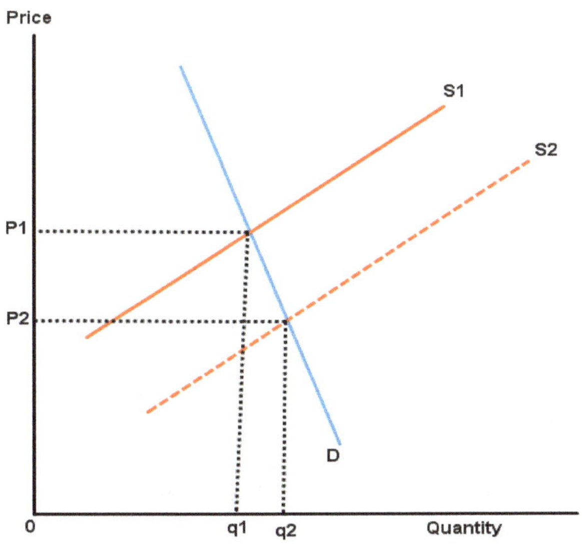

The demand for farm products is quite inelastic as shown in the diagram by the relatively steep demand curve D. The original supply curve is S1. The initial equilibrium price and quantity are P1 and q_1 respectively.

Now suppose that the supply of farm products increases from S1 to S2 as shown in the diagram. This increase in supply causes the price to fall from P1 to P2. At the same time, the quantity rises only slightly from q1 to q2. The substantial fall in price does not stimulate a corresponding increase in quantity and as a result, farmers' incomes fall.

An arithmetic example will illustrate the point. Suppose the initial equilibrium price and quantity are \$7 and 4,000 units respectively. Total revenue for the farmers will be (\$7 × 4000) = \$28,000. Now, suppose the increase in supply causes the equilibrium price to fall to \$4 and the equilibrium quantity to increase to only 5,000. The total revenue for the farmers would be (\$4 × 5000) = \$20,000. Farmers' income would fall by \$8,000.

Problem 18-5

What is Engel's law? What is the relationship of this law to the incomes of farmers?

Requirement and Clue: *This is a two-part problem. Solve each part in order. The first part of the problem is definitional. You are required to give a clear and precise statement of Engel's law. For the second part of the problem, focus on the income elasticity of demand for farm products.*

Solution:

Engel's law states that as income rises, the percentage spent on food declines. Because farm products have a low income elasticity of demand, income from farm operations does not increase as fast as total income does.

Problem 18-6

The price elasticity of demand for farm products has been estimated to be about 0.2. What light does this information throw on the farm problem?

Requirement and Clue: *Focus on the meaning of a price elasticity of demand of 0.2 and on the farm problem.*

Solution:

The demand for farm products is price inelastic. Now the problem states that the elasticity coefficient is 0.2. This means that a 10a5 fall in the prices of farm products results in only a 2% increase in the quantity of farm products demanded. In order to induce a 10% increase in consumer purchases of farm products, the prices of farm products would have to fall by 50%. Clearly, this is a colossal problem for farmers.

Problem 18-7

The following schedule shows the demand for grain.

Price per ton	Quantity demanded (000 000 tons)
$3.00	5.0
2.80	5.5
2.60	6.0
2.40	6.5
2.20	7.0
2.00	7.5
1.80	8.0
1.60	8.5
1.40	9.0
1.20	9.5
1.00	10.0
0.80	10.5
0.60	11.0
0.40	11.5
0.20	12.0

(a) *Assume that farmers grow 9.5 million tons of grain, regardless of the price of grain. Show the supply schedule in a column to the right of the demand schedule.*

(b) *What price will farmers get for their grain?*

(c) *Calculate the total revenue of farmers from grain.*

(d) *Assume now that the supply of grain increases to 11.5 million tons, show the new supply schedule.*

(e) *What price will farmers now get for their grain?*

(f) *Calculate the total revenue of farmers at this new price.*

Requirement and Clue: *This problem has multiple parts. Answer each part in order. The problem involves basic market demand/supply analysis.*

Solution:

The quantity supplied at each and every price is 9.5 million tons as shown in the third column of the table below. The first and third columns represent the supply schedule.

Price (per ton)	Quantity demanded (10^6 tons)	Quantity supplied (10^6 tons)	New Quantity supplied (10^6 tons)
$3.00	5.0	9.5	11.5
2.80	5.5	9.5	11.5
2.60	6.0	9.5	11.5
2.40	6.5	9.5	11.5
2.20	7.0	9.5	11.5
2.00	7.5	9.5	11.5
1.80	8.0	9.5	11.5
1.60	8.5	9.5	11.5
1.40	9.0	9.5	11.5
1.20	9.5	9.5	11.5
1.00	10.0	9.5	11.5
0.80	10.5	9.5	11.5
0.60	11.0	9.5	11.5
0.40	11.5	9.5	11.5
0.20	12.0	9.5	11.5

(a) The price that farmers will get is the price at which quantity demanded and quantity supplied are equal. In this case, that price is **$1.20**.

(b) Total revenue is price × quantity. That is, ($1.20 × 9.5) million = **$11.4 million.**

(c) See column 4 in the table above.

(d) Farmers will now get a price of **$0.40** for their grain. This is the price at which quantity demanded and quantity supplied are equal.

(e) The total revenue of farmers will now be $0.40 × 11.5) = **$4.6 million.**

Problem 18-8

Explain how a price support program will benefit farmers.

Requirement and Clue: *It would be useful to define a price support program. Focus on the effect of a price support program on the price and quantity of farm products.*

Solution:

A price support program is a system whereby the government sets the prices of certain farm products so that they do not fall below a certain level. The following diagram will help to illustrate how a price support program will benefit farmers.

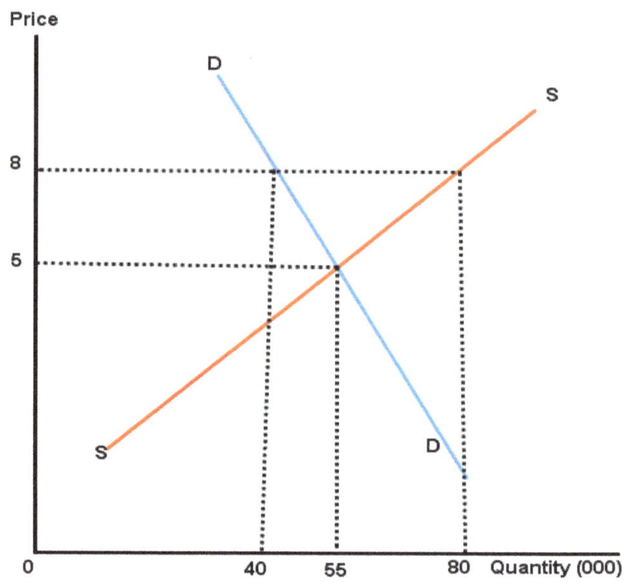

Suppose the government wants to support the price of a certain agricultural product. The initial demand and supply curves are DD and SS respectively. The equilibrium price and quantity are $5 and 55,000 units respectively. Suppose now that the government sets a price of $8. At this price, consumers are willing to buy only 40,000 units of the product, while producers are willing to offer 80,000 units for sale. There will therefore be a surplus of 40,000 units (80,000 – 40,000). At a price of $8, the value of the surplus is $320,000.

Clearly, if a program of price supports is initiated, the farmers gain. In the absence of the price-support program, they would produce 55,000 units at a price of $5, and receive a total revenue of

$275,000, that is (55,000 × $5). With the price support program, they produce 80,000 units at a price of $8, and receive a total revenue of $640,000, that is (80,000 × $8). The price support increases the farmers' revenue by $365,000 ($640,000 – $275,000).

Problem 18-9

Briefly discuss direct income subsidies as a means of helping farmers.

Requirement and Clue: *A definition of direct income subsidies should be provided. Focus on the advantages and disadvantages of income subsidies.*

Solution:

Direct income subsidies are monies given to farmers to augment their incomes from agriculture. Under this scheme, the determination of prices for agricultural products would be left entirely up to the market. The advantage of direct income subsidies is that the market is allowed to work, eliminating surpluses and shortages. One disadvantage of income subsidies is the difficulty of determining the criteria on which to base the subsidy.

Problem 18-10

Discuss market quotas as a solution to the agricultural problem.

Requirement and Clue: *Clearly, you must know what market quotas are and you should show some familiarity with the agricultural problem. Include any problems with this scheme in your discussion.*

Solution:

The agricultural problem relates to the wide fluctuations in the prices of farm products and in the incomes of farmers. The setting of market quotas is one way of dealing with this problem. A market quota is a limit placed on the amount of a crop that farmers can produce. It is a way of controlling the price by restricting supply. Under a quota system, each producer is given a prescribed number of marketing certificates for each product. Thus, a producer who has 50 certificates for peas can sell only 50 units of peas. In this way, the supply of any particular farm product is controlled. Price fluctuations can therefore be greatly reduced. Two major problems are encountered with the use of this policy. First, the direct restriction of output in order to raise the price of the product may be socially undesirable. Second, farmers have shown a strong tendency to resist this type of control.

Problem 18-11

Which of these policies—price supports, income subsidies to farmers, or market quotas—is best from the consumers' point of view, assuming that the tax burden is equal in all cases?

Requirement and Clue: *Familiarity with each policy is essential. Focus on the effect of each policy on consumers.*

Solution:

A price support is a price that is set above the market equilibrium in an attempt to assist producers. Income subsidies are monies given to farmers to augment their incomes from agriculture. Market quotas are limits placed on the amount of a crop that farmers are allowed to produce. Price supports result in higher prices for consumers. Market quotas result in both fewer farm products and higher unit prices. Subsidies, on the other hand, allow consumers to have more agricultural products at lower unit prices. Therefore, from the consumers' point of view, subsidies to farmers are better than either of the other two policies.

Problem 18-12

Comment on the following statement:

"Food is a necessity, and its demand is inelastic. On this basis, economic theory predicts that farmers can increase their revenues by raising their prices. The fact that farmers have relatively low incomes is something that economic theory just cannot explain."

Requirement and Clue: *Read the statement carefully, looking out for any errors in concepts, ideas, etc. Focus on whether economic theory can explain the relatively low incomes of farmers.*

Solution:

Economic theory can easily explain the relatively low incomes of farmers. Because the demand for farm products is inelastic, an increase in the supply of farm products results in a relatively large fall in prices which causes farm income to decline. Moreover, the income elasticity of demand for farm products is relatively low, hence, when total income in the economy rises, the demand for farm products increases by a smaller proportion. This means that farmers do not benefit much from general economic prosperity. Contrary to the statement given, economic theory is well able to explain the relatively low incomes of farmers.

Problem 18-13

Briefly describe each of the following terms with reference to agriculture:

(a) *Income elasticity*
(b) *Surplus*
(c) *Price supports*

Requirement and Clue: *This problem is largely definitional. Give a clear and precise meaning of each of the concepts. It is important to relate the concepts to agriculture.*

Solution:

(a) Income elasticity (of demand) is the extent to which quantity demanded responds to a small change in income. With reference to agriculture, income elasticity tells how much the quantity of agricultural products demanded will change as a result of small changes in the prices of agricultural products. If income rises by 10%, and the demand for agricultural products rises by only 3%, then the income elasticity of demand for agricultural will be defined as being low.

(b) A surplus exists when, at some particular price, the quantity demanded of an item is less than the quantity supplied. The operation of a free market system will eliminate surpluses. With reference to agriculture, government policy to assist farmers may result in a surplus of agricultural products on the market.

(c) A price support is a price that is set above the market equilibrium in an attempt to assist producers. With reference to agriculture, the producers are farmers. The government guarantees that they will be able to sell their products at the set price. This often means that the government buys up any surplus resulting from the set price.

Problem 18-14

One way of assisting farmers is to increase the demand for farm products. What are some ways whereby a government can help to increase the demand for farm products?

Requirement and Clue: *Think of policies that a government can implement that would increase the demand for food.*

Solution:

The following are some ways whereby a government can increase the demand for farm products. First, the government can subsidize the incomes of low-income earners who spend a large portion of their incomes on food. Second, the government can purchase large quantities of farm products for distribution to qualified consumers. A food stamp program is an example of such a plan. Third, a government can remove taxes from food items, making it cheaper for consumers to purchase food. Fourth, the government can launch advertising campaigns that encourage the use of agricultural products. Fifth, the government can support industries that use agricultural products as inputs. Finally, through research, the government can find alternative uses for agricultural products. All these are ways whereby a government can help to increase the demand for farm products.

Problem 18-15

Describe some ways in which agriculture differs from manufacturing industries.

Requirement and Clue: *Agriculture has different properties that distinguish it from manufacturing industries. Focus on these special properties.*

Solution:

The following are some ways in which agriculture differs from manufacturing industries. First, food is an absolute necessity. Without it, we die. Thus the demand for food is very highly inelastic compared with the demand for almost any other product. If the price of a manufactured product such as an electric kettle or a guitar changes, the quantity demanded is likely to change noticeably. That is not the case with food whose demand is highly inelastic. Second, the demand for food has a relatively low income elasticity. When income rises, the demand for most manufactured goods rises to some noticeable degree. In the case of food, when income rises, the demand for food hardly increases at all. Third, it is relatively easy for manufacturing industries to respond to changes in price. Not so with agriculture. When the prices of agricultural products rise, farmers cannot easily increase the quantity supplied in the short run. Fourth, agricultural output is subject to wide fluctuations because of weather conditions and seasonal factors that are beyond the control of farmers. Manufacturing industries don't suffer from these drawbacks.

Problem 18-16

Show that a bumper crop might reduce farmers' incomes.

Requirement and Clue: *Focus on the price elasticity of demand. A diagram would be helpful here.*

Solution:

A bumper crop is an unusually large crop. It can be seen as a huge increase in the supply of some particular farm product. The demand for farm products is highly inelastic as shown as DD in the following diagram.

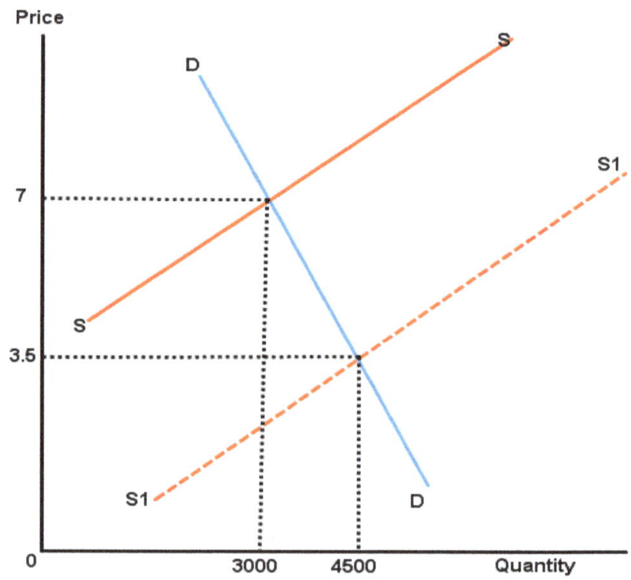

The initial supply is represented by the supply curve SS in the diagram. The market for this product is in equilibrium at a price of \$7 and a quantity of 3000 units. The bumper crop shifts the supply curve from SS to S1S1 as shown in the diagram. As a result of the low price elasticity of demand for this product, the price falls significantly from \$7 to \$3.50 and the quantity increases from 3,000 to 4,500. Before the bumper crop, the farmer's income was (\$7 × 3000) = \$21,000. Now with the bumper crop, farmer's income is (\$3.5 × 4,500) = \$15,750. Thus, because of the bumper crop, the farmer's income fell by (\$21,000 – \$15,750) = 5,250.

Multiple-Choice

In each case, circle the letter that corresponds with the correct answer.

1. The agricultural sector is especially important because:

a. it is the most difficult to manage
b. all the farms are owned by people living below the poverty line
c. it produces food for the population
d. it is the largest of all the economic sectors.

Answer: c

Reason: *Without food, the population cannot survive.*

2. As a general rule, as an economy develops, the share of agriculture in total output tends to:

a. decline
b. increase
c. remain constant
d. grow exponentially

Answer: a

Reason: *During the early stages of development, agriculture tends to be dominant. As development proceeds, other industries develop, and they tend to reduce the share of agriculture in total production.*

3. As a general rule, as an economy develops, the proportion of the labour force employed in agriculture tends to:

a. decline
b. increase
c. remain constant
d. grow exponentially

Answer: a

Reason: *As development proceeds, new industries such as manufacturing and service industries develop and draw labour away from agriculture. Also, the use of machines in agriculture tends to free up labour for other industries.*

4. Which of the following is correct?

a. Agriculture is the largest industry in most advanced economies
b. In all countries, the agricultural sector is the largest employer, by far
c. International law prevents international trade in agricultural products
d. None of the above

Answer: d

Reason: *Choices a, b, and c are all incorrect, leaving d and the correct choice.*

5. The farm problem refers to:

a. the excessively high incomes earned by farmers for little or no work
b. stable farm prices during economic fluctuations
c. wide fluctuations in the prices of farm products and in the incomes of farmers
d. none of the above

Answer: c

Reason: *Farm prices and incomes fluctuate widely from year to year.*

6. The demand for farm products is:

a. very elastic
b. perfectly elastic
c. highly inelastic
d. none of the above

Answer: c

Reason: *Because food is a necessity, a small increase in price will not result in a huge fall in quantity demanded. A small fall in price will not cause people to buy a great deal more food.*

7. The prices of agricultural products tend to be:

a. very predictable from year to year
b. uncertain because of wide fluctuations
c. set by farmers with no regard for demand
d. none of the above

Answer: b

Reason: *Farm prices tend to fluctuate widely from year to year.*

8. If the demand for agricultural products is inelastic, an increase in supply will cause:

a. a relatively small increase in the prices of farm products and farm incomes
b. a relatively small increase in the prices of farm products and a relatively large increase in farm incomes
c. a relatively large decrease in the prices of farm products and farm incomes
d. a relatively large increase in the prices of farm products and a relatively small increase in farm incomes.

Answer: c

Reason: *The resulting fall in price is so huge that it reduces farm revenue.*

9. Engel's law states that:

a. farm products have an inelastic demand
b. the percentage of income spent on food declines as income increases
c. farm products have a high income elasticity of demand
d. farm products are inferior goods.

Answer: b

Reason: The law implies that as income rises, expenditure on food does not keep pace with the increase in income.

10. Price supports:

a. can result in surpluses that the government buys
b. often result in shortages which drive the price up even higher
c. benefit consumers of farm products more than producers of farm products
d. benefit consumers and producers to the same extent.

Answer: a

Reason: *Because the support price is set above the equilibrium price, the quantity supplied exceeds the quantity demanded at that price, leading to a surplus.*

11. Payment of income subsidies to farmers:

a. prevents the market mechanism from working
b. results in surpluses which the government must buy
c. forces farmers to restrict their output
d. leaves the prices of agricultural products to be determined by the market.

Answer: d

Reason: *Income subsidies allow the market to work and then the government tweaks the market results to obtain the desired outcome.*

12. Market quotas:

a. always result in surpluses
b. result in lower prices for consumers
c. result in higher prices of farm products
d. none of the above

Answer: c

Reason: *Setting market quotas is a way of restricting output in order to raise price.*

True-False

Determine whether each of the following statements is true or false.

1. As an economy develops, the share of agriculture in total output tends to increase.

Answer: False

Explanation: *The share of agriculture tends to decline as other industries develop.*

2. As economic growth proceeds, the proportion of the labour force employed in agriculture tends to decline.

Answer: True

3. The price elasticity of demand for farm products is greater than 2 (demand is elastic); hence the prices of farm products and farm incomes are quite stable.

Answer: False

Explanation: *The demand for farm products is inelastic and farm prices and farm incomes fluctuate considerably.*

4. A relatively small increase in the supply of agricultural products will result in a relatively large decrease in the prices of farm products and farm incomes because the demand for agricultural products is inelastic.

Answer: True

5. The farm problem refers to declining prices of farm products and farm incomes, and low farm incomes in relation to other incomes.

Answer: True

6. Engel's law states that as income increases, the percentage spent on food will diminish.

Answer: True

7. According to Engel's law, as people's incomes increase, they will spend less on food.

Answer: False

Explanation: *The law states that as incomes increase, people will spend a smaller percentage of their incomes on food. They could buy more food even though the percentage spent declines.*

8. Price supports for farm products increase the allocative efficiency of the market mechanism.

Answer: False

Explanation: *Price supports establish prices other than those determined by the market.*

9. Income subsidies to farmers result in surpluses because they cause high prices for farm products. These high prices in turn reduce the demand for farm products.

Answer: False

Explanation: *Income subsidies do not cause surpluses because the market is allowed to work, and it eliminates surpluses. Note also that high prices will reduce quantity demanded, not demand.*

10. Market quotas restrict output in order to cause economic scarcity. This scarcity results in high prices.

Answer: True

11. A price-support program should be avoided if the demand for the product is elastic with respect to price.

Answer: True

12. The use of a deficiency-payment system should be avoided if the demand for the product is inelastic with respect to price.

Answer: True

Completion

(Fill in the blanks)

Use each word or combination of words from the list exactly once.
*(**Hint**: Proceed by elimination)*

Word list

Decreases — Law — Food — Unstable — Inelastic x 2 — Fall — Engel's — Surplus — Allows — Reduce

Questions

1. It can be stated as a general rule that as an economy develops, the share of agriculture in total output ___________ [increases, decreases]
2. The agricultural sector is important in any economy because it provides ___________ for the population.
3. Farm prices and farm incomes tend to be ___________ [stable, unstable].
4. In terms of price elasticity of demand, the demand for farm products is ___________.
5. In terms of price elasticity of supply, the supply of farm products will likely be ___________.
6. If the supply of farm products increases, prices of farm products will tend to ___________ [rise, fall] substantially.
7. According to ___________ ___________, farm products have a low income elasticity of demand.
8. Price supports result in a ___________ which the government must buy.
9. The payment of subsidies ___________ ___________ [allows, does not allow] prices to be determined by demand and supply.
10. Market quotas tend to ___________ [increase, reduce] fluctuations in the prices of farm products.

Solution

1. (Decreases)
2. (Food)
3. (Unstable)
4. (Inelastic)
5. (Inelastic)
6. (Fall)
7. (Engel's Law)
8. (Surplus)
9. (Allows)
10. (Reduce)

19 PUBLIC FINANCE

SYNOPSIS

Through its powers to spend and to tax, the government exerts significant influence on the economy. **Public finance** is that branch of economics that studies government spending and taxation. Government expenditure has grown significantly over the past several years. Government expenditures include purchases of goods and services by the government, and government **transfer payments.**

Wagner's law states that government spending would rise faster than total spending. The experiences of many countries support Wagner's law. The rate of growth of government spending has consistently exceeded that of total spending.

Government expenditure has grown partly because of increasing government responsibilities, partly because of inflation, and partly because of population growth. Large expenditure items include social services, protection of persons and property, health, and education.

Taxation is the main source of revenue for the government. The benefit principle of taxation states that the amount of taxes people pay should be proportional to the benefits they receive. The ability-to-pay principle of taxation states that people should be taxed according to their ability to pay.

A **progressive tax system** is one where the percentage of income paid in taxes increases as income increases. A **proportional tax system** is one where the percentage of income paid in taxes remains constant as income increases. A **regressive tax system** is one where the percentage of income paid in taxes decreases as income increases.

The **Laffer curve** shows the relationship between tax rate and tax revenue. As the tax rate increases, tax revenue increases. After a while, however, further increases in the tax rate discourage economic activity and thus lower tax revenue. The optimum tax rate is that rate that maximizes tax revenue.

The economic effects of a tax depend on the type of tax. Sales and excise taxes tend to increase income inequality, reduce consumption and production, and alter resource allocation. High corporate income taxes may impede economic growth. Personal income taxes, being progressive, reduce income inequality, but they may also reduce work incentive.

LEARNING OBJECTIVES

In connection with this module, you should be able to:

1. explain the growth in government expenditure
2. discuss the role of government in society
3. discuss the expenditures of various levels of government
4. discuss sources of government revenue
5. distinguish between different taxation systems
6. explain the Laffer curve
7. analyze the effects of taxes

DEFINITIONS & CONCEPTS

You should be able to define the following terms and concepts:

public finance	transfer payments
Wagner's law	tax
personal income tax	benefit principle
corporation tax	ability-to-pay principle
consumption tax	sales tax
progressive tax	proportional tax
regressive tax	excise tax
Laffer curve	property tax
Incidence (of a tax)	goods and services tax

19

PUBLIC FINANCE

Concepts, Definitions & Problems

Problem 19-1

What is public finance and why is public finance an important area of study in economics?

Requirement and Clue: *This is a two-part problem. Answer each part in order. The first part of the problem is definitional. State clearly the meaning of the concept. For the second part of the problem, focus on the role of government in an economy.*

Solution:

Public finance is the study of government behaviour in the areas of spending and taxation. The government provides a wide variety of services to the population. The government pays for these services via taxation. That is the subject of public finance.

Government spending exerts a significant impact on the economic life of the country. A student of economics should have some idea of the spending activities of the government in order to understand certain aspects of the operation of the economy. In a free enterprise economic system, the government protects individual freedom, enforces contracts, and implements policies that improve the operation of the economy. Also, the government provides education, health services, and protection of persons and property. Taxation also affects the economy both directly and indirectly. For example, a tax on income affects people's spending, and a tax on certain products affects both the quantities demanded and supplied. Public finance is clearly an important area of economic study.

Problem 19-2

Briefly discuss four items of major government expenditure?

Requirement and Clue: *Focus on government activities and don't forget to be brief.*

Solution:

Four items on which the government spends a considerable amount of money are: social services, health, education, and national security.

Social services

Social services are services designed to improve the quality of life of people in the society. These services include, among others: child care and protection, housing, financial support, community development, transportation, and long-term adult care.

Health care

Health care has grown to be a very expensive item in the government's budget. This is especially the case in an aging population. It is generally agreed that the government should assume some responsibility for providing health services, especially to the needy.

Education:

Education is considered to be a public good, and as such, it is generally accepted that the government should contribute to the education of the population.

National security:

Like education and sanitation and health services, national security is a public good. Most people would agree that police protection and national defence are necessary and should be provided by the government and paid for out of taxation.

Problem 19-3

Distinguish between government purchases of goods and services and government transfer payments.

Requirement and Clue: *Your solution should emphasize the difference between the two concepts. Examples should be used to distinguish one from the other.*

Solution:

Government purchases of goods and services refer to government expenditure on goods and services. Examples of government purchases of goods and services include payment for uniforms, food, and office furniture and supplies. Government transfer payments on the other hand, do not represent payment for goods and services but transfers of purchasing power from one group to another. Examples of government transfer payments are family allowances, old age security payments, and government subsidies. These payments represent income to the recipients, but they do not represent payments for goods produced or services rendered.

Problem 19-4

State Wagner's law. How can one determine whether or not Wagner's law applies to a particular country?

Requirement and Clue: *This is a two-part problem. Answer each part in order. For the second part of the problem, think of the situation that would have to exist to make Wagner's law valid.*

Solution:

Wagner's law states that the rate of increase in government spending would eventually outstrip the rate of growth of total spending on goods and services. This would be due to the increasing complexity of government activity, thus making government spending more expensive.

The applicability of Wagner's law to any particular economy can be determined by taking growth rates in government spending for a recent period of years and comparing them with the rate of growth of total spending for the same period.

Problem 19-5

Discuss possible reasons for the growth in government spending over time.

Requirement and Clue: *Focus on possible changes in the economy that can have an impact on government spending.*

Solution:

Several factors are responsible for the growth of government spending over the years. Among them are increasing government responsibilities for certain services, inflation, and population growth.

Increasing responsibilities

The government has assumed increasing responsibility for providing certain services such as health care, education, and social services. Total expenditure on these items has increased significantly over the years.

Inflation

Relatively rapid rates of price increases over the years mean that the government has had to pay higher prices for the goods and services that it purchases. Also wages and salaries have risen substantially over the years, and this means that the government must pay more to civil servants and other government employees for their services.

Population growth

An important factor in the growth of government spending is the increase in population. Obviously, we can expect the government's budget to increase as population increases, because there will be a larger number of people for whom services must be provided. Also, as the population ages, there are increasingly more people who depend on government for financial assistance, and this implies an increase in government spending.

Problem 19-6

Government expenditure is tied to its role in the economy. Discuss the role of government in a modern economy.

Requirement and Clue: *Focus on the services that the government provides and on its regulatory activities.*

Solution:

It is generally agreed that it is the responsibility of the government to provide the services that would not be profitable for private firms and individuals to provide but that are socially desirable. It is also generally agreed that the government should engage in those activities where government is more efficient than private enterprises. Thus, the provision of law and order and the protection of persons and property are considered the province of government.

It is now an accepted view that education benefits the society and not just the individual who receives that education. Hence, most people would probably agree that the government should provide at least elementary and secondary education out of the public purse. In many instances, the government pays for elementary and secondary education, and it subsidizes college and university education quite heavily.

It is also considered desirable for the government to provide sanitation and health services and social welfare services. Such services, it is felt, should not be left in the hands of private enterprise. It is also believed that it should be the responsibility of the government to build and maintain water supply systems, roads, and sewage systems.

Finally, the government does play an important role in the efficient operation of the economy. It may play this role by regulating certain industries, by using its power to impose taxes, and by conducting fiscal and monetary policies.

Problem 19-7

What impact would you expect an aging population to have on government expenditure?

Requirement and Clue: *Focus on the implications of an aging population on government programs.*

Solution:

A significant portion of government spending is allocated to social service programs, including old age security payments. As the population ages, one expects expenditure for this function to increase. Government pension plans also provide benefits to persons who have reached retirement age. In addition, expenditure on health services is likely to rise with an aging population.

Problem 19-8

What is a tax? List some desirable properties of a tax.

Requirement and Clue: *This is a two-part problem. Answer each part in order. The first part of the problem requires a clear and precise statement of the meaning of a tax. The second part requires only a listing of desirable properties of a tax. A list of four properties should suffice. No discussion is called for.*

Solution:

A tax is a compulsory payment levied by a government to pay for goods and services provided for the benefit of the community.

The following are some desirable properties of a tax.

1. A tax should yield adequate revenue.
2. A tax should be perceived as being fair.
3. A tax should not impede the operation of the market system.
4. A tax should be as convenient as possible to pay.
5. A tax should be simple enough to be understood by taxpayers.

Problem 19-9

Discuss the two main criteria for assessing the equity of a tax.

Requirement and Clue: *The problem is a test of your knowledge of the criteria for equity or fairness of a tax. Therefore, you should state the principles and comment on each one.*

Solution:

The two main criteria for assessing the equity of a tax are the benefit principle and the ability to pay principle. The benefit principle states that the tax paid should be proportional to the benefit received. This implies that if citizen A benefits more than citizen B from the provision of a certain service, then citizen A should be taxed more for the service. This criterion faces the problem posed by determining the amount of benefit received by each person from any particular service. It may also be difficult to identify which groups benefit. For example, a playground or a park obviously benefits those who use the facilities, but it also benefits other residents who do not like the noise of children playing in the streets, or who have no patience for the accidents—like broken windows—caused by children playing in inappropriate places.

The ability to pay principle states that people in similar circumstances should be affected similarly by the tax. This criterion implies also that high-income earners should pay more than low-income earners. That is, taxpayers should be taxed according to their abilities to pay. Using this criterion, an income tax is equitable if people with similar incomes and exemptions are taxed similarly. One problem with this criterion is the difficulty of determining whether or not people are in similar economic circumstances. For example, it may not be accurate to conclude that people with similar incomes and exemptions are in similar circumstances. Moreover, some forms of incomes are not easily identified.

Problem 19-10

Describe each of the following types of taxes:

(a) *Progressive tax*
(b) *Proportional tax*
(c) *Progressive tax*

Requirement and Clue: *Your description of each type of tax should be clear and precise.*

Solution:

(a) A progressive tax is one for which the percentage of income paid in taxes increase as income rises. Thus a progressive tax claims a higher percentage from high-income earners. If income doubles, the amount paid in taxes more than doubles.

(b) A proportional tax is one for which the percentage of income paid in taxes remains constant as income increases. An example of proportional tax is a property tax. If the property tax is 1.5% of the value of the property, then regardless of the value of the property, the tax rate will remain the same. The tax on a property valued at $40,000 will be $600 while the tax on a property valued at $150,000 will be $2250.

(c) A tax is said to be regressive if the percentage of income paid in taxes decreases as income increases. A tax of $10 imposed on each passenger who boards an aircraft is regressive. For passengers with incomes of $100 per week, the tax represents 10% of their income. For passengers with incomes of $200 per week, the tax paid is only 5% of their income.

Problem 19-11

Use tables and graphs to illustrate the difference among progressive, proportional, and regressive taxes.

Requirement and Clue: *You could construct a table with various income levels and then show the tax and tax rate that would be associated with each tax level for a progressive, proportional, and regressive tax. Don't forget to use graphs also.*

Solution:

With a progressive tax, the percentage of income paid in taxes increases as income rises. With a proportional tax, the percentage of income paid in taxes remains constant as income rises. With a regressive tax, the percentage of income decreases as income rises. The following table illustrates the difference among progressive, proportional, and regressive tax.

	Progressive		Proportional		Regressive	
Income ($)	Tax ($)	Rate (%)	Tax ($)	Rate (%)	Tax ($)	Rate (%)
100	10	10	10	10	10	10.0
200	24	12	20	10	18	9.0
300	42	14	30	10	24	8.0
400	64	16	40	10	28	7.0
500	90	18	50	10	30	6.0
600	120	20	60	10	33	5.3

Progressive, proportional, and regressive taxes are illustrated in the following graph.

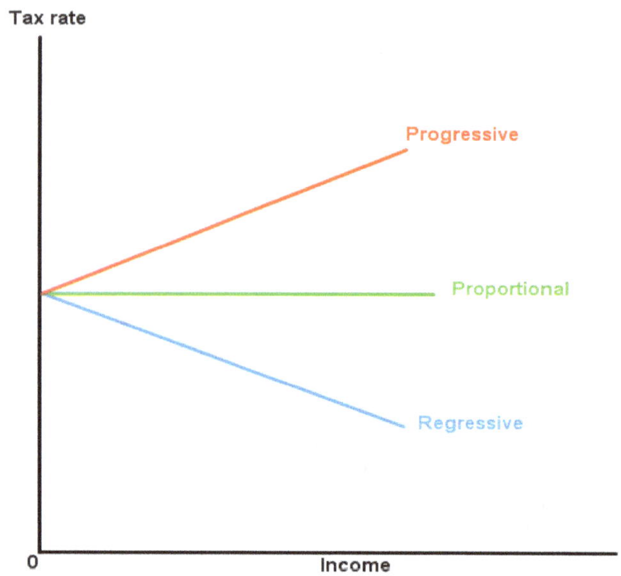

Problem 19-12

Define:

(a) *The Laffer curve*

(b) *Optimum tax rate (for a revenue tax).*

Requirement and Clue: *This is a definitional problem. Give a clear and precise meaning of each of the concepts.*

Solution:

(a) The Laffer curve is a curve that shows the relationship between total tax revenue and the tax rate. Specifically, the curve shows that as the tax rate increases, tax revenue will increase, but as the tax rate continues to rise, tax revenue will eventually decline.

(b) The optimum tax rate (for a revenue tax) is the rate that maximizes tax revenue. A higher or lower rate will lower tax revenue.

Problem 19-13

"A government can always raise additional tax revenues by simply raising the tax rate." Comment on this statement.

Requirement and Clue: *You are to determine whether or not the statement is true or false and defend your position. Focus on the effect of continually rising tax rates.*

Solution:

The effect of increasing the tax rate depends on the effect of the higher tax rate on economic activity and hence on income. If the increase in the tax rate does not result in a corresponding decrease in economic activity and income, then tax revenues will increase. If, however, the increase in the tax rate acts as a disincentive to work, then total income may fall to the extent that the higher rate yields a lower—rather than a higher—tax revenue.

Problem 19-14

What are the advantages and disadvantages of the personal income tax?

Requirement and Clue: *The problem assumes that you are familiar with the personal income tax. Start with a brief definition and then focus on those aspects of the tax that are considered to be desirable. Think of what may be undesirable about the tax.*

Solution:

Personal income tax is a tax that is imposed on individuals' incomes. The personal income tax has certain advantages and disadvantages.

The personal income tax has certain obviously desirable characteristics. It produces a fairly adequate and dependable revenue. It is relatively fair in the sense that people with equal incomes and deductions pay the same amount of tax. Tax deductions by the employer make the personal income tax convenient. It is relatively easy to collect. And in most cases, even though the actual calculations may present some difficulty, it is sufficiently simple for most taxpayers to understand the basic principle.

The personal income tax also has some defects. Various loopholes make tax avoidance possible, and many people feel that high-income earners are most able to take advantage of tax avoidance. A second disadvantage of the personal income tax is that it may be so progressive that it discourages individuals from earning extra income and so restricts economic activity.

Problem 19-15

What criticisms have been made against the corporate income tax?

Requirement and Clue: *A definition of the corporate income tax is relevant here. You are expected to be able to reproduce the arguments that have been raised against the corporate income tax.*

Solution:

A corporate income tax is a tax imposed on the profits of corporations.

One criticism against the corporate income tax is that it discourages new investment by firms, and may thus slow down economic activity. It is also argued that the corporate income tax represents a double taxation of income since the profit of the corporation is taxed and the income of the shareholders is taxed again when it is distributed to them as dividends. A third criticism that has been made against the corporate income tax is that it is passed on to consumers in the form of higher prices for goods and services.

Problem 19-16

What is a consumption tax? What are its advantages and disadvantages?

Requirement and Clue: *This is a two-part problem. Answer each part in order. State clearly and precisely what a consumption tax is. Focus on the properties of a good tax and try to apply them to the consumption tax.*

Solution:

A consumption tax is a tax imposed on consumer goods and services. It includes excise tax and sales tax. An excise tax is a tax levied on a specific commodity, while a sales tax is a tax levied on broad groups of goods and services. Excise taxes are levied, for example, on gasoline and tobacco products.

Consumption taxes produce a dependable revenue. They are convenient to collect (the consumer pays them at the time of purchase since they are added to the price of the product. The only way for the taxpayer to avoid these taxes is to refrain from purchasing the goods and services on which the tax is levied. The major disadvantage of these taxes is that they tend to be regressive. For example, although the sales tax is expressed as a given percentage of total purchases, high income earners will pay a smaller percentage of their income in sales taxes than low income earners will.

Problem 19-17

Discuss the economic effects of taxes.

Requirement and Clue: *Since different taxes have different effects, it is well to examine the effects of different taxes. Focus on the effects of these taxes on prices, resource allocation, business investment, etc.*

Solution:

Sales taxes and excise taxes tend to take a larger percentage of the incomes of low-income earners and hence to increase income inequality. Also, because these taxes are consumption taxes, they tend to reduce consumption (and hence production) of goods on which the taxes are levied. Resources will tend to shift away from industries producing the taxed goods and into other industries. Hence, these taxes affect resources allocation.

Sales and excise taxes definitely result in higher prices for the consumer. But there is little agreement on the extent to which firms are able to shift the incidence of corporate income taxes onto consumers in the form of higher prices. The effect of corporate income taxes on prices, however, is not expected to be significant. But high corporate income taxes do restrict business expansion, and impede economic growth.

If personal income tax is progressive, it will tend to reduce income inequality. This is so because, other things being equal, high-income groups are taxed more heavily than low-income groups. If the personal income tax rate is too steeply graduated, it will tend to reduce incentive. Individuals will be reluctant to expend effort to earn extra income if most of that extra income will be taxed away.

Property taxes have two main economic effects. First, they cause relocation of private homes and businesses as individuals and firms try to avoid the high property tax areas. Second, property taxes leave less money in the hands of consumers and firms to pursue their objectives of maximizing satisfaction and profits.

Problem 19-18

How can a consumption tax reduce production?

Requirement and Clue: *Focus on the effect of a consumption tax on consumption and then examine how changes in consumption affect production.*

Solution:

A tax imposed on a commodity will tend to reduce the quantity of that commodity that consumers will buy. If producers continue to produce the same quantity as they did before the imposition of the tax, they will notice that their stocks (inventories) will begin to pile up as consumers reduce their purchases of the commodity. In response to this situation, producers will reduce their level of production.

Problem 19-19

The following table shows tax and income information.

Income	Tax paid	% of income paid in taxes
$ 0	$ 0	
5,000	500	
10,000	1,100	
15,000	1,800	
20,000	2,600	
25,000	3,500	
30,000	4,500	

(a) *Complete the table.*

(b) *What kind of tax structure does this table illustrate?*

Requirement and Clue: *This is a two-part problem. Make sure that you answer each part in order. For the second part of the problem, remember the nature of each type of structure.*

Solution:

(a)

Income	Tax paid	% of income paid in taxes
$ 0	$ 0	0
5,000	500	10
10,000	1,100	11
15,000	1,800	12
20,000	2,600	13
25,000	3,500	14
30,000	4,500	14

(b) Since the percentage of income paid in taxes increases as income rises, the tax structure is progressive.

Problem 19-20

The following table shows tax and income data. The marginal tax rate is defined as the change in taxes divided by the change in income.

Income	Tax paid	Income after tax	% of income paid in taxes	Marginal tax rate (%)
$ 0	$ 0			
2,000	200			
4,000	480			
8,000	1,200			
16,000	3,200			
32,000	8,960			
50,000	20,000			

(a) *Complete the table.*

(b) *What kind of tax structure does the table illustrate?*

(c) *On the basis of the data contained in the table, if Jane Peters' pre-tax income is $8,000 and she wants to increase her after-tax income by $900, how much extra income must she earn?*

Requirement and Clue: This is a multiple-part problem. You should answer each part in order. For part (b), remember the nature of the various tax structures. For part (c) focus on the marginal tax rate.

Solution:

(a) See table below.

Income	Tax paid	Income after tax	% of income paid in taxes	Marginal tax rate (%)
$ 0	$ 0	$ 0	0	10
2,000	200	1,800	10	14
4,000	480	3,520	12	18
8,000	1,200	6,800	15	25
16,000	3,200	12,800	20	36
32,000	8,960	23,040	28	61
50,000	20,000	30,000	40	

(b) Since the percentage of income paid in taxes increases as income rises, the tax structure is progressive.

(c) Since the marginal tax rate at $8,000 is 25%, Jane's extra after tax income of $900 represents 75% of the extra income she must earn. The extra income she must earn is therefore:

$$\frac{(\$900 \times 100)}{75} = \mathbf{\$1,200}$$

Problem 19-21

A government believes that by lowering the tax rate, work incentive will increase, thereby increasing productivity, income and tax revenue.

Draw a Laffer curve and indicate a point on the curve where the government believes the economy to be operating.

Requirement and Clue: *An understanding of the Laffer curve and its implication is necessary to solve this problem.*

Solution:

See the graph that follows.

Any point on the curve to the right of the maximum revenue point (such as A) would indicate the government's belief with respect to where the economy is operating. If the tax rate is lowered from t_a to t*, tax revenue will increase from TRa to TR*.

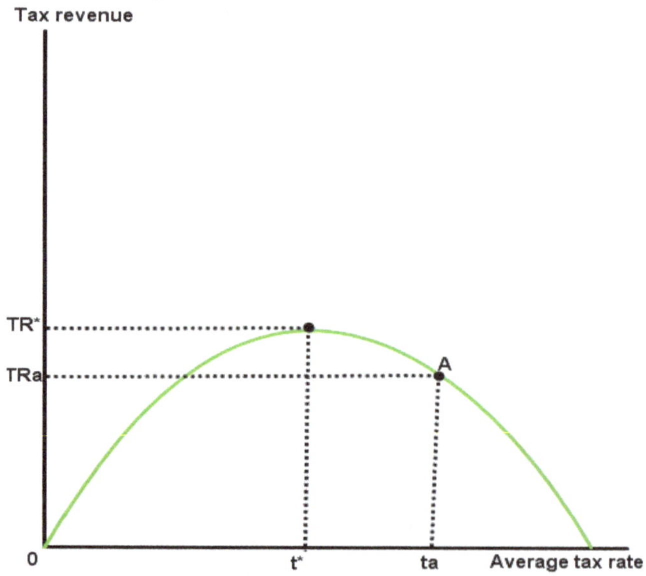

Problem 19-22

"A good word can be said about sales taxes. Because they are expressed as a percentage of total purchases, they affect all buyers equally. They are fair since the rich are likely to buy more than the poor and will thus pay more taxes."

Comment on the above statement.

Requirement and Clue: *Read the statement carefully and if you detect any errors, identify them and offer a correction. Focus on the nature of sales taxes.*

Solution:

Sales taxes do not affect all buyers equally. The rich may pay more in absolute terms but they pay a smaller proportion of their income in sales taxes than do the poor. In that sense, sales taxes tend to be regressive.

Multiple-Choice

In each case, circle the letter that corresponds with the correct answer.

1. Public finance refers to:

a. the expenditures of individuals and firms of goods and services and resources
b. how organizations raise funds from the public
c. the public's donations to political parties during elections
d. the study of government's behaviour in the areas of spending and taxation.

Answer: d

Reason: *Public finance is that area of economics that deals with government spending and taxes.*

2. The government spends much of the taxes it collects on:

a. assisting farmers and small businesses
b. social services, health, and education and protection of persons and property
c. making sure that government ministers are all millionaires
d. none of the above

Answer: b

Reason: *Expenditures on the items in b account for a large share of total government spending.*

3. Government transfer payments are:

a. payments for goods and services
b. monies paid out in the form of old age security pension, guaranteed income supplement, and unemployment insurance benefits
c. payments made by the government to transfer goods and services throughout the country in an attempt to redistribute income
d. all of the above

Answer: b

Reason: *Transfer payments do not represent payments for goods and services.*

4. Government transfer payments include:

a. purchases of uniforms for the military
b. civil servants' salaries
c. social security payments and family allowances
d. all of the above

Answer: c

Reason: *Government transfer payments are transfers of purchasing power from one group to another. They do not represent payments for goods and services.*

5. The law that states that government spending will grow faster than total spending is called:

a. Murphy's law c. Marshall's law
b. Wagner's law d. Engel's law

Answer: b

Reason: *Wagner's law states that the rate of government spending will eventually outstrip the rate of growth of total spending.*

6. Wagner's law states that:

a. the government should not engage in economic activity but should confine its activities strictly to the political sphere
b. it is illegal for people (other than government) to give transfer payments
c. government spending as a percentage of total spending would fall as income rises
d. government spending would rise faster than total spending

Answer: d

Reason: *Choice d is an accurate statement of Wagner's law.*

7. Reasons for the growth in government spending include:

a. increasing government responsibilities
b. inflation
c. population growth
d. all of the above

Answer: d

Reason: *Choices a, b, and c have necessitated increased government spending.*

8. Which of the following accounts for the increase in government spending over time?

a. Inflation and population growth
b. The decline in the birth rate
c. The rapid increase in international trade
d. All of the above

Answer: a

Reason: *Choice a is the only option that can explain growth in government spending.*

9. It is generally agreed that the government should be responsible for:

a. education c. sanitation and health
b. law and order d. all of the above

Answer: d

Reason: *These are public goods and should be provided by the government for the benefit of society.*

10. Of the following, the federal government spends the most on:

a. social services c. police protection
b. transportation d. subsidies to farmers

Answer: a

Reason: *Federal government expenditures of transportation, police protection, and subsidies to farmers are small in relation to expenditures on social services.*

11. Of the following, the provincial governments spend the most on:

a. protection of persons and property
b. environment
c. health services
d. housing

Answer: c

Reason: *Provincial governments' expenditures on the other three functions are small in relation to expenditures on health services.*

12. Of the following, the local governments spend the most on:

a. education c. regional planning
b. housing d. health

Answer: a

Reason: *Local governments' expenditures on the other three functions mentioned are small relative to expenditures on education.*

13. A compulsory payment levied by a government to pay for goods and services provided for the benefit of the population is called:

a. a fee c. a tax
b. a price d. none of the above

Answer: c

Reason: *A tax is a compulsory sum of money levied by a government on income, goods and services, or property.*

14. Which of the following is a desirable property of a tax?

a. If it's a revenue tax it should yield adequate revenue.
b. It should be fair
c. It should not impede the operation of the market system
d. All of the above

Answer: d

Reason: *In general, taxes that have the properties mentioned are preferred to those that don't.*

15. The benefit principle of taxation states that:

a. all taxpayers should benefit equally from a tax
b. taxes paid should be proportional to the benefits received from the tax
c. people with equal incomes should be taxed equally
d. none of the above

Answer: b

Reason: *According to the benefit principle of taxation, those who benefit more from government expenditure should pay more **taxes** to support such expenditure. This is consistent with choice b.*

16. The ability-to-pay principle of taxation states that:

a. all taxpayers should pay the same amount of tax
b. all taxpayers should benefit equally from a tax
c. taxpayers should be taxed according to their ability to pay
d. the ability to pay should not be used as a criterion of equity

Answer: c

Reason: *The ability-to-pay principle is the proposition that those who have the greatest income should pay the most taxes. This is consistent with choice c.*

17. If taxes on taxable incomes of $500, $800, and $1200 are $100, $160, and $240 respectively, then the tax is:

a. proportional c. regressive
b. progressive d. cumulative

Answer: a

Reason: *At each level of income, the tax is 20% of taxable income.*

18. According to the Laffer curve:

a. increases in the tax rate will always increase tax revenue
b. increases in the tax rate can reduce tax revenue
c. reductions in the tax rate will always result in lower tax revenue
d. reductions in the tax rate will always result in greater tax revenue.

Answer: b

Reason: *The effect of changes in the tax rate on tax revenues depends on the economy's position on the Laffer curve.*

19. Which of the following definitely results in higher prices for consumers?

a. Personal income taxes
b. Excise taxes
c. Property taxes
d. Corporation income taxes

Answer: b

Reason: *Excise taxes are levied on particular goods and thus raise the prices of such goods for consumers.*

20. The main source of revenue for the federal government is:

a. personal income taxes
b. property taxes
c. sales taxes
d. corporation income taxes

Answer: a

Reason: No other tax yields as much revenue for the federal government as do personal income taxes.

21. The largest tax revenue source for provincial governments is:

a. personal income taxes
b. alcohol and tobacco taxes
c. property taxes
d. corporate income taxes

Answer: a

Reason: No other tax yields as much revenue for the provincial governments as do personal income taxes.

22. The main source of revenue for local governments is:

a. personal income taxes
b. general sales taxes
c. employment insurance contributions
d. transfers from other levels of government

Answer: d

Reason: Transfers from other levels of government to local governments exceed all other sources of funds for local governments.

True-False

Determine whether each of the following statements is true or false.

1. In most countries, the government finances its expenditures from the profits made from its investments.

Answer: False

Explanation: The government finances its expenditures mainly from taxation.

2. Public finance is the branch of economics that studies how the general public earns and spends money.

Answer: False

Explanation: Public finance is the study of government's spending and taxes.

3. Taxes constitute the largest source of revenue for the government.

Answer: True

4. Governments make sure that they levy enough taxes and curtail their spending so that they never have any occasion to borrow.

Answer: False

Explanation: Governments often borrow because they spend more than the amount they collect in taxes, thus creating a debt.

5. Principal expenditure items for the government include social services, interest on the public debt, health, and education.

Answer: True

6. Transfer payments are funds transferred from the government to individuals and firms for services and goods provided to the government.

Answer: False

Explanation: Transfer payments are transfers of purchasing power from one group to another. They do not represent payment for goods or services.

7. Examples of government transfer payments are old age security payments, family allowances, and employment insurance benefits.

Answer: True

8. Wagner's law states that government should spend money only on essential services which cannot be provided by private enterprise.

Answer: False

Explanation: Wagner's laws states that government spending would rise faster than total spending in an economy.

9. It is generally agreed that the government should pursue economic policies that reduce inflation and unemployment.

Answer: True

10. Reasons for the growth in government spending over the years include increasing government responsibilities, inflation, and population growth.

Answer: True

11. As the population ages, more people dies so government spending falls because there are fewer people to take care of.

Answer: False

Explanation: As the population ages, there are increasingly more people who depend on government for financial assistance, and this implies an increase in government spending.

12. Among the largest expenditure items of the federal government are transportation and communications, the environment, international trade promotion, and regional planning and development,

Answer: False

Explanation: Major expenditure items of the federal government include social services, debt charges, and protection of persons and property.

13. A tax is a compulsory payment levied by a government to pay for goods and services provided for the benefit of the population.

Answer: True

14. The only desirable property of a tax is that it should yield adequate revenue.

Answer: False

Explanation: In addition to yielding adequate revenue (for a revenue tax) the tax should be fair, should not impede the operation of the market system, should be convenient, and should be simple.

15. The benefit principle of taxation states that people should be taxed according to the benefits they receive from taxes.

Answer: True

16. The ability-to-pay principle states that people should be taxed according to their ability to pay.

Answer: True

17. Any tax that increases as income increases is necessarily progressive.

Answer: False

Explanation: Even a regressive tax increases as income increases. In determining whether a tax is progressive, proportional, or regressive, one must look at the percentage of income paid in taxes as income changes.

18. A tax is said to be proportional if the amount paid in taxes remains constant as income rises.

Answer: False

Explanation: A proportional tax is one for which the percentage of income paid in taxes remains constant as income increases.

19. The Laffer curve implies that there exists a tax rate that maximizes tax revenue, and this rate is not necessarily the highest rate.

Answer: True

20. The optimum tax rate for a revenue tax is that rate with which taxpayers are most comfortable.

Answer: False

Explanation: The optimum tax rate is that rate that maximizes tax revenue.

21. One disadvantage of a highly progressive income tax is that it tends to reduce work incentive.

Answer: True

22. Personal income taxes and general sales taxes are important sources of revenue for the provincial governments.

Answer: True

Completion

(Fill in the blanks)

Use each word or combination of words from the list exactly once.
*(**Hint**: Proceed by elimination)*

Word list

Ability-To-Pay — Benefits — Consumption — Corporate — Decrease — Double — Education — Excise x 2 — Federal — Finance — Health — Increase — Loopholes — Optimum — Personal — Progressive — Property — Proportional — Provincial x 2 — Public — Regressive x 2 — Sales — Services — Social — Tax — Transfer — Transfers — Value-Added — Wagner's

Questions

1. The branch of economics that studies government taxation and the use of taxes is called ____________ ____________.
2. The notion that government spending will grow faster than total spending in an economy is referred to as ____________ law.
3. Old age security payments, family allowances, and employment insurance benefits are examples of ____________ payments.
4. The federal government spends most of our tax dollars on ____________ ____________.
5. The provincial governments' largest expenditure item is ____________.
6. By far, the largest expenditure item of local governments is ____________.
7. A(n) ____________ tax is one where the percentage of income paid in taxes increases as income rises.
8. A(n) ____________ tax is one where the percentage of income paid in taxes remains constant as income increases.
9. A(n) ____________ tax is one where the percentage of income paid in taxes decreases as income increases.
10. A tax imposed on a domestically produced good is called a(n) ____________ ____________.
11. The Laffer curve suggests that as the tax rate increases, tax revenue will ____________ [increase, decrease]. But as the tax rate increases further, tax revenue will eventually ________________ [increase, decrease] (increase, decrease)
12. Personal income taxes are paid to two levels of government. These levels are the ____________ and the ____________. (
13. A(n) ____________ tax is a tax levied on a specific commodity. A(n) ____________ tax is a tax levied on broad groups of goods and services. These taxes are referred to collectively as ____________ taxes.
14. The main sources of revenue for the federal government

are ___________ income taxes and ___________ income taxes.

15. Local governments receive most of their revenues in the form of ___________ from the ___________ governments. Their most important tax revenue source is ___________ taxes.

16. Bob earns $3,000 a year and pays $350 in taxes. Joan earns $10,000 a year and pays $1,000 in taxes. This tax structure is ___________.

17. The proposition that people should be taxed according to their economic position is called the ___________ principle of taxation.

18. The idea that people should be taxed according to the benefits they receive from the tax is called the ___________ principle of taxation.

19. Provisions in the tax laws that allow incomes to escape taxation or to be taxed at a lower level are called tax ___________.

20. For a revenue tax, the tax rate that yields the most revenue is called the ___________ tax rate.

21. ___________ taxation refers to the fact that dividends are taxed both as corporate income and as personal income.

22. A(n)___________ tax is a tax that is imposed on a product at each stage of production.

Solution

1. (Public Finance)
2. (Wagner's)
3. (Transfer)
4. (Social Services)
5. (Health)
6. (Education)
7. (Progressive)
8. (Proportional)
9. (Regressive)
10. (Excise Tax)
11. (Increase, Decrease)
12. (Federal, Provincial)
13. (Excise, Sales, Consumption)
14. (Personal, Corporate)
15. (Transfers, Provincial, Property)
16. (Regressive)
17. (Ability-To-Pay)
18. (Benefits)
19. (Loopholes)
20. (Optimum)
21. (Double)
22. (Value-Added)

20 INTERNATIONAL TRADE

SYNOPSIS

International trade is extremely important to many economies. Through trade, residents of one country can consume goods produced in other countries. International trade allows nations to concentrate on producing those goods in which they have an absolute advantage or a comparative advantage. In addition, international trade results in increased efficiency and **economies of scale**.

Country A has an **absolute advantage** over country B in the production of a certain commodity if country A is more efficient than country B in the production of that commodity. If country A is more efficient than country B in the production of X and Y, and if country A's efficiency is greater in the production of X than it is in the production of Y, then country A has a **comparative advantage** over B in the production of X. Determinants of comparative advantage include natural endowment, acquired advantage, and special knowledge.

LEARNING OBJECTIVES

In connection with this module, you should be able to:

1. discuss the basis for international trade
2. explain the gains from trade
3. explain the principle of absolute advantage and the principle of comparative advantage

DEFINITIONS & CONCEPTS

You should be able to define the following terms and concepts:

international trade
regional specialization
absolute advantage
comparative advantage
terms of trade
trading curve
geographical determination

20 INTERNATIONAL TRADE

Concepts, Definitions & Problems

Problem 20-1

What is the basis for international trade?

Requirement and Clue: *Focus on reasons that it may be advantageous for countries to engage in international trade.*

Solution:

The basis for international trade is the realization that because of certain conditions existing in different countries, trade can be beneficial to trading partners. Different countries are differently endowed with resources and technical know-how. Some, for instance, are heavily endowed with natural resources. Others are less favourably endowed. Some countries are rich in capital. Others suffer from a lack of capital relative to other resources. And human resources vary among countries. Some countries have a more highly skilled labour force than do others. Some countries have larger populations than others. Moreover, technological capabilities are not evenly distributed across countries. Country A may have a technological edge over country B in the production of telecommunication equipment while country B may have a technological advantage over country A in the production of books.

A country well endowed with labour can be expected to have lower wage rates than a country with scarce labour resources. Consequently, we can expect the cost of manufacturing a product requiring a large amount of labour to be lower in a labour-abundant country than in a labour-scarce country, other things being equal. Similarly, we would expect the cost of growing tropical fruits such as oranges and bananas in a tropical climate to be much lower than it would be in a temperate climate.

Problem 20-2

Carefully explain the principle of absolute advantage.

Requirement and Clue: *You are required to state the principle clearly. An illustrative example of the principle will be helpful.*

Solution:

The principle of absolute advantage states that a country should specialize in the production of the commodity in which it has an absolute advantage. One country has an absolute advantage over another in the production of a commodity if it can produce the commodity with fewer resources than the other country can. If country A is more efficient than country B in the production of a certain commodity, then country A has an absolute advantage in the production of that commodity.

The following simple example will illustrate the concept of absolute advantage. Suppose that a worker in country A can produce five cars per year while a worker in country B can produce only two cars per year. Suppose also that a worker in country A can produce only eight tons of grain per year while a worker in country B can produce ten tons of grain per year. For convenience, the data are presented in the following table.

Country	Cars (units)	Grain (tons)
A	5	8
B	2	10

A worker in country A is 2.5 times as efficient as a worker in country B in car production, but a worker in country B is 1.25 times as efficient as a worker in country A in grain production. In this case, country A has an absolute advantage in the production of cars, while country B has an absolute advantage in the production of grain.

Problem 20-3

Is there any relation between trade flows and income levels in different countries?

Requirement and Clue: *A simple yes or no answer will not suffice. You are required to explain. Focus on the effects of changes in income domestically and in foreign countries on flows of exports and imports.*

Solution:

The term "trade flows" refers to the flows of exports and imports. Let us first consider exports from a particular country that we will call country X. If the level of income rises in foreign countries, people in those countries will buy more goods and services, including imported goods and services, hence exports from country X will likely increase. If the level of income in country X increases, consumers in country X will buy more goods and services, including imported goods and services; thus imports into country X will increase. This means that exports of other countries will increase. We can conclude therefore, that a direct relation exists between income levels and trade flows.

Problem 20-4

Explain the principle of comparative advantage.

Requirement and Clue: *You should state the principle clearly. An illustrative example would be helpful.*

Solution:

A country has a comparative advantage in the production of a commodity if it can produce that commodity at a lower opportunity cost than another country. Let us consider two countries, country A and country B. Suppose a worker in country A can produce 10 cars or five tons of grain per year, while a worker in country B can produce either three cars or three tons of grain per year. The data are contained in the following table.

Country	Cars (units)	Grain (tons)
A	10	5
B	3	3

The worker in country A is more efficient than the worker in country B in the production of cars and grain. Country A has an absolute advantage in the production of both commodities.

Instead of producing 10 cars, the worker in country A could have produced five tons of grain. Hence, the opportunity cost of a car in country A is 0.5 tons of grain. On the other hand, instead of producing three cars, a worker in country B could have produced three tons of grain. Hence, the opportunity cost of a car in country B is one ton of grain. Since the opportunity cost of a car in country A is less than the opportunity cost of a car in country B, country A has a comparative advantage in the production of cars.

The opportunity cost of a ton of grain in country A is two cars, while the opportunity cost of a ton of grain in country B is one car. Since the opportunity cost of grain in country B is less than the opportunity cost of grain in country A, country B has a comparative advantage in the production of grain.

The principle of comparative advantage states that trading countries will benefit mutually if each country specializes in the production of the commodity in which it has a comparative advantage, and trades with each other.

Problem 20-5

Define each of the following concepts:

(a) *Terms of trade*

(b) *Trading curve*

Requirement and Clue: *This is a definitional problem. Once you have given a clear and concise meaning of the concepts, you have solved the problem.*

Solution:

The terms of trade are the rates at which one country's exports are exchanged for its imports. For example, if a car is traded for 10,000 kg of beef, then the terms of trade would be 1:10,000.

A trading curve is a graphical depiction of all combinations of goods and services available through specialization and trade.

Problem 20-6

Discuss the main determinants of comparative advantage?

Requirement and Clue: *A brief definition of comparative advantage is in order. Focus on factors that bestow production advantage on a country.*

Solution:

The main determinants of comparative advantage include natural endowment, acquired advantage, and special knowledge.

Natural Endowment: The Caribbean islands have numerous white and pink sandy beaches and a warm climate all year round, naturally. They therefore are a *natural* attraction for tourists who want to get away for a week or two between December and March, when it is cold and snowing in much of North America and Europe. The comparative advantage enjoyed by the Caribbean islands in this area is a matter of natural endowment. In this case, the comparative advantage is geographically determined.

Acquired Advantage: In the same way that some individuals work hard to develop and improve whatever abilities may have been bestowed on them, so too can nations, by their own efforts, acquire comparative advantage in certain lines of production. Japan is often cited as the classic example of a nation that has compensated for of lack of natural endowments by saving and by making huge investment in capital, both physical and human.

Special Knowledge: Whether by accident or design, some countries have special knowledge that gives them a comparative advantage in the production of certain products. A country that comes to mind in this regard is Switzerland, with its reputation for watch-making. There is little doubt that Switzerland's expertise in watch-making is partly a result of many years of concentration on that activity.

Problem 20-7

Discuss the role of international trade in facilitating economies of scale and increasing efficiency.

Requirement and Clue: *Clearly, you must be familiar with the concepts of economies of scale and efficiency mentioned in the problem. Focus on how international trade can lead to economies of scale and greater efficiency.*

Solution:

Economies of scale exist when long-run average cost decreases as output increases. Because of increased output resulting from specialization and international trade, production costs may fall. This may not have been possible without international trade. Efficiency is a measure of the amount of output that can be produced with a given amount of inputs. The higher the level of output that can be produced with a given amount of inputs, the more efficient the production process is. As a country specializes in the production of a commodity, it will likely acquire greater skills and expertise in the production of that commodity. This increase in efficiency may not have occurred in the absence of international trade.

Problem 20-8

Explain how international trade tends to equate the prices of resources in trading countries.

Requirement and Clue: *Focus on the effects of international trade on the demand for and supply of resources, applying the principle of comparative advantage.*

Solution:

Let us consider two countries that are differently endowed with capital and labour. Country A is well endowed with capital while country B is well endowed with labour. In country A, the price of capital will be relatively low while the price of labour will be relatively high. In country B, the price of labour will be relatively low while the price of capital will be relatively high. The principle of comparative advantage suggests that country A will specialize in the production of capital-intensive activities while country B will specialize in labour-intensive activities. As country A specializes in the production of capital-intensive industries, the demand for capital will rise and so will the price of capital, other things being equal. As country B specializes in labour-intensive industries, the demand for labour will rise and so will the price of labour. Thus, the prices of capital and labour will tend to be equalized in the trading countries.

Problem 20-9

Can there be gains from trade in the absence of comparative advantage? Explain.

Requirement and Clue: *Clearly, a simple yes or no will not suffice. You are required to explain. Think of anything other than comparative advantage that could motivate exchange.*

Solution:

To answer this question, let us assume that two countries have identical opportunity costs so that neither country has a comparative advantage in the production of any commodity. Let us assume also that tastes and preferences differ in each country. Differences in tastes and preferences could provide a motive for exchange via international trade thus enabling specialization. International trade increases the size of the market and may enable the trading countries to benefit from economies of scale, specialization and increased efficiency.

Problem 20-10

The following table shows hypothetical demand and supply schedules for desk sets in country A and country B.

	COUNTRY A		COUNTRY B	
Price ($)	Quantity Demanded (000)	Quantity Supplied (000)	Quantity Demanded (000)	Quantity Supplied (000)
10	14	5	7	4
12	12	6	6	6
14	10	7	5	8
16	8	8	4	10
18	6	9	3	12

(a) *Without trade, what will be the price in country A?*

(b) *Without trade, what will be the price in country B?*

(c) *Now, suppose free trade exists between country A and country B. What will be the price of desk sets?*

(d) *Which country will export desk sets?*

(e) *How many desk sets will the country export?*

Requirement and Clue: *This is a multiple-part problem. Answer each part in order. Recall that the equilibrium price is determined by the equality of quantity demanded and quantity supplied. Note that a country will export any surplus and import any shortage that it faces.*

Solution:

(a) In country A, at a price of $16, the quantity demanded and the quantity supplied are equal. The equilibrium price is therefore **$16.**

(b) In country B, at a price of $12, the quantity demanded and the quantity supplied are equal. The equilibrium price is therefore **$12.**

(c) With free trade, the total quantity demanded and supplied at each price are shown in the following table:

Price ($)	Quantity demanded	Quantity supplied
10	21,000	9,000
12	18,000	12,000
14	15,000	15,000
16	12,000	18,000
18	9,000	21,000

The price will be $14, where the quantity demanded and the quantity supplied are equal.

(d) At a price of $14, there will be a shortage in country A and a surplus in country B. Therefore, country B will export desk sets.

(e) At a price of $14, the surplus in country B is 3,000 desk sets. Country B will export **3,000** desk sets.

Problem 20-11

Country A can produce 40 clocks or 2,000 units of clothing with a certain amount of resources. Country B can produce 20 clocks or 1,500 units of clothing with the same amount of resources.

(a) *Is this an example of absolute or comparative advantage?*

(b) *Will free trade be beneficial to each of these countries?*

(c) *If these countries engage in free trade, which country should specialize on clothing?*

Requirement and Clue: *This is a three-part problem. Answer each part in order. Focus on the difference between absolute advantage and comparative advantage.*

Solution:

(a) This is an example of comparative advantage. In country A, the opportunity cost of a clock is 50 units of clothing. In country B, the opportunity cost of a clock is 75 units of clothing.

(b) Free trade will be beneficial to both countries because the opportunity cost is different in each country.

(c) Country B should specialize in clothing because it has a comparative advantage in the production of clothing.

Problem 20-12

A and B are two countries that use a common currency. Country A can produce 50,000 TV sets and 10,000 tons of wheat per year. Country B can produce 10,000 TV sets and 30,000 tons of wheat per year.

(a) *Complete the following table.*

Country	TV sets	Wheat (tons)
A		
B		
Total		

(b) Production costs in country A are $200 for a TV set and $300 for a ton of wheat. Production costs in country B are $800 for a TV set and $200 for a ton of wheat. Suppose country A specializes in TV sets while country B specializes in wheat.

Complete the following table.

Country	TV sets	Wheat
A		
B		
Total		

Requirement and Clue: *This is a two-part problem. Answer each part in order.*

Solution:

(a)

Country	TV sets	Wheat (tons)
A	50,000	10,000
B	10,000	30,000
Total	60,000	40,000

(b) Instead of producing 10,000 tons of wheat at a cost of $300 per ton (total cost of $3,000,000), country A could produce 15,000 TV sets at a cost of $200 per TV set. If country A produces no wheat, it could produce 65,000 TV sets. Instead of producing 10,000 TV sets at a cost of $800 each (total cost of $8,000,000), country B could produce 40,000 tons of wheat. If country B produces no TV sets, it could produce 70,000 tons of wheat. See the following table.

Country	TV sets	Wheat (tons)
A	65,000	0
B	0	70,000
Total	65,000	70,000

Problem 20-13

Comment briefly on the following statement:

"Economists have realized, for a very long time now, that international trade can be beneficial to all trading partners. They realize that the benefits of specialization and trade result from a greater consumption mix (i.e., a greater variety of products for the trading partners) rather than from an increase in the volume of output."

Requirement and Clue: You are required to examine the statement carefully to see if it contains any errors. If you detect any errors, you should identify them and offer a correction. Note that brevity is a requirement.

Solution:

International trade allows trading countries to consume a greater variety of products, some of which would be quite costly to produce in some countries. But contrary to the statement, international trade also results in a greater volume of output as countries become more efficient through specialization and as they reap the benefits of economies of scale.

Multiple-Choice

In each case, circle the letter that corresponds with the correct answer.

1. International trade is:

a. the flow of people between countries through immigration and emigration
b. the exchange of goods, services, and resources between nations
c. negotiations between sovereign states regarding trading policies
d. all of the above

Answer: b

Reason: *Choice b correctly defines the essence of international trade.*

2. The main reason for international specialization is:

a. economic stability
b. economic self-sufficiency
c. differences in resources endowment
d. none of the above

Answer: c

Reason: *Because countries are differently endowed with different resources, they can benefit by specialization and trade.*

3. The basis for international trade is the fact that:

a. some nations are rich while others are poor
b. some countries operate under a free enterprise system while others do not
c. countries are differently endowed with resources
d. some countries are large while others are small.

Answer: c

Reason: *Different resources give different countries productive advantages over others and allow countries to benefit from trade.*

4. Country A has an absolute advantage over country B if country A can:

a. produce a good using less resources than can country B
b. produce a good using more resources than can country B
c. sell a good at a higher price than can country B
d. none of the above

Answer: a

Reason: *Choice a correctly defines absolute advantage.*

5. The principle of absolute advantage states that:

a. no country can ever have an absolute advantage in anything
b. a country should specialize in the production of the commodity in which it has an absolute advantage
c. absolute advantage is irrelevant as far as international trade is concerned
d. none of the above

Answer: b

Reason: *Two countries can gain by trading if each specializes in the production of the commodity in which it has an absolute advantage. This is the principle of absolute advantage.*

6. A country is said to have a comparative advantage in those products:

a. that it can sell more cheaply
b. in which its efficiency relative to other countries is highest
c. in which its efficiency relative to other countries is lowest
d. none of the above

Answer: b

Reason: *Comparative advantage is the ability of one country to produce a commodity at a lower opportunity cost than another country can. This is consistent with choice b.*

7. Specialization and trade lead to:

a. higher prices and higher output
b. higher prices and lower output
c. lower prices and lower output
d. lower prices and higher output

Answer: d

Reason: *The combined output of trading partners will increase because of specialization and lower prices will result.*

8. Company A can produce 5 units of tea or 18 units of clothing with 1 unit of resources. Country B can produce 10 units of tea or 20 units of clothing with I unit of resources. We would expect:

a. country A to specialize in producing tea
b. country A to produce neither tea nor clothing
c. country B to export tea and import clothing
d. country B to import tea and export clothing

Answer: c

Reason: *Country B has a comparative advantage in producing tea.*

9. If country C can produce 50 tons of corn or 30 books with one unit of resources, and country D can produce 10 tons of corn or 20 books with I unit of resources, then:

a. country C should specialize in the production of books
b. country C has a comparative advantage in the production of books
c. country D has a comparative advantage in the production of corn
d. country C has a comparative advantage in the production of corn

Answer: d

Reason: *The cost of a ton of corn in country C is only 0.6 books, compared with 2 books in country D.*

10. Which of the following is not a reason for specialization and trade?

a. Self-sufficiency   c. Economies of scale
b. Increased efficiency   d. All of the above

Answer: a

Reason: Specialization and trade involve reliance on trading partners, not self-sufficiency.

11. Which of the following statements is correct?

a. Only comparative advantage can result in trade benefits

b. Both absolute advantage and comparative advantage can result in benefits from trade

c. Only absolute advantage can result in trade benefits

d. Trade cannot result in mutual benefits to trading partners: if one gains, someone must lose.

Answer: b

Reason: Both absolute advantage and comparative advantage can lead to mutual benefits from trade if each country specializes in the production of the commodity in which it has either an absolute advantage or a comparative advantage.

12. The terms of trade refer to:

a. the terms and conditions governing the exports of goods from a country

b. the conditions that must be met before importers can bring goods into the country

c. the rate at which exports are exchanged for imports

d. the regulations governing trade between countries.

Answer: c

Reason: The terms of trade tell how much exports are required to pay for imports. This matches choice c.

13. Geographical determinism explains:

a. country location　　c. country size

b. population growth　　d. comparative advantage

Answer: d

Reason: Geographical determinism, along with acquired advantage and special knowledge, helps to explain comparative advantage.

14. The trading curve shows:

a. the pattern of exports from a country

b. the pattern of imports from other countries

c. items that can be traded and items that cannot be traded

d. all combinations of goods and services made possible through specialization and trade.

Answer: d

Reason: Specialization and trade offer greater combinations of goods and services than would be possible by the country's production-possibility curve. These greater combinations are represented by the trading curve.

15. Which of the following is a determinant of comparative advantage?

a. Natural endowment　　c. Acquired knowledge

b. Special knowledge　　d. All of the above

Answer: d

Reason: Choices a, b, and c can cause a country to have a cost advantage over another country in the production of certain products.

True-False

Determine whether each of the following statements is true or false.

1. The basis for international trade is the fact that nations are endowed differently with resources.

Answer: True

2. International trade refers to trading trade secrets among independent nations.

Answer: False

Explanation: International trade refers to the exchange of goods, services, and resources between nations.

3. International trade is sometimes used to refer to the study of the flows of goods, services, and resources between nations.

Answer: True

4. We can expect the cost of manufacturing a product requiring a large amount of labour to be lower in a labour-abundant country than in a labour-scarce country.

Answer: True

5. A country has an absolute advantage over another country if that country can produce a good with fewer resources than can the other country.

Answer: True

6. If country A is more efficient than country B in producing both wheat and automobiles, then trade between A and B cannot be beneficial to both.

Answer: False

Explanation: Trade between A and B can be mutually beneficial if one has a comparative advantage over the other.

7. If country A has a comparative advantage over country B in producing transistor radios, then trade between A and B will benefit only country A.

Answer: False

Explanation: Country A and country B can both benefit from trade if country B has a comparative advantage in come other good.

8. The principle of comparative advantage states that each country can benefit from international trade if each specializes in the production of the commodity in which it has a comparative advantage.

Answer: True

9. Gains from trade include increased efficiency and economies of scale.

Answer: True

10. The trading curve is just another name for the production possibility curve.

Answer: False

Explanation: The trading curve shows all combinations of goods and services available to a country trough specialization and trade. The production possibility curve, on the other hand, shows all combinations of goods and services that an economy can produce, given its resources and technology.

11. International trade allows a country to move off its production possibility curve outward to its trading curve.

Answer: True

12. The terms of trade refer to the rules and regulations governing the flows of exports and imports between countries.

Answer: False

Explanation: The terms of trade define the rate at which a country's exports exchange for its imports.

13. Geographical determinism refers to the notion that most nations try to locate their major cities near sea ports.

Answer: False

Explanation: It refers to the idea that comparative advantage is determined by natural endowment.

14. International trade is beneficial because it facilitates increased efficiency and economies of scale.

Answer: True

Completion

Fill in the blanks.

Use each word or combination of words from the list exactly once. (***Hint***: Proceed by elimination)

Word list

Absolute — Advantage x 2 — Comparative — Computers — Corn — Cost — Curve — Determinism — Downward — Eighty — Fifty — Gadgets — Geographical — International x 2 — Low — Opportunity — Right — Terms — Trade x 3 — Trading — Widgets

Questions

1. The area of economics that studies the flows of goods, services, and resources among nations is called ____________ ____________.
2. ____________ ____________ refers to the exchange of goods, services, and resources among nations.
3. A country that is well endowed with labour resources is likely to have a relatively ____________ [high, low] wage rate.
4. A country is said to have a(n) ____________ ____________ over another country in the production of a commodity if it can produce the commodity with fewer resources than the other country can.
5. Country A has a comparative advantage in producing widgets and country B has a comparative advantage in producing gadgets. If country A specializes in ____________ and country B specializes in ____________, the combined output of widgets and gadgets will be greater than if each produced both widgets and gadgets.
6. With a certain amount of resources, Capitaland can produce 100 computers or 5,000 tons of corn. With the same amount of resources, Landania can produce 50 computers or 4,000 tons of corn. In Capitaland, the opportunity cost of a computer is ____________ tons of corn. In Landania, the opportunity cost of a computer is ____________ tons of corn. Capitaland should specialize on ____________ and import ____________ from Landania.
7. The ____________ of ____________ refer to the rate at which a country's exports exchange for its imports.
8. The principle of ____________ ____________ states that each trading can benefit from international trade if each specializes on the commodity that it can produce at a lower opportunity cost.
9. The trading curve is ____________ [upward, downward] sloping and lies to the ____________ [right, left] of the production possibility curve.
10. A line showing all combinations of goods and services made available through specialization and trade is called a(n) ____________ ____________.
11. The theory that states that comparative advantage is determined by natural endowment is called ____________ ____________.
12. Relative efficiency can be measured in terms of ____________ ____________.

Solution

1. (international trade)
2. (International trade)
3. (low)
4. (absolute advantage)
5. (widgets, gadgets)
6. (50, 80, computers, corn)
7. (terms of trade)
8. (comparative advantage)
9. (downward, right)
10. (trading curve)
11. (geographical determinism)
12. (opportunity cost)

21 TARIFFS & TRADE POLICY ISSUES

SYNOPSIS

A **tariff** is a tax levied on imported goods. Nations impose tariffs for a variety of reasons, including raising revenue, redistributing income, improving the country's balance of payments position, reducing unemployment, restricting consumption, and protecting domestic industries.

A **specific tariff** is expressed as a dollar amount on each unit imported. An **ad valorem tariff** is expressed as a percentage of the value of the imported item. A **compound tariff** is a combination of specific and ad valorem tariffs.

Supporters of tariffs claim that they protect **infant industries**, that they create employment, that they improve the **terms of trade**, and that they promote industrialization and diversification. Opponents of tariffs claim that they interfere with the principle of comparative advantage, and that they are inefficient.

Non-tariff restrictions on international trade include import quotas and voluntary restrictions. In practice, **import quotas** are more effective than tariffs in keeping out imports.

There are no tariffs on goods within a **free trade area,** but each member country maintains its own tariffs against non-member countries. A **customs union** eliminates trade barriers among member countries but maintains a common tariff with non-member countries. A **common market** allows goods and factors of production to move freely between member countries. An **economic union** allows the free movement of goods and factors, and leads towards harmonization of economic policies. Complete economic integration is achieved when monetary, fiscal, and social policies become the responsibility of a supra-national authority acting for the integrated group.

Economic integration results in trade creation and trade diversion. Trade creation causes resources to be shifted into more efficient uses. Trade diversion shifts resources into less efficient uses. Economic integration may improve the terms of trade increase competition, promote technological change, and lead to economies of scale.

LEARNING OBJECTIVES

In connection with this module, you should be able to:

1. explain the reasons for tariffs
2. identify different types of tariffs
3. discuss tariff structure
4. present arguments in favour of tariffs
5. present arguments against tariffs
6. explain the optimum tariff
7. describe other restrictive and control devices
8. explain economic integration

DEFINITIONS & CONCEPTS

You should be able to define the following terms and concepts:

tariff or import duty
specific tariff
ad valorem tariff
compound tariff
infant industry
terms of trade
import quotas
voluntary restrictions
economic integration
comparative advantage
economic cooperation
free trade area
tariff evasion
customs union
common market
economic union
complete economic integration
trade creation
trade diversion

21

TARIFFS & TRADE POLICYISSUES

Concepts, Definitions & Problems

Problem 21-1

What is a tariff and what is its effect on buyers?

Requirement and Clue: *This is a two-part problem. Solve each part in order. For the first part of the problem, give a clear and precise meaning a tariff. For the second part of the problem, focus on how a tariff affects the price of the good that is taxed.*

Solution:

Citizens of one country may import goods from another country. The government may levy a duty or a tax on those goods. Such a tax is called a tariff. Therefore, a tariff is a tax imposed on foreign goods.

A tariff raises the prices of the taxed goods, thus making them more expensive for buyers of those goods.

Problem 21-2

List four reasons that nations impose tariffs?

Requirement and Clue: *You can think of several reasons that nations might impose tariffs. You are asked to list four of them. Focus on arguments in favour of tariffs.*

Solution:

There are numerous reasons for the imposition of tariffs. The following is a list of four of those reasons.

1. To support certain industries that are considered to be critical from an economic, a military, or a political point of view.
2. To raise revenue for the government.
3. To restrict the consumption of certain foreign goods that may be considered socially or economically undesirable.
4. To protect certain industries from the full force of international competition.

Problem 21-3

Define each of the following types of tariffs:

a. *a specific tariff*
b. *a revenue tariff*
c. *a protective tariff*
d. *a compound tariff*
e. *an ad valorem tariff.*

Requirement and Clue: *This is a multiple-part problem. Be sure to answer each part in order. Give a clear and precise meaning of each concept. There is no need for any discussion of these concepts.*

Solution:

a. A specific tariff is a tax or duty expressed as a fixed amount per unit of the imported item. Thus a tariff of $1.00 imposed on each litre of a certain substance imported would be an example of a specific tariff.

b. A revenue tariff is a tariff whose main objective is to raise revenue for the government. Tariff on clothes and food items could be examples of revenue tariffs if the main aim is to raise funds for the government's coffers.

c. A protective tariff is a tariff whose main objective is to protect domestic industries or producers. An example of a protective tariff is a tariff on chicken and eggs designed to protect a fledgling domestic poultry industry.

d. A compound tariff is a combination of specific and ad valorem tariffs. A tariff expressed as $0.5 per kilogram for the first 50 kilograms and 10% of the value of any amount over 50 kilograms is an example of a compound tariff.

e. An ad valorem tariff is a duty levied on an imported item, expressed as a fixed percentage of its value. A tariff of 25% of the value of textiles imported into a country is an example of an ad valorem tariff.

Problem 21-4

Discuss the infant industry argument in favour of tariffs.

Requirement and Clue: *Here, you are required to state the argument as succinctly as you can and then discuss any arguments against it.*

Solution:

According to the infant industry argument, new or young domestic industries cannot compete with those that are older and better established in foreign countries; hence, new domestic industries, especially those that show great promise of success, need to be protected by tariffs from the full blast of competition. New domestic industries, moreover, may have the potential to develop a comparative advantage, if given a chance. This potential may never be realized unless such industries are allowed to grow to maturity with the assistance of tariffs.

For this argument to be valid, the tariff would have to be temporary—in place only until the protected industry matures. Also, protecting infant industries is justified only if the gains from such protection cannot be claimed exclusively by the firms' owners in the form of eventual profits. The infant industry argument is significantly strengthened when external economies, in the form of benefits to the society, are present.

Problem 21-5

State the "terms of trade argument" in favour of tariffs. Is there any flaw in this argument?

Requirement and Clue: *This is a two-part problem. State the argument as clearly and as precisely as you can. Study the argument carefully and see if you can detect any flaw.*

Solution:

The terms of trade argument in favour of tariffs is that a country can improve its terms of trade by imposing tariffs on goods imported from other countries, thus making the country better off. The "terms of trade" refers to the rate at which a country's exports can be exchanged for its imports. The imposition of a tariff means that a larger quantity of imports will be required for any given quantity of exports.

That a tariff can improve a country's terms of trade is true. It is not necessarily true, however, that the country will be better off because of higher tariffs. It is possible for the tariff to be so high that it chokes off all imports making the country worse off than if the tariff had not been imposed.

Problem 21-6

What are the main economic arguments against tariffs?

Requirement and Clue: *Focus on the advantages of free trade.*

Solution:

There are two main economic arguments against tariffs. First, they interfere with the operation of comparative advantage. Thus, they reduce or negate the gains from specialization and trade. International trade benefits each trading partner and increases total production. The imposition of tariffs, conversely, can result in each trading partner being worse off.

Another economic argument against tariffs is that, in many cases, the objectives that they are designed to achieve, can be achieved by other, more efficient means. For example, the objective of industrialization can be achieved more efficiently by subsidization than by the imposition of tariffs. This occurs because if, for example, the objective of the tariff is to increase the production of a certain item, a subsidy will likely produce the desired result without discouraging the total consumption of the item by raising its price as a tariff does.

Problem 21-7

With the help of appropriate diagrams, analyze the effects tariffs.

Requirement and Clue: *Demand and supply graphs can be used to solve this problem. Focus on the impact of tariffs on price and quantity.*

Solution:

The following diagram shows demand and supply curves for wheat. At the world price of wheat (Pw), this country produces Q1 bushels of wheat, but the quantity demanded at this price is Q2 There is a shortage of (Q2 – Q1) which the country can import from the rest of the world (ROW). If a tariff is imposed on imported wheat, the price will rise from Pw to Pw + t as shown in the diagram. The country now produces Q3 bushels of wheat, but the quantity demanded at this higher price falls from Q2 to Q4. There is now a shortage of (Q4 – Q3) bushels which the country can import.

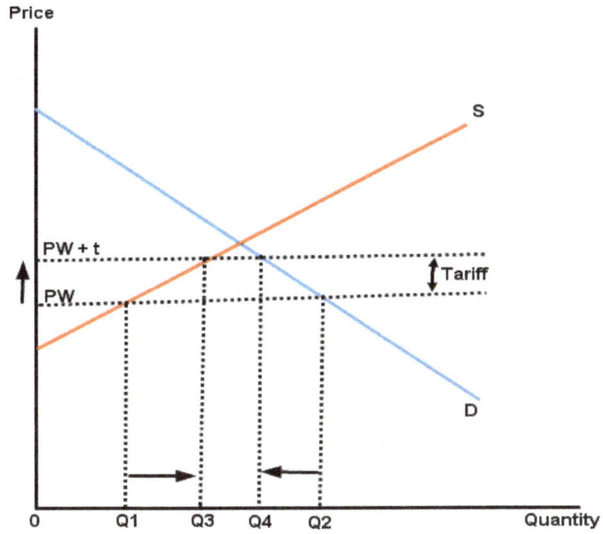

The effect of the tariff is that consumers in the country are paying a higher price and getting a smaller quantity of wheat. But wheat farmers in the country are getting a great deal more money: Q3(Pw + t) instead of (Pw × Q1). Wheat farmers in ROW are selling less wheat to this country.

Problem 21-8

Could consumers benefit from a gradual elimination of the tariff on shoes?

Requirement and Clue: *A simple yes or no solution will not suffice. You are expected to defend your position. Focus on the effects of the reduction or elimination of the tariff on producers, domestic consumers, and on resource allocation.*

Solution:

A gradual reduction and ultimate elimination of the tariff on shoes will lead to the importation of relatively inexpensive shoes. Domestic producers, in order to compete with foreign producers, will have to be more efficient and reduce their prices. This means that domestic consumers will benefit from a reduction in the price of shoes.

Problem 21-9

Briefly explain each of the following:

(a) *import quota*

(b) *export subsidy*

(c) *voluntary export restraints.*

Requirement and Clue: *This is a three-part problem. Answer each part in order. You are required to demonstrate that you are familiar with each of the concepts.*

Solution:

(a) An import quota is the maximum amount of a commodity that may be permitted to enter the country during a given period of time. To ensure that the quota is adhered to, the government requires each importer of the commodity to obtain an import licence for the amount to be imported.

(b) An export subsidy is any of the variety of means used by a government to help exporters. Export subsidies reduce the domestic exporters' costs, thus enabling them to reduce their prices and so compete more effectively with foreign producers

(c) Voluntary export restraints (VER) are non-tariff barriers to trade in which an importing country persuades another country to voluntarily reduce its exports of a commodity. This non-tariff device may prevent a flood of low-priced goods on the market, thus enabling domestic industries to compete.

Problem 21-10

Discuss the differences between tariffs and quotas in terms of their effects.

Requirement and Clue: *Two or three differences should suffice. Focus on the relative effectiveness of each device, and the effects on government, consumers and producers.*

Solution:

First, import quotas are likely to be more effective than tariffs in limiting the quantity of imports entering a country. If the desire for an imported good is very strong, some amount of that good is likely to be imported in spite of a high tariff. Some consumers may be willing to pay the price to have the item. In the case of an import quota, the quota establishes the limit and it cannot be exceeded.

Second, a tariff raises the price of the imported product and thus reduces the quantity demanded of that product. The proceeds from the tariff accrue to the government as revenue. The tax burden is borne by consumers of the imported product in the form of higher prices, and also by the foreign exporters in the form of reduced quantities demanded. Domestic producers of the product are thus at an advantage because the tariff does not apply to their product. A quota, on the other hand, reduces the supply of the product on the domestic market, and hence pushes up its price. The higher prices are paid to foreign exporters of the product and also to domestic producers. They do not accrue to the government as tax revenues as in the vase of a tariff.

Finally, a tariff is non-discriminatory in the sense that it applies equally to all foreign exporters. Thus, all domestic importers of the product pay the same tariff. On the other hand, import licences may be awarded on the basis of criteria that have nothing to do with efficiency. For example, import licences may be granted to some importers for political reasons, while more efficient importers may be denied import licences. In such cases, the consumers will be the main losers.

Problem 21-11

What is the difference between economic integration and economic cooperation?

Requirement and Clue: *You are required to show some familiarity with both concepts and to demonstrate that you can identify the difference between them.*

Solution:

Economic integration is an arrangement between two or more countries to abolish certain discriminatory practices between them. Economic cooperation, on the other hand, is an arrangement between two or more countries to reduce certain forms or discrimination among them. In economic integration, discriminatory practices are *abolished*; in economic cooperation, they are *reduced*. An example of economic integration would be an agreement between Canada and the United States to abolish trade barriers between the two countries. An example of economic cooperation would be an agreement to reduce tariff barriers between the two countries.

Problem 21-12

Define each of the following terms:

(a) *free-trade area*

(b) *customs union*

(c) *common market*

(d) *economic union*

Requirement and Clue: *This is a multi-part problem. Answer each part in order. Clearly state the meaning of each concept without elaboration.*

Solution:

(a) A free-trade area is a trading arrangement in which goods and services flow freely (without tariff) between the member countries. Each member country however, maintains its own tariff against the rest of the world.

(b) A customs union is a form of economic integration in which members countries agree to remove all tariffs among themselves, but erect a common tariff against the rest of the world.

(c) A common market is a trading arrangement in which goods flow freely between member countries. A common tariff exists with non-member countries, and there are no restrictions on the movement of labour and capital between the members.

(d) An economic union is a form of economic integration in which there is free movement of goods and factors of production and some degree of harmonization of national economic policies.

Problem 21-13

Discuss the concept of tariff evasion.

Requirement and Clue: *You should first demonstrate your knowledge of the concept. You should then show how tariff evasion may come about.*

Solution:

Tariff evasion is an attempt to evade a tariff by rerouting imports. This is a common problem with free-trade areas. Tariff evasion may occur in the following manner. Let us suppose that two countries, A and B, agree to form a free-trade area. Let us assume also that countries A and B impose tariffs of 20% and 30% respectively on the value of goods imported from a third country, C. An importer in country B who wishes to import a product from country C can arrange for the imported product to enter the free-trade area at A, where the tariff is lower than at B. The importer can then transport the product to B and thus avoid B's higher tariff. Such an arrangement will benefit the importer only if transportation costs from A to B are sufficiently low to make the arrangement worthwhile.

Problem 21-14

What problems are associated with a customs union?

Requirement and Clue: *You should first demonstrate your familiarity with the concept and then discuss briefly, two or three problems associated with it.*

Solution:

A customs union is a form of economic integration in which member countries remove all tariffs among themselves, but erect a common tariff on goods imported from outside the customs union. The levying of a common tariff may be problematic. If each country's tariff structure is consistent with its own agenda, negotiations for a common tariff are likely to be difficult. Each participating country will try to secure a tariff that protects its own industries.

Another problem with a customs union is that agreeing on how to distribute joint customs revenues among the participating countries can be very difficult. At first glance, an obvious solution appears to be to divide the proceeds proportionately according to each member country's volume of imports. But the formation of the customs union is likely to affect the volume of imports of each member of the union. This must be taken into account.

Yet another problem with customs unions is the difficulty of ensuring that the rules of the common tariff structure are interpreted and applied in the same manner in each member country. If countries interpret and administer the customs union laws differently, then the problem of tariff evasion will become an issue.

Problem 21-15

Briefly explain trade creation and trade diversion.

Requirement and Clue: *You are required to state clearly the meanings of these concepts. Do not ignore the term "briefly" in the problem.*

Solution:

Trade Creation: Trade creation results from a shift from high-cost domestic production to low-cost production in a member country because of economic integration. Thus, if country A is high-cost producer of a certain item and country B is a low-cost producer of the same item, country A may produce the item under tariff protection. If these two countries now decide to eliminate tariffs between them, country A will find it more economical to import supplies of the item from country B. This is trade creation.

Trade Diversion: Trade diversion results from a shift from the lowest-cost external producer to a higher-cost member producer because of economic integration. Trade is considered to be beneficial since it involves shifting resources into more efficient uses. Trade diversion, on the other hand, is considered to be harmful if it shifts resources into less efficient uses.

Problem 21-16

Discuss three advantages of economic integration.

Requirement and Clue: *Focus on effects such as terms of trade, competition, technological change, market stability, and economies of scale.*

Solution:

(You can select any three of the following).

- One advantage of economic integration is that it may have favourable effects on the terms of trade. A group of countries negotiating as a unit can win trade concessions from the rest of the world—concessions that probably could not be won if each country bargained individually. These concessions contribute to improved terms of trade.
- Another advantage of economic integration is that it increases competition. Sometimes, industries are established behind high tariff walls. Because of the high degree of protection offered to these industries, they do not have to compete with similar industries in other countries. This can result in high-cost, inefficient production. Competition forces industries either to seek more efficient methods of production or to leave the market. Lack of competition allows industries to produce inefficiently and at high cost. Now, suppose some industries agree to integrate. This will jeopardize the high-cost inefficient firms because imports can now come from member countries without a tariff. The increase in competition among member countries will result in a more efficient use of resources. Costs and prices will then tend to decrease.
- Economic integration promotes technological change. Limited domestic markets, on the other hand, tends to impede technological change. In response to a larger market made possible by economic integration, existing firms will tend to expand. Resources may then flow into research and development (R & D). Possibly, latent comparative advantage may also be realized, and the area could become an exporter to non-member countries. All in all, technological change is a positive force because it promotes economic growth.
- Economic integration is advantageous because it dispels fears that markets may disappear because of changes in tariffs, quotas, and other forms of trade restrictions. The market stability ensured by economic integration reduces risk and uncertainty, and promotes a more favourable climate for domestic investment. Foreign investment may also increase as a result of economic integration.
- A final advantage of economic integration is that it provides an opportunity to taje advantage of economies of scale. Economic integration promotes the development of a larger domestic market. The larger domestic market encourages firms to set up plants and equipment that facilitate economies of scale, since these firms will be supplying a larger regional market.

Multiple-Choice

In each case, circle the letter that corresponds with the correct answer.

1. A tariff is:

- a. a means of encouraging imports into a country
- b. a tax on goods produced domestically
- c. also called an import duty
- d. a device for lowering the prices of imported goods

Answer: c

Reason: *A tariff is a tax or duty on imported goods.*

2. Which of the following is a reason for imposing a tariff?

- a. To protect certain domestic industries
- b. To create employment
- c. To improve the country's terms of trade
- d. All of the above.

Answer: d.

Reason: *Countries impose tariffs for all of the reasons listed.*

3. Tariffs are categorized as:

a. revenue tariffs	c. compound tariffs
b. protective tariffs	d. all of the above

Answer: d

Reason: *The tariffs listed are all different types of tariffs.*

4. A revenue tariff is:

- a. a tariff imposed on the revenues of firms
- b. a tax on revenues exceeding a certain amount
- c. any tariff that affects the revenues of firms
- d. none of the above

Answer: d

Reason: *A revenue tariff is any tariff that is designed mainly to raise revenue for the government.*

5. A tariff of $0.75 imposed on each barrel of oil imported is an example of:

a. a compound tariff	c. an ad valorem tariff
b. a specific tariff	d. a prohibitive tariff

Answer: b

Reason: *A specific tariff is expressed as a dollar amount on each unit imported.*

6. Which of the following is not an argument in favour of a tariff?

- a. It lowers prices
- b. It increases domestic production
- c. It protects infant industries
- d. It improves the terms of trade

Answer: a

Reason: *Tariffs raise prices. They do not lower them.*

7. The optimum tariff is that tariff which:

a. maximizes tariff revenue
b. is easiest to collect
c. maximizes the country's welfare
d. maximizes evasion

Answer: c

Reason: *Tariffs are intended to make the country better off. A tariff that does this best is the optimum tariff.*

8. An import quota is:

a. the greatest amount of imports that a country can afford to buy
b. the amount of imports that is just equal to the amount of exports
c. the maximum amount of imports permitted to enter the country
d. none of the above

Answer: c

Reason: *An import quota imposes a limit on the amount of goods that importers can bring into the country.*

9. Which of the following are restrictive trade devices?

a. Tariffs
b. Import quotas
c. Voluntary restrictions
d. All of the above

Answer: d

Reason: *Choices a, b, and c all impose restraints on imports.*

10. An agreement between two countries to reduce the tariff on a particular item is an example of:

a. economic cooperation
b. economic integration
c. free trade
d. economic conspiracy

Answer: a

Reason: *Economic cooperation is an agreement between countries to reduce trade discrimination between them.*

11. Suppose there are only three countries in the world: A, B, and C. Goods are allowed to flow freely between A and B, but these two countries have a common tariff on goods imported from C. Which of the following describes the arrangement between A and B?

a. Free trade area
b. Customs union
c. Common market
d. Economic union

Answer: b

Reason: *A customs union eliminates trade barriers among member countries but maintains a common tariff with non-member countries.*

12. Which of the following is not an advantage of economic integration?

a. Trade diversion
b. Trade creation
c. Economies of scale
d. Competition

Answer: a

Reason: *Trade diversion shifts resources into less efficient uses, and that cannot be considered to be an advantage.*

True-False

Determine whether each of the following statements is true or false.

1. A tariff is a small charge for the use of government services.

Answer: False

Explanation: *A tariff is a tax or duty imposed on imported goods.*

2. A tariff increases the price of the good to the buyer.

Answer: True

3. Reasons for imposing tariffs include the protection of domestic industries, an improvement of the country's terms of trade, and raising revenue for the government.

Answer: True

4. All tariffs are revenue tariffs because they all raise revenue for the government.

Answer: False

Explanation: *Although a tariff may raise revenue for the government, it is a revenue tariff only if its main objective is to raise government revenue.*

5. A protective tariff is one designed to protect the government's revenue from declining.

Answer: False

Explanation: *A protective tariff is one whose main objective is to protect domestic industries.*

6. Import quotas are the most widely used restrictions on free trade.

Answer: False

Explanation: *Tariffs are much more widely used than import quotas.*

7. An ad valorem tariff is a tariff that adds value to the item that is being traded.

Answer: False

Explanation: *An ad valorem tariff is one that is expressed as a certain percentage of the value of the imported item.*

8. An infant industry is one that is set up by a government to ensure that the needs of children are fully met.

Answer: False

Explanation: *An infant industry is one that is considered to be in its early developmental stages.*

9. A tariff can improve a country's terms of trade and this increase its gains from international trade.

Answer: True

10. The infant-industry argument for tariffs is that new domestic industries cannot compete with older industries in foreign countries. Hence they need tariff protection.

Answer: True

11. Tariffs restrict international trade and specialization, and thus cause resources to be more efficiently allocated.

Answer: False

Explanation: It is true that tariffs restrict international trade, but such restrictions on free trade hamper efficient allocation of resources.

12. Tariffs may increase a country's terms of trade, but they reduce the volume of trade.

Answer: True

13. Protective tariffs keep domestic industries profitable and create jobs, thus they benefit the entire country.

Answer: False

Explanation: Protective tariffs do help some industries, but usually at a cost to the entire economy.

14. The optimum tariff is that tariff that effectively shuts out all imports, beca use then it is most effective.

Answer: False

Explanation: The optimum tariff is that tariff that maximizes the country's welfare.

15. Trade creation occurs when production shifts from a high-cost domestic producer to a lower-cost producer in an integration economic arrangement.

Answer: True

16. Economic integration is likely to weaken each member's bargaining power in trade negotiations with non-member countries. Thus it worsens the terms of trade.

Answer: False

Explanation: On the contrary, economic integration builds a stronger bargaining unit that might be able to win trade concessions that a single country might not be able to win.

17. Tariff evasion is an attempt to avoid a tariff by re-routing imports into a country with a lower tariff.

Answer: True

13. One of the problems with a customs union arrangement is tariff evasion.

Answer: False

Explanation: There is no tariff evasion in a customs union because there is a common tariff on goods imported from outside the customs union.

18. A free-trade agreement between countries may enable countries to take advantage of economies of scale.

Answer: True

19. A possible cost of a free-trade agreement is the closure of certain firms in member countries, resulting in unemployment.

Answer: True

Completion

(Fill in the blanks)

Use each word or combination of words from the list exactly once. (Hint: Proceed by elimination)

Word list

Ad Valorem — Area x 2 — Compound Tariff — Cooperation — Creation — Customs x 2 — Decreases — Diversion — Economic x 3 — Employment — Free — Free Trade Area — Improves — Industrialization — Infant Industry — Integration — Protective — Quotas — Revenue — Specific — Tariffs — Terms of Trade — Trade x 4 — Union x 3

Questions

1. A tariff whose main objective is to raise revenue for the government is called a(n)______________ tariff.
2. A tariff whose main objective is to protect domestic industries is called a(n) ______________ tariff.
3. A(n) ______________ tariff is expressed as a given amount per unit of the imported item.
4. A tariff of 10% of the value of an imported item is called a(n) ______________ tariff.
5. A tariff expressed as 10 cents per litre for the first 100 litres, and 15% of the value thereafter is called a(n) ______________ tariff.
6. The main economic arguments in favour of tariffs are (in any order): (i) the ______________, (ii) the ______________, (iii) the ______________, and (iv) the ______________ arguments.
7. Comparing tariffs and quotas, ______________ are more effective in restricting the volume of imports, but ______________ raise more revenue for the government.
8. As a country raises its tariffs, its terms of trade ______________ [improves, worsens], but the volume of trade ______________ [increases, decreases]
9. An arrangement between countries to allow the free flow of goods between them while each maintains its own tariffs with the rest of the world is called a(n) ______________.
10. An arrangement between countries to abolish tariffs and other restrictive trade devices is called ______________ ______________.
11. An agreement between countries to reduce tariffs is called ______________ ______________.
12. An agreement among countries to allow the free flow of goods among them while each maintains its own tariffs with the rest of the world is called a(n) ______________ ______________ ______________. If, in addition to the free movement of goods, the countries establish a common

tariff with the rest of the world, then the arrangement is a(n) ______________ ______________.

13. A common market is a level of integration that is just higher than a(n) ______________ ______________, and just lower than a(n) ______________ ______________.

14. When economic integration causes a shift from high-cost domestic production to lower-cost production in a member country, we say that ______________ ______________ has occurred.

15. When economic integration causes a shift from the lowest cost external producer to a higher-cost member producer, we say that ______________ ______________ has occurred.

Solution

1. (revenue)
2. (protective)
3. (specific)
4. (ad valorem)
5. (compound tariff)
6. (infant industry, employment, terms of trade, industrialization)
7. (quotas, tariffs)
8. (improves, decreases)
9. (free trade area)
10. (economic integration)
11. (economic cooperation)
12. (free trade area, customs union)
13. (customs union, economic union)
14. (trade creation)
15. (trade diversion)

About the Author

Elijah M. James is a professor in the Department of Economic at Dawson College in Montreal, Quebec, Canada. He has also taught at McGill University, John Abbott College, and Concordia University. Dr. James studied economics at Memorial University of Newfoundland, University of Western Ontario, Concordia University (Montreal), University of Toronto, and California Western University. Professor James has published extensively in the area of economics and his textbooks on microeconomics and macroeconomics are well-known to Canadian students.

Professor James won the Teaching Excellence award in 2009-2010 at Dawson College and has been awarded the *Association québécoise de pédagogie collégiale (AQPC) Honourable Mention 2017.* He has been recognized for his contribution to education.

www.ingramcontent.com/pod-product-compliance
Lightning Source LLC
LaVergne TN
LVHW060027210926
848481LV00013B/3805
* 9 7 8 1 9 2 6 7 1 6 4 4 2 *